175544

# NEW DIRECTIONS IN PUBLIC ADMINISTRATION

Edited by
## Barry Bozeman and Jeffrey Straussman
THE MAXWELL SCHOOL, SYRACUSE UNIVERSITY

350
N532

BROOKS/COLE PUBLISHING COMPANY
MONTEREY, CALIFORNIA

Brooks/Cole Publishing Company
A Division of Wadsworth, Inc.

Printed in the United States of America

10 9 8 7 6 5 4 3 2 1

**Library of Congress Cataloging in Publication Data**
Main entry under title:

New directions in public administration.

1. Public administration—Addresses, essays, lectures.
I. Bozeman, Barry.   II. Straussman, Jeffrey D.

JF1321.N47      1984            350            83-26210

ISBN 0-534-03266-4

Sponsoring Editor: *Marquita Flemming*
Production Editor: *Carol Rost*
Manuscript Editor: *Vicki Nelson*
Permissions Editor: *Carline Haga*
Interior and Cover Design: *Vernon T. Boes*
Art Coordinator: *Rebecca Ann Tait*
Interior Illustration: *John Foster*
Typesetting: *Omegatype Typography, Inc.*
Cover Printing, Printing and Binding: *R. R. Donnelley & Sons Co.*

# NEW DIRECTIONS
## IN
## PUBLIC ADMINISTRATION

# PREFACE

The objectives of this book are to identify some of the problems of Public Administration, including not only the lasting issues but some new and rapidly developing ones; to present some of the scholarly work addressing these problems; and in general to represent the state of the art in Public Administration. Among these objectives, one is preeminent. Simply stated, it is finding out "what's new" in Public Administration. By any strict test, we are doomed to fail in our attempt to determine what's new. There are too many new trends and research topics in Public Administration for a single volume to do justice to them. Nevertheless, the selections included here seem to us to reflect some especially far-reaching trends. Public Administration is changing so rapidly that the best one can hope to do is to provide a clear snapshot of a body in motion. We feel this volume provides a reasonably clear picture of today's Public Administration.

We gratefully acknowledge the assistance of the following reviewers: Richard W. Campbell, University of Georgia; Greg Daneke, Arizona State University; Richard Higgins, The American University; Kenneth J. Meier, The University of Oklahoma, Norman; Stuart Nagel, University of Illinois; James L. Perry, University of California, Irvine; Hal Rainey, Florida State University; and Stephen R. Rosenthal, Boston University.

Several persons at Brooks/Cole Publishing Company have contributed much to this book. We are especially grateful to Henry Staat, Marquita Flemming, Carol Rost, Vernon Boes, and Vicki Nelson.

*Barry Bozeman*
*Jeffrey Straussman*
Syracuse University

# CONTENTS

CONTENTS

# NEW DIRECTIONS
# IN
# PUBLIC ADMINISTRATION

# INTRODUCTION

*There was a time, in the '20s and '30s, when public administration was scientific management, elegant systems hidden from the ugly face of politics[.] . . . There was a time, in the '40s and '50s, when public administration was considered the art and science of getting-it-done, after someone else had decided what to do and why.[1]*

## NEW DIRECTIONS AND OLD DIRECTIONS

There was a time, not so long ago, when "Made in Japan" produced more punch lines than bread lines; when there was more concern with the evils of the technological fix than with fixing technology; when cutbacks were something managed by football players in the open field. But the social environment of public administration has dramatically changed. Since the public administration of the eighties (and the public administration of the earlier decades) is a mirror of social change, one finds that new directions in the field very much resemble the new directions of society.

Public administration is not only a mirror. It reflects action, but it also shapes action. The reactive part of public administration ensures that it will evolve and adapt to social and economic trends, but the active part ensures that it will help determine those trends. Thus, public administration charts some of its own new directions and, in so doing, helps determine the course of social change.

Much of what is new in public administration can be understood as reaction to change, much else as initiation of change. But public administration is not all reformation and no substance. There is a set of timeless core issues in public administration, and these enduring concerns provide stability in the midst of change. These core issues are perhaps the most secure bond uniting the diverse community of public administration practitioners, academics and "pracademics." It is no more possible to identify a discrete set of core issues than it is to enumerate a complete and valid list

of "scientific principles" of public administration. Still, public administrationists might agree that any list of core issues should at least include political accountability in administration, the role of the public interest (or some other expression of the place of values in administration), and the assessment of efficiency and effectiveness. Moreover, public administration's concern with the abiding issues ensures that many of the new directions are set by old problems. Public administration is inexorably old, just as it is inexorably new.

## PUBLIC ADMINISTRATION: A CRAFT AND A DISCIPLINE

Public administration is a craft and it is a field of study. Sometimes it is not easy or even meaningful to draw boundaries between the two. Nevertheless, it is useful to distinguish between public administration and Public Administration; we use the lower case version of the term to refer to the practice of public administration and the upper case version to refer to the discipline or field of study. We distinguish between them, in part, to show how they are related. Public Administration, the body of theory and research, is based on observation or ideas about the practice of public administration. But Public Administration also seeks to influence practice. Even in the days in which Public Administration was viewed as a science, it was a science of *practice*. Unlike many traditional social sciences, Public Administration has never been dominated by theorists posing as detached and disinterested observers.

The reliance of Public Administration and public administration on each other has never been equal. While theory and research have influenced practice in important ways, developments in public administration practice have had more influence on theory and research. There are several reasons. In the first place, the practice of public administration often proceeds at such a whirlwind pace that there is little time to give much consideration to theory and research. The external political and social environment makes demands that must be quickly heeded. Sometimes this haste affords little time for reflecting on theory or research evidence. Second, while public administration research and theory are growing, there are many issues critical to the practice of public administration not given much consideration by researchers and theorists. Some of the theory and research produced is not perceived by practitioners as relevant to their needs—especially those needs that are highly particular, dependent on

context, and nonroutine. Furthermore, Public Administration competes with other fields of study for the attention of practitioners. Sometimes those competing fields impress more easily if they have a stronger body of theory and an impressive set of analytical techniques. The fact that Public Administration is not a field with sharp boundaries is both a blessing and a curse. Public Administration builds upon the work of management theorists, psychologists, and sociologists, among others. But practitioners look to these disciplines for guidance as often as they do to the amalgamated social science of Public Administration.

Public Administration bears little resemblance to conventional social science disciplines. There is a core set of issues that have captivated Public Administration scholars over the years—enduring issues such as the nature of the public interest, accountability, the role of values in administration, effectiveness, and efficiency—but there is little theoretical consensus.

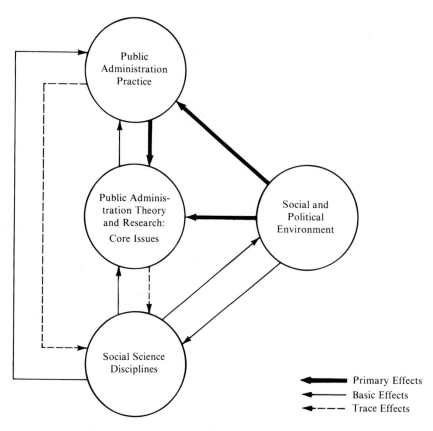

Factors Influencing the Growth of Knowledge in Public Administration

2

Public Administration has no counterpart to sociologists' structural-functionalism, economists' Keynesian theory, or psychologists' behaviorism. There are core issues but no core theory. For the most part, Public Administration scholars have chosen to borrow relevant theories from other disciplines rather than developing indigenous theory. In part, this is because Public Administration, more than most fields, is interested in keeping abreast of significant developments in the practice of public administration and in the social and political environment. Practical problems frame much of Public Administration scholarship.

Our view of the factors influencing the growth of knowledge in Public Administration is summarized in the simple model illustrated. The model inspires humility about the place of Public Administration and its effects on the world of ideas and the world of action. But Public Administration is still a young field, even among the youthful social sciences, and its influence will grow as its body of research and theory progresses. At present, the gaps in our knowledge are enormous. Public Administration is often inconclusive, and theories are often so broad that there is little likelihood that they will be put to the test. Theories are accumulated, but few are forsaken for demonstrably better theories. But the gaps are not all attributable to the relative lack of explanatory power of Public Administration theories. Public Administration has a broad intellectual dominion, with fewer researchers and theorists than important research problems.

## NOTES

1. Cleveland, Harlan. The future of public administration. *The Bureaucrat*, 1982, *11*, 3.

# PART ONE

# THE CHANGING FACE

# OF

# THE PUBLIC SECTOR

By all criteria, the public sector is different now from the past—even the not too distant past. Conventional ways of comparing the public sector today from yesteryear use quantitative indicators such as the *size* of government, the *number* of new governments (especially at the local level), and the *scope* of government activity. Government is indeed bigger, as reflected in the number of people who work for government, or as measured by the financial resources of government. Government organizations are continually created to grapple with problems that seem intractable. Governments spend money on a multitude of problems from agriculture to zoological research, and, lest we forget, governments regulate practically everything!

This image of government can be found in any textbook on public administration. But it is yesterday's description of the public sector. Tomorrow's public sector will be different. How?

In "The Future of Management," Dwight Waldo gives us some insight into the changing demands on the public manager. In moving from an industrial society (based on land, labor, and capital) to a post-industrial society (where knowledge is the central resource), the manager's job and requisite skills have changed. Tomorrow's public organizations require more expertise and more specialization of tasks. Yet the need for managers to coordinate, to become the "great integrators," is stronger than ever before. The task of integration requires a *strategic* orientation. This means that tomorrow's public managers will have to be able to anticipate organizational complexity, interorganizational relations, and the linkages between organiza-

tions and their external environments. Managers will be the "human glue" binding together diverse specialists.

Another important respect in which the public sector is changing is in the very meaning of "public." In the past, a major distinction between public and private sectors was that the former was service oriented and the latter was production oriented. But in a post-industrial service-oriented economy, the manufacturing plant is no longer the stereotypical private organization.

There was a time when the boundaries of private and public sectors were sharply delineated. No one mistook Chrysler Corporation for a branch of the federal government. Today this mistake could not only be made, it may not even be a totally incorrect assumption. When the government provides a corporation with a loan guarantee to ensure the corporation's financial survival, we can say that the corporation takes on "public" overtones. In contrast, when the U. S. Army advertises to "be all that you can be" on national television, it is marketing itself in ways that are not fundamentally different from Ivory Soap. In short, we have been experiencing the *blurring* of sectors in the United States. Some public organizations have become more businesslike. And some businesses have become more like government organizations.

The authors come to somewhat different conclusions about the implications of sector blurring. Graham Allison ("Public and Private Management: Are They Fundamentally Alike in All Unimportant Respects?") suggests that public management continues to require skills different from private sector management, the blurring of sectors notwithstanding. Bozeman's "Dimensions of Publicness" is not aimed squarely at the issue of public versus private management, but nevertheless implies that there are few, if any, hard-and-fast sector-based differences in organizations.

One of the chief causes of sector blurring is the widespread recognition of scarcity. Both the evolution of organizational forms and the emphasis on resource management are in part attributable to scarcity. Both Waldo and Laurence Rutter ("Strategies for the Es-

sential Community") emphasize the role of managers in coping with decline and husbanding resources. But Bozeman and Slusher ("Scarcity and Environmental Stress in Public Organizations") observe that public organizations are not well equipped to deal with scarcity and may fall into the trap of sacrificing long-term managerial strategy for short-run gains.

Part One includes articles that explore the sources of public sector change, the consequences of change, and the options available to public organizations.

# CHAPTER ONE

# The Prospects
# of
# Public Organizations

## The Future of Management

Dwight Waldo

Management began when civilization began and in some form will continue as long as civilization endures. However, management technique, style, and spirit are subject to great variation. These are changing and will change further in response to social stresses and change.

Some say that social stresses are now so great and the pace of change so rapid that management, viewed by these persons as a way of conducting group enterprises under stable conditions, will disappear. But while transformations are certain, disappearance is impossible barring only two alternatives. One is the disappearance of the enterprise of civilization, with which management is so intimately entwined. The other is the arrival of the anarchist utopia in pure form: Things somehow run themselves without the interventions indicated by such terms as organization, administration, management.

To say that management is closely intertwined with civilization is not to speak carelessly. The development of the arts and technologies of management was essential to the rise of early civilizations as many studies, including E.N. Gladden's two-volume *History of Public Administration* (1972), fully demonstrate. Of course, some charge that civilization was a false start, a wrong turn, in the human experience, responsible

for the violence and oppression that have plagued humanity since the rise of the first river-centered civilizations. But while this view of history has a certain poetic truth and critical value it is essentially irrelevant: Civilization did happen and this fact is decisive, one way or another, for all subsequent experience.

In no civilization does management exist as art and technology apart from the major components of that civilization; but in early and simpler civilizations the interactions were especially close—or in time's perspective are especially visible. "Civic" centers, concerned with such matters as public works and public records, were as well religious and military centers. These centers also fostered the development of agriculture, art, engineering, law, and metallurgy. They were central in the development of mathematics and the early sciences. For all such enterprises management was matrix and mortar, supplying sustenance, providing stability, insuring continuity.

In the several millennia of history the arts and technologies of management have sometimes regressed, even lapsed. But there has also been something of a secular growth. In various ways the management experience of the New Kingdom, of the Roman Empire, of the Church, of the Renaissance merchants and bankers, of the early modern monarchs, has been woven into the fabric of contemporary life.

### THE ARRIVAL OF SELF-CONSCIOUSNESS

Sometimes, we can see in retrospect, the imparting of management skills (or at least the imparting of skills, such as law or accounting, useful in management) was the objective of educational or training arrangements, the eighteenth-century Prussian program of Cameralist studies being a notable example. But it is only in the recent modern period, approximately in the last 100 years, that management has achieved "self-consciousness"; that managers or persons connected with management have come to believe that management "as such" exists, and thus can be developed and improved, studied and taught. Such an arrival of self-consciousness is not unique, of course. As there were managers before Management, so there were historians before History, scientists before Science, artists before Art.

Speaking centrally for the United States, the arrival of management self-consciousness was associated with the rise of industrialization and urbanization, with the quickening of technological change and its consequences, with increasing respect for the achievements of science and rising hopes for its future beneficence, with the growth of specialization and professionalization, with the rise of the contemporary university, with the attainment of self-consciousness on the part of several social sciences—to name some of the more obvious stimulating and molding phenomena. Two developments early in the century were of critical importance. One was the Scientific Management movement, the other the rise of schools of business administration.

The Scientific Management movement began and centered in industry, but its spirit and techniques spread to all major institutions; in fact, it became an international movement, important not only in the capitalist countries but in shaping the communist approach to management after the Russian Revolution. The central postulate of Scientific Management—as the name indicates—was that the scientific method is applicable in management itself, just as it is applicable in the movement and transformations of materials by industry: Through study the "one best way" to perform a particular function can be identified, learned, and taught.

Responding in part to the spread of Scientific Management but also to other impulses, the idea that "business is a profession"—or ought to be and can be—became increasingly popular. Special schools and institutes to train personnel in "commercial" skills such as bookkeeping were not enough; it was necessary to establish college and university level programs to convey to would-be and future managers a range of knowledge from corporation law and the techniques of marketing to personnel management and organiza-

tion theory. By mid-century not only were there hundreds of college and university programs in business administration, there were many special programs as well to train for administrative positions in public administration and for positions in institutional areas, particularly education, that embraced both public and private categories.

In the sixties the full logic of the idea that management or administration is an identifiable function that lends itself to study and teaching received institutional form. "Schools of Administration" were established, sometimes de novo, sometimes by renaming and somewhat broadening a School of Business Administration. These "generic" schools are premised, not only on the idea that management can be studied and taught, but on the idea that the skills of management are essentially independent of knowledge of the institution (factory, school, hospital, or whatever) to be managed.

Management, conceived as an identifiable, important function, for which special education is possible and desirable, had now arrived, and would henceforth be regarded as a normal, even necessary, aspect of a complex modern civilization. Or so it would seem. Not only were the idea and its institutional embodiment a generally accepted aspect of American life, there was a widespread movement in the same direction in other countries. This movement often responded to indigenous impulses and reflected indigenous knowledge. But the idea that the "American Challenge" was not so much scientific-technical in a traditional sense, but represented rather the development of a higher level of expertise in management, became widely accepted. The competition, it was concluded, must be met at this level.

## CONTINUING DOUBTS

The picture just sketched ignores continuing doubts and complications. And in recent years doubts—and assertions—of a new and more fundamental nature have placed a question mark over the future of the management function itself. The continuing doubts and complications cannot be explored adequately here. It must suffice to note two of fundamental import. The more recent doubts and assertions will then receive attention.

The first continuing doubt concerns the "scientific" status of management knowledge. This has been repeatedly if not continuously challenged by those claiming that management is a practical skill only, a combination of personal attributes and experience. Attacks of quite a different nature have been mounted from the vast literature of "philosophy of science" and of scientific method as developed and perceived in the physical sciences. Defenders have countered in various ways. For example: that the social sciences are different from physical sciences, and must have an interpretation of science appropriate to them; that management as an applied field, or perhaps "profession," compares fairly well with other applied fields (say, medicine) in the coherence of its theories, the firmness and permanence of its factual base, the relationship of training to performance.

The second continuing doubt concerns the "culture" problem, which has both factual and normative dimensions. As to the first, the core question is: Is it possible to attain "management knowledge" that is firm and valid irrespective of time and place? Or is it not, rather, that what is "true" or "works" will vary with the people concerned, according to their history, their culture, their circumstances? The normative dimensions of the culture problem are many, and are practical (and sometimes personal) as well as theoretical. For example: Is "management science" really a covert class-based ideology, seeking to control or change in the interests of the managers? Or a national, or Western, ideology? Can management science be introduced in any country where it is not indigenous without profound implications for the culture of that country? If not, by what right, by whose warrant, is it introduced?

## NEW CHALLENGE

Some recent books suggest not just that management has continuing problems, but that futility and failure threaten what generally has become accepted as an idea and institutionalized in practice. These are not hostile books, written by "outsiders" and directed against business or management on principle. Rather, they are books by persons experienced in management, typically management consultants. In general their message is: We must stop pretending that accepted practices and theories will "work" in the present and emerging world. Classical management theory and techniques presumed a continuity and stability of the social environment that have disappeared. The problems now posed are what to do when science falters, how to cope with swift and often unpredictable change as well as turmoil and conflict, how to survive and

even succeed through the use of new modes of thought and styles of action.

Three books will serve to illustrate. Roger A. Golde's *Muddling Through: The Art of Properly Unbusinesslike Management* (1976) is advertised as "the guide to conscious, creative, nonlogical forms of thinking that succeeds where management 'theory' fails." Arguing that the higher up the organization hierarchy the more uncertainty and the more "muddling," it sets forth a range of "strategies" which are most likely to be productive and successful: "muddling strategies designed to help managers find answers to sticky problems."

One discovers as he proceeds that these strategies are not in fact unknown either in the world of management or of psychology. Indeed, they have a certain long-recognized respectability and credibility. But the important circumstance is that here they are presented as ways of dealing with a world in which accepted ways are gone and established rules futile.

Charles H. Tavel's *The Third Industrial Age: Strategy for Business Survival* (1975; published earlier in French as *L'Ere de la Personnalité, Essai sur la Stratégie Créatrice*) aims to make "a tactician into a strategist" in a world of swift change over which single enterprises, even large ones, will have little or no control. The first industrial age was that of the entrepreneur, who created the industries; the second was that of the strategist, who will be charged with preserving and extending what has been created. "Strategy" reaches beyond conventional management, beyond planning, organizing, and directing. What is it, more precisely? Well, while not forsaking such virtues as common sense and moderation, it is characterized (not surprisingly) by such qualities as foresight and creativity; it selects the proper objectives realistically and devises workable schemes to reach them. To make strategists of his readers, Tavel takes them on a global tour to present the relevant emerging world as he sees it, and then offers advice on how to survive and prosper. Not exactly "despite all": The creative personality will find opportunities where others experience impossible difficulties.

Stewart Thompson's *The Age of the Manager Is Over!* (1975) argues forthrightly just that. Golde and Tavel do not so much dismiss management as demote it, but Thompson directly challenges "today's obsolete management theories and practices." The "very idea of professional management is a sham," and to attempt to practice it only "exhausts and depletes." A "well-managed" corporation today can only be one blind both to the dangers and opportunities of its environment, for the world moves too fast and changes too quickly to permit "management." In 21 chapters the theme is illustrated—and repeated. What then, if management is futile? Well, we must use our intelligence, be free and creative, develop a new "sense of touch."

These three books are hardly "scholarly" or "scientific" by the criteria of contemporary social science (though there *is* a large social science literature emphasizing the passing of the "stable state"). But this is to miss the point. Their writers are persons of considerable experience, the books are published by reputable publishers, and the message is directed toward corporate management. What is significant is that such books are written, sold, and read. What do they signal? An End of Management?

As indicated above, this, to me, cannot be the case. They represent, rather, a certain type of reaction, in some ways "extreme," to real developments and problems. I shall set forth briefly my own version of the developments and problems. I shall indicate some of the more "moderate" responses that others in or concerned with management have been and are making to these developments and problems. These responses may not be proper in all cases, or collectively adequate to meet the needs. But they advance beyond conventional management and do not simply enjoin us to be free, intelligent, and creative.

## FORCES SHAPING FUTURE MANAGEMENT

A statement of the "forces shaping future management" cannot but smack of pretentiousness and fatuousness, since it must be a statement of "what is happening" in the world. This acknowledged, nevertheless I set forth the following as a summary view of what seem to me main forces (movements, tendencies —the proper designation is not clear) shaping the future of management.

First, a transition from industrialism to postindustrialism. A considerable amount of the Futures literature of the past two decades concerns an alleged transformation of the condition of man from the industrial era of approximately the past 200 years to a new condition of man designated negatively as "postindustrial." Some of the key arguments include the following: that knowledge, particularly codifiable, scientific-technical knowledge, is emerging as the critical factor in pro-

ductivity, supplementing and perhaps leading the traditional triad of land, labor, and capital; that accompanying the increasing knowledge, contributing to it and multiplying its effects, is the emergence of new technologies for gathering, storing, manipulating, transmitting, and applying knowledge; that new power elites and power centers accompany these changes, since those who produce knowledge and are charged with its transmission, storage, and so forth, occupy strategic positions; that the factory, as the archetypical institution of industrialism, is being replaced with more sophisticated and flexible methods of production, requiring more skilled and less unskilled labor; that the new means of production, being machine based and even increasingly machine directed, are extremely efficient, and that therefore the "problem of production" has been or can be solved, enabling us to turn our attention to problems of distribution; that implied in the changes specified is a general shift from "production" occupations to "service" (or "knowledge") occupations, as well as an increase in leisure time as against work time.

The turmoil and social dislocations of the late sixties, the economic downturn of the early seventies, the development of an energy shortage, and other factors have led the postindustrialists to modify some of their projections. Indeed, it is clear that what was projected will not come to pass without significant modification. However, despite contrary events and second thoughts, the projections of a new human situation have considerable force; the postindustrialists have sketched *some* of the features of the human future.

Second, a conflict between a Revolution of Rising Expectations and a Revolution of Lowering Expectations. The Revolution of Rising Expectations refers, first of all, to the phenomenon giving rise to the name: the expectation on the part of hundreds of millions of persons that their standard of living both should rise and can rise, enabling them to live in a manner more or less like that of prosperous persons in the advanced industrial nations. The Revolution of Rising Expectations may also be used to designate raised expectations on the part of populations within the industrial nations that have been "disadvantaged" and now seek and expect an improved status. Back of both of these is a long-term secular phenomenon: In the West now for generations there has been both an expectation that the material standard of living will rise and, giving substance to the expectation, a secular rise in the standard of living.

10

The Revolution of Lowering Expectations I use to designate the complex of interests and concerns indicated by such expressions as: the energy crisis, environmental pollution, the exhaustion of nonrenewable resources, destruction of the biosphere, Spaceship Earth. This complex of interests and concerns has a tremendously increased salience as against a decade ago.

It seems obvious that the Revolution of Rising Expectations and the Revolution of Lowering Expectations must in various ways, at various times, in various places, come into conflict: The former says "more," the latter says "less"—or at least "different." Indeed, one can see them coming into conflict day by day, both nationally and internationally.

Third, contradictions in and challenges to the nation-state system. The nation-state system as a way of organizing the political aspects of our lives has existed only a short time in man's experience, even in his relatively brief historical experience. There is no reason to assume that it is the final method of structuring the political factor. Indeed, there are reasons to presume that the nation-state system is under stress and in transition—though to what is very problematical.

One factor here is a rise in ethnicity which, along with other factors, has resulted in a three-fold multiplication in the number of independent states in the last generation. The relationship of ethnicity to nationalism is murky. But certainly the two cannot be equated; and it is arguable that ethnicity has been gaining over nationalism as an "organizing principle" since the end of World War I.

It is notable also that the number of international-multinational-transnational organizations has been increasing rapidly. While the most visible of these are the large transnational economic corporations, some of which are larger in resources and membership than some of the independent states, what is little appreciated is that the increase extends also to organizations of nearly every variety.

Fourth, the growth of a large "gray" area, mixing the "public" and the "private." One of the distinguishing characteristics of the modern era (as against the medieval period) has been a distinction between the categories of the public and the private. We see now, however, the constant enlargement of a "gray" area in which these categories are mixed and mingled, and the distinction confused or lost. In conducting the large enterprises of contemporary life it seems sensible, indeed necessary, to create complex "mixes"; otherwise it is impossible to put together what must be put together in performing recognized functions and in dealing with what are regarded as problems. Governments alone through traditional bureaucracies cannot perform the tasks laid upon them by legislative mandate; private corporations, even those jealous of their private status and eager to guard it, increasingly find it impossible to function without government support and even regulation.

Fifth, the decline of traditional sources and styles of authority. Patterns of organization and administration are inextricably linked to the sources and styles of authority of the society in which they exist. There is now a voluminous literature dealing with particular aspects of the "decline of authority," or addressing what is perceived as a "crisis of authority" of a general nature. More broadly still, some sociologists profess to perceive a "demodernization of the world," an erosion or evaporation of the core beliefs and attitudes that have given the modern world its distinguishing institutions and ethos.

Perhaps I have not set forth what will prove to be the chief forces affecting management in the future. Certainly each of the "forces" set forth is involved with the others; and it is difficult to tell cause from effect, how best to "cut into" complex reality in an attempt to understand it. Certainly, too, one can make a much longer list of "things" that will affect future management. There is, for example, the general speeding up of the processes of technological and social change, so well advertised in Alvin Toffler's *Future Shock*.

But enough has been said to indicate that beyond doubt the environment of management in the future will be uncertain, swiftly changing, characterized by stress and turmoil. And this listing takes no account of the unpredictable yet certain events: the wars, revolutions, catastrophes, whatever, that will add uncertainty to uncertainty.

## MANAGEMENT ADAPTATION AND EVOLUTION

From what has been said so far, it might be presumed that twentieth-century management is a mature set of techniques for achieving organizational control and insuring operating efficiency under conditions of relative social stability. But management, rather, is a constantly evolving complex of attitudes, arts, and techniques; and in the past generation, and particularly in the past decade, there has been a notable attempt to adapt management to a world of more rapid change, great complexity, and increased stress. The nature of these developments should be indicated. But it will be useful, first, to sketch a picture of "bureaucracy," for it is in contrast to bureaucracy that the changes in management can be appreciated.

The classic "picture" of bureaucracy is that of Max Weber, presented in his ideal-typical delineation early in this century. As pictured, a fully-developed bureaucratic organization is characterized by such qualities as: hierarchy, the direction of subordinates by superordinates, the profile of the organization being pyramidal; a clear specification of the functions and responsibilities of each position in the hierarchy; regular routines and the conduct of activities according to rules; appointment and promotion according to merit (education, experience, etc.); the existence of career ladders in the organization and the expectation of a career within the organization.

Patently, such organizational features are familiar to anyone who has lived in an industrialized, urban society (even though departures from the "ideal" are also familiar). One need not accept at face value Weber's view that bureaucracy is the most rational and efficient mode of group activity to achieve goals, and hence has a certain inevitability, to conclude that bureaucracy has had a plausible "fit" to conditions and expectations in the late modern period. How else to account for the spread of bureaucratic organizational styles around the world, so cogently discussed in Henry Jacoby's recent *The Bureaucratization of the World* (1973)?

But, perhaps in its triumph, bureaucracy creates the conditions that lead to its transformation if not to its demise. (On this there is keen observation in Daniel Bell's recent *The Cultural Contradictions of Capitalism,* 1976.) At least, for whatever reasons, in some places—certainly in the United States—during recent decades organizational forms and styles have increasingly departed from rather than advanced toward the bureaucratic formula.

Unquestionably, though the number of organizations continues to grow and the "organizationness" of life does not diminish, there is under way something of a "*de*bureaucratization" of some parts of the world at the same time that bureaucratization continues a significant advance worldwide. Overall, in the United States (and in the West generally) as against a few decades ago: Hierarchy is less strict, or to put the matter differently, there are more recognized sources

of authority (unions, for example) and the principles of authority (expertise, for example) that impinge upon official authority; there is more personal mobility, both within organizations and between organizations; the pace of organizational change (reorganizations, recombinations, and so forth) has accelerated; more attention is given to affect—to the springs of motivation and even to "fulfillment"—as against the economic and rational interpreted in a narrow way; interorganizational relations have assumed greater importance, with managers becoming more sensitive to the complex environment to which they must respond.

Some of the change in organizational form and style owes no particular debt to self-conscious management. Organizations and environment have evolved together, in complex, subtle cause-and-effect relationships, and management has often been responding to urgent promptings from the environment even when crediting itself with foresight and imagination. However, whatever the causal chain or the attribution of credit, management has responded and evolved. It is appropriate to note some of the responses, as past and present adaptivity give some indication of future ability to cope with an environment, external and internal, as changing and stressful as that indicated above.

1. *The Human Relations and Organizational Humanism movements.* The Human Relations movement that began in the twenties and was active into the fifties was both an extension of and a corrective to the Scientific Management movement, extending the study of efficient production and effective management from motion to emotion, from the physical to the social. The Organizational Humanist movement grew out of Human Relations and is active today. It represents a broadening and a "softening" of Human Relations, as its name suggests; it seeks not just productivity and efficiency, but modes of management and interaction that simultaneously insure organizational effectiveness and participant self-fulfillment.

Critics charge that the Organizational Humanists have not really solved the problem set: to make organizational and member interests congruent. But a complete solution to the problem of making the interests of the collectivity and its individual members completely compatible—*the* central problem of social science—is probably not possible.

2. *Systems Theory.* Systems Theory has been one of the main intellectual currents of recent decades. Focusing on the "systematic" behavior of phenomena

ostensibly of great variety, it has sought understanding and control by seeking to identify the behavior of systems by virtue of the fact that they *are* systems. A protean movement, Systems Theory has developed a range of interests from the narrowly technical to the broadly philosophical.

Management technology has drawn extensively upon Systems Theory; indeed, the study of organization and management, one way and another, has been an important part of that complex of interests. Systems Theory has provided conceptual links in such management technologies as Planning, Programming, Budgeting System; in the area of organization theory, the "open system" concept has been invaluable in helping to understand interchanges between organizations and their environments (including other organizations).

3. *Computer technology.* In a single generation the electronic computer, together with the complex of technologies that surround it, has transformed human potentialities for the accumulation, storage, manipulation, and transmission of information. Management not only has responded by putting computer technology to work in management, but management working in and through organizations is in large part responsible for the development and widespread use of the computer.

4. *Organizational Futurism.* One of the significant intellectual developments of the recent period—spawning institutes, societies, publications—has been Futurism: an attempt to project, foresee, plan, and anticipate the future, to move into the future intelligently rather than stumble into it blindly. As with Systems Theory, management has played an active role in the movement, seeking to discern the implications of social and technical changes for organizational change, recommending the adoption of organizational styles and management techniques calculated to achieve objectives under newly emerging conditions.

The management literature interpreting present and projecting future developments is indeed large, but five representative items may be cited: Warren Bennis, *Beyond Bureaucracy: Essays on the Development and Evolution of Human Organization* (1966); Harlan Cleveland, *The Future Executive; A Guide for Tomorrow's Managers* (1972); Peter F. Drucker, *The Age of Discontinuity: Guidelines to Our Changing Society* (1969); Jong S. Jun and William S. Storm, editors, *Tomorrow's Organizations* (1973); James D. Thompson, *Organizations in Action: Social Science Bases of Administrative Theory* (1967). While these books are cited as an introduction to the literature of Organizational Futurism, they provide commentary as well upon Organizational Humanism, Systems Theory, and the impact and implications of the computer. How, indeed, could the future of management be interpreted without relation to these matters?

The responsiveness and adaptivity of management presumably have been illustrated by these examples. What needs emphasis is that these are examples only. A full discussion would include attention to training techniques (the case method, executive seminars, and so forth) and interactions of management theory and practice with the several social sciences, as well as with psychology and statistics. It would as well give attention to the clustering of concepts and techniques indicated by such terms as decision theory, organization development, participative management, policy science, contingency theory—the latter, as might be surmised, being directed toward management in a changing, uncertain situation.

## DOES MANAGEMENT HAVE A FUTURE?

Presumably the reader will have observed some interrelations between the several "forces shaping future management," set forth above, and this brief look at recent and contemporary management adaptation. Organizational Humanism, for example, represents a response to the shift from the discipline of the factory and of classical bureaucracy to the more flexible, knowledge-based organizations envisaged by the post-industrialists, as well as a response to the decline of traditional sources of authority. Systems Theory is used in accommodating to a world of increasing numbers of organizations that have varied and changing relationships. Organizational Futurism represents an attempt to see, globally, the forces acting on and the challenges to management. In its close engagement with computer technology management itself participates in the postindustrial transition.

This is not to assert, of course, that management is satisfactorily addressing—or even addressing—all the problems posed by the forces that move and change the world (whatever they are). There are a number of these problems that, in my view, are "heroic" and deserving of the most serious and concentrated effort it is possible to muster.

One of these is the future of the venerable and honorable concept of the Public Interest. What meaning does it have, and how should it be institutionalized and realized, in a world increasingly "gray" and "horizontal"? Another is how to effect a reconciliation between or a merger of the concept(s) of economic rationality and the concept(s) of political rationality, if it is a given that these two worlds will be increasingly blended. (In this connection it may be observed that some economists assert that economics, usually judged the most advanced and scientific of the social sciences, must start anew from different premises.) These two "heroic" problems may in fact be the *same* problem.

On the evidence, management is not a fixed set of techniques related to a stable world but a focus of attention and center of action that displays considerable creativity and adaptability. In fact, it is clear that management has actively participated in the creation of the fluidity and instability some now predict cannot be "managed." But does management have *enough* creativity and adaptability?

For this question there is no answer. There is no answer because there are so many unknowns and imponderables, and because the future can only be guessed, not foretold. More fundamentally, however, there is no answer because the question is not a proper question: there is no definition or measure of "enough." Enough of what, for what?

Answering such questions is of course what the fundamental enterprises of religion, science, and philosophy are about. What is certain is that when these have spoken—and blind chance as well—management will still be there. As long, that is, as civilization is still there.

---

# Strategies for the Essential Community
## Local Government in the Year 2000

Laurence Rutter

How will cities, counties, and regional councils of governments meet the challenges posed by economic changes, demographic shifts, new urban patterns, and technological and political changes in the next two decades? The International City Management Associ-

From *The Futurist* (June, 1971), Vol. 13, pp. 19–28. Copyright 1981, World Future Society. Reprinted by permission.

ation's Committee on Future Horizons of the Profession, in a recent study, concluded that the best approach is what they called nurturing the essential community through four strategies: getting by modestly, regulating demand, skeptical federalism, and finding the proper scale and mix for government services.

## GETTING BY MODESTLY

The prevailing view of local government—what can be called its current paradigm—assumes future growth. This expectation pervades our thinking about cities, counties, and councils of government (COGs). The paradigm calls for budgets to grow, federal grants to increase, incrementalism to reign, wealth to rise, roles to expand, and benefits to improve. Nearly every decision made in city halls or county courthouses has been based on the assumption that growth is inevitable.

The paradigm has been relatively valid for the last 30 years or so. Cities and counties have grown steadily and, it seems, inexorably. Local governments were inadequately prepared for a great deal of the growth; "better" governments were those that prepared for growth better.

Reality may be outstripping the paradigm, however. Straws in the wind indicate that growth—both economic and demographic—is not inevitable. Holding the line indefinitely may become the order of the decade for public sector organizations. For successful negotiation of the 1980s and 1990s, policy strategies will be based on the assumption that the scope of local government can just as easily contract or remain constant as grow.

### Budgets

Getting by modestly will translate into budgeting strategies that are not based on the assumption of incremental growth. These strategies do not yet have names, but they will be in great demand and will be difficult to implement. The difficulty arises because without incrementalism it will be hard, if not impossible, to cover up who wins and who loses—the politics of the shrinking pie. If the pie grows, losses can be masked because everyone's slice increases at least a little even though proportions change. No growth means it is harder to buy off the losers.

Emerging budgeting strategies must be based on the recognition that it will be much harder to reallocate resources in both the short and the long run. Surprising though it may seem, when inflation is brought under control the problems for municipal budgets will be exacerbated. Inflation at least gives the appearance—a false and pernicious one, admittedly—of growth.

## Public/Private Cooperation

Getting by modestly also will require increased involvement of the private sector in traditionally public sector concerns—meaning greater pressures to transfer services from one sector to the other. Contracting out will be much more popular, but writing these contracts with the good of the public in mind will test local government ingenuity. Private sector support will become much more important in local government decision-making. And cities and counties will have an interest in improving the climate for the private sector, especially in the area of unnecessary regulation and red tape.

## Volunteers

The trend toward professionalization of the municipal work force will be halted. Volunteerism will become necessary if not fashionable.

The key to use of volunteers is to distinguish between truly professionial and quasi-professional services and between essential and nonessential activities. Volunteers can perform quasi-professional and nonessential services in the interest of getting by with less.

Quasi-professionalism is not the same as unskilled activity. Volunteers can be trained, as thousands of volunteer firefighters can testify. They can perform medical, patrol, maintenance, and other functions on a par with paid employees.

## Self-help

Another way in which local governments can get by with less is to help people do for themselves what they have come to expect local government to do for them.

This is not volunteerism, where people contribute to the common good, but rather individual self-help, where people take control of their own lives—a control that could be even more tenuous in the future. Local government can help people recognize their own skills, resources, and abilities to deal with the problems that beset them.

Citizens are losing the opportunity to help themselves, to learn about their own capacities to cope and grow. Machines and government have taken over, and both are likely to take over more unless checked in the future.

The programs and the machines have laudable objectives and frequently are necessary. But they have contributed to people's loss of control. People remain passive toward the machine, which cannot provide sympathy, cannot be reasoned with, and cannot handle capricious or out-of-the-ordinary activities.

People increasingly assume that their personal problems can, or at least should, be handled by government. But consumer protection is no substitute for caveat emptor. Safety helmets are not tantamount to defensive driving. Safety regulations are not a substitute for prudence.

There is every indication that people's sense of powerlessness will increase in the future. The demographic projections for the next 20 years suggest a real possibility of great atomization—smaller families, fewer marriages, and more divorces. And the growth of telecommunications as a substitute for personal contact will increase the tendency toward anomie among individuals.

At the same time, local governments and the public sector at large will no longer be able to assume a great many social burdens. Surely one solution will be for cities and counties to help citizens themselves shoulder some of the responsibilities for their lives.

With some initial assistance, citizens and commercial establishments can undertake a great many activities for which they may not be willing to pay taxes. They can sweep the streets in front of their homes or buildings, especially if receptacles for the sweepings are readily available. If proper tools are provided, they can trim and spray trees in front of homes or businesses and even maintain neighborhood parks and clean up after their animals. In a few cases, local governments have succeeded in changing from back door to curbside refuse pickup, but with considerable protest.

Political and civic leadership is the key to changing the psychology from "this is someone else's responsibility" to "this is my responsibility." And leadership should primarily be by example.

## Risk

Getting by modestly also may require coming to grips with what might be called the zero-risk ideal, the tendency to overprotect at the expense of taxpayers. The question to examine is how many public policies and standards for municipal services are based on the belief that the risk of failure or of an undesirable event should be zero. The question is, Can the public sector afford to pay for reducing the risk to zero?

In fire safety, for instance, should we work toward zero risk of property loss? Or is some degree of risk acceptable—providing we continue to reduce loss of life? Is having a community volunteer fire company more important than a certain small loss of property? How much do we pay for a decrease of 1% in the risk of property loss? In police protection, how much patrolling would be necessary to reduce the incidence of mugging? Can we afford the cost? Or is there an acceptable level of risk given the cost?

The answers to such questions do not preclude a city or county from working toward zero risk. But it may cause them to assess the cost more accurately and appreciate the cost of government generally. It also may make people recognize that they are willing to run certain risks, that such risks are implicit in almost all public policies, and that exposing the public to some risk is not inhumane.

## Labor

Getting by modestly involves some important challenges for the public employer and employee. One of the straws in the wind is a reduction of upward mobility in the work force. Too many people will be competing for too few jobs at the top.

The new paradigm will require facing up to the fact that within each jurisdiction the possibilities for advancement will decrease. The problem can be ameliorated only through finding ways to improve working conditions, involve employees in management-level decisions, and encourage interjurisdictional mobility.

Rigid job classifications must be relaxed so that employees can change the nature of the tasks they perform, learn new skills, and have an opportunity for variety if not upward mobility in their work.

Advancement in the future also will require the ability to move between jurisdictions. Patrol personnel wanting to become sergeants should be able to change jurisdictions to advance when opportunities arise. To permit such mobility, a great many local personnel policies and traditions will have to be changed. Pension requirements will need to be altered. Future entrance and examination requirements should not penalize outside applicants. Department managers will need to appreciate the importance of at least not discouraging mobility among personnel.

Few of these policies are going to be easy to implement. Yet the lack of growth in the public sector and the economic adjustments and demographic changes in the future make them necessary.

## REGULATING DEMAND

Some of the same forces—economic and demographic —that will require local governments to get by modestly will also require them to find ways to influence the demand for both public and private goods and services.

### Price

One important and under-utilized way to reduce demand for government services is the use of a pricing system. A price on a service increases the threshold of use. People learn to think twice about taking advantage of a city or county service if there is a personal, out-of-pocket cost. The cost need not reflect the full cost of the service, but it should be high enough to discourage unnecessary or spurious use. It also causes users to take more personal interest in the delivery of the service.

Prices or fees can be associated with services in numerous ways. Weekly trash pickup may be viewed as a necessity in some communities, twice weekly pickup a useful service, and three times weekly a luxury. It may be possible by imposing fees on a block-by-block basis to allow people to choose the level of service they prefer. Wealthier neighborhoods may want pickups three times a week. Others may be satisfied with a weekly pickup at no charge—the cost being borne by taxes.

The same may apply to police patrol. In Maryland, for instance, the state police literally lease their officers on a county-by-county basis in a "resident trooper program." Some counties are willing to pay for resident troopers; some are not. There is no reason to preclude the same kind of program with municipal or county police on a neighborhood-by-neighborhood basis for patrol purposes.

The price creates a threshold to dampen demand; yet it allows all citizens to receive at least a minimum level of service. Taxes can be minimized and government held to a market-determined size.

Prices also can be used to reduce aggregate demand for consumer and industrial goods and to reduce the side effects of this demand. For example, pricing systems can be built into land subdivision policies to reduce urban sprawl (and the high governmental costs associated with sprawl) and to better control both initial and long-range costs for transportation, water and sewer services, and other services that will be provided in the new area. Much of this pricing is not new: most cities for many years have required land developers to install streets, sewer and water lines, sidewalks, street lights, and other facilities at their own expense for the land within the subdivision boundaries.

Pricing also can be used by local governments to reduce waste and pollution, the costs of which are eventually passed on to citizens through the tax system. Instead of building waste treatment plants, local governments could concentrate on placing a price on collection of effluent and solid waste from both residential and commercial establishments, a price large enough to discourage the waste itself. The price could be based on a unit of waste collected.

Two caveats must be offered here.

One is to recognize the complexity of the market system itself, a system in which prices are a prime ingredient. Price levels can affect all facets of the economic system and cause ripples throughout the community. Prices should not be imposed without analysis of the possible consequences far beyond the immediate goods or services involved.

The second caveat relates to equity. Prices can deprive people of services they badly need. Local governments must be careful to use highly targeted subsidies to prevent the very poor from choosing to forgo vital services.

## Energy

Energy is the most important area in which demand needs to be reduced throughout society. Local government has a role to play, a role that is part regulation, part pricing, and part leadership.

Building codes need to be updated to reflect community concerns for energy conservation, and they need to be flexible enough to accommodate unanticipated future technological developments. New buildings especially are susceptible to codes that set standards for insulation, site, and types of heating units. Codes can specify that buildings should be capable of being retrofitted for solar energy when it becomes more competitive with oil and electricity. A number of communities, such as Davis, California, have already updated their codes.

It may be that the process of enforcing energy-related building codes needs to be updated along with the codes themselves. Some communities are using "energy audits," whereby inspectors use visual inspection and/or computers to identify opportunities to save energy costs in heating and cooling. One community in Minnesota uses federally supported employees to help citizens identify ways to make their homes and business establishments more energy-efficient.

Many local governments are directly involved in supplying energy to citizen-customers through their own public utilities. These governments can increase energy efficiency over the next two decades by establishing pricing systems that reduce peak load demand for electricity or penalize users for excessive energy consumption.

Many other local governments have taken the view that leadership by the city, county, or COG is an important element in encouraging individual conservation. The new city hall in Vineland, New Jersey is an example of what has been called a "smart building," with a computer-based system that constantly monitors and adjusts temperatures to conserve energy. Sherman, Texas has developed a comprehensive plan of energy use designed to help identify short- and long-term conservation opportunities for the city. Springfield, Missouri has converted a bus into a mobile educational lab, teaching citizens how to conserve energy.

These activities are the wave of the future for local governments as they mobilize to limit demand.

## SKEPTICAL FEDERALISM

Still other strategies for nurturing the essential community should be considered by local citizens, elected officials, and their management staffs.

One is a skeptical federalism, one that contemplates buying back local independence from the national government. It will be no easier than getting by modestly. And it could be very costly.

The committee believes that cities, counties, and COGs run considerable risk of being swallowed up by the central government. They run the risk of losing the ability to determine their own priorities, run their own programs, hire their own personnel, and fashion their communities in the way their citizens desire.

It is conceivable that by the year 2000 most local governments will get substantially more than one-half their revenue from the central and state governments and raise few of their resources locally. Moreover, it is conceivable that if local governments raised no resources independently, the vast majority of their essential activities would be circumscribed by the central government.

There is only one way to prevent this from happening with any certainty, and that is for local governments to buy back their independence from the central government while they have the resources to do the job.

In simple terms, it is a matter of money. Given the interpretation of the Constitution by the courts, when local governments accept federal money, they are subject to any conditions that might legally be placed on that money. The trend in recent years has been for Congress to impose more and more conditions, and as yet no court has declared a condition unconstitutional. The more dependent local governments become, the bolder will be the Congress and the president in imposing conditions on them.

A reversal is vastly easier said than done. Short-term political considerations make it extremely difficult to turn down grants from the central government. Yet some way needs to be found at least to make programs, from revenue sharing to historical preservation, less attractive.

### Taxes

First, locally raised taxes should be made more palatable. The property tax as it is currently structured in most places is a very unpopular tax—and with good reason.

Many local governments make annual reassessments of real property, a policy intended to keep the property tax equitable. But experience in California and other states has shown that annual reassessments force assessed property values to keep in step with market prices and, therefore, with the relentless forces of inflation.

Another frequently cited problem with the property tax is that it measures only the present market value of the property and not the owner's current ability to pay tax on it. Thus, the tax falls most heavily on the poor and those living on fixed incomes, except in places that have some sort of circuit breaker for these groups.

Many people have called for the abolition of the property tax because it is widely perceived to be one of the most unfair taxes currently levied. Yet without it,

many local governments would be at a loss to replace that local revenue base and would further lose their independence. And a persuasive argument can be made that land and buildings are an appropriate base for many local taxes and the services these taxes pay for. Many essential local government functions exist for the maintenance and protection of property. Water and sewer services, zoning, and waste collection maintain or enhance the value of property. Police and fire services protect property. Zoning and land use controls and building and occupancy codes regulate the use of property.

The nature, value, and dispersion of property are important determinants of the nature, cost, and intensity of a great many municipal services. A community with all frame homes has different fire suppression and code enforcement problems and services from one in which homes are brick or masonry. Apartments have a police protection problem different from that of single-family dwellings.

So it may not be entirely wise or equitable for local governments to abandon this tax. But changes are needed to make any tax in which property is a factor more equitable and politically palatable.

Cities and counties may want to consider:

- A property tax that is scaled to income as determined by a state or federal income tax.
- A property tax that delays the effects of rapid inflation—and perhaps rapid deflation as well—in land values (income averaging on the federal income tax may be a model for consideration).
- A tax that is levied on the sale of property.
- A tax that distinguishes more between land itself and the improvements on the land.

The fee-for-service concept also needs full exploration by local governments; it uses price to affect demand and is compatible with the notion of public/private cooperation.

### Grants

Maintaining a local tax base is only one part of the price of skeptical federalism. The other price is taking a particularly cold look at grants from the central government.

The governing body may want to set an annual ceiling on the level of federal and/or state money in the community. And it may want to consider reducing the level of this ceiling annually until it reaches a satisfactory minimum. Every community would have a different ceiling.

Skeptical federalism, in short, means knowing how and when to look a gift horse in the mouth, even when the family thinks the nag is charming—and then finding the money to get your own mount when the "free" horse looks suspicious.

## SCALE AND MIX OF GOVERNMENT

The fourth facet of the strategy for local governments over the next 20 years is finding the proper scale and mix for government services.

### Scale

The scale of services has been debated for years. The issue is whether local citizens, elected officials, and professional staff people should work to regionalize and/or decentralize the level at which local government programs and services are delivered.

The answer is that it all depends. The future, we believe, requires both regionalization and decentralization. But if there should be a pattern, it will be in the direction of decentralization of local services and programs.

#### REGIONALISM REEXAMINED

Regionalism is undergoing reexamination. For decades, the doctrine among urbanists was that local government should be regionalized. That consensus has broken down. Now some argue with equal conviction that small is always better, that smaller government is closer to the citizen and can operate municipal services more effectively.

The committee was impressed, but not completely convinced, that small is always better. It did come to realize, however, that many virtues of small-scale policymaking and service delivery have been overlooked. At the same time, however, large metropolitan areas have a compelling need for some regional units and decision-making bodies.

#### DECENTRALIZATION

The most important trend in terms of the scale of local government services will be in the other direction—decentralization.

Today a great many cities and counties are experimenting with decentralization. Administratively, the neighborhood "city hall" has been tried in Dayton, Ohio; Boston, Massachusetts; and other cities. The neighborhood planning commission is being tried in Washington, D.C. Politically, some communities are experimenting with having neighborhoods construct their own annual budgets, allocating funds among various services according to their preferences. Citizen groups naturally will focus on the neighborhood, following the decentralization of administrative and political activities.

The objective of decentralization should be to facilitate access of citizens to local government.

As with regionalism, however, decentralization eventually has limits. Some decisions must be made uniformly for the entire jurisdiction. Major zoning decisions cannot, and should not, be dealt with in isolation; but many variances are only neighborhood matters. The basic requirements for hiring police patrol personnel should be standard; but some neighborhoods may need specialized skills. Solid waste requires centralized collection control, but collection schedules can vary by neighborhood. Overall budget decisions must be made at the city or county council level, but neighborhoods can have many options within the framework of these decisions.

There are, in short, no easy rules. As a general proposition, localities should concentrate on the question of decentralization over the next decade or so. Yet a time will come when they will reach the limits of this important action. At the same time, they cannot ignore the regional picture and the need to strengthen their COGs. But the rules will invariably apply differently in every region and for every jurisdiction within the region.

#### CITIZEN INVOLVEMENT

One of the important keys to adjusting the scale of government to provide more direct access by citizens is the mechanisms to be used. Traditional methods will still be needed—public hearings, citizen representatives, complaint offices, neighborhood meetings, advisory committees, boards, commissions. But the telecommunications revolution offers added possibilities for reducing both the physical and the psychological distance between citizen and government.

Cable TV is a natural for increasing access. Experiments in Columbus, Ohio with the QUBE system, which offers two-way communication between subscriber and studio, open entirely new horizons. Cable systems can bring into everyone's home a forum for two-way discussions of vital community issues—zoning, land use, budgets, important ordinances, or whatever.

Cable TV also can allow more direct access by citizens to information from local governments. Video display terminals could be used by citizens in their own homes, or in nearby neighborhood offices, to renew drivers' licenses, check tax records, record complaints, change addresses, request special services, and perhaps even engage in some forms of personal counseling.

There are some obvious, and perhaps unobvious, problems inherent in this adaptation of telecommunications to citizen involvement. People have learned to trust television (through Walter Cronkite, for instance) and to take numbers (such as opinion polls) at face value. But there is nothing inherently authoritative about a TV screen. Misinformation can be communicated as easily as correct information. Viewers may or may not be a representative sample—and they may or may not be recording their true reactions. Moreover, there may be a great temptation with these systems to encourage direct as opposed to representative democracy. They could serve to bypass elected officials rather than assist them in reflecting the views of the public.

Another problem is confidentiality. Local governments should be particularly sensitive to this problem because much of the data held locally is of the most personal nature: personal property tax declarations, medical records, and so on.

## Mix

The mix of services provided by cities, counties, and COGs in the next 20 years will be determined in large part by the mix of people they serve. Demography is destiny. As the populations served by local governments change, so, too, will the priorities of the governing bodies.

We only can speculate about the effect population changes might have on local government priorities. But the speculation is important because some of these changes in priorities should be anticipated before they overtake our cities, counties, and COGs.

### THE ELDERLY

The specter of "gray power" has been sighted on the horizon as associations of retired people begin to gain local clout. The form such clout will take in the future

depends on what makes this population group unique. Will it have a separate and distinct set of needs that local governments can serve? Will it cause distinct problems? Here the committee finds itself of two minds. On one hand, it can identify a number of unique needs of the elderly, needs that will have to be given more attention in the next two decades. On the other hand, it questions whether the definition of "elderly" that we use today will apply in 2000.

Today we think of the elderly as those over 65 years of age, because they are very likely to be retired, to live on fixed incomes, to have high mortality rates from disease, and to be approaching the limits of their life expectancy.

It is not at all clear that those over 65 in the year 2000 will be so easily categorized. Given the continuing trend toward elimination of mandatory retirement, the fact that life expectancy is probably increasing, and the inability of the working part of the population to pay for early retirement and a sustained income throughout life, it is possible that what we once defined as elderly—65 and older—may no longer fit. It may be 70 and older. Or 75.

If "elderly" is redefined, the population with similar needs will become smaller. Nonetheless, local governments will need to begin now anticipating some changes in the mix of services based on the aging of the population.

Transportation is one area of major concern. The jitney bus, the short-run shopping bus, and the subsidized cab may all be in considerable demand. The elderly probably will require this service, because most will be highly mobile, probably gainfully employed part time, but unable to afford the very expensive automobile fuels of the future.

In housing, there will be an even greater demand for multihousehold dwellings, conveniently located close to shopping and entertainment facilities. The dwellings need not be publicly subsidized, but they will present some challenges, especially in land use planning. It is conceivable that single complexes will be devoted exclusively to the elderly who are dependent on public transportation and who need to be within walking distance of major commercial areas and medical care facilities. This demand may require specialized police patrol and assistance programs and specially equipped fire service personnel.

The elderly, no matter what their age, will have special recreation needs that have been largely overlooked by most local governments. Swings, jogging tracks, and, in some cases, swimming pools may not fill the bill.

Another problem is clearly pensions. The growth in the percentage of the work force that will be retired in the next 20 years is alarming. Politically and economically, it will be very difficult for pension programs to require, as many do today, that current workers pay for the currently retired.

This will hit local governments' own pension programs hard. Those not fully funded now will find it increasingly difficult to shoulder the burden.

The result almost certainly will be that current workers will contribute some more, but retirees will be getting relatively less in the way of retirement benefits. This alone will present local councils with some nasty political decisions. Another result will be that people who once planned to stop working at retirement age will have to return to the work force at least part time.

Employment opportunities will be one order of the problem, largely for the public sector. But the support services to sustain part-time employment will be a local problem. Transportation has been mentioned. Now we support those who work on a full-time basis by rush-hour bus service and automobile traffic control measures. With more part-time elderly, the non-peak hours of the present will become peak hours of the future. Recreation facilities, too, may need more flexible hours.

As the elderly increase in number, political influence, and personal freedom, we may see some changes in local politics. Many more of the elderly may be interested in seeking public office, serving on boards and commissions, and presenting their cases to councils. Some observers allege that today's officeholders are younger than they once were. Tomorrow the reverse may be true, thus bringing different orientations, values, expectations, time horizons, and energy to public life.

### THE YOUNG

There will be proportionately fewer young people in the year 2000 than today. We can see this happening already, with the closing of schools throughout the country for lack of sufficient enrollment. This was a trend that took most of us by surprise, and we are determined that similar trends should not do so in the future. To that end, the committee urges communities not to dispose of their school buildings and youth recreation centers too quickly. Between 1982 and 1992 —depending on what assumptions are made—the Bu-

reau of the Census, in *Social Indicators, 1976,* sees an upswing in the number of people under 24 years of age. These people will be needing the schools that are being closed today.

### WOMEN

Women will continue to be a larger proportion of the population than men and to enter the work force in increasing numbers. Their effect on the mix of services provided by local governments will change accordingly.

The day of the woman volunteer subsidizing vital local services is about to end. Local leaders should recognize the growing unpopularity of volunteering among many women, who now are demanding full pay for such activity. This may serve as a counterforce to the desire of local governments to change many services from a professional to a volunteer basis. But as women become more independent and need independent income, they will find volunteering less attractive.

Day care is no passing need. In the future, day care is likely to play an even greater role in the lives of children than it did in the past. It will extend beyond preschool to school-age children who require care in the early mornings or late afternoons—and to children of mothers who travel on the job or on weekends. Recreational facilities may assume the job of providing day care-type services seven days a week, eight to twelve hours a day, to accommodate the needs of these mothers.

Male underemployment may be another consequence of women's growth spiritually, politically, and economically in society, especially if the economy does not produce sufficient jobs for both sexes. The result, once the considerable problems of personal adjustment are mastered, may be that men will become the volunteers of the future—and campaigns to recruit, train, and deploy volunteers to help the community should begin planning for such an adjustment.

### MINORITIES

Over the next 20 years, as today, minorities will be concentrated in certain areas. A great proportion of blacks will be in the Northeast, the Midwest, and the South. Hispanics will be found in large numbers in the Southwest; Native Americans in the Midwest and West.

Affirmative action among all these groups will still be needed, but its implementation in 2000 may be unrecognizable by today's standards. Although we

21

must not slack off our current local governments' commitment to bring minorities into the work force of our cities, counties, and COGs, the new affirmative action will be focused more on preventing slippage and dealing with the problems of people at midcareer, who will then be part of the baby-boom cohort competing for limited jobs.

Beyond affirmative action, local governments will need to be aware of the needs of Hispanics in particular. Language will be the most important problem, as many Hispanics will not speak English adequately to compete in the labor market.

Special efforts will be needed on two fronts. The first will be to make every effort to help Hispanics compensate for language barriers by installing bilingual signs; hiring bilingual local government employees, especially in reception areas; and producing special printed and broadcast material for Hispanic communities. The second should be a strong effort to provide English-language training for non-native speakers. This will mean incorporating language instruction into adult education and recreation programs and building it into special regular school curricula.

### SMALLER HOUSEHOLDS

The declining size of the household will bring about some changes similar to those required for the elderly —the need for multifamily dwellings, for example. Indeed, the change in household size may revamp many traditional images of the ideal home setting for a large number of Americans.

We can see the image changing from the half-acre lot with the four-bedroom house and two-car garage in the planned unit development. In its place will be much smaller homes, many garden apartments, and town houses. People will make much more use of recreation and social settings outside the home (since no one will be home in many more cases).

Smaller homes and lots will have several implications for local governments. The number of water and sewer hookups will continue to grow, but the use of these facilities per thousand population may decline. At any given time, fewer homes will be physically occupied by the tenant, making neighborhood security and patrolling by police more important. In some suburbs with very large houses, there may be more demand to use the houses for "group homes" or even to subdivide them into apartments.

As local governments enter the 1980s and 1990s, these are just a few of the changes in the mix of services provided, changes brought about by the fluctuating demographics of urban living.

So the mix of local services as well as the scale of their delivery will need adjustment over the next 10 to 20 years. This will be another strategy for nurturing the essential community, along with learning how to get by modestly, beginning to regulate demand for services, and buying back independence from the national government.

All this is a very complex, difficult, and challenging agenda for the future horizon of citizens, elected leaders, and their top professional managers.

---

## Scarcity and Environmental Stress in Public Organizations
### A Conjectural Essay

Barry Bozeman
E. Allen Slusher

*Some observers, including many "doomsday" futurists, have contended that a predominant characteristic of future society will be extreme scarcity. Viewing this assumption of extreme scarcity as plausible (though not necessarily most probable), this conjectural essay considers some of the possible effects of sustained scarcity, particularly sharp declines in public spending and public employment, on public organization behavior. The focus is on the effects of scarcity on four types of strategic choices in public organizations: domain selection, development and deployment of technology, organization structure, and organization process. Arguments are developed that public organizations facing sustained scarcity could be expected to: constrain their domain definition, allow domain selection to dictate technology, seek clientele suited to existing technologies, and in general, take actions that will ensure that existing technologies are employed at capacity. Further, we argue that narrow efficiency criteria will become paramount and will give rise to more formal, centralized, and rigid organization structures and a habituation of organizational responses to environmental change.*

---

From *Administration & Society,* Vol. 11, No. 3, pp. 335–356. Copyright 1979 by Sage Publications, Inc., with permission.

"Thinking about the unthinkable," to borrow Kahn's (1960) well-turned phrase, has been the fashion for some time now. Kahn's original unthinkable was thermonuclear war, but recently futurists have concerned themselves with additional unthinkables relating to such perils as population explosion, depletion of natural resources, and unbridled pollution (Meadows et al., 1972; Mesarovic and Pestel, 1974; Forrester, 1971; Renshaw, 1976).

Public administrators are among those captivated and, one supposes, influenced by such studies. But if public administrators have been stimulated by studies of global unthinkables, they have been jolted by a new unthinkable that strikes closer to home—sustained decline in public spending. Understandably, public administrators are likely to find a tax revolt (or any other stimulus to widespread cutbacks) more gripping than even the most apocalyptic computer-based model of planetary doom.

Students of public administration have also been attentive to trends toward decline and have provided helpful analyses and prescriptions (McCaffery, 1978; Levine, 1978). Most of these studies have addressed current or intermediate-term problems of decline and provided realistic assessments of present conditions or trends. They have been, by and large, concerned with our current "age of inconvenience." In this essay we ponder some of the possible effects of sustained, long-range economic decline on public organization behavior. What if current shortfalls and cutbacks are exacerbated and extreme scarcity comes to be taken as a given? How might we expect public organization behavior to differ in an "age of unrelenting scarcity"?

We do not argue, let us hasten to note, that such an extreme scarcity scenario is *most* probable, only that it is sufficiently plausible to demand our attention. Our aim is to move toward "surprise-free scenarios" (to borrow again from futures studies parlance) rather than to develop a "most-probable scenario."

Our assumptions are gross and simple. We assume a precipitously declining rate of economic growth (in the United States and the industrialized world). We assume that general economic decline will be accompanied by a sharp decline in public spending, in the number of public employees, and in the number of public organizations. We further assume that the government can do nothing to reverse the trend.[1] Since our purpose is not prediction but speculation, we are not interested in providing more specific (and constraining) assumptions and we are not concerned with

providing clear-cut linkages between our highly general assumptions and our somewhat more specific conclusions. We contend that such broad license is appropriate, given that: (1) our chief aim is to stimulate reflection, discussion, and argument; (2) for purposes of *speculation* we need care little about the causes of scarcity so long as it is sustained and so long as the government can do little to remedy the condition; (3) any forecast is so ensnared in logical problems (Rescher and Helmer, 1959; Bozeman, 1977) that higher degrees of specification lend nothing to the verifiability of the forecast. Moreover, our concern is with the suggestive value of our conjecture.

## SCARCITY, STRESS, AND STRATEGIC CHOICE

Our focus is on the impact of increasing scarcity and stress on organizational choice, particularly as a function of changes in available technology and resources. Organizations can be viewed as facing four types of strategic choices (Child, 1972; Miles et al., 1974):

1. What portion of the organization's environment should be selected as its area of activity, or *domain*?
2. What *technology* should be developed to enable the organization to manage the constraints and opportunities in its domain?
3. What *structure* is most appropriate to control the organization's technology?
4. What *processes* must be established to insure the organization's adaptation to environmental change?

Although it will be convenient in some instances to think of the organization as a self-conscious decision unit making strategic choices (just as it is sometimes convenient for psychologists to conceptualize human choice in terms of a "mind"), in reality strategic choices are made by individuals—often in a halting, haphazard, and only partly self-conscious manner—and "outcomes" reflect the aggregation of such individual choices as matched to available resources (see Weick, 1969). Strategic choices are best viewed as broad commitments based on streams of administrative decisions, actions, and resources converging in response to choice opportunities. Often, organizational processes proceed according to the "garbage can" model: solutions seeking problems, decision makers seeking (and framing) decision-making opportunities (Cohen et al., 1972).

## ORGANIZATION DOMAINS

Early, closed-system views of organizations ignored the environment because it was generally simpler and posed fewer problems for administration than internal factors. As environments became more complex and problematic, theorists adopted an essentially reactive view of organization-environment relations (Scott, 1961). This reactive approach focused on how the organization reacts internally to forces which impinge upon it from the environment. For example, a highway department reacts to an urban growth pattern by constructing new highways. Of course, a more proactive stance by the organization may also be taken. A highway department can certainly influence urban development by its plans for highway construction. Organization theorists have begun to adopt a primarily proactive view of the organization in relation to its environment. However, organizations exercise varying degrees of control over environmental elements. Although most administrators would probably agree with this conclusion, it is less certain that they would see themselves as having a role in selecting their organization's domain.

Implicit in the concept of organization domain is the assumption of a proactive organization. However, the domain concept is more basic and inclusive. Whereas the reactive-proactive perspective is concerned with which environmental elements or forces are controllable and which are uncontrollable, domain is concerned with which elements are actually considered by the organization. That is, the organization has the ability, within limits, to define or enact its own environment (Weick, 1969). This choice of domain has pervasive and fundamental effects on the organization. Although legislative acts or executive orders typically provide broad outlines for the public organization's domain, the organization usually retains some ability to interpret and operationalize its domain.

Perrow (1970) provides an instructive illustration. He contrasts two homes for juvenile delinquent boys (i.e., with the same general domains), one defining its mission as custodial and the other seeing its mission as rehabilitative (i.e., with different specific domains). These divergent definitions led to different technologies, structures, and administrative processes. The custodial home used a routine technology, centralized de-

cision making, and few staff personnel. In contrast, the rehabilitative home had a more flexible technology and more open structure in transforming human input. We can imagine quite different domains for the two homes. The rehabilitative home probably existed in an environment where community action groups, schools, and job-training programs were relevant elements. For the custodial home, police, probation officers, and courts were surely more important.

Administrators typically do not recognize their role in choosing a domain because in actuality it is the culmination of many decisions regarding the environment rather than a discrete choice. Thus, to understand the effects of future trends on domain selection, it is necessary to examine how these trends would affect a multiplicity of administrative decisions. Among the most important of such decisions are those which establish and maintain independence with other organizations.

Many observers have noted that the relevant environment for complex organizations is increasingly consisting of other organizations (see, for example, Pfeffer, 1972). The economy of scarcity should intensify this development. With resource scarcity, we would expect: (1) organizations to represent less varied interests, (2) greater heterogeneity among these organizations (Aldrich, 1971), and (3) competition among organizations. In short, the public organization's environment will become more complex, dynamic, and interdependent. Such turbulent environments result in more demands on the organization (Terreberry, 1968; Emery and Trist, 1965). These conclusions are hardly surprising, but we must also examine the effects of scarcity on organizations' strategic choices.

As their growth rate declines, public organizations will become more concerned about survival. Such concerns for survival, muted in a more munificent environment, conduce the organization to move from an emphasis on social problem solving to a position of more narrow self-interest (Bozeman and McAlpine, 1977; Straw and Szwajkowski, 1975). There will be more pressure to match the internal capability of the organization with its defined domain. That is, the organization will emphasize what it views as its "distinctive competencies." With fewer resources available, the public organization will have a lower perceived internal capability (Hall and Mansfield, 1971) and will therefore act to constrain its domain definition (Jurkovich, 1974). Even if the *level* of controlled environmental interaction stays constant or increases, the *scope* will be narrowed. Minority coalitions will not be able to substantially affect the organization's domain choice and the proportional size required for minimal winning coalitions is likely to increase (Cyert and March, 1963). Thus the constriction of domain is likely to accentuate internal conflict rather than build consensus around perceived distinctive competencies.

When the effects of scarcity on the external environment and the organization itself are jointly considered, a paradox arises. The public organization's turbulent environment is essentially demanding an increased domain. However, the organization's response is to constrict (or at least avoid expanding) its domain. That is, the organization's response is opposite that which would be predicted by usual adaptation models for dealing with environmental turbulence. Significantly, this is related to one of the chief differences in expectations of public and private organizations' response to scarcity. The firm can expand domain in the face of increasing environmental stress because it may be possible to overcome scarcity by generating profits that might be expected from diversification and increased market penetration. The public organization cannot expect a one-to-one correspondence between "market penetration" and "profit" (in the form of increased appropriations or other revenues). The incentive for domain expansion is reduced. Also, even during periods of scarcity, the public organization can expect that a failure to appropriately expand or adjust its domain will not necessarily be fatal to the organization. In terms of both reward and punishment for modification of the domain, the private organization can expect that effects will be more direct and more swiftly realized.

## TECHNOLOGY

We define *technology* in the broadest sense, referring to the skills, equipment, and knowledge necessary to transform materials, information, and people into desired outputs. As available public revenues shrink and the reservoir of available human resources becomes depleted, the public organization will shift from relatively labor-intensive technologies. This shift will have two basic effects. First, the movement represents a change from a more generally applicable technology to more specific forms. The equipment, employee skills, and operating procedures are more specialized. The major implication of this technological specialization is that the organization will be less able to respond

to changing environmental demands. We have already argued that the public organization will attempt to narrow its domain. The organization is therefore able to screen out those environmental elements for which the technology is ill-suited. Constraining the domain definition allows (and often requires) the organization to move toward more specialized technologies.

A second and related effect of more specialized technology (and constricted domain) is to reverse the direction of causality between domain choice and technology choices. Under less stressful conditions we expect the organization to develop technology that is responsive to domain. For example, we would expect programs (part of the organization's technology) to be developed to serve client demands (an aspect of domain). But there is good reason to expect that the sequence will be reversed under assumptions of extreme scarcity. Given assumptions of scarcity, there is little hope that a highly developed technology will be enhanced by additional resource inputs. The problem for the organization is to maximize the productive capacity of the technology, thereby avoiding "technological slack" (underutilized productive capacity) that might be expected to lead to further decrements in available resources. It is not only cost efficient, but it is in all likelihood politically expedient to operate the technology at capacity and to avoid modifications. The organization can be expected to pursue a strategy of playing to past technological success. One upshot of this strategy is that public organizations will seek to serve clients (or problems) for which a technology exists. Indeed, organizations will seek to create a perception of need for the technology among clients. One can expect vigorous marketing of existing, well-developed and under-utilized technologies because "technological slack" is to be avoided at all costs.

At another level, a psychological interpretation for this behavior can be provided. We have predicted that organizations will seek to minimize modifications in existing specialized technologies and will respond to change by seeking to implement existing technologies in repetitive fashion. We expect this behavior on efficiency grounds, but we can also expect this behavior on the grounds that it is a characteristic response set to stress. Cowen's (1952) study of the effects of stress on problem-solving rigidity indicated that prolonged stress is related to increasing decision-making rigidity. In another laboratory study, Moffit and Stagner (1956) reported that subjects under stress exhibited habitual response and inflexibility in decisional behavior. Additionally, in a study of the relationship between human information processing and stress, Smock (1955) found that subjects under stress were more intolerant of ambiguous information and more likely to disregard communications that were not clearly coded. While the relevance of these findings for organization behavior under assumptions of resource scarcity cannot be straightforwardly demonstrated, clearly strategic choice in organizations is an aggregation of human decisions and we might well expect that stress would have patterned effects on those decisions.

To summarize, we expect that increasing specialization of technology and the organization's attempts to shelter core technologies will lead to behaviors that are woefully maladaptive. The organization responds to a more turbulent environment by habitually applying well-developed technologies (that are likely to be less responsive to a broad range of environmental demands), thereby further constraining choice of domain. Dysfunction builds upon dysfunction.

Another aspect of technology deserves attention. When Thompson's (1967) typology for technology (i.e., long-linked, mediating, intensive) is applied, the importance of mediating technology is seen as increasing in public organizations. Since public organizations are less capable of providing desired services, external groups are more likely to become involved in activities that fill residual demand. The public organization may emerge as a broker that links clients with privately developed programs. The reason for the shift from public provider to private provider is straightforward. Given reduced demand, it is often easier for a number of small private firms to move into a highly segmented and declining market than it is for a large public organization to quickly reduce its scale and diversify its services. The shift from a provider to a broker role has the advantage of allowing the public organization to exploit well-developed (but no longer serviceable) technologies in a new fashion. This might also help rationalize the continued employment of individuals whose programs have been abolished.

## ORGANIZATION STRUCTURE

As public organizations shift to more specialized technologies, their structures will be affected (Woodward, 1965; Child, 1973). Theorists have argued that organic and "free-form" structure is often suitable when the organization is required to adapt to a highly turbulent environment (Burns and Stalker, 1961; Lawrence and

Lorsch, 1967). We argue that public organizations responding to environmental stress created by extreme scarcity will erect more formalized and centralized structure. More formal and centralized structure is a reasonable response in that it matches the new specialized technology and organization form that emphasizes efficiency. In a turbulent but affluent environment, with organizations having considerable freedom to modify technology in the face of environmental change, we would expect the public organization to move toward organic or more flexible structure. But under conditions posited, the public organization is caught in a vicious cycle of "trained incapacity" (Jurkovich, 1974): Pressures cause the highly structured organization to become even more structured by habitual response. Eventually, the inadequacy of these responses may produce enough internal and external conflict to halt, or even reverse, the cycle. In the meantime the cost to both the organization and society may be great.

Despite the fact that public organizations will develop more rigid, hierarchical, and centralized structures, they will share one feature with most free-form organizations: heavy reliance on information technology. It has been observed that the only organization structure in the more fluid free-form organizations is the management information system (Ericson, 1972). Public organizations confronted with scarcity will also rely greatly on computer-based management information systems (MIS) but for different reasons. In free-form organizations the MIS is employed to route information among highly decentralized and changeable decision centers. Since no structure is allowed to "freeze," it is necessary to channel information along an elaborate and dynamic communications loop. One of the basic purposes of the MIS in this instance is to provide information that enables repeated structural modification. But in the public organization constrained by scarcity, the MIS serves a different purpose.

In the first place, the adoption and widespread use of the computer-based MIS is consistent with our assumption of a shift from labor-intensive technology. Furthermore, computer systems not only enable the administration to more effectively monitor and respond to change (Galbraith, 1973) but also allow more effective integration and coordination. Ultimately the MIS can be employed as a means of furthering centralization by channeling information to a single decision nexus and making possible a greater degree of managerial control. The computer's speed and ability to synthesize prodigious amounts of data permit decision making to be more centralized and hierarchical. Without such an MIS, organization response requires that decisions be diffused to lower organizational levels.

It should also be pointed out that extensive use of computer MIS can accentuate domain contraction and habitual response. The computer is useful for handling factual, quantitative data rather than qualitative, judgmental data. Thus it can be quite useful for monitoring delivery of existing technology and currently engaged domain but is of little help in exploring uncharted areas of the organization's environment. Also, any highly structured MIS has the effect of defining organizational reality according to the parameters of the system and has the potential, particularly in the absence of aggressive managerial leadership, of foreclosing decisional options that are outside its programmed definition of reality.

## INTERNAL ORGANIZATIONAL PROCESSES AND ADAPTATION

Throughout the discussion thus far has run a basic theme, that scarcity-induced stress will cause public organizations to behave as if their complex, dynamic, and interrelated environments are in fact, simple, static, and unrelated. These behaviors include narrower domain definitions, reduction in labor-intensive technology, increasing specialization of technologies, and more mechanistic structures with tighter administrative control. Anticipated changes in organizational processes will serve only to accelerate this closed system reaction.

Short-run administrative decisions are greatly influenced by whether the decision maker perceives the decision environment as relatively certain or relatively uncertain (Duncan, 1972). Just as the organization can select its own domain, individual administrators have the freedom to perceive their environments uniquely. Therefore, it is crucial that we consider the forces that affect administrative perceptions.

As the growth rate of public organizations declines and human resources become scarce (Wurzburg, 1970), the public sector work force will begin to stabilize.[2] For each individual public organization, the work force will be much more stable. Beyond its personnel management implications, this work force stability will greatly affect how the organization perceives its environment. Long-term employees are more likely to share common norms and values, reach consensus more easily, and become committed to their organization (Starbuck, 1976). That is, long-term employees are more likely to have similar perceptions of their organizational world. Thus we would expect narrow domain definition, inflexible technology, mechanistic structure, emphasis on accountability, and tight controls to impact somewhat uniformly on administrative perceptions. In particular, we would expect habitual or routine ways (March and Simon, 1958) of perceiving the environment to predominate. Moreover, such habitual perceptions cause the public organization to be relatively insensitive to environmental change. There is some support in the empirical research literature for the proposition that high degrees of organizational identification and low levels of employee turnover are negatively related to certain measures of effectiveness and creativity (Rondini, 1975).

The ability to adapt to an uncertain environment is largely a function of information processing capacities (Terreberry, 1968). Moreover, information processing depends on: (1) advance information, (2) active search, and (3) available memory store. Although computer-based administrative systems (an aspect of more specialized technology and a control orientation) are likely to increase the organization's memory capacity, they are less useful in dealing with the first two issues. The development of advance information requires effective monitoring of the environment. We have already argued that public organizations will perceive their environments in a more habitual fashion. Such habitual perceptual processes are insensitive to change and make for poor monitoring where sensitivity is essential. Advance information about the environment also depends on the feedback received from novel responses to the environment by the organization. However, the pressures for accountability will make it increasingly likely that compromise (or even computational) responses will push out inspirational approaches to the environment (Thompson, 1967). Search processes will be hampered because "novel informational inputs, as well as novel communication channels, often derive from change in personnel inputs" (Terreberry, 1968) and such personnel inputs to public organizations will be limited. Limited resources imply the centralization of authority and restriction of communication channels (Hermann, 1963), which limit search capability. Under conditions of scarcity there will be few rewards available for those administrators who attempt to actively engage their environments. Administrators will be preoccupied with playing an internal zero-sum game to protect their own sub-group's goals (March and Simon, 1958). Coalition struggles, particularly in the budgeting process (Pondy, 1970), can be expected to develop.

Conflict will be suppressed by the increasing symmetry of perceptions of the environment. But there will be greater divergence in individual and group abilities to affect internal distribution of resources. Thus, there are countervailing pressures, one serving to increase conflict, the other to reduce conflict. The effects of conflict on individual satisfaction and goal attainment (at all levels) will be best predicted by reinforcement theory (Cherrington, 1973). Organizations may, therefore, experience similar levels of conflict, but the conflict can be expected to have different effects (Schneider and Snyder, 1975).

Accountability, control, and long-range planning are organizational responses which assume that efficiency is paramount. However, in a turbulent environment, short-run efficiency may be purchased at the cost of long-run effectiveness. For example, "excess managerial capacity" may be inefficient, but it does provide resources, not committed to operating the technology, which are likely to push for an expanded organizational domain. Such expanded domains imply greater sensitivity to the changing environment and concern for adaptive responses.

## CONCLUSIONS

In our speculations about the impact of scarcity-based environmental stress on future public organizations, we have portrayed public organizations as, in many ways, congenitally maladaptive. The hypothesized effects are summarized in Table 1. The essential message is that environmental stress of the variety and magnitude assumed could be expected to breed structural rigidity, formalization, habitual response, and increasing interorganizational conflict—all potentially maladaptive. We should point out that not all our hypothesized responses to environmental stress are viewed as maladaptive; we expect that organizations will be encouraged by scarcity to take certain steps that could be useful even under assumptions of affluence (e.g., attempting to broker clients' needs with private providers' capacities).

Although the chief purpose of this essay has been to suggest some of the implications of scarcity for the structure and operations of public agencies, we would be remiss if we failed to suggest possible strategies for optimizing the social utility of organizations. There are two basic approaches that would be most fruitful —policy process innovation and organizational design. And we argue that the former should, conceptually and instrumentally, subsume the latter.

Organization design, as we use the term, refers to the systematic and self-conscious creation, adaptation,

**TABLE 1**
**Effects of extreme scarcity on public organizations**

| Domain | Technology | Structure | Process |
|---|---|---|---|
| 1. Greater heterogeneity between organizations in the domain | 1. Shift from labor-intensive to more specialized technologies | 1. More formalized, centralized, and rigid structure | 1. Habituation of responses to environment |
| 2. Greater competition and inter-organizational conflict | 2. Less adaptability of technology | 2. Closed, hierarchical decision-making | 2. Emphasis on accountability |
| 3. Constrained domain definition | 3. Domain choices dictated by technology | 3. Strong reliance on computer-based MIS | 3. Fewer rewards for engaging the environment, focus on internal zero-sum games |
| 4. Little internal participation in domain selection | 4. Seek (or establish) clientele suited to existing technology | 4. Structure constrains organizational choice | |
| | 5. Serve as broker (mediating technology) between clients and private groups | | |

and manipulation of organization structures, technologies, and processes in pursuance of social, organization, and/or individual goals. Policy process, by our usage, refers to patterns of behavior (by both organization members and relevant external actors) through which resources are converted into public programs and other binding decisions. By and large, we believe that organization design is important as a means of "coping" but is less significant than policy process innovation as a means of manipulating the environment from which the stress emanates. While organizational designs *can* have significant effects on policy, we view organization design as one component of policy processes. Since we believe that the problems presented by scarcity are best treated holistically, our approach to designing organizations is to treat organizations as a significant component of the whole (the policy process) and to consider the significance of organization design not only for efficiency of the organization but also (and predominately) for the contribution to policy effectiveness. This approach to analysis of organizations is not offered as *the* valid approach or, necessarily, as the approach that is of the greatest theoretical significance. We simply argue that for certain clusters of issues, particularly issues related to organizational ecology, it is often useful to consider the policy process as the essential unit of analysis, subsuming the organization.

Given this approach, what strategies might be suggested for managing scarcity-induced stress? First, attention must be given to decision or policy *types* that are conduced by stress. For example, our conclusions lead us to believe that regulatory policies (as a form) will increasingly dominate policy making. Such policies often require fewer of the organization's resources, can be more easily tailored to fit cases, and have considerably lower administrative costs than transfer or distributive policies. Much of the cost for regulation is shifted to the private sector.[3] If we assume that regulatory policies will be the predominant decision form, then there are implications for organizational design. Organizational technologies will increasingly be mediating technologies (this is consistent with other assumptions that we have made), and organization design should center on needs of mediating technologies.

Another example of our "policy process contingency" approach to organizational design: We feel that policy process innovations that promote information sharing and diffusion among public agencies might be

one of the keys to allaying the more unfortunate responses to environmental stress that we have predicted. A policy process innovation that might promote information sharing among public agencies—which now are prone to view information in almost as proprietary a fashion as private R&D firms (Allen, 1977)—would be to institute penalties for exclusionary treatment of policy-relevant information. The design implications that would sustain information sharing policy are numerous (we have discussed those implications elsewhere; see Bozeman, Slusher, and Roering, 1978).

In conclusion, we argue that the most suitable approach to coping with environmental stress brought about by resource scarcity is neither organizational design nor policy process innovation but a strategy that systematically (but creatively) integrates organizational design and policy process issues. Economists have long included policy response functions in economic models. It is time for organization designers to begin to think about incorporating policy response functions into the design of organizations. It is not enough to assume that organizational evolutions will provide a suitable "natural selection"; it is not enough (though it is certainly difficult) to design organizations to cope satisfactorily with undesirable environmental conditions. It is important to develop concepts, and later theories, that help us understand the reciprocal influence of policies, policy processes, and organization design. Until we develop such a body of knowledge we may have to be content designing adaptive but socially dysfunctional public agencies—a task for which we seem well prepared (Kaufman, 1976).

## NOTES

1. One might assume that an appropriate government response to general economic decline would be to increase public spending so as to stimulate economic growth. Such a response would be dictated by modern public finance theory, and, moreover, this response proved successful in coping with the Depression and subsequent recessions. But it must be remembered that this policy response is constrained by the existing ratio of public to private spending. In earlier times public spending was a relatively small percentage. A better parallel for modern times is the experience of the British and Scandinavian governments. Economists and public officials alike have discovered that there is a threshold effect, that at a certain level increases in public spending (as a proportion of GNP) not only fail to stimulate growth but

may have the opposite effect. We argue that the United States is approaching that threshold that has already been passed by many European governments and, therefore, a "prime-the-pump" approach to remedying economic decline will be (and will be perceived to be) an inadequate response to extreme scarcity in the future.

2. Some colleagues who have read this paper have suggested that public personnel unions can employ their increasing power to stem any effort to reduce the size of the public work force. We disagree with this position because we feel that public employee unions will have little impact on a reduction-in-forces (RIF) approach to reducing the public work force (aside from insisting that such reductions are made on a seniority basis, thus reinforcing our proposition about the stability and homogeneity of the work force). There is some evidence supporting our contention (Cebulski, 1977; Rosenbloom, forthcoming) and little evidence that public employee unions have been successful in quashing RIFs.

3. The private sector is becoming increasingly aware of the redistributive effects of regulation, and such groups as the Business Roundtable have taken steps to measure the costs of regulation. Also litigation is currently pending that would limit the ability of government to impose the costs of regulation on business. Obviously we are assuming that these efforts will not have important long-run effects. But if the costs of public regulation become a significant item on the policy agenda, our arguments regarding shifts in policy forms would have to be modified substantially.

*We are grateful for comments provided by David Rosenbloom, Steve Loveless, and two anonymous referees. This is a revised version of a paper presented at the annual meeting of the American Society for Public Administration, April 9–12, 1978, Phoenix, Arizona.*

## REFERENCES

ALDRICH, H. (1971) "Organizational boundaries and inter-organizational conflict." Human Relations 24: 279–293.

ALLEN, T. (1977) Managing the Flow of Technology. Cambridge, MA: MIT Press.

BOZEMAN, B. L. (1977) "Epistemology and futures studies: how do we know what we can't know." Public Administration Rev. 37: 544–549.

BOZEMAN, B. L. and W. E. McALPINE (1977) "Goals and bureaucratic decision-making: an experiment." Human Relations 30: 417–429.

BOZEMAN, B. L., E. A. SLUSHER, and K. ROERING (1978) "Social structure and the flow of scientific information in public agencies." Research Policy.

BURNS, T. and G. STALKER (1961) The Management of Innovation. London: Travistock.

CEBULSKI, B. (1977) Affirmative Action Versus Seniority —Is Conflict Inevitable? Berkeley: University of California Institute of Industrial Relations.

CHERRINGTON, D. J. (1973) "Satisfaction in competitive conditions." Organizational Behavior and Human Performance 19 (August): 47–71.

CHILD, J. (1973) "Predicting and understanding organizational structure." Administrative Sci. Q. 18: 168–185.

CHILD, J. (1972) "Organizational structure, environment, and performance: the role of strategic choice." Sociology 6, 1: 1–22.

COHEN, M., J. MARCH and J. OLSEN (1972) "A garbage can model of organizational choice." Administrative Sci. Q. 17: 1–25.

COWEN, E. L. (1952) "The influence of varying degrees of psychological stress on problem-solving rigidity." J. of Abnormal Psychology 47: 512–519.

CYERT, R. M. and J. MARCH (1963) A Behavioral Theory of the Firm. Englewood Cliffs, N J: Prentice-Hall.

DUNCAN, R. (1972) "Characteristics of organizational environments and perceived environmental uncertainty." Administrative Sci. Q. 17: 313–327.

EMERY, F. E. and E. L. TRIST (1965) "The causal texture of organizational environments," Human Relations 18: 17–27.

ERICSON, R. F. (1972) "Visions of cybernetic organizations." Academy of Management J. 15: 427–443.

FORRESTER, J. W. (1971) World Dynamics. Cambridge, MA: Wright-Allen.

GALBRAITH, J. (1973) Designing Complex Organizations. Reading, MA: Addison-Wesley.

HALL, D. J. and R. MANSFIELD (1971) "Organizational and individual response to external stress." Administrative Sci. Q. 16: 533–547.

HERMANN, C. (1963) "Some consequences and crises which limit the viability of organizations." Administrative Sci. Q. 8: 61–82.

JURKOVICH, R. (1974) "A core typology of organizational environments." Administrative Sci. Q. 19: 380–394.

KAHN, H. (1960) On Thermonuclear War. Princeton, N J: Princeton Univ. Press.

KAUFMAN, H. (1976) Are Government Organizations Immortal? Washington, D C: Brookings Institution.

LAWRENCE, P. and J. LORSCH (1967) Organization and Environment. Homewood, IL: Irwin.

LEVINCE, C. H. (1978) "Organization decline and cutback management." Public Administration Rev. 38: 316–332.

MARCH, J. and H. SIMON (1958) Organizations. New York: John Wiley.

McCAFFERY, J. [ed.] (1978) "A Symposium: Budgeting in an Era of Resource Scarcity." Public Administration Rev. 38: 510–544.

MEADOWS, D. H., D. L. MEADOWS, J. RANDERS, and W. BEHRENS (1972) The Limits to Growth. New York: Universe.

MESAROVIC, J. and E. PESTEL (1974) Mankind at the Turning Point. New York: Universe.

MILES, R., C. SNOW, and J. PFEFFER (1974) "Organization-environment: concepts and issues." Industrial Relations 13: 244–264.

MOFFIT, J. W. and R. STAGNER (1956) "Perceptual rigidity and closure as functions of anxiety." J. of Abnormal Psychology 52: 146–150.

PERROW, C. (1970) Organizational Analysis. Belmont, CA: Wadsworth.

PFEFFER, J. (1972) "Interorganizational influence and managerial attitudes." Academy of Management J. 15: 317–330.

PONDY, L. (1970) "Toward a theory of internal resource-allocation," in M. Zald (ed.) Power in Organizations, Nashville: Vanderbilt Univ. Press.

RENSHAW, E. F. (1976) The End of Progress. North Scituate, MA: Duxbury Press.

RESCHER, N. and O. HELMER (1959) "On the epistemology of the inexact sciences." Management Sci. 6 (October): 25–52.

RONDINI, T. (1975) "Organizational identification: issues and implications." Organizational Behavior and Human Performance 13 (February): 95–109.

ROSENBLOOM, D. (forthcoming) "City personnel: issues for the 1980s" in D. Nachmias and J. Blair (eds.) Urban Politics in Transition: Beverly Hills: Sage.

SCHNEIDER, B. and R. A. SNYDER (1975) "Some relationships between job satisfaction and organizational climate." J. of Applied Psychology 60, 3: 131–142.

SCOTT, W. (1961) "Organization theory: an overview and appraisal." Academy of Management J. 4: 7–26.

SMOCK, C. (1955) "The influence of psychological stress on the intolerance for ambiguity." J. of Abnormal Psychology 50: 177–182.

STARBUCK, W. (1976) "Organizations and their environments," in M. Dunnette (ed.) Handbook of Industrial and Organizational Psychology. Chicago: Rand-McNally.

STRAW, B. and B. SZWAJKOWSKI (1975) "The scarcity-munificence component of organizational environments and the commission of illegal acts." Administrative Sci. Q. 20: 345–354.

TERREBERRY, S. (1968) "The evolution of organizational environments." Administrative Sci. Q. 12 (March): 590–613.

THOMPSON, J. (1967) Organizations in Action. New York: McGraw-Hill.

WEICK, K. E. (1969) The Social Psychology of Organizing. Reading, MA: Addison-Wesley.

WOODWARD, J. (1965) Industrial Organization: Theory and Practice. London: Oxford Univ. Press.

WURZBERG, F. (1970) "Bureaucratic decay." J. of Comparative Administration I: 387–397.

# CHAPTER TWO

# Blurred Boundaries
# of
# the Public Sector

## Public and Private Management: Are They Fundamentally Alike in All Unimportant Respects?

Graham T. Allison, Jr.

My subtitle puts Wallace Sayre's oft-quoted "law" as a question. Sayre had spent some years in Ithaca helping plan Cornell's new School of Business and Public Administration. He left for Columbia with this aphorism: Public and private management are fundamentally alike in all unimportant respects.

Sayre based his conclusion on years of personal observation of government, a keen ear for what his colleagues at Cornell (and earlier at OPA) said about business, and a careful review of the literature and data comparing public and private management. Of the latter there was virtually none. Hence, Sayre's provocative "law" was actually an open invitation to research.

Unfortunately, in the 50 years since Sayre's pronouncement, the data base for systematic comparison of public and private management has improved little. Consequently, when Scotty Campbell called six weeks ago to inform me that I would make some remarks at this conference, we agreed that I would, in effect, take up Sayre's invitation to *speculate* about similarities

and differences among public and private management in ways that suggest significant opportunities for systematic investigation.

To reiterate: This paper is not a report of a major research project or systematic study. Rather, it is a response to a request for a brief summary of reflections of a dean of a school of government who now spends his time doing a form of public management—managing what Jim March has labeled an "organized anarchy"—rather than thinking, much less writing.[1] Moreover, the speculation here will appear to reflect a characteristic Harvard presumption that Cambridge either is the world, or is an adequate sample of the world. I say "appear" since as a North Carolinean, I am self-conscious about this parochialism. Nevertheless, I have concluded that the purposes of this conference may be better served by providing a deliberately parochial perspective on these issues—and thereby presenting a clear target for others to shoot at. Finally, I must acknowledge that this paper plagiarizes freely from a continuing discussion among my colleagues at Harvard about the development of the field of public management, especially from Joe Bower, Hale Champion, Gordon Chase, Charles Christenson, Richard Darman, John Dunlop, Phil Heymann, Larry Lynn, Mark Moore, Dick Neustadt, Roger Porter, and Don Price. Since my colleagues have not had the benefit of commenting on this presentation, I suspect I have some points wrong, or out of context, or without appropriate subtlety or amendment. Thus, I assume full liability for the words that follow.

Paper prepared for Public Management Research Conference, Brookings Institution, Washington, D.C. Reprinted by permission.

This paper is organized as follows:

- Section 1 frames the issue: What is public management?
- Section 2 focuses on similarities: How are public and private management basically alike?
- Section 3 concentrates on differences: How do public and private management differ?
- Section 4 poses the question more operationally: How are the jobs and responsibilities of two specific managers, one public and one private, alike and different?
- Section 5 attempts to derive from this discussion suggestions about promising research directions and then outlines one research agenda and strategy for developing knowledge of and instruction about public management.

## SECTION 1: FRAMING THE ISSUE WHAT IS PUBLIC MANAGEMENT?

What is the meaning of the term "management" as it appears in Office of *Management* and Budget, or Office of Personnel *Management?* Is "management" different from, broader or narrower than "administration"? Should we distinguish between management, leadership, entrepreneurship, administration, policy making, and implementation?

Who are "public managers"? Mayors, governors, and presidents? City managers, secretaries, and commissioners? Bureau chiefs? Office directors? Legislators? Judges?

Recent studies of OPM and OMB shed some light on these questions. OPM's major study of the "Current Status of Public Management Research" completed in May 1978 by Selma Mushkin of Georgetown's Public Service Laboratory starts with this question. The Mushkin report notes the definition of "public management" employed by the Interagency Study Committee on Policy Management Assistance in its 1975 report to OMB. That study identified the following core elements:

1. *Policy management:* The identification of needs, analysis of options, selection of programs, and allocation of resources on a jurisdiction-wide basis.

2. *Resource management:* The establishment of basic administrative support systems, such as budgeting, financial management, procurement and supply, and personnel management.
3. *Program management:* The implications of policy or daily operation of agencies carrying out policy along functional lines (education, law enforcement, etc.).[2]

The Mushkin report rejects this definition in favor of an "alternative list of public management elements." These elements are:

- Personnel Management (other than work force planning and collective bargaining and labor management relations)
- Work Force Planning
- Collective Bargaining and Labor Management Relations
- Productivity and Performance Measurement
- Organization/Reorganization
- Financial Management (including the management of intergovernmental relations)
- Evaluation Research, and Program and Management Audit[3]

Such terminological tangles seriously hamper the development of public management as a field of knowledge. In our efforts to discuss public management curriculum at Harvard, I have been struck by how differently people use these terms, how strongly many individuals feel about some distinction they believe is marked by a difference between one word and another, and consequently, how large a barrier terminology is to convergent discussion. These verbal obstacles virtually prohibit conversation that is both brief and constructive among individuals who have not developed a common language or a mutual understanding of each other's use of terms. (What this point may imply for this conference, I leave to the reader.)

This terminological thicket reflects a more fundamental conceptual confusion. There exists no overarching framework that orders the domain. In an effort to get a grip on the phenomena—the buzzing, blooming confusion of people in jobs performing tasks that produce results—both practitioners and observers have strained to find distinctions that facilitate their work. The attempts in the early decades of this century to draw a sharp line between "policy" and "administration," like more recent efforts to mark a similar divide between "policy making" and "implementation," reflect a common search for a simplification that allows one to put the value-laden issues of politics to one side (who gets what, when, and how), and focus on the more limited issue of how to perform tasks more efficiently.[4] But can anyone really deny that the "how" substantially affects the "who," the "what," and the "when"? The basic categories now prevalent in discussions of public management—strategy, personnel management, financial management, and control—are mostly derived from a business context in which executives manage hierarchies. The fit of these concepts to the problems that confront public managers is not clear.

Finally, there exist no ready data on what public managers do. Instead, the academic literature, such as it is, mostly consists of speculation tied to bits and pieces of evidence about the tail or the trunk or other manifestation of the proverbial elephant.[5] In contrast to the literally thousands of cases describing problems faced by private managers and their practice in solving these problems, case research from the perspective of a public manager is just beginning.[6] . . . But the paucity of data on the phenomena inhibits systematic empirical research on similarities and differences between public and private management, leaving the field to a mixture of reflection on personal experience and speculation.

For the purpose of this presentation, I will follow Webster and use the term management to mean the organization and direction of resources to achieve a desired result. I will focus on *general managers,* that is, individuals charged with managing a whole organization or multifunctional subunit. I will be interested in the general manager's full responsibilities, both *inside* his organization in integrating the diverse contributions of specialized subunits of the organization to achieve results, and *outside* his organization in relating his organization and its product to external constituencies. I will begin with the simplifying assumption that managers of traditional government organizations are public managers, and managers of traditional private businesses, private managers. Lest the discussion fall victim to the fallacy of misplaced abstraction, I will take the Director of EPA and the Chief Executive Officer of American Motors as, respectively, public and private managers. Thus, our central question can be put concretely: In what ways are the jobs and re-

sponsibilities of Doug Costle as Director of EPA similar to and different from those of Roy Chapin as Chief Executive Officer of American Motors?

## SECTION 2: SIMILARITIES
## HOW ARE PUBLIC AND
## PRIVATE MANAGEMENT ALIKE?

At one level of abstraction, it is possible to identify a set of general management functions. The most famous such list appeared in Gulick and Urwick's classic *Papers in the Science of Administration.*[7] Gulick summarized the work of the chief executive in the acronym POSDCORB. The letters stand for:

- Planning
- Organizing
- Staffing
- Directing
- Coordinating
- Reporting
- Budgeting

With various additions, amendments, and refinements, similar lists of general management functions can be found through the management literature from Barnard to Drucker.[8]

I shall resist here my natural academic instinct to join the intramural debate among proponents of various lists and distinctions. Instead, I simply offer one composite list (see Table 1) that attempts to incorporate the major functions that have been identified for general managers, whether public or private.

These common functions of management are not isolated and discrete, but rather integral components separated here for purposes of analysis. The character and relative significance of the various functions differ from one time to another in the history of any organization, and between one organization and another. But whether in a public or private setting, the challenge for the general manager is to integrate all these elements so as to achieve results.

## SECTION 3: DIFFERENCES
## HOW ARE PUBLIC AND
## PRIVATE MANAGEMENT DIFFERENT?

While there is a level of generality at which management is management, whether public or private, functions that bear identical labels take on rather different

**TABLE 1**
**Functions of general management**

*Strategy*

1. **Establishing objectives and priorities** for the organization (on the basis of forecasts of the external environment and the organization's capacities).
2. **Devising operational plans** to achieve these objectives.

*Managing Internal Components*

3. **Organizing and staffing:** In organizing the manager establishes structure (units and positions with assigned authority and responsibilities) and procedures (for coordinating activity and taking action); in staffing he tries to find the right persons in the key jobs.*
4. **Directing personnel and the personnel management system:** The capacity of the organization is embodied primarily in its members and their skills and knowledge; the personnel management system recruits, selects, socializes, trains, rewards, punishes, and exits the organization's human capital, which constitutes the organization's capacity to act to achieve its goals and to respond to specific directions from management.
5. **Controlling performance:** Various management information systems—including operation and capital budgets, accounts, reports and statistical systems, performance appraisals, and product evaluation—assist management in making decisions and in measuring progress toward objectives.

*Managing External Constituencies*

6. **Dealing with "external" units** of the organization subject to some common authority: Most general managers must deal with general managers of other units within the larger organization—above, laterally, and below—to achieve their unit's objectives.
7. **Dealing with independent organizations:** Agencies from other branches or levels of government, interest groups, and private enterprises that can importantly affect the organization's ability to achieve its objectives.
8. **Dealing with the press and public** whose action or approval or acquiescence is required.

*Organization and staffing are frequently separated in such lists, but because of the interaction between the two, they are combined here. See Graham Allison and Peter Szanton, *Remaking Foreign Policy* (Basic Books, 1976), p. 14.

---

meaning in public and private settings. As Larry Lynn has pointed out, one powerful piece of evidence in the debate between those who emphasize "similarities" and those who underline "differences" is the nearly unanimous conclusion of individuals who have been general managers in both business and government. Consider the reflections of George Shultz (former Director of OMB, Secretary of Labor, Secretary of the Treasury; now President of Bechtel), Donald Rumsfeld (former congressman, Director of OEO, Director of the Cost of Living Council, White House Chief of Staff, and Secretary of Defense; now President of GD Searle and Company), Michael Blumenthal (former Chairman and Chief Executive Officer of Bendix, Secretary of the Treasury, and now Vice Chairman of Burrows), Roy Ash (former President of Litton Industries, Director of OMB; now President of Addressograph), Lyman Hamilton (former Budget Officer in BOB, High Commissioner of Okinawa, Division Chief in the World Bank and President of ITT), and George Romney (former President of American Motors, Governor of Michigan and Secretary of Housing and Urban Development).[9] All judge public management different from private management—and harder!

## Three Orthogonal Lists of Differences

My review of these recollections, as well as the thoughts of academics, has identified three interesting, orthogonal lists that summarize the current state of the field: one by John Dunlop; one major *Public Administration Review* survey of the literature comparing public and private organizations by Hal Rainey, Robert Backoff, and Charles Levine; and one by Richard E. Neustadt prepared for the National Academy of Public Administration's Panel on Presidential Management.

John T. Dunlop's "impressionistic comparison of government management and private business" yields the following contrasts.[10]

1. *Time perspective:* Government managers tend to have relatively short time horizons dictated by political necessities and the political calendar, while private managers appear to take a longer time perspective oriented toward market developments, technological innovation and investment, and organization building.

2. *Duration:* The length of service of politically appointed top government managers is relatively short,

averaging no more than 18 months recently for assistant secretaries, while private managers have a longer tenure both in the same position and in the same enterprise. A recognized element of private business management is the responsibility to train a successor or several possible candidates while the concept is largely alien to public management since fostering a successor is perceived to be dangerous.

3. *Measurement of performance:* There is little if any agreement on the standards and measurement of performance to appraise a government manager, while various tests of performance—financial return, market share, performance measures for executive compensation—are well established in private business and often made explicit for a particular managerial position during a specific period ahead.

4. *Personnel constraints:* In government there are two layers of managerial officials that are at times hostile to one another: the civil service (or now the executive system) and the political appointees. Unionization of government employees exists among relatively high-level personnel in the hierarchy and includes a number of supervisory personnel. Civil service, union contract provisions, and other regulations complicate the recruitment, hiring, transfer, and layoff or discharge of personnel to achieve managerial objectives or preferences. By comparison, private business managements have considerably greater latitude, even under collective bargaining, in the management of subordinates. They have much more authority to direct the employees of their organization. Government personnel policy and administration are more under the control of staff (including civil service staff outside an agency) compared to the private sector in which personnel are much more subject to line responsibility.

5. *Equity and efficiency:* In governmental management great emphasis tends to be placed on providing equity among different constituencies, while in private business management relatively greater stress is placed upon efficiency and competitive performance.

6. *Public processes versus private processes:* Governmental management tends to be exposed to public scrutiny and to be more open, while private business management is more private and its processes more internal and less exposed to public review.

7. *Role of press and media:* Governmental management must contend regularly with the press and media; its decisions are often anticipated by the press. Private decisions are less often reported in the press, and the press has a much smaller impact on the substance and timing of decisions.

8. *Persuasion and direction:* In government, managers often seek to mediate decisions in response to a wide variety of pressures and must often put together a coalition of inside and outside groups to survive. By contrast, private management proceeds much more by direction or the issuance of orders to subordinates by superior managers with little risk of contradiction. Governmental managers tend to regard themselves as responsive to many superiors while private managers look more to one higher authority.

9. *Legislative and judicial impact:* Government managers are often subject to close scrutiny by legislative oversight groups or even judicial orders in ways that are quite uncommon in private business management. Such scrutiny often materially constrains executive and administrative freedom to act.

10. *Bottom line:* Governmental managers rarely have a clear bottom line, while that of a private business manager is profit, market performance, and survival.

Second, the *Public Administration Review's* major review article comparing public and private organizations, by Rainey, Backoff, and Levine, attempts to summarize the major points of consensus in the literature on similarities and differences among public and private organizations.[11]

Third, Richard E. Neustadt, in a fashion close to Dunlop's, notes six major differences between Presidents of the United States and Chief Executive Officers of major corporations.[12]

1. *Time horizon:* The private chief begins by looking forward a decade, or thereabouts, his likely span barring extraordinary troubles. The first-term President looks forward four years at most, with the fourth (and now even the third) year dominated by campaigning for reelection. (What second-termers look toward we scarcely know, having seen but one such term completed in the past quarter century.)

2. *Authority* over the enterprise. Subject to concurrence from the Board of Directors which appointed and can fire him, the private executive sets organization goals, shifts structures, procedure, and personnel to suit, monitors results, reviews key operational decisions, deals with key outsiders, and brings along his Board. Save for the deep but narrow sphere of military movements, a President's authority in these respects is

shared with well-placed members of Congress (or their staffs); case by case, they may have more explicit authority than he does (contrast authorizations and appropriations with the "take-care" clause). As for "bringing along the Board," neither the Congressmen with whom he shares power or the primary and general electorates which "hired" him have either a Board's duties or a broad view of the enterprise precisely matching his.

3. *Career system:* The model corporation is a true career system, something like the Forest Service after initial entry. In normal times the chief himself is chosen from within, or he is chosen from another firm in the same industry. He draws department heads et al. from among those with whom he's worked, or whom he knows in comparable companies. He and his principal associates will be familiar with each other's roles— indeed he probably has had a number of them—and also usually with one another's operating styles, personalities, idiosyncracies. Contrast the President who rarely has had much experience "downtown," probably knows little of most roles there (much of what he knows will turn out wrong), and less of most associates whom he appoints there, willy nilly, to fill places by Inauguration Day. Nor are they likely to know one another well, coming as they do from "everywhere" and headed as most are toward oblivion.

4. *Media relations:* The private executive represents his firm and speaks for it publicly in exceptional circumstances; he and his associates judge the exceptions. Those aside, he neither sees the press nor gives its members access to internal operations, least of all in his own office, save to make a point deliberately for public-relations purposes. The President, by contrast, is routinely on display, continuously dealing with the White House press and with the wider circle of political reporters, commentators, columnists. He needs them in his business, day by day, nothing exceptional about it, and they need him in theirs: The TV network news programs lead off with him some nights each week. They and the President are as mutually dependent as he and Congressmen (or more so). Comparatively speaking, these relations overshadow most administrative ones much of the time for him.

5. *Performance measurement:* The private executive expects to be judged, and in turn to judge subordinates, by profitability, however the firm measures it (a major strategic choice). In practice, his Board may use more subjective measures; so may he, but at risk to morale

and good order. The relative virtue of profit, of "the bottom line" is its legitimacy, its general acceptance in the business world by all concerned. Never mind its technical utility in given cases, its apparent "objectivity," hence "fairness," has enormous social usefulness: a myth that all can live by. For a President there is no counterpart (except *in extremis* the "smoking gun" to justify impeachment). The general public seems to judge a President, at least in part, by what its members think is happening to them, in their own lives; Congressmen, officials, interest groups appear to judge by what they guess, at given times, he can do for or to their causes. Members of the press interpret both of these and spread a simplified criterion affecting both, the legislative box-score, a standard of the press's own devising. The White House denigrates them all except when it does well.

6. *Implementation:* The corporate chief, supposedly, does more than choose a strategy and set a course of policy; he also is supposed to oversee what happens after, how in fact intentions turn into results, or if they don't to take corrective action, monitoring through his information system, acting, and if need be, through his personnel system. A President, by contrast, while himself responsible for budgetary proposals, too, in many spheres of policy, appears ill-placed and ill-equipped to monitor what agencies of states, of cities, corporations, unions, foreign governments are up to or to change personnel in charge. Yet these are very often the executants of "his" programs. Apart from defense and diplomacy the federal government does two things in the main: It issues and applies regulations and it awards grants in aid. Where these are discretionary, choice usually is vested by statute in a Senate-confirmed official well outside the White House. Monitoring is his function, not the President's except at second-hand. And final action is the function of the subjects of the rules and funds; they mostly are not federal personnel at all. In defense, the arsenals and shipyards are gone; weapons come from the private sector. In foreign affairs it is the *other* governments whose actions we would influence. From implementors like these a President is far removed most of the time. He intervenes, if at all, on a crash basis, not through organizational incentives.

Underlying these lists' sharpest distinctions between public and private management is a fundamental *constitutional difference.* In business, the functions of general management are centralized in a single individual: the Chief Executive Officer. The goal is authority commensurate with responsibility. In contrast, in the U.S. government, the functions of general management are constitutionally spread among competing institutions: the executive, two houses of Congress, and the courts. The constitutional goal was "not to promote efficiency but to preclude the exercise of arbitrary power," as Justice Brandeis observed. Indeed, as *The Federalist Papers* make starkly clear, the aim was to create incentives to compete: "The great security against a gradual concentration of the several powers in the same branch, consists in giving those who administer each branch the constitutional means and personal motives to resist encroachment of the others. Ambition must be made to counteract ambition."[13] Thus, the general management functions concentrated in the CEO of a private business are, by constitutional design, spread in the public sector among a number of competing institutions and thus shared by a number of individuals whose ambitions are set against one another. For most areas of public policy today, these individuals include at the federal level the chief elected official, the chief appointed executive, the chief career official, and several congressional chieftains. Since most public services are actually delivered by state and local governments, with independent sources of authority, this means a further array of individuals at these levels.

## SECTION 4:
## AN OPERATIONAL PERSPECTIVE
## HOW ARE THE JOBS AND
## RESPONSIBILITIES OF DOUG COSTLE,
## DIRECTOR OF EPA, AND ROY CHAPIN,
## CEO OF AMERICAN MOTORS,
## SIMILAR AND DIFFERENT?

If organizations could be separated neatly into two homogeneous piles, one public and one private, the task of identifying similarities and differences between managers of these enterprises would be relatively easy. In fact, as Dunlop has pointed out, "the real world of management is composed of distributions, rather than single undifferentiated forms, and there is an increasing variety of hybrids." Thus for each major attribute of organizations, specific entities can be located on a spectrum. On most dimensions, organizations classified as "predominantly public" and those "predomi-

nantly private" overlap.[14] Private business organizations vary enormously among themselves in size, in management structure and philosophy, and in the constraints under which they operate. For example, forms of ownership and types of managerial control may be somewhat unrelated. Compare a family-held enterprise, for instance, with a public utility and a decentralized conglomerate, a Bechtel with ATT and Textron. Similarly, there are vast differences in management of governmental organizations. Compare the Government Printing Office or TVA or the Police Department of a small town with the Department of Energy or the Department of Health and Human Services. These distributions and varieties should encourage penetrating comparisons within both business and governmental organizations, as well as contrasts and comparisons across these broad categories, a point to which we shall return in considering directions for research.

Absent a major research effort, it may nonetheless be worthwhile to examine the jobs and responsibilities of two specific managers, neither polar extremes, but one clearly public, the other private. For this purpose, and primarily because of the availability of cases that describe the problems and opportunities each confronted, consider Doug Costle, Administrator of EPA, and Roy Chapin, CEO of American Motors.[15]

### Doug Costle, Administrator of EPA, January 1977

The mission of EPA is prescribed by laws creating the agency and authorizing its major programs. That mission is "to control and abate pollution in the areas of air, water, solid wastes, noise, radiation, and toxic substances. EPA's mandate is to mount an integrated, coordinated attack on environmental pollution in cooperation with state and local governments."[16]

EPA's organizational structure follows from its legislative mandates to control particular pollutants in specific environments: air and water, solid wastes, noise, radiation, pesticides, and chemicals. As the new Administrator, Costle inherited the Ford Administration's proposed budget for EPA of $802 million for federal 1978 with a ceiling of 9,698 agency positions.

The setting into which Costle stepped is difficult to summarize briefly. As Costle characterized it:

- "Outside there is a confusion on the part of the public in terms of what this agency is all about: what it is doing, where it is going."

- "The most serious constraint on EPA is the inherent complexity in the state of our knowledge, which is constantly changing."
- "Too often, acting under extreme deadlines mandated by Congress, EPA has announced regulations, only to find out that they knew very little about the problem. The central problem is the inherent complexity of the job that the agency has been asked to do and the fact that what it is asked to do changes from day to day."
- "There are very difficult internal management issues not amenable to a quick solution: the skills mix problem within the agency; a research program with laboratory facilities scattered all over the country and cemented in place, largely by political alliances on the Hill that would frustrate efforts to pull together a coherent research program."
- "In terms of EPA's original mandate in the bulk pollutants we may be hitting the asymptotic part of the curve in terms of incremental clean-up costs. You have clearly conflicting national goals: energy and environment, for example."

Costle judged his six major tasks at the outset to be:

- Assembling a top management team (six assistant administrators and some 25 office heads);
- Addressing EPA's legislative agenda (EPA's basic legislative charter—the Clean Air Act and the Clean Water Act—were being rewritten as he took office; the pesticides program was up for reauthorization also in 1977);
- Establishing EPA's role in the Carter administration (aware that the administration would face hard tradeoffs between the environment and energy, energy regulations and the economy, EPA regulations of toxic substances and the regulations of FDA, CSPS, and OSHA. Costle identified the need to build relations with the other key players and to enhance EPA's standing);
- Building ties to constituent groups (both because of their role in legislating the agency's mandate and in successful implementation of EPA's programs);
- Making specific policy decisions (for example, whether to grant or deny a permit for the Seabrook Nuclear Generating Plant cooling system. Or how the Toxic Substance Control Act, enacted in October 1976, would be implemented: This act gave EPA new responsibilities for regulating the manufacture, distribution, and use of chemical substances so as to prevent unreasonable risks to health and the environment. Whether EPA would require chemical manufacturers to provide some minimum information on various substances, or require much stricter reporting requirements for the 1,000 chemical substances already known to be hazardous, or require companies to report all chemicals, and on what timetable, had to be decided and the regulations issued);
- Rationalizing the internal organization of the agency (EPA's extreme decentralization to the regions and its limited technical expertise).

No easy job.

### Roy Chapin and American Motors, January 1977

In January 1967, in an atmosphere of crisis, Roy Chapin was appointed Chairman and Chief Executive Officer of American Motors (and William Luneburg, President and Chief Operating Officer). In the four previous years, AMC unit sales had fallen 37 percent and market share from over 6 percent to under 3 percent. Dollar volume in 1967 was off 42 percent from the all-time high of 1963 and earnings showed a net loss of $76 million on sales of $656 million. Columnists began writing obituaries for AMC. *Newsweek* characterized AMC as "a flabby dispirited company, a product solid enough but styled with about as much flair as corrective shoes, and a public image that melted down to one unshakeable label: loser." Said Chapin: "We were driving with one foot on the accelerator and one foot on the brake. We didn't know where the hell we were."

Chapin announced to his stockholders at the outset that "we plan to direct ourselves most specifically to those areas of the market where we can be fully effective. We are not going to attempt to be all things to all people, but to concentrate on those areas of consumer needs we can meet better than anyone else." As he recalled: "There were problems early in 1967 which demanded immediate action, and which accounted for much of our time for several months. Nonetheless, we began planning beyond them, establishing objectives, programs and timetables through 1972. Whatever happened in the short run, we had to prove ourselves in the marketplace in the long run."

Chapin's immediate problems were five:

- The company was virtually out of cash and an immediate supplemental bank loan of $20 million was essential.
- Car inventories—company owned and dealer owned—had reached unprecedented levels. The solution to this glut took five months and could be accomplished only by a series of plant shutdowns in January 1967.
- Sales of the Rambler American series had stagnated and inventories were accumulating: A dramatic merchandising move was concocted and implemented in February, dropping the price tag on the American to a position midway between the VW and competitive smaller U.S. compacts, by both cutting the price to dealers and trimming dealer discounts from 21 percent to 17 percent.
- Administrative and commercial expenses were judged too high and thus a vigorous cost reduction program was initiated that trimmed $15 million during the first year. Manufacturing and purchasing costs were also trimmed significantly to approach the most effective levels in the industry.
- The company's public image had deteriorated: The press was pessimistic and much of the financial community had written AMC off. To counteract this, numerous formal and informal meetings were held with bankers, investment firms, government officials, and the press.

As Chapin recalls, "with the immediate fires put out, we could put in place the pieces of a corporate growth plan—a definition of a way of life in the auto industry for American Motors. We felt that our reason for being, which would enable us not just to survive but to grow, lay in bringing a different approach to the auto market—in picking our spots and then being innovative and aggressive." The new corporate growth plan included a dramatic change in the approach to the market to establish a "youthful image" for the company (by bringing out new sporty models like the Javelin and by entering the racing field), "changing the product line from one end to the other" by 1972, acquiring Kaiser Jeep (selling the company's nontransportation assets and concentrating on specialized transportation, including Jeep, a company that had lost money in each of the preceding five years, but that Chapin believed could be turned around by substantial

cost reductions and economies of scale in manufacturing, purchasing, and administration).

Chapin succeeded: For the year ending September 30, 1971, AMC earned $10.2 million on sales of $1.2 billion. Recalling the list of general management functions in Table 1, which similarities and differences appear salient and important?

## Strategy

Both Chapin and Costle had to establish objectives and priorities and to devise operational plans. In business, "corporate strategy is the pattern of major objectives, purposes, or goals and essential policies and plans for achieving these goals, stated in such a way as to define what business the company is in or is to be in and the kind of company it is or is to be."[17] In reshaping the strategy of AMC and concentrating on particular segments of the transportation market, Chapin had to consult his Board and had to arrange financing. But the control was substantially his.

How much choice did Costle have at EPA as to the "business it is or is to be in" or the kind of agency "it is or is to be"? These major strategic choices emerged from the legislative process which mandated whether he should be in the business of controlling pesticides or toxic substances and if so on what timetable, and occasionally, even what level of particulate per million units he was required to control. The relative role of the President, other members of the Administration (including White House staff, Congressional relations, and other agency heads), the EPA Administrator, Congressional committee chairmen, and external groups in establishing the broad strategy of the agency constitutes an interesting question.

## Managing Internal Components

For both Costle and Chapin, staffing was key. As Donald Rumsfeld has observed:

the single most important task of the chief executive is to select the right people. I've seen terrible organization charts in both government and business that were made to work well by good people. I've seen beautifully charted organizations that didn't work very well because they had the wrong people.[18]

The leeways of the two executives in organizing and staffing were considerably different, however. Chapin closed down plants, moved key managers, hired and fired, virtually at will. As Michael Blumenthal has written about Treasury, if you wish to make substantive changes, policy changes, and the Department's employees don't like what you're doing, they have ways of frustrating you or stopping you that do not exist in private industry. The main method they have is Congress. If I say I want to shut down a particular unit or transfer the function of one area to another, there are ways of going to Congress and in fact using friends in the Congress to block the move. They can also use the press to try to stop you. If I at Bendix wished to transfer a division from Ann Arbor to Detroit because I figured out that we could save money that way, as long as I could do it decently and carefully, it's of no lasting interest to the press. The press can't stop me. They may write about it in the local paper, but that's about it.[19]

For Costle, the basic structure of the agency was set by law. The labs, their location, and most of their personnel were fixed. Though he could recruit his key subordinates, again restrictions like the conflict of interest law and the prospect of a Senate confirmation fight led him to drop his first choice for the Assistant Administrator for Research and Development, since he had worked for a major chemical company. While Costle could resort to changes in the process for developing policy or regulations in order to circumvent key office directors whose views he did not share, for example, Eric Stork, the Deputy Assistant Administrator in charge of Mobile Source Air Program, such maneuvers took considerable time, provoked extensive infighting, and delayed significantly the development of Costle's program.

In the direction of personnel and management of the personnel system, Chapin exercised considerable authority. While the United Auto Workers limited his authority over workers, at the management level he assigned people and reassigned responsibility consistent with his general plan. While others may have felt that his decisions to close down particular plants or to drop a particular product were mistaken, they complied. As George Shultz has observed: "One of the first lessons I learned in moving from government to business is that in business you must be very careful when you tell someone who is working for you to do something because the probability is high that he or she will do it."[20]

Costle faced a civil service system designed to prevent spoils as much as to promote productivity. The Civil Service Commission exercised much of the responsibility for the personnel function in his agency.

Civil service rules severely restricted his discretion, took long periods to exhaust, and often required complex maneuvering in a specific case to achieve any results. Equal opportunity rules and their administration provided yet another network of procedural and substantive inhibitions. In retrospect, Costle found the civil service system a much larger constraint on his actions and demand on his time than he had anticipated.

In controlling performance, Chapin was able to use measures like profit and market share, to decompose those objectives to subobjectives for lower levels of the organization and to measure the performance of managers of particular models, areas, divisions. Cost accounting rules permitted him to compare plants within AMC and to compare AMC's purchases, production, and even administration with the best practice in the industry.

## Managing External Constituencies

As Chief Executive Officer, Chapin had to deal only with the Board. For Costle, within the executive branch but beyond his agency lay many actors critical to the achievement of his agency's objectives: the President and the White House, Energy, Interior, the Council on Environmental Quality, OMB. Actions each could take, either independently or after a process of consultation in which they disagreed with him, could frustrate his agency's achievement of its assigned mission. Consequently, he spent considerable time building his agency's reputation and capital for interagency disputes.

Dealing with independent external organizations was a necessary and even larger part of Costle's job. Since his agency's mission, strategy, authorizations, and appropriations emerged from the process of legislation, attention to Congressional committees, and Congressmen, and Congressmen's staff, and people who affect Congressmen and Congressional staffers rose to the top of Costle's agenda. In the first year, top level EPA officials appeared over 140 times before some 60 different committees and subcommittees.

Chapin's ability to achieve AMC's objectives could also be affected by independent external organizations: competitors, government (the Clean Air Act that was passed in 1970), consumer groups (recall Ralph Nader), and even suppliers of oil. More than most private managers, Chapin had to deal with the press in attempting to change the image of AMC. Such occasions were primarily at Chapin's initiative, and around events that Chapin's public affairs office orchestrated, for example, the announcement of a new racing car. Chapin also managed a marketing effort to persuade consumers that their tastes could best be satisfied by AMC products.

Costle's work was suffused by the press: in the daily working of the organization, in the perception by key publics of the agency and thus the agency's influence with relevant parties, and even in the setting of the agenda of issues to which the agency had to respond.

For Chapin, the bottom line was profit, market share, and the long-term competitive position of AMC. For Costle, what are the equivalent performance measures? Blumenthal answers by exaggerating the difference between appearance and reality:

> At Bendix, it was the reality of the situation that in the end determined whether we succeeded or not. In the crudest sense, this meant the bottom line. You can dress up profits only for so long—if you're not successful, it's going to be clear. In government there is no bottom line, and that is why you can be successful if you appear to be successful—though, of course, appearance is not the only ingredient of success.[21]

Rumsfeld says:

> In business, you're pretty much judged by results. I don't think the American people judge government officials this way. . . In government, too often you're measured by how much you seem to care, how hard you seem to try—things that do not necessarily improve the human condition. . . . It's a lot easier for a President to get into something and end up with a few days of good public reaction than it is to follow through, to pursue policies to a point where they have a beneficial effect on human lives.[22]

As George Shultz says:

> In government and politics, recognition and therefore incentives go to those who formulate policy and maneuver legislative compromise. By sharp contrast, the kudos and incentives in business go to the persons who can get something done. It is execution that counts. Who can get the plant built, who can bring home the sales contract, who can carry out the financing, and so on.[23]

This casual comparison of one public and one private manager suggests what could be done—if the issue of comparisons were pursued systematically, horizontally across organizations and at various levels within organizations. While much can be learned by examining the chief executive officers of organizations, still more promising should be comparisons among the much larger numbers of middle managers. If one compared, for example, a Regional Administrator of EPA and an AMC division chief, or two Comptrollers, or equivalent plant managers, some functions would appear more similar, and other differences would stand out. The major barrier to such comparisons is the lack of cases describing problems and practices of middle-level managers.[24] This should be a high priority in further research.

The differences noted in this comparison, for example, in the personnel area, have already changed with the Civil Service Reform Act of 1978 and the creation of the Senior Executive Service. Significant changes have also occurred in the automobile industry: Under current circumstances, the CEO of Chrysler may seem much more like the Administrator of EPA. More precise comparison of different levels of management in both organizations, for example, accounting procedures used by Chapin to cut costs significantly as compared to equivalent procedures for judging the costs of EPA mandated pollution control devices, would be instructive.

## SECTION 5: IMPLICATIONS FOR RESEARCH ON PUBLIC MANAGEMENT

The debate between the assimilators and the differentiators, like the dispute between proponents of convergence and divergence between the U.S. and the Soviet Union reminds me of the old argument about whether the glass is half full or half empty. I conclude that public and private management are at least as different as they are similar, and that the differences are more important than the similarities. From this review of the "state of the art," such as it is, I draw a number of lessons for research on public management. I will try to state them in a way that is both succinct and provocative:

• First, the demand for performance from government and efficiency in government is both real and right. The perception that government's performance lags private business performance is also correct. But the notion that there is any significant body of private management practices and skills that can be transferred directly to public management tasks in a way that produces significant improvements is wrong.

• Second, performance in many public management positions can be improved substantially, perhaps by an order of magnitude. That improvement will come not, however, from massive borrowing of specific private management sales skills and understandings. Instead, it will come, as it did in the history of private management, from an articulation of the general management function and a self-consciousness about the general public management point of view. The single lesson of private management most instructive to public management is the prospect of substantial improvement through recognition of and consciousness about the public management function.

Alfred Chandler's prize-winning study, *The Visible Hand: The Managerial Revolution in American Business,*[25] describes the emergence of professional management in business. Through the nineteenth century most American businesses were run by individuals who performed management functions but had no self-consciousness about their management responsibilities. With the articulation of the general management perspective and the refinement of general management practices, by the 1920s American businesses had become competitive in the management function. Individuals capable at management and self-conscious about their management tasks—setting objectives, establishing priorities, and driving the organization to results—entered firms and industries previously run by family entrepreneurs or ordinary employees and brought about dramatic increases in product. Business schools emerged to document better and worse practice, largely through the case method, to suggest improvements, and to refine specific management instruments. Important advances were made in technique. But the great leaps forward in productivity stemmed from the articulation of the general management point of view and the self-consciousness of managers about their function. (Analogously, at a lower level, the articulation of the salesman's role and task, together with the skills and values of salesmanship made it possible for individuals with moderate talents at sales to increase their level of sales tenfold.)

The routes by which people reach general management positions in government do not assure that they will have consciousness or competence in management. As a wise observer of government managers has written,

One of the difficult problems of schools of public affairs is to overcome the old-fashioned belief—still held by many otherwise sophisticated people—that the skills of management are simply the application of "common sense" by any intelligent and broadly educated person to the management problems which are presented to him. It is demonstrable that many intelligent and broadly educated people who are generally credited with a good deal of "common sense" make very poor managers. The skills of effective management require a good deal of uncommon sense and uncommon knowledge.[26]

I believe that the most significant aspect of the Civil Service Reform Act of 1978 is the creation of the Senior Executive Service: the explicit identification of general managers in government. The challenge now is to assist people who occupy general management positions in actually becoming general managers.

• Third, careful review of private management rules of thumb that can be adapted to public management contexts will pay off. The 80-20 rule—80 percent of the benefits of most production processes come from the first 20 perent of effort—does have wide application, for example, in EPA efforts to reduce bulk pollutants.

• Fourth, Chandler documents the proposition that the categories and criteria for identifying costs, or calculating present value, or measuring the value added to intermediate products are not "natural." They are invented: creations of intelligence harnessed to operational tasks. While there are some particular accounting categories and rules, for example, for costing intermediate products, that may be directly transferable to public sector problems, the larger lesson is that dedicated attention to specific management functions can, as in the history of business, create for public sector managers accounting categories, and rules, and measures that cannot now be imagined.[27]

• Fifth, it is possible to learn from experience. What skills, attributes, and practices do competent managers exhibit and less successful managers lack? This is an empirical question that can be investigated in a straightforward manner. As Yogi Berra noted: "You can observe a lot just by watching."

• Sixth, the effort to develop public management as a field of knowledge should start from problems faced by practicing public managers. The preferences of professors for theorizing reflects deep-seated incentives of the academy that can be overcome only by careful institutional design.

In the light of these lessons, I believe one strategy for the development of public management should include:

• *Developing a significant number of cases on public management problems and practices.* Cases should describe typical problems faced by public managers. Cases should attend not only to top-level managers but to middle and lower-level managers. The dearth of cases at this level makes this a high priority for development. Cases should examine both general functions of management and specific organizational tasks, for example, hiring and firing. Public management cases should concentrate on the job of the manager running his unit.

• *Analyzing cases to identify better and worse practice.* Scientists search for "critical experiments." Students of public management should seek to identify "critical experiences" that new public managers could live through vicariously and learn from. Because of the availability of information, academics tend to focus on failures. But teaching people what not to do is not necessarily the best way to help them learn to be *doers.* By analyzing relative successes, it will be possible to extract rules of thumb, crutches, and concepts, for example, Chase's "law": Wherever the product of a public organization has not been monitored in a way that ties performance to reward, the introduction of an effective monitoring system will yield a 50 percent improvement in that product in the short run. GAO's handbooks on evaluation techniques and summaries suggest what can be done.

• *Promoting systematic comparative research:* management positions in a single agency over time; similar management positions among several public agencies; public management levels within a single agency; similar management functions, for example, budgeting or management information systems, among agencies; managers across public and private organizations; and even cross-nationally. The data for this comparative research would be produced by the case development effort and would complement the large-scale development of cases on private management that is ongoing.

• *Linking to the training of public managers.* Intellectual development of the field of public management should be tightly linked to the training of public managers, including individuals already in positions of significant responsibility. Successful practice will appear in government, not in the university. University-based documentation of better and worse practice, and refinement of that practice, should start from problems of managers on the line. The intellectual effort required to develop the field of public management and the resources required to support this level of effort are most likely to be assembled if research and training are vitally linked. The new Senior Executive Service presents a major opportunity to do this.

The strategy outlined here is certainly not the only strategy for research in public management. Given the needs for effective public management, I believe that a *major* research effort should be mounted and that it should pursue a number of complementary strategies. Given where we start, I see no danger of overattention to, or overinvestment in the effort required in the immediate future.

Any resemblance between my preferred strategy and that of at least one school of government is not purely coincidental.

*This article was presented as part of the Public Management Research Conference, Brookings Institution, Washington, D. C., November 1979.*

## NOTES

1. In contrast to the management of structured hierarchies, for which the metaphor of a traditional football game in which each team attempts to amass the larger number of points is apt, an organized anarchy is better thought of as a soccer game played on a round field, ringed with goals; players enter and leave the field sporadically, and while there vigorously kick various balls of sundry sizes and shapes toward one or another of the goals, judging themselves and being judged by assorted, ambiguous scoring systems. See Michael Cohen and James March, *Leadership and Ambiguity* (McGraw-Hill, 1974).

2. Selma J. Mushkin, Frank H. Sandifer, and Sally Familton, *Current Status of Public Management: Research Conducted by or Supported by Federal Agencies* (Washington, D. C.: Public Services Laboratory, Georgetown University, 1978), p. 10.

3. Ibid., p. 11.

4. Though frequently identified as the author who established the complete separation between "policy" and "administration," Woodrow Wilson has in fact been unjustly ac-

cused. "It is the object of administrative study to discover, first, what government can properly and successfully do, and, secondly, how it can do these proper things with the utmost possible efficiency . . ." (Wilson, "The Study of Administration," published as an essay in 1887 and reprinted in *Political Science Quarterly,* December 1941, p. 481. For another statement of the same point, see Brooks Adams, *The Theory of Social Revolutions* (Macmillan 1913), pp. 207–208.

5. See Dwight Waldo, "Organization Theory: Revisiting the Elephant," *PAR* (November–December 1978). Reviewing the growing volume of books and articles on organization theory, Waldo notes that "growth in the volume of the literature is not to be equated with growth in knowledge."

6. See *Cases in Public Policy and Management* (Spring 1979) of the Intercollegiate Case Clearing House for a bibliography containing descriptions of 577 cases by 366 individuals from 79 institutions. Current casework builds on and expands earlier efforts of the Inter-University Case Program. See, for example, Harold Stein, ed., *Public Administration and Policy Development: A Case Book* (Harcourt, Brace, and World, 1952), and Edwin A. Bock and Alan K. Campbell, eds., *Case Studies in American Government* (Prentice-Hall, 1962).

7. Luther Gulick and Al Urwick, eds., *Papers in the Science of Public Administration* (Institute of Public Administration, 1937).

8. See, for example, Chester I. Barnard, *The Functions of the Executive* (Howard University Press, 1938), and Peter F. Drucker, *Management: Tasks, Responsibilities, Practices* (Harper and Row, 1974). Barnard's recognition of human relations added an important dimension neglected in earlier lists.

9. See, for example, "A Businessman in a Political Jungle," *Fortune* (April 1964); "Candid Reflections of a Businessman in Washington," *Fortune* (January 29, 1979); "A Politician Turned Executive," *Fortune* (September 10, 1979); and "The Ambitions Interface," *Harvard Business Review* (November–December, 1979) for the views of Romney, Blumenthal, Rumsfeld, and Schultz, respectively.

10. John T. Dunlop, "Public Management," draft of an unpublished paper and proposal, Summer 1979.

11. Hal G. Rainey, Robert W. Backoff, and Charles N. Levine, "Comparing Public and Private Organizations," *Public Administration Review* (March–April, 1976).

12. Richard E. Neustadt, "American Presidents and Corporate Executives," a paper prepared for a meeting of the National Academy of Public Administration's Panel on Presidential Management, October 7–8, 1979.

13. *The Federalist Papers,* No. 51. The word "department" has been translated as "branch," which was its meaning in the original papers.

14. Failure to recognize the fact of distributions has led some observers to leap from one instance of similarity between public and private to general propositions about similarities between public and private institutions or management. See, for example, Michael Murray, "Comparing Public and Private Management: An Exploratory Essay," *Public Administration Review* (July–August, 1975).

15. These examples are taken from Bruce Scott, "American Motors Corporation" (Intercollegiate Case Clearing House #9-364-001); Charles B. Weigle with the collaboration of C. Roland Christensen, "American Motors Corporation II" (Intercollegiate Case Clearing House #6-372-350); Thomas R. Hitchner and Jacob Lew under the supervision of Philip B. Heymann and Stephen B. Hitchner, "Douglas Costle and the EPA (A)" (Kennedy School of Government Case #C94-78-216); and Jacob Lew and Stephen B. Hitchner, "Douglas Costle and the EPA (B)" (Kennedy School of Government Case #C96-78-217). For an earlier exploration of a similar comparison, see Joseph Bower, "Effective Public Management," *Harvard Business Review* (March–April, 1977).

16. U. S. Government Manual, 1978/1979, 507.

17. Kenneth R. Andrews, *The Concept of Corporate Strategy* (Dow Jones-Irwin, 1971), p. 28.

18. "A Politician-Turned-Executive," *Fortune* (September 10, 1979), p. 92.

19. "Candid Reflections of a Businessman in Washington," *Fortune* (January 29, 1979), p. 39.

20. "The Abrasive Interface," *Harvard Business Review* (November–December 1979), p. 95.

21. *Fortune* (January 29, 1979), p. 36.

22. *Fortune* (September 10, 1979), p. 90.

23. *Harvard Business Review* (November–December 1979), p. 95.

24. The cases developed by Boston University's Public Management Program offer a promising start in this direction.

25. Alfred Chandler, *The Visible Hand: The Managerial Revolution in American Business* (Belknap Press of Harvard University Press, 1977).

26. Rufus Miles, "The Search for Identity of Graduate Schools of Public Affairs." *Public Administration Review* (November 1967).

27. Chandler, op. cit., pp. 277–279.

# Dimensions of "Publicness"
## An Approach to Public Organization Theory

Barry Bozeman

Most students of public organizations would find little fault with Donald Warwick's admonition that "it is not enough to pack a briefcase with concepts and measures developed in other settings, unload them in a public agency, and expect them to encompass all of worthwhile reality to which they are exposed."[1] Yet despite widespread agreement that the "publicness" of organizations implies something germane to theory and practice, there is less agreement on the nature and significance of that something.

One of the major obstacles to the development of public organization theory is the blurring of public and private sectors. Business firms are increasingly interdependent with government agencies, but at the same time many government agencies have begun to resemble business firms as user charges and other quasimarket approaches become more common. The result is that traditional distinctions between public and private organizations are less meaningful. Further contributing to complexity is the fact that government organizations are sometimes quite "public" (i.e., closely resembling stereotypes) in some respects but not in others. Likewise, business firms often retain some aspects of their traditional market orientation but not others. When we consider the "publicness" of business organizations and the "privateness" of government agencies along with the increase in avowedly hybrid organizations (such as government-sponsored enterprises and not-for-profit organizations), the real world of organizations presents an ever-greater challenge to the concepts of organization theorists.

My objective is to provide a conceptual approach that allows organization theorists to deal more realistically with the blurring of sectors and the publicness of organizations. The approach employs a concept of publicness based on the degree of external governmental constraint imposed on the basic activities of organizations. The novelty of this approach is that the concept of publicness is applicable not only to government organizations but business firms and not-for-profit organizations as well. With this approach we can not only speak of the publicness of business organizations and the privateness of government organizations but can also view the relative publicness/privateness of sets of organizations regardless of sector affiliation. I refer to this as a *dimensional approach* because each of the organization's essential activities is viewed as a dimension of publicness (i.e., in terms of the external governmental constraint of the activity). Thus, it is possible that an organization could be quite public in certain dimensions and not at all in others.

Before outlining the approach and suggesting applications, it is useful to elaborate the publicness problem and document the need for a different approach to organization theory.

## WANTED: A MORE SATISFYING APPROACH TO THE PUBLICNESS PROBLEM

Operating on the assumption that public organizations are distinct entities, a number of organization analysts have set out to compare public and private (usually meaning government and nongovernment) organizations.[2] But not everyone is convinced that the public status of organizations is of much significance, especially if one's purpose is construction of organization theory. While some organization theorists (chiefly those trained in political science or public administration) feel that publicness is often a crucial determinant of organizational behavior, others are unimpressed. Many organization theorists, perhaps even a majority, argue that public status, if important at all, is no more significant than a host of other characteristics such as size, resources, complexity, and technology. Some argue that even in those cases where public organizations seem to be distinct entities, the public status of the organization is actually only a surrogate for its more basic features.[3]

### The Publicness Problem

Organization theorists are faced with the *publicness problem*, which, simply stated, is knowing when publicness is a problem. That is, does the public status of organizations significantly affect their behavior? As matters stand, the publicness problem is unresolved. There are strongly held beliefs, but empirical evidence is scant.[4] Studies comparing public and private organizations are few in number, are often based on small samples, and employ a wide variety of concepts and measures. While most studies of public organizations focus on government organizations, there is not even a consensus on the definition of public organization or public character.

The limited progress toward resolution of the publicness problem is disappointing because the issues hanging in the balance are critical to theorists and managers. Are innovations in private organizations transferable to government organizations and, if so, under what circumstances?[5] Are public organization environments really more turbulent?[6] Most agree that public and private organizations are political, but are public organizations *more* political or political in a different manner? It is commonly argued that evaluating the effectiveness of government organizations is more difficult because there is no bottom line. But what of business organizations that seek multiple objectives such as profit, growth, and stability? And how does one go about assessing the effectiveness of government or nonprofit organizations?[7]

These are only a few of the problems of publicness. Many issues have an immediacy to practitioners, but there are a good many others that are just as compelling to researchers, issues having to do with such matters as approaches to aggregation and sampling, choice of unit of analysis, application of research methods, and so forth.[8] For those interested in research on organizations (and not just public organizations), the problem of publicness is often a significant deterrent to the advance of knowledge. Thus, a failure to deal adequately with publicness hinders research and theory and poses problems for those interested in a variety of practical matters pertaining to the management of organizations and the making and evaluation of policy.

## The Blurring of Sectors: Implications for the Publicness Problem

A number of factors account for limited progress toward resolution of the publicness problem, but none is more fundamental than the absence of a more encompassing and realistic concept of publicness. In one of the more helpful attempts to identify critical differences between public and private organizations, Rainey, Backoff, and Levine review a number of approaches to distinguishing between "private" and "public" and conclude that "none of these approaches can succeed in drawing a clear line between sectors;

there are always intermediate types, and overlaps on various dimensions."[9] Theorists have not yet found a way to deal adequately with one of the most significant developments in the real world of organizations, namely, the blurring of sectors and the proliferation of hybrid organizations.

Forces promoting the blurring of government and nongovernment organizations are well known and require little discussion. Business firms operate within the boundaries of a legal government and are subject to very general and sometimes quite specific governmental controls. Large corporations and even many small family-owned businesses are dependent on government at their birth (e.g., chartering, licensing, zoning), death (e.g., bankruptcy laws, merger, antitrust policies), and points in between (e.g., resources from government contracts, loans). Firms also receive direct services (e.g., assistance of the Small Business Administration) and indirect services (e.g., police protection).

At the same time, many government organizations are beginning to take on characteristics usually associated with business firms. A most obvious businesslike practice is setting user charges, but government agencies are increasingly involved in advertising and marketing (though they avoid use of those terms). Also, approaches to compensation, collective bargaining, and financial management are beginning to resemble business practice.

A development related to the convergence of business and government organizations' attributes and practices is the rise of hybrid organizations such as the government-sponsored enterprise (GSE). As one student of GSEs observes, the existence of "an either/or, public/private world, separating the government and for-profit enterprises, has long ceased to exist, if it ever really did."[10]

Government-sponsored enterprises are difficult to classify and contribute further to the publicness problem. Even the fundamental legal status of the GSEs is subject to great variation. Just focusing on those organizations created by Congress, legal status includes private for-profit corporations, government-sponsored private corporations, government ownership, private nonprofit corporations, public corporations, and multiorganization enterprises with myriad encompassing legal statuses.

A major assumption of this essay is that researchers interested in developing generalizable, cumulative knowledge about organizations can ill afford to treat lightly the *blurring* phenomenon. In the absence of a useful approach for publicness—one that goes beyond simple distinctions between government and nongovernment status—important theoretical problems will remain unresolved.

## THE DIMENSIONS OF PUBLICNESS APPROACH

The dimensions of publicness (hereafter referred to as *dimensional*) approach focuses not on the legal status, sector affiliation, or ownership of the organization but on the extent to which the organization's activities are constrained by government and policies and decisions. The focal organization may itself be a government organization, a business organization, or a mixed type.

An external constraint view of organizations is not novel. Organizations are constrained by dependency relationships with other organizations.[11] All organizations exercise some degree of autonomy not only in operations and management but also in domain selection,[12] application of technology, and direction of resources.[13] But all organizations are dependent (to varying degrees and in different respects) on their environment. My focus is exclusively on constraints imposed by governmental entities.[14] Further, it is not sufficient to gauge the absolute level of governmental constraint on the focal organization; we must also consider the extent to which particular activities of the organization are externally constrained. This point is worth emphasizing because *a major assumption of the dimensional approach is that an organization may be public (i.e., constrained by government entities) in some of its activities but not others.*

### Theoretical Roots of the Dimensional Approach

While the dimensional approach has much in common with a variety of approaches to organization theory, it is perhaps closest in its theoretical assumptions to political economy and systems theories of organization. With a few conspicuous exceptions, political economy approaches have not had as much influence in organization theory as one might expect.[15] Political economy approaches have been much more influential in public policy analysis and theory of bureaucratic politics.[16] But there is potential for greater application in organization theory. Political economy approaches allow the researcher to go beyond simplistic distinctions among organizations (e.g., government versus nongovernment). As Buchanan has pointed out, few organizations' goods and services are exclusively public in character according to economists' view of what is public (one's consumption of a good or service does not diminish its availability to others; user charges are not conveniently established).[17]

Evans observes that "goods can be placed in a spectrum according to their external effects, the pure private goods at the one end of the spectrum and the pure public goods at the other."[18] We may say, then, that the character of goods and services provided by organizations is best thought of as dimensional in character.

If there is a difficulty with public goods approaches, it is that certain aspects of organization behavior are not easily or well described in economic terms. Nevertheless, the economic character of goods and services is an important consideration and public goods theory is useful in guiding organization theorists to a more sophisticated view of organizational "products" (and also of financing arrangements and distributional costs). Wamsley's and Zald's work not only underscored the relevance of political economy to the study of organizations but also demonstrated that, with some conceptual adaptation, political economy approaches can be applied to a broader range of organization problems.

The dimensional approach shares assumptions with political economy approaches to organizations, but the focus is somewhat shifted—namely, it is assumed that a variety of organization behaviors can be perceived in terms of dimensions and only some of these behaviors are economic in character. The lineage of the dimensional approach can also be traced to recent work in open systems theory, especially new developments in resource dependency and organization environment perspectives.[19] A useful summary of the work of this genre is provided by Scott:

> The rational models that have dominated our theories since the early 1960s are being challenged by a set of open, natural models. . . . These models place great emphasis on the importance of the environment in determining the behavior and life chances of organizations: they are clearly open systems models. However, the assumption that organizations behave as rational systems is strongly challenged in this work. To begin, organizations are believed to place their own survival over goal attainment . . . [and] the meaning of effectiveness is transformed.[20]

The resource dependency literature is not unrelated to more familiar systems theory approaches to the study of organizations, but its concepts of organization effectiveness and autonomy represent a departure. Pfeffer and Salancik's view that "effectiveness of an organization is a sociopolitical question"[21] distances the approach from traditional ones. Likewise, the idea that compliance with externally imposed rules is more important than production efficiency challenges rational models.[22]

It is important to note that the term *constraint* has a special meaning in this paper. The term often takes on a pejorative meaning in management literature. Even if theorists omit such qualifying adjectives as *undue*, *unnecessary*, or *burdensome*, their usage makes clear that constraints are to be avoided. My usage of *constraint* carries no such connotation in this paper, and I assume that *constraints can be viewed by the organization or the manager as positive, negative, or neutral in value*. Take, for instance, the changing role of the Interstate Commerce Commission (ICC) in regulating the railroad industry. During the early history of the ICC, its regulations were viewed as limiting, and railroad barons took a dim view of ICC constraints. Later, ICC regulations provided an economic shelter for railroads and constraints had a positive value for owners and investors. Both sets of regulatory policies, those limiting monopolistic practices as well as those sheltering the railroad from a transportation market in which it could no longer compete successfully, are constraints in my use of the term.

In sum, the dominant assumptions of the dimensional approach owe much to political economy and resource dependency approaches. Specifically, it is assumed that: (1) the publicness of organizations is not an absolute quality but a matter of degree; (2) much of organization behavior is poorly explained by rational choice models and is better accounted for in terms of the constraints imposed by external actors; (3) while a variety of external influences constrain the organization, those influences flowing from government entities account for the public character of organizations; (4) the publicness of organizations requires a redefinition of organization effectiveness, a definition that views the organization less as an agent for achievement of internally devised rational goals than as an entity serving multiple constituencies (both internal and external).

## Publicness and the Essentials of Organization Behavior

If we are to take external governmental constraint of the organization's processes as a focus, we must identify the processes that are of interest. There is at least some potential for external governmental constraint of virtually any organizational activity, but as a starting point we might wish to restrict the analysis to the essential processes of the organization. But, of course, the key question is begged: What are the essential processes? One meaning of *essential* is "defining." The question, then, becomes: What is the set of attributes and activities without which the concept *organization* begins to lose its meaning? This is, of course, not the only means of identifying essentials, but such a stipulative approach seems at least to provide a beginning and can help focus conceptual analysis.

The next step is to establish a satisfactory definition of *organization* so that essentials can be derived. Rather than simply positing a definition, I choose to review a number of definitions and distill common terms. Even a cursory review of basic works in organization theory yields a great many technical definitions of the term. There is enough variation in technical definitions to place some strain on those accustomed to thinking of organizations in nontechnical terms. I offer the following as a definition that seems to capture the most common elements of technical definitions as well as natural language (i.e., in use) definitions: *Organizations are formally structured social collectivities established to attain goals by acquiring resources from the environment and directing those resources to activities perceived as relevant to the goals.* This formulation draws from a number of definitions provided in some of the better-known works in organization theory.[23] It should be emphasized that this is a purposeful but not necessarily rational view of organization. The goals may or may not be formalized and they may be in the public interest, the collective interest, and/or the interest of one or more individuals; resources may be directed toward conflicting and even mutually exclusive goals; direction of resources may or may not be efficacious. I would argue that such a view of organizations is basic enough to encompass not only Weberian-style organizations but also "organized anarchies."[24]

To repeat, the purpose of this definitional exercise

is to derive the essential processes of organization with a view to arguing the relevance of a dimensional concept of publicness. According to the definition, the essential (i.e., defining, irreducible) processes in organization behavior are: (1) establishing and maintaining the organization, (2) structuring the organization, (3) acquiring and managing resources, (4) setting and seeking goals.[25]

Each of the essential processes within an organization entails numerous organization behaviors, and there are many factors, some internal in origin and others imposed from outside, that constrain organization behaviors. The focus here is on just one category of constraint—those imposed by governmental actors. The argument that publicness can be viewed in terms of dimensions of external governmental constraint on organization processes requires that we specify not only the dimensions but also polar values. Figure 1 depicts the various dimensions of publicness (for the essential processes stipulated) and establishes polar values.[26]

In some cases, it is easy to identify intermediate values in addition to polar values. For example, in the case of the life cycle dimension, some organizations are created by government; the creation of others is constrained only by market forces. But the creation of many organizations is to some degree subject to government constraints even if the government is not a formal party to the creation process. Sometimes the government's role is of central importance, such as regulation of entry into the marketplace. Other times government constraint is less direct and somewhat less crucial, such as the constraints tax policies impose on creation of new firms.

The remainder of the essay builds on this basic outline of the dimensional approach. The dimensions are elaborated, examples are provided, and implications for public organization theory and research are discussed.

## RESOURCE PROCESSES AND PUBLICNESS

No activity of organizations is more vital than resource acquisition and management. The essential activities of organizations presume a resource base, and much of the energy of the organization is directed toward expanding, safeguarding, or deploying resources. Also, the maintenance of the organization and its goal-directed activities are closely related to resource acquisition and management. There is a primacy to resource processes.

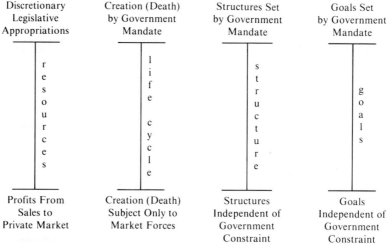

**Figure 1** Dimensions of Publicness for Essential Organizational Processes

Resource processes are not only complex but also multifaceted.[27] Since several aspects of resource processes are potentially subject to governmental constraint, a comprehensive approach to assessing the publicness of organizations' resource processes would require considerable conceptual development. As a starting point, however, we can focus on a single aspect, the resource mix of the organization. *Resource mix* is a simple enough concept but one that has received little attention in organization theory and research.

If all private organizations were at one pole of the resource dimension (i.e., receiving 100 percent of their resources from sales to private consumers in competitive markets) and all government organizations were at the other, there would be no need for a dimensional approach to resource processes. But organizations derive financial support from a variety of sources: profits from private markets, profits from government contracts, government subsidies, trust funds, user charges, special earmarked revenues, and so forth. These sources vary in the extent of government constraint implied.

Simple measures of resource mix are easily devised. By arraying sources of income in terms of implication for external governmental constraint and calculating the mix of revenues for a given organization, a rough index of publicness can be developed. Even granting problems in operationalization and measurement, it seems a potentially useful approach, certainly more useful than simply classifying organization into dichotomous categories of profit making and nonprofit. Figure 2 provides histograms for two hypothetical firms and illustrates one approach to depicting the resource publicness of organizations. The histograms allow us to rank the resource publicness of the organizations, but only a few additional steps are required to move from these histograms to a more precise measure.[28]

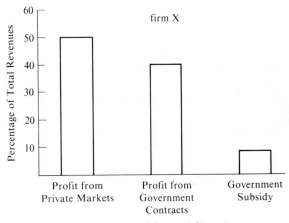

Resource Mix

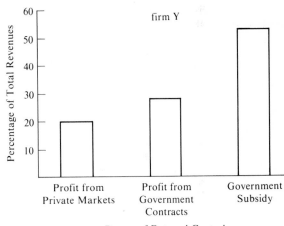

Resource Mix

**Figure 2**   Index of Publicness of Resource Mix

## RESOURCE PUBLICNESS: THE AEROSPACE INDUSTRY AS AN EXAMPLE

Figure 2 shows the possibilities for assessing the publicness of government organizations' resources, but it is also possible to use a similar approach to assess the publicness of business firms' resource mix. The resource dependency of business firms is well illustrated in the case of the aerospace industry, an industry that has had close ties to government since its inception.[29]

Dependency on government resources is a basic characteristic of the aerospace industry (indeed, one observer describes the industry as "the virtual ward of government"[30]), but in actuality there is much variance among firms in regard to degree of dependence on government. It is this variance that makes the aerospace industry an especially attractive case.

Seven aerospace firms account for more than 90 percent of the production of U.S. aircraft (measured by airframe weight). In the simplest of ordinal scales—a scale with only two values—we can consider the percentage of sales receipts derived from sales to, respectively, commercial firms and U.S. government contracts (including foreign and military sales which are under the control of the U.S. government). Figure 3 gives the percentages of sales receipts for these two categories and demonstrates the considerable variance in firms' dependence on government contracts. While Figure 3 illustrates one approach to measuring the publicness of business firms' resources, this is only a single measure for an industry pervaded by publicness. Reliance on government sales contracts represents only one aspect of the publicness of aircraft manufacturers' resource processes. Firms' sales profits are subject to limitations imposed under the Vinson-Trammell Act, which provides for government financial review of the profits gained through government contracts. It is also worth noting that the aerospace-government connection is not limited to sales. Firms are very much dependent on government for research and development funds.[31] Several industries rely on government funds or tax credits for research and development, but the aerospace industry's degree of dependence is exceptional. Even more noteworthy is the industry's dependence on government resources for financing capital improvements. In most instances, business firms' decisions about construction of new facilities are both made and financed independently.

It is tempting to agree with the assessment that the aerospace industry is the "virtual ward of government." But this is not the basic lesson of the dimensional approach. While it is true that organization theorists who fail to note the publicness of the aerospace firms' resource processes seriously distort reality, there is little theoretical advantage in jumping to the other extreme:

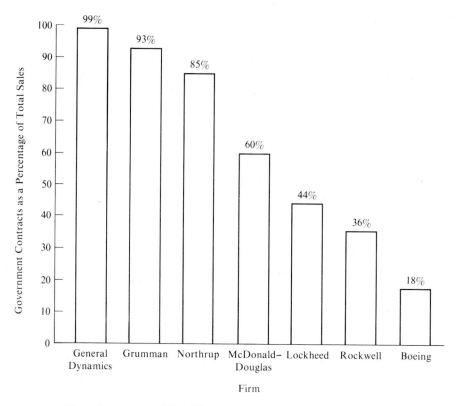

**Figure 3**   Aerospace Firms' Dependency on Government Contracts

ignoring the substantial variation in firms' publicness and treating these organizations as essentially public. The advantage of the dimensional approach is that it encourages a more differentiated view of the organizations comprising the aerospace industry and, for that matter, all organizations that are not "purely" public or private.

## Theoretical Implications of Resource Publicness

To this point, it has been demonstrated that both business and government organizations vary in respect to the publicness of their resource base and that simple measures of publicness can be developed from existing data. But to what end? Granted, more than 90 percent of Grumman's sales and only 18 percent of Boeing's are derived from government contracts—but does this difference result in significantly different patterns of organization behavior? That is, of course, an empirical question best addressed by research, but for present purposes we can consider some of the likely theoretical implications of resource publicness.

The chief theoretical implications of resource publicness relate to the sometimes conflicting values of autonomy and stability. Organizations that remain relatively free from external constraints typically retain greater flexibility not only in managing resource processes but in strategic decision making as well. Autonomy allows the organizations to adjust to the market, as conditions require, by expanding production, limiting production, initiating new products or services, stockpiling resources, creating slack resources, and so forth. Further, organizations relatively free from external constraints can sometimes manipulate the market and in many instances create demand through advertising, aggressive marketing, expansion of sales resources, or development of new clients.

It is not always the case that government and nongovernment resource acquisition strategies differ in a fundamental way (since government organizations can mobilize support for activities in much the same manner that nongovernment firms can create consumer demand). The important distinction between government and nongovernment organizations on this dimension of publicness is that executives in government organizations have a limited ability to control the means of acquiring resources and (just as importantly) managing the flow of resources. Most government organizations do not set prices and levy user charges (though of course there are trends in that direction, especially in local government).

Yet the limited ability of government organizations to control resource acquisition and flow directly is not always of great significance for the study of organizations. Students of public budgeting and appropriations have shown that government organizations are not passive supplicants.[32] Nor does the formal dependency of government organizations imply that they are blown hither and yon by prevailing political winds. Dependence on legislative and executive superiors does not necessarily result in unpredictability of resources. In the first place, budgeting is often incremental[33] and appropriations curves are rarely jagged, given the importance of the base.[34] Prior to our current extraordinary times, most agencies planned programs assuming that appropriations would match or exceed the previous year's. Even now, in an environment of fiscal austerity, there are few great surprises for agency officials. Legislators, budget examiners, and executive superiors provide cues on likely appropriations outcomes and agency officials are sensitive to these cues. Additionally, the budgeting process in the federal government (and many of the states) proceeds two to three years ahead of actual commitment of obligational authority. Finally, a good portion of government agency resources can be counted as "uncontrollable" in the sense that they are derived from trust funds, earmarked taxes, or indexed statutory entitlements and involve little discretion.

The point is that external governmental constraint of resource acquisition is often a force for stability. Dependency can offer some advantages. The "most private" firms (those sustained by profits generated from private markets) enjoy all the freedom associated with autonomy—including freedom in management and investment of financial resources—but must typically operate in a more uncertain environment. Thus, a major implication of the dimensional approach is that publicness of organization resource processes is not intrinsically good or bad but instead a variable that is judged in relation to management strategies and characteristics of the organization's environment. As Thompson notes, organizations seek strategies that shelter their core technology from environmental stress and uncertainty. In some instances, publicness is an effective shelter; in others, it is an effective shackle.[35]

## LIFE CYCLE PROCESSES AND PUBLICNESS

Establishing and maintaining the organization is a basic process common to all organizations. Organizations come into existence, seek to maintain themselves, and ultimately perish; thus, they can be said to have a life cycle. In line with the approach outlined here, organization life cycles are considered in terms of the degree to which external governmental constraints affect the creation, maintenance, and dismantling of organizations. At one end of the life cycle dimension are organizations whose existence is completely subject to governmental control; at the other end are those whose existence is completely independent from government constraints.

Government organizations are not only subject to legal requirements but are dependent on legal superiors for their creation. Government organizations—whether created by statute, executive order, or superior entities in the bureaucracy—are not (at least in a formal sense) self-initiating. While this formal difference between government and nongovernment organizations is important, one must also consider that nongovernment organizations rarely spring into existence all at once, unfettered by charter requirements, licensing procedures, antitrust laws, or similar governmental constraints. There is considerable variance in external governmental constraint of the birth/death processes of nongovernment organizations.[36] Small voluntary organizations often have almost no external constraints imposed at the time of formation, but (at another extreme) processes for establishing and incorporation of a large firm operating in an oligarchic market and heavily constrained by antitrust laws often involves substantial external constraint.

In addition to direct external constraints (such as antitrust legislation), life cycle dependence often results from government regulation of markets. Pfeffer provides evidence of the effects of Civil Aeronautics Board regulations on the entry of new airlines into the industry.[37] Also, tax incentives often play an important role in the establishment of organizations.[38] Thus, we can consider the effects of external governmental constraint on the creation of organizations even in cases where there is no direct legal constraint on creation. This is not to say that the differences in legal requirements are unimportant. The point is that we can differentiate *nongovernment* organizations on the basis of the external governmental constraints on their creation.

### Publicness and Organization Life Cycles: Lessons from the Aerospace Industry

Just as the aerospace industry serves as a good illustration of resource publicness, it also provides us with insights concerning governmental constraints on organizational life cycles. The most familiar case is the role of government bodies in maintaining aerospace firms that have floundered in the marketplace. The federal government's bailout of Lockheed is especially well known and widely documented.[39] Most observers agree that the federal guarantee of $250 million in bank loans prevented the bankruptcy of the firm—a firm that only a few years earlier had been responsible for devastating cost overruns in the production of the C-5A aircraft.[40]

The Lockheed episode provides one of the most dramatic studies of government constraint of the life cycle of a private firm, but it is important to note that the aerospace industry has from its inception been closely tied to government. The creation processes for the industry were perhaps even more constrained than the maintenance processes. It is common knowledge that the early aircraft industry was a child of World War I, but less well known is the extraordinary (especially for the time) steps taken by the federal government in midwifing the birth of the industry. Not only did government contracts bankroll the industry, but the federal government also provided for exceptional patenting procedures, unprecedented cross-licensing arrangements, and technical assistance. As a result, an industry that had attracted very little investor interest when subject to normal viscissitudes of the market managed to increase investment tenfold in a single year. As late as 1914, only about 50 aircraft were produced; government-spurred production had brought that figure to more than 14,000 only four years later.[41] Moreover, during the next five decades the growth of the industry was largely a function of a variety of government initiatives including, for example, the Air Mail Act of 1925, the Air Commerce Act of 1926, and various policies of the Army Air Corps and the Navy. The only significant growth *not* attributable to policy initiatives and government demand was the growth in civilian aircraft ushered in by the "Lindbergh Boom" during the late 1920s.

The Lockheed case and the early history of the industry underscore the same point. An understanding of organizational life cycles requires an encompassing view of publicness. Government organizations' and business organizations' life cycles are often shaped in similar ways by government constraints.

## The Mortality of Business and Government Organizations: Some Conflicting Findings

The fact that private firms, like government organizations, are subject to government constraints affecting their life cycles does not imply that there are no differences between business and government organizations' life cycles. Kaufman's study of the growth and decline of government organizations provides evidence of the exceptional longevity of many government agencies[42]; Department of Commerce statistics show that a high percentage of new business ventures fail during their first year. Government organizations do not live by the "natural laws" of profit and growth.

Nevertheless, the distinction in the growth and decline process of government and nongovernment organizations is not so great as it appears and it is easy to overemphasize the significance of legal status. The failure rates for new businesses are deceptive statistics because so many businesses are small operations; business firms of about the same size as the median size government organizations exhibit considerable longevity. Furthermore, Starbuck's and Nystrom's reinterpretation of Kaufman's data gives a different view of the explanatory power of legal status in regard to organizations' longevity. Starbuck and Nystrom argue that "Kaufman biased his classifications toward demonstrating stability: he classified agencies as being lineal descendants even if they had different names, performed substantially different functions, belonged to different departments, and had no personnel in common with their ancestors."[43] Starbuck and Nystrom applied a different framework to government organizations and corporations and concluded that "the similarity [in survival rates] between federal agencies and corporations is amazing ... agencies and business firms appear about equally stable."[44]

What are we to conclude from such conflicting studies? The conclusion that a dimensional approach to publicness suggests is that questions of the longevity of organizations might be clarified by considering not only legal status (government/nongovernment) but also the effects of government constraints of various types and intensities. This does not, of course, imply that legal status is insignificant. Differences in the respective maintenance, growth, and decline processes of government and nongovernment organizations may

have been overemphasized in the past, but legal status remains an important factor in understanding organizational life cycles. Lockheed has not yet vanished because of periodic failure to show a profit, but profit is not incidental to the corporation. Likewise, the fact that some government organizations can be dismantled only by an act of Congress is surely consequential. The central point is that while organizations may share many life cycle determinants (such as size, resource munificence, and productivity) that have little to do with external governmental constraint, a dimensional approach to publicness can contribute to the understanding of organization life cycles.

## STRUCTURAL/MANAGERIAL PROCESSES AND PUBLICNESS

Another basic element of organizations is structure, and here, too, there are implications for publicness. There are a number of centralizing features in government that might be lumped together in the category of structural/managerial constraints.

In the federal government, two of the most significant agencies in promoting structural/managerial dependency are the General Services Administration (GSA) and the Office of Management and Budget (OMB). The centralization of procurement in the GSA has no true counterpart in nongovernment organizations though, of course, in those instances where a single vendor is dominant there are certain similarities in external constraint. Also, the policies of GSA directly affect many government contractors. The OMB promulgates regulations that set management procedures for federal agencies, and, like GSA, OMB also has substantial impact on the structuring and management of nongovernment organizations. A recent illustration of the effects of external constraint exerted by the OMB is the provision for full-time accounting in research grants and contracts, OMB circular A-21.[45] Through this requirement and related mandated procedures, OMB has the power to greatly affect the operations, management, and structuring of nongovernment research and development organizations.

Another familiar set of government constraints that could be viewed as elements of structural/managerial publicness pertain to personnel management. Most evident are the constraints imposed by government entities on other government entities: Agencies are constrained by the availability of personnel lines, by hiring freezes, and by civil service requirements. But nongovernment organizations have found themselves subject to governmental constraint in their recruitment, advancement, and management of personnel. Affirmative Action and Equal Employment Opportunity guidelines have sometimes had significant impacts on business firms' hiring practices. Also, regulations imposed by such agencies as Occupational Safety and Health Administration have constrained organizations in the management and direction of employees. Minimum wage legislation and social security requirements are further elements of publicness. Most importantly, organizations differ somewhat in the degree to which personnel practices are constrained. For example, organizations that rely heavily on government contracts often find that conformance to government personnel standards is a precondition for contract awards. Universities (including private universities) are particularly vulnerable because it is legally possible to withhold all federal money from a university because a single department or even a single project has been found in violation of Affirmative Action guidelines. Moreover, governmental constraint not only has direct consequences on hiring, promotion, and personnel procedures, but also affects the structure and operation of personnel and even line units.

A potentially significant distinction between government and business organizations is the degree to which authority to impose sweeping structural change is vested in the organization. In a formal sense, government organizations have little authority to impose major reorganization plans unilaterally (though there is considerable flexibility at the Department level to impose changes in bureaus). But within a given organization (at the level of the bureau or the independent agency), there is typically considerable freedom to manipulate organization structures. Certainly, legislative oversight is rarely concerned with the structuring of organizations and, typically, executive superiors grant considerable discretion.[46]

### Structural/Managerial Publicness in the Aerospace Industry

The publicness of structure and managerial practice is well illustrated in the aerospace industry. Previously, I observed that there is no private-sector counterpart to the GSA and its procurement practices. But government procurement and facilities management can have

a significant impact on business firms. An obvious example is the effect of government contracting and accounting procedures on financial structures and financial management practices in aerospace firms. But another example comes from facilities management. During World War II, no less than 92 percent of the aircraft industry's facilities expansion was underwritten by the federal government. In 1944, the federal government actually owned 90 percent of the facilities for the manufacture of aircraft.[47] This posed an interesting problem at the end of the war, namely, how to dispose of billions of dollars of surplus equipment without gutting the industry. Due to government constraints, the disposal of surpluses was not simply a market problem. A contemporary account noted:

> Since complete assembly lines for the production of [civilian aircraft] consist of government-owned tools and equipment, the manufacturers cannot proceed with construction until some disposition is made of these tools. On the government side of the picture, however, is the necessity for disposal to be carried out along democratic lines, i.e., all interested parties must be given an equal opportunity to participate in the sale of government equipment. The surplus disposal problem, both aircraft and facilities, thus, is a complex problem which can be solved only through the establishment and execution of a broad, over-all policy.[48]

The postwar surplus problem illustrates some of the ramifications of government dependency on the publicness of firms' structure and management practices. While the postwar example is extreme, the aerospace industry is even today highly dependent on government-owned facilities and equipment. Moreover, the aerospace industry is not alone in its sensitivity to government constraints on contracting, procurement, facilities management, accounting procedures, and personnel practices.

## GOAL PROCESSES AND PUBLICNESS

Mohr makes a distinction between *transitive goals* and *reflexive goals*. A transitive goal is "one whose referent is outside the organization in question . . . an intended impact of the organization upon its environment."[49] Reflexive goals, by contrast, are internally oriented, deal with system maintenance, and most generally, involve inducements aimed at evoking member contributions to the organization:

. . . Within the general framework of the reflexive goals, each organization works out its own rules of the game. The criteria used in partitioning organizational resources and the resultant distribution of inducements —money, power, status, psychological experience, etc.—will certainly differ from organization to organization.[50]

It is useful to think of both types of goals in terms of the degree to which external constraint may be exerted, though there is typically greater variability in the publicness of transitive goals. A distinction between government and nongovernment organizations is that the former are established with one or more transitive goals in place, usually stated in the agency's enabling legislation or executive order. As Mohr points out, nongovernment organizations frequently do not profess transitive goals but instead may exist solely for the achievement of reflexive goals (such as the economic benefit of organization members).

Nevertheless, despite the existence in government organizations of formal transitive goals, students of bureaucratic politics are well aware that transitive goals sometimes have limited significance for understanding organization behavior. Government agencies may be assumed to have formal goals that transcend the organization, but that assumption should not unduly color expectations about behavior. As Downs observes, "[public] bureaucratic officials, like all other agents in society, are significantly—though not solely—motivated by their own interests.[51] This does not, of course, imply that the public manager's goals are necessarily incompatible with the organizations' transitive goals. Downs recognizes that public managers have a "complex set of goals including power, income, prestige, security, convenience, loyalty (to an idea, an institution, or the nation), pride in excellent work, and desire to serve the public interest."[52]

Moreover, transitive goals may be of considerable consequence in some instances but may be of relatively little importance in understanding behavior in cases where the transitive goals have been displaced, ignored, or used as convenient rationalizations for reflexive goals. While government organizations can be assumed to possess formal transitive goals, it is important to remember that: (1) any organization may profess transitive goals, and (2) government/nongovernment status tells us little about the empirical significance of transitive goals.

Formal transitive goals are sometimes of little use in explaining the behavior of organizations but are critically related to *expectations* about behavior. An important distinction between government and business organizations relates to the sharing of transitive goals. It is not enough for a particular government agency to achieve its goals, either reflexive or transitive, if in achieving the goals the agency has undermined a broader public policy objective (i.e., a more significant transitive goal) it shares with other organizational actors. If an agency's success is at the expense of broader policy goals (e.g., crime prevention, technological innovation, full employment), the agency is "effective" only in a narrow sense. In government organizations, organizational effectiveness takes a back seat to policy effectiveness. The goals of business organizations, even firms in the same industry, are rarely linked in the same *way* even in those rare instances where they are linked to a similar *degree*.

## SHARED GOALS IN THE AEROSPACE INDUSTRY: DIFFERENCES IN BEHAVIOR VERSUS DIFFERENCES IN EXPECTATION

Let us consider yet another example from the aerospace industry to illustrate that business organizations, even those that are public in many respects, are rarely linked in the same manner as government organizations. Beginning in the mid-1950s, there was a sharp decline in the demand for military aircraft and the industry was faced with a crisis shared by every major airframe manufacturer.[53] There were three characteristic responses: scaling down production and closing facilities, diversifying into fields far removed from airframe production, and positioning the firm to compete for now-abundant missile design and production contracts. Most of the larger firms chose the third alternative. However, the competition for missile contracts was, at least initially, quite different than that for aircraft contracts. Since the 1940s, aircraft production had been dominated by just a few firms, and experience, equipment, and vendor familiarity had by this time begun to serve as a significant barrier to the entry of new firms.[54] The picture was abruptly changed as firms competed for missile contracts. No one had any experience building missiles, there were no vendor "track records," and even the aircraft manufacturers' plants would have to be completely overhauled. The aircraft manufacturers could claim technical expertise, but so could electrical firms, electronics firms, and even automobile manufacturers. Indeed, even as late as 1956, less than 30 percent of missile contracts had been awarded to aircraft manufacturers.[55] The major firms in the aircraft industry found themselves linked by a critical goal: the need to "sell" the industry's advantages for missile production in order to expand the industry's base. For a period, aircraft manufacturers closed ranks against electronics firms and other potential missile vendors, shared technical expertise, and pursued common promotional strategies. Their success is reflected in the aircraft firms' ability to procure most of the major missile contracts during the 1960s.[56]

What are we to make of this episode? In the first place, private firms, even those locked in life-or-death competitive struggles, sometimes find themselves linked by goals that reflect the firms' shared interest. But even if firms are linked to a similar or even a greater degree than government agencies, they are not linked in the same manner. In this example, the linkage is one dictated by survival, not by a need to achieve some goal that transcends the aggregated interests of the individual firms. Government organizations are *expected* to behave in the public interest (i.e., in service to broad transitive goals); business firms are *expected* to pursue their own interests. This is not to say that government organizations necessarily behave in the public interest; no empirical generalization is implied. Moreover, it is in the realm of normative expectations, rather than empirical behavior, that distinctions between government organizations and business organizations take on greater importance, even if the business organizations are substantially public, such as those in the aerospace industry.

## SUMMARY AND CONCLUSIONS

The central arguments of this essay are uncomplicated and easily summarized. Organization theory and research has made little progress in solving the publicness problem; there is little agreement about the significance of publicness as a determinant of organizations' behavior. There are few convincing theoretical rationales for guiding *public* organization research, and comparative research on public/private organizations is, typically, poorly justified. Furthermore, comparative research has, for a variety of reasons, provided inconclusive findings. I have argued that one obstacle to theoretical progress on the publicness problem is the absence of a publicness concept that deals realistically with the blurring of sectors and with government pene-

tration of organizations traditionally viewed as private. My view is that it is helpful to think of publicness in terms of external government constraint on organizations' activities. Further, an organization may (by this concept of publicness) be quite public in some respects but not in others. A related point is that we can view business and mixed-type organizations, as well as government organizations, in terms of degree of publicness. While such an approach raises its own problems in conceptualization and measurement, a widely applicable dimensional approach would seem to hold more promise than traditional approaches of shedding light on the publicness problem.

### Public Organization Theory and Error Reduction

To put the dimensional approach in some perspective, we can compare it to other approaches. While approaches to publicness are many and varied, just a few archetypal categories seem to capture most approaches. For convenience sake, these categories can be called *aggregate, binary,* and *comparative.* The first assumes that publicness is of little significance, the second assumes that it is of paramount significance, and the third suspends judgment. The approaches vary not only in assumptions but in objectives.

Research and theory in the aggregate category is typically more concerned with broad generalization and development of encompassing theories of organization. The population of interest is *all* organizations. If publicness is considered at all, it is viewed as having secondary importance; in effect, it is a single term or an intervening variable in a more general model. The approach is appropriate insofar as the assumption about the limited significance of publicness is valid.

The binary approach assumes that public organizations usually defined as government organizations are unique (not just that they tend to be different) and that government organizations' behavior cannot, therefore, be explained by more general models. The population of interest is all government organizations or, in some instances, a subset of government organizations. The approach is appropriate insofar as the assumption about the primacy of publicness is valid.

The comparative approach assumes that publicness is potentially a significant determinant of organizations' behavior and sets out to determine empirically the relevant differences between public and private organizations. The approach is productive provided that adequate constructs of publicness have been developed.

Each of these approaches (or, more accurately, categories) plays a role in development of public organization theory, but each has weaknesses. In my view, a central task of public organization theory is elimination of error in assumptions about the significance of publicness. The task is to eliminate Type A and Type B error where *Type A (aggregation) error* is the probability of incorrectly assuming that publicness is *not* a significant determinant of organization behavior and *Type B (binary) error* is the probability of incorrectly assuming that publicness *is* a significant determinant.

There is as little a priori justification for distinguishing among organizations on the basis of public status as there is for assuming that so obvious a distinction is trivial. The approach that can come closest to resolving the publicness problem is the comparative approach.

Figure 4 shows the relationship of the three predominant approaches to the probability of Type A and B error. It is important to emphasize that any of the three approaches can be useful provided its basic assumption is valid. Even the comparative approach can be inappropriate if it wastes researchers' time and energy in pursuit of dead ends. In those cases where publicness is of no importance, the comparative approach is at best inefficient.

Where does the dimensional approach fit into this scheme? It is a reconstruction of the comparative approach, a reconstruction that replaces traditional comparative foci (government/nongovernment) with a publicness concept altered to take into account the public (*and* private) dimensions of all organizations. In my view, the dimensional approach is a means to facilitate comparison and, at the same time, an approach that facilitates the generalizations central to organization theory.

## An Agenda for Theory and Research

The first step in developing the dimensional approach is refinement of concepts. As presented here, external governmental constraint is a concept that has intuitive appeal but not as much substance as needed for research applications. Some crude approaches to measuring external government constraint were suggested, especially in connection with the resource processes dimension, but further development of concepts and measures is required.

Despite these problems, the agenda is expansive. It provides at least as many possibilities as the binary approach; in each case one might compare the publicness of organizations instead of, or in addition to, government/nongovernment status. But if the dimensional approach is applicable to a prodigious number of research questions, there are some it seems to emphasize. Perhaps at the top of an empirical and conceptual research agenda is the relation of publicness to organization effectiveness. My assumption is that the relation of publicness to organization effectiveness varies considerably according to the particular dimension of publicness and according to the concept of effectiveness that is of interest. One might hypothesize, for example, that an organization that is "more public" in resource processes is likely to prove more effective in stability, organizational maintenance, and "smoothness" (in Cameron's terms),[57] but less effective by those measures pertaining to goal attainment. The dependence implied by publicness might serve to inhibit change in personnel, procedures, and level of resources and thus reinforce stability. That same dependence might, however, constrain and complicate organizational goal attainment activities and thus inhibit goal-related effectiveness.

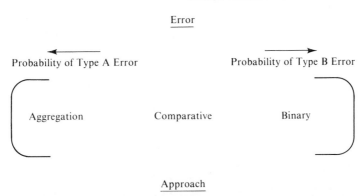

Error

Probability of Type A Error      Probability of Type B Error

Aggregation     Comparative     Binary

Approach

**Figure 4**   Error Reduction and Approaches to Publicness

Another line of investigation suggested by the dimensional approach to publicness is the transferability of management techniques and innovations among sectors. For example, are government agencies that are "more private" on relevant dimensions of publicness more receptive to business management techniques than those agencies that are "more public"? As is the case with a number of potentially fruitful applications of the dimensional approach, researchers and theorists interested in this question will need to exercise great care to avoid problems of definitional dependence when considering this question.

Another question suggested by the dimensional approach involves public accountability and citizen satisfaction. One might hypothesize, for example, that business firms that are "more public" are more responsive to citizen demands and to the public interest (by one or another definition) than firms that are "more private." One might assume that the greater dependence on government organizations would lead to an increased concern with the public interest and citizen satisfaction. (Conversely, one might assume that organizations relying solely on profits from private markets might have a greater stake in citizen and consumer satisfaction).

These are simply a few of the theoretical and research issues that are facilitated by a dimensional approach to publicness. The chief point is that an approach that goes beyond legal and formal distinctions in its concept of publicness can contribute to the clarification, and possibly even the resolution, of a good many gaps in organization theory. This essay has simply been a first step in the development of a dimensional approach to publicness.

*A number of people have contributed to this essay. Hal Rainey read two drafts and offered several useful suggestions. Michael Crow commented on two drafts and helped provide examples. Others who have read all or part of a draft and contributed helpful suggestions include Howard Aldrich, Richard Hall, Steve Loveless, Ken Ruscio, and Bill Starbuck.*

## NOTES

1. D. Warwick, *A Theory of Public Bureaucracy* (Cambridge, Mass.: Harvard University Press, 1975), p. 204.

2. An especially useful synthesis of the literature comparing public and private organizations is presented in Hal Rainey, Robert Backoff, and Charles Levine, "Comparing Public and Private Organizations," *Public Administration Review* 36 (1976): 223–244. More recent but less comprehensive overviews are presented in Barry Bozeman, "Organization Structure and the Effectiveness of Public Agencies," *International Journal of Public Administration* 3 (1982): 235–296; Graham Allison, "Public and Private Management: Are They Fundamentally Alike in All Unimportant Respects?" paper prepared for the Public Management Research Conference, Brookings Institution, Washington, D. C., November 19–20, 1979; and Laurence Lynn, Jr., *Managing the Public's Business* (New York: Basic Books, 1981).

3. M. W. Meyer and R. O. Williams, *Comparison of Innovation in Public and Private Sectors: An Exploratory Study,* unpublished study prepared for the National Science Foundation under grant PRA-19967, n.d.

4. Most empirical studies focus on individual-level (microorganizational) behaviors. Some especially useful comparative studies include: Bruce Buchanan, "Government Managers, Business Executives and Organizational Commitment," *Public Administration Review* 35 (1975): 533–546; H. G. Rainey, "Public Agencies and Private Firms: Incentive Structures, Goals, and Individual Roles," *Administration and Society* (in press); Bruce Buchanan, "Red-Tape and the Service Ethic," *Administration and Society* 6 (1975): 423–444; H. G. Rainey, "Perceptions of Incentives in Business and Government," *Public Administration Review* 15 (1983): 207–242.

5. See David Roessner, "Incentives to Innovate in Public and Private Organizations: Implications for Public Policy," *Administration and Society* 9 (1977): 341–365.

6. Louis Gawthrop, *Administrative Politics and Social Change* (New York: St. Martin's Press, 1971), chap. 5; see Orion White, "The Problem of Urban Administration and Environmental Turbulence," in H. G. Frederickson (ed.), *Neighborhood Control in the 1970's* (San Francisco: Chandler, 1970), pp. 117–137.

7. An overview of the problems of assessing the effectiveness of public organizations is presented in B. L. Bozeman, "Organization Structure and the Effectiveness of Public Agencies," *International Journal of Public Administration* 4 (1982): 235–296.

8. For discussion of problems of aggregation in organizational research, see J. H. Freeman, "The Unit of Analysis in Organization Research," in Marshall Meyer and Associates, *Environments and Organizations* (San Francisco: Jossey-Bass, 1978), pp. 335–351; John Kimberly, "Issues in the Design of Longitudinal Organization Research," *Sociological Methods and Research* 4 (February 1976): 321–347; K. H. Roberts, C. L. Hulin, and D. M. Rosseau, *Developing an Interdisciplinary Science of Organizations* (San Francisco: Jossey-Bass, 1978). An overview of methodological problems in research comparing public and private organizations is given in Hal Rainey, James Perry, and Barry Bozeman,

"Empirical Comparisons of Public and Private Organizations: Conceptual and Methodological Issues," paper prepared for the Annual Meeting of the American Society for Public Administration, Honolulu, Hawaii, March 21–25, 1982.

9. Hal Rainey, R. Backoff, and Charles Levine, "Comparing Public and Private Organizations," *Public Administration Review* 36 (1976): 234.

10. G. S. Finney, "Public-Private Partnerships," paper prepared for National Academy of Public Administration Conference on Governments' Use of Non-Profit Agencies to Manage Social Research and Demonstration, Washington, D. C., November 1978, pp. 77–78.

11. Peter Blau and W. R. Scott, *Formal Organizations* (San Francisco: Chandler, 1962).

12. Marshall Meyer, "Organizational Domains," *American Sociological Review* 40 (1973): 599–615.

13. B. L. Bozeman and E. A. Slusher, "Scarcity and Environmental Stress in Public Organizations," *Administration and Society* 11 (1979): 335–356.

14. Two disclaimers are now in order. First, I do not assume that constraints imposed by government entities are necessarily more important than constraints flowing from other elements of the organization's environment. Second, while it seems to me useful to define publicness in terms of government constraint, this is clearly only one of many possible approaches. The chief advantage of this definition is that it seems to have the potential to help resolve certain problems in organization theory. Its chief disadvantage is that it ignores many of the connotations of public that have less to do with institutions of government than with community (public) interest, symbols of legitimacy, and collective values. At present I am willing to sacrifice some of the broader connotations of public in an effort to achieve some degree of conceptual clarity.

15. One familiar work seeking to employ political economy approaches in developing organization theory is Gary Wamsley and Mayer Zald, *The Political Economy of Public Organizations* (Lexington, Mass.: Lexington Books, 1973).

16. See, for example, Anthony Downs, *An Economic Theory of Democracy* (New York: Harper & Row, 1957); William Niskanen, Jr., *Bureaucracy and Representative Government* (Chicago: Aldine-Atherton, 1971).

17. James Buchanan, *The Demand and Supply of Public Goods* (Chicago: Rand-McNally, 1973).

18. A. Evans, "Private Good, Externality, Public Good," *Scottish Journal of Political Economy* 22 (1970): 80.

19. See, for example, J. Pfeffer and G. Salancik, *The External Control of Organizations* (New York: Harper & Row, 1978).

20. W. Richard Scott, *Organizations: Rational, Natural and Open Systems* (Englewood Cliffs, N. J.: Prentice-Hall), p. 131.

21. Ibid., p. 11.

22. J. W. Meyer and Brian Rowan, "Institutionalized Organizations: Formal Structure as Myth and Ceremony," *American Journal of Sociology* 83 (1977): 340–363.

23. Works consulted include D. Katz and R. Kahn, *The Social Psychology of Organizations,* 2nd ed. (New York: Wiley, 1978); Richard Hall, *Organizations: Structure and Process,* 2nd ed. (Englewood Cliffs, N. J.: Prentice-Hall, 1977); A. Etzioni, *Modern Organizations* (Englewood Cliffs, N. J.: Prentice-Hall, 1964); Peter Blau and W. R. Scott, *Formal Organizations* (San Francisco: Chandler, 1962).

24. M. Cohen, J. March, and J. Olsen, "A Garbage Can Model of Organizational Choice," *Administrative Science Quarterly* 17 (1972): 1–25.

25. In identifying these essential dimensions, I do not mean to imply that this is a comprehensive list of organization properties, only that it is a list of defining attributes. As a biologist might say, these are the diagnostic characteristics for the organism, those without which it would be some other organism. Also, these should not be viewed as orthogonal or mutually exclusive dimensions. It is quite likely that these are important relationships among the dimensions. For example, the relationship between resource processes and maintenance of the organization is patent.

26. In part for analytic convenience, and in part out of ignorance, I have simplified the dimensions. Obviously, there is much more to organizational resource processes than source of revenue. Later work should concentrate on elaborating the dimensions and examining the relation of a wider array of processes to government constraint.

27. My focus here is only on financial resources and even then only on some aspects. For a more comprehensive treatment, see Barry Bozeman and Jeffrey D. Straussman, "Organizations' 'Publicness' and Resource Management Strategies," in Richard Hall and Robert Quinn, eds., *Organization Theory and Public Policy* (Beverly Hills, Calif.: Sage, 1983).

28. This could be done in a number of ways, but one example should suffice. We could begin by ordering funding sources according to the degree of external control implied and assigning an ordinal value to each source (e.g., private sales receipts = 1; government contract receipts = 2, government subsidy = 3; trust funds and earmarked revenues = 4; legislative appropriations = 5). A value for this index of publicness might then be obtained by taking the product of (1) the revenue source as a percentage of total revenues for the organization, and (2) the ordinal value (or alternatively the weight) assigned to a revenue category. Clearly, there are

major operational problems with such a measure, but it serves to illustrate one means of deriving a distribution of values for the publicness of organizations' financial resources.

29. Howard Mingos, "The Rise of the Aircraft Industry" in G. R. Simonson (ed.), *The History of the American Aircraft Industry* (Cambridge, Mass.: MIT Press, 1968), pp. 23–73.

30. Herman Stekler, *The Structure and Performance of the Aerospace Industry* (Berkeley: University of California Press, 1965).

31. Data for research and development funding are less easily obtained than for sales receipts. Nevertheless, some relevant figures are in the public domain. Rockwell International reported in 1979 that of the $1.3 billion spent on research and development, $152.6 million was provided from internal sources (the remainder was derived from government research and development contracts). Of the $152.6 million put up by the firm, $98.4 million was actually charged as expenses to the firm; the remainder was recoverable through contracts or overhead cost allowances. Thus, for a firm with 36 percent of its sales derived from government contract, we find that approximately 99 percent of its research and development effort is also government financed. While the research and development contract figures are somewhat above the average for the industry, they do reflect a pronounced tendency for firms to rely heavily on government for the financing of research and development.

32. Aaron Wildavsky, *The Politics of the Budgetary Process,* 2nd ed. (Boston: Little, Brown, 1974).

33. Ibid.

34. John Wanat, "The Bases of Budgetary Incrementalism," *American Political Science Review* 68 (1974): 122–129.

35. James Thompson, *Organizations in Action* (New York: McGraw-Hill, 1967).

36. See John Kimberly, Raymond Miles, and Associates, *The Organizational Life Cycle* (San Francisco: Jossey-Bass, 1980) and John Kimberly, "Issues in the Creation of Organizations," *Academy of Management Journal* 22 (1979): 437–457.

37. J. Pfeffer, "Administrative Regulation and Licensing: Social Problem or Solution?" *Social Problems* 17 (1974): 218–228.

38. For a review of literature pertaining to tax policy and barriers to market entry, see B. Bozeman and A. Link, *Investments in Technology: Corporate Strategies and Public Policy* (New York: Praeger, 1983).

39. For a description of government actions in the Lockheed case, see "Lockheed: Loan Guarantee for Defense Contractor," *Congressional Quarterly,* May 21, 1971, pp. 1124–1128; F. V. Fowlkes, "Foes of Lockheed Loan Guarantee Challenge Basic Premises Behind Proposal," *National Journal,* May 24, 1971, pp. 1151–1155.

40. An overview of the problems surrounding the production of the C-5A is given in Berkeley Rice, *The C-5A Scandal* (Boston: Houghton Mifflin, 1971).

41. For the early history of the aircraft industry, see G. R. Simonson (ed.), *The History of American Aircraft Industry* (Cambridge, Mass.: MIT Press); *The Aircraft Year Book,* published yearly by the Aircraft Industries Association since 1919; W. W. Axe, *The Aviation Industry in the U. S.* (New York: Houghton Economic Studies, 1938); W. A. Schrader, *Fifty Years of Flight: A Chronicle of the Aviation Industry in America* (Cleveland: Eaton, 1953); J. K. Northrop, *Aviation History* (Washington, D. C.: U. S. Library of Congress, 1949).

42. Herbert Kaufman, *Are Government Organizations Immortal?* (Washington, D. C.: Brookings, 1976).

43. William Starbuck and Paul Nystrom, "Designing and Understanding Organizations," in Paul Nystrom and William Starbuck (eds.), *Handbook of Organizational Design* (London: Oxford University Press, 1981), p. 18.

44. Ibid., p. 21.

45. S. MacLane, "Total Reporting for Scientific Research," *Science* 210 (1980): 158–163.

46. B. L. Bozeman, "Organization Design in Public Bureaucracy," *American Review of Public Administration* 15 (1981): 107–118.

47. W. G. Cunningham, *The Aircraft Industry: A Study in Industrial Location* (Los Angeles: Morrison, 1951).

48. R. M. Cleveland and F. Graham (eds.), *The Aviation Annual of 1946* (Garden City, N. J.: Doubleday, Doran, 1945), pp. 94–95.

49. Lawrence Mohr, "The Concept of Organizational Goal," *American Political Science Review* 67 (1973): 476.

50. Ibid., p. 476.

51. Anthony Downs, *Inside Bureaucracy* (Boston: Little, Brown, 1966), p. 2.

52. Ibid., p. 2,

53. G. R. Simonson, "Missiles and Creative Destruction in the American Aircraft Industry, 1956–1961," *Business History Review* 38 (1964): 302–314.

54. Ibid.

55. Ben Lee (ed.), *Aviation Facts and Figures, 1957* (New York: McGraw-Hill: 1957).

56. *The Aerospace Yearbook, 1967* (Washington, D. C.: Aerospace Industries Association of America, 1967).

57. Kim Cameron, "Critical Questions in Assessing Organizational Effectiveness," *Organization Dynamics* (Autumn 1980): 66–80.

# Beyond Corporate Responsibility
## Toward a Fundamental Redefinition of the Roles of the Public and Private Sectors

Robert P. Kogod
Stephen C. Caulfield

For most of this country's history a process has been underway that has defined increasingly separate domains for the public and private sector, and perhaps most significantly has expanded the mandate of the public sector. In the course of this process, incentives, or the lack thereof, have led to different executive and managerial styles in each sector.

The resources of the public sector are now both contracting, as a function of tax cuts and the recession, and being reallocated to improve our defense capacity. The ability of states to increase tax revenues has been limited by voter rebellion in recent years, and our tolerance for deficits at both the state and federal level is shrinking.

The confluence of these factors with the rising costs for public programs, a heightened awareness of corporate responsibility, and a generalized public acceptance that some fundamental institutional reforms may be appropriate, provides us with a unique challenge and opportunity to examine how our public and private institutions might better serve our needs. The process will be difficult, for our choices will be constrained by our inability to pay for everything, and in the near term, by low productivity and the relatively high cost of capital. If, however, we can make these difficult choices well, a new and substantially different relationship between the public and private sector can emerge, one where opportunity for decent employment, housing, environment and education are available to all, where some government programs may be replaced by smaller enterprises using risk capital rather than grants, and where the individual at all levels of our society not only feels self worth, but also self-determination.

This opportunity should be seized quickly, for many believe that unless the task is well begun in the next twelve to eighteen months, the opportunity will pass us by, with a return to costly government programs, rapidly increasing taxation and regulation, and a further decline in productivity and efficiency in both sectors.

## REDEFINITION OF PUBLIC/PRIVATE RESPONSIBILITIES

Corporate responsibility is a Rorschach-like image; individuals offer widely varying interpretations of the concept. The emerging consensus, however, is expressed in the Business Roundtable's 1981 "Statement on Corporate Responsibility" which concludes with these thoughts:

> A corporation's responsibilities include how the whole business is conducted every day. It must be a thoughtful institution which rises above the bottom line to consider the impact of its actions on all, from shareholders to society at large. Its business activities must make social sense just as its social activities must make business sense.

We submit that at this time in our history this definition is laudable, but must be viewed in its widest context. We believe that leaders in both business and government can and must step out of their existing institutions, view the whole social system from the capitalistic, private enterprise philosophy that has made our country great, and restructure our programs and institutions accordingly. We further submit that anything short of this comprehensive review and redefinition will lead to a further erosion of the democratic system by missing the opportunity to create flexible, incentive-induced, service programs in the place of more monolithic structures.

## DETERMINATION OF NEED AND THE CREATION OF INCENTIVES

How will this be accomplished? Two ways: first, each and every program supported by tax dollars should be tested against three tough questions, questions well known in the private sector.

- Is there a real need?
- What are the minimum resources (capital and human) required to satisfy that need?
- What is the most efficient organization to obtain and convey these resources to those who need them?

Second, once we decide which programs are needed, incentives must be developed. Incentives for action, not inaction, must be woven into the government's approach to these problems. Tax benefits should be earned, with specific program objectives in mind, not granted in the hopes that "the rising tide will raise all ships." The importance of positive incentives seems obvious; all democratic peoples, and especially the American business community, are more responsive to positive incentives and resent being backed into corners.

## IMPEDIMENTS OF HISTORICAL DIFFERENCES

Even if the government moves towards a system of positive incentives, the assessment of the merits of existing programs may be extraordinarily difficult, not so much because of data problems, but because those in executive positions in the public and private sectors have been taught and conditioned by very different environments, largely attributable to incentives and rewards. They will perceive the needs differently, define the resources differently and conceptualize different organizational solutions. Consider the following:

*Goals, Objectives and Incentives:* In the public sector, success is often not measured against programmatic goals. Input and process measurements are frequently used where outcome measurements are required, with the opposite being equally true. Tough evaluation and meaningful legislative oversight are often absent in public sector programs. In the private sector this is less true. Incentives are often used to keep goals focused and to motivate production. Such incentives are rarely used in the public sector.

*Generalist/Specialist:* In the private sector, managers are expected to be flexible and fungible, while in the public sector specialization is often encouraged.

*Planning:* In the public sector, with appropriations on a yearly cycle, congressional elections on a two-year cycle and legislation continually changing, long-range planning is rare. In the private sector, two- to five-year planning is the norm. Public sector programs are often "reactive" in nature, determined by external factors. The fact that many social programs are called "uncontrollable"

is instructive. Consider how many private sector programs would be so characterized.

*Program Development:* In the private sector, programs are usually built on "cleared sites," adequately capitalized and staffed, and under the general assumption that the program will be accepted for what it is and not "gamed" to achieve alternative ends. In the public sector, it is quite different.

Austin Sullivan, Jr., now Vice President for Public Affairs for General Mills, who worked for a number of years as the legislative director for a congressional committee, described the problem this way:

> In part, this is because some of these programs are built on false premises. The process of reconciling different interests and points of view during the legislative process has encumbered the authorizing statutes with administrative requirements that would defeat even the most creative and efficient business manager; and, those same legislators have tended to overprescribe which constituencies are to be provided with which services in which ways and by whom, just as they have not been clear enough in identifying the central objective of the program which should serve as the measure of its performance.

> In short, a substantial amount of the ineffectiveness found in government programs can be traced to the statutes themselves. This, in turn, is compounded by the further layers of complication and regulation that are layered on by the bureaucracy in its administration of government programs, reflecting its fundamental lack of confidence in the capacity of local people to make sound judgements.

• *Retrenchment:* The public sector is often reluctant to cut its losses, close programs, lay off employees and generally "manage" retrenchment. The management of decline in the public sector is often characterized by budget and spending freezes, attrition, or across-the-board cuts. The private sector is more likely to target retrenchment, i.e. close entire operations, to preserve growth in the rest of the enterprise.

• *The Management of Change:* In the private sector, executives and managers are expected to constantly adjust their enterprise to changes in markets, technology, the economy and a score of other factors. In the public sector consistency, not change, is the virtue. As former Treasury Secretary W. Michael Blumenthal said in an interview in *Fortune* in January 1979:

Another example of how . . . different that is in government as compared to in a corporation—has to do with the risk of changing your mind. A businessman is entitled and expected to change his mind, and there is no particular approbation attached to that at all. You get new facts, conditions change, the markets change, industries change, you get a new contract or you lose one, you talk to more people . . . What counts in the end is how you come out, not whether you've changed your mind or not. In the government, if you change your mind you're accused of inconsistency. That's one reason there's a lot of doubletalk in Washington.

• *Executive Workload, Delegation and Decision Making:* In the private sector, a well-run corporation allows decisions to be made at the level where the data are, delegates most operating decisions down the line and reserves for the executive those few broad policy decisions that shape the future of the enterprise. In the public sector, because of specialization and policy interests rather than managerial or operating interests, decisions tend to rise several levels above where the data are; policy decisions are often formulated at the mid-level with the executives often left with a crushing operational work load. As Hale Champion, now the Executive Dean at the Kennedy School of Government at Harvard and former Under Secretary of Health, Education and Welfare told us:

When Joe (Califano) and several others of us were running HEW we had virtually no time to be reflective, to think through policy options and to plan. We were working 14 to 16 hours a day just to keep the department going. While we tried to structure it differently we often could not succeed because the accountability structure in the public sector will not accept delegation, even where the variance in management inherent in delegation would make no difference. You can pick up the paper daily and read about public officials being called to task for delegating decisions that deviated slightly from the perceived path of perfect implementation. Thus you have the anomalous situation where there is no big picture, long-term accountability (except for history), while narrowly the public sector demands perfect equity.

The private sector understands the cost of delegation which allows many CEOs to have at least a third of his or her time free from operating demands to evolve a coherent management approach and, equally important, to think about the broad social and cultural context in which the enterprise operates.

These are but a few of the "cultural" differences that may make the collaborative process of redefinition difficult, but not as difficult as one might expect. People are remarkably resilient and change can often be achieved by simply restructuring the incentives. Indeed, the three illustrative quotes above are from individuals who have been very successful in both the public and private sector and who have adapted with ease to the incentives of the private sector. By the proper structuring of incentives, it is possible to create effective private management of public programs.

## MANAGEMENT OPTIONS: TOWARDS AN INCENTIVE BASED, PRIVATE NON-PROFIT MODEL

If one distinguishes between the management function and the financing structure, the spectrum between public and private has two organizational models:

1. Public management with public financing (social security, public education and public housing)
2. Private management
   • Non-profit with publicly subsidized financing (Amtrak, etc.)
   • Profit with publicly subsidized financing (government service contracts)
   • Non-profit with private financing (private schools, colleges and universities)
   • Profit with private financing (private industries)

The process of redefining roles and responsibility can be initiated by either government or the private sector. We believe government has the responsibility to test every public program against private alternatives. While we favor government initiative, many of the successful examples of redefinition have occurred without it when a private competitive force perceives that public sector programs have failed in either service or cost or both. Consider, for example, the range of private sector alternatives to the U. S. Postal Service; the development of private education programs, not just private and parochial schools, but private, for-profit reading centers, remediation services for the structurally unemployed, and specialized services for the learning disabled. While the market share of these programs has remained relatively small, they do demonstrate that competition can be created in programs historically designated as the public domain.

This leads us naturally and directly to a central definitional question: Are there functions that for reasons of equity, efficiency, or national security must remain the unique and sole responsibility of the public sector? While clearly there are such functions, we will not attempt to answer this question definitively here. What is important is that we intuitively believe there are vast areas now under the so-called public domain that are open to privatization.

In testing public programs against private alternatives, the government should understand that the private sector not only includes the for-profit corporations, but also, as we have noted above, that vast array of non-profit institutions that are structured to deliver goods and services outside of government, albeit often with government funds. This non-profit sector—churches, hospitals, social agencies and cultural enterprises—has historically been supported by government and philanthropy in a manner that has been both stable and generally uncritical. As the director of a large corporate trust told us:

> I am held to a very different and looser standard of performance than my colleagues in line operations or in our venture capital group. In this changing environment I suspect I, and the programs I recommend for funding, will be held to stricter performance standards. I welcome this change because it represents an ongoing evaluative corporate involvement after the grant has been made.

It is our vision that this not-for-profit sector can lead the way towards a new definition of both responsibility and management style for programs serving broad social needs, for these not-for-profit corporations can often break free from the limitations of tenure, politicized constituencies, and the monolithic characteristics of large public programs. Indeed, with appropriate incentives, particularly compensation incentives for management, these institutions may well become the social program entrepreneurs of the 1980s. They would be supported not by charity but by venture capital from the private sector with a mandate of operating at maximum efficiency even if maximum efficiency fails to yield any return on equity, and with the flexibility to incorporate in response to demand, to change as needs change, and to cut back or close as needs diminish.

To achieve the development of the not-for-profit private sector as the "engine" for the redefinition of public and private functions and as one of the operational entities by which this is to be achieved, the corporate world will need to refocus its social responsibility programs from "giving" to "investing," not investing in the same sense of other acquisitions or venture capital investments, but investing in social enterprises that will have low or no return on equity and may have substantial risk associated with them. Here tax incentives should be used to encourage this new concept of venture capital.

This suggestion runs counter to many current trends in the private sector. This is a time when corporate America is not a risk-taker; when entrepreneurial and executive instincts have been replaced by managerial skills as the sought-after virtue in business; and when long-term strategic planning is often sacrificed for earnings per share per quarter. Most large corporations today that wish to diversify do so by acquisition, not by creation. And yet to accomplish the fundamental task of redefining public and private functions, some risk will be required. What is involved, in our view, is not the more efficient running of the public sector, but a rethinking of whether the functions are necessary and who is in the best position to provide these necessary services.

## THE PURSUIT OF PROFITS/
## THE REDUCTION OF COSTS

The growth of democratic capitalism has been premised on the efficient delivery of goods and services to profitable markets. Those necessary residual unprofitable enterprises became the public sector's responsibility. And, as products and markets changed over time, so too did the definition of public responsibility. Consider, for example, railroads. For generations, the nation's railroad system was exclusively the domain of the private sector and for good reason: It generated vast wealth. Today, portions of our rail system still generate substantial profit, but other sectors have become the public responsibility, at tremendous costs in terms of tax subsidies. In the opposite direction, consider the hospital business. For years U. S. hospitals were virtually all public or non-profit. Today, more than 10 percent of all beds are investor owned and generate substantial return on equity, but they are not the large urban public hospitals like Cook County (Chicago) and Bellevue (New York) that continue to require substantial tax subsidies.

It would be unrealistic to expect this process to stop and it would probably be detrimental to our society if it were even slowed. Thus, we advocate the continuing aggressive pursuit of profitable enterprises, but with it the development of a strong private sector commitment to the unpopular and unpleasant task of helping to decide which public tax-subsidized programs can be closed without significantly damaging our basic social values. For as important as profits are to the private sector, eliminating duplicative and ineffective programs is essential to the public sector.

Closing programs is not easy—you can always get politicians to a ribbon-cutting ceremony, but they are never seen at a boarding-up event. The reductions in public programs necessitated by reductions and reallocations of public resources will be large and in many communities will pit the symphony against day care programs, a capital drive for a new Y against training for the structurally unemployed, the renovation of a school against housing for the destitute. We neither endorse nor decry these budget cuts: We challenge the leadership in the public and private sector to set aside rhetoric and politicization and make some very difficult choices, and to make thoughtful and realistic commitments.

Not only do these times force us to re-examine roles, they tempt us to extremes. In the public sector the obvious extreme is doomsaying . . . without this or that program, our cities will burn in riots, our youth will be malnourished, our educational system will be bankrupt and the truly disenfranchised—the destitute —will be abandoned. The private sector may be equally tempted to respond in extremes. Indeed, the President has repeatedly suggested that the private sector can pick up much of the slack of his program cutbacks. The danger, of course, is overpromising and underdelivering, or retreating in fright, overwhelmed by the magnitude of the problem.

## DECISION AVOIDANCE

It is widely accepted that critical policy decisions must be made at the highest level in an organization. Even at high levels, however, there are a multitude of ways of avoiding difficult decisions. Consider these:

*Do We Have Enough Data?* Do we know enough to make such serious decisions as closing programs?

We believe in most instances we do, either cognitively or viscerally. Data collection for executives can be like pencil sharpening for the student— postponement of action. We do not suggest whimsical or cavalier decisions, but rather a commitment to thoughtful action. Inaction compounds most problems.

*Can We Run It Better?* If the operation were better managed, would I be so tempted to close it? A typical private sector pitfall—avoid the executive decision of "Is this a business to be in?", in favor of the management decision—"How to run it better"—whether it is needed or not.

*Can We Get An 11th Hour Reprieve?* Obviously a program like this cannot be abandoned or even reorganized. All that is needed is active and thoughtful lobbying and some savior will arrive.

*Can We Run It Smaller?* If we can't afford the whole loaf, let's try half a loaf. This kind of reasoning sidesteps the fundamental question of whether the program is needed in the first place and may often create a situation where a marginally adequate program becomes totally useless (for half the cost or more).

Despite these options for avoiding the difficult decisions of what programs will survive, how they will be funded and who will run them, we believe that around this country there is an increasing understanding that the decisions must be made, made well and made quickly.

## MEETING THE CHALLENGE AND OPPORTUNITY AT HAND

Several writers, among them Peter L. Berger, have recently noted that corporate responsibility will be driven by an increasing need for "legitimacy." Berger in a recent *Harvard Business Review* comments, "Restoration of legitimacy will depend as much on successful competition of ideas as on successful competition in the market. From a sociological point of view, business must learn to speak a new language. It knows economics and politics; now it must address meaning and value."

Independent of the need for legitimacy, there is a more urgent agenda for change. The government by both choice and necessity is moving out of a number of social programs. An expectation has been created that the private sector can assume responsibility for many of these programs. As a society we have substantial, but still finite, resources in the private sector. We must now ask how they are to be allocated, what will be our mechanisms for both decisions and delivery, and ultimately what will be the quality of our lives and the lives of our communities.

These are difficult and critical choices. They must be made quickly, with care and with a new combination of prudence and compassion. It is our belief that the private sector can best meet this challenge if a new concept of the non-profit sector emerges which understands the task and has the incentives to carry it out efficiently—a non-profit sector that is as committed to efficiency and effectiveness as the business community traditionally has been, while, at the same time, being committed to programs and markets that are inherently unprofitable. Tax and other incentives can be designed to replace return on equity considerations, so that the private for profit sector may also be induced to participate. Therein lies the challenge of this process of redefinition: if not doing well by doing good, to at least do the best while doing the essential. After all, we are but one people with similar needs and differing resources. To move that allocation of resources to the private sector is an opportunity that cannot be passed by.

The goal is clear. We must preserve a caring, humane society within the context of our free enterprise system.

# PART TWO

# ORGANIZATION BEHAVIOR

Some of the most prominent officials in Washington came from positions of executive leadership. In the administration of Ronald Reagan, both the Secretary of Defense, Caspar Weinberger, and the Secretary of State, George Schultz, were senior executives from the Bechtel Corporation. President Carter's Secretary of Treasury, Michael Blumenthal, was a vice-president of the Bendix Corporation.

The movement between the world of business and the world of government has been going on for many years. When these "in-and-outers" put their experiences down on paper, they invariably say that public management is both different, and more difficult, than management in the private sector. But the contrary view—management is management—still has currency. Sometimes called *generic management,* this notion, one with a long-standing intellectual history in public administration, is based on the belief that the basic "principles" of management—regardless of organizational environment—can be taught to the aspiring managers of tomorrow.

Even if different managerial approaches ("solutions") are required in public and private sectors, there are nevertheless some common problems. We can identify three problems faced by all organizations: the design of organizations, people, and organization ineffectiveness.

*Are* some organizational forms *inherently* more appropriate than others? Does form follow function? That is, do the tasks of organizations dictate particular organization designs? Much of the speculation on this question has focused on private organizations. But as sector blurring continues, public and nonprofit organi-zations will also undergo alterations in their organizational arrangements.

Louis Davis ("Evolving Alternative Organization Designs") suggests some criteria for understanding organizational designs and the impact of organization structure on behavior. Perhaps the trendiest of organization designs is the "Type Z" organization that characterizes many Japanese organizations. Ouchi and Jaeger ("Type Z Organization") identify some of the elements of this much-ballyhooed design and assess its potential for improving the management of organizations.

There is a certain looseness in language when we speak about organizations. For instance, when we say something about "organizational behavior," we often really want to make a statement about *people* in organizations. After all, people do make up organizations! People have beliefs, attitudes, and different degrees of motivation and competence. One of the tasks of management, identified many years ago by Chester Barnard in his classic, *The Functions of the Executive,* is to stimulate cooperative behavior among individuals to achieve an organizational mission.

Often there are sources of friction among individuals when they must work together in groups. Encouraging cooperative behavior is a major objective of a branch of organization development (OD). OD is really a series of techniques used to uncover the source of administrative problems and intervene in the work environment to solve or at least reduce the conflict. OD usually requires the intervention of a third party, often an outside consultant. Widely used in industry, it has gained some stature in the public sector as well—as readings in Part Two make clear. Warner Burke ("Organization Development and Bureaucracy in the 1980s") provides an overview of the contemporary role of OD. In "Increasing Productivity and Morale in a Municipality," Paul and Gross evaluate the effects of an OD intervention on the productivity and job satisfaction of a group of public employees in San Diego.

It is one thing to ensure that your subordinates are cooperating with one another and are productive as individuals; it is something else to determine whether their cooperation and productive activity leads to anything useful. When we move from the behavior of individuals to the "behavior" of organizations, we are really asking about *organizational effectiveness.* How well has the organization performed its mission? As Richard Hall ("Effectiveness Theory and Organizational Effectiveness") shows, this question can be rather vexing. Consider the military establishment: One criterion of effectiveness might be the ability to win a war. But how would we evaluate the effectiveness of an army that has not fought a war in decades? In other words, performance standards are difficult to determine, and even more difficult to apply in practice. As you will learn in Part Two, evaluating the performance of public organizations remains as elusive as ever. But evaluate we must!

# CHAPTER THREE

# Organization Design
# and
# Effectiveness

## Evolving Alternative Organization Designs

### Their Sociotechnical Bases

Louis E. Davis

*The implicit assumptions underlying dominant or classical organization designs and the present forces in society are examined as a background for rise of alternative organization designs. Some fourteen attributes commonly shared by the new designs are presented. These include systematic structure and roles, organizations as open systems, design by joint optimization, organizational uniqueness, stated organizational values or philosophy, quality of working life as an essential objective, comprehensive roles, self-maintaining social units, flat structure, participation, minimal status differences, make large small, iterative evolutionary development, and minimal critical specifications. Some attributes are a response to needs for institutional survival, others for long-term economic survival, and still others for enhanced institutional effectiveness. A postscript compares evolving alternative organization designs with proposals of proponents of intermediate technology.*

From *Human Relations* (March, 1977), Vol. 30, pp. 261–273. Copyright 1977 by Tavistock Institute of Human Relations. Reprinted by permission.

## INTRODUCTION

Formal organization design, or deliberate as opposed to informal or evolved organization design, is part of the evolution of both Western and Eastern civilizations. In Exodus, the Old Testament records the deliberate design to organize a mass who had lost their organizational forms during a long servitude as slaves. There are other reports in Western and Eastern history as well. Modern Western industrial organizations were first reported about 200 years ago and are intimately linked with the rise of capitalism and its dominant organizational triumph—the factory system. For these reports we are indebted to Adam Smith and Charles Babbage, who laid down the fundamentals of how people are to be used in structuring industrial work. Remarkably, their recommendations have gone largely unchallenged to this day and served as a basis for the development of the culture of Western industrial society. Only recently has the dominant structural form of modern organizations, that of scientific management-bureaucracy, been subject to critical examination leading to the evolution of alternative forms, to a deeper understanding of the assumptions and concepts underlying the classic forms, and to the evolution of new designs and theories. While raising important questions at all levels of organization, the major previous challenge, that of Karl Marx in the 1860s, has resulted largely in new forms of ownership. However, with the exception of Yugoslavia, the basic form of internal industrial organization is almost identical in communist, socialist, and capitalist countries. More organizational innovations, or development of alternative organization forms, are occurring in Western or capitalist countries than elsewhere today.

What are the bases of the organizational innovations or alternative organizations now being considered? To answer this question, we must go back to the implicit or unstated assumptions underlying the dominant or classic organization designs, and must examine present demands and forces in society that are giving rise to alternative forms of organization as a response. The position taken here is that organizational forms both conform to the prevailing culture and influence further development of the culture. So, when new forms or alternative organizations evolve, they do so in response both to internal institutional needs and to changes in the environments of organizations.

In a recent paper, Herbst (1975) has provided a concise review of the underlying assumptions of the bureaucracy-scientific management models that are so dominant in organizational forms.

## INTERNAL INSTITUTIONAL NEEDS

Internal institutional needs derive from the mismatch between implicit assumptions underlying classic organization forms and the changing reality surrounding both those who work in organizations and how the organization will accomplish those activities upon which its survival depends. Raised here are issues about power and governance, structure, man-machine relations, skills, roles, rewards, careers, management prerogatives, union rights, and other issues that now dominate management and industrial relations discussions.

A central implicit concept underlying classic organization has been that ownership carried with it absolute authority. The resulting authoritarian organizations embedded within democratic societies continue to be a growing source of difficulty between those members of an organization who represent the owners and the rest of the members. These difficulties stimulate growing concern with the purposes and social objectives of organizations. A few more assumptions are in need of emphasis. Others have been the object of discussion in countless books and articles in the last few years (Davis, Cherns, and Associates, 1975; Davis and Taylor, 1972). The implicit success strategy of classic organizations was based upon—and continues to require—men being or becoming cheap, unreliable, single-skilled, or single-purpose instruments, narrowly self-centered, and immediately responsive to simple rewards. The continued implementation of this strategy has served to develop apathy, hostility, fragmented tasks and services, and overblown bureaucratic superstructures.

Present assumptions concerning technology probably were realistic 200 years ago. Machines were then and still are dear and reliable; what needed to be done and how it was to be done were thought to be determined by logical and scientific means that were accepted as rational and applied in the work place. Revisionist or radical economists (Dickson, 1974) studying the history of the origin of the industrial revolution indicate that fractionated work was developed in the first factories, not so much to use the new machines, particularly the steam engine, but to stamp out craftsmanship as a way of working so that men could be fully controlled by owner-managers. Organizations operating under the above assumption are so structured that men are the spare parts and staff specialists are the repository of learning from organizational experience, with a consequent loss of talent on the one hand, and a loss of organizational learning on the other. The fractionation of tasks required, and continues to require, an organizational superstructure of many layers to both cement together the disjointed pieces and deal with the internal and external disturbances that arise. The needs, abilities, aspirations, and ideals of society brought by individuals into the work place have served as a constant and growing source of difficulty, irritation, disaffection, and malfunction in classically structured organizations based on the bureaucratic-scientific management assumptions stated above.

## EXTERNAL ORGANIZATIONAL ENVIRONMENTS

The single most descriptive term for organization environments is change. This characteristic in itself is the basis for innovation of alternative organizations, since the implicit assumption of classic organization was high stability or placidity of the environment. Organizations designed on the basis that changes will not be necessary find themselves developing new forms where response to continuous changes in the political, social, technological, and economic environments is the order of the day.

In the social environment perhaps the most significant change has been in educational levels; the average length of schooling for the entire work force will be 12 years by 1980. What is crucial here is not the specific skills that are acquired through an average of 12 years of schooling, but the socialization into expectations and rewards as well as ways of living and working in a school society. Most American organizations are based on concepts taken from scientific management, an organizational form 75 years old, proposed at a time when the average length of schooling of the work force was three years. Other changes in the social environment include the shift from privileges to entitlements, to rights, including the right to have meaningful careers, to control one's work life, etc.; these are placing new pressures on relationships between workers and managers. On the whole, members of our society are prepared to give control of only a very small part of their life space to the organizations for which they work.

Related to changes in the social environment are changes in the political environment. These are placing on most organizations social responsibilities that were unheard-of a few years ago, bringing into the purview of organizations a whole host of external factors that were thought to be safely ignored in the past. These extended responsibilities increase the turbulence of the environment of organizations and require them to be responsive to more and more changes if they are to survive.

Changes in the technological environments of organizations have represented both a continuation of the mechanization trend and a change in kind. The change in kind, which until recently was misunderstood as the issue of automation, is now much better understood as continuous processing. The latter is now seen to require different organizational forms and roles. The impact of the changes in technology on organizations is bringing about an expansion of the field of organization study to encompass technology, which may explain the widespread interest in sociotechnical systems (Davis, 1971; Maitland, 1975).

Changes in product technology have brought in train changes in market requirements of the sort leading to greater market instability. This calls for more rapid response to the market on the part of the organization. Changes in process technology are of the sort that call for very large capital investments in plant and equipment, which require such a long payout period that presently designed organizations will have to be suitable to the needs of a period 10 years in the future. This is stimulating intensive organization design efforts in parallel with technology design.

In the face of these changes the responses of organizations are very mixed. A growing number are deliberately embarking upon the development of innovations in organization structure and in job structure in response to the needs and pressures of the situations in which they find themselves. The consequences of their attempts are alternative organizations different not only in specific particulars, but reflecting a systemic view of internal organizational life and relations with the external environment.

## ATTRIBUTES OF ALTERNATIVE ORGANIZATION DESIGNS

Alternative organization designs cannot be discussed in specific, since each design represents the consequences of the choices made to achieve a fit with internal needs and external environments. However, if we look at the objectives that the alternative organization designs seek to satisfy, we begin to get some insights into the differences from classic structures. An examination of alternative organization designs, particularly those based in socio-technical systems concepts, reveals attributes or characteristics commonly shared by most, if not all of them. A brief examination of these inferred attributes can provide insights as to the directions in which alternative organization designs are developing. What are referred to here as attributes do not always have physical manifestations; some are abstractions reflecting the structural and operational characteristics of the organization. Similarly, design processes that supported and reinforced the organizational attributes were followed by most of the alternative organizations. In addition, in such organizations one sees behaviors that derive from structure, and aspects of the local and national environments permeate the organization. With general regard for order of importance, the attributes of alternative organization designs are given below, each with a brief description.

1. *Systemic.* The structure of the organization and its roles reflect the recognition that all aspects of organizational functioning are interrelated; the organization design process maintains the integrity of interrelated roles and structures.

2. *Open System.* Recognition of the need for continuous adaptation to requirements flowing from environments usually resulting in flexible structural features and to requirements for capturing and using organizational learning; the properties of the organization are reflective of the salient properties of its internal and external environments.

3. *Joint Optimization.* Recognition that in terms of meeting its output and service objectives, an organization is a sociotechnical system. As such, it is required to evaluate the impact of the technology design on the social system and of the requirements of the social system on the design and operation of the technical (work) system by jointly considering the best in either the technical or social system and its effect on having the best in the other.

4. *Organizational Uniqueness.* Structure of the organization or its components and its roles suit the specific individual organization's situation requiring individualized design based on general design principles (Cherns, 1976) in place of imported solutions.

5. *Organizational Philosophy.* The process of organizational design and the organization's structures and roles are congruent with agreed organizational values explicitly stated as an organizational philosophy.

6. *Quality of Working Life.* Explicit organizational values respecting the integrity, values, and needs of individual members are reflected in the roles, structure, operations, and rewards of the organization.

7. *Comprehensive Roles of Individuals or Groups.* Roles encompass tasks, activities, or functions required to accomplish objectives or meet goals; specific content of roles at any one time is determined by the individual or group in response to perceived needs.

8. *Self-Maintaining Social Systems.* Structure of organization, content and scope of roles, reward systems, design of technology, and functions of social systems are such that organizational units can carry on without external coercion; individuals or groups are provided the requisite response capabilities and authorities to regulate and control variances or disturbances without having to rely on external interference to achieve desired objectives, i.e., they are or can become self-regulating.

9. *Flat Structure.* Fewer organizational layers or levels.

10. *Participation.* Participation mechanisms and structures are extensive for problem solving, learning, and governance. Some refer to this and minimal status differentials as democratization of the work place.

11. *Minimal Status Differentials.* Artificial status differences are absent, i.e., there are minimal differences in privileges and status that are unrelated to role and organizational needs.

12. *Make Large Small.* Organizational and physical structures provide both smaller, more intimate organizational boundaries and a feeling of smaller physical environment for individuals or groups.

13. *Organizational Design Process.* Technical, managerial, and personal components of the organization evolve in a participative, iterative manner, only partially determined by advance planning.

14. *Minimal Critical Specification.* A prominent principle of the organizational design process; designers specify (design or select) the crucial relationships, functions, and controls, leaving to role-holders the evolutionary development of the remainder.

15. *Action Research* (this is not an attribute, but refers to the principal source of organization data). Knowledge for organization design is based on organizational behavior data that are obtained from actual change instances in functioning organizations studied by means of action research approaches.

Growing numbers of managements, and occasionally but increasingly the unions as well, are prepared to risk the unknowns of alternative organizational forms and undertake the considerable changes in leadership and collaborative behaviors that are required. They have recognized that the dominant organizational forms are increasingly ill-suited to the perceived needs for institutional survival, economic survival, institutional effectiveness, and quality of working life.

## INSTITUTIONAL SURVIVAL

A number of the attributes of alternative organizations are a response to the needs for institutional survival in a society where the confidence in individual leaders and private and public institutions is not very high.

The designs are directed at providing congruence between evolving societal ideology and organization structure and behavior. Organization and job structures are directed at providing more participative, self-regulating, democratic roles and standards. Both operationally and structurally, differentials in status and privileges are minimized, and there is greater sharing of power and equalizing of influence. Many designs provide for participative systems of governance and social justice. Members of such organizations are found to be engaged in activities as a consequence of their competence rather than membership in a managerial class or a worker class. Of course, there are snags and hangups.

Participative systems (Pateman, 1970) call for new understandings and relationships between managements and unions. Few such have developed so far and there is a distinct possibility that direct participation on the part of employees, which is a growing demand, may become an area of conflict between unions and managements. Direct participation competes with representative participation—the basis of the union's role in relation to management. Both are needed and if the former is used or seen to be used to drive out the latter, action to protect the union's hard-won role may be expected to ensue. The working through of changed roles for each of the parties and the building of appropriate trust is one of the major developments needed in the present era.

Where survival is related to the regulation and control of pollution, for example, control is found to be in the hands of those who either can contribute to or avoid pollution. Alternative organizations have avoided falling into the conventional organization trap of creating a special function, i.e., pollution controller or pollution inspector, to handle a crucial need. Theoretically, what we see here is a reduction in the traditional management role of filtering and insulating members of the organization from needs or requirements coming from the external environment.

## ECONOMIC SURVIVAL

Long-term economic survival is a requirement in cases of intensive capital investment in plant and facilities. This may be an underlying reason helping to explain why so many new alternative organization designs are for continuous process industries. As one board chairman indicated, "We can only afford to build new plants with very costly new technologies based on the economic justification that they will maintain effective performance over a very long time period. Therefore, we cannot risk designing 'old organization structures,' whose defects we know, in conjunction with new technologies."

A principal organizational objective sought in these instances is that of adaptability, and design of organization structure is seen as the means by which it is to be attained. By providing structure, adaptive behaviors can develop not dependent upon chance or goodwill. In such organizations, the principle of redundant skills or wide training is the practice. Organizational units are so structured that, as appropriate, they are on the boundary of the organization and as such, deal with internal and external problems, carrying on their work as directly affected by environmental forces. Again, we see that management does not (and perhaps cannot) insulate and filter environmental pressures. What we have here, from the point of view of organizational analysis and design, is an interesting set of issues concerned with boundary location. Further, in such organizations all jobs from top to bottom of the organization are multiskilled jobs. Structures exist for capturing organizational learning whether through immediate feedback, the control of data at the lowest point in the organization at which the data are generated, the development of deliberate learning experiences around the performance of various activities, or through widely shared data from top to bottom without restriction as to status or class of the data receiver. In sum, workers know a great deal more about the functioning of the organization, about what is happening to it in terms of its environments, and as multiskilled members of organizational units, they develop the understandings of the exigencies at levels usually seen to exist only among managers.

The structure of such organizations is usually characterized by the requirements to control and regulate the critical variances or disturbances affecting performance. In response, whether within teams or groups, or within individual jobs, one sees joint maintenance and operations, joint quality control or inspection and operations, and frequently a matrix structure to deal with emergencies or major disturbances. In support of such structural arrangements is the delegation of the necessary authority to act—what may be called widely dispersed work authority. Additionally, one finds in such settings decentralized laboratories for inspection or control, decentralized maintenance workshops, etc. In capital-intensive settings, particularly in process industries, the organizational characteristics reviewed above are seen to be linked to economic survival. Even in matters of operational effectiveness, economic survival is seen to be much more dependent on minimizing and avoiding down time than on increasing the speed of operations.

## INSTITUTIONAL EFFECTIVENESS

Some innovations are directed at enhancing institutional effectiveness. In alternative organizations one sees team ownership of work process, by which is meant an identifiable part of the process is assigned to a group or team of people who are responsible for achieving the outcomes desired, regulating the disturbances, etc. The design of the structure of the team, its jobs, duties, etc., is generally based on the notion of minimal critical specifications, permitting evolutionary self-development to take place in support of autonomy or self-regulation. Usually within a team or group there are ill-defined boundaries between the jobs or, more precisely, roles of team members. What members do is subject to self-generated change from time to time to suit the demands that arise. Additionally, one finds that an essential part of the role of members of such teams is the maintenance of the team's social system, so that both the team or group and its members have duties to perform and functions to carry out, related to maintaining the social system and to the work it does. This is of course very much the attribute of self-regulating, semiautonomous, or autonomous work groups. Additionally, one sees vastly expanded roles for members including not only work activities, but teaching activities and others as well. In addition, members may and do frequently serve on ad hoc problem-solving groups created to deal with production, performance, and other difficulties.

Another characteristic of alternative organizations is that individuals progress through the organization largely on the basis of the acquisition of skills, knowledge, and competence rather than by being advanced to or appointed to the specific jobs, usually on the occasion of the release of the job by its incumbent. To support a system or progression, such organizations have deliberate and specific means of providing learning and involving others in the teaching of colleagues, so that they can progress. Of course such organizations have reward systems that support and reinforce such progression; namely, people are rewarded for the knowledge and the competence they have rather than on the job title they may possess or the specific tasks that they are assigned to carry out.

## QUALITY OF WORKING LIFE

Alternative organizations reflect the position that enhancing the quality of working life of their members is an essential objective. This is seen as responding to changes in the external social environments of organizations by their members. Rising expectations in our society, and expectations and experiences flowing from long years of schooling, to name a few, are making themselves felt in the work place in demands for individuality, autonomy, shared power, careers, meaningfulness, appropriate rewards, and recognition as well as equitable rewards, etc. Many of the attributes of alternative organization designs previously reviewed work to provide for such needs, which are receiving growing emphasis, particularly by younger members of organizations.

The emphasis on individuality has led a number of organizations to make provision for individual differences, one of the objectives in enhancing the quality of working life. When provision of options for satisfying individual differences is taken as a design requirement, alternative organization designs are in complete antithesis to both bureaucratic practice and ethos and to the organizational and job standardization central to F.W. Taylor's scientific management. Such organization and job designs are characterized by many career paths, localized structuring of work, different organization structures among work groups, departments, and so on, options for progressing at different rates, etc. Organization design to support individual differences is an area in great need of research and development.

Many designs of alternative organizations, particularly at the level of jobs, incorporate various attempts to provide better security, equity, and rewards, and to satisfy the growingly articulated psychological needs of all who work. These needs have been stated before (Davis, 1975; Englestad, 1972) and the list given below is enlarged to include individual differences.

1. The need for the content of the work to be reasonably demanding in terms other than sheer endurance, yet provide a minimum of variety (not merely novelty).
2. The need to be able to learn on the job and go on learning, which requires standards and knowledge of results.
3. The need for some area of decision making that an individual can call one's own in which one can exercise one's own discretion.

4. The need for social support in the work place, i.e., the need for an individual to know that one can rely on others for help needed in performing the job as well as for sympathy and understanding.
5. The need for an individual to have recognition within the organization for one's performance and contributions.
6. The need for an individual to be able to relate what one does and what one produces to one's social life.
7. The need to feel that the job leads to some sort of desirable future.
8. The need for an individual to know that choices are available in the organization by which one can satisfy one's needs and achieve one's objectives.

Designing jobs in support of satisfying these needs is seen in the effect it has on design or choice of machines, layout, work systems, training, rewards, careers, and other aspects of life in the work place.

## SUMMARY

This review of alternative organizations began by indicating that new organizations are evolving that are systemic. An examination of all the attributes and characteristics described reveals that they are interrelated, one supporting another. Rewarding individuals for knowledge and competence has a bearing on adaptability. Team ownership of work process has a bearing on control of critical variances, etc.

The effectiveness of such organizations and the support that they are receiving from their members raise the question as to their general applicability to other situations not characterized by the deliberate and specific pressures coming from the various external environments. It is our view that there is widespread applicability for these alternative organizations. They not only are proving themselves to be suitable to new demands and conditions, but they provide the beginnings for examining long-standing issues regarding industrial and business organizations in democratic societies.

Some time ago Davis (1971) indicated that "the social and the technological forces can be seen working toward the same end, for 'job characteristics that develop commitment' and thus promote the economic goals of the highly automated enterprise are exactly those that are beginning to emerge as demands for meaningfulness from the social environment—

participation and control, personal freedom and initiative." What was becoming visible in 1970 is a well-established trend in 1976.

## POSTSCRIPT

From a societal standpoint, it may be instructive to turn to another literature, one that openly challenges the ethos and underlying assumptions of industrial society as now developed. In his book *Small Is Beautiful: Economics As If People Mattered,* Schumacher (1975) takes up the issue of large-scale organization design. To stem the evergrowing Parkinsonian bureaucracies, he indicates that "the fundamental task is to achieve smallness within large organizations." Every "organization has to strive continuously for the orderliness of 'order' and the disorderliness of creative 'freedom.' The specific danger inherent in large-scale organization is that its natural bias and tendency favor order, at the expense of creative freedom." Schumacher lays down five "principles" for design of large-scale organizations:

1. The Principle of Subsidiarity or of Subsidiary Function: "The higher level must not absorb the functions of the lower one, on the assumption that, being higher, it will automatically be wiser and fulfill them more efficiently."

"Loyalty can grow only from the smaller or lower levels to the larger or higher ones, not the other way around." "The burden of proof lies always on those who want to deprive a lower level of its function, and thereby of its freedom and responsibility in that respect." "The higher level will gain in authority and effectiveness if the freedom and responsibility of the lower levels are carefully preserved."

2. The Principle of Vindication: With carefully defined exceptions "the subsidiary unit must be defended against reproach and upheld by central authority." "Good government is always government by exception." Application of the principle requires very few criteria for accountability; otherwise, creativity and entrepreneurship cannot flourish in the smaller lower units.

3. The Principle of Identification: "Each subsidiary unit must have both a profit and loss account and a balance sheet." "It is not sufficient to have one balance sheet for the organization as a whole." "A unit's success should lead to greater freedom and financial scope for the unit and failure should lead to restriction and disability."

4. The Principle of Motivation: "Although it is a trite and obvious truism that people act in accordance with their motives, motivation is the central problem of large organizations given the incomprehensibility that stems from large size and its bureaucratic structure, remote and impersonal controls and abstract rules and regulations." Particularly at lower levels "many have no desire to be in the work stream because their work does not interest them, providing them with neither challenges nor satisfaction, and has no other merit in their eyes than that it leads to a paycheck at the end of the week."

5. The Principle of the Middle Axiom: "Neither the soft method of government by exhortation nor the tough method of government by issuing specific instructions is adequate." "Required is something in between, a middle axiom, an order from above that leaves freedom of choice to those doing the job."

Not surprisingly these "principles" are not so strange when examined in the light of the evolving structures of alternative organizations.

## REFERENCES

CHERNS, A. B. The principles of sociotechnical design. *Human Relations,* 1976, *29* (8), 783–792.

DAVIS, L. E. The coming crisis for production management. *International Journal of Production Research,* 1971, *9,* 65–82.

DAVIS, L. E. Work revamping can help workers and efficiency. *LMRS Newsletter* (National League of Cities, Washington, D. C.), 1975, *6* (12), 3.

DAVIS, L. E., CHERNS, A. B., & ASSOCIATES. *Quality of working life: Problems, prospects, and state of the art* (Vol. 1). New York: Free Press, 1975.

DAVIS, L. E., & TAYLOR, J. C. *Design of jobs.* London: Penguin Books, 1972.

DICKSON, D. *Alternative Technology.* London: Fontana, 1974.

ENGLESTAD, P. H. Socio-technical approach to problems of process control. In L. E. Davis & J. C. Taylor (Eds.), *Design of jobs.* London: Penguin Books, 1972, p. 353.

HERBST, P. G. The logic of bureaucratic hierarchies. *National Labor Institute Bulletin,* 1975, *I* (11), 1–7.

MAITLAND, R. P. Is technology a constraint on humanization of work? *Proceedings, International Federation of Automatic Controls Sixth Triennial World Congress,* Boston, 1975.

PATEMAN, C. *Participation and democratic theory.* Cambridge University Press, 1970.

SCHUMACHER, E. F. *Small is beautiful: Economics as if people mattered.* New York: Harper Colophon Books, 1975, Part IV, chap. 2.

---

# Type Z Organization
## Stability in the Midst of Mobility

William G. Ouchi
Alfred M. Jaeger

*Aspects of the "ideal types" of American (Type A) and Japanese (Type J) forms of organization are compared and related to their socio-cultural roots. A hybrid organizational "ideal type" (Type Z), which is particularly appropriate for many situations in today's changing American society, is presented.*

> Now all the evidence of psychiatry . . . shows that membership in a group sustains a man, enables him to maintain his equilibrium under the ordinary shocks of life, and helps him to bring up children who will in turn be happy and resilient. If his group is shattered around him, if he leaves a group in which he was a valued member, and if, above all, he finds no new group to which he can relate himself, he will under stress, develop disorders of thought, feeling and behavior . . . The cycle is vicious; loss of group membership in one generation may make men less capable of group membership in the next. The civilization that, by its very process of growth, shatters small group life will leave men and women lonely and unhappy . . . (11, p. 457).

Society traditionally has relied upon kinship, neighborhood, church, and family networks to provide the social support and normative anchors which made collective life possible. As Mayo (16) pointed out, the advent of the factory system of production and the rapid rate of technological change produced high rates of urbanization, mobility, and division of labor. These forces weakened the community, family, church, and friendship ties of many Americans. Social observers point to this weakening of associational ties as the basic cause of increasing rates of alcoholism,

---

From *Academy of Management Review,* (1978), Vol. 3, No. 4, pp. 305–314. Copyright 1978, Academy of Management. Reprinted by permission.

divorce, crime, and other symptoms of mental illness at a societal level (2, 3, 10).

While worrying over the disappearance of family, church, neighborhood, and the friendship network, predispositions can blind us to the most likely alternative source of associational ties or cohesion: the work organization. The large work organization which brought about urbanization and its consequent social ills can also provide relief from them. Donham notes:

> Mayo shows us for the first time in the form of specific instances that it is within the power of industrial administrators to create within industry itself a partially effective substitute for the old stabilizing effect of the neighborhood. Given stable employment, it might make of industry (as of the small town during most of our national life) a socially satisfying way of life as well as a way of making a living (16, Foreword).

Employment already defines many aspects of people's lives: socio-economic status, their children's education, kinds and length of vacations, frequency and severity with which they can afford to become ill, and even the way in which pension benefits allow them to live their retirement years. From childhood to the grave, the work organization plays a central role identifying people and molding their lives. Japan (1), Poland (14), and China (28), provide models of work systems which organize life and society, but we have been unwilling to borrow these models, because they do not permit the individual freedom that is valued in American life.

With memories of the totalitarian paternalism of the mines and plantations still not healed by time, Americans have been reluctant to even consider the work organization as the social umbrella under which people can live free, happy, and productive lives. The ideology of independence that is part of the basic fabric of the American persona recoils at the thought of individual freedom subordinated to collective commitment. American idols are the rough, tough individualists, the John Waynes, the Evel Knievals, the Gloria Steinems. Our most pitiable figures are those who lose their individuality in some larger, corporate entity and become "organization men," faceless persons "in gray flannel suits."

We must discover that ideologically unique American solution which allows individual freedom while using the work organization to support and encourage the stability of associational ties.

The beginnings of this solution were found in a study by one of the authors (12). Interviews were con-

ducted with employees of all level of Japanese and American firms which had operations in both the U.S. and Japan. In Japanese companies in Japan were found the now familiar characteristics first reported by Abegglen (1): almost total inclusion of the employee into the work organization so that the superior concerns himself or herself with the personal and family life of each subordinate; a collective, non-individual approach to work and responsibility; and extremely high identification of the individual with the company. These characteristics are largely the result of the lifetime employment system which characterizes large companies in Japan (1, 7, 8, 9, 10).

The surprising finding was that Japanese companies with operations in the U.S. are applying a modified form of the pure Japanese type with some success. While they do not provide company housing or large bonuses as in Japan, they attempt to create the same sort of complete inclusion of the employee into the company. Supervisors are taught to be aware of all aspects of an employee's life; extra-work social life is often connected to other employees; corporate values are adjusted to reflect employee needs as well as profit needs, and high job security is protected above all else. The American employees expressed liking for this "atmosphere" or "climate," with the managerial staff in particular noting the difference from their previous employers.

The study gave evidence that, while Americans probably do not want a return to old-style paternalism, they favor a work organization which provides associational ties, stability, and job security. The Japanese-American mixed form suggested the model which may simultaneously permit individual freedom and group cohesion.

Some American companies, by reputation, have many of the characteristics of this mixed model. Best known are Kodak, Cummins Engine Company, IBM, Levi Strauss, National Cash Register, Proctor and Gamble, and Utah International. Their historical rates of turnover are low; loyalty and morale are reputed to be very high, and identification with the company is reputed to be strong. In addition, each company has been among the most successful of American companies for many decades, a record which strongly suggests that something about the form of organization, rather than solely a particular product or market position, has kept the organization vital and strong. It is widely believed that these companies have been co-opted by their employees; they do not express goals of short-term profitability but rather pay some cost in order to maintain employment stability through difficult times. These work organizations may have created the alternative to village life to which Mayo referred.

Compare persons associated with this mixed model to the "ideal type" of bureaucrat described by Toennies (23), Weber (27), and Merton (17)—a person involved in the limited, contractual, only partially inclusive relationships that characterize traditional American organizations. In a sense, the scheme being proposed here is an organizational analogue of Toennies' *Gemeinschaft* and *Gesellschaft* (23). Just as societies suffer from poor mental health as a result of size, density, and heterogeneity which lead to contractualism and segmentalism in life, work organizations also can become segmented and contractual as they grow. This is what Weber (27) expected. He advocated development of a contractual *Gesellschaft* in work organizations to shield the meritocracy from outside ascriptive values and ties (24, 25). In a stable society, individuals can develop ties outside work to complement the impersonal nature of participation in a contractual organization. But in a mobile and changing society, societal values and outside ties are weaker, posing less threat to the efficiency of the organization. More individuals are less likely to have developed personal ties outside of work which satisfactorily complement the impersonal interactions engaged in at work. Thus, organizations whose goals and philosophy are in tune with today's general societal values can survive and even thrive by being more "personal."

## THE IDEAL TYPES:
## TYPE A, TYPE J, AND TYPE Z

This section describes three ideal types of work organization. It is argued that each type is an integrated system and will yield either positive or negative outcomes for the society depending on certain environmental conditions. Type A represents the Western organization, especially the North American and Western European forms. Type J represents the Japanese and mainland Chinese forms, and Type Z is an emergent form which is particularly suited to the United States of America today.

Each ideal type contains seven dimensions. Length of employment refers to the average number of years served within the corporation, considering all employees. This is important in two respects. First, if mean number of years of tenure is high, employees will be more familiar with the workings of the organi-

zation and more likely to have developed friendship among their co-workers; second, if the new employee anticipates a long career within one organization, he or she will be willing to incur greater personal costs in order to become integrated into the culture of the organization.

### TABLE 1
### Characteristics of two familiar organizational ideal types A and J

| Type A (American) | Type J (Japanese) |
| --- | --- |
| Short-term employment | Lifetime employment |
| Individual decision-making | Consensual decision-making |
| Individual responsibility | Collective responsibility |
| Rapid evaluation and promotion | Slow evaluation and promotion |
| Explicit, formalized control | Implicit, informal control |
| Specialized career path | Nonspecialized career path |
| Segmented concern | Holistic concern |

The mode of decision-making refers to typical ways of dealing with nonroutine problems. Individual decision-making is a mode by which the manager may or may not solicit information or opinions from others, but he or she expects and is expected by others to arrive at a decision without obligation to consider the views of others. Under consensual decision making, the manager will not decide until others who will be affected have had sufficient time to offer their views, feel they have been fairly heard, and are willing to support the decision even though they may not feel that it is the best one (21).

Although responsibility is not easily distinguished from decision making style in all cases, it represents an important, independent dimension. Individual responsibility as a value is a necessary precondition to conferring rewards upon individuals in a meritocracy. A manager possibly could engage in consensual decision making while clearly retaining individual responsibility for the decision. Indeed, the Type Z organization exhibits just this combination. In the J organization, responsibility for overseeing projects and for accepting rewards or punishments is borne collectively by all members of a sub-unit. American companies in Japan which have attempted to introduce the notion of individual responsibility among managers and blue-collar workers have found strong resistance from their employees. But in the United States individual responsibility is such a central part of the national culture that no organization can replace it with the collective value of the J type.

The speed of evaluation and promotion category is self-explanatory, but its effects are subtle. If promotion is slow, managers have time to become acquainted with the people and the customs which surround their jobs: Workers will be shaped by and ultimately assimilated into the corporate culture. For better or worse, the maverick will not be promoted until he or she has learned to abide by local customs. An organization with a history of rapid promotion will not have as unified a culture as an organization with slower rates of upward mobility.

Speed of evaluation also has significant effects upon the character of interpersonal relationships. In an achievement-oriented organization, evaluations of performance must be free of dimensions such as friendship or kinship. The only solution open to an evaluator is an impersonal relationship. If evaluations occur rapidly, for example once each six months, the subject of the evaluation will typically be known only to the direct supervisor, who will be charged with the responsibility of rendering the evaluation. The supervisor is thus blocked from forming personal, friendship ties with the subordinate. But if major evaluations occur only once every five or ten years (as is common in Japanese firms), the evaluation is no longer explicitly rendered by one superior but emerges through a non-explicit process of agreement between the many superiors who know the subordinate. Being one among many judges, the direct superior is freed from the need to preserve an "objective" attitude toward the subordinates and thus can take a personal interest in him or her.

The dimension of control is represented in an oversimplified manner. In a sense, the whole idea type represents a form of social control, and each ideal type achieves this social control in a different manner. But we can identify in Type A organizations the use of explicit standards, rules and regulations, and performance measures as the primary technique of ensuring that actual performance meets desired performance. In Type Z, expectations of behavior or output are not explicitly stated but are to be deduced from a more general understanding of the corporate philosophy.

For example, during one of the author's visits to a Japanese bank in California, both the Japanese president and the American vice-presidents of the bank accused the other of being unable to formulate objectives. The Americans meant that the Japanese president could not or would not give them explicit, quantified targets to attain over the next three or six months,

while the Japanese meant that the Americans could not see that once they understood the company's philosophy, they would be able to deduce for themselves the proper objective for any conceivable situation.

The degree to which a career path is typically specialized according to function differs greatly between organizational types. In the A organization, an upwardly mobile manager typically remains within a functional specialty, for example going from bookkeeper to clerical supervisor to assistant department head of accounting to head of the accounting department. In the J organization, the typical career path is not specialized by function, but may go from bookkeeper to supervisor of the planning department.

A specialized career path yields professionalization, decreases organizational loyalty, and facilitates movement of the individual from one firm to another. A non-specialized career path yields localism, increases organizational loyalty, and impedes inter-firm mobility. Career specialization also increases problems of coordination between individuals and sub-units, while non-specialization eases the coordination problem. Career specialization also yields the scale economies of task specialization and expertise, whereas non-specialized career paths often sacrifice these benefits. A and J organizations may be the same in formal structure—having equal divisional separation, for example—but individuals will move through those sub-units in quite different patterns.

Concern refers to the holism with which employees view each other and especially to the concern with which the supervisor views the subordinate. In the A organization, the supervisor regards the subordinate in a purely task-oriented manner and may consider it improper to inquire into her or his personal life. In comparison to this segmented view of people, the J organization manager considers it part of the managerial role to be fully informed of the personal circumstances of each subordinate.

Each ideal type represents a set of interconnected parts, each dependent on at least one other part. The systematic nature of each type is best understood by putting it in an environmental context.

The type A has developed in a society characterized by high rates of individual mobility, in a culture which supports norms of independence, self-reliance, and individual responsibility. A work organization in such a setting must contend with high rates of inter-firm mobility and a short average tenure of employment. It reduces interdependence between individuals, avoiding the start-up costs of replacing one part of a team. Individual decision making and individual responsibility provide an adaptive response to rapid change of personnel. If inter-firm mobility is high, it becomes impossible to integrate new members into the organization on a large number of dimensions. It is simpler to attend to only the one or two necessary task dimensions of the new member and integrate those. Thus a segmented concern evolves, because a concern for the whole person presents an impossible problem to an organization with high turnover. But as a result, the employee has only limited, contractual ties to the organization, has not internalized its values, and must be dealt with in a compliant relationship, in which control is explicit and formalized.

The A type organization has a relatively short time in which to realize productive benefits from the necessary investment in an individual employee (costs of search and training). It can best realize these benefits by having the person follow a highly specialized career path in which necessary learning can occur rapidly and scale economies are soon achieved. Finally, rapid turnover requires replacement of managers and thus rapid promotion of those at lower levels. Because promotion must be preceded by evaluation, to preserve the impression if not the fact of a meritocracy, evaluation also will occur rapidly.

Ideal Type J organizations evolved in a society in which individual mobility has been low in a culture which supported norms of collectivism. Through historical accidents which preserved a feudal society in Japan into the 19th century and then, after the Meiji restoration, rushed Japan into full-blown industrialism (19), feudal loyalties were transferred to major industrial institutions, with owners and employees taking the appropriate historical roles of lord and vassal. Because employees are expected to be in the same firm for a lifetime, control can be implicit and internalized rather than explicit and compliant (as in the A type). This form of control evolves because it is more reliable and can account for a wide variety of task- and personally-oriented actions, whereas no explicit system of rules and regulations could be sufficiently comprehensive to encompass that range of behavior.

Type J employees need not follow specialized career paths, because the organization can invest in them for a long period of time and be assured of repayment in later years. By following non-specialized career paths, they become experts in the organization rather than experts in some function. They are no longer inter-changeable with other organizations, since their particular set of skills and values is unique to one firm, but that is not a cost to them or to the firm. Rather, their loyalty to the firm has increased and the firm need not monitor them closely, thus saving managerial overhead.

Furthermore, coordination problems are reduced, since employees have the information and inclination to accommodate each other in jointly taking action. Since they are to spend a lifetime together, they have an interest in maintaining harmonious relationships and engaging in consensual decision making. The larger culture supports norms of collectivism which are mirrored in the organization. No individual can properly take credit or blame for actions, since organizational action by its very nature is a joint product of many individuals. Given joint responsibility, rapid evaluation would be difficult, since the task would be like that of performing a multivariate analysis with a sample of one observation. But since turnover and promotion occur slowly, evaluation need not proceed quickly. Many observations of the individual are accumulated over a period of years before the first major evaluation is made. This slow evaluation takes the pressure off a single superior and frees him or her to take a holistic concern for the employee.

The complex relationships between elements of the ideal types are not yet completely specified; that is one task of the present research, which will be aided through empirical analysis. But clearly, the major driving force behind development of the ideal types is the rate of inter-firm mobility, which is closely related to the cultural values which aid or inhibit mobility. It can be argued that the A type is an adaptive response to high rates of social mobility while the J type is a response to low rates of social mobility, both forms fitting naturally with their environments. The work organization in this view represents just one way in which members of a society are integrated; it is both influenced by and influences the structure of its surrounding society.

Having concluded that each ideal type represents a natural adaptation to a particular environment, how is it that the J type apparently has succeeded in the United States (12)? The U. S. provided the social environment in which the A type evolved. Americans are highly urbanized, move about, lead segmented lives, and thus have created a situation in which a work organization must be able to rely on people who are strangers to each other and still get coordinated effort

## TABLE 2
### Characteristics of organizational Type Z

---

*Type Z ( Modified American)*

---

Long-term employment
Consensual decision-making
Individual responsibility
Slow evaluation and promotion
Implicit, informal control with explicit, formalized measures
Moderately specialized career path
Holistic concern, including family

---

out of them. The answer was the A type, which is contractual, formalized, and impersonal. How can a very different type, the J, flourish in this same social environment?

Interviews with managers from a large number of companies over the past two years were focused on companies which, by reputation, have many characteristics of Type J. Out of these interviews came a conception of a third ideal type, which initially appeared to be the J but differs from it in some essential characteristics.

The ideal Type Z combines a basic cultural commitment to individualistic values with a highly collective, non-individual pattern of interaction. It simultaneously satisfies old norms of independence and present needs for affiliation. Employment is effectively (although not officially) for a lifetime, and turnover is low. Decision-making is consensual, and there is often a highly self-conscious attempt to preserve the consensual mode.

But the individual still is ultimately the decision-maker, and responsibility remains individual. This procedure puts strains on the individual, who is held responsible for decisions singly but must arrive at them collectively. These strains are mitigated by the fact that evaluation and promotion take place slowly and that the basic control is implicit and subtle. Thus the complexities of collective decision making are taken into account in rendering personal evaluations, but there are explicit measures of performance as in Type A. In the Z organization, although there are lots of formal accounting measures of performance, the real evaluation is subjective and highly personal. No one gets rapidly promoted or punished solely because their performance scores are good or bad. In an A organization, by contrast, people's careers often succeed or fail solely on explicit performance measures, as must be the case in any purely formalized system.

Career paths in the Z organization tend to be mod-

erately specialized, but quite non-specialized by comparison with the Type A organization. The slowness of evaluation and the stability of membership promote a holistic concern for people, particularly from superior to subordinate. This holism includes the employee and his or her family in an active manner. Family members regularly interact with other organization members and their families and feel an identification with the organization.

## IMPLICATIONS FOR SOCIETY AT LARGE

Why is the Z type useful in thinking about American organizations if the A type is the natural adaptation to a society and culture? If a second ideal type can be accommodated, social conditions must have changed.

The critical aspect of the environment is its ability to provide stable affiliations for individuals. Traditional sources of affiliation in American society (family, church, neighborhood, voluntary association, and long-term friendship) have been weakened by urbanization and geographical mobility. Figure 1 represents the combination of societal and organizational sources of affiliation. It includes only ideal types A and Z; ideal type J, the pure adaptation to a Japanese society, is not useful as a representation of American organizations.

Throughout most of its history, this nation has been high in sources of affiliation outside of the work place. Under this condition, Type A organizations evolved, creating a stable, integrated state in which most people devoted most of their energies to affiliative networks away from the workplace and were only partially included in the work organization. Had the work organization been Type Z, each employee would have been torn between two mistresses and in an overloaded state (Cell I). In the past few decades, much of American society has moved from the "High" to the "Low" affiliation state (13, 20, 22, 26). High mobility has broken the traditional patterns of interaction, but the values which supported those patterns will change more slowly. Those values support the notion of partial inclusion, of individuality, of the Type A organization. Thus many find themselves largely in the Underloaded cell (Cell IV), with society unable to provide affiliation and work organizations not organized to do so. To return to a balanced state, affiliation will have to come mostly from the organization and not from society at large.

| Affiliation in the Organization | Affiliation in Society | |
|---|---|---|
| | High | Low |
| High (Type Z) | I Overloaded | II Integrated |
| Low (Type A) | III Integrated | IV Underloaded |

**Figure 1**  Societal and Organizational Sources of Affiliation

Because not all people need the same level of affiliation (or achievement or power), each person will respond differently to being in each of the cells I through IV. According to Maslow (15), all people have a need for affiliation, belongingness, or love, which can be satisfied through feeling that they are part of a group or company. On the average, people in Cell IV ("Underloaded") will have unfulfilled needs for affiliation. They will experience "anomie," the sensation that there are no anchors or standards, and thus a feeling of being lost.

All these elements can be combined in one model which describes how the organization interacts with its social environment and with the needs of its individual members to produce high or low loyalty for the organization and high or low mental health for the employees (See Figure 2).

If American society is moving from high to low affiliation, people who are employed in a Type Z organization should be better able to deal with stress and should be happier than the population at large. Certainly the Type Z organization will be more appropriate for that segment of society which lacks stable and strong affiliative ties. That is not to suggest that the work organization will in any way replace or compete with other national institutions. Quite the opposite: If the company provides a strong basic stability in people's lives, then the family, church, and neighborhood can all flourish.

Some may object that they will never support a Type Z approach in their company or that it would never work in their industry. They may be right. So-

ciety contains a range of people and environments; some prefer an employer who leaves them alone, evaluates them purely on objective measures, and recognizes achievement through rapid promotion even over the heads of others. There will always be organizations for such people and such tastes. Stability of employment is not possible in some industries. Aerospace is one example of an industry where a Type Z organization would be harmful; if people built rich ties with each other and a control system based on personal knowledge, both would be wrenched and destroyed when the contract came to an end and massive layoffs became necessary. The Type Z form will not be for everyone.

Due to chance, some models of the Type Z organization are available to study and learn from. Until recently, the Type A organization was the most successful form in American society. When people had relatives, neighbors, and churches, they did not need Dr. Spock to tell them why the baby was purple, and they did not need a company that provided them with a rich network of social contacts. But in a few cases, companies grew up in small towns, or in places like California that were populated by emigrants, or in industries which required frequent re-location of employees. In all three cases, one side-effect was that people had no immediate form of social contact available except through their employer. The extreme case is the military base, which looks, feels, and smells the same whether it is in Hawaii, Illinois, or New York. To make life possible under conditions of high geographical mobility, the military has developed a culture

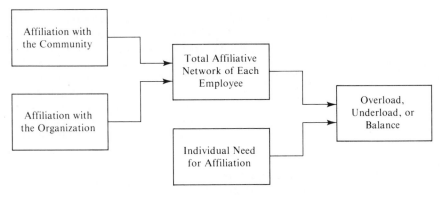

**Figure 2**  A Model of Organizational and Individual Affiliation Needs

which is immediately familiar and secure no matter where its employees go. These organizations, public and private, created a social vacuum for their employees and then had to develop internal sources of support to replace what had been taken away. Now the rest of the country is "catching up" with them as stable sources of support disappear elsewhere. One can look to such models for ideas about how to cope with the new society.

The future problem confronting the work organization seems relatively clear. American society, which has been in a constant process of change during its turbulent 200 years, has reached a critical point. Church membership is declining; violent crimes increasingly involve a victim who is completely unknown to the assailant; workers feel less commitment to employers; all of us long for stability and structure in our lives. These changes signify a decline in belongingness and suggest the fate assigned by Homans (11) to societies which lose the feeling of membership: we will become ". . . a dust heap of individuals without links to one another."

*The ideas expressed here were shaped through discussions with many managers and academics. We are particularly indebted to Melvin B. Lane, L. W. Lane, Jr., Patricia James Lyman, Alan Wilkins, Alice Kaplan, Raymond Price and David Gibson. This research was supported by grants from the Stanford University Research Development Fund, the Alcoa Foundation, and the E. I. du Pont de Nemours and Company, for which we are grateful.*

## REFERENCES

1. Abegglen, J. C. *The Japanese Factory: Aspects of its Social Organization* (Glencoe, Ill.: Free Press, 1958)

2. Angell, R. C. *The Moral Integration of American Cities* (Chicago: University of Chicago Press, 1951).

3. Angell, R. C. "The Moral Integration of American Cities, Part II," *American Journal of Sociology,* Vol. 80 (1974), 607–629.

4. Aries, P. *Centuries of Childhood: A Social History of Family Life* (New York: Knopf, 1962).

5. Blau, P., and W. R. Scott. *Formal Organizations* (Scranton, Pa.: Chandler, 1962).

6. Bradburn, Norman M. *The Structure of Psychological Well-Being* (Chicago: Aldine, 1969).

7. Cole, R. *Japanese Blue Collar: The Changing Tradition* (Berkeley: University of California Press, 1971).

8. Cole, R. "Functional Alternatives and Economic Development: An Empirical Example of Permanent Employment in Japan," *American Sociological Review,* Vol. 38 (1973): 424–438.

9. Dore, R. *British Factory—Japanese Factory* (Berkeley: University of California Press, 1973).

10. Form, W. H. "The Social Construction of Anomie: A Four Nation Study of Industrial Workers," *American Journal of Sociology,* Vol. 80 (1975), 1165–1191.

11. Homans, G. C. *The Human Group* (New York: Harcourt, Brace and World, 1950).

12. Johnson, R. T., and W. G. Ouchi. "Made in America (Under Japanese Management)," *Harvard Business Review,* Vol. 52, No. 5 (1974), 61–69.

13. Kasarda, J. D., and M. Janowitz. "Community Attachment in Mass Society," *American Sociological Review,* Vol. 39 (1974), 328–339.

14. Kolarska, L. "Interorganizational Networks and Politics: The Case of Polish Industry." Unpublished manuscript (1975).

15. Maslow, A. H. *Motivation and Personality* (New York: Harper, 1954).

16. Mayo, E. *The Social Problems of an Industrial Civilization* (Boston: Harvard Business School, 1945).

17. Merton, Robert K. *Social Theory and Social Structure,* 2nd ed. (Glencoe, Ill.: Free Press, 1957).

18. Mousseau, J. "The Family, Prison of Love: A Conversation with Phillipe Aries," *Psychology Today,* Vol. 9, No. 3 (1975), 52–54.

19. Nakane, C. *Japanese Society,* rev. ed. (Middlesex, England: Penguin Books, 1973).

20. Reissman, L. *The Urban Process* (Glencoe, Ill.: Free Press, 1964).

21. Schein, E. *Process Consultation* (Reading, Mass.: Addison-Wesley, 1969).

22. Short, J. F. *The Social Fabric of the Metropolis* (Chicago: University of Chicago Press, 1971).

23. Toennies, Ferdinand. *Gemeinschaft and Gesellschaft,* trans. by Loomis (New York: American Book Company, 1940).

24. Udy, S. "Bureaucracy and Rationality in Weber's Organization Theory: An Empirical Study," *American Sociological Review,* Vol. 24 (1959).

25. Udy, S. "Administrative Rationality, Social Setting and Organizational Development," *American Journal of Sociology,* Vol. 68 (1962), 299–308.

26. Warren, R. L. *The Community in America* (Chicago: Rand McNally, 1972).

27. Weber, Max. *The Theory of Social and Economic Organization,* trans. by A. M. Henderson and T. Parsons, (Glencoe, Ill.: Free Press and Falcon's Wing Press, 1947).

28. Whyte, M. K. "Bureaucracy and Modernization in China: The Maoist Critique," *American Sociological Review,* Vol. 38 (1973), 149–163.

# Effectiveness Theory and Organizational Effectiveness

Richard H. Hall

Organizational effectiveness is the ultimate question in any form of organizational analysis. Regardless of the ideological, political, or organizational bias

From *Journal of Applied Behavioral Science,* (1980), Vol. 16. Copyright 1980, JAI Press. Reprinted by permission.

of the investigator, effectiveness remains the dependent variable to be explained, sought, or opposed. Most approaches to effectiveness have been justifiably labeled as administrative-technical (Benson, 1977) or pro-managerial. This is fully understandable given the sources of funding, academic affiliation, and data sources of the vast majority of organizational theorists. I will argue here that while there may be a pro-managerial orientation on the part of investigators, all too seldom are the realities faced by managers taken into account in the construction of organizational theory. As a corollary, the realities faced by workers and organizational clientele are seldom addressed in effectiveness considerations.

As a data base for this analysis, I will draw upon a comprehensive empirical analysis of effectiveness (Hall & Clark, 1980) among a set of social service organizations and my own experience as a university vice-president. It is my belief that the implications drawn from these data can be generalized to a wide variety of organizations.

## THEORIES OF ORGANIZATIONAL EFFECTIVENESS

There are two basic approaches to organizational effectiveness—the goal model and the resource acquisition model (see Hall, 1977; Goodman & Pennings, 1977, for fully developed statements of these models). A third model, dealing with participant satisfaction (Georgiou, 1973; Cummings, 1977) is not sufficiently developed for consideration here.

The goal model of organizational effectiveness has its roots in Weber's (1947) seminal work. It is essentially a rational model of organizations that is both simple and complex. In its simple version, effectiveness has been defined as "the degree to which [an organization] realizes its goals" (Etzioni, 1964, p. 8). Complexity enters the picture as soon as it is realized that most organizations have multiple and frequently conflicting goals. Kochan, Cummings, and Huber (1976) have noted that structural differentiation in organizations is related to goal diversity and goal incompatibility. Since most organizations are structurally differentiated, goal multiplicity and incompatibility can almost be taken for granted in most organizations. In the Hall and Clark (1980) study, for example, one set of organizations included in the analysis was juvenile detention centers. One of their goals involved "maintaining secure custody" of youths while another involved "providing healthy living arrangements." Activities directed at securing the first goal would be exactly the opposite of activities in pursuit of the second goal. Obviously, organizations will vary in the degree to which they emphasize and act upon their diverse goals, but the existence of such diversity means that it is not reasonable to conceive of organizations as rational, (single) goal-seeking entities.

Today the goal model continues to be a focus of much analysis. Two decades ago Perrow (1961) made the important distinction between official and operative goals, with the latter involving what the organization is actually attempting to do, regardless of official statements. Most analyses utilize the operative goal approach. Most also recognize that goals are not static.

Three sources of goal change have been identified (Hall, 1977). One source of change is interaction with environmental elements. Thompson and McEwen (1958) suggested that competition, bargaining, co-optation, and coalition formation contributed to goal change. Goals also change because of internal dynamics. Internal political processes can move an organization toward oligarchy (Michaels, 1949), and internal accounting procedures can lead an organization to emphasize the easily quantifiable (Gross, 1968). Finally, indirect influences from the environment contribute to goal shifts. For example, the technological development of safe vaccines for polio contributed to a major (both official and operative) goal shift for the March of Dimes organization (Sills, 1957).

Hannan and Freeman (1977a) made a comprehensive analysis of the goal model. They noted that it was plagued with three basic problems, but at the same time noted that it would be a mistake to drop goals from organizational analysis since they are one of the major defining characteristics of organizations. The first problem Hannan and Freeman note is multiplicity of goals. They suggest that the "imagination is boggled" by the multiplicity and diversity of goals in large federal agencies (p. 112). The same boggling would occur with organizations in other sectors. Secondly, organizational goals are usually general rather than specific, making analysis difficult. Thirdly, the temporal dimension is too seldom considered. Effectiveness in the short run could lead to disaster in the long run, while an emphasis on the longer term could contribute to more immediate problems. Hannan and Freeman conclude that goals should be retained in organizational analysis and used much like individual preferences are in micro-economics: that is, as the basis of testable hypotheses.

The measurement of effectiveness when using the goal model is also difficult. A major difficulty is the "bounding system" (Hannan & Freeman, 1977a, p. 116) used in the analysis. This involves the problem of disentangling events that happen outside and inside the organization. Qualities of inputs may or may not be subject to organizational controls. It is well known that some social service organizations, for example, are very successful in shunting difficult tasks to other organizations or to "cracks" between organizations and thus enhancing their own treatment effectiveness. In a similar manner, it is very difficult to determine the contributions of many internal activities. It could be argued that the personnel selection process is more critical than the accounting process, or vice versa—or neither. The point here is that organizational analysts are not yet in a position to specify the contributions of organizational components to organizational actions.

A second major difficulty with measuring effectiveness from the goal perspective involves the question of which party's views are to be utilized. Our (Hall & Clark, 1980) research has shown that quite different answers are given by organizational participants, members of other organizations, and by organizational clients. Similar differences have been found between hierarchical levels in universities (Gross, 1968).

Quite obviously, effectiveness is measured in the mind of the beholder. Pennings and Goodman (1977) have suggested that the "dominant coalition" of an organization is the key in the determination of effectiveness. This is correct from a managerial perspective, but begs the issue of the impact of organizations on other constituents.

Despite the problems associated with it, the goal model remains as a dominant perspective on effectiveness. Its dominance is linked to the fact that organizations do in fact utilize goals, as witnessed by annual reports and planning documents. While these can be labeled as rationalizations for past actions, goals remain as a central component of most theories of organizations and of organizational effectiveness.

The resource acquisition model has been developed as an alternative approach in the study of organizational effectiveness. The primary impetus for this model comes from the work of Yuchtman and Seashore (1967) and Seashore and Yuchtman (1977) although it can be traced to earlier writings (Gouldner, 1959) and be seen in later analyses which take an ecological perspective (Stinchcombe, 1965; Aldrich & Pfeffer, 1976; Hannan & Freeman, 1977b). From this perspective Seashore and Yuchtman define the effectiveness of an organization as "the ability to exploit its environment in the acquisition of scarce and valued resources to sustain its functioning" (p. 393). Such resources can take many forms, including raw materials, money, clients, personnel, and so on.

Seashore and Yuchtman developed "penultimate" criteria of effectiveness, claiming that ultimate criteria, such as survival or death, can only be considered over very long time periods. The penultimate criteria that were developed were tested on a set of insurance firms and are specific to this particular kind of organization. The criteria included such things as growth in business volume and the youthfulness of the organizational members.

Few would argue that resource acquisition is not important for all organizations. Whether or not this is an appropriate model for analyzing effectiveness has been subject to debate. I (Hall, 1977, p. 91) suggest that resource acquisition does not just happen, but rather is based upon what the organization is attempting to achieve. Decisions are based on goals as well as resource acquisition. Such acquisition can be viewed as a necessary prerequisite for goal attainment. At the same time, it seems foolish to view organizations as acquiring resources for their own sake. Rather, resources are sought on the basis of the paths or goals established by the dominant coalition of the organization.

Scott (1977, p. 67) suggests that Seashore and Yuchtman essentially recognize this point when they suggest that the criteria for determining effectiveness must be identified. The identification of effectiveness criteria must be done on the basis of some understanding of where the organization is attempting to go. Scott also notes that the Seashore-Yuchtman approach is overly narrow inasmuch as it only utilizes the interests of the organizational directors. In the case of insurance firms, potential customers could withhold resources, but there are many forms of organizations in which potential customers do not have this option.

Campbell (1977, p. 44) notes an additional difficulty with the resource acquisition approach. Seashore and Yuchtman utilized a factor analysis technique in deriving their penultimate criteria. This is a sound methodological technique, but it does not permit the arrangement of the factors in any hierarchy. Campbell suggests that some of the penultimate criteria may be more important than others and that choices may thus have to be made among the criteria. In the example of the insurance firms, a choice might have to be made between the criteria of increasing business volume or increasing market penetration. When stated in these terms, the argument becomes strikingly like the goal model.

Two additional points regarding the resource acquisition approach should be noted. First, it has not generated any coherent line of research (Pennings & Goodman, 1977, p. 4). Despite this, the second point is that the resource acquisition approach remains a dominant theoretical perspective in the study of organizational effectiveness. It holds a prominent position apparently because of recognition of the intuitive sense that the approach makes which is clear linkage to the environmental orientations that more general organizational theory has taken.

Pennings and Goodman (1977) have attempted to bring the goal and resource acquisition models together, with resource acquisition being termed constraints that must be met before goals can be attained. This is probably a sensible resolution to the continuing debate among advocates of the alternative models, but still misses some important components of the situations which organizations face.

## SOME NEGLECTED ISSUES

Both of these "traditional" effectiveness models contain an important assumption. They suggest that the decisions of organizational management, or the dominant coalition emergent from political processes, are guided by goal or resource acquisition considerations. This is surely true, but there are other crucial considerations which do not appear in these formulations, or in more general organizational theory.

A major consideration is the fact that many critical contingencies of organizations are beyond management's control. Energy crises and general economic downturns or upturns are uncontrollable realities of organizational existence. While it can be argued that oil firms and some financial institutions are capable of controlling even these phases of their environments, this point seems to be stretched when the total scope of international political, economic, and social arrangements are considered. For the vast majority of private and public organizations, such control is out of the question, and the organization must be simply viewed as the recipient (not necessarily passive) of externally derived forces. Organizations have to cope with such developments. Colleges and universities, for example, are facing overriding demographic and economic conditions in the 1980s which are beyond their control. It is impossible to control the changes, yet such changes weigh heavily in decision making. At my own university fiscal austerity is being confronted as it is by all agencies within the state. Similarly, a shrinking population of traditional college-aged individuals presently confronts the administration of colleges and universities throughout the country.

These are not surprising events. At the same time, organizational theory, even with the current emphasis upon the environment, tends not to consider these external, but penetrating, phenomena. They cannot be controlled by the organization.

A second category of phenomena which are not typically considered are the externally mandated contingencies with which an organization must deal. These primarily involve economic and regulatory phenomena. On the economic side, for example, costs of energy, which may or may not be related to the energy shortage, are imposed on organizations. In most energy related or, more generally, monopolized situations, the receiving organization can do little but receive. Noneconomic examples include the vast array of federal and state regulations which are imposed on organizations, with little or no input from the organizations involved. At present, for example, colleges and universities are developing plans for the implementation of federal regulations with the acronym "A-21." These regulations are designed to ensure that federally funded research and other projects receive the time and effort for which they are budgeted. Countless (and at times pointless) meetings are being held at *all* colleges and universities in regard to A-21. The point here is not A-21, but rather that an externally imposed mandate impinges upon these organizations to an extreme extent. The same thing occurs with respect to other external mandates, such as Affirmative Action, occupational health and safety regulations, minimum wage provisions, and so on. Regardless of whether the content of such regulations is seen as good or evil, their organizational consequences are largely the same.

Lest this analysis appear to be concerned with only governmental regulations, I must add that externally imposed mandates also come from the private sector. Computer manufacturers, for example, change the language capabilities of their computers, making certain operations obsolete and forcing users to adapt to new language requirements. While this achieves goals and acquires resources for the computer manufacturer, the recipient organization simply has to absorb the external mandates.

These mandates are imposed upon the organization and the organization must deal with them. Not dealing with them contains the threat of loss of funds, loss of business, loss of certification, or loss of personnel. In New York State, for example, "truth-in-testing" legislation, aimed at reducing the advantages of the advantaged, is having the effect of making student selection at the graduate and undergraduate levels much less certain (although not necessarily worse), and definitely much more difficult.

The third kind of phenomena to be considered are internally generated norms which minimize the range of options open to organizational decision makers or dominant coalitions. Union contracts, tenure rules, and the force of tradition are notable examples. Organizations simply do not have a complete range of decisions open to them. While it might appear advantageous, for example, for a university to close down a department with no students and no majors and with unproductive faculty members, this cannot be done, except under very dire economic conditions calling for "retrenchment." . . .

The discussion thus far has focused on the limitations faced by organizations. It also must be noted that the uncontrollable contingencies and external and internal mandates can create opportunities where they did not previously exist. Suppose, for example, that an automobile firm developed a highly fuel-efficient engine. At the time of its development, it was too expensive for successful competition, but rising fuel prices could make it become economically viable. A market could be entered where none existed before. The growing number of adults who were born during the baby boom of the 1940s now represent a new market for recreational industries and education. Increases in longevity have provided the consumers for the old-age industry.

The point of all this is that uncontrollable contingencies and internally and externally imposed mandates are central aspects of the reality which organizational decision makers must face. Ideas of goal attainment and resource acquisition are carried on within a framework of coping with these constraints. While the contingencies and mandates are certain, the methods of coping are not. A great deal of time and effort are spent on dealing with these phenomena. Alternative coping strategies are discussed, reductions in service are contemplated, and potential consequences are evaluated. On the basis of my observations, a good part of contemporary organizational theory does not deal with the kinds of issues which have been discussed here.

## ORGANIZATIONAL THEORY RECONSIDERED

In this final section, two points in regard to organizational theory will be made and a suggestion for future research will be offered. The first point is a relatively minor one, but is worth noting. Many writers have discussed the importance of dealing with uncertainty (Hickson, Hinings, Lee, Schneck & Pennings, 1971; Pennings & Goodman, 1977). Yet, it would appear that in many ways, the crucial issue for organizations is dealing with *certainty*. Externally imposed mandates are presented in writing. There may be uncertainty in the interpretation of the mandated regulations, but these too can be provided by the mandator. Rising fuel costs are certain; it is the coping technique which is uncertain. Organizational environments do contain elements of uncertainty to be sure. The elements of the environment that are beyond an organization's control are surely uncertain. I would argue that very few organizational members have a first crack at position openings on another campus in the state system. This, in turn, potentially limits the decision making freedom of the second campus. As another example, it is not too far-fetched to suggest uncertainty in a quite different light than most analysts would suggest.

The second point is more general. Organizational theory must begin to include events beyond organizational control. Whetten and Aldrich (1979) have found that the size and diversity of organizational sets are variables over which administrators have little control. The argument here is that this finding must be generalized to the total range of organizational phenomena, including effectiveness. I would argue, for example, that the current interest in ecological phenomena is misdirected. Instead of searching for factors that contribute to organizational survival or death, it would be wiser to search for those phenomena which emerge to impinge upon the ongoing operations of the organization and examine the manner in which organizations cope with these certainties.

Rather than asking whether or not decisions are made on the basis of a set of goals or resource acquisi-

tion needs, the question should be—how are goals achieved and resources acquired in the face of the external and internal mandates which have been discussed. It should be stressed that this approach goes beyond the notion of "constraints" developed by Pennings and Goodman (1977). They suggest that "*Constraints* are conditions that must be satisfied if an organization is to be considered effective. . ." (p. 160). In their view, constraints are standards developed by the dominant coalition. In many ways, these constraints are cast in terms of standards for resource acquisition, with goal achievement seen as the key for effectiveness. The argument here is that both resource acquisition and goal achievement can best be viewed in terms of a prior consideration of coping with external contingencies and external and internal mandates.

Finally, this analysis suggests that organizational research and theory will be best served by increased attention to the realities which organizational decision makers face. If the research emphasis is on effectiveness, and it is recognized at the outset that the perspective will be that of the dominant coalition (admitting the administrative-technical bias), then insights into, and information from, the dominant coalition are needed. Secondary data will not do here, nor will data from the rank and file. It is a mistake to impose goal or resource acquisition issues in advance. Rather, research and theory must be informed by the range of considerations actually taken into account by the dominant coalition. Toward this end, in my view, the considerations raised in this paper have received insufficient attention.

## REFERENCES

Aldrich, H. E., & Pfeffer, J. Environments of organizations. *Annual Review of Sociology*, 1976, 2, 79–105.

Benson, J. K. Innovation and crisis in organizational analysis. *The Sociological Quarterly*, 1977, 18, 3–16.

Campbell, J. P. On the nature of organizational effectiveness. In P. S. Goodman & J. M. Pennings (Eds.), *New perspectives on organizational effectiveness*. San Francisco, Calif.: Jossey-Bass, 1977. Pp. 13–55.

Cummings, L. L. Emergence of the instrumental organization. In P. S. Goodman & J. M. Pennings (Eds.), *New perspectives on organizational effectiveness*. San Francisco, Calif.: Jossey-Bass, 1977. Pp. 56–62.

Etzioni, A. *Modern organizations*. Englewood Cliffs, N. J.: Prentice-Hall, 1964.

Georgiou, P. The goal paradigm and notes toward a counter paradigm. *Administrative Science Quarterly,* 1973, 18, 291–310.

Goodman, P. S. & Pennings, J. M. (Eds.). *New perspectives on organizational effectiveness.* San Francisco, Calif.: Jossey-Bass, 1977.

Gouldner, A. W. Organizational analysis. In R. K. Merton, L. Broom, & L. S. Cottrell, Jr. (Eds.), *Sociology today.* New York: Basic Books, 1959. Pp. 400–428.

Gross, E. Universities as organizations: A research approach. *American Sociological Review,* 1968, 33, 518–544.

Hall, R. H. *Organizations: Structure and process.* Englewood Cliffs, N. J.: Prentice-Hall, 1977.

Hall, R. H., & Clark, J. P. An ineffective effectiveness study and some suggestions for future research. *The Sociological Quarterly,* 1980, 21, 119–134.

Hannan, M. T., & Freeman, J. Obstacles to comparative studies. In P. S. Goodman & J. M. Pennings (Eds.), *New perspectives on organizational effectiveness.* San Francisco, Calif.: Jossey-Bass, 1977. Pp. 106–132. (a)

Hannan, M. T., & Freeman, J. The population ecology of organizations. *American Journal of Sociology,* 1977, 82, 929–964. (b)

Hickson, D. J., Hinings, C. R., Lee, C. A., Schneck, R. E., & Pennings, J. M. A strategic contingencies theory of intraorganizational power. *Administrative Science Quarterly,* 1971, 16, 216–229.

Kochan, T. A., Cummings, L. L., & Huber, G. P. Operationalizing the concepts of goals and goal incompatibility in organization behavior research. *Human Relations,* 1976, 29, 527–544.

Michaels, R. *Political parties: A sociological study of the oligarchical tendencies of modern democracy.* New York: Free Press, 1949. (Originally published 1911)

Pennings, J. M., & Goodman, P. S. Toward a workable framework. In P. S. Goodman & J. M. Pennings (Eds.), *New perspectives on organizational effectiveness.* San Francisco, Calif.: Jossey-Bass, 1977. Pp. 146–184.

Perrow, C. The analysis of goals in complex organizations. *American Sociological Review,* 1961, 26, 854–866.

Scott, W. R. Effectiveness of organizational effectiveness studies. In P. S. Goodman & J. M. Pennings (Eds.), *New perspectives on organizational effectiveness.* San Francisco, Calif.: Jossey-Bass, 1977. Pp. 63, 95.

Seashore, S. E., & Yuchtman, E. Factorial analysis of organizational performance, *Administrative Science Quarterly,* 1977, 12, 377–395.

Sills, D. L. *The volunteers.* New York: Free Press, 1957.

Stinchcombe, A. L. Social structure and organizations. In J. G. March (Ed.), *Handbook of organizations.* Chicago, Ill.: Rand McNally, 1965. Pp. 142–193.

Thompson, J. D., & McEwen, W. J. Organizational goals and environment: Goal setting as an interaction process. *American Sociological Review,* 1958, 23, 23–30.

Weber, M. *The theory of social and economic organization.* (A. M. Henderson & T. Parsons, trans.). New York: Free Press, 1947.

Whetten, D., & Aldrich, H. E. Organizational set size and diversity: People processing organizations and their environments. *Administration and Society,* 1979, 11, 251–281.

Yuchtman, E., & Seashore, S. E. A system resource approach to organizational effectiveness. *American Sociological Review,* 1967, 32, 891–903.

# CHAPTER FOUR

# Organization Development

## Organization Development and Bureaucracy in the 1980s

W. Warner Burke

Even though organization development may:

a. represent nothing more than a convenient rubric for a conglomeration of activities (Kahn, 1974),
b. suffer from problems of diffusion of success (Walton, 1975),
c. now be confused with or merely serve as another name for quality of working life,
d. be considered a taboo term in certain organizations (better to say "human resource development"),
e. disappear by being absorbed into other organizational functions such as "human resource management" (Tichy, 1978), and
f. never have a comprehensive theoretical base,

the field is alive and well. The OD Network numbers more than 2,000 members, the OD Division of the American Society for Training and Development has even more, and the OD Division of the Academy of Management has approximately 1,000 members. There is overlapping membership among these three primary OD groups, but it is reasonable if not conservative to assume that the number of people in the United States who call themselves OD practitioners or OD consultants is near 5,000. The total number of OD practitioners outside the U. S. is probably smaller than this

From *Journal of Applied Behavioral Science,* (1980), Vol. 16. Copyright 1980, JAI Press. Reprinted by permission.

estimate of 5,000, but the number is increasing especially in Western Europe and Japan.

The number of organization development courses in universities and books on the subject continues to increase, and the job market is as active as ever. At this writing I know of a dozen positions to be filled in the greater New York City area alone—and the employing organizations are using the OD label for these openings. OD practitioners still come from a variety of backgrounds—not just psychology, sociology, and education—but they presently have more opportunity for training in the applied behavioral sciences, at least at universities, than was the case a decade ago.

Though diverse in background and wide-ranging in skills and competencies, OD practitioners have choice since the job market remains healthy. And even though external consultants in OD have more autonomy than their internal counterparts, the latter nevertheless have more freedom of action, as a rule, than many other groups inside organizations. Internal practitioners do have restrictions, however. For example, they rarely consult with the top management group of the total organization (a limitation that may be appropriate), or get involved with top management succession planning or corporate planning in general. But if they feel too restricted by their employing organization, they can strike out on their own—I continue to be amazed at the number who choose to take this step and actually "make it"—or, of course with the job market continuing to be healthy, join another organization.

Although there has not been a substantial increase in new methods and techniques in recent years, people in the field remain quite busy, and they continue to have more choice in their careers than many other groups.

## OD IN BUREAUCRACIES

Organization development practitioners in bureaucracies, however, have not had an easy time of it. Earlier there was optimism (Bennis, 1967; Slater & Bennis, 1964). Bennis (1966) went so far as to predict "the coming death of bureaucracy." He gave it another 25 years or so. Bennis believed that bureaucracy was vulnerable because of:

1. Rapid and unexpected change—a bureaucracy could not cope with the accelerated pace of change;
2. Growth in size—with growth organizations becoming more complex and not as amenable to the bureaucratic simplicities of division of labor, hierarchy, standardization, roles, procedures, and so forth for effectively coping with their environments;
3. More diverse and highly specialized competence is now required—with increases in size and complexity, organizations require greater and different specializations whereas bureaucracy demands standardization, common policy and procedures, routine, and well-defined jobs; and
4. A change in managerial behavior—rather than the impersonality in human relations characteristic of bureaucracies, a newer philosophy is emerging which is based on changing concepts of:
   a. the human being—more complex with recognized needs,
   b. power—collaboration and reason being more highly valued than coercion and threat, and
   c. organizational values—based more on humanistic and democratic ideals than the depersonalized, mechanistic value system of bureaucracy.

Others shared much of these same beliefs especially with respect to changes in values (e.g., Tannenbaum & Davis, 1969).

Then there was pessimism (Bennis, 1970). As a result of his experience as an academic administrator (a bureaucratic situation if there ever was one), Bennis came to the view that human nature being what it is, bureaucracies were not amenable to the kinds of changes

in organizational life that he had previously predicted. He reluctantly declared that people as a rule are more concerned with: (a) power and personal gain than with openness and love, (b) clarity of organization than with ambiguity, and (c) self-interests than with the good of the organization or public interest. No doubt many readers of Bennis's change in attitude commented, "I could have told you so."

Later came pragmatism (Perrow, 1977; Schein & Greiner, 1977). Perrow has paradoxically argued that the efficient bureaucracy can centralize in order to decentralize. His ideas are not as far-fetched as this statement may sound. In fact, his argument is based primarily on the accepted and valid principle of management in any organization—delegation. Schein and Greiner have addressed more directly the applicability of organization development (OD) to bureaucracies. They pointed out that the basic ideology of OD is that organizations in response to their changing environments should become more organic systems and therefore more capable of responding to rapid change. Organic systems were characterized by Schein and Greiner as having structures such as matrix or project rather than functional designs and as having open communications, interdependence among groups, considerable trust, joint problem solving, and employees who take risks. Schein and Greiner (1977, p. 49) did not believe that many of these kinds of organizations exist:

> Despite OD's preoccupation with organic practices, we contend . . . that the millennium of organic organizations is not on the horizon, which in turn causes us to question the relevance of the present OD movement for the great bulk of business and public organizations. The preponderance of evidence, by contrast, shows that bureaucratic structures are still the dominant organizational form, either for an entire firm or for product groups.

They assumed that different organizational structures develop unique and inherent behavioral problems and that "behavioral diseases" emerging from bureaucracies differ from those which emanate from organic structures. Accordingly, they argued for a contingency model of OD and proposed a "fine tuning" approach in dealing with bureaucracies. By fine tuning Schein and Greiner meant using OD techniques as a way of sharpening "the operations of an organization" and freeing it from "dysfunctional behaviors" (p. 53). For bureaucracies, then, OD consultants should not attempt to bring about significant change but rather work to improve or fine tune the operations of the system.

Schein and Greiner were specific in their recommendations for fine tuning bureaucracies. They used two criteria for the selection of OD techniques for fine tuning: that the quality of working life will be enhanced as a result, but the situations bounded by the environmental and technological realities of the organization will not be the prime focus of change. They went on to specify four "behavioral diseases" of bureaucracies and to suggest certain OD techniques as potential cures. The four diseases are:

1. *Functional myopia and suboptimization*—results from high division of labor and individuals' allegiance to their specialty;
2. *Vertical lock-in and incompetency*—promotions stay within a single function, emphasis on rank and seniority;
3. *Top-down information flow and problem insensi-*

*tivity*—authority, problem solving, plans, and objectives are defined at the top;

4. *Routine jobs and dissatisfaction*—results from bureaucratic need for economics of scale and labor being considered a variable cost.

Table 1 is a summary of Schein and Greiner's behavioral diseases in bureaucracies, the associated behavioral symptoms, and the cures from OD for purposes of fine tuning the operations of the system.

Schein and Greiner's final recommendations were that OD consultants:

- adopt a more positive and accepting attitude toward bureaucratic organizations;
- acquire a more thorough knowledge of bureaucratic operations;
- adopt a more conceptual and realistic orientation for understanding bureaucratic behavior; and
- develop a more versatile range of OD techniques that apply to bureaucracies.

**TABLE 1**

**A summary of "behavioral diseases" of bureaucracies, their symptoms, and OD cures (from Schein & Greiner, 1977)**

| Critical behavioral diseases of bureaucracies | Behavioral symptoms | OD cures for fine tuning |
|---|---|---|
| Functional myopia and suboptimization | Interdepartmental conflict<br>Lack of planning coordination<br>Lack of adequate communication across functions | Team building for top management groups<br>Off-site meeting of top two or three levels of management for participative planning and budgeting session<br>Limited structural intervention designed to facilitate goal integration, e.g., senior coordination group<br>Job rotation of high potential managers |
| Vertical lock-in and incompetency | Frustration<br>Boredom<br>Technical knowledge valued more than managerial ability | Assessment center<br>Job posting<br>Manpower information system<br>Career counseling<br>Management training |
| Top-down information flow and problem insensitivity | Lack of innovation<br>Minor problems become major by the time they reach top management | Develop "shadow" structure<br>• reflective (Greiner)<br>• collateral (Zand)<br>• parallel (Carlson)<br>Junior board of middle managers<br>Ombudsman |
| Routine jobs and dissatisfaction | Absenteeism<br>Boredom<br>First-line supervisors feel caught between workers' problems and management's pressure for production | Job enrichment<br>Job rotation<br>Vary work schedules<br>Flexi-time<br>Supervisory training<br>Scanlon plan<br>Salary instead of hourly wages<br>Employee stock ownership plans |

Where is OD today vis-à-vis bureaucracies, and what about the next decade? The remainder of this paper is an attempt to respond to these questions.

## CURRENT OD IN BUREAUCRACIES

It is difficult to know precisely, but from what is known it seems reasonable to generalize that very little OD is being practiced today in bureaucracies whether they be in the private or public sector. To the extent that OD is practiced in bureaucracies, it is much as Schein and Greiner described: Techniques are used to respond to system ills. But this use of OD techniques is really not organization development. If we subscribe to Beckhard's (1969) definition (no doubt the most popular one), what is practiced in bureaucracies is not "system-wide, planned change managed from the top." And if one chooses my definition—i.e., change in the organization's culture (Burke, 1971)—then the actual practice of OD in bureaucracies may be even more limited.

There is at least one exception to the above generalization. If we can agree that General Motors Corporation is a bureaucracy, then OD in such a system, now under a new name, QWL, is in place (Carlson, 1978). Carlson (in press) now sees organization development as a part of GM's quality of working life effort; an integral part but subsumed under its QWL umbrella nevertheless. In any case, GM's practice of QWL does appear to be a system-wide change effort primarily because:

a. its effects are regularly surveyed and fed back among a wide range of employees,
b. managers' performances are partially assessed and rewarded as a function of how well their units rate on these surveys of the employees' (including management) perceived feelings regarding their quality of work life, and
c. these QWL efforts are strongly supported by the UAW.

I know of no other such examples from private industry, and I know of none at all in the public sector. The U.S. Army is active with its organizational effectiveness (OE) program, and perhaps in time this entire segment of the Department of Defense may be affected. But for now the OE consultation, while proving to be helpful, is rather limited in scope and impact.

Robert Golembiewski is one of the more experienced consultants in the field of OD with bureaucracies, especially in the public sector. He tends to be optimistic about such consultation and has even provided 19 guidelines for consulting effectively with bureaucracies (Golembiewski, 1978). To the extent that he has been successful as a consultant, he may be an exception to my remarks about the absence of OD in the public sector. Most OD consultants find working with bureaucracies, especially public ones, to be difficult at best (Goodstein, 1978). And there are enough failures on record (Bennis, 1977; Crockett, 1977; Glaser, 1977; Goodstein & Boyer, 1972) to give one pause.

Apparently, most OD consultants have either become more pragmatic and realistic or they have given up when it comes to working with large, bureaucratic organizations. Tichy (1978) has found that both internal and external consultants in OD have: (a) become rather doubtful about the possibilities of their consultation having any significant impact toward system-wide change, and (b) come to recognize that what they espouse regarding organizational change and what they actually practice as consultants differ rather dramatically. Tichy's sample was quite small—11 external and 17 internal consultants—and generalizing to all OD consultants is obviously inappropriate. Tichy's sample included, however, OD consultants experienced in the field (some for 15 or more years), and therefore these results should not be ignored.

So, whether present OD consultation with bureaucracies can be characterized as pragmatic and realistic or as tinkering with the system and fundamentally changing nothing depends on how you choose to define organization development. Is OD a process of helping the client organization to adapt and cope with its environment and internal workforce more effectively or is it a process of bringing about some fundamental changes in the organization's culture—i.e., its way of doing things? Is it single-loop learning or double-loop (Argyris & Schön, 1978)?

Although there is a question of definition here, there is a deeper concern than merely attempting to redefine OD. As far as I am concerned, the definitions we have are adequate. Some of my preferred definitions, in addition to my own, include those by Beckhard (1969), Golembiewski (1979), Hornstein, Bunker, and Hornstein (1971), Margulies and Raia (1978), and Weisbord (1978). Thus, I am not calling for a conference to define or redefine OD.

The deeper concern to which I wish to draw attention is not merely a matter of whether OD techniques are used in organizations. They are. Moreover, it seems that more and more people are calling themselves OD consultants. The fundamental question concerns what these people are accomplishing: Is planned organizational change resulting from their efforts or not? I believe the answer is that very little or no fundamental change is occurring in bureaucratic organizations.

In spite of heavy criticism especially from the humanistic perspective (e.g., Argyris, 1964, 1973; Bennis, 1966; Emery, 1974; Singer & Wooten, 1976), bureaucracy as a form of organization persists. I think this persistence will increase during the 1980s, assuredly for the first half of the decade. A number of facts support this prediction. Perhaps the most important one comes from economics. Inflation is obviously persistent and large organizations (and small ones) are searching for ways to economize. Managers are being rewarded not only for the amount of gross income they can show, but also for how much cost savings they can demonstrate as well. A concurrent and natural inclination is to centralize. It is generally believed—and there is supportive evidence—that centralization will help to cut costs. When duplication (often a consequence of decentralization) can be eliminated, significant savings will frequently be realized. Three examples should support the prediction of increased bureaucracy.

General Motors, paragon of the huge but decentralized organization, has recently centralized its purchasing function. Formerly, the purchasing function was located in each division, and gradually each corporate unit has transferred its purchasing operations to corporate headquarters. Considerable conflict between corporate and the divisions had to be managed for these transfers to occur, but the "numbers" were clear —with the greater volume of purchasing power, significant cost savings could be realized.

At AT&T, a corporation consisting of relatively autonomous operating companies and similarly autonomous supporting units (e.g., Western Electric), more centralization is under consideration. Billions of dollars are spent annually on training and education. Each of these relatively autonomous units has its own training function—and so does AT&T corporate. People in the system who know agree that there is considerable duplication of effort. It therefore seems clear that centralizing at least more of training would save money. A kind of OD consultation, incidentally, is being used to help with this decision-making process.

The National Aeronautics and Space Administration has become more centralized in recent years. In the days of the Apollo mission, NASA centers competed for the same project. With less money available today, more centralization of decision making assures that costly competition does not occur.

Typically, centralization breeds bigger bureaucracy. Standardization may save, but more people and functions have to conform to the same rules. As one manager in AT&T put it, "Managing is not as much fun as it used to be. Everything has to go upward through one layer of committees after another, just to make sure we are going to do it 'the right way.'"

In summary, today OD in bureaucracies can be characterized at best as fine tuning the system. Although OD techniques are used, fundamental changes in large organizations rarely occur. Change in General Motors, in spite of some centralization and potential increase in bureaucratization, seems to be occurring. But other examples are hard to find. Furthermore, since centralization will probably be on the increase, dismantling the bureaucratic structure of large organizations is not in the offing.

## WHAT'S AN OD CONSULTANT TO DO?

If my analysis of the situation is correct, we must ask: "What is an OD consultant to do?" Continuing to fine tune and tinker with the system is one obvious choice for organizational consultants. This option allows OD consultants to provide help to client organizations, and consultants may realize satisfaction as a result. I am not opposed to this option. I have exercised it myself and will probably continue to do so. In fact, I enjoy helping, but I also worry.

The source of my uneasiness grows from Hart and Scott's (1975) discussion of the "organization imperative." They make the obvious but very substantive case that our society has gradually shifted from an individual base to an organizational one. To oversimplify their point a bit—you can't do anything without an organization. Specifically, they state that our cultural values have shifted in the following ways:

- from individuality to obedience,
- from the indispensability of the unique individual to dispensability,
- from community to specialization,
- from spontaneity to self-conscious planning,
- from voluntarism to an organizational paternalism.

In helping organizations to "renew, improve, and become more effective," we OD consultants may be doing nothing more than responding to and facilitating the organizational imperative. The client is the system, right? Golembiewski (1979) puts it this way:

> However noble the professed goals underlying OD interventions, some danger—or perhaps an absolute inevitability—exists that those values will be perverted by the inexorable demands of the organizational system. (p. 115)

Referring to Walton and Warwick (1973), Golembiewski goes on to state that:

> OD interventions may be tolerated only when they basically serve to stabilize the system, as in "cooling out" those members who develop antagonistic feelings toward some system. Human needs will be responded to, in this view of the world, only (or mostly) when they happen to coincide with the organizational imperative. (1979, p. 115)

These remarks may spell out the consequences of the first option: tinkering with existing bureaucracies. They also suggest a second option for OD consultants: they may quit. Some have and are now managers, trainers and educators, personnel specialists, academicians, entrepreneurs, and real estate agents. But for many a commitment to changing organizations continues, and dropping out is not the preferred option.

The third option, albeit the most difficult one, is to try to do OD—to attempt to change the system itself, especially its culture, to stem the tide of the organizational imperative at least to the point where the individual is not sacrificed. I honestly cannot say that with my accumulated knowledge of and experience in organization development, I know how to stem this tide and eliminate the inhumane aspects of bureaucracy. At the risk of sounding like Don Quixote or perhaps Sisyphus, I will nevertheless make three recommendations. These recommendations are somewhat strategic and in any case emphasize particular interventions. Strategically, I am recommending certain OD interventions aimed toward the decentralization of power. These interventions already have precedence, so we are dealing with a matter of emphasis.

1. *Group interventions.* These interventions are critical because: (a) they are based on the key strengths of OD knowledge: group dynamics and process consultation, and (b) because the organizational work group is one, if not the only, primary linkage between the individual employee and the organization. In other words, more may be done for the individual via his or her work group than through any other medium or organizational juncture. Two kinds of group interventions hold promise for dealing with bureaucracies: autonomous (or semi-autonomous) work groups and the so-called quality control (QC) circles.

Based on Bion's (1961) theory concerning authority issues in small groups and its application in sociotechnical systems (Emery & Trist, 1960; Rice, 1958), "autonomous" or "self-managing" work groups are designed to alleviate problems associated with supervisor-subordinate relationships by encouraging group members to: (a) share leadership functions among themselves rather than depend on a formal leader (i.e., supervisor), and (b) work collaboratively. The work of these groups is designed to include whole tasks, skill variety among group members, worker discretion regarding methods, schedules and division of labor, and pay and feedback on performance based on the group as a whole (Hackman & Oldham, 1980).

> The attributes are intended to provide the work group with the task boundary, autonomy, and feedback necessary to control variances from goal achievement within the unit rather than external to it. This self-regulating capacity is hypothesized to lead to greater productivity and worker satisfaction. (Cummings, 1978, p. 625)

And there is evidence to support that hypothesis (Cummings & Molloy, 1977).

My purpose here is to point out that supervisory functions change significantly as a result of this kind of intervention. If indeed a first-line supervisor is needed at all, his or her job would not be "the exercise of power over individuals, but the coordination of the group's legitimate requirements to do its job with the resources and objectives of the organization" (Emery, 1974, p. 12). Supervisors become managers rather than "the person in the middle."

It is interesting to learn that even though quality control circles (quality circles or simpy QC groups as they are frequently called) were developed in Japan, the technical foundation for such groups—e.g., statistical methodology for determining quality control—was provided by Americans, W. Edwards Deming and Joseph Juran, who lectured in Japan during the early 1950s (Gregerman, 1979). QC groups are problem-solving groups composed of volunteer workers who meet periodically—typically once a week—to discuss work problems, especially those concerned with quality. These discussions are usually chaired by a supervisor but are participative in nature. That is, solutions to work problems proposed by the groups are then implemented via the regular managerial and operational process. QC groups are becoming popular in the United States. For example, with only 15 circle groups in operation, the Lockheed Corporation has documented savings of more than a quarter million dollars over a two-year period. Moreover, 97% of those who participated in the QC circles showed a strong preference for continuing the program (Yager, 1979). The Buick Division of General Motors has been active with QC groups as well.

As an intervention, quality control circles facilitate the solving of problems at the level where most of the information can be found and simultaneously decentralize some of the power in the organization. The effectiveness of autonomous work groups and quality circles is generally improved via the more traditional forms of OD work—team building and process consultation.

2. *Participative management.* More research and evidence is accumulating to support OD consultants' authoritatively advocating this approach to management (Burke, 1979). Also, Ackoff's (1974) circular organization, in which every manager has a board, clearly demonstrates the possibility of having a certain amount of democracy within a hierarchical system. I believe we are in a stronger position now to advocate with supportive data that, in general, a participative approach to management will certainly be more fruitful than a unilateral one and probably more effective than even a consultative approach. I am using the term "authoritatively" in the same sense that Argyris (1971) has suggested: OD consultation can at times take the form of recommending certain directions for change. The authority of the recommendation is based on sound research and theory from the behavioral sciences. I believe we now have a sound case.

3. *Reward systems.* It is a fact that people will tend to do in the future what they have been rewarded for doing in the past, and behavior in organizations is no exception to the rule. In addition to interventions that decentralize power, OD consultants should look to changes in reward systems as ways of changing an organization's culture. Inherent within these latter interventions should be processes for providing employees with choice (Argyris, 1970). Lawler (1977) has summarized much of what is known about the pros

and cons of certain rewards in organizations, especially those that are classified as extrinsic. Along with this summary, Lawler provides an explanation of some of the newer alternatives in rewards for organizational members. These include job posting, cafeteria-style fringe benefits, pay based on skill evaluation rather than job evaluation, all salary as opposed to salary and hourly paid, lump sum increases instead of monthly or biweekly increases, and the Scanlon Plan, an older innovation that is now receiving renewed attention. Many of these newer aspects of reward systems provide more choice for individuals and thereby place more control in their hands rather than management's. Lawler also points out the merits of openness in organizations rather than secrecy with respect to pay and compensation and participation by employees in the decision-making process regarding changes in the reward system.

## CONCLUSION FOR THE 80s

Bureaucracies will remain, at least for the foreseeable future. We should also keep in perspective the fact that bureaucracies have been around for quite some time—much longer than organization development. To assume that OD can affect bureaucracy is to believe that all or most OD consultants are Davids facing Goliath. The analogy is about right for age and size comparisons but not for level of skill and quality of instrument. And since we are not as skillful as David, we should not rely on only one instrument anyway. Just to work with groups particularly at the "shop floor" is to intervene at the micro-level and is therefore limited. I have recommended the above three interventions for emphasis and as a priority, but at the same time I view them as a minimum and as supplementary —not as the only ones.

OD consultants should continue fine tuning, keeping in mind the risk of furthering the organizational imperative, but they should also attempt to change bureaucracy in some fundamental ways. OD is one way that is still worth pursuing.

## REFERENCES

Ackoff, R. L. *Redesigning the future.* New York: Wiley, 1974.

Argyris, C. T-groups for organizational effectiveness. *Harvard Business Review,* 1964, 42, 60–74.

Argyris, C. *Intervention theory and method.* Reading, Mass.: Addison-Wesley, 1970.

Argyris, C. *Management and organizational development.* New York: McGraw-Hill, 1971.

Argyris, C. *On organizations of the future.* Beverly Hills, Calif.: Sage Publications, 1973.

Argyris, C., & Schön, D. A. *Organizational learning: A theory of action perspective.* Reading, Mass.: Addison-Wesley, 1978.

Beckhard, R. *Organization development—strategies and models.* Cambridge, Mass.: Addison-Wesley, 1969.

Bennis, W. G. The coming death of bureaucracy. *Think,* 1966, Nov.–Dec., 30–35.

Bennis, W. G. Organizations of the future. *Personnel Administration,* 1967, Sept.–Oct., 6–19.

Bennis, W. G. A funny thing happened on the way to the future. *American Psychologist,* 1970, 25, 595–608.

Bennis, W. G. Bureaucracy and social change: An anatomy of a training failure. In P. H. Mirvis & D. N. Berg (Eds.), *Failures in organization development and change.* New York: Wiley, 1977. Pp. 191–215.

Bion, W. F. *Experiences in groups.* New York: Basic Books, 1961.

Burke, W. W. A comparison of management development and organization development. *Journal of Applied Behavioral Science,* 1971, 7, 569–579.

Burke, W. W. Leaders and their development. *Group and Organization Studies,* 1979, 4(3), 273–280.

Carlson, H. C. GM's quality of work life efforts . . . an interview. *Personnel,* 1978, July–Aug., 11–23.

Carlson, H. C. Improving the quality of work life. In P. Mali (Ed.), *Management handbook.* New York: Wiley (in press).

Crockett, W. J. Introducing change to a government agency. In P. H. Mirvis & D. N. Berg (Eds.), *Failures in organization development and change.* New York: Wiley, 1977. Pp. 111–147.

Cummings, T. G. Self-regulating work groups: A socio-technical synthesis. *The Academy of Management Review,* 1978, 3(3), 625–634.

Cummings, T. G., & Molloy, E. S. *Improving productivity and the quality of work life.* New York: Praeger Publishers, 1977.

Emery, F. E. Bureaucracy and beyond. *Organizational Dynamics,* 1974, 2(3), 2–13.

Emery, F. E., & Trist, E. L. Socio-technical systems. In C. W. Churchman & M. Verhulst (Eds.), *Management sciences: Models and techniques, Vol. 2.* London: Pergamon Press, 1960.

Glaser, E. M. Facilitation of knowledge utilization by institutions for child development. *Journal of Applied Behavioral Science,* 1977, 13, 89–109.

Golembiewski, R. T. Managing the tension between OD principles and political dynamics. In W. W. Burke (Ed.), *The cutting edge: Current theory and practice in organization development.* La Jolla, Calif.: University Associates, 1978. Pp. 27–46.

Golembiewski, R. T. *Approaches to planned change. Part I: Orienting perspectives and micro-level interventions.* New York: Marcel-Dekker, 1979.

Goodstein, L. D. Organization development in bureaucracies: Some caveats and cautions. In W. W. Burke (Ed.), *The cutting edge: Current theory and practice in organization development.* La Jolla, Calif.: University Associates, 1978. Pp. 47–59.

Goodstein, L. D., & Boyer, R. K. Crisis intervention in a municipal agency: A conceptual case analysis. *Journal of Applied Behavioral Science,* 1972, 8, 318–340.

Gregerman, I. B. Introduction to quality circles: An approach to participative problem solving. *Industrial Management,* 1979, Sept.–Oct., 21–26.

Hackman, J. R., & Oldham, G. R. *Work redesign.* Reading, Mass.: Addison-Wesley, 1980.

Hart, D. K., & Scott, W. G. The organizational imperative. *Administration & Society,* 1975, 7(3), 259–284.

Hornstein, H. A., Bunker, B. B., & Hornstein, M. G. Some conceptual issues in individual- and group-oriented strategies of intervention into organizations. *Journal of Applied Behavioral Science,* 1971, 7, 557–568.

Kahn, R. L. Organization development: Some problems and proposals. *Journal of Applied Behavioral Science,* 1974, 10, 485–502.

Lawler, E. E. III. Reward systems. In J. R. Hackman & J. L. Suttle (Eds.), *Improving life at work.* Santa Monica, Calif.: Goodyear Publishing Company, 1977. Pp. 163–226.

Margulies, N., & Raia, A. P. *Conceptual foundations of organizational development.* New York: McGraw-Hill, 1978.

Perrow, C. The bureaucratic paradox: The efficient organization centralizes in order to decentralize. *Organizational Dynamics,* 1977, 5(4), 3–14.

Rice, A. K. *Productivity and social organization: The Ahmedabad experiments.* London: Tavistock Publications, 1958.

Schein, V. E., & Greiner, L. E. Can organization development be fine tuned to bureaucracies? *Organizational Dynamics,* 1977, 5(3), 48–61.

Singer, E. A., & Wooton, L. M. The triumph and failure of Albert Speer's administrative genius. *Journal of Applied Behavioral Science,* 1976, 12, 79–103.

Slater, P., & Bennis, W. G. Democracy is inevitable. *Harvard Business Review,* 1964, 42, 51–59.

Tannenbaum, R., & Davis, S. A. Values, man, and organizations. *Industrial Management Review,* 1969, 10(2), 67–83.

Tichy, N. M. Demise, absorption or renewal for the future of organization development. In W. W. Burke (Ed.), *The cutting edge: Current theory and practice in organization development.* La Jolla, Calif.: University Associates, 1978. Pp. 70–88.

Walton, R. E. The diffusion of new work structures: Explaining why success didn't take. *Organizational Dynamics,* 1975, 3(3), 2–22.

Walton, R. E., & Warwick, D. P. The ethics of organization development. *Journal of Applied Behavioral Science,* 1973, 9, 681–698.

Weisbord, M. R. Input- versus output-focused organizations: Notes on a contingency theory of practice. In W. W. Burke (Ed.), *The cutting edge: Current theory and practice in organization development.* La Jolla, Calif.: University Associates, 1978. Pp. 13–26.

Yager, E. Examining the quality control circle. *Personnel Journal,* 1979, Oct., 682–684, 708.

# Increasing Productivity and Morale in a Municipality
## Effects of Organization Development

Christian F. Paul
Albert C. Gross

*A year-long organization development project in the Communications and Electrical Division of the City of San Diego was completed and assessed. The goals of the project were to increase productivity and to improve morale, without allowing either goal to interfere with achievement of the other. The treatment group received an intervention that consisted of personal interviews of all employees, team-building workshops, counseling, process consultancy, and training in management skills. Measures of productivity (number of tasks performed, efficiency in both time and money) and job satisfaction (three surveys: absenteeism, turnover, grievances filed) as well as customer satisfaction (mail and telephone surveys) were taken both before and during the intervention period. Data from suitable comparison groups were collected for several of the dependent measures. The results lent strong support to the notion that both productivity and morale can be increased by means of organization development techniques.*

From *Journal of Applied Behavioral Science,* (1981), Vol. 17. Copyright 1981, JAI Press. Reprinted by permission.

This paper reports the outcome of a year-long organization development (OD) project conducted in the City of San Diego, California.[1] During fiscal year 1978 (FY 78), the OD and Training Section of the City's General Services Department conducted and evaluated an intervention in the Communications and Electrical (C&E) Division. Consistent with their values, the management of C&E and the OD consultants who conducted the project established the following goals: *to increase productivity, to improve morale, and to maintain or improve customer satisfaction.* While such projects are not particularly rare, adequate evaluation of them is quite uncommon.

Porras and Berg (1978) reviewed the OD evaluation research for the period 1959 to 1975. While Porras and Berg disconfirmed the notion that OD projects have not been scientifically evaluated, their article nevertheless suggests how difficult it is to find rigorous quantitative evaluations of OD projects. By exhaustively searching journals, bibliographies, and abstracts, Porras and Berg found 160 articles that reported evaluation of OD interventions. Approximately 130 of those articles (Porras, personal communication, May 14, 1979) met two criteria: *(a) that the intervention be concerned with people and processes rather than with technology and organization structure, and (b) that the projects involve real-life organizations.* Only 35 of the 130 articles (Porras, personal communication, May 14, 1979) met two additional criteria: *(c) that the evaluation measure at least organizational (as opposed to solely project or output) variables, and (d) that the research use quantitative evaluation techniques.* Only 27 of the 35 studies used methods that Campbell and Stanley (1963) classified as quasi-experimental in nature, rather than pre-experimental. That is, of the 160 articles initially identified by Porras and Berg, only 27 (16.9%) employed a design adequate for investigating the effects of the intervention with some degree of scientific precision.

Apparently, effective evaluation of OD projects is rare. Even rarer still, however, is rigorous evaluation of public sector OD interventions, although many municipalities have conducted OD projects. Of the 35 articles that met all four criteria of Porras and Berg, none reported an intervention in a municipal government setting. There were eight projects in public organizations (six were school districts or groups of administrators and teachers; one was a hospital; one was a group of religious communities), and the remaining 27 articles evaluated interventions in such private sector organizations as businesses, sales groups, and restaurants.

Although Porras and Berg demonstrated that OD projects can be scientifically evaluated, the myth persists, especially among OD practitioners themselves, that the efficacy of the process has not been (and perhaps cannot be) adequately demonstrated. Katzell and Yankelovich (1975) reported, on the basis of surveys, that managers and labor leaders generally believe that job satisfaction and work performance are positively correlated; hence the myth must not be the product of "hard boiled" resistance of line personnel to humanistic approaches to organization improvement. A statement typical of the strange self-doubt of OD practitioners was made by Farkash (1979) in a paper investigating the beliefs of OD consultants:

> Research has yet to prove that there is a positive relationship between OD activities and objective organizational outcomes like: productivity, profits and decreased turnover and absenteeism. (Farkash, 1979, n. p.)

Of course, research results never prove causal relationships; rather they provide evidence concerning one or more hypotheses (Crano & Brewer, 1973). We believe that the results of the San Diego OD project reported here support the hypothesis that both productivity and morale can be improved simultaneously by OD intervention. We attempted to avoid the pitfalls for which similar research efforts have been justly criticized (Porras & Berg, 1978). We employed a quasi-experimental design; took care to obtain high-quality comparison groups; made frequent measurements; used eclectic data-collection methods; and sought appropriate statistical methods for analyzing the data. The evaluation of this project was decided in advance of the intervention. Whereas many similar projects employ *post hoc* evaluation procedures, in the present study all dependent measures were chosen before the project had commenced.

## METHOD

### Overview

We applied the OD treatment to the experimental group and gathered data from that group and from a variety of other (comparison) groups. Not all forms of data were available from all the comparison groups, so the design of the present study is in reality several designs, each one applicable to a few dependent measures. Therefore, the study may be most easily understood by considering in turn the nature of the treatment, the character of the comparison groups, and the measures taken.

### Experimental Group

The experimental group was the Communications and Electrical Division of the City of San Diego. The C&E Division is primarily a service organization that maintains several electronic systems that directly or indirectly benefit the public. Briefly, the C&E Division is responsible for the following:

1. Maintenance of all city radio systems and communication equipment used by the Police, Fire, Lifeguard, General Services, Transportation, and Utilities departments. This equipment includes mobile and fixed radios, pocket pagers, intercoms, speaker systems, and so on.
2. Maintenance of a radio communications center for all radio-equipped vehicles except Police, Fire, and Lifeguard vehicles. The center operated 24 hours a day during the OD intervention.
3. Maintenance and operation of all traffic-signal equipment and systems in the city. This includes handling customer service calls, relamping, repair, routine maintenance, and so on. There are approximately 12,500 lights in service.

4. Maintenance of all outside lighting of city-owned grounds—playgrounds, recreation centers, and the like—and all city street lights.
5. Maintenance and coin collection of all parking meters (approximately 5,200).

This division ordinarily employs about 90 people. Its budget for FY 77 totaled $3.95 million, 43% of which was spent on power for exterior lighting and traffic signals.

## OD Treatment

The OD treatment given to the C&E Division consisted of a rigorous application of the action research model (Chein, Cook & Harding, 1948). Briefly, the action research model progresses through stages of gathering data, feeding information back to the organization's personnel, planning and implementing change, and evaluating the results of the entire intervention with a view toward repetition of the process in order to deal with new and unresolved issues. The OD intervention team[2] and the C&E Division management used the findings of the data gathering to jointly plan a series of specific project activities. The activities included interviewing, team-building workshops, counseling, process consultancy, and classroom training in management skills; all activities occurred during FY 78.

### INTERVIEWS

Members of the intervention team individually interviewed each employee of the C&E Division, including the superintendent, to discover employee perceptions of the organization's climate. Both open-ended questions (e.g., "What makes cooperation between work groups difficult?") and Likert-scale questions (e.g., "On a scale of 1 to 5, how satisfied are you with your job?") were included. These one-on-one interviews required approximately 30 to 45 minutes each. While the interviews were conducted informally and in a style intended to establish rapport between the interviewer and the employee, an interview question guide was used to impose a measure of standardization. In order to encourage candor, employees were assured that their individual responses would be treated confidentially. No tape recorders were used, but the interviewers noted answers and other relevant information on a data-collection form. Subjective and objective data from the interviews were used in planning later project activities.

### TEAM-BUILDING WORKSHOPS

The top management group of the C&E Division participated in a three-day, team-building workshop. This group consisted of the Division Superintendent and his immediate subordinates. Diagnostic data obtained from the interviews, employee attitude surveys, and the organization's management information system guided the design of the workshop. At the workshop, the participants:

a. received training in communication and management skills;
b. were briefed on the overall results of the earlier data gathering, employee attitude surveys, and interviews;
c. went through a role-clarification exercise in which each person had an opportunity to enumerate the duties of his or her position and to verify that role perception with the Division Superintendent; and
d. engaged in formal exercises designed to identify specific organizational problems and to plan solutions for them.

In this initial workshop, the Division Superintendent served as the focus for the role clarification and problem identification. In subsequent, two-day workshops, each of the Superintendent's direct subordinates also served as the leader/focal point for his/her immediate subordinates. Those subordinates in turn served as hosts in workshops attended by their work groups. Substantially the same workshop was repeated for each immediately subordinate work group until each employee had participated in a workshop with his or her supervisor. Likert (1961, 1967) has called this process "linking down the organization."

The most important result of the team-building workshops was the identification of organization problems and the formulation of plans to solve them. During the remainder of the project, managers, supervisors, and other employees of the division were assigned individual and group responsibility for solving specific problems.

### COUNSELING

Throughout the intervention, the OD team provided C&E's top managers with individual advice and counseling on how to implement the OD program and solve problems identified in the workshops. A major purpose of the counseling was to provide objective insight on the division's functioning—an outsider can often provide a fresh perspective on problems. Another major purpose of the counseling was to allow the OD specialists to expand available alternatives by describing problem solutions that had worked in other settings. The counseling was designed to facilitate the organization's solution of its own problems by providing support without usurping any of the power of the division's managers.

### PROCESS CONSULTANCY

OD specialists attended numerous meetings of division personnel in order to act as process consultants. The role of OD process consultants is to provide meeting participants with insights and feedback concerning decision making, problem solving, and communication within the group. The consultants are supposed to focus on group processes, making only minor contributions to the content of a conference. Process consultants are not required to be devoid of personal opinions, but their role in meetings is to subordinate expression of their own attitudes to the task of facilitating the expression of ideas and attitudes by the meeting's other participants. Their role is to make the conference more effective.

### MANAGEMENT-SKILLS TRAINING

C&E's managers identified a need to train division supervisors on several management skills and City of San Diego administrative procedures. The intervention team agreed to present a series of two-hour training events on topics which the supervisor had identified. Specifically, the division received training on the City Manager's expectations of supervisors, methods for conducting effective meetings, stress reduction, effective discipline, leadership style, employee motivation, performance evaluation, solving organizational problems, effective time management, and the city's Memorandum of Understanding with employee labor unions.

The assistance requested was traditional skill training. However, the manner in which the needs had been assessed and the manner in which the skill building had been incorporated into the project make this traditional training an integral part of the OD treatment. Many of the skills taught in the training sessions were related to resolving specific issues from the workshops. The desired result of the training was more than cognitive knowledge; the meetings were designed to lead to

organizational improvement. To keep the training from becoming "just a supervisory skills course," we varied the time of the meetings, set an informal participative tone, and encouraged supervisors to use the meetings to solve real-life organizational problems.

### Comparison Groups[3]

Pains were taken to secure data from comparison groups wherever possible. Since random assignment of groups was impossible, it was important to find the most similar comparison groups available. While each group had some attributes to recommend it as a good comparison group, it was unfortunately not possible to obtain data on all measures from all groups. For example, productivity data from the Long Beach comparison group was simply not available, and job satisfaction data could not be collected from CALTRANS employees.

### BUILDINGS DIVISION

We chose the Buildings Division of the City of San Diego as a comparison group because its employees work at crafts and trades similar to those practiced by C&E personnel and because the division works under administrative regulations and political conditions virtually identical to those in the C&E Division. The Buildings Division thus was the best available comparison group within the City of San Diego. This group received both administrations of the three surveys discussed below.

### LONG BEACH COMMUNICATIONS AND ELECTRICAL WORKERS

The personnel in the City of Long Beach, California, who provide the same services as San Diego's C&E Division, constituted a second comparison group. This group was chosen for comparison because the people perform the same tasks as the C&E employees but under slightly different institutional policies and procedures. While the Long Beach group was not identical to C&E on administrative procedures, it was in a city strikingly similar to San Diego in demographic, geographic, climatic, political, and economic characteristics; and its employees performed the same tasks as C&E's employees. This group, like the Buildings Division, received both administrations of the surveys but experienced no OD treatment.

## SIMILARITY OF BUILDINGS, LONG BEACH, AND C&E GROUPS

The Survey of Organizations contained several demographic questions. Respondents were asked to give their sex, age, tenure on the job, level of education, and type of community where reared. Chi-square analysis of the demographic variables suggests that C&E, Buildings, and Long Beach differed on only sex ($\chi^2(2) = 8.46$, $p < .02$) and job tenure ($\chi^2(10) = 20.22$, $p < .03$). The significant difference in the proportion of male and female workers can be attributed to the fact that there were no women in the Buildings Division sample, while C&E included 12% women and Long Beach included 7% women. The significant tenure difference was caused by the fact that 69% of the Long Beach sample had been on the job for less than 10 years, while approximately 47% of the Buildings and C&E samples had less than 10 years of tenure. It should be noted that the shorter job tenure at Long Beach was not reflected in a difference in age. In short, this analysis means that these groups were not appreciably different from one another on most demographic variables.

## CALTRANS DISTRICT 11

The traffic-signals and street-lamps crews of District 11, California State Department of Transportation (CALTRANS), constituted a third comparison group. District 11, which encompasses the City of San Diego, had a crew that maintained street lamps and traffic signals. That crew was used as a comparison group for the productivity-index measurements compiled on the sections in C&E which performed the same functions.

## OTHER CITY OF SAN DIEGO GROUPS

Six groups of city employees were used as comparison groups for the absenteeism and turnover measures. These groups were Buildings Division, General Services Department, Fire Department, Police Department, Park and Recreation Department, and total of all city groups.

## Dependent Measures

### PRODUCTIVITY

Productivity was measured by simple tabulation of the number of specific tasks completed by two sections of the C&E Division during both the year preceding and the year of intervention. The tasks performed by the street-lamping section were number of street lights relamped, number of outages repaired, and total amount of preventive maintenance performed. The tasks performed by the traffic-signals section were number of emergency repairs begun within an hour and number of nonemergency repairs begun within one day. No similar data were available from any of the comparison groups.

### EFFICIENCY MEASURES

The ratio of productive work hours to available work hours was obtained for the C&E traffic-signals and street-lamps sections combined. A total count of specific tasks completed by employees in these sections was taken in biweekly periods coinciding with pay periods. This information was available on individuals' daily work cards and so was a relatively unobtrusive measure of efficiency.

For each task, the total volume of work done by all employees in the section was multiplied by the task's "time guideline," a fair-work time standard in minutes generated by time-and-motion studies that had been completed just prior to the OD project. For example, wiring a traffic signal takes 76.8 minutes. If the traffic-signals section repaired the wiring on four signals in one pay period, the total productive time for that task during that period would be 307.2 minutes. The productive times for all tasks were totaled to arrive at a grand total of productive time achieved during the pay period. This total was adjusted for unavoidable process losses as determined by the time-and-motion studies (e.g., clean-up time, transportation time) and converted to total hours earned. When divided by total work hours available, this figure yielded an efficiency index totaled for two sections.

The California State Department of Transportation compiles records of work output for crews performing the same tasks as the two sections in the C&E Division. Because District 11 includes the City of San Diego, that district's lighting crew often works under conditions identical to those encountered by the C&E Division's street-lamps and traffic-signals sections. For that reason, we also compiled efficiency indices for the CALTRANS lighting crew to use for comparison.

Differences in the two reporting systems necessitated computing the CALTRANS efficiency index in a manner slightly different from that of the C&E group. Mileage records and correction factors for unavoidable delays differed somewhat between the two groups, but otherwise the computations were identical. Therefore, while it is legitimate to compare trends in productivity between C&E and CALTRANS, it would be misleading to directly compare actual efficiency ratios.

JOB SATISFACTION: SURVEYS

Three widely used and previously validated surveys were administered to the C&E personnel, to employees of Buildings Division, and to Long Beach communications/electrical workers. These surveys all have job satisfaction scales; there were seven such scales in all.

1. The Survey of Organizations (SO) includes 124 questions eliciting reactions to organizational climate, leadership, peer influence, group dynamics, and satisfaction. Development of the SO began in 1966, and the instrument has been submitted to several validity and reliability studies (see Taylor & Bowers, 1972). The survey provides a profile of an organization. Many of the 32 subscales which the instrument yields are more useful for guiding the actual intervention than for evaluating the intervention's effect on morale, organizational climate, and job satisfaction. Consequently, here we report results only from the satisfaction scale of the SO. (See Hausser, Pecorella, and Wissler, 1975, for a complete description of the SO and its subscales.)

2. In the short form of the Minnesota Satisfaction Questionnaire (MSQ), Weiss, Dawis, England, and Lofquist (1967) diagnose morale by eliciting respondents' satisfaction with 20 aspects of their jobs (e.g., chances for advancement, feelings of accomplishment, pay, and workload). The questions are clustered into three scales: intrinsic satisfaction, extrinsic satisfaction, and general satisfaction. Factor analysis of the long form of the MSQ had revealed two factors—intrinsic and extrinsic satisfaction—and general satisfaction is the sum of the two. All three scales were used in the present study.

3. The Job Diagnostic Survey (JDS) (Hackman & Oldham, 1974) was designed both to diagnose jobs and to assess effects of job redesign. The 20 scales of the instrument are divided into three classes:
   a. those that assess objective job attributes (e.g., amount of skill required to perform the job);
   b. those that assess affective reactions to the performance of the job (essentially satisfaction and motivation); and
   c. those that assess "critical psychological states" thought to be necessary for positive affective reactions to occur.

Since some of the scales are used primarily for job redesign, only the scales most relevant to measuring job satisfaction and employee morale are presented in this report. The relevant scales are the satisfaction, pay satisfaction, and supervisor satisfaction scales.

JOB SATISFACTION: UNOBTRUSIVE MEASURES

The City of San Diego Civil Service Commission routinely compiles data on all city departments and divisions. These data are known simply as "Personnel Statistics." Released quarterly, these data are basically tabulations of the number of persons employed, total number of days of sick leave taken, and number of employees separated per quarter per division or department. We computed mean number of days of sick leave taken and percent of employees resigning for the seven city work groups for the six quarters prior to and the six quarters after the onset of the intervention. These data constituted unobtrusive measures of absenteeism and turnover. C&E records of employee grievances filed during FY 77 and FY 78 were also available.

CUSTOMER SATISFACTION

In order to assess the changes in the ability of the C&E Division to serve the public effectively, both private citizens and institutional customers were asked to evaluate the service. The general public's opinion of C&E Division was found by conducting a telephone survey of a random sample ($n = 20$) of private citizens who had previously reported malfunctioning traffic signals or street lamps. The institutional users of C&E's services were surveyed by mail. Both the telephone survey and the mail survey questioned the respective customers at two times, once at the beginning of the intervention and once at the end. Comparison group data were not available on this dependent measure.

## Summary

A standard OD intervention, made up of interviews, workshops, counseling, process consultancy, and classroom training, was applied to the C&E Division of the

City of San Diego. Data were unobtrusively collected to assess changes in productivity, job satisfaction, and customer satisfaction attributable to the intervention. Unobtrusively collected efficiency data were also available for both the experimental group and the CALTRANS District 11 comparison group for the entire period of the intervention. Finally, pre- and postintervention survey results assessing job satisfaction were collected from the experimental group and two appropriate comparison groups, Long Beach and Buildings Division. Table 1 summarizes the dependent variables.

## RESULTS
## Productivity

Productivity in the C&E Division generally increased from FY 77 to FY 78. The increase in amount of work done by the street-lamping section is reflected in the number of lights re-lamped (2,767 in FY 78 vs. 2,422 in FY 77) and in the number of outages repaired (494 vs. 431) as well as in the total amount of preventive maintenance re-lamping/re-cleaning accomplished (11,291 vs. 9,494). Similarly, the traffic-signals section showed an increase in the number of emergency repairs begun within one hour (1,422 in FY 78 vs. 1,070 in FY 77), although there was a drop in the number of nonemergency repairs begun within one day of notice (3,198 vs.

3,740). Clearly, more work was done by the C&E Division during the year of OD intervention than during the previous year, but lack of any comparison group data for this particular measure prevents us from venturing beyond that simple observation.

### Efficiency
#### WORK HOURS

Data on the number of work hours required for the completion of specific tasks in the C&E Division support the expectation that the employees' efficiency rose during the intervention period. Fewer hours were required for repair of both stationary FM components (5.31 vs. 5.43) and mobile FM components (2.67 vs. 4.47). Similarly, less time was needed to complete 100 communications (1.00 vs. 2.08 hours) and slightly less time was spent per 100 parking meter collections (.99 vs. 1.03 hours). On the other hand, repair of parking meters required more time both in the field (.21 vs. .16 hours) and in the shop (1.17 vs. .62), and so did repair of microwave components (7.38 vs. 5.94 hours). However, even though group re-lamping of street lamps, a time-saving practice, was suspended during FY 78, mean work hours for that task increased only from .06 to .07 during the intervention period. On balance, then, it would seem that efficiency, as measured by time spent per task, did improve during the period of intervention.

#### COST

The cost per year to repair and maintain street lights increased by 5% in FY 78, from $23.26 to $24.42. At the same time, the repair and maintenance of a signal intersection fell from $829.00 in FY 77 to $723.24 in FY 78, a decline of 13%. This is a substantial saving.

#### EFFICIENCY INDEX

A plot of the efficiency index data over time for the C&E group shows a slow decline in efficiency prior to intervention followed by an increase during the intervention period (see Figure 1). This picture is supported by the slopes of the regression lines: The pre-intervention slope is indeed negative ($b = -.0003$), while the slope during the intervention is positive ($b = .0002$). However, 95% confidence intervals indicate that these gradients do not differ significantly from zero or from each other. Nevertheless, analysis of variance applied to the means suggests that efficiency did increase dramatically in the C&E Division during

#### TABLE 1
**Summary of dependent measures available from the C&E group and from various comparison groups**

| Variable | Measure | Frequency of measure | Comparison groups |
|---|---|---|---|
| Job Satisfaction | SO | Before/After | Long Beach, Buildings |
| | JDS | Before/After | Long Beach, Buildings |
| | MSQ | Before/After | Long Beach, Buildings |
| | Absenteeism | Quarterly | Six City groups |
| | Turnover | Quarterly | Six City groups |
| | Grievances | FY 77/FY 78 | None |
| Production Efficiency | Five Tasks | FY 77/FY 78 | None |
| | Time | FY 77/FY 78 | None |
| | Cost | FY 77/FY 78 | None |
| | Efficiency Index | Monthly | CALTRANS |
| Customer Satisfaction | Telephone Survey | Before/After | None |
| | Mail Survey | Before/After | None |

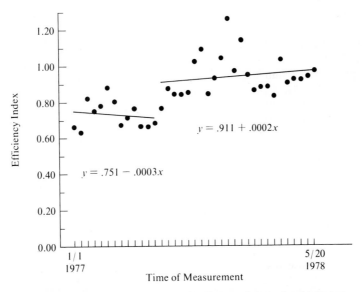

The increments on the horizontal axis are the biweekly pay periods mentioned in the text.

**Figure 1** Efficiency in Communications and Electrical Division (Intervention Group)

the period of intervention. The pre-intervention mean of .728 rose by 29% to .939 during the intervention, $F(1, 35) = 36.35, p < .001$. Hence we may safely conclude that efficiency did increase during the intervention period.

Data from the CALTRANS comparison group, plotted the same as the C&E data, show just the opposite trends; but again the trends were not statistically significant (see Figure 2). The pre-intervention slope of .0002 did not differ from zero or from the postintervention slope of −.0007. The means (.727 and .721, respectively) did not differ from one another either, $F(1,22) < 1$.

These results lend support to the belief that efficiency improved in the C&E Division as a result of OD intervention. Savings in both time and money were made during the intervention period, and efficiency (as measured by the efficiency index) increased substantially for the C&E group but not at all for the similar CALTRANS comparison group.

### Job Satisfaction: Surveys

Survey responses[4] for the seven job-satisfaction scales were submitted to nonorthogonal, repeated-measures analyses of variance (Woodward & Overall, 1976) with group (C&E, Long Beach, and Buildings) and time (pre-intervention, postintervention) as factors, and re-

peated measures on the time factor. Only four of the 21 F values proved reliable: Two were associated with the main effect of group, and two were associated with the two-way interaction effect.

The main effect of group was significant for both the JDS general satisfaction scale and the JDS pay satisfaction scale, $Fs(2, 110) = 5.52$ and 6.54, respectively, $ps < .01$. The order of means for the JDS general-satisfaction scale was C&E ($M = 5.10$), Long Beach ($M = 4.91$), Buildings ($M = 4.43$), but these means were not reliably different from one another by Newman-Keuls test. The order of means for the JDS pay satisfaction scale was Long Beach ($M = 4.68$), C&E ($M = 3.86$), Buildings ($M = 3.12$); the Newman-Keuls test indicated that Long Beach and Buildings were reliably different from each other, with C&E intermediate.

The significant interaction effects appeared in the MSQ extrinsic satisfaction scale, $F(2, 107) = 3.90$, $p < .05$, and the JDS supervisor satisfaction scale, $F(2, 107) = 3.30, p < .05$. The means appear in Table 2, where it can be seen that, for the former scale, the C&E group experienced an increase in extrinsic satisfaction over time, while the comparison groups reported less satisfaction. For the latter scale, the error term was too high for the multiple-comparison test to detect any differences.

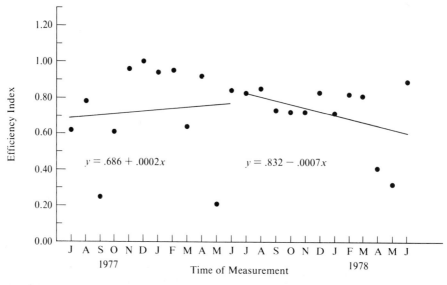

The increments on the horizontal axis are months of the year, beginning with July. The horizontal axis is on the same scale as that of Figure 1.

**Figure 2**   Efficiency in CALTRANS District 11 (Comparison Group)

These survey results are not overly impressive evidence for the efficacy of the OD intervention, although they are not by any means damaging. The repeated-measures analysis of variance is an excellent statistical test for this kind of data, but in the present case there is good reason to inspect the data in other ways as well. The main problem with the present analysis is that only those individuals who answered a sufficient number of questions on both administrations of the surveys (see note 4) and identified themselves the same way both times are represented in the repeated-measures analysis. Therefore, these results may represent only the least disgruntled, most compulsive, least distrustful, most consistent employees.

To compensate for these shortcomings, we re-analyzed these survey data, submitting them to one-way, unweighted-means analyses of variance.[5] The group means and particulars about the tests appear as Table 3. We note that job satisfaction was fairly high in the C&E group to begin with, falling even with or below the Long Beach group on all seven scales prior to intervention. By the second administration of the surveys, the C&E group means exceeded the comparison group means in absolute value on every scale but one.

These results lend credence to the notion that the intervention program helped to improve satisfaction with a variety of aspects of the job for C&E employees.

## Job Satisfaction: Unobtrusive Measures
### ABSENTEEISM

A two-way analysis of variance, with time (pre-intervention, postintervention) and group (the seven city comparison groups) as factors failed to yield any significant effects. The grand mean number of days of sick leave taken per employee was 2.16. The mean for C&E was 1.92.

### TURNOVER

The analysis of variance on the turnover data produced significant main effects of time, $F(1,70) = 18.53$, $p < .001$, and group, $F(6,70) = 3.69$, $p < .01$, but no significant interaction, $F(6,70) = 1.55$. This analysis was therefore rather uninformative. The grand mean probability of quitting was .0131; that for C&E was .0146. The range for the seven groups was .0036 (Fire Department) to .0212 (Buildings Division).

### GRIEVANCES

C&E employees filed seven grievances in FY 77 and seven in FY 78. Whereas in FY 77 one complaint was resolved at the first level, one at the second, and the

**TABLE 2**
**Satisfaction scale means from three groups taken**
**before and during the OD intervention**

| Scale | Time | Buildings | Group Long Beach | C&E |
|---|---|---|---|---|
| MSQ Extrinsic | Pre-intervention | 2.76 | 3.19 | 2.93 |
| Satisfaction | Postintervention | 2.72[a] | 2.96[b] | 3.13[ab] |
| | | (28)[a] | (22)[ab] | (60)[b] |
| JDS Supervisor | Pre-intervention | 4.87 | 5.11 | 4.85 |
| Satisfaction | Postintervention | 5.05 | 4.52 | 5.01 |
| | | (29) | (22) | (59) |

*Note:* Means sharing no subscript differ at the .05 level by Newman-Keuls test. The JDS means did not differ from each other by that test. Cell *n*s appear in parentheses.

**TABLE 3**
**Job satisfaction data from three groups collected before and during the OD intervention**

| Scale | Time | Buildings | Group Long Beach | C&E | F value | df | p |
|---|---|---|---|---|---|---|---|
| SO | 1 | 1.87$_a$ | 2.40$_b$ | 2.22$_b$ | 7.04 | 2,200 | .002 |
| Satisfaction | 2 | 1.97$_a$ | 2.18$_{ab}$ | 2.38$_b$ | 3.50 | 2,182 | .04 |
| MSQ | 1 | 2.26$_a$ | 2.56$_b$ | 2.59$_b$ | 5.48 | 2,197 | .005 |
| General | 2 | 2.52$_b$ | 2.22$_a$ | 2.68$_b$ | 7.62 | 2,167 | .001 |
| MSQ | 1 | 1.65$_a$ | 2.15$_b$ | 1.93$_{ab}$ | 6.13 | 2,201 | .005 |
| Extrinsic | 2 | 1.89 | 1.79 | 2.13 | 2.58 | 2,173 | .08 |
| MSQ | 1 | 2.62$_a$ | 2.82$_{ab}$ | 2.95$_b$ | 4.36 | 2,202 | .02 |
| Intrinsic | 2 | 3.86$_b$ | 3.47$_a$ | 3.92$_b$ | 8.14 | 2,170 | .001 |
| JDS General | 1 | 2.12$_a$ | 2.62$_b$ | 2.69$_b$ | 10.86 | 2,195 | .001 |
| Satisfaction | 2 | 2.26$_a$ | 2.43$_{ab}$ | 2.69$_b$ | 4.51 | 2,180 | .02 |
| JDS Pay | 1 | 1.52$_a$ | 2.58$_c$ | 1.96$_b$ | 15.75 | 2,197 | .001 |
| Satisfaction | 2 | 1.25$_a$ | 2.14$_b$ | 1.86$_b$ | 8.91 | 2,179 | .001 |
| JDS Supervisor | 1 | 2.29$_a$ | 2.75$_b$ | 2.55$_{ab}$ | 3.31 | 2,196 | .04 |
| Satisfaction | 2 | 2.54$_{ab}$ | 2.18$_a$ | 2.69$_b$ | 3.56 | 2,178 | .04 |

*Note:* All means scaled to 0–4. Within rows, means with no common subscript differ at the .05 level by Newman-Keuls test. Time 1 refers to measurement prior to intervention; Time 2, to measurement during intervention.

remainder at the fifth level, in FY 78 the grievances were resolved much earlier: three at the first level, three at the second level, and one at the third level. These data point to an increased responsiveness to employees' complaints.

### Customer Satisfaction
#### TELEPHONE SURVEY

Responses to the three questions, scaled from 1 to 5, were submitted to *t* tests. None of the test results were significant (all *t*s < 1), indicating no change in customer satisfaction during the nine-month interval. Re-

sponses to these questions were positive. Customers reported that they had been treated courteously ($M = 3.54$) and had had little trouble locating the right person to help them ($M = 4.28$).

#### MAIL SURVEY

As with the telephone survey, highly favorable responses characterized both pre-intervention and postintervention data from the mail survey. The only significant finding indicated a more favorable attitude on the second administration than on the first. Asked to indicate the amount of influence that the C&E Division had on the way the respondent's agency does its work, these customers' replies moved from a mean of 2.85 to 3.04, where 2 = *too much influence* and 3 = *about the right amount,* paired $t(26) = 2.00, p < .05$. A summary of the results appears as Table 4.

## DISCUSSION

The present study supports the notion that OD intervention can produce both increased productivity and increased job satisfaction in municipal government employees. With respect to productivity, the C&E group seems to have benefited by the treatment. The amount of work done increased for four of five specific tasks, and less time was required to complete four of eight tasks that could be assessed. Of two cost measures, one—street-lamp maintenance—increased at less than the rate of inflation, whereas the other—traffic-signal maintenance—fell by some $100 per intersection. Furthermore, a dramatic increase in rated efficiency, from 73% to 94%, occurred for the intervention group but not for a comparison group, whose efficiency was rated on a highly similar scale at 73% and 72% during the same periods.

These important increases in productivity were by no means accompanied by any decrease in morale or service rendered to the customers of the intervention group. To the contrary, both verbal responses and unobtrusive measures of job satisfaction indicate improvement in morale for a group that already had relatively well-satisfied employees. The survey results for seven self-report scales show that the C&E employees' job satisfaction rose after the onset of the intervention period, to exceed that of two comparison groups. The unobtrusive measures of satisfaction (absenteeism, turnover, and grievances) showed no reliable changes. Finally, both private citizens and agency representatives remained highly satisfied with the service they received from the C&E Division.

These results illustrate the efficacy of OD intervention precisely because there was comparatively little room for upward movement on the measures we employed. At the beginning of the OD project, the C&E Division employees were already well satisfied with their jobs, and they already performed at adequate levels of efficiency. Nevertheless, on a variety of measures, we found substantial improvements that may reasonably be attributed to the intervention treatment.

The present study shows that it is feasible to assess the effects of OD intervention projects that are conducted in municipal government settings. Even though there is no product or service sold to a specific market, as is the case in many private sector organizations that undergo OD treatment, organizations within municipalities do produce both goods and services for their customers, including other governmental agencies, private organizations, and the general public. As mentioned earlier, such projects in municipal governments, although frequent, seem rarely to be adequately assessed. We see this oversight as unfortunate and increasingly difficult to justify. It is unfortunate in that those who invest time, energy, and money to accomplish certain goals via an OD project can never know whether those goals have been reached unless they make some effort to evaluate the project. In a time of increasing demand for accountability to a cost-conscious public, government agencies that conduct OD projects will very likely find it harder and harder to gain approval for those projects that lack adequate evaluation.

**TABLE 4**
**Summary of the impact of the OD treatment on C&E morale and efficiency**

| Variable | Measure | Outcome |
|---|---|---|
| Job Satisfaction | SO | Increased satisfaction |
| | JDS | Increased satisfaction |
| | MSQ | Increased satisfaction |
| | Absenteeism | No difference over time |
| | Turnover | Mixed result |
| | Grievances | Earlier resolution of grievances |
| Production Efficiency | Five Tasks | More work done |
| | Time | Less time needed for four tasks |
| | Cost | Substantial savings |
| | Efficiency Index | Significant increase |
| Customer Satisfaction | Telephone Survey | No decrease over time |
| | Mail Survey | No decrease over time |

## REFERENCES

Campbell, D. T., & Stanley, J. D. *Experimental and quasi-experimental designs for research.* Chicago: Rand McNally, 1963.

Chein, I., Cook, S., & Harding, J. The field of action research. *American Psychologist,* 1948, 3, 43–50.

Crano, W. D., & Brewer, M. B. *Principles of research in social psychology.* Reading, Mass.: Addison-Wesley, 1973.

Farkash, A. *An empirical investigation of organization development beliefs, activities and outcomes.* Selected Paper No. 8, American Society for Training and Development. Madison, Wisc., March 1979.

French, W. L., & Bell, C. H. *Organization development: Behavioral science interventions for organization improvement.* Englewood Cliffs, N. J.: Prentice-Hall, 1973.

Friedlander, F., & Brown, D. Organization development. *Annual Review of Psychology,* 1974, 25, 313–341.

Hackman, J. R., & Oldham, G. R. *The job diagnostic survey: An instrument for the diagnosis of jobs and the evaluation of job redesign projects.* Technical Report No. 4, Yale University Department of Administrative Sciences, May 1974.

Hausser, D. L., Pecorella, P. A., & Wissler, A. L. *Survey-guided development: A manual for consultants.* Ann Arbor, Mich.: University of Michigan Institute for Social Research, 1975.

Katzell, R. A., Yankelovich, D., and others. *Work productivity and job satisfaction: An evaluation of policy-related research.* New York: The Psychological Corporation, 1975.

Likert, R. *New patterns of management.* New York: McGraw-Hill, 1961.

Likert, R. *The human organization.* New York: McGraw-Hill, 1967.

Porras, J. I., & Berg, P. O. Evaluation methodology in organization development: An analysis and critique. *Journal of Applied Behavioral Science,* 1978, 14, 151–173.

Taylor, J., & Bowers, D. *The survey of organizations: A machine-scored standardized questionnaire instrument.* Ann Arbor, Mich.: Institute for Social Research, 1972.

Weiss, D. J., Dawis, R. V., England, G. W., & Lofquist, L. H. *Manual for the Minnesota Satisfaction Questionnaire.* University of Minnesota: Industrial Relations Center Work Adjustment Project, 1967.

Woodward, A. J., & Overall, J. E. Nonorthogonal analysis of variance in repeated measures experimental designs. *Educational and Psychological Measurement,* 1976, 36, 855–859.

*This project was funded by the City of San Diego and by U. S. Department of Housing and Urban Development Innovative Projects Program Grant No. H-2579-RG to the OD and Training Section, General Services Department, City of San Diego. We gratefully acknowledge the support of George Simpson, Bob Walter, Terry Flynn, and Richard L. Hays.*

*We are indebted to David Greene and George Barbour of Stanford Research Institute for their valuable advice at various stages of the project and to Jerry Porras for both a helpful critique of the manuscript and his kind assistance in providing us with data. Thanks also to two anonymous reviewers for their helpful comments.*

## NOTES

1. We do not wish to add to the already large number of definitions of OD (see Friedlander & Brown, 1974; French & Bell, 1973; Porras & Berg, 1978), but for the benefit of the reader unfamiliar with OD, we will venture what we see as the common element in such definitions. OD intervention is an intentional effort to improve some dimension of an organization by using applied behavioral science techniques. Often, as in the present case, the "action research" model (see Method section) is followed in the OD project.

2. The intervention team included Albert C. Gross, Haywood H. Martin, and C. Greg Wright, assisted by consultant Peter Gregg.

3. We appreciate the assistance of Bob West (Buildings Division), Robert Kennedy (Long Beach), and Dean Burns (CALTRANS), who facilitated the data collection from the comparison groups.

4. Scores on these seven scales consist of the mean of the responses to the questions constituting the scales. No scale score was computed for any subject who answered fewer than half the questions for that scale. Naturally, since there were repeated measures, no subject is represented on a given scale who did not have both a pre-intervention score and a post-intervention score. The scores had the following possible ranges: SO, 1–5; MSQ, 1–5; JDS, 1–7.

5. For these analyses, all data were transformed to a 0–4 scale.

# PART THREE

# RESOURCES

# OF

# PUBLIC MANAGEMENT

"Money is power." "Information is power." "Command over people is power." Or is control over technology power? The answer? They all may contribute to power. Why? Because each one is a *management resource.*

Consider money first. A manager may have great ideas, powerful leadership skills. But to put ideas and leadership skills into action, a manager needs financial resources, and in the public sector, financial resources come from the budget. It is no wonder that managers have identified the budget as one area of management responsibility that occupies a considerable amount of their time. The budget may not be a sufficient criterion of management success, but it is a necessary resource for all managers who aspire to success. It is an indispensable link between their programmatic wishes and the prospects of turning management dreams into reality. In this era of fiscal scarcity, the attention given to the budget has become even more pronounced than ever before and, as Naomi Caiden ("Public Budgeting Amidst Uncertainty and Instability") suggests, the rigors of managing a budget are different than in bygone days of "built-in" predictability.

But money is not everything. People are resources, too. Sometimes personnel can create headaches as well. The reason is that managers must hire, train, motivate, and yes, occasionally fire employees; consequently, personnel management is one of the timeless jobs of public administrators. These traditional responsibilities, from hiring to firing, are still very much a part of the world of the public manager. The task of personnel management has been made more challenging by recent developments such as the legal constraints on civil servants, new applications of motivational techniques, and incentives for higher-level civil servants. Tomorrow's managers will be responsible for ensuring that their subordinates are productive *and* accountable—all within the context of a shrinking budget pie.

Two of the three articles in the personnel section deal with issues that were of little concern to public personnel managers until recently, but the third deals with an issue that has been on the public agenda at least since the 1880s and the passage of the Pendleton Act. Godwin and Needham ("Reforming Reform") challenge the venerable assumptions upon which recent reforms (and many earlier ones as well) have been based. The selection by Hildreth and his coauthors ("The Liability of Public Executives") deals with an issue that has received much attention of late—the vulnerability of public employees to litigation. Recent court decisions have expanded the liability of public employees. In "The Impact of Flexitime on Performance and Attitudes in 25 Public Agencies," Ronen and Primps provide a positive assessment of the implementation of a personnel management innovation in government.

Money and people alone do not public management make! The essence of public management is decision making, and making decisions requires information. There was a time when it was assumed that much public management took place in an atmosphere of ignorance: "If we only had more information, our decisions would be better." In reality, it is not the dearth of information that confounds public managers.

Rather, selecting and interpreting the most appropriate information is the real challenge for the managers of tomorrow. Computers, be they main frames, minis, or microprocessors, allow managers to store, retrieve, and analyze much more information than ever before. So public managers do not have too little information. On the contrary, they are often swamped with information and must select what they really need from an array of data—an array that includes much that is of questionable value. *Managing information,* then, is a major task of public management. The alternative? One could fall prey to a common managerial malady: information overload. As Bozeman and Bozeman ("Technical Information and Policy Choice") note, more and more information does not necessarily lead to a better and better decision. Sometimes it leads to no decisions at all. Nor can we expect that computers will be the panacea for all our information ills. There is no question that computer and information processing will play a critical role in public management, but there is some evidence that computers do not always live up to their advance billing. James Danziger ("Computers, Local Governments, and the Litany to EDP") exposes some of the myths of mechanized management.

In sum, Part Three includes articles that discuss the varied resources of public management. Be prepared to have some myths exposed, to learn, for example, that resources provide challenges, opportunities, but, alas, pitfalls as well. One thing is virtually certain: Managing the resources available to public administrators will be more difficult tomorrow than it was yesterday.

# CHAPTER FIVE

# Public Budgeting

## Public Budgeting Amidst Uncertainty and Instability

Naomi Caiden

The world of budgeting which we had grown to know well in the past fifty years, since the advent of the Keynesian revolution in public economies and the rapid expansion of the administrative state, is fast being disoriented by new and unexpected events. Familiar landmarks are being obliterated. The rules of the budgeting game are rapidly changing, and many public authorities are in danger of losing their way unless they adjust to the new context. The credibility of secure public financing which has for so long been taken for granted is at stake. Certainty and stability are giving way to uncertainty and instability.

Budgeting processes may be said to thrive on stability. Since budgeting is concerned with making financial provision for future activities, it depends on accurate prediction of the amount of revenues available and of the cost of expenditures. In its more sophisticated forms, it demands knowledge of future output or achievement related to given resources, preferably over a long period of time. Budgeting works best where year-to-year adjustments are marginal, where it is possible to make firm commitments in advance of expenditures, where the recent past is a good guide to the immediate future, and where results may be easily and promptly evaluated.

Classical budget theory tried to keep uncertainties within bounds through insistence on annual budgets (foreshortening the time period), budget unity (keeping all expenditures under a single control), strict appropriation (preventing unauthorized changes), and timely audit (checking past performance). The budget process in itself brought a measure of stability and predictability previously lacking in state finance, but its efforts to impose order could never entirely make the world according to its own rules or exclude all uncertainties. Budgeters have traditionally guarded against surprises by such informal strategies as underestimating revenues and overestimating costs of expenditures, and limiting spending in the first part of the year. Policies of incrementalism, of regular additions to the budget base, have also helped to accommodate change and increase predictability from year to year. Generally buoyant revenues for many jurisdictions have provided a measure of redundancy, cushioning uncertainties, and allowing for flexibility and correction of errors.

Now the traditional means of coping with uncertainty appear inadequate, while the uncertainties themselves are multiplying to an unprecedented extent. The symptoms are marked. The value of the American dollar has been declining for nearly two decades and no relief is in sight. State and local governments are increasingly dependent on federal subventions without which many would face bankruptcy; already several have had to be rescued from the brink. Growing resistance to rising public expenditures and taxes is being translated into expenditure ceilings and tax revolts. Public authorities cannot predict from one year to the next what they will have to spend and where they will find the money. They still cannot prove convincingly that they spend money wisely and that the public receives value from public expenditures.

The task of public budgeting has become infinitely more complex, complicated and worrisome. Current budget theory and practice lag behind operational requirements. A new agenda is urgently needed to bridge the gap and provide better instruments to cope with uncertainty and instability. Its items should avoid rehashing traditional proposals that fail to reflect the changing environment of public budgeting.

## THE CHANGING ENVIRONMENT OF BUDGETING

For a long time, it was believed that the major challenges in public budgeting had been met and that all that remained was some tinkering around with the form of the budget to match inputs and outputs, costs and benefits, resources and results. Public needs were conceived as finite and public resources infinite. The ability of governments to raise revenues and manage large expenditures was accepted as a matter of course. Given modern techniques of taxation and borrowing, the amounts of money that could be generated seemed virtually limitless, while social problems seemed amenable to solution through the mechanisms of the administrative state. It is now quite apparent that the administrative state often merely encourages new public demands, without ensuring that effective use is made of public resources at its disposal or dispelling resentment of taxation. We now have to work on a different assumption, namely, that public resources are finite and public needs infinite.

The ability of public authorities to raise any given level of revenues without serious resistance can no longer be taken for granted. Historically, the ability to tax on a substantial scale has been a function of industrialization and democratization. It has depended on maintaining a high level of economic activity and retaining public confidence in an efficient, effective and accountable public administration capable of delivering quality goods and services. Lately, concern about the amount and equity of taxation, fears that the public sector is reaching its limits in a mixed economy, and mistrust of proliferating public bureaucracy indicate that the era of expanding public revenues may be coming to a close. Inflation temporarily obscures the

longer-term effects of greater financial pressures on taxpayers, demands for tax relief and a decline in the real value of tax receipts relative to the costs of expected services. All these make rising real revenues more problematical, particularly if taxpayers succumb under inflationary pressure to temptations to avoid or evade paying taxes, and more people join the underground economy beyond the reach of government control and taxation.

If these complications were not enough, a dramatic new factor has arisen to affect governmental capacity to raise revenues, namely, numerous public initiatives to restrict revenues and/or expenditures constitutionally. They immediately impact on expected fund levels because of speculation whether they will pass and their unpredictable effects. Administrators have to prepare several budgets to meet different possible outcomes. Even without formal limitations, politicians, responding to what they believe is the mood of the public, put tax relief and lower budgets near the top of their priorities, restricting expenditure growth to the rate of inflation or below.

In contrast, demands for public goods and services do not abate. They can be expected to rise in the future. America's aging population will entail large increases in social expenditures on the elderly just when the labor force will decline. Hopes that poverty would be susceptible to a one-time solution have given way to somber realization that it is a structural problem that will take generations to resolve. Burgeoning technology requires heavy public investment in research and development and increasing public expenditures on safety measures and environmental protection. The hardening habit of turning to the administrative state to fulfill needs unmet by the market system is creating new legal rights. Consequently, in many areas of public administration, such as health, education, social welfare, urban renewal, crime control and consumer protection, there is no clearly defined and acceptable level of public expenditure. Money can be poured indefinitely into defense, environmental protection, police, schools, hospitals, job retraining and recreation facilities. They are all open-ended expenditures in the sense that there is no limit to the potential amount of public funds which may be devoted to improving them.

More and more public administrators find themselves working in conditions of fiscal stress in which they must try to accomplish unlimited goals with fewer real resources. It is increasingly difficult for them to provide for contingencies through disguised surpluses and reserves, or compensate for mistakes and faulty judgment, or spread resources to satisfy as many parties as possible. They cannot avoid hard choices any longer. Already they find it harder to forecast revenues and costs, and their budget plans are upset by economic problems. With potential resource levels more variable and objectives more complex, past experience is less relevant in budgeting. Meantime competition for resources intensifies among pressure groups, levels of government and public agencies. Alignments disintegrate, shift and reform with baffling fluidity. The budget game is being played with more conflict and the rules are giving way under the strain. It becomes more difficult to agree on and stick to budgets.

When the environment becomes increasingly uncertain and more stringent, budgets are more complex, more difficult to control and less predictable. Revenue uncertainties promote multiple budgets and dysfunctional tactics by administrators protecting themselves. As programs have to be undertaken and maintained without guarantee of funding until the last minute, administrators have to take countervailing protective action. They seek out new revenue resources, switch expenditures between categories, pad estimates, cut essential items to favor others knowing that cuts will have to be made up later, and engage in a whole host of ploys familiar to students of budgetary politics. Unfortunately, in trying to create more certainty for themselves, they probably compound uncertainty for everybody else as the general pool diminishes and information becomes increasingly suspect.

Imbalances of resources and responsibilities at different government levels vastly complicate the intergovernmental system and make it virtually impossible to track funding through the maze. Once a fairly clearcut stratification of types of government matched to specific functions, the intergovernmental system has become an inextricable jumble of interdependent responsibilities and finances. Budgets at all levels now reflect a complex maze of intergovernmental grants, subsidies and reimbursements designed for different purposes and disbursed according to different criteria and formulae. It is hard to discover just what is being spent and by whom on any particular function. Further, because many intergovernmental programs are funded conditionally or subject to frequent renewal, continued funding is not assured. Recipients have to deal with the red tape engendered by efforts of donors to target funds to areas of greatest need and to ensure that funds are used effectively and for the purposes for which they are intended. Meantime, the donors discover that existing technologies are inadequate to prevent seepage and that their intelligence is soon overtaken by events. To discipline apparently "uncontrollable" budgets, they devise new and increasingly sophisticated methods which further compound complexity and uncertainty in formulating and carrying through budget policies.

The injection of new values such as forward planning, participation, formal program evaluation, prioritizing and zero base considerations into the budget process has enormously complicated the life of budget formulators. Budget documents have expanded from single binders to sets of volumes occupying several feet in shelving. Participation has added to the number of steps and pairs of hands through which a budget must travel. Technical innovations entail conversions from one system of budgeting and accounting to another, and then back again. With integrated budgeting systems, a change in one figure requires wholesale alterations across the board. To meet requirements of formal planning and lengthier budget processes, the lead time of federal budgets has been extended two years or more in advance of the budget year. Budget formulators find they have to work on three future budgets at once, using information that is bound to be outdated before they finish.

Even when the budget has been passed, uncertainties continue to plague implementation and execution. In the past we could assume that once a budget document had been approved, expenditures would follow the printed figures. A routine audit at year's end would ensure correspondence of purpose and expenditure. In a turbulent environment, the predictions of an annual budget cannot keep pace. Transfers of appropriations between categories have considerably increased and are now routine in some agencies. Spending toward the end of the budget year is common as agencies hold on to money at the beginning, fearing later overruns, or financial management authorities refuse to release it or agencies overestimate and then panic in fear of cuts the following year. Thus even the agencies themselves find it more difficult to track expenditures, to know what is spent and to control funds. The growth of intergovernmental disbursements, multipocket budgeting, contracting and third party payments poses major problems for control.[1]

It should hardly surprise that budget formulators and financial managers should evince a mood of doubt and pessimism. Even in the best of times, they have come to realize that a substantial portion of governmental budgets is uncontrollable, or that is what budget experts tell them.[2] But they have been thrown off balance by the disappearance of certainty and stability. They do not have adequate hard data on which to base realistic forecasts of revenues and expenditures. They do not have clear benchmarks for expenditure categories. They can barely link the achievement of social objectives with the public money spent on them. Problems of control and tracking expenditures in a complex budgeting system create new opportunities for fraud, abuse, waste, extravagance and corruption. Yet they are mindful that many proposals now being made to remedy the situation may actually aggravate it further. They are challenging traditional theories which have structured our ways of looking at budgeting and produced these suspect solutions, because they feel that they are not the only ones overtaken by current events.

## THE QUEST FOR BUDGET REFORM

Even before budgeting concepts were upset by recent events, budgeting was the focus for reform efforts. Although traditional budgeting was acceptable, it suffered several defects that advocates of PPB and ZBB were quick to point out. In any event, it has always been a target for reformers. Budget management is an activity in which all governments must engage, for in a money economy it is the crucial element in carrying out public policies. The budget represents the outcome of competition for political power. As success is having one's claims written into the budget, the structure and process of budgeting must concern any interest group attempting to influence governmental policy. Further, budgets are also major weapons for controlling governments. After all, the wresting of financial power from arbitrary rulers was a key constitutional issue in the evolution of representative governmental institutions.

As a result of all this interest in budgeting, there now exists an impressive array of budget reforms that cover:

1. The mobilization of resources for public use and employment;
2. The consolidation and control of available resources to prevent seepage and monitor their location at all times;
3. The allocation of resources among competing demands;

4. The prompt and economic disbursement of public funds;
5. The improvement of skillful and proficient financial management;
6. The institutionalization of honest, open and careful accounting practices;
7. The establishment of independent audit; and
8. The scientific evaluation of public expenditures and projects.

Many have been incorporated successfully into practice with impressive results. Others are being tried out with more variable success. Cost benefit analysis, for example, is still in its infancy. Performance auditing is proving fertile ground for budget innovations. Too much attention has been focused on the novelties, such as PPB and ZBB, which are only a small portion of current contemporary efforts to improve budgeting.

Many budget experiments disclose a distressing gap between theory and practice. As with other administrative reforms, it is difficult to convince conservative administrators to try something different and to get them to persist with new ways of doing things when they hanker after the old with which they were comfortable no matter what the evidence shows. They cherish the hallowed principles of accountability—annuality, unity, appropriation, balance and audit—even though they are observed in the breach as governments grow. In the massive budgets of contemporary national government detailed accountability to the public or the public's representatives is largely a fiction. Even leaving aside hidden accounting for secret intelligence agencies and other politically sensitive areas, budgets are too complex for ready understanding. Off-budget trust funds and multi-year appropriations create large uncontrollable accounts which infringe annuality and budget unity. Balancing the budget has virtually been abandoned in practice, given consistent deficits at the federal level and the extensive use of capital budgeting and borrowing powers of special districts by public authorities at state and local levels. Similarly, external auditing has given way to internal checks. Yet public administrators continue to pay lip service to principles on which they no longer operate. They are reluctant to replace them with principles that better suit the new reality.

This reluctance has been partially responsible for recent failures to gain acceptance for more sophisticated techniques designed to accomplish efficiency, rationality and planning in the budget process. The most elaborate effort along these lines, program budgeting or PPB, has been largely abandoned at the federal level. Its successor, zero base budgeting or ZBB, is fading from the scene. Accumulating evidence suggests that its effectiveness in influencing decision making and outcomes is in doubt.[3] The history of these new budget concepts has been told too many times to bear recounting here.[4] Suffice it to say that the great expectations raised by across-the-board changes in budgeting methods have been punctured, leaving behind a skeptical mood in the face of an intractable budget situation seemingly beyond control.

The failure of such budget reforms cannot be attributed to lack of willingness to experiment, or lack of appreciation of what the reforms were supposed to achieve, or sheer obstinacy by smug, complacent bureaucrats too set in their ways to try something new. Reviewing the welter of specific circumstances which may have defeated these particular reforms, some major reservations can be drawn. One is that the whole notion of budget reform may be misconceived and doomed to failure. A second is that budgeting goals have been misunderstood and that reform has overconcentrated on form without considering that ultimate goals may be unattainable or in conflict. A third is that budget systems are intrinsically fragile and cumulative reform cannot be expected. Finally, reformers pay insufficient attention to the environment in which budgeting, conceived as a purely technical process, is conducted. If the mistakes of the past are to be avoided in coping with uncertainty in public budgeting, these reservations should be carefully considered.

## Budget Reform Is Misconceived

Budget reform has often been conceived as the rationalization of budget outcomes through the incorporation of programming and planning techniques and restructuring of budget processes. Emphasis has been placed on formal determination of objectives, evaluation of alternatives and authorization of programs on the basis of systematic analysis. The aim of budgeting is seen as the maximization of societal return from public expenditures.

Budgets may also be seen somewhat differently as a reflection of politics.[5] Budgets are put together by political and bureaucratic actors pursuing their own strategies and reacting to their perceptions of public needs and priorities. The process follows certain rules, expressed formally in regulations but more importantly in informal practices, the foremost of which has

been incrementalism, that is, basing each budget on that of the previous year with regular, limited additions. Incrementalism describes both decision processes and outcomes. If budgeting is politics in the raw, its forms reflect current political realities and enable political processes, such as competition bargaining, accommodation and compromise, to work.

These two views are often juxtaposed. Procedural rationality is contrasted with incrementalism and political dynamics. Reforms of techniques and processes, it is alleged, will inevitably be undermined by the rationale of politics and bureaucratic behavior. Moreover it is asserted that budget reform represents an improper dictation of policies and purposes of government which should be the prerogative of democratic politics. Budget reform might therefore be regarded not only as foredoomed to failure, but in some measure as illegitimate.

Such a sharp dichotomy is misleading. There is no reason why improved budget techniques should not inform, clarify and strengthen political financial decision making. Similarly, a rationality which takes no account of political conditions or subordinates the practicality of budget outcomes to formal processes is not really rational at all. But successful budget reform has to elucidate its aims over and beyond incorporation of techniques and processes. It must also heed the political climate and take into account the inertia and rationale of existing budget methods.

## Process Subordinates Substance

Budget reformers seem to belive that behavior follows form since they concentrate so much on the formal processes of budgeting and rarely deal with budgeting behavior. The trouble with this view is that new procedures may simply be subverted by old ways instead of mandating real changes in decision-making behavior. Reforms are formally instituted but the old ways continue in practice. Further, alterations in the formal processes may miss the real aim of budget reform which is a change in budget allocations. Process reforms, such as PPB and ZBB, are only intermediate steps. Through them, it is hoped to incorporate certain values (rationality, planning, prioritizing) into budgetary decision making. Unfortunately, in the effort to get the formal processes right the values are subordinated. Should good budgetary decision making be judged by the process by which it is arrived at or by the substantive outcomes? Even if process goals are conceded, they may be inconsistent. For example, the continuity and predictability required for planning may clash with the need for management flexibility.[6]

## Reforms Are Not Cumulative

Reformers appear to believe that new reforms build on earlier ones. Reform resembles a path marked with regular signposts which indicate the right direction and the progress so far made toward it. Reforms once accomplished, stay accomplished. Unfortunately, this is not so. The path requires constant repair and maintenance. We cannot assume, for instance, that once we have learned how to structure budget systems for control purposes that control in practice is an accomplished fact which requires no further attention. Circumstances may so change that older methods for maintaining control or management efficiency no longer suffice. The very introduction of new methods cannot be achieved without changing existing emphases or outcomes. Budgeting is a dynamic process depending as much on habits of thought and mutual expectations as on formal regulations. Budget institutions are built on trust, probity and a spirit of public service and guardianship of the public purse, none of which can be legislated. These qualities are not constant. They change according to popular morality, perceptions of public role, institutional reactions to external pressures, and a host of other imprecise and poorly understood factors. In short, budget processes cannot be conceived as a set of fixed techniques which remain in place irrespective of what is happening around them. Constant monitoring and reevaluation is needed to ensure that well-tried methods are still appropriate for reaching desired ends.

## Reforms Are Not Universal

Because budgeting is such a pervasive activity of governments, reformers have readily assumed that a single set of prescriptions applies in all circumstances. Reform failures have been blamed on faulty implementation. Little attention has been paid to contextual supports of budget systems. For instance, the part played by complex redundancy in the smooth working of budgeting in rich countries has been inadequately appreciated. Such redundancy provides greater reliability, allows for looser estimating and calculation, and increases the number of current and future options. Now that such redundancy is diminishing and cannot cushion an increasingly uncertain budgeting environment, public authorities in rich countries are beginning

to experience problems similar to those of their counterparts in poor countries.[7] Budgets disappear as earmarked funds and special authorities are established to gain and hold revenues. Cash flow management in the form of repetitive budgeting or preauditing of expenditures replaces the regular budgeted flow of funds. In the frenzied scramble for funds, the apparently neutral and universal stipulations of budgetary technology fail to work. Successful budgeting techniques seem to depend as much on their environment as on their own internal perfection.

We have not inherited an encouraging legacy to help us with current budget problems. So-called rationalists and incrementalists are locked in combat. Significant reform failures have brought disillusion, cynicism and exhaustion. Practitioners are suspicious of innovative budget theorists. The immediate outlook is not promising. But the dawning realization that there is no quick fix through mechanical changes may enhance receptivity to a more realistic agenda for public budgeting and aid adaptation to uncertainty and instability.

## COPING WITH UNCERTAINTY AND INSTABILITY

Clearly budgeting should move beyond sterile exercises in the application of techniques. Budgeting should be seen again as an integral part of a complex learning process through which public administrators come to understand the constraints and opportunities of their environment. When contemporary budgeting systems emerged in the early nineteenth century with the advent of the administrative state, they were seen by their progenitors as instruments both of control and choice. Before then, governments had been at the mercy of their financial environments. They had little control or choice over methods. Their finances were a jumble of indiscriminate taxes levied opportunistically, a maze of debts, and a variety of mind-boggling expedients. All the elements of modern budgeting—forecasting, planning, balancing revenues and expenditures, calculation of tax burdens or worth of expenditures—were missing.

As government administration became accountable to elected legislatures, the annual budget became an instrument of deliberate choice. Expenditures were forecast and provided for by revenue measures. Taxes were levied according to criteria of relative yield and equity. Through the budget, public finance became a matter for public debate, and gradually by experience the limits and possibilities of public revenues and expenditures came to be appreciated. Such knowledge was never exact; errors and misjudgments were made. But there was confidence that the public budget was an effective tool manipulable in the public interest. Such confidence is lacking today.

Nevertheless budget officials have to cope with the effects of these uncertainties in carrying out their functions. The following list of some of these uncertainties and possible ways of dealing with them may be of some aid. At this point suggestions are necessarily generalized; they represent areas to which attention should be directed, not a set of solutions for all times and places. Their development or application would require further research, diagnosis, discussion and cooperation on the part of those concerned.

1. *Uncertainties arising from novelty.* A major source of uncertainty in budgeting today is the feeling that we are coping with unique and unprecedented problems. The future is unclear and policy choices have to be made without benefit of previous experience. Hence a persistent casting around for novel solutions.

This preoccupation with the novel may be exaggerated, particularly in the area of budgeting where knowledge of how other budget systems work is often fragmentary. Systematic studies among several jurisdictions are a rarity.[8] This valuable tool for research has been neglected. Yet if we want to learn about what works in budgeting and what doesn't, it is indispensable and preferable to constructing systems a priori and imposing them in blanket fashion irrespective of circumstances. The comparative approach, marred in the past by collections of descriptions of formal budget processes from exotic places, broadens the learning experience by focusing on how finance officials deal with their problems and reviewing their diverse experiences to discover apposite lessons of wider applicability. There is no need to travel far to do this. Cities, counties, states and government corporations can pool ideas and learn from one another. A wealth of historical evidence waits to be tapped. It should provide valuable insights into the relationship between changes in formal structures and budgeting behavior and outcomes, and between environmental changes and budget processes. Analysis should not be confined solely

to the public sector, for valuable lessons can also be obtained from comparing private and public practices. For example, public administrators can study the possibilities of applying such concepts as flow of funds, opportunity costs in capital budgeting, and accounting indicators of future financial problems. By studying environments other than their own, budget theorists and practitioners may find similarities to their own experiences and be encouraged to innovate and experiment.

2. *Uncertainties arising from an annual perspective.* Financing the activities of governments is a continuous process, which budgeting fits into an annual framework for purposes of accountability, assessment of past and future expenditures and orderly provision of funding and fiscal policy. Annual budgeting brings greater certainty to government financing by imposing periodic check and review upon transactions, ensuring appropriation of funds in advance of obligations, and allowing comprehensive oversight of the financial position.

But precisely because annual budgeting uses a static framework to control a continuous and dynamic flow of activities, it may become a source of uncertainty. Where, as is commonly the case today, programs extend beyond a single year, the annual period of accounting and review is too short. Such programs require stable long-term commitment of funds so that persons, agencies and authorities depending on them can plan ahead in the knowledge that the end of each budget year will not bring about a sudden cut-off in funds.

In practice provision is made to deal with programs which extend beyond a single year through setting up entitlements, multi-year authorizations and permanent appropriations. But these practices create a different kind of uncertainty relating to control of programs for which provision has already been made in advance of the annual budget. These form an "uncontrollable" budget, which lies outside the discretion of legislators formally responsible for deciding annual allocations of funds.

This uneasy dilemma between the uncertainties of commitment and control[9] arises from reliance on an annual framework to impose accountability where the majority of government programs extend over a number of years. The appropriateness of repetitive annual budgeting in such cases seems open to question. It is possible that adoption of differential time spans for program review according to need may be a more realistic response to this problem. Such periodic appropriations and reviews might allow greater concentration on fewer areas, different kinds of scrutiny over the life of a program, and better monitoring of program progress and effectiveness.[10]

3. *Uncertainties arising from problems in forecasting.* The literature on budgeting often gives the misleading impression that once a budget has received assent according to due process, there is nothing more to be discussed. The grand debates about budgeting are concerned mainly with how budget totals are arrived at, not with what happens to them after that. But in a fast changing environment and high inflation, forecasts of costs and revenues become more difficult. At the beginning of the year, it is harder to envisage the financial position at the end. Increasingly budget allocations require readjustment during the year. Programs which have been underestimated may run out of money and require supplementary appropriations. Alternatively where attempts have been made to do too much too quickly, unrealistic overallocations to popular programs may result in underspending and large balances at the end of the year. The changed nature of government outlays no longer fits into an even and regular apportionment schedule.[11] Irregular disbursements, frequent adjustments, under or over spending in various categories, all represent divergences from initial budgetary intentions and may involve serious inefficiencies in the use of public funds. The initial allocation of funds through the annual budget process can no longer be relied upon to ensure that spending will be exactly in accordance with its mandates.

The implementation phase of the budget should not be ignored. The annual budget can no longer be expected to last in unaltered form for a whole year. It is therefore essential that serious consideration be given to planning budget implementation processes, reviewing how officials work with budgets during the year, the arrangements made for ensuring cash flow at critical periods, self-pacing disbursement schedules and incentives for compliance with budget mandates.

4. *Uncertainties arising from centralization and bureaucratic controls.* One of the major changes in budgeting in recent years is that few budgets are made in isolation. Local governments in particular have become heavily dependent on resources distributed by other levels of government. Federal agencies increasingly find themselves in a donor role, while state governments are sometimes donors and sometimes recipients. Recipient governments have suffered loss of control over their budgets where financial transfers are channeled into ear-marked funds beyond local decision making, though they may have ramifications on other local government activities. They also suffer from uncertainties of commitment where donor governments hold up transfers for one reason or another, or will not commit funds for more than a limited period. Donor governments for their part have trouble determining eligibility requirements or need for aid, and also in tracking the use and effectiveness of indirect outlays.

The response to these uncertainties by donor governments has generally been toward increased bureaucratic control, which has been regarded as the linchpin of financial accountability. But particularly in the case of intergovernmental financial relations, bureaucratic controls have become increasingly hard to administer, and often seem counterproductive. The redoubling of efforts at control and integration increases red tape and makes information more difficult to obtain and interpret. It may be that this approach is misconceived. Now that accounting techniques and computerized operations offer new possibilities for comparing, tracking and assessing expenditures, it may be feasible to achieve greater decentralization as well as more effective accountability by means other than centralized controls.

5. *Uncertainties arising from size and complexity.* The explosive growth in size and complexity of government budgets in recent years is an obvious source of uncertainty. Both bureaucratic and legislative oversight become more difficult because of the sheer volume of transactions involved. Efforts to maintain independence from budget discipline have created a tendency to separate budgets and accounts which conceal more than they reveal.

In several jurisdictions considerable effort has gone into simplifying presentations and processes for purposes of clarification, and also into bringing all relevant accounts into the budget. Special analyses, and special budgets to deal with fringe areas such as regulatory costs and tax expenditures, have been undertaken or suggested. Legislative research efforts and new legislative procedures have provided more information and a sharper focus for legislators. Yet size and complexity often obfuscate, and simplification should remain on the agenda. The need is particularly urgent in view of growing attempts to boost program staff participation in the budget process. If these financial amateurs are to understand what they are doing, procedures should be designed for maximum clarity and precision.

6. *Uncertainties arising from erosion of accountability.* A major problem undermining public confidence in government is the difficulty in ensuring that public money is spent wisely and efficiently. The vogue for public expenditure controls is an indication of this unease. But these may prove a blunt instrument for achieving official responsibility in handling public resources. They penalize both good and bad areas alike, and the avoidance technique they encourage may actually make for worse decision making. Yet if legitimate public purposes are to be fulfilled, it is essential that steps be taken to ensure that the public feels that it is getting its money's worth.

It is imperative to examine government budgets to determine what has been achieved for given revenue outlays. We need to find out the total amounts which have been spent on various government functions, and establish indicators of performance. We need more exact ideas about how much of a public service can be provided for a given outlay. Some work of this kind has already been undertaken, but all too often a simple inquiry about levels of expenditure and results cannot be answered. Measures for ensuring accountability need to be built into program design. New incentives for good performance should be instituted. At the same time, it is necessary to cut down the probability of waste or corruption by examination of procedure for contracting, disbursements and auditing.

On the other side of the budget, questions of revenue need to be tied into issues of expenditure. For too long, the literature of budgeting has tended to separate the two. While budget discussions have concentrated on expenditure policies and classification, revenue raising has been regarded as the province of public finance experts. Budget management needs to be regarded as a unitary function in which revenues and expenditures figure in a single equation. Further, as pressures mount on budgets, attention has to be given to finding new sources of revenues (new kinds of taxes or loans) and restructuring taxation to accord with economic goals, yet meet public demands for greater equity and fairness. Existing sources of revenues should be made more effective. The growth of a significant underground economy represents an important loss of tax revenues and adds to the burden of those

who do not participate in it. It also corrupts public administration and worsens the seepage of public funds. Research into the underground economy and illegal markets and their impact on public finance is long overdue.

## CONCLUSION

These six areas of uncertainty and suggestions for their alleviation, by no means exhaustive of what needs to be done in public budgeting, are merely manifestations of a deeper crisis in American society. Public finance is the center of the controversy over the future role of the administrative state. An agenda for public budgeting amidst uncertainty and instability cannot be drawn without reference to the public purposes it serves. As long as these are in doubt, the proper allocation of public funds will remain beyond the grasp of public budgeting. Financial administrators will continue to receive mixed and perplexing signals. They will not know how to prioritize let alone make sense out of the confusion that passes for budget formulation and execution or satisfy conflicting and contradictory claims on them. They won't even know what direction to take. However, if they assess their own practices in the areas presented here, they may be better able to find their bearings and realize not only the real constraints upon their actions but also what new opportunities are open to them.

Public administrators cannot solve by themselves the bigger issues raised here. They can do much better in the special field of their own competence. To improve budgeting, a good look has to be taken at current budget institutions. Are they adaptive enough to apparent changes in the environment? Are they performing well enough? Are they capable of assuming new roles? Do they take advantage of all available techniques?

In particular, we need to encourage innovation and creativity in public finance as the traditional landmarks fade amidst uncertainty and instability. We still do not have sufficient incentives in the public sector to prevent waste and encourage economy. We still do not have adequate means of dealing with large-scale capital expenditures on risky, long-term public projects. We still do not know how to manage what amount to open-ended contracts to private organizations to deliver important public goods and services. We still do not have proper tools to tackle tax evasion and expenditure seepage. We have numerous momentary fads and fancies, many half-baked and untested theories, and a continuous flow to refinements to traditional budgeting, when what really may be needed is a new budgetary system more in keeping with the new context of public finance, more appropriate to current technological capability, and more attuned to public expectations, not managerial convenience.

## NOTES

1. Allen Schick, "Contemporary Problems in Financial Control," *Public Administration Review,* Vol. 38, November/December 1978, pp. 513–519.

2. Joseph A. Pechman and Robert W. Hartman, "The 1980 Budget and the Budget Outlook," in Joseph A. Pechman (ed.), *Setting National Priorities: The 1980 Budget* (Washington, D. C.: The Brookings Institution, 1979), p. 54.

3. Allen Schick, *Zero Base '80* (Washington, D. C.: National Governors Association, 1980).

4. Allen Schick, "The Road to PPB: The Stages of Budget Reform," *Public Administration Review,* Vol. 26, December 1966, pp. 243–258; Allen Schick, "The Road from ZBB," *Public Administration Review,* Vol. 38, March/April 1978, pp. 177–180.

5. See Aaron Wildavsky, *The Politics of the Budgetary Process,* 3rd ed. (Boston: Little Brown, 1979).

6. Aaron Wildavsky, "A Budget for All Seasons? Why the Traditional Budget Lasts," *Public Administration Review,* Vol. 38, November/December 1978, p. 501.

7. Naomi Caiden and Aaron Wildavsky, *Planning and Budgeting in Poor Countries* (New York: Wiley, 1974, and Transaction Books, 1980).

8. See Aaron Wildavsky, *Budgeting: A Comparative Theory of Budgetary Processes* (Boston: Little Brown, 1975). See also the section on "Comparative Budgeting" in Albert C. Hyde and Jay M. Schafritz, *Government Budgeting: Theory, Process and Politics* (Oak Park, Illinois: Moore Publishing Company, 1978).

9. Statement of Elmer B. Staats, Comptroller General of the United States, before the Budget Process Task Force Committee on the Budget, House of Representatives, *The Federal Budget Process,* December 11, 1979, p. 24.

10. See scheme for biennial review for R & D activities in Statement of Elmer B. Staats, Comptroller General of the United States, before the Committee on Science and Technology, House of Representatives, *H. R. 7178, The Research and Development Authorization Estimates Act,* June 4, 1980.

11. Elmer B. Staats, *Effectiveness of the Federal Apportionment Process and Implications for Budget Execution* (Washington, D. C.: General Accounting Office, November 1979), p. 5.

## Congress and Budget-Making

Robert W. Hartman

Federal budget decisions not only reflect views about fiscal and social policy, but also are substantially shaped by electoral politics and by the processes of government. Breaking a budget stalemate appears to require that a compromise between quite divergent views be worked out by the president and the two houses of Congress in this election year using a still-evolving budget process. It will not be easy. Moreover, in the past year such actions as reconciliation and closing the government for a day have left the public more confused than ever at a time when calm judgment is needed to deal with the serious substantive issues raised by this year's budget.

This article tries to provide a background for understanding some of the procedural developments of the past and alternatives for the future. It first discusses legislative developments through President Reagan's first year in office, then examines prospects for avoiding a stalemate, and concludes with a look at alternative future budgetary procedures, ranging from relatively weak budget controls to a constitutional amendment to balance the budget.

### EVOLUTION OF BUDGET REFORM

"The president proposes and the Congress disposes" is shorthand for the American system of handling federal laws, including the budget. While budgetary procedures of the executive branch changed little in the 1970s, those of the Congress underwent significant change.

#### The Executive Branch

The preparation of the president's budget proposal each January has been more or less the same for the last twenty-five years. In the spring preceding the

Reprinted with permission from the *Political Science Quarterly,* 97 (Fall, 1982): 381–402.

budget's submission, the Office of Management and Budget (OMB) conducts a spring preview, a series of meetings and presentations involving OMB and agency officials, in an attempt to identify the issues likely to have a major impact on the upcoming budget. These reviews may lead to further study, to directives to agencies to prepare specific proposals, and to the development of planning ceilings for the agencies. By the fall, the OMB's attention turns more directly to the budget. Ordinarily the OMB director holds meetings to review all parts of the budget. Decisions are made on the administration's economic assumptions and overall fiscal policy. These are translated into firm budget guidance to each government agency. As the calendar year draws to a close, there is a series of exchanges of budget submissions between the OMB and the agencies, culminating in final negotiations between the White House and the agency heads. Various presidents have involved themselves in the process in greater or lesser detail, but the president is always the final arbiter.

When a new president comes to office, the transition imposes a need for supplementing procedures in the executive branch. At the start of both the Carter and Reagan presidencies in 1977 and 1981, budget amendments were hurriedly put together for delivery to the Congress by March to meet the congressional budget calendar. Obviously, the telescoped amending process cannot involve as much agency consultation or give-and-take as there is in the ordinary budget deliberations. In 1981 there was almost none, in part because OMB Director David Stockman was knowledgeable and had a comprehensive program and in part because in early 1981 there was little expert opposition either in the White House or in the agencies. Thus President Reagan's first-stage budget proposal in 1981 was conceived and born in the OMB. The fiscal 1983 budget, which had a full year to develop, was not an all-OMB product. Stockman's power had been eroded by his candid observations in a magazine article,[1] and several forceful cabinet officials had developed power and influence with the president. Thus the 1983 budget was more a joint product of the agencies and the OMB.

The OMB's main role usually ends with the submission of the president's budget to Congress. Although the OMB monitors the budget's progress and clears officials' testimony, the brunt of the responsibility for defending the president's proposals falls to agency chiefs. While the appearance of unswerving loyalty to the president is always maintained by agency officials who want to keep their jobs, deals that depart from the president's proposals are often cut between agency heads, who may be acting on behalf of outside interest groups, and committee chairmen. There was little evidence that this "iron triangle" of interest group, agency, and congressional committee exerted influence in 1981, in part because the OMB took a much stronger interest than customary in the budget's progress through Congress. Indeed, because most of the key budget legislation was encompassed in a single bill, the Omnibus Budget Reconciliation Act of 1981, the iron triangle would have had to have been designed by a computer. Stockman was able to exert full control over President Reagan's spending plans because the OMB played a large part in drafting the "bipartisan" Gramm-Latta proposals that later became law.[2] The interdependence of the parts of the fiscal 1983 presidential budget proposal or a possible compromise package makes it likely that the OMB will continue to play a central role in negotiations with Congress.

### Congressional Budgetary Procedures

Before 1974 the Congress did not deal with the president's budget submission in a systematic or well-coordinated manner. The legislative proposals in the president's budget were simply parceled out to the various committees in each house.[3] Proposed *appropriations* (which set dollar limits, usually called *budget authority,* on the commitment of funds for any particular government activity) were sent to the appropriations committee in each house, which then allocated the requests to its subcommittees. Proposed *authorizations,* which establish the legal basis for the federal government to engage in an activity, such as the Vocational Education Act, and set an upper limit on appropriations for that activity, usually over several years, were sent to the pertinent authorizing committee (for example, the Senate Labor and Human Resources Committee) for consideration. Tax change proposals went to the House Ways and Means Committee and later to the Senate Finance Committee. Each committee worked at its own pace, and after each piece of legislation cleared both houses and a conference committee to reconcile differences, it was sent to the president for signature. The "budget" that emerged was the uncoordinated sum of the spending consequences of all these laws.[4]

No committee of Congress was in charge of the

budget as a whole. Although the Ways and Means and Finance Committees were in command of the laws governing taxes, they acted independently and often in ignorance, of actions taken by the spending committees. The appropriations committees did give some overall guidance to their subcommittees and usually cut spending below the president's request. Authorizing committees were totally uncoordinated and often circumvented the appropriations committees by establishing and liberalizing *entitlements*. Entitlements are authorizing laws that establish a beneficiary's claim to a government payment (for example, food stamps), thereby making the subsequent appropriation an *uncontrollable* item in the sense that the appropriations committees have no discretion over it. Aside from the lack of coordination and of a central accountable entity, this congressional process lacked timeliness. Some appropriations became law before the start of the fiscal year; others did not. When a regular appropriation had not been passed, an agency would be financed under a *continuing resolution,* a stopgap measure that left much to be desired.

## The Congressional Budget and Impoundment Control Act of 1974

Most of these procedures remain intact today, but the Congressional Budget and Impoundment Control Act of 1974 made several important changes in budgetary procedures while building on the existing structure of legislative activity. The act created a Committee on the Budget in each house to coordinate budget policy and a Congressional Budget Office to provide staff expertise. The coordinating role of the Budget Committees can best be understood through the procedural calendar also established by the 1974 act. Under the new procedures, the proposed laws implementing the president's budget are still parceled out to the authorization, appropriation, and tax committees, but action on the floor of Congress is not permitted until certain milestones are passed. The cycle begins in mid-March, when each committee sends a report to the Budget Committee containing its recommendations for budgetary action in its domain of expertise.

The Budget Committees draft and report out by April 15 a *first concurrent resolution on the budget.* This resolution specifies aggregate targets for budget authority, outlays, revenues, and deficits, as well as for the cumulative debt subject to statutory limit.[5] The

resolution also sets forth targets for budget authority and outlays in each function (national defense, health, and so forth). Budget Committee staff translate them into targets for each committee that has jurisdiction over some part of the budget. Once a common first concurrent resolution has passed each house, scheduled for May 15, the authorizing and appropriating committees, acting under the guidance of the first resolution, may bring bills to the floor.[6] All the while, the Congressional Budget Office keeps track of the progress of legislation and aids the budget committees in informing members if the targets in the resolution are likely to be breached. Thus during the summer, when most spending legislation is being enacted, the committees of Congress are under only one (nonbinding) constraint—the target for spending or taxing allocated to them as a result of the first concurrent resolution.

The congressional budgetary process culminates in September, just before the start of the fiscal year, which was shifted to October by the 1974 act. The act requires Congress to pass a *second concurrent resolution* in September and, if necessary, to revise the limits contained in the first resolution. The estimates for spending and taxing in the second resolution are "binding" in this sense: Once the resolution has been passed, any member can kill legislation that raises the outlays and budget authority above their ceiling or reduces revenues below the revenue floor by objecting to its consideration. Before any such legislation can be passed, a *third concurrent resolution* is required to change the limits. Thus the final binding budget under the new procedures constrains only *legislative action;* it does not limit the budgetary outcomes themselves. Indeed, the budget resolutions are only a set of rules for Congress; they are not signed by the president and have no status as laws. Also, if at the time the second concurrent resolution is adopted the previous actions of any committee are found to be inconsistent with the dollar limits of the second resolution, the situation would be rectified by the *reconciliation process.* In the second resolution itself, committees would receive reconciliation instructions that directed them to amend or to rescind appropriations or other spending legislation or to change the tax laws. The legislation drafted by the committees given these directives would be packaged (without change) by the budget committees into a single *budget reconciliation act.* The budget reconciliation act must clear Congress by September

25, to give the president time to sign it before the fiscal year begins.[7]

## HOW THE REFORMED PROCESS WORKED

These procedures operated pretty much as the legislation intended between 1976 when the new procedures were first fully implemented, and 1978—covering the budgets for fiscal years 1977–79. As shown in Table 1, the budget calendar was adhered to in that period, and the first resolution outlay targets were not breached by either committee legislative activity or subsequent events. Revenues were slightly overestimated in fiscal 1977 but underestimated in 1978 and 1979, and the ac-

tual budget deficit came in well under initial estimates.

This propitious start for a new procedure was facilitated by the state of the economy and the reaction to it in Congress. In 1977 and 1978, recovery from the recession of the mid-1970s was the central economic preoccupation of the country. President Carter's first budgetary actions, amending the 1978 budget, were explicitly designed to stimulate the economy. The substantive committees of Congress supported him, and the budget committees made little challenge, thus establishing their place in the legislature without disturbing continuing power relationships.

Fiscal 1979 represented a transition for the economy and for budget policy. When Carter first proposed his

**TABLE 1**
**Outlays and revenues under Congressional budget resolutions and actual outcomes,**
**fiscal years 1977–82**

| Item | Date of conference agreement | Outlays[a] | Revenues[a] | Deficit |
|---|---|---|---|---|
| **Fiscal 1977** | | | | |
| First resolution | 5/13/76 | 413.3 | 362.5 | 50.8 |
| Second resolution | 9/16/76 | 413.3 | 362.5 | 50.6 |
| Actual | — | 401.9 | 356.9 | 45.0 |
| Overrun or shortfall[b] (−) | — | −11.4 | −5.6 | −5.8 |
| **Fiscal 1978** | | | | |
| First resolution | 5/17/77 | 461.0 | 396.3 | 64.7 |
| Second resolution | 9/15/77 | 458.3 | 397.0 | 61.3 |
| Actual | — | 449.9 | 401.1 | 48.8 |
| Overrun or shortfall[b] (−) | — | −11.1 | 4.8 | −15.9 |
| **Fiscal 1979** | | | | |
| First resolution | 5/17/78 | 498.8 | 447.9 | 50.9 |
| Second resolution | 9/23/78 | 487.5 | 448.7 | 38.8 |
| Actual | — | 493.7 | 465.9 | 27.7 |
| Overrun or shortfall[b] (−) | — | −5.1 | 18.0 | −23.2 |
| **Fiscal 1980** | | | | |
| First resolution | 5/24/79 | 532.0 | 509.0 | 23.0 |
| Second resolution | 11/28/79 | 547.6 | 517.8 | 29.8 |
| Actual | — | 579.6 | 520.0 | 59.6 |
| Overrun or shortfall[b] (−) | — | 47.6 | 11.0 | 36.6 |
| **Fiscal 1981** | | | | |
| First resolution | 6/12/80 | 613.6 | 613.8 | 0.2[c] |
| Second resolution | 11/20/80 | 632.4 | 605.0 | 27.4 |
| Actual | — | 657.2 | 599.3 | 57.9 |
| Overrun or shortfall[b] (−) | — | 43.6 | −14.5 | 58.1 |
| **Fiscal 1982** | | | | |
| First resolution | 5/21/81 | 695.5 | 657.8 | 37.7 |
| Second resolution | 11/19/81 | 695.5 | 657.8 | 37.7 |
| Actual[d] | — | 725.3 | 626.8 | 98.6 |

Source: Congressional Budget Office.
a. Actual outlays and revenues in each year use the definitions in force at the time. In fiscal 1982 the actual reflects new definitions adopted after the budget resolutions for that year were voted.
b. From first resolution.
c. Surplus.
d. Estimated in *Budget of the United States Government, Fiscal Year 1983*, pp. 2–14.

budget for that year in January 1978, the centerpiece was a tax cut intended to maintain the growth of the economy. As time passed, however, it became clear that the economy was improving significantly and that inflation was worsening. The president narrowed the proposed tax cut, and these lower limits were incorporated in the second concurrent resolution passed in September. In October, when the tax bill reached the floor of the Senate, several proposals to deepen the tax cut beyond the limits of the second resolution were defeated when Senator Edmund S. Muskie, Budget Committee chairman, objected and was upheld by the Senate.

Beginning with the 1980 budget, attention turned to fighting inflation, and budgetary difficulties began to develop. The 1980 budget proposed by President Carter in January 1979 was billed as an austerity budget. It included what seemed then to be unusually large spending cuts, and the deficit was limited to under $30 billion, a figure Carter had promised in the fall of 1978. For the first time, the new budgetary procedures had to deal with unpleasant choices, and the results were not encouraging. Because President Carter had proposed a $30 billion deficit and because inflation was raging in early 1979, the Budget Committees felt obliged to issue a first concurrent resolution with a deficit no larger than the president had proposed. The first resolution therefore assumed that certain savings, amounting to about $5.6 billion, would be made by authorizing committees. These were referred to in the conference report on the first resolution but not in the resolution itself. As the summer wore on these legislative savings failed to materialize in committee actions, and a deep division developed between the two houses.[8] For the second concurrent resolution, the Senate Budget Committee decided to carry out the reconciliation procedures and called for $4 billion in mandatory savings, and the full Senate agreed. The House Budget Committee could not agree to implement reconciliation, and after a protracted delay in conference the second budget resolution passed in late November 1979 with no reconciliation. This resolution still projected a fiscal 1980 deficit of under $30 billion, even though all indications were that such a level could not be reached without further deficit-reducing legislation. The failure to implement reconciliation meant that such legislation would not be enacted. The Budget Committees were becoming convinced that the weak mechanism for enforcing legislative savings assumed in the first concurrent resolution needed strengthening.

## The Budget Prelude of Fiscal 1981

The procedural developments in the 1981 budgetary process were a turning point. In January 1980, President Carter sent Congress his budget proposal, tailored to election-year politics. It dropped the austerity theme and tried to offend no important constituency. Perhaps because of the public's awareness that the second budget resolution for fiscal 1980 was phony in the sense that its assumptions were not likely to be realized, a sharp eye was cast on Carter's January proposal. The reaction was skepticism, and this contributed to plummeting financial markets early in 1980. Interest rates on three-month Treasury bills rose from 12 to 15.5 percent between January and March. Bond and stock prices fell precipitously.

President Carter withdrew his budget seven weeks after it was submitted and began an extensive series of conferences with members of Congress on an acceptable alternative. The chairmen and members of the Budget Committees played a major role along with the leadership of Congress in these negotiations. After Carter submitted his revised budget in March, the Budget Committees took advantage of this enhanced role and supported a first concurrent resolution that included reconciliation instructions directing eight House and ten Senate authorizing committees to report legislation reducing outlays by over $6 billion in 1981. Tax committees were instructed to raise more than $4 billion in revenues. These actions were only a small part of those needed to balance the budget as promised in the resolution.[9] The committees were instructed to report legislation within a few weeks of the first resolution, which passed in June 1980.

The move to cut spending stalled in the middle of 1980. The recession coupled with an election led to a stalemate. The Senate passed a reconciliation bill in July, and the House passed its quite different bill in September. The conference committee, which numbered over one hundred, repeatedly deadlocked and did not pass the reconciliation act until early December after the long-delayed second budget resolution was voted.

The Omnibus Budget Reconciliation Act of 1980 was a disappointing piece of legislation. Since the reconciliation instructions included in the first concurrent resolution specified savings targets for fiscal 1981 only, a number of committees "complied" by drafting changes in law that shifted expenditures from 1981 to future years. Other committees included legislation that actually raised spending in some programs in part to offset cuts made. A reduction in cost-of-living adjustments for federal civilian and military retirees that passed the Senate was dropped by the conference. In all, the Omnibus Budget Reconciliation Act provided $4.6 billion in outlay reductions and $3.6 billion in new taxes, for a total deficit-reduction package of about $8 billion, well under the action needed to balance the budget as originally intended.

Two additional innovations in the fiscal 1981 congressional budgetary process are worth noting. First, both houses of Congress made a start on multiyear budgeting. The budget resolutions incorporated budget targets for the out-years fiscal 1982 and 1983 as well as for the budget year 1981, but each house set different targets for future years. Second, for the first time, levels of federal credit activity were specified. This "credit budget" attempted to curb the total volume of both new direct loans and guaranteed loan commitments of federal agencies by requesting that appropriation limitations be extended to all federal credit activity. Such actions were intended to increase control since many federal credit activities are subject to weak limits imposed by authorizing legislation that sets the terms of loans by executive discretion, or even by market demand. As in the early years of the new budgetary process, however, these "credit limits" were revised during fiscal 1981 to conform to what was happening to federal credit, rather than the other way around.

## THE REAGAN REVOLUTION IN THE BUDGET PROCESS

In many ways the stage had been set for President Reagan's entrance. Over time, the Budget Committees had increasingly extended their roles in and influence over budgeting outcomes. A major procedural breakthrough had been made in 1980 when reconciliation instructions were incorporated in the first concurrent resolution. Yet the Stockman-directed progress of President Reagan's budgetary legislation through the summer of 1981 is regarded by many as a revolution because of the size and scope of the changes made and the threat they posed to hallowed congressional procedures.

Within about seven weeks of taking office, President Reagan sent Congress a full-blown set of budget revisions for fiscal 1982 and beyond. The most controversial proposals were an increase in spending for national defense, a reduction in business and personal taxes, and a huge cut in federal non-defense spending. The administration, with the support of the Republican-controlled Senate Budget Committee, sought to carry out as much of the spending reduction program as possible in the form of reconciliation action. The Senate in late March—just a few days after the president's budget revisions were submitted—passed a resolution instructing its committees to make major budget cuts.

These instructions were incorporated in the Senate's first concurrent resolution, which passed in May. The House proceeded along a more conventional track. The budget committee reported a first concurrent resolution that included reconciliation instructions. This resolution, bearing the stamp of Chairman James R. Jones, was challenged on the floor of the House by a substitute resolution cosponsored by Delbert L. Latta, the ranking Republican on the House Budget Committee, and Phil Gramm, a Democratic member of the committee and a leader of a group of conservative Democrats called "Boll Weevils." Gramm-Latta I, as the budget resolution became known, passed the House in late May, after an apparently effective presidential television plea for it. The Senate passed an equivalent resolution the next day.

Gramm-Latta was monumental in a number of respects. First, it contained instructions for budget reductions addressed to fifteen House committees and fourteen Senate committees. The instructions specified amounts to be saved for fiscal years 1982, 1983, and 1984. This multiyear focus was designed to avoid the temporary cosmetic cuts of the previous year's legislation and to complement the administration's multiyear tax-cutting plan. Second, the outlay reductions totaled $36 billion, $47 billion, and $56 billion for the three fiscal years, over eight percent of non-defense, non-interest outlays. These sums were several times larger than previous reconciliation actions. Third, the reconciliation savings were to be made in two types of authorizing legislation: entitlements and discretionary programs. For entitlement spending, a reconciliation directive to the authorizing committee is recognized as the only way to impose restraint since subsequent appropriations are perfunctory. But spending for other programs—for example, grants to states for education programs—can be limited either by proposing limits on annual appropriations or by the much stronger measure of directing the committee that authorized the program to lower the authorization ceiling over several years. The latter arrangement was a feature of

Gramm-Latta and was not part of the Jones proposal that was defeated.

The congressional committees responded to the reconciliation instructions by submitting legislation affecting 250 different federal programs.[10] Arguing that some of the changes proposed in the House showed a "clear danger of Congressional backsliding and a return to spending as usual,"[11] the administration quickly fashioned an alternative reconciliation bill, called Gramm-Latta II, to replace the work of several committees. Gramm-Latta II, like its predecessor, narrowly passed the House, after gaining support from the Boll Weevils and a group of moderate Republicans called "Gypsy Moths" who demanded and received certain concessions from the administration. After an efficiently run conference, the president in August signed the Omnibus Budget Reconciliation Act of 1981, an inch-thick compendium of twenty separate titles covering a range from Agriculture and Forestry to Health Professions. The law changed entitlement program eligibility rules (for example, for food stamps), limited the amounts authorized in scores of programs for 1982–84, rewrote major parts of substantive law having little effect on the budget (for example, for radio and TV broadcasting), and probably did a few other things that have not been discovered yet.

This extraordinary law was debated on the floor of the House for two days. There were no hearings at all on some sections of the law. The possibility of amending the bill was strictly limited, and it was voted on in a single vote, not section by section.

The reconciliation act's companion legislation, the Economic Recovery Tax Act of 1981, was meanwhile wending its way through the Senate Finance Committee and the House Ways and Means Committee. The first concurrent resolution had set targets for tax cuts for 1982–84. A period of negotiation between the White House and the Democratic chairman of the Ways and Means Committee, Congressman Dan Rostenkowski, had produced no agreement, especially on the size and phasing-in of a personal income tax. Accordingly, the administration decided to attract enough Boll Weevil votes to its side to command a majority in the House by offering to include tax changes that would appeal to them. Rostenkowski countered with additional lures to keep the Boll Weevils in the fold. OMB Director Stockman characterized the resulting scramble as: "The hogs were really feeding. The greed level, the level of opportunism, just got out of control."[12] Despite this, the Economic Recovery

Tax Act complied with the revenue reduction limits in the first concurrent resolution, although the act's tax cut for 1985, which was deepened by adding indexation of the individual income tax in that year, probably went beyond what the supporters of the concurrent resolution had envisioned.

## Aftermath

Congress adjourned in August. The members heard from constituents about high interest rates, and they had time to think about what had transpired in the first half year of budget policy under President Reagan. Congress prides itself on being a deliberative body. The helter-skelter of enacting reconciliation and the tax bill was the opposite of a careful legislative process. The modus operandi of the Congress had for a long time been that the work is done by committees that share power. In 1981 the Senate had ceded full control to the Budget Committee, and in the House the committee proposals for reconciliation had been thrown out. The main function of Appropriations Committee members had been as watchdog on the Treasury. But the reconciliation process had given the play to the Budget Committees and the authorizing committees, leaving Appropriations a cipher. Members of Congress like to show their expertise and independence by sponsoring amendments and the like, but the whole legislative show in 1981 had boiled down to two votes for or against President Reagan's entire program. These concerns, as well as uneasiness about the economy, presaged trouble ahead.

The president's initial budget plan had contemplated program cuts to be made in areas not covered by reconciliation. So had the first concurrent resolution on the 1982 budget. The exact size of these cuts was a matter of confusion, in part because the president's cuts were measured from a baseline different from that used in reconciliation. Moreover, some of the members of Congress who had been lured into the administration's camp for the reconciliation thought they had been promised some relenting in the pursuit of further cuts.

Against this backdrop came the Reagan administration's fall offensive. A new package of budget cuts encompassing entitlement reductions, appropriations reductions, and even some "revenue enhancement" was announced by the administration on September 24— incidentally making it absolutely impossible to meet the deadlines set by the 1974 act. The program was not well received by Congress. The entitlement package was never even formally introduced and the tax enhancers were withdrawn. The administration decided, however, to make yet another fight over its proposed across-the-board (with some exceptions) reductions in appropriations.

When the fiscal year began on October 1, no appropriations bills had been signed into law.[13] As a result, the entire government was being funded under a continuing appropriation law. The first continuing appropriation resolution, signed into law on September 30, is a relatively short document setting limits on the commitment of funds for the first part of the year. Instead of specifying appropriations on a line-by-line basis as in ordinary appropriations laws, the resolution sets spending limits by mechanical rules. Thus the limit on spending for each program is as follows: If both houses have passed an appropriation for that program, it may operate at the lesser of the two appropriated amounts; if only one house has passed an appropriation, spending may continue at the lesser of the appropriated amount or the "current rate." The current rate generally means the rate of the previous fiscal year.[14] The first continuing appropriation set an expiration date of 20 November 1981, in the expectation that regular appropriations laws, which supersede continuing appropriations, would be on the books by that time.

As it turned out, very few appropriations—and none of the major ones—had been passed by Friday, November 20, because of the continuing controversy over the administration's fall-offensive cuts, and a second continuing appropriation was needed. The Congress agreed on such a bill at the final hour and sent it to President Reagan. Over the weekend of November 21–22, President Reagan decided to veto the continuing resolution and did so on Monday, November 23. As a result, federal offices throughout the country closed that day, nonessential workers were sent home, and President Reagan and members of Congress (who stayed on the job—their appropriation had passed) got together that same day on a compromise extension of the continuing resolution until December 15. On December 15, with few appropriations yet enacted, still another continuing appropriation was passed until 15 February 1982.

By the end of December 1981, most appropriations laws—though not the biggest non-defense one, for the Departments of Labor, Health and Human Services, and Education—had been signed into law. As indicated in Table 2, the administration was forced to accept some increases over its fall proposals in the appropriations that passed. In defense and foreign aid, appropriations were below the administration's request; but the Agriculture, Interior, and combined Housing and Urban Development, Veterans Administration, and National Aeronautics and Space Administration appropriations exceeded the administration's request. While it is probably true that these appropriations would have been even higher if the administration had not waged a fall offensive, it is clear that President Reagan's total mastery over budgeting began to erode in the appropriations process. It is also evident that the patent disregard for the Appropriations Committees' prerogatives in the reconciliation process stiffened these committees' resistance to further cuts.

It is universally agreed that operating a large part of the government under continuing appropriations is a most unsatisfactory way of doing the public's business. First, because the continuing resolution is simply a set of general rules to limit spending, it tends to perpetuate spending patterns that conform to no one's preferences, and it can lead to unintended consequences. For example, if one house of Congress passes a low appropriation for a particular program, quite conceivably as a result of a vendetta by one member of the Appropriations Committee, that low appropriation governs the program no matter how high the other house sets it. On a regular appropriation, matters such as this as well as simple mistakes are taken care of in conference before a final bill is approved. Second, continuing appropriations lead to even greater managerial inefficiency than is customary in government activities. When an agency manager does not know what level of funds will be available for the whole fiscal year, the inevitable tendency is to be cautious in committing funds. Contracts are not let early in the year, to ensure that funds will be available later in the year. Then when the full appropriation is finally voted, there is frantic activity to commit funds before they expire. On some accounts, particularly those pertaining to salaries and expenses of employees, the tendency is to be optimistic: Don't fire anybody until it is absolutely necessary. If the optimism proves to have been false when the full appropriation becomes law, the agency may have to fire too many people or furlough (put on unpaid leave) an entire staff. There is ample evidence that this kind of behavior was developing as fiscal 1982 unfolded.

The legislative history of the 1982 budget ended on a sour note. In November, in the midst of the dispute

**TABLE 2**
**Status of fiscal year 1982 appropriations, as of 15 March 1982**
Budget authority in billions of dollars

| Title of appropriation | Date enacted | September administration request | House bill | Senate bill | Final action | Difference between final action and administration request |
|---|---|---|---|---|---|---|
| Agriculture and related agencies | 12/23/81 | 22.3 | 22.7 | 22.9 | 22.6 | +0.3 |
| Defense Department | 12/29/81 | 200.9 | 197.4 | 203.7 | 199.9 | −1.0 |
| District of Columbia | 12/4/81 | 0.6 | 0.5 | 0.6 | 0.6 | * |
| Energy and Water Development | 12/4/81 | 12.1 | 13.2 | 12.8 | 12.5 | +0.4 |
| Foreign Aid | 12/29/81 | 7.8 | 7.4 | 7.3 | 7.5 | −0.3 |
| HUD, Veterans, NASA | 12/23/81 | 58.7 | 62.6 | 60.5 | 60.4 | +1.7 |
| Interior and related agencies | 12/23/81 | 6.4 | 11.1 | 7.4 | 7.2 | +0.8 |
| Legislative Branch | 10/1/81 | 1.4 | 1.1[a] | 0.9[a] | 1.3 | −0.1 |
| Military Construction | 12/4/81 | 7.3 | 6.9 | 7.3 | 7.1 | −0.2 |
| Transportation and related agencies | 12/23/81 | 9.8 | 11.1 | 10.4 | 10.1 | +0.3 |
| Subtotal | | 327.3 | 334.0 | 333.8 | 329.2 | +1.9 |
| Labor, HHS, Education | — | 82.5 | 85.2 | 84.8[b] | — | — |
| State, Justice, Commerce, Judiciary | — | 8.2 | 8.7 | 8.6[b] | — | — |
| Treasury, Postal Service, General Government | — | 9.1 | 9.7 | 9.4[b] | — | — |

Sources: *Congressional Quarterly Weekly Report* 40 (16 January 1982), p. 103; and *Weekly Compilation of Presidential Documents* 17, nos. 43–53 (26 October 1981–4 January 1982).
*Less than $100 million
a. House bill excludes cost of Senate operation and vice versa.
b. Committee approved amount.

over the administration's reductions in appropriations and well after it had become evident that economic events had transformed the projected budget outcomes of the first concurrent resolution, both houses passed a second concurrent resolution. Instead of acknowledging the sharply changed economic circumstances and reaching some decision on appropriations still outstanding, the second concurrent resolution simply rubberstamped the outdated first resolution. In effect, Congress decided to put over into calendar 1982 any further decisions on the budget.

## PROSPECTS FOR PEACEFUL REFORM

The six years that the new congressional budget has been in effect cover a rough period in the nation's economic history, encompassing a recovery from the worst recession since the 1930s, the onset of high and highly variable inflation and interest rates, and the beginning of a period of retrenchment in federal spending. The congressional budgetary process has emerged from this period with some scars, but with the solid achievement of having proved resilient to changing

needs. Stimulating the economy called for accommodative Budget Committees, but as the economic and political trend moved toward spending restraint, the control mechanism was strengthened. When a president needed support in making a credible budget, the budgetary process provided an opportunity for joint action with the Congress, but it also provided room for a confrontation when the parties differed sharply. Such resilience could be interpreted as a lack of discipline, a process with no firm direction. But a more accurate lesson to be learned is that economic and political circumstances do change, and a flexible procedure is needed to allow changes in direction.

The budgetary history of the last few years raises two kinds of questions for the future. First, how will budget procedures affect the decisions to be made in the coming year? Second, what modifications in budgetary processes should be made in the longer term?

### Stalemate and Its Alternatives, 1983

Congressional final action on President Reagan's 1983 budget is uncommonly difficult to forecast. The public and Congress seem to agree that the projected deficits

—especially if adjusted to more realistic economic assumptions than those of the administration—are too high, but there is little evidence of a consensus on how to lower them. The major disagreements are over whether to raise revenues or lower outlays and which types of spending and taxing should bear the brunt of the burden. The prospects for a repeat performance by President Reagan in securing substantially complete acceptance of his budget seem remote. On the other hand, expecting Congress to fashion a budget entirely on its own is unrealistic. Any group in Congress that takes the lead on formulating a package—which would necessarily involve both higher taxes and major program cuts—would face the attendant political danger of being blamed (possibly by the president) for being the enemy of the elderly or the taxpayer, among others. It is hard to imagine that many congressmen would relish that role, and it is nearly inconceivable that the Democratic chairmen of the House Budget Committee and the Ways and Means Committee, who lost out to President Reagan in 1981, would voluntarily take that chance again.

Another possibility is that the president and Congress will agree to compromise. A bipartisan coalition in the Congress and the president would concur on a set of budgetary actions perceived as being built on the president's plan but with significant modifications. The agreed-upon package would almost certainly require a single vote since the individual parts of it could not pass in an election year; accordingly, such a package would probably take the form either of firm reconciliation instructions or even of specific legislation attached to some other bill, such as an impending act to raise the limit on the public debt. These shortcuts would further erode the conventional way of doing business in Congress; thus, opposition should be expected not only on substantive and partisan political grounds but also on procedural ones. This is a substantial number of hurdles to get over.

If any agreement is not reached, a stalemate is possible. Unlike other legislative action, a budgetary stalemate does not mean that nothing happens. In this case it would probably mean passing a first concurrent resolution on the budget that did not contain mandatory instructions to authorizing committees to come up with budget-saving legislation, and it might mean passing some appropriations that would greatly exceed the president's proposals, which would then be vetoed. Or the appropriations committees could fail to act at all. By October 1, a continuing resolution covering spending for most of the agencies and extending through the November election would be needed. Essentially, stalemate means that the difficult budget decisions of early 1982 would be pushed ahead to a post-election session of Congress, where a clearer consensus might emerge. This scenario appears to be fraught with great risks to the economy as uncertainty about the budget stretches out over months, and it greatly increases the possibility of a radical reaction to what will be perceived as an intractable budget mess. One such radical solution—a constitutional amendment to balance the budget—is discussed below.

It is important to end this account with the reminder that, if there were a solution to the budgetary impasse that commanded strong popular support, the budgetary process in the Congress would not stand in its way. Even with presidential opposition, one can imagine the congressional leadership riding the crest of a popular wave to beat back whatever fragmentary congressional opposition to a popular outcome developed. The Congressional Budget and Impoundment Control Act is proof that Congress, acting alone, can undertake changes that roil customary legislative relationships. Only when an attempt is made to preempt traditional legislative procedures with legislation that does not enjoy wide popular support does the system seem to fail. Should stalemate ensue in 1982, the blame should rest more on the failure to reach a consensus than on a shortcoming of the budgetary process. Indeed, the only hope of a better outcome lies in the budgetary process forcing all parties to attempt to reach such an agreement.

## Longer-Run Reforms

When the current budget crisis subsides, attention will turn to reexamination of the procedures by which Congress tackles the budget. Many members of Congress object to the steps taken in recent years as being an effort to make the Budget Committees all-powerful, thereby challenging the shared-power tradition and even raising questions about the role of party leadership in Congress. These members would like to curb the Budget Committees and make them responsive to the views and actions of other committees.

Such a revision to past procedures makes the most sense if future Congresses are uninterested in budgetary control but are mainly concerned with retuning priorities in a growing budget. In that case, enhancing the power of specialized committees would build on their strength in conducting full reviews of existing and proposed programs, considering legislative alternatives in detail, ascertaining the views of interest groups, and building constituent coalitions for government programs. These are functions that a budget committee, no matter how hard-working, cannot accomplish as effectively. The Budget Committees' role in this more traditional congressional arrangement would be to set fiscal policy and dollar limits on broad priorities. This primary function of coordination probably implies some revision of the congressional calendar to allow time for a sensible debate on priorities, some consideration of the process of setting economic assumptions so that the fiscal plans of each Budget Committee and the president's proposal are not being measured differently, and some better system for reducing each committee's incentives to get as much of the budget pie as it can. These changes would be marginal; the budgetary process could revert to what it was in 1976–79.

Procedural changes directed toward strengthening budget control, on the other hand, make the most sense if one envisions the environment of the future as one of heightened attention to slowing expenditure growth and cutting deficits. The crucial procedural innovation of the last few years—reconciliation early in the budget decision process—seems essential to any move to strengthen control. Because the predominant message for the congressional committees in this austerity scenario is that spending be cut and taxes raised, it is unrealistic to expect such measures to be put into effect unless committees are forced to act. This is the primary function of reconciliation: It allows Congress as a whole to order its committees to take actions.

Early reconciliation does not have to follow the pattern set by Stockman in 1981. The coverage of reconciliation instructions, in particular, may have gone overboard in that year. To control entitlement programs, there is general agreement that early reconciliation is a must. Authorizing committees are the only agents that can effect restraint by rewriting the laws, and they need external direction and adequate time. For the parts of federal spending that are not governed by entitlements, the most direct avenue of control is appropriations, not underlying laws, as in the 1981 reconciliation. Efforts to control appropriations by reconciling them in the second concurrent budget resolution at the end of a budget cycle are futile. Effective control of appropriations would mean that mandatory limits would have to be moved up to the first concurrent resolution. Since current budgetary procedures already contain a mechanism for providing dollar guidance to the Appropriations Committees,[15] all that would have to be done is to make such guidance mandatory, probably by moving the dollar limits into the budget resolution and stating them as instructions rather than as guidance. Naturally, this procedural reform would not solve the problem of the Appropriations Committees' shifting funds out of one budget year into the next; the simplest solution would be to move toward two-year appropriations bills and two-year mandatory instructions in the first budget resolution in pertinent parts of the budget.

Early reconciliation and early mandatory limits on appropriations would strengthen budgetary procedures, but they might create new problems that require further adjustments in the process. One of these is the timing of the first budget resolution. If the first resolution is to be the vehicle for mandatory spending cuts and tax increases, a case can be made for pushing the deadline for the resolution beyond May to give the budget committees time to digest the views of the president and of the committees. A case can also be made that the resolution should be issued before May to give working committees time to hold hearings, consult experts, and deliberate before writing the laws. No one wants to repeat the haste of legislation in 1981. Since the length of a year is immutable, both of these timing changes cannot be made.[16] One school of thought holds that the solution is a biennial budget. The first year would be devoted to events leading up to a first concurrent resolution and the second to carrying out that resolution by issuing two-year appropriations. This idea has some obvious problems relating to economic forecasts (see note 16) and to the timing of elections and presidential transitions.[17]

Another aspect of budget reform intended to strengthen existing procedures relates to the coverage of the budget and the scope of its control. The most obvious, though not widely recognized, weakness here is that current budgetary procedures are asymmetrically weak in dealing with taxation. Budget resolutions spell out spending limits by function while the only tax guidance offered is a single number for the amount revenues are to be raised or lowered. While there is a legislative structural reason for this imbalance[18] and the tax committees' hegemony inspires awe, stronger budget control implies greater detail in the budget resolution on the kind of tax changes it seeks. This could be accomplished by specifying broad targets by tax type (for example, income tax or excise tax) or by functional breakdown of tax expenditures (for example, to eliminate subsidies that the tax system gives to health and to housing). Along the same lines, centralized budget control could be strengthened by tighter controls on federal credit activities. For example, Congressmen Norman Y. Mineta and Edwin R. Bethune, Jr. (and 150 cosponsors) have suggested in House bill 2372 that targets for new direct loan obligations and loan guarantee commitments be incorporated in the first budget resolution and that the second resolution set binding limits on legislative activity pertaining to loans. The Mineta-Bethune bill would also require extensive reports on the status of federal credit activity and its relation to monetary policy from the Treasury and the Federal Reserve Board. Of equally serious concern for control are off-budget entities, but here the major activity is that of one organization, the Federal Financing Bank, and it can be dealt with in a number of ways that do not entail revamping budgetary procedures.[19]

The long list of reforms considered under this heading of strengthening budgetary procedures requires two cautionary notes. First, if all the reforms were implemented, the process might fall from its own weight. The work load from existing procedures is already heavy, and a new calendar, stronger directions, broader coverage, and so on could bring sheer confusion and weaken the whole structure. Second, it seems ludicrous to fortify congressional procedures for pinpointing fiscal policy decisions and fine-tuning federal credit activities without giving serious consideration to how these decisions interact with monetary policy. Setting standards for fiscal policy requires some understanding of, and presumably influence over, general monetary and credit conditions. There are now only weak links between Federal Reserve decisions and the budgetary process—mostly consisting of the central bank informing Congress of its goals and accomplishments—and no forum for arriving at the appropriate policy mix. This, of course, stems from a long tradition, but since we are breaking with the past in so many ways, maybe it is time for a review of congressional control over money and credit.

## A Constitutional Amendment to Balance the Budget

The most radical approach to changing budgetary procedures would be replacing the annual assessment of fiscal alternatives with a fixed external rule, such as a constitutional requirement that the budget be balanced each year. This approach is generally favored by those

who feel that the present system is biased toward excessive growth of government and deficit financing of public expenditures. The adoption of a constitutional amendment to balance the budget would considerably change existing budgetary procedures and other aspects of running the government.

One version of a constitutional amendment has passed the Senate Committee on the Judiciary and seems to gain momentum each time a budgetary target is missed or a deadline is not met. The amendment also seems to have election-year appeal because it offers members of Congress a chance to vote for the popular balanced budget without having to cut programs or raise taxes. Senate Joint Resolution 58 provides for a balanced budget by requiring Congress to adopt before the start of each fiscal year a "statement" (budget) in which planned outlays are no greater than total receipts. It also requires that the planned receipts of the budget grow no faster than national income grew in the previous calendar year. The final control is that "the Congress and the President shall ensure that actual outlays do not exceed the outlays set forth" in the budget statement. The amendment would allow a simple majority of each house of Congress to waive the receipts-growth clause, while a 60 percent vote in each house would be needed to approve a planned deficit.[20]

Obviously many facets of such a balanced budget amendment warrant extended discussion. Several criticisms can be listed. Eliminating discretionary fiscal policy might spur undue reliance on other aggregate control measures. Strict control of spending could shift attention to regulation as an alternative or to credit activities unless control over them was strengthened. The amendment's weak guidance for the rate of growth of receipts could make estimating receipts an even more political exercise than it is now. The case for the amendment boils down to a belief that history demonstrates that nothing less will bring about a balanced budget.[21]

One aspect of Senate Joint Resolution 58 directly impinges on budgetary procedures. The stipulation that the president and Congress ensure that actual outlays do not exceed planned outlays would seem to require a whole new set of budget-policing procedures. Currently the entire budgetary process is based on guiding legislation (authorizations or appropriations) that set upper limits on the commitment of funds over a certain period. The actual amount spent as a result of such commitments—outlays—is not directly controlled by existing procedures. Actual outlays either for a particular program or in the aggregate may exceed planned outlays for any number of reasons: an unforeseen economic or natural event; unexpectedly rapid completion of contracts; incorrect projections of case loads, prices, or interest rates; and so on. These factors would still exist under a constitutional amendment, so there would have to be an enforcement mechanism to ensure that if a preponderance of the uncontrolled items were overrunning the planned outlay level, some underruns would be available for offset. In practice, this would almost certainly mean that Congress would have to delegate to the president the power to make such adjustments.[22] If Congress made such a delegation with no constraints, this would give a president broad license to impound (not spend appropriated) funds, which ironically was the "abuse of power" (by President Nixon) that brought on budget reform in the first place. Giving the president a line-item veto, a measure favored by President Reagan, would have a similar effect. An alternative would be for Congress to delegate the power to impound subject to limits on how much any particular program could be cut. This, in turn, is the equivalent of agencies living under an insecurity similar to that of a continuing resolution: not knowing in advance how much they will have to spend.[23]

A constitutional amendment would greatly change federal budgeting. It would inevitably shift more power to the executive branch and would focus more attention on matters such as the budget being on target—just as public attention now focuses on money supply growth being on target—and less attention on broad budget policy goals. For more than just the obvious reasons a constitutional amendment would therefore open a new chapter on how the federal government conducts its operations.[24]

## CONCLUSION

The preoccupation of this article with budgetary decision-making processes should not divert attention from the real issues behind the policy crisis. Government officials are seeking to find a non-inflationary way to move massive amounts of resources from consumer industries to investment and defense industries, from the public to the private sector, from Washington to the state capitals, from the dole to wages and dividends, from the current standard of living to the nation's future well-being. Under the best circumstances, these changes would be hard to bring off. The fact that we are attempting to move very fast only heightens the dislocations that change always brings. Add a partisan political environment and a Hippocratic ethic for politicians ("Do no harm") and you have a recipe for stalemate or a hypocritical compromise ("Do no electoral damage").

No budgetary process or external imperative can make tough decisions easy. The present procedures have proved flexible enough in the past to accommodate a variety of economic circumstances. As economic and political changes have made a shift to greater restraint in public spending seem desirable, budgetary control procedures have been strengthened and the shift has been carried out. The budgetary process would help any grand compromise reached in 1982 between the president and Congress by providing a legislative vehicle that forced all parties to such an agreement to join. And the process can be strengthened for future years by formally incorporating early reconciliation and increasing the scope of budget resolutions. Or it can be put back to the guidance procedures of budget reform's early years. The choice will depend on the expected need for tightness of budgetary control.

A constitutional amendment to balance the budget at bottom expresses a lack of faith that Congress can achieve budgetary control and a strong belief in the importance of such an achievement. The difficulties of reaching a budget compromise in 1982 have apparently created a climate where voting for a constitutional amendment to balance the budget is an easy vote for an esteemed goal. In reality, such an amendment would bring about profound changes in the government, not all of which are intended by its proponents.

*This article is adapted from the author's essay in the recent book* Setting National Priorities: The 1983 Budget, *published by the Brookings Institution and edited by Joseph A. Pechman. The author thanks Henry J. Aaron, Arthur M. Hauptman, Darwin G. Johnson, and Robert D. Reischauer for helpful comments, Alice M. Rivlin for research assistance, and Jane R. Taylor for secretarial assistance.*

## NOTES

1. See William Greider, "The Education of David Stockman," *Atlantic Monthly,* December 1981, pp. 27–54.

2. Dale Tate, "Reconciliation's Long Term Consequences in Question as Reagan Signs Massive Bill," *Congressional Quarterly Weekly Report* 39 (15 August 1981): 1463–1466.

3. The budget document itself is not a proposed law. It is accompanied by proposed laws that are very specific. There is no single law that can be called "the budget." See the discussion in the text of budget resolutions.

4. And of laws passed earlier which established "permanent appropriations" (such as for interest on the national debt) that do not require annual legislation.

5. The debt subject to statutory limit includes virtually all Treasury debt whether owned by the public or by federal agencies. The unified budget deficit ("the deficit" in everyday parlance), on the other hand, nets out the annual surplus of federal trust funds (almost always held in the form of Treasury securities), and it does not include the deficit of off-budget entities, which are financed by the issue of Treasury debt. Thus the annual increase in the debt subject to statutory limit (except for small adjustments relating to cash accounts) equals the unified budget deficit plus the trust fund surplus plus the deficit of off-budget entities. The debt subject to statutory limit will rise even if the budget, as conventionally defined, is balanced; it will cease rising only if there is a surplus on non-trust fund accounts ("federal funds") equal to or greater than the deficit of off-budget entities. See *Budget of the United States Government, Fiscal Year 1983, Special Analysis E: Borrowing and Debt* (Washington, D.C.: Government Printing Office).

6. The 1974 act required that authorizing legislation be reported by committees no later than May 15, but numerous waivers of procedure have weakened this constraint.

7. See Allen Schick, *Reconciliation and the Congressional Budget Process* (Washington, D.C.: American Enterprise Institute for Public Policy Research, 1981).

8. The legislative savings were supported by the Carter administration, but its influence with Congress was low in mid-1979, the period in which the president went on a solitary retreat and then fired several members of the cabinet.

9. Further savings were assumed to be made on appropriations. As a safeguard, the first resolution called for delaying the transmittal to the president of appropriations bills that exceeded the resolution targets until a second resolution had been approved.

10. One committee, the House Energy and Commerce Committee, could not agree on a response. Its chairman forwarded Democratic proposals to the House Budget Committee. It is not clear what sanctions can be taken against a committee that refuses to comply—other than the Budget Committee writing its own legislation.

11. Ronald Reagan, "The President's News Conference of June 16, 1981," *Weekly Compilation of Presidential Documents* 17 (22 June 1981), p. 632.

12. As quoted in Greider, "Education of David Stockman," p. 51.

13. The legislative branch appropriation was incorporated into the first continuing appropriation resolution.

14. Even so, "current rate" is an ambiguous term because "the" rate of the previous fiscal year may be quite different rates for each quarter (which is generally the period over which the OMB apportions appropriations to agencies) and the final quarter of the fiscal year may not reflect what the Appropriations Committee intends as the limit for the next period.

15. The mechanism is the allocation of dollar limits by committee under section 302 of the Congressional Budget and Impoundment Control Act.

16. Starting the new fiscal year in January rather than October to lengthen the decision period is regarded as out of the question, if only because economic forecasts would have to be made so far in advance that they would be less credible than they are now.

17. If a two-year cycle commenced in October of even-numbered years, President Reagan's first budget proposal made with the help of a full staff would be for the two years starting in October 1984, only a few months before his term expires. Starting in an odd year interposes a congressional election in the middle of the two-year deliberative process.

18. A single spending number could not be allocated among the various committees, but the functional breakdown in the budget resolutions makes this feasible. However, there is only one tax committee in each house, so a single revenue target can be allocated to its proper committee.

19. See Congressional Budget Office, *The Federal Financing Bank and the Budgetary Treatment of Federal Credit Activities* (CBO, 1982); and Andrew S. Carron, "Fiscal Activities outside the Budget," in Joseph A. Pechman, ed., *Setting National Priorities: The 1982 Budget* (Washington, D.C.: Brookings Institution, 1981), pp. 261–269.

20. There is also a specific waiver for a declaration of war and a section forbidding Congress to require states to "engage in additional activities" unless the federal government puts up all the necessary funds. See U.S. Congress. Senate. *Balanced Budget—Tax Limitation Constitutional Amendment.* 97th Cong., 1st sess. S. Rept. 97-151, p. 2.

21. For a fuller discussion of the pros and cons of a balanced budget amendment, see Bruce K. MacLaury, "Proposals to Limit Federal Spending and Balance the Budget," in Joseph A. Pechman, ed., *Setting National Priorities: The 1980 Budget* (Washington, D.C.: Brookings Institution, 1979), pp. 213–223; and Alvin Rabushka and William Craig Stubblebine, eds., *Constraining Federal Taxing and Spending* (Stanford, Calif.: Hoover Institution, forthcoming).

22. Congress could assign a committee the power to ensure that actual outlays stayed on target or it could regularly appropriate so little that an overrun could not occur. Neither

approach would last long: committees have no executive power, which is necessary to control outlays, and sham outlay estimates are sitting ducks for frustrated spending committees.

23. It is actually a greater insecurity because a continuing resolution creates uncertainties about the level of funds an agency can *commit* while the balanced budget amendment creates uncertainty about *spending,* something that most agencies have much less ability to control.

24. If two-thirds of both houses of Congress approved an amendment like Senate Joint Resolution 58, it would then have to be ratified by three-quarters of the state legislatures and would take effect in the second fiscal year after ratification. Since the amendment takes spending and taxing for the preceding year as a base, budgeting up to the effective date would probably be very divisive.

# Budget Control Is Alive and Well
## Case Study of a County Government

Jane Massey
Jeffrey D. Straussman

The period from 1975 to the present has hardly been dull for students and practitioners of public budgeting. A major preoccupation has been a search for strategies and tactics to shrink the size of government. Indeed, a number of articles have appeared on the general theme of "cutback management."[1]

While these articles help us consider the alternatives available for a fiscally strained public sector, they treat cutback strategies as a reaction to an identifiable crisis. There is good reason for this. We tend to identify resource scarcity at the state and local level with episodes like California's Proposition 13, Massachusetts' Proposition 2½, and President Reagan's budget retrenchment. In addition, the financial woes of New York City, Cleveland, and Detroit reinforce the concept of cutback management as a response to a specific series of events.

But fiscal stress also can affect governments gradually. When revenue growth lags pressures to spend, public officials face an insidious fiscal constraint—creeping scarcity, if you will—that may characterize the public sector during the 1980s.[2]

From *Public Budgeting and Finance,* Vol. 1, pp. 3–11. Copyright 1981. Reprinted by permission.

Traumatic fiscal stress is likely to elicit a different cutback response than insidious fiscal constraint. For one thing, public officials may find it easier to justify more radical solutions to financial problems. An illustration comes from Detroit where Mayor Coleman Young's "get tough" stance toward the municipal unions in the wake of the city's financial crisis was facilitated by the need for quick action. The mayor demanded that the unions accept a two-year wage freeze as part of an overall financial plan to bring the city back to solvency. The unions balked. The mayor threatened to lay off city workers, and the unions backed down.[3] But most public officials never get an opportunity to take center stage in a financial drama. Their humdrum world of insidious fiscal constraint goes largely unnoticed. Yet there are many more budgetary belt-tightening situations than dramatic fiscal crises.

In the spring and summer of 1981, the authors discussed budget control practices with department heads and elected officials of a nonmetropolitan county in New York State. By studying this county, we hoped to gain a better understanding of the responses to resource scarcity and to consider the potential consequences of those responses for budget control and service delivery. While we realize the dangers of generalizing from one case, we believe that thousands of local governments share many characteristics with this county. The county's fiscal problems and its attendant responses are not as dramatic as those of governments facing traumatic crises, but we think they are more typical of the setting in which most budgetary actions are taken.

The county we visited didn't fit the textbooks. There is no budget office, no budget analysts, not even a chief executive. Rather, the county is governed by a board composed of elected town supervisors. Decisions are made by the Board of Supervisors (led by a chairman) through a weighted voting system based on the population of the towns in the county. The board is divided into committees that oversee policies in their respective domains and the county departments responsible for administering county programs. The chief financial official is an elected county treasurer who also acts as a budget officer. County officials are politically and fiscally conservative. It appeared that budget control would come naturally to these folks.

There are two dimensions to the county's budget control orientation. While this county, like other local governments, has been forced to increase spending by state and federal mandates, it remains concerned with providing basic services at a moderate level. When Ronald Reagan talked about "getting government off our backs," he was playing this county's theme song. The county's budget control orientation is in keeping with its general orientation toward limited government.

But the control orientation goes beyond fiscal philosophy. The need to hold down spending in the county because of fiscal stress is increasingly important and a top priority. There are three basic reasons for the county's financial difficulties. First, county officials are unwilling to raise additional local revenues by increasing property taxes. Like the city councillors in Oakland, California, described by Arnold Meltsner in *The Politics of City Revenue,*[4] the members of the Board of Supervisors feel that property taxes have reached their upper political limit. They still talk about the political fallout from an outraged citizenry when taxes were increased sharply in 1976. They do not want to face an angry electorate again.

Second, like other local governments, the county faces sharp reductions in state and federal aid. (Forty percent of the county's revenues now come from intergovernmental aid.) Recent federal budget cutbacks will worsen this revenue squeeze. Third, the county must meet rising costs for labor, energy, and many other goods and services.

The budget control orientation of the county is reminiscent of early budget reforms. Line itemization is practiced faithfully, and careful scrutiny of departmental spending requests is made to ensure that the proposed spending is in accord with legislative intent, and that the proposed spending is "really necessary." Faced with new challenges to curb spending, county officials instinctively turn to the standard approaches to hold down expenditures: travel restrictions, personnel controls, and transfer controls. County officials use these control mechanisms much in the same way that budgetary reformers did decades earlier.

## WATCH YOUR PENNIES AND THE DOLLARS WILL TAKE CARE OF THEMSELVES

Watching your pennies as an operating budgetary philosophy for local governments epitomizes a budget control orientation. Pennypinching is what the county does best. This is illustrated by the use of three traditional budget control procedures: travel, personnel, and budget transfers.

Consider travel controls. Out-of-state trips, generally to conferences and other meetings, require prior approval by the Board of Supervisors. The board reviews every travel request even though travel funds have been appropriated for the fiscal year in question. The review procedure serves two basic purposes. If the board does not feel that the proposed travel is necessary or adequately justified, the request is likely to be denied. In a sense, this is the board's version of legislative oversight. But the second purpose is clearly more important. By reviewing each travel request, the Board of Supervisors can slow spending if it threatens to outstrip available revenues. Naturally, the travel policy is irritating to a few department heads. One department head, probably the one most affected by it because of the number of professionals in his agency, considers the board's approach to travel an obstacle to good management. Yet, the travel policy forces managers to consider more carefully the justification for having employees attend seminars, workshops, or conferences.

Since this county is experiencing insidious fiscal constraint, expenditures for travel are viewed as a luxury. The county therefore requires employees to share a portion of the cost of attending a conference by paying for their own transportation. One might question whether this is the most effective way to impose travel controls on county personnel. Nevertheless, it saves the county some money, probably discourages travel, and is in keeping with the supervisors' attitude that the employee receives as much, or more, of the benefits from travel as does the county.

There is nothing unique about the county's approach to travel. Travel controls have usually been imposed during periods of budgetary stringency and relaxed when the budget climate brightens. In other words, cyclical variation in the financial health of governments has been accompanied by similar fluctuations in control patterns. Yet, the very character of insidious fiscal constraint has produced a modicum of certainty in travel policy. Many county professionals who would like to travel to meetings know the attitude of the Board of Supervisors toward travel. They may not like it, they grumble, but they are not surprised by it because it is nothing new. In many ways, the approach toward travel symbolizes the pennypinching that is a logical outgrowth of insidious fiscal constraint.

The largest single cost for the county is labor. So it comes as no surprise that county officials try to curb personnel growth. To some supervisors this seems like a losing battle, since, in the 1970s, county personnel went from 300 to 681 positions. The explanation for this growth is not difficult to find. Much of it is in federal and state-mandated social services and mental health programs. Still, even this politically conservative county has not been immune from local pressures to spend. The county has added a personnel department and a fire control department, and it has expanded the public health and planning departments. While supervisors are aware of this growth in personnel, they find it difficult to identify all of the causes of the expansion. They are trying to halt the trend through a policy of personnel vacancy review.

The vacancy review policy consists of a four-step approval process which must be satisfied before a department head can fill a vacancy (or create a new position). First, the department head must obtain approval from the committee which oversees the department. Committee approval allows the department head to submit a request with accompanying justification to the director of personnel. After studying the request and consulting with the board's personnel committee, the director of personnel makes a recommendation to the county's version of a ways and means committee. This committee makes its recommendation to the full board. The final action is passage by the board of a resolution authorizing the department head to fill the vacancy. While the process sounds extremely bureaucratic, in this small county government it could be completed in two to four weeks.

Unlike the travel controls discussed earlier, the vacancy review procedure represents a more deliberate effort to curb county spending. This is not obvious at first glance. Like many governments faced with insidious fiscal constraint, the county has always had a vacancy review procedure. The new policy simply adds one step to the old procedure; that is, the department head's request to fill the vacant position is reviewed by the director of personnel who makes a recommendation. This additional hurdle is disliked by some department heads. But the supervisors feel that the involvement of a professional personnel specialist will allow them to make more informed decisions on county positions. From a budgetary perspective, the vacancy review procedure has a simple logic. It causes some delay in filling positions, which saves the county some money. And saving money is what the county's control techniques are all about. The county's approach to position vacancies is much like the pattern of "repetitive budgeting" that Naomi Caiden and Aaron Wildavsky found in poor countries.[5] Like finance ministers in developing countries, the Board of Supervisors curbs spending through delay—a rational response to insidious fiscal constraint.

The control orientation of the county is carried even further through budget classification and transfer controls. Recent budget innovations in the county are being used to strengthen the control capabilities of county officials. This is illustrated by the computerization of the county's budget.

The county uses a detailed line-item budget which reinforces the existing expenditure control emphasis. Each budgeted position is listed separately. So is each type of equipment to be purchased. The current budget provides a great deal of information on county expenditures. A computer printout of the adopted county budget now allows managers, the county treasurer, and supervisors to track spending during the year. The system also allows the county to keep accounts with unencumbered funds open after the end of the fiscal year rather than closing all accounts at the end of the year as was done in the past. With the added capability of the computerized system, the treasurer is experimenting with increasing the detail in the accounts. Instead of having a line-item called "office supplies" or "publications," a sub-item showing each type of office supply or each specific journal subscription would be listed. The treasurer believes that more detail would increase managerial accountability and aid the Board of Supervisors in making budget decisions.

The treasurer also believes that computerization could be applied to limit the discretion of department heads over funds within an account. Currently, department heads do not need approval for within-account line-item transfers (e.g., from "office supplies" to "postage"). The treasurer would support a move to require department heads to obtain authorization prior to modifying any of their budget line-items. He believes that the more closely a manager can be held to the original budget, the higher the level of accountability and the less waste there will be. The treasurer's interest in accomplishing these changes is in keeping with the county's penny watching orientation. It also indicates the current direction of change. Like the new vacancy review policy, computerization is viewed as a way to improve the capacity to exercise better budget control. What does "better" mean in this context? Saving more money is the obvious answer.

## THE LIMITS OF CONTROL

There is a long-standing joke in government that when you are up to your hips in alligators, it is hard to remember that your original objective was to drain the swamp. Like many governments, the county seems to have a problem keeping its central mission of service delivery in mind while trying to fight off the alligators of insidious fiscal constraint. The county is in a difficult position. If it could take a broad look at service delivery in respect to its priorities, the swamp might be drained and the alligators would go away. But the need to cut costs quickly, coupled with a lack of financial and political resources to make service decisions, deprives the county of that perspective.

In addition to the control measures discussed earlier, the county has taken other alligator-fighting measures. The county no longer patrols county lakes or provides security services for charitable fund raising events. It has delayed some resurfacing work on county roads. It is considering a change to equipment leasing rather than purchase. But the budget controls and cuts such as these are offset by strong pressures to spend.

The county budget grew substantially in the 1970s. What has caused the growth? Like other local governments, a great part of the expansion comes from intergovernmental programs and state and federal mandates. The programs and mandates are not unique to the county. Social services, mental health and public health, are largely responsible for the growth. Moreover, much of the law enforcement activities are mandated by the state. The county must meet expensive state mandates for jail staffing, and the aging jail facilities will have to be replaced in the near future—an unpopular expense that will create a substantial financial burden for this small county.

Intergovernmental programs and federal and state mandates are largely beyond the control of the county. So are the cuts in revenue sources. Specifically, the state has reduced state aid; the federal government has reduced revenue sharing funds and eliminated the CETA Program. These two pressures on the county— pressures to spend coupled with revenue shortfalls— are likely to worsen. While budgetary belt tightening has been the dominant response of county officials to

these outside pressures, they will soon require action that goes beyond the routines of budget control.

Pressures to spend are also generated by efforts to professionalize county government. The most important move toward professionalization has been the hiring of a director of personnel, a new position for the county. The county now has a professional to represent it at the bargaining table. The director hopes to improve the personnel classification system, to make wage and salary surveys, to stimulate employee development, safety and orientation programs, and to devise incentive systems to reduce absenteeism and improve efficiency. While the cost of these professional innovations is not known, surely any improvements in the county's efficiency or effectiveness would take some time to be realized. In the short run, the changes will cost money for the personnel director's salary and necessary equipment, supplies, and staff.

There is some sentiment among the supervisors for hiring a county administrator. Currently, the board and its chairman have little staff support and must spend considerable time in meetings. The burden of managing county government is increasingly heavy on these part-time legislators. There is also some concern about the board's reliance on recommendations from department heads, especially on matters in which the department heads have a vested interest. Hiring a county administrator would enable the board to spend less time on administrative matters and might provide it with an improved source of information and assistance. But again, the positive results of improved administration would be felt in the long term, while the costs would be borne at once.

There are other examples of the county's move toward increased professionalization. The county treasurer put a trained accountant on his staff. He is also interested in meeting with area county treasurers on a regular basis to talk about mutual problems. The sheriff's department has been going through growing pains during the last ten years as it has become more professional.

The atmosphere in the county is one of "creeping professionalism." Public officials want better government. But above all they want cheaper government. However, professionalism is geared toward the long term. Not only is it unlikely to produce short-term savings, it is likely to increase short-run costs. This problem may not be apparent to county officials who want both more professionalism and less spending.

The long-term versus short-term perspective is illustrated by the vacancy review policy. As a short-term budget control device it cannot be faulted. But it may not be the best way to undertake a review of county positions. Control is clearly a part of the annual budget cycle. On the other hand, a thorough review of county personnel positions, even in a small county like this one, is a major undertaking that can better be conducted apart from the budget process.

## CONCLUSION

Are there any lessons that could be drawn from this study of a small county that has been wrestling with insidious fiscal constraint for many years? We think so. Books have been written about the price, real and imagined, that a city like New York paid when it was on the brink of financial collapse.[6] In our case study, the price is smaller, but there are more local governments that resemble this little county than the New Yorks, Clevelands, and Detroits.

Local governments afflicted with insidious fiscal constraint are likely to turn to budget control procedures to hold down spending. There is a good reason for this; controls tend to be effective. Budget controls *do* save money. Public officials in the county we studied did not suddenly turn to budget controls for a financial quick fix. The traditional controls on travel, personnel, and budgetary transfers were always in place. As pressure to curb spending increased, controls were used more extensively. While budget control is a constant struggle, county officials are willing to expand control procedures, as illustrated by the new vacancy review procedure and the computerization of the budget. They have every reason to believe that these additional control procedures are effective—and they are probably correct in this assessment.

Can one justifiably criticize the county for its preoccupation with budget control? Consider a possible by-product of the severe limitations on travel. It is conceivable that the savings generated by the travel controls would be offset by losses in employee productivity. The relationship between travel and productivity is subject to debate, but that is exactly the point. A similar argument can be made about the treasurer's infatuation with computerization of the county budget, to exert more expenditure control mainly by restricting the transfer authority of department heads. Again, we might hypothesize that a reduction in managerial discretion is dysfunctional. Specifically, we might argue

that excessive controls on travel, personnel, and budget transfers adversely affect efficiency and are therefore counterproductive.

If we criticize the county—and by implication thousands of local governments that behave as it does—along the lines suggested above, a fundamental justification for budget control is ignored. A recent article by Fred Thompson and William Zumeta reminds us that expenditure controls try to achieve three objectives: efficiency, compliance with legislative intent, and a balanced budget.[7] These three objectives are not always compatible, and they may not be equally obtainable at a given point in time. Which control objective is predominant? Thompson and Zumeta argue that balancing the budget is more important to budgetary decision makers than the other two. The county we studied reflects this orientation. To the extent that insidious fiscal constraint forces local government officials to search for ways to avoid budget deficits, the stress on budget balancing makes sense—even when it is at the expense of efficiency. Moreover, there is a lesson here for local governments that face more dramatic, acute attacks of financial stress. Cities like Detroit, Cleveland, and New York obviously are different from local governments that have lived with insidious fiscal constraint for years. But they must also begin pennypinching budget control, especially with the objective of balancing the budget foremost in mind. Budget control is not sufficient, but it is clearly necessary.

Why isn't a control orientation sufficient for a county that has faced insidious fiscal constraint for years? The county has pressures on it that require a perspective that goes beyond budget control. Intergovernmental programs coupled with state and federal mandates are especially onerous when fiscal constraint worsens. A preoccupation with control alone does not allow local government officials to step back and evaluate broader multiyear ramifications of decisions that are largely beyond their immediate control. In fact, budget controls may be used to cut locally funded programs and activities much more severely than programs with significant amounts of intergovernmental aid. If this happens, an overbearing control orientation could produce unintended changes in program priorities.

The early reformers who wrote about budgeting were aware of the limits of budget control. It is instructive to return to the writings of A.E. Buck,[8] Frederick Cleveland,[9] and Lent Upson[10] to appreciate this point. From their perspective, control, by itself, was not sufficient for sound public budgeting. Recall the lament by Upson in his 1924 article in *The Annals*:

> The average city official confronted with the budget finds nothing in it that enables him to determine in a large way the value of the activities that are rendered the public, or in a lesser way the degree of efficiency with which such activities are conducted.[11]

Upson was, of course, pushing for a public budgeting perspective that would go beyond control to include a management orientation. Upson and the other early reformers described public budgeting in terms which we all recognize through Allen Schick's classic typology of control, management, and planning.[12] Yet, when we compare the views of the early reformers with the county we investigated, it seems that the control route is predominant. Insidious fiscal constraint requires this emphasis. Still, external pressures, creeping professionalism, and even innovation as symbolized by the computerization of the budget process all suggest that management and budget planning need to be acknowledged and developed. The fiscal challenges of the coming years will likely force the county officials beyond their budget control orientation.

Insidious fiscal constraint, by definition, is ongoing. It afflicts many local governments today. Yet, insidious fiscal constraint is not static. In a county like the one we studied, insidious fiscal constraint is unlikely to improve. Given a few "bad breaks"—increasingly severe state and federal cutbacks, a judicial mandate to improve the jail, a couple of plant closings—the county could easily slip into a more traumatic period of stress. Budget controls were never meant to resolve underlying causes of fiscal stress. But the first step toward alleviating resource scarcity may well lie in local governments' ability to use control to preserve short-term financial health.

## NOTES

1. See Charles H. Levine, "Organizational Decline and Cutback Management," *Public Administration Review*, Vol. 38, No. 4 (July/August 1978), pp. 316–325; and Carol W. Lewis and Anthony T. Logalbo, "Cutback Principles and Practices: A Checklist for Managers," *Public Administration Review*, Vol. 40, No. 2 (March/April 1980), pp. 184–188.

2. For a classification of types of resource scarcity and their implications for budgeting, see Allen Schick, "Budgetary Adaptations to Resource Scarcity," in *Fiscal Stress and Public Policy*, eds. Charles H. Levine and Irene Rubin (Beverly Hills: Sage Publications, 1980), pp. 113–134.

3. John Holusha, "Detroit Rescue Plan Seems to Clear Union Hurdle," *The New York Times* (July 30, 1981), p. 14.

4. Arnold J. Meltsner, *The Politics of City Revenue* (Berkeley: University of California Press, 1971).

5. Naomi Caiden and Aaron Wildavsky, *Planning and Budgeting in Poor Countries* (New York: Wiley and Sons, 1974), p. 71.

6. There is no shortage of interpretations of New York's financial crisis. Two different ones are Ken Auletta, *The Streets Were Paved With Gold* (New York: Random House, 1979), and Charles R. Morris, *The Cost of Good Intentions* (New York: W. W. Norton and Company, 1980).

7. Fred Thompson and William Zumeta, "Control and Controls: A Reexamination of Control Patterns in Budget Execution," *Policy Sciences*, Vol. 13 (February 1981), pp. 25–50.

8. A. E. Buck, "The Development of the Budget Idea in the United States," *The Annals*, Vol. CXIII (May 1924), pp. 31–39.

9. Frederick A. Cleveland, "Evolution of the Budget Idea in the United States," *The Annals*, Vol. LXII (November 1915), pp. 15–35.

10. Lent D. Upson, "Half-Time Budget Methods," *The Annals*, Vol. CXIII (May 1924), pp. 69–74.

11. Ibid, p. 72.

12. Allen Schick, "The Road to PPB: The Stages of Budget Reform," *Public Administration Review*, Vol. 26, No. 5 (December 1966), pp. 243–258.

# CHAPTER SIX

# Personnel

## Reforming Reform
### Challenging the Assumptions for Improving Public Employees' Performance

Phil Godwin
John Needham

### INTRODUCTION

New York Mayor Edward Koch, in addressing a gathering of representatives of local and state government personnel agencies and state legislatures, called public personnel management reform "the most pressing problem in American government today."[1] Mayor Koch's statement is representative of a growing interest at the state and local levels of government in improving their service to the public by reforming their personnel systems.[2] The Federal Government's Civil Service Reform Act of 1978 (CSRA) has been the catalyst for much of this interest.

This article will examine three critical assumptions upon which the Civil Service Reform Act and many state and local reform efforts are based. The assumptions, we believe, are weak and poorly supported, and are too dependent upon the notion that certain private sector management principles can improve performance in public sector organizations. The first assumption we will challenge is that the political executive (e.g., President, Governor, Mayor), when functioning as head of government, has duties, powers, and re-

From *Public Personnel Management,* (Summer, 1981), Vol. 9, No. 3, pp. 233–242. Copyright 1981, International Personnel Management Association. Reprinted by permission.

sponsibilities like those of a chief executive officer of a private business when dealing with matters of personnel administration. The second assumption inherent in civil service reform efforts is that public managers have too little authority in managing their employees. This assumption is closely linked with the third—that "merit pay" in public sector organizations can improve managerial performance.

These assumptions are examined in terms of their potential impact on the Federal Government and on those state and local governments which have implemented, or are planning to implement, similar personnel management reforms.

### THE POLITICAL EXECUTIVE AS CHIEF EXECUTIVE OFFICER

The first key assumption upon which the civil service reform efforts are based is that a political executive is elected to implement an electoral mandate and is, therefore, accountable to the people for the success or failure of executing this mandate. Since public employees are responsible for implementing the executive's programs and because the public workforce is governed by the personnel system, that system must be accountable to the executive. Alan Campbell, former Director of the Office of Personnel Management, clearly stated the Carter Administration's case during the debate on CSRA:

New policy makers arrive with mandates for change and find that though they can change structures and appearances, it is very difficult to make dramatic changes in direction. In signing the bill which granted him general reorganization authority, therefore, President Carter expressed his commitment to "move as quickly as possible to improve the efficiency and the effectiveness and the sensitivity of the federal government bureaucracy in dealing with the needs of the American people." This, he believes, "was one of the campaign issues that induced the American people to give [him] their support."[3]

President Carter strongly supported the view concerning the personnel system when he said in announcing civil service reform that:

> The single most important step that we can take [in improving the operations of the government] is a thoroughgoing reform of the civil service system.[4]

Public policy experts outside the Carter Administration also supported the assumption that the civil service should be accountable to the political executive. James Sundquist, representing the National Academy of Public Administration, in testimony before the Senate committee that considered the reform legislation, said that the legislation

> . . . seeks to give the President the means for leadership over the government. He has the responsibility for executing the laws. He needs to be able to upgrade and direct and manage the personnel systems of the government in order to do that.[5]

With this view, Sundquist pointed out the deficiencies that existed before reform. He continued:

> . . . adverse relationships arise now from the rigidities of the [civil service] system. A political officer comes in with the responsibility to get the job done. He finds a staff of career civil servants frozen into their jobs and if he can't get along with them, he finds he can't move them, he has to organize around them.[6]

This assumption is the natural outgrowth of over 50 years of Government reform in the area concerned with the Executive management of public programs both at the Federal and state levels of Government—especially at the state level where emphasis has been on strengthening the powers of the Governor's office.

In the Federal Government, of course, this assumption culminated in CSRA, which is now 2 years old. This assumption has not been questioned seriously at the national level and now is forming the basis for reforms at both state and local levels.[7]

Frederick Thayer puts forth a powerful argument that private sector efficiency ethics dominate this concept of accountability as embodied in CSRA. He states:

> . . . the theory of the President and his advisors holds that public and business administration are different, but the difference lies in the superiority of business administration. The authors of the *Final Staff Report* indicate time and again that government personnel management can best be improved by searching out and copying . . . the methods that are used widely and effectively in private industry.[8]

## Differences Between Public and Private Executives

The notion that the political chief executive should be the equivalent of a private sector chief executive officer ignores the public sector concept of separation of powers. The Presidency, which has generally served as the model for both state and local governments in structuring their executive functions, is a co-equal of the Congress in managing the government and its personnel. This fact disputes the contention that the executive function of a government is similar to that of a private corporation. The recent book *American Bureaucracy* points to this equality by comparing the actual powers of the Congress with those of the President in the following three critical areas of management:

### ORGANIZATIONAL STRUCTURE

Congress has the principal powers in organizing the bureaucracy. Congress establishes and abolishes agencies and it determines where they are to be located in the executive branch. This is one of the major powers of the Congress regarding administrative organization.

### ORGANIZATIONAL RESOURCES

Congress also has the final authority in supplying resources to the bureaucracy. It exercises this authority in two ways. First, it can and does establish personnel ceilings for agencies and second, it has the power of appropriation. Congress, once it establishes an agency, can, through the power of appropriation, be sure that the agency carries on with its original congressional mandate. It is the legislative branch which determines what an agency can or cannot do.

### PERSONNEL

The Constitution gives Congress the power to take part in certain Presidential appointments, which are to be "by and with the advice and consent of the Senate." Congress may, of course, extend the sharing of the appointive power when it sets up new agencies.[9]

The political executive's role is primarily one of policy leadership; the elements of this role comprise the following: setting objectives, formulating policies to meet these objectives, securing legislative support to implement the policies and appointing personnel to carry out the adopted policies. While this description may ostensibly resemble the role of the private sector manager, it is not substantially similar. The reasons for this are clear. The political executive will devote much of his/her time and energy to seeking agreement among the legislative, bureaucratic and external principles on what the policy should be, while the private sector manager will devote most of his/her time and energy in the implementation of policies that were decided upon in a far less complex process. The private sector executive, subject to the concurrence of the Board of Directors, can set the organization's goals, and shift and change structures, procedures, and personnel to suit personal and organizational needs. The private sector executive also monitors results and reviews key operation decisions as well as deals with the principal outsiders for the organization. With the possible exception of the military, the President has none of these powers often held by the private sector executive. The programs which the political executive must implement are established by law—particularly at the state level, where there are numerous boards and commissions over which the chief executive has little or no control. This is far from the model of the private sector executive.

### The Merit System

The notion that industry should provide the model for public executives is also contradicted by the merit system principles which dominate Federal and state civil service operations. Since the mid 1880s, when civil service concepts came into being, the predominant ethic that has governed the civil service has been the concept of "merit." Bernard Rosen, former Executive Director of the U. S. Civil Service Commission, in a monograph prepared for the House Committee on Post Office and Civil Service, states the reasons for the merit system in public employment. He points to the principal differences between the public and private sector concepts of personnel management. Rosen writes:

Numerous, well-supported reasons for having a merit system include the following:

- Assures needed expertise for continuity in government regardless of changes in Administration or times of crises.
- Makes more certain that laws are carried out and public services are delivered on a fair and impartial basis thus strengthening the people's confidence in our form of government.
- Attracts and retains well-qualified, honest people in the public service thereby increasing efficiency and enhancing the quality of government operations.
- Provides a sound basis for equal employment opportunity.
- Establishes a good foundation for effective relations with unions by making clear the Government's commitment to deal fairly on all matters of employment.

These reasons arise from several needs vital to our nation: the effective continuity of government operations in a very complex industrial society; citizen confidence in competent and impartial administration of laws; and fair treatment for government workers as well as those seeking government jobs.[10]

These principles were established precisely because of the need to manage Government differently from private industry.

State and Federal civil service reform efforts are based, in part, upon an assumption that is not appropriate for public sector personnel management. The reasoning behind the assumption that public employees should be accountable to the political executive is faulty on two counts:

- The Executive shares its powers over the bureaucracy with the Legislative Branch which is a co-equal partner in the management of the administrative functions of the Government.
- Merit, not efficiency, is the principal ethic which governs public sector personnel management practices while efficiency is the principal ethic that guides private sector personnel practices.

## INCREASED MANAGERIAL FLEXIBILITY

A second assumption of civil service reform efforts is that if public managers have more flexibility to manage their personnel, as private sector managers do, they will be able to use their human resources to better achieve program goals.

Proponents of reform argue that rigid civil service laws and regulations deny managers the flexibility they need to use their staffs effectively. Constraints on their ability to pay, promote, remove and reassign their employees prevent optimum use of human resources to achieve program goals. As Alan Campbell stated before CSRA passage: "Federal managers have too little authority to hire, reward, develop and discipline their employees—in short, to manage."[11]

This philosophy led President Carter's Personnel Management Project, which initially designed CSRA, to conclude that

> . . . many well-intentioned managers and personnel officers who are earnestly trying to attain program objectives believe that strict adherence to (personnel) procedures makes timely decisions difficult if not impossible. They must . . . be free to manage or there will be little accountability . . .[12]

This inability of managers to use personnel tools, reformers argue, results in long-term disadvantages to the agency. Personnel management decisions, such as hiring and developing good career staff and demoting or removing incompetent employees, comprise an investment in the agency's future, which rigid civil service systems prevent public managers from making.

The response to this concern in public civil service reform movements consists of provisions for increased agency and management flexibility in hiring, firing, promoting, demoting, reassigning and, in some cases, paying civil servants.

The basis for these decisions in CSRA is to be the new performance appraisal system that the Act mandates. This appraisal system—which requires performance standards that employees are able to help set and are responsible for achieving—is tailored by each agency to meet its unique program objectives once OPM sets minimum requirements. It is supposed to provide the information on employee performance that managers need to make decisions on using human resources to make their operations more efficient and effective in the short run, and to improve the agency's long-term quality.[13]

## Why Managers Do Not Manage

The problem with this assumption is that it attacks a symptom by focusing on what may not be its cause. By assuming that managers do not manage because they lack tools and flexibility, reform fails to address what may be more fundamental causes of management problems. While civil service laws may indeed be rigid, managers have always been free to manage, but have

not done so for two deeply rooted reasons. First, managers traditionally view personnel functions as unrelated to program results—as impediments to effective program management. Second, the political environment of public sector activities leads to disincentives to managing people to develop the long-term potential of an agency.

## Managers' View of Personnel Management

What civil service reform fails to recognize is that the problem may not lie as much with managers' *opportunity* to manage as with their *willingness* to manage. A staff study by Howard Goheen for the Defense Manpower Commission concludes that complaints about civil service rigidity are largely unfounded. Goheen found that:

> The problem with respect to management's authority to transfer or reassign Federal employees appears to be one of the manner in which it is perceived rather than of preventive legislation or restrictive regulations. Short of actions which are arbitrary, capricious, or in gross error, management has complete authority in this area . . . [The] regulations [also] appear adequate to deal with . . . marginal or unproductive employees. Present regulations are more helpful than restrictive. Management has the tools but they are not being used . . .[14]

Yet line managers do not tend to use personnel management as a means to improve organizational performance. Indeed, they often view such activities as obstacles—as time away from the job. As Elmer B. Staats, former Comptroller General of the United States, writes:

> Federal managers often perceive personnel activities . . . as roadblocks to progress in achieving objectives. It is difficult for them to see a relationship between personnel efforts, such as training and development, and mission accomplishments.[15]

If managers have failed to use the tools already available to them to manage, it is doubtful that granting them more tools will make them any more inclined to manage. Hal Rainey cites empirical evidence suggesting that it is questionable whether increasing public managers' flexibility over personnel functions will provide incentives for them to improve performance. He states that precious little research exists on whether rigid civil service laws are truly impediments to effective management.[16]

Most personnel experts would agree that if increased managerial flexibility is to be useful, it must be supported by a strong performance appraisal system. Performance appraisal experts largely agree that effective appraisal requires tremendous time and personal commitment from managers if it is to provide useful information.[17] Effective appraisal is a rigorous process which can succeed only if managers believe it will help them manage better. They must be willing to take the time to use it to obtain information on employees' skills, abilities, needs, and contributions and translate this information into decisions that will improve organizational performance.

Managers, however, do not appear to have this commitment. Carroll and Tosi, among others, point to a reluctance of and lack of commitment by managers to spend time at performance appraisal.[18] Appraisal is not seen as contributing to getting the job done. It is a requirement that "must be done," and is given only *pro forma* attention.[19] Federal managers bear this out by their reluctance to use the appraisal process that has been a legal requirement for 30 years (hence the perceived need for the appraisal provisions in CSRA). The 1950 Performance Rating Act, in fact, already requires appraisals based on standards communicated to employees to help improve their performance (similar to, albeit much less inclusive than, CSRA's fundamental appraisal requirements).[20] One wonders why managers would be any more committed to using the new appraisal system (or any less committed to finding ways to circumvent it by giving it only *pro forma* attention) than they have the past one.

While the preceding discussion focuses on problems with managerial *commitment* to appraisal, Herbert Meyer questions whether supervisors are even *capable* of making objective, valid distinctions among individuals' performance levels which can be used to make useful personnel decisions. He notes that unions—even of professional employees—generally reject the validity of supervisor judgements.[21]

Requiring a new appraisal system does not guarantee that managers will be committed to using it as a basis for personnel decisions. Indeed, the perceived need to mandate a new appraisal system is itself an admission that managers do *not* have this commitment.

## Political Constraints

No matter how many new opportunities or requirements for managing a new law may provide, the political environmental of government agencies creates dis-

incentives for line managers to spend time on personnel functions. In a world of transient leaders and goals, concern centers more around achieving short-term political ends than investing in the long-term capabilities of an agency through personnel activities.[22]

As discussed earlier in this article, political appointees who make up government agencies' top management layer arrive at an agency with the intention of implementing a political mandate in a short amount of time. They are brought to an agency to lobby Congress, change regulations, attract new constituencies, etc.—*not* to spend time developing the foundations of a strong agency that can function more effectively in 5 or 10 years. Their interest in personnel functions is generally shaped by their immediate political goals. They do not have the incentive to be concerned with creative personnel policies which can help develop an effective career staff. As Hugh Heclo states:

> Political appointees generally are not interested in the implications of their personnel actions for the civil servants' careers, much less for the civil service as an enduring system. In fact, there is every incentive for any appointee to "milk" civil servants for his own short-term advantage . . . Using career people as a strategic resource may help particular appointees, but it is no real help in establishing the civil service as an instrument of reliable government performance.[23]

Another political obstacle to managing in the public sector is the innate, mutual lack of trust between the political and career levels of the bureaucracy. Problems ostensibly resulting from inadequate flexibility for political appointees over career staff may actually result more from this lack of trust. The appointee often arrives expecting the entrenched bureaucracy to resist any change in direction or policy while the career employee assumes the new politico lacks expertise and understanding in an area in which the careerist has had years of experience.[24]

As a result, political appointees often complain of a lack of flexibility in obtaining or reassigning people in the best way to achieve their goals. This, in fact, is one of the arguments put forth in favor of civil service reform.

The problem, though, is not with personnel management procedures. The appointee cannot, after all, no matter how flexible the civil service laws, turn out all the careerists and still expect to manage effectively. The career staff possesses the technical expertise, the relationships with congressional committee staff, and the knowledge of detailed procedures necessary to run programs effectively. Also, as shown in the first section of this article, career bureaucrats' loyalty is not reserved totally for the political head of an agency, but must be shared with Congress, and with a commitment for dealing with problems that transcend the terms of short-term appointees. The appointee has no choice but to depend on these people to a great extent, for they have a great deal to do with whether he succeeds or fails in office.[25]

Blaming the problem at the political-career interface on rigid personnel procedures again results in attacking the symptom rather than its cause. Civil service reform can create false hopes for improved management. Granting increased flexibility in personnel management neither removes the political disincentives against managing people effectively, nor insures that the flexibility will be used to improve political appointees' ability to use people to achieve their goals.

By assuming that insufficient attention to personnel concerns is a function of rigid civil service systems, reformers ignore what may be more fundamental causes—i.e., a lack of understanding of how personnel management can improve program management, a lack of commitment to spending the time necessary to effectively use personnel tools, and a political environment that makes personnel management a low priority. Reformers should spend more effort examining what the causes are of the lack of emphasis on personnel management rather than on implementing reforms based on assumptions whose validity has not been determined.

## MERIT PAY AS A MEANS TO IMPROVE MANAGERIAL PERFORMANCE

The third assumption in civil service reform is that merit pay can be used in public sector organizations, as it is in many private sector organizations, to improve managerial performance.

Proponents of merit pay argue that pay systems rewarding longevity, with automatic annual step increases, rather than performance, provide no incentive for high quality performance. As the Personnel Management Project's final report states, in referring to the pre-CSRA system for Federal employees:

> Existing procedures make it extremely difficult to provide a meaningful reward for high quality performance or to withhold pay increases for low quality performance. This situation tends to foster mediocre performance.[26]

Performance pay has already become, or soon will become, reality for most Federal managers under provisions in CSRA. Up to one-half of the members of the new Senior Executive Service can qualify for one-time bonus payments of up to 20 percent of their base pay in any year. Supervisors and management officials in grades GS 13–15 must compete for permanent increases in salary through a new merit pay system that eliminates within-grade step increases. This system provides each agency with a merit pay fund comprised of the total amount that would normally be spent on step increases, and one-half or less of the annual comparability adjustment. (OPM determines how much— to one-half—the comparability adjustment will be included in the merit pay pool. The remainder—at least one-half—the adjustment will automatically go to all employees.) The new performance appraisal systems, as described in the preceding section, are to serve as the basis for merit pay decisions.[27]

Few would argue against basing managers' pay on their contribution to the employing organization. It makes sense that if two people hold the same position, the one who performs better should be paid more. Yet, pay and personnel experts cannot agree on whether pay for performance has been effective—even in private industry, which is often held up by proponents of public sector merit pay as a model. And many argue, as discussed below, that even if it did work in industry, special public sector constraints make its feasibility even more questionable in government organizations. In any case, research on how to apply pay for performance to government organizations is scant at best, and probably should be improved significantly before the concept is applied to the public sector.

### Problems in Linking Pay and Performance

The most fundamental question about merit pay is: Can merit pay achieve the goal of improving performance? Even merit pay's greatest critics would probably argue that, given perfect circumstances, it could work, but that it usually does not.

Herbert Meyer writes: "Despite the apparent soundness on which merit pay is based, experience tells us that it does not always work with such elegant simplicity." He points out that managers are usually unwilling to make large distinctions in salary decisions, even if differences in performance are great, and that merit pay plans are, therefore, difficult to administer. This problem, however, seems almost superficial compared to the more fundamental questions Meyer raises about reward theory. He cites research showing "strong evidence that we should *not* focus attention on money as the primary motivator . . . to the extent that pay is attached directly to the performance of the task, intrinsic interest in the task itself decreases." Meyer also questions whether supervisors' judgments of employee performance provide a reasonable basis for merit pay decisions.[28] He points out problems relating to the mechanics of appraisal systems, such as setting up valid procedures and forms. "Unless you appraise performance," Lawler writes, "unless you do it well, it is impossible to relate pay to performance."[29]

Clay Hamner, in his article titled "How to Ruin Motivation with Pay," cites numerous studies on the failure of merit pay systems. Among other problems, he points out that merit pay increases or lack of increases do not often succeed in communicating what it is about the recipient's performance that is being encouraged or discouraged. As a result, employees have misperceptions about their performance.[30] When this is the case, merit pay could conceivably have as much of a negative effect as a positive effect on managerial performance.

These problems with merit pay are not necessarily arguments that merit pay is impossible to administer successfully. But these pay experts cite over thirty years of research on the failures of merit pay systems which raise serious questions that should be addressed before public sector organizations attempt to use pay to improve performance. Specific constraints in the public sector raise additional doubts about merit pay's usefulness in government.

### Special Constraints in the Public Sector

The argument against the second assumption already pointed out that several constraints in the public sector could prevent increased managerial flexibility in personnel matters from improving organizational performance. It was argued that, at a minimum, performance appraisal systems must be capable of providing useful, accurate information if increased flexibility is to pay off. This is certainly the case with merit pay, as both Lawler and Meyer agree. But, as pointed out earlier, public managers have generally not done a good job of appraising performance, and it is doubtful that "reformed" appraisal systems will be much more successful.

Another problem with merit pay in public sector organizations is the size of merit increases that can be awarded. Lawler argues that if pay is to be used to improve performance, relatively large increases must be attached to good performance. If an organization cannot do this, he states, "it should probably forget about using pay to motivate performance."[31] Yet, governments tend to have salary ceilings at each grade level which limit the size of increases that can be paid. CSRA provides such a constraint for Federal employees and also limits an agency's total merit pay fund to the total of what would have been paid for step increases plus up to one-half of comparability under the old system.[32] Thus, it may be impossible to reward truly outstanding performers with large increases without holding average or just above average performers at lower levels than their supervisors would prefer. As a result, if increases are evened out to avoid "cheating" other employees, performers whose ratings show they are outstanding may be discouraged by what they perceive as inadequate increases. On the other hand, if outstanding performers receive what they deserve, other employees whose performance may be adequate will receive smaller increases than they were used to getting before merit pay was implemented, and may no longer be motivated to perform well.

Before merit pay is introduced in public sector organizations, a great deal of research should be performed on how it can truly be used to improve performance. Governments should insure that pay is adequately considered along with other rewards and that performance is accurately appraised. Rewards and their effects on immediate performance and long-term effects on agency goals should be totally understood.

## CONCLUSION

Federal, state, and local governments should reexamine the assumptions upon which their efforts to improve personnel management have been based. The three assumptions that this article examined—that the political executive should function in a way that is similar to the private sector executive; that public managers have too little authority in managing their employees; and that merit pay can be used to improve public managers' performance—have been widely accepted as the basis for personnel reform. Many reforms have been undertaken with little or no assurance that they can lead to improved performance by public sector employees.

Governments committed to improving the public service through personnel management reforms should question whether private sector management principles can be successfully applied to the management of public organizations.

## NOTES

1. News item from *Management* (Office of Personnel Management, September 1979, Volume 1), p. 28

2. For a complete listing of these efforts see "State and Local Notes" in *Management* (Office of Personnel Management, September 1979 and Fall 1980), pp. 29 and 32, respectively.

3. Campbell, Alan K., *Civil Service Reform: A New Commitment,* (Public Administration Review, March/April, 1978, Washington, D. C., 1978), p. 102.

4. Carter, Jimmy E., *Address Before the National Press Club,* (Public Papers of the President, March 2, 1978, Government Printing Office, 1978), p. 435.

5. Sundquist, James, *Testimony Before the U. S. Senate Committee on Governmental Affairs,* April 4, 1978, (U. S. Government Printing Office, Washington, D. C.), p. 383.

6. Ibid, p. 384.

7. See note 2 and the items it references.

8. Thayer, Frederick, *The President's Management "Reforms": Theory X Triumphant,* (Public Administration Review, July/August 1978), pp. 309–312.

9. Woll, Peter, *American Bureaucracy,* (W. W. Norton & Co., 1977, New York), pp. 62 and 63.

10. Rosen, Bernard, *The Merit System in the United States Civil Service,* (U.S. Government Printing Office, 1975, Washington, D. C.), p. 8.

11. Campbell, Alan K., "Civil Service: Is Management Reform Possible?" *The Personnel Administrator* (June 1978), p. 24.

12. U. S. President's Reorganization Project, Personnel Management Project, Volume 1, *Final Staff Report,* Washington: Government Printing Office, December 1977, v–vii. (Hereafter *Final Staff Report*)

13. Civil Service Reform Act of 1978 (U.S. Government Printing Office, October 13, 1978), Title V.

14. Goheen, Howard W., "Limitations on Managers Brought About by Restrictions of the Federal Civil Service System: A Staff Issue Paper for the Defense Manpower Commission, in

*Defense Manpower Commission Staff Studies,* Washington: Government Printing Office, May 1976.

15. Staats, Elmer B., "Accountability for Career Development—A Must for Improved Program Management," *The Bureaucrat,* 8, 3 (Fall 1979), pp. 2 and 3.

16. Rainey, Hal G., "Perceptions of Incentives in Business and Government: Implications for Civil Service Reform," *Public Administration Review,* (September 1979), pp. 441 and 445.

17. Carroll, Stephen J., Jr. and Tosi, Henry L., Jr., *Management by Objectives: Application and Research* (New York: The McMillan Company, 1973), chapter 3.

18. Ibid, p. 329. Also see Ellig, Bruce R., "Compensation Management: Its Past and Its Future," *Personnel* 54, May–June 1977, p. 35; Staats, p. 3.

19. Krieger, H. L., "Performance Appraisal: An Opportunity for Improved Management," *GAO Review* 15 (1980), pp. 33–36.

20. *Changes in Federal Performance Ratings,* (U. S. General Accounting Office, Washington, D. C., FPCD-77-80, March 3, 1978).

21. Meyer, Herbert H., "The Pay-for-Performance Dilemma," *Organizational Dynamics* (Winter 1975), pp. 39–41.

22. Stanley, David, "The Quality of Senior Management in Governments of the U. S." unpublished, 1979.

23. Heclo, Hugh, *A Government of Strangers: Executive Politics in Washington,* (Washington: The Brookings Institution, 1977), pp. 218–220.

24. Ibid, pp. 182–187.

25. Staats, op. cit., p. 4; Heclo, op. cit., chapter 4.

26. *Final Staff Report,* op. cit., p. 147.

27. CSRA, op. cit., Title V.

28. Meyer, op. cit., pp. 39–41.

29. Lawler, Edward E., "Performance Appraisal and Merit Pay," *Civil Service Journal* (April/June 1979), pp. 14 and 15.

30. Hamner, W. Clay, "How to Ruin Motivation With Pay," *Compensation Review* (Third Quarter 1975), pp. 17–27.

31. Lawler, Edward E., *Pay and Organizational Effectiveness: A Psychological View* (New York: McGraw-Hill, 1971), p. 72.

32. Civil Service Reform Act of 1978 (U.S. Government Printing Office, October 13, 1978), Title V.

# The Liability of Public Executives
## Implications for Practice in Personnel Administration

W. Bartley Hildreth
Gerald J. Miller
Jack Rabin

*This article provides an overview of the law of tort liability as it applies to personnel administrators. Starting with the premise that personnel practitioners can avoid liability pitfalls by familiarizing themselves with current statutory and case law, the authors analyze trends in the development of personal and official liability. The impact of tort liability upon the personnel profession is exemplified through reference to four personnel topics: employee non-discrimination; union activity; disciplinary policy; and supervisory practices. The authors conclude with several recommendations intended to assist practitioners in avoiding liability problems, including the careful design of bias-free rules and regulations, and the establishment of training programs and monitoring systems to avoid and/or remedy potential liability risks.*

## INTRODUCTION

Damage suits against public personnel administrators have raised concerns among professionals who view this newly created jeopardy with the hope that it will simply go away. Danger resides in a lack of concern, evident in the paucity of discussion in personnel journals, about the liability of public executives for personnel-related activities.[1] The legal complexities of the issue realistically restrain personnel managers' attempts to grapple with the problem. Yet, neither lack of concern nor the legal issue's complexities need compound the jeopardy.

Does liability pose an unresolvable threat? We think not. Liability suits need not threaten the personal assets of decision makers nor government budgets. Protection can be found in a basic knowledge of the law and the use of management strategies which are

From *Review of Public Personnel Administration,* (Fall, 1980), Vol. 1, pp. 45–46. Copyright 1980, Bureau of Governmental Research and Service, University of South Carolina. Reprinted by permission.

built upon already-existing personnel management concerns. This essay first considers the legal issues confronting state and local executives. Subsequently, by focusing upon several personnel issues, we pinpoint some slices of the liability question which intersect with programs already facing today's public personnel managers.

## AN OVERVIEW OF LIABILITY

Liability has emerged from court action in two forms: personal liability and official liability. Personal liability concerns the individual public official's responsibility for both his own acts and subordinates' erroneous acts and omissions resulting in damage or injury to another. Injury may be caused by physical action but courts have increasingly looked at the violation of constitutional rights and those rights guaranteed by federal laws as a primary liability claim. Public officials, found personally liable, pay damages to the injured party from their own pocket.

Official or governmental liability refers to the governmental unit or agency's responsibility for unlawful policies. Policies formulated or executed by personnel managers may lead to a liability suit if these policies violate protected rights. In official liability cases, the courts hold the government entity—essentially, the executive as an official, not as an individual—responsible for the injury. The payment of damages comes from the government's resources rather than the individual official.

## PERSONAL LIABILITY

Of significance in the area of personal liability of public executives is the changing balance between the need for effective administration of government policies and the need for protection of the individual citizen's rights. Several factors have affected the balance through the past few years.

First, the common law as interpreted and applied by the courts has historically tended to favor protection of public officials. Courts' interpretations have relied on two components, the scope of an officer's duties and the distinction between offices.

Duties of public officials are often considered relative to the amount of discretion required. Officials who routinely exercise considerable discretion have been generally granted latitude in making decisions and absolute immunity from suit. Otherwise, "The burden of a trial and the danger of its outcome would dampen the ardor of all but the most resolute or the most irresponsible" (*Gregoire v. Biddle,* 1949: 579).

On the other hand, one who has specific tasks in executing policies and has no opportunity to exercise discretion is said to have ministerial duties. If such an administrator does not perform his assigned tasks or is negligent in performing them, he is liable for the consequences. Immunity is not granted since performance is either in accordance with or fails to conform to legal responsibilities (negligence or failure to act). The distinction between ministerial and discretionary duties is clearer in legal theory than in actual practice, however, since most jobs require some discretion.

The courts have also considered the office itself in determining liability. Using "settled principles of common law," courts have granted judges absolute immunity. (See *Bradley v. Fisher,* 1872: 335; *Pierson v. Ray,* 1967: 547). Legislators have received similar protection.[2] As long as these officials have acted within the scope of legitimate authority and jurisdiction, they have been free from threat of damages. Again, the stated purpose was to keep such public officials from being concerned with reprisals for their activity.

The common law rulings have not met with complete acceptance when the courts have more recently examined the personal liability question concerning local, state and federal executives. The primary legislative mandate for the personal liability of administrators at local and state levels comes from the Civil Rights Act of 1871. As codified in Title 42, Section 1983 of the U.S. Code, this section states:

> Every person who, under color of any statute, ordinance, regulation, custom, or usage, of any State or Territory subjects, or causes to be subjected, any citizen of the United States or other person within the jurisdiction thereof to the deprivation of any rights, privileges, or immunities secured by the Constitution and laws, shall be liable to the party injured in an action at law, suit in equity, or other proper proceeding for redress.

In recent years, the U.S. Supreme Court has used Section 1983 to rule that officers with discretionary duties are subject to liability for activities arising out of their conduct in office. A decision by the Court in *Scheuer v. Rhodes* (1974), in fact, held that state executive officers using discretionary authority might have only qualified immunity from damage suits. Liability would be ascertained, the Court said, on the basis of

not only the scope of the official's discretionary authority—the traditional rule—but also evidence as to whether the officer acted reasonably and in good faith. Later the Court held in *Wood v. Strickland* (1975) that an executive officer would be liable if he reasonably could have known that his actions were unconstitutional.

Federal executives, unlike their local and state counterpoints, observe no legislative mandate regarding personal liability, but have the same qualified immunity. In *Bivens v. Six Unknown Named Agents of the Federal Bureau of Narcotics* (1971), the U.S. Supreme Court, interpreting the Constitution, ruled that a federal official can neither act outside authority nor abuse that authority by violating constitutional rights. Later, the Court applied the standard of conduct conceived for local and state officials to federal officials: An official will be liable for his conduct if he knew or should have known his acts would violate constitutional rights (*Butz v. Economou,* 1978).

The Court, therefore, fashioned an objective test for all public officials' conduct. Instead of relying on officials to act as they believed they should act, the Court forces judges and juries to evaluate the alleged misconduct on the basis of what the official should have known at the time were clearly established legal rights. Disregard for "settled, indisputable" law places a good faith defense beyond the official's reach.[3]

## OFFICIAL LIABILITY

Only recently has the Court added another type of liability—official liability, we call it—to the pressures facing public administrators. Official liability is governmental liability. That is, managers making policy face damage suits against the governmental unit when policies transgress citizens' rights. The government pays, but, of course, the officials making the offending policy ultimately account for their action to the constituents they serve.

For example, in *Monell v. Department of Social Services* (1978) the U.S. Supreme Court held the City of New York liable. The Court ruled that the city had to pay female employees for wages lost when the city's unconstitutional pregnancy leave policy forced them out of their jobs temporarily.

Moreover, the City of Independence, Missouri (*Owen v. City of Independence,* 1980) recently was ruled potentially liable for a personnel action. The

Court ruled that Independence officials could not defend with good faith their refusal to grant a police chief a name-clearing hearing after summarily firing him. Although the Supreme Court had ruled on the hearing issue in another case more than two months *after* the Independence city manager fired the police chief (holding that government entities must provide a name clearing hearing), the Court decided in *Owen* that Independence officials could be held responsible anyway for the damaged reputation caused the chief in the episode. Clearly, anticipating U. S. Supreme Court rulings will become a major new activity for public managers.

## WHAT ACTS CREATE LIABILITY?

Liability has traditionally followed when a public official has, through intent or neglect, physically harmed an innocent victim. Today's public official faces the threat of suit, in addition, when he or she violates the legally guaranteed rights of citizens. Furthermore, even the definition of "legally guaranteed rights" continues to broaden. In 1980, for example, the U. S. Supreme Court ruled that the Civil Rights Act of 1871 covered not only *constitutionally* guaranteed rights such as due process and equal protection, but also rights guaranteed by *federal statute* (*Maine v. Thiboutot,* 1980). Federal statutory rights, of course, cover many activities in local and state government. Certainly, equal employment opportunity, comprehensive employment and training, and rights of the disabled or handicapped merely begin a long list of rights for whose violation a public official may be held liable.

## PERSONNEL ISSUES

The wide scope of liability law and the seeming volatility of court action make even a brief review of personnel issues hazardous. However, many of the legal issues creating potential liability for local and state officials are not entirely new. These legal issues, in fact, have appeared on the personnel administrator's agenda for quite some time. Liability is merely a newer, more extreme method for creating change and ensuring administrative responsibility.

To illustrate how personal liability revives some contemporary personnel issues, this essay will sample four common areas dealt with in personnel administration:

1. Employment non-discrimination;
2. Unionizing activity;
3. Disciplinary policy; and
4. Supervisory practices.

In all areas the focus is on clarifying why personal liability has become a management problem which should be handled in conjunction with other ongoing personnel programs.

## EMPLOYMENT NON-DISCRIMINATION

Public officials and employees face liability under the Civil Rights Act of 1871 for their acts or policies resulting in employment discrimination. We address both the standard Section 1983 approach and the more recent mode of attacking employment discrimination through federal statutes and Section 1983. Two factors form the basis of the standard Section 1983 damage claim: bad faith and unreasonable action.

A bad faith effort in employment discrimination considers intent of purposeful behavior (*Washington v. Davis,* 1976). Normally, most employment policies and practices seem to favor no particular group or person. As proof of discrimination, besides an admission of intentional discrimination, of course, courts will allow use of objective evidence to infer violation of the law. The courts reason that the actor is presumed to have intended the actual discriminatory act, or more importantly, the natural consequences of his deeds. Thus, the impact of the discriminatory practice and its magnitude provide the needed inference. For example, a continual disregard by an employer of available blacks and women for key jobs provides support for the claim of intentional deprivation of rights (*Williams v. Anderson,* 1977).

The unreasonable action requirement is the other element necessary to prove employment discrimination cases under Section 1983. As a result of *Wood v. Strickland* (1975) the court has defined unreasonable action as action contrary to "settled" law, or law over which courts agree. If the courts find that a certain practice is unconstitutional and a personnel manager continues that practice, the injured person has sufficient evidence to show that the official acted unreasonably or should have known his or her action was unconstitutional. Courts, for example, use settled principles of law developed under Title VII of the Civil Rights Act of 1964, as amended in 1972, to help define employment practices which are discriminatory. Continuing practices previously overruled by the Courts can lead to liability. The Equal Employment Opportunity Commission (EEOC) guidelines on employee selection procedure, for example, provide the settled law basis for use in Section 1983 cases in even greater detail (see *Crockett v. Green,* 1975).

Following the thrust of the recent *Maine v. Thibotout* decision, a personal liability complaint may also be directly based upon a violation of the 1972 EEO Act. As is well known, the 1972 Act prohibits state and local governments from using employment practices which discriminate on account of race, sex, color, religion, and national origin. Under the 1972 Act, courts allow *objective* evidence, such as disparate work force statistics, to prove that an employment practice actually discriminates against one of the above five protected classes. Does this new linkage remove the need, under Section 1983 decisions, to show *both* bad faith (a subjective prong) and unreasonable action (an objective prong) to find an executive liable for certain employment practices? A definitive court ruling is needed to clarify this question. Suffice it to say, Section 1983 provides a way to hold executives accountable via monetary damages and other methods for violation of the rights of individuals in employment.

## UNIONIZING ACTIVITY

State and local governments also face an increasing number of unionizing efforts by public employees. The chance of a personal liability suit arises if public officials attempt to stop the unionization movement.

Public employees enjoy the right to form or join labor unions when the purpose is to promote a legitimate, legal interest. Union membership is protected by the right of association under the First and Fourteenth Amendments to the United States Constitution (*McLaughlin v. Tilendis,* 1969).

Courts have limited the status of a union, however. The Constitution, courts have held, does not require the public employer to recognize or bargain with the union.

Deprivation of constitutionally protected rights of association may result in a suit under the Civil Rights Act of 1871. State and local public officials and executives may be sued personally for damages if they deny these constitutional rights, by restraining union activity under at least three circumstances.

First, dismissal of an employee due to membership in a union is a reason for a personal liability suit against a public official. To illustrate, a city commissioner in charge of the street department of the City of

North Platte, Nebraska, discharged two workers who had joined a newly formed union. The Eighth Circuit Court of Appeals, in 1969, ruled that the city commissioner could be sued for his denial of First Amendment rights to city employees (*AFSCME v. Woodward,* 1969).

Courts reject the idea that a public official can be ignorant of such fundamental rights as freedom of association and speech. In a Texas case, a fire chief, believing he was acting in concert with state law, denied a fireman the right to belong to a union and to speak in its behalf. After being suspended from his job, the fireman brought a personal liability suit against the fire chief. In this case the fire chief had to pay the lost wages of the fireman he had suspended for union activity (*Castleberry v. Langford,* 1977).

Second, departmental rules which forbid membership or participation in associations or unions face severe scrutiny in the courts. Courts have held a rule such as this unconstitutional on its face, absent a showing of actual, detrimental characteristics of the union (*Vorbeck v. McNeal,* 1976).

Third, the courts allow segregation of supervisors and subordinates, but hold liable officials who attempt to forbid supervisors' unionization. Thus the courts allow restrictions on membership by rank and file members of a public organization and supervisors in the same bargaining unit. For instance, the city of Tupelo, Mississippi could exclude fire department supervisors from membership in a rank-and-file union, according to a district court ruling (*Local 2263 IAFF v. City of Tupelo,* 1977). Despite this prohibition, however, the city could not prevent supervisors from organizing a union local which did not include rank-and-file members of the department. In this case, the district court pointed out that First Amendment rights are broad, limited only by the public interest in keeping supervisors and subordinates out of the same union.

## DISCIPLINARY POLICY

Adverse actions against employees have consequences for the initiating official. Violation of an employee's due process rights can rise to the level of a constitutional infraction which can prompt a damage claim against the supervisor and/or the personnel officer.

Courts' views of due process in conjunction with adverse actions lack a single, simple guideline for all cases. Rather, as one observer describes the case law, courts have adopted an idiographic approach—one based on individual cases (Rosenbloom, 1975: 52). The necessity for such an approach rests on the complexity of such questions as, for instance, who enjoys a legitimate claim for due process protections to his or her job and what process is *due*?

Generally, due process safeguards include such procedures as adequate notice, a full and fair hearing, and a way by which to appeal the initial decision. Violation of any or all of these generally accepted procedural due process guidelines can lead to a claim of deprivation of a constitutionally protected right. The recent case of *Owen v. City of Independence* provides one example. The city police chief fired without a name clearing hearing could press his damage claim against the city, the Court ruled.

A progressive disciplinary policy enjoying elements of procedural due process conforms to "good" personnel procedures, advanced management strategies, and the necessary action to avoid personal or official liability claims.

## SUPERVISORY PRACTICES

Supervisors in public agencies have a critical responsibility to deal with subordinates who violate constitutional rights. The supervisor who fails to supervise, in other words, faces liability.

Why supervisory liability? Many suits are brought against public officials as supervisors because supervisors who get paid more can better afford the costs of judgment. Also, the injured citizen may not know or be able to identify the offending lower level official who actually caused his injury; suing the supervisor ensures a responsible defendant. Finally, suing the supervisor may better encourage change or the end of unconstitutional acts by subordinates since the supervisor has the power to change or alter subordinate behavior.

The law on supervisory liability involves several different rules. Specifically, suits against supervisors have led courts to interpret a supervisor's liability in two different ways: (1) personal involvement in wrongdoing, or (2) personal knowledge and failure to act.

### Personal Involvement

Some courts require that a person suing a supervisor prove that the supervisor had personal involvement in the unconstitutional acts of his or her subordinates. Under this rule, the supervisor must have participated in, encouraged or directed the illegal conduct of sub-

ordinates ("Developments in the Law", 1977: 1206–1207). Evidence must show that the supervisor was present when subordinates committed an illegal act, and could have prevented or ended that conduct.[4]

### Personal Knowledge and Failure to Act

A far broader interpretation of supervisory liability rests on the idea that inaction by supervisors is as dangerous as action. In other words, supervisors are liable for a subordinate's act when they know or should have known of civil rights violations by a subordinate and failed to take reasonable steps to halt the action or prevent its recurrence (*Sims v. Adams,* 1976). The lack of disciplinary action against an offending subordinate or even the lack of retraining may subject a supervisor to liability.

In many organizations supervisors receive special training opportunities. Using a training approach to focus on the responsibilities of supervisors offers one way to deal with the added personal liability questions.

## THE FUTURE

How can personnel administrators respond to the personal liability situation? Of course, one can deny the problem. Or, when the problem reaches litigation, one can face the charge and defend one's action to the end, over the constitutional issues. Still another approach counsels personnel administrators to seize the opportunity by following at least three major steps: (1) constructing sound personnel practices for dealing with such areas as nondiscriminatory employment practices; (2) even-handed responses to unionizing activity; and (3) observing due process considerations in a disciplinary policy and special programs dealing with responsible supervisory management.

Three major steps are available. The first ingredient is the construction of rules and procedures to define what may be done and how the individual's rights will be taken into consideration. Initially, this will involve a survey to find out how a particular problem is currently handled. One might then evaluate current policy in light of legal trends and assess the policy through other indicators such as citizen complaints. In personnel administration, for example, this would involve validated selection instruments and appropriate affirmative action procedures.

Moreover, the due process rights of employees deserve special attention. When considering discipline or dismissal actions, local government officials should practice caution. Rash action in cases of employee misconduct should be tempered with thorough investigation and application of penalties consistent with past cases.

In each area where the need for regulation arises, the public official studies the problem at length and attempts to deal with it reasonably and in good faith. Whether an official's effort attempts to solve a problem, meet a demand or comply with court orders, he or she must clearly determine the purpose of the regulation and design appropriate and reasonable rules. This step is crucial because all procedures, training and monitoring will by definition be based on the efforts to grapple with this problem.

Comprehensive, on-going training, the second step, provides a special opportunity. Through training, personnel managers can address personal liability questions constructively. Training programs can be instituted to familiarize employees with established policies and procedures which conform to settled constitutional law. Using cases which outline potential risks, employees get special warning of the specific areas which can result in damage suits.

Two types of programs can be designed: one for skill updating, and another for new employees. In each program the basic rules and procedures gain visibility and employees learn to use these rules and procedures with more facility.

A variety of training methods may be employed in the two programs, of course. For example, role-playing exercises efficiently illustrate the dynamics of liability situations and provide experience in decision making under liability constraints. One such approach has been designed by these writers in conjunction with colleagues and practitioners.[5] The approach has met with success in providing experimental training to a wide cross-section of public administrators. A byproduct of training sessions such as these could well be the identification of previously undetected risks, adding an unexpected feedback element to the first step of constructing and reviewing rules and procedures.

Complementing this effective, but incidental, feedback is information which comes through the process of monitoring. Establishing monitoring systems will help officials check employees' performance, gain internal organization feedback, and govern the implementation of policies. Monitoring employees' compliance will strengthen the training process, demonstrate unclear training methods, reveal gaps in understanding, and isolate individuals who are unable to comprehend the risks being taken. Internal organization feedback can help change managerial practices before their inadequacy leads to disruption and litigation. Finally, monitoring the effect of policies and procedures will permit policy makers to adapt rules to the needs of clientele and point out unfamiliar ways of dealing with problems.

By addressing these and other personnel areas,[6] the threat of a liability suit can be factored into existing personnel management programs which reduce risks. While employment discrimination, unionization, disciplinary policy, and supervisory practices have so far emerged as special cases creating potential liability, the personnel officer should consider the current liability approach to correction of personnel practices as indicative of both the rate of change and content of the future state of public personnel administration. The current court decisions presage further federalization or nationalization of state and local personnel management.[7] Recognizing the sweeping decisions that may lie ahead, managers would be wise to conduct a thorough examination of all personnel management practices to determine the extent of liability risks.

## NOTES

1. The personnel literature remains sparse with but one tangential exception. A general discussion of management liability was presented by Stanton, 1978: 43–48.

2. Generally, the rule follows *Tenney v. Brandhove,* 1951: 367.

3. Although efforts have been made to amend the Civil Rights Act of 1871 to lower this standard of conduct, it seems likely that should legislative efforts succeed, the courts will continue to use the standard by inferring a remedy directly under the constitution, as illustrated by cases involving federal officials. Simply, the injured party could allege a deprivation of federal rights, assert a federal question, and demand the federal court take jurisdiction under federal law 23 U. S. C. 1331.

4. From a statement by Drew S. Days III before the Subcommittee on the Constitution, Committee on the Judiciary, U. S. Senate. Civil Rights Improvements Act of 1978. Hearings, February 8, 9 and May 3, 1978. 95th Congress, 2nd Session: 61.

5. See Nigro et al., 1978.

6. Other topics relevant to Section 1983 claims include such areas as grievance procedures and hair and dress codes, re-

viewed quarterly in *Personal Liability Digest* (P. O. Box 4361, Montgomery, Alabama 36101).

7. This important insight was provided by an anonymous reviewer.

## REFERENCES

*AFSCME v. Woodward* (1969). 406 *F. 2d* 137.

*Bivens v. Six Unknown Named Agents of the Federal Bureau of Narcotics* (1971). 403 *U. S.* 388.

*Bradley v. Fisher* (1872). 13 *Wall* 335.

*Butz v. Economou* (1978). 438 *U. S.* 478.

*Castleberry v. Langford* (1977). 428 *F. Supp.* 676.

*Crockett v. Green* (1975). 388 *F. Supp.* 912.

*Davis v. Passman* (1979). 442 *U. S.* 228.

*Gregoire v. Biddle* (1949). 177 *F. 2d* 579.

*Harvard Law Review* (1977). "Developments in the Law — Section 1983 and Federalism." Volume 90: 1133–1361.

*Local 2263 IAFF v. City of Tupelo* (1977). 439 *F. Supp.* 1224.

*McLaughlin v. Tilendis* (1969). 398 *F. 2d* 287.

*Maine v. Thiboutot* (1980). 48 *U. S. L. W.* 4859.

*Monell v. Department of Social Services of the City of New York* (1978). 436 *U. S.* 658.

Nigro, F. A., J. Rabin, W. B. Hildreth and G. J. Miller (1978). *Personal Liability in Government: A Workbook in the Tort Liability of Government Officials.* Montgomery, Alabama: American Society for Public Administration.

*Owen v. City of Independence* (1980), 43 *U. S. L. W.* 4389.

*Pierson v. Ray* (1967). 386 *U. S.* 547.

Rosenbloom, D. H. (1975). "Public Personnel Administration and the Constitution: An Emergent Approach." *Public Administration Review* 35 (January–February): 52–59.

*Scheuer v. Rhodes* (1974). 416 *U. S.* 232.

*Sims v. Adams* (1976). 537 *F. 2d* 829.

Stanton, R. A. (1978). "Professional Managers and Personal Liability." *Public Personnel Management* 7 (January–February): 43–48.

*Tenney v. Brandhove* (1951). 341 *U. S.* 367.

*Vorbeck v. McNeal* (1976). 407 *F. Supp.* 733.

*Washington v. Davis* (1976). 426 *U. S.* 229.

*Williams v. Anderson* (1977). 562 *F. 2d* 1081.

*Wood v. Strickland* (1975). 420 *U. S.* 308.

# The Impact of Flexitime on Performance and Attitudes in 25 Public Agencies

Simcha Ronen
Sophia B. Primps

With the recent passage of flexitime and part-time legislation (S. 517 and S. 518) authorizing experimentation with alternative work schedules in the Federal Government, the real effects of flexible working hours on the organization and on the individual have become an important concern to personnel managers and policymakers. The advantages of flexible scheduling have been associated with such issues as the organizational effectiveness, life stage of the employee, improvements in the quality of work life and quality of life through increased control over the interface between the work and personal life domains (Ronen, Primps, and Cloonan, 1978). This bill allows the relaxation of regulations requiring the payment of wage premiums for work in excess of specified maximum work periods (usually 8 hours per day), creating the possibility of experimentation in these areas through variations in the number of hours worked per day. For example, an employee might work 9 hours on one day and 7 on another, averaging out to 8 hours worked each day. Before the laws were relaxed, the organization would have been required to pay the employee 1 hour of overtime for the day that he worked 9 hours, although the decision to work 9 hours was the employee's, not the organization's.

Prior to the passage of the flexitime legislation, close to 100 bureaus and agencies had experimented with various forms of flexitime, the earliest starting in about 1972. Approximately 25 of these completed studies on the impact of flexitime on employee attitudes and effectiveness. We have taken these studies, analyzed and categorized the results, and summarized them for presentation here. These results should be particularly relevant in light of the passage of S. 517 and the increased popularity of flexitime among both employees and managers. In order to assist in the decision to implement flexitime, evaluative data on the results of existing flexitime programs should be available to de-

From *Public Personnel Management,* (Summer, 1981), Vol. 9, No. 3, pp. 201–207. Copyright 1981, International Personnel Management Association. Reprinted by permission.

cisionmakers. We should also note that since flexitime has been fully described in recent issues of this journal (Finkle, 1979; Stevens and Elsworth, 1979), we will assume that the reader is familiar with the basic aspects of the concept.

## RESULTS

The experiments conducted at each agency were not standardized; the criteria for evaluation were determined internally by each organization. Even those agencies reporting the same dependent variables used varying criteria for their measurement. With this in mind, we have chosen to report four broad categories of information. Because our purpose is to indicate general trends, the measurements taken from agency reports have been grouped into these categories, at times, somewhat arbitrarily. The four major categories of information are presented as follows: Table 1—Organizational Effectiveness; Table 2—Attitudes; Table 3—Membership; Table 4—Time Management. The results have been evaluated for each organization and the direction of change reported as "Positive," "Negative," "No Change," or "Inconclusive." It was not possible to report amount of change for each agency in this type of summary because of the many different methodologies and degrees of rigor employed in the 25 agencies. The breakdown of results from each agency including amount of change, is presented in detail in Ronen (1981).

There are two types of findings which are reported in these studies: objective data and attitudinal (subjective) results. In some cases, the information source is strictly attitudinal; for example, Table 2 describes attitudes towards the schedule and changed attitudes towards the job and employing organization. In other categories such as Organizational Effectiveness (Table 1), the types of results reported include both objective and attitudinal data. In each table, the results are differentiated between these two types, and the number of organizations providing data in the category is reported.

### Organizational Effectiveness

Table 1 contains all measures pertaining to organizational effectiveness. It is subdivided into the categories: Productivity, Work Environment, and Costs to the organization. Under Productivity, we have summarized all measures which were defined in the agency

**TABLE 1**
**The impact of flexitime on organizational effectiveness in 25 public agencies**

|  | Objective data | Subjective data |
|---|---|---|
| Productivity | N = 11<br>9 positive<br>2 inconclusive | N = 17<br>14 positive<br>1 no change<br>2 inconclusive |
| Work environment: access/relations | N = 1<br>1 positive | N = 10<br>6 positive<br>3 no change<br>1 inconclusive |
| Work environment: control of hours/ quiet time | N/A | N = 7<br>6 positive<br>1 no change |
| Costs | N = 9<br>6 positive<br>2 negative<br>1 no change | N = 4<br>1 negative<br>1 no change<br>2 inconclusive |

studies, including criteria such as quality of work, quantity produced, accuracy, efficiency, ability to meet schedules, and increases in interdepartmental or interorganizational communications, as reflected in both exempt and non-exempt employee behavior. Both objective and survey results are positive; there are *no reports* of decreased productivity.

There is, however, one finding which is not indicated on Table 1 that should be mentioned. When reports of employees and supervisors were compared within the same organization, it was found that employees perceived greater improvements in productivity than supervisors (although the supervisors were consistently positive as well). In general, employees perceive flexitime as influencing performance more positively than do their supervisors, although both groups report that flexitime has positive effects on productivity. Perhaps, the most obvious explanation of this observation is that an employee's favorable attitude towards flexitime colors his/her perception of the impact on performance. Employees may generalize or exaggerate the benefits as an expression of their positive experience, and as a reflection of their desire to make the system work. On the positive side, distortions of this type represent evidence for the employee's positive attitudes towards the program. He/she may feel more productive for a variety of reasons: Communications levels with peers and superiors may be improved, feedback from these groups have increased, the employee may enjoy a greater sense of autonomy and may actually perform a greater range of job tasks. All of these would be contributing factors to the perception of increased productivity. On the negative side, such perceptions may mean that the data is somewhat suspect. However, there is little reason to suspect significant exaggeration concerning productivity, since most agencies make it clear to employees that the purpose of introducing flexitime is to improve the quality of work life, the overall organizational climate and work/nonwork fit for the employees and their families. Often, issues of transportation, commuting and congestion in parking lots and elevators provide the impetus for the initial consideration of a flexible schedule. Thus, the organization may be prepared to accept *no change* in productivity as acceptable. As long as there are no decreases, the other benefits of flexitime justify its implementation.

Another possibility exists which may explain this difference in perceptions between supervisors and employees. It may be that supervisors' perceptions about flexitime's impact on productivity are less positive, reflecting less favorable attitudes towards flexitime itself. The adjustment necessary for first-line supervisors can be considerable because flexitime is often perceived as causing a decrease in autonomy and control and, in certain cases, an increased work load. These concerns may bias the supervisors' reports on productivity.

In Table 1, the subcategory, Work Environment, was further divided into two areas of results: Access to, or relations with, supervisors and co-workers; and Control over work hours or quiet time. Most of this information was the result of employee or supervisor opinion, rather than objective data. Of the 11 agencies reporting on work relations, 7 of the agencies indicated an overall improvement, 3 reported no change, and 1 reported inconclusive results. In the latter case, the organization reported information obtained from employees, supervisors and agency heads. While the supervisors and employees tended to report positive results or no change, the agency heads were more negative. It should also be noted that two organizations reported some supervisory problems (one reported a small decrease in supervisory skills), although their overall reports were positive. This apparent disparity between managers and employees is most easily explained as adjustment difficulties. Inadequate preparation for implementation, consideration of new work flows, and changing work process or scheduling demands may result in less positive evaluations of flexitime at the management level.

From the positive results, it appears that the provision of control over work and time scheduling allows the employee to schedule greatly-needed quiet time. This opportunity to work without interruptions can only mean a more effective employee, if he/she is willing to take advantage of the opportunity.

The Cost category reflects all aspects of flexitime implementation which increased or decreased costs mentioned in the agency reports. These include night differential expenses, plant operation, power consumption, maintenance and overtime. There was evidence from a few organizations that overtime costs were decreased. In general, however, no organization assessed the full impact of flexitime on costs, including, for example, costs of a time recording system. A systematic study and analysis is necessary before any generalizations can be made in this area.

## Attitudes

Table 2 presents changes in employee attitudes resulting from flexitime. These attitudes are grouped into two general categories: changes in attitudes *towards the job* expressed as morale or job satisfaction, and attitudes *towards the flexitime program* itself. Because of the nature of attitudes as perceptions, all information in the table is recorded as subjective.

Reports in both of these categories are consistently positive. However, two potential problem areas, as reflected in the reports from two agencies, should be mentioned. First if some number of employees are for task-related reasons unable to participate in the FWH program, management should expect a drop in morale and job satisfaction in that group. The effects of this discrimination can be minimized through careful education and explanation but will have to be considered a possible negative side effect in the overall evaluation of flexitime. Second, the only nonpositive response in FWH attitudes came from a group of supervisors who reported no change in satisfaction over time. It is difficult to draw conclusions, except to express the concern that the impact on supervisors' attitudes is very much contingent upon the style of implementation in the organization, including the training and help received in coping with new demands as a result of the schedule.

Despite these concerns, the positiveness of these results can only mean an improved work environment, including enhanced employee-supervisory relations. If

**TABLE 2**
**Changes in employee attitudes***

| | |
|---|---|
| Morale/job satisfaction | N = 17 |
| | 17 positive |
| Attitudes toward flexitime | N = 15 |
| | 14 positive |
| | 1 inconclusive |

*All data is subjective.

**TABLE 3**
**The impact of flexitime on membership behavior**

| | Objective data | Subjective data |
|---|---|---|
| Absenteeism | N = 11 | N = 6 |
| | 7 positive | 6 positive |
| | 1 negative | |
| | 2 no change | |
| | 1 inconclusive | |
| Tardiness | N = 9 | N = 5 |
| | 9 positive | 5 positive |

these attitudes prove to be stable over time, the implications for the work climate are significant.

### Membership Behavior

Membership includes behaviors such as absenteeism, whether in the form of personal leave or sick leave and tardiness. While this is certainly a criteria for organizational effectiveness, membership behavior is reported as a separate table (Table 3) because such results were generally available and reported separately in the agencies. Absenteeism includes all the forms of absence reported by the organizations, such as sick leave, short-term leave and personal leave usage. No attempts were made to subcategorize absenteeism further, as the types of leave granted with and without pay, and sick leave policy, varied from organization to organization. As shown in Table 3, the types of absenteeism reductions most frequently reported were short-term leave usage and sick leave usage. These favorable results confirm the notion that flexitime alleviates the need for employees to call in sick when they have personal business to attend to, or when an extra hour of sleep would suffice.

The impact of flexitime on tardiness is consistently positive, for both objective and subjective measures. This is one of the most consistent reported benefits of flexible scheduling. It is interesting to note that none of the organizations reported any problems with employee arrival after core time had begun. Perhaps this is reflective of employee arrival patterns—in almost all organizations surveyed, 80%–90% of employees tend to arrive during the early portion of the morning flexband.

### Personal Time Management

Table 4 describes some of the aspects of the employee's life outside the job which are affected by flexitime. The categories which we have chosen to present here are Personal Time Usage, including time for family, recreation and control over personal life, and Transportation.

This first category is quite broad, including a number of facets of the employee's personal life, as well as home/work fit. Examples of the types of aspects investigated included ease of child care, time available for family, control over work and personal life (through control over hours), community, educational, and social activities, satisfaction with work/nonwork fit, individual freedom and leisure time, and ability to conduct personal business. The results reflected improvement in all areas reported.

The Transportation section included information on changing the mode of transportation, the use of carpools, fuel consumption, and changes in the ease or difficulty of getting to work after flexitime implementation.

It was clear from the reports that employees were already beginning to realize benefits in terms of decreased commuting time and gas utilization, although flexitime schedules had been implemented in a very limited basis in their geographic areas of work. If flexitime were to be adopted on a widespread basis, especially in large cities, the benefits could become quite substantial.

### CONCLUSIONS

The general conclusions which can be drawn from the data are the following:

1. The organization as a unit can improve its level of effectiveness through flexitime implementation. Objective data on productivity, and subjective data on performance and interpersonal relations support this conclusion.
2. Individual employees have reported improved control over work scheduling and work process, as well as an increase in uninterrupted work

**TABLE 4**
**Implications of flexitime for personal time management**

|  | Objective data | Subjective data |
|---|---|---|
| Personal time usage | N/A | N = 9<br>9 positive |
| Transportation | N = 3<br>3 positive | N = 12<br>11 positive<br>1 inconclusive |

periods. These benefits contribute to improved organizational as well as individual effectiveness.

3. With respect to membership behavior, absenteeism can be significantly reduced and tardiness virtually eliminated following the implementation of a flexitime schedule.

4. Employee attitudes toward his job and the work environment are improved, although supervisors/managers tend to be somewhat less positive.

5. Employees experience an improvement in the interrelationship between their work and non-work domains—specifically, the impact of work on personal life. This includes increased flexibility in allocating time for recreation and leisure, educational and community activities, as well as the opportunity to take a more active role in family life and child rearing.

6. We do feel that flexitime has the potential to improve the employee commuting and thus, his state of relaxation upon arrival. However, the data as presented here is inconclusive. Additional studies are necessary to confirm this hypothesis.

Although the results are so positive, there are a few problem areas indicated in the data which can be avoided through rigorous planning and well-thought-out implementation. Organization change techniques should be utilized—especially for the training and preparation of first-line supervisors. Often, this particular group is less receptive towards the concept and needs special attention.

In general, *all* levels of employees are more receptive to a new concept if they have had the opportunity to be included during the planning stages, and to contribute their ideas. Useful insights may be obtained which might be overlooked at higher levels of management. In the same context, it is important to design *each* flexitime installation around the demands of the immediate work environment. This may mean different flexitime designs within an organization, or even within a department.

Although these results are promising, the lack of uniformity in the data creates constraints for rigorous analysis. There is a critical need for the standardized controlled experimentation proposed here, so that more reliable results can be obtained.

The passage of S. 517 will certainly prompt further investigation of the impact of flexitime. It will be interesting to compare future results with the results presented here, to investigate differences based on the additional flexibility in scheduling now possible.

*We wish to thank Ms. Barbara Fiss and Mr. Tom Cowley for their help and cooperation in making their data available and to all the agencies that provided additional information directly.*

## REFERENCES

Finkle, A. L. Flexitime in Government. *Public Personnel Management*, Vol. 8, No. 3, May–June, 1979, p. 152.

Ronen, S. *Flexible Work Hours: An Innovation in Quality of Work Life*. New York: McGraw-Hill, 1981.

Ronen, S., Primps, S. B. and Cloonan, J. Testimony submitted to the Senate Committee on Governmental Affairs. Hearings before the Committee on Governmental Affairs, U. S Senate, 95th Congress, Second Session on S. 517, S. 518, H. R. 7814, June 29, 1978.

Stevens, E. D. and Elsworth, R. Flexitime in the Australian Public Service: Its Effects on Non-Work Activities., *Public Personnel Management*, Vol. 8, No. 3, May–June 1979, p. 196.

# CHAPTER SEVEN

# Technology
# and
# Information Management

## Computers, Local Governments, and the Litany to EDP[1]

James N. Danziger

*Given the serious problems facing urban/suburban local governments, the search for a* deus ex machina *solution has centered upon the extensive use of computers and electronic data processing (EDP). For a variety of information-processing tasks, the contributions of EDP have been substantial. However, there has developed among many local government actors a "litany" to EDP. This consists of certain canons about the beneficial impacts of computers on local government operations. This article on the basis of case study analysis in 12 cities and counties, identifies major components of the litany to EDP. These include the beliefs that EDP is staff-reducing and cost-reducing, that EDP provides better information for decision makers, that EDP increases the superordinate's ability to monitor subordinates, and so on. The evidence suggests that the litany is often misleading and occasionally incorrect. The article presents generalized findings meant to temper the uncritical acceptance of the litany to EDP.*

The demands and problems facing local governments in metropolitan areas have increased so dramatically since 1960 that the notion of an "urban crisis" is commonplace. In most urban and suburban jurisdictions,

the scope and cost of goods and services provided by local governments have risen enormously while there has been no corresponding increase in fiscal capacity. And the greater complexity and interdependence of problems has vastly increased the decision makers' cognitive costs in gathering information, searching for solutions, and implementing and monitoring policies. Under these "crisis" conditions, the longing for some *deus ex machina* is strong. To this point, the prime candidate for this role is the computer and the use of electronic data processing (EDP).

City and county governments are currently spending more than $1 billion per year on EDP. With the broad capabilities of third generation hardware and with the development of sophisticated software, the computer's potential for aiding local government seems great. Moreover, the success or at least the promised success of the use of EDP for particular activities in particular city or county governments has been well publicized. A body of largely promotional information has been transmitted by the literature in the computer field and in the fields of local government professionals. As a result, the perceptions and expectations about the benefits of EDP are generally high among local government officials.

This article will suggest that a litany to EDP has developed. The article is meant to stimulate critical thinking and research about the litany by presenting controversial observations which merit systematic analysis. Only recently has empirical social science research been directed to a reasoned analysis of the impact of local government EDP.[2] This article presents findings derived from exploratory case studies in 12 cities and counties around the United States. These findings are not based on the execution of a rigorous case study design. In particular, there was no set of hypotheses specified for explicit testing in the field. The selection of research sites was informed by a classificatory scheme (using the level of EDP sophistication and the politico-demographic characteristics of the city or county as dichotomous variables in a 2 × 2 table). Data collection, based upon numerous open-end interviews and the analysis of written documents, was not systematic, though it was extensive.[3] The findings are based on the author's deduction and insight and are supported in the text by a limited amount of evidence. While substantial evidence underlies the findings, it is relatively subjective. Thus the findings should be viewed as exploratory and suggestive.

## EDP AND LOCAL GOVERNMENT OPERATIONS

The capability to store, to retrieve, and to analyze information is fundamental to the success of all organizations. It is obvious that the kinds of information which are currently processed effectively by computers are only a sub-set of the total information utilized in the determination and implementation of local government activities. Other important kinds of information include insight concerning political values and constraints, understandings accumulated through experience, and verbal and written communications.

There are, however, a variety of "information processing tasks" in local government where the use of EDP is particularly valuable. For these tasks, the computer might contribute to the information system by providing data that are: (1) stored more efficiently and economically; (2) more accurate; (3) more comprehensive; and (4) more easily retrieved and transferred. Moreover, the computer facilitates manipulation and analysis of data at a level of sophistication, speed, and magnitude that was not possible prior to EDP. There are several types of information processing tasks where EDP has made fundamental and valuable contributions to the activities of city and county governments. Table 1 presents a typology of these tasks[4] and a few representative examples of their use.

## THE LITANY TO EDP

This array of capabilities of EDP is most impressive. It seems clear that, under appropriate conditions, most local governments should make effective and beneficial use of EDP for various information processing tasks. However, there has been little effort by practitioners and researchers to specify either the full range of impacts of EDP or the conditions for effective use of the technology.

Rather, the literature on local government computing is characterized by a promoter's bias.[5] This bias is manifest in reports that, *inter alia*: (1) focus on the success of a single system in a single jurisdiction; (2) tend to discuss impacts in a future-oriented verb tense ("will be" or "is becoming") rather than in the present tense ("is"); (3) infrequently examine automated tasks that are evaluated as failures or major disappointments; (4) examine real costs of EDP, financial and human, in a perfunctory manner and imply (with impressionistic evidence or none at all) that such costs are surely outweighed by payoffs.

The obvious potential of EDP has combined with this promotion-oriented flow of evaluative information to create a favorable climate of opinion among high-level staff about EDP in local governments. There are several components which underlie this climate. One is that there are many legitimate examples of beneficial EDP uses in cities and counties. Another component is that, given the "urban crisis" and the pervasive search for help, local government actors willingly suspend their disbelief about EDP. A third component is the paucity of readily available information about negative impacts of EDP.[6]

These phenomena have given rise to a sort of litany to EDP in local government—a broadly circulated and generally accepted credo about the impacts of computers. Although there is some variation in the content of the litany by place and by person, there is a striking recurrence of certain themes when those involved in local government computing discuss EDP. These views are particularly evident among members of the unit providing EDP services. But recitation of the litany is also prevalent among top policy makers and administrators.[7] The following is a catalogue of some central canons of the EDP litany:

1. EDP tends to be staff reducing and cost reducing.
2. EDP turns mountains of data into molehills.
3. EDP provides better information for decision makers.
4. EDP increases the supervisor's ability to manage subordinates.
5. Inadequate utilization of EDP is primarily a function of either the user's resistance to or the user's failure to understand computers.

**TABLE 1**
**A typology of information processing tasks characterization**

| Type | | Examples |
|---|---|---|
| 1. Record-keeping | Activities which primarily involve the *entry, updating, and storage of data,* with a secondary need for access; the computer facilitates manageable storage and easy up-dating for nearly unlimited amounts of information. | Inventories, such as voter registration files and land use files; statistics-keepers, such as Uniform Crime Reports data; throughput systems, such as accounting ledgers. |
| 2. Calculating/printing | Activities which primarily involve *sorting, calculating, and printing of stored data* to produce specific operational outputs; utilizes the computer's capabilities as a high-speed data processor. | Payroll processing, utility billing, preparation of mailing lists, simple budget preparation. |
| 3. Record-searching | Activities where *access to and search of data files* is of primary importance; by defining parameters, relevant cases can be retrieved from a file with speed and comprehensiveness; on-line capability of computer is particularly useful. | Regional, state and national wanted warrant files among police agencies; parking ticket "scofflaw" systems; jury selection. |
| 4. Record restructuring | Activities which involve *reorganization, reaggregation, and/or analysis of data*; the computer is used to link data from diverse sources or to summarize large volumes of data as management and planning information. | Social services information and referral systems; program budgeting systems; geoprocessing systems, such as ACG/DIME. |
| 5. Sophisticated analytics | Activities which utilize *sophisticated visual, mathematical, simulation, or other analytical methods* to examine data; the special capabilities of computers make possible the manipulation of data about complex, interdependent phenomena. | Computer mapping and graphics systems such as SYMAP, regression models to estimate the appraised value of real property, planning simulation models, revenue and expenditure forecasting. |
| 6. Process control | Activities which *approximate a cybernetic system*; data about the state of a system is continually monitored and fed back to a human or automatic controller which steers the system toward a performance standard; the computer's capability for real-time monitoring and direction of activities is utilized. | Police, fire, and ambulance dispatch; budget monitoring and control; traffic signal control; water and power distribution control. |

6. Transfer of computer technology among local governments will prevent the continual reinvention of the wheel.

Each of these canons is assessed briefly in the following section. Given such brevity in the examination of complicated issues, conclusive assessment is not possible. Moreover, by selective use of the case study evidence, one could support or dispute any of these themes. An anti-computer polemic is wholly inappropriate since EDP can be and is being put to many effective uses in local governments. But the purpose here is to examine each canon critically—to serve as counter-point to the rather uncritical acceptance of the EDP litany and to temper the sanguine perceptions of many local government actors by focusing upon some of the problematic aspects of the EDP-local government interface.

## ASSESSING THE LITANY TO EDP

1. EDP tends to be staff reducing and cost reducing.

One of the most attractive anticipated consequences of automating many local government operations has been the reduction of staff. The speedy efficiency of the computer, it is argued, can replace the staff required for many of the routinized information processing tasks. Such staff reductions are evident on many of the printing/calculating and record-keeping functions. In some cases, the number of staff has remained constant while the number of transactions has increased. In other cases, EDP has enabled an operating unit to expand the scope of a task or undertake new tasks.

However, staff reductions are the exception on most of the more complex tasks which have been computerized.[8] Data coding and entry often involve more staff time per transaction than did the manual system. In many cases, new or expanded data collection is undertaken, at least some of which has questionable utility. Moreover, substantial technical staff time is required to service computer operations and software.

More broadly, political jurisdictions usually face important constraints on staff reduction. In those units where patronage continues to be an important resource, there is a reluctance to eliminate the kinds of jobs automation might affect. And in most settings, local government personnel have some job protection through civil service. For those above the clerical level, EDP normally affects the nature of a person's job rather than eliminating the job or clearly altering productivity.[9]

It is extremely difficult to evaluate the claim that EDP is cost reducing for local government. First, the cost-savings argument is often linked closely to purported staff reductions. But if reduction of staff is not substantial and if the EDP staff command moderately high salaries, this aspect of cost-reduction is problematic. Second, there are analytical problems in doing the kind of cost-benefit studies which would assess this claim.[10] It is difficult to measure the real cost of EDP, given the many hidden costs related to development, maintenance, modification, and training. Estimating the dollar value of benefits is particularly slippery. The tasks initially automated, like billing systems, were often revenue producing; but an increasing proportion of the computerized tasks do not directly generate revenue. As these kinds of uses proliferate, the value of EDP, if it is assessed at all, is established by revelation rather than evaluation.

A third aspect of the cost puzzle is that EDP tends to create a kind of artificial slack resources. Normally, a local government expands its programmer and analyst staff to meet the work demands of a development phase in which the automation of most tasks appears cost-effective. After these systems are built, there seems to be underutilization of technical staff, since maintenance is less time consuming. In addition, most jurisdictions acquire hardware with capacity substantially exceeding current needs. All of this "underutilization" inspires a solution: initiate new projects. Over time, the momentum of the development/redesign cycle takes control. One consequence of this cycle is that attention to the intrinsic cost-effectiveness of automating a task is diminished. The central question relating to EDP development/redesign becomes: what next? rather than: anything next?

2. EDP turns mountains of data into molehills.

There is no doubt that EDP facilitates the storage, manipulation, and retrieval of large amounts of information. For local governments, a number of information processing tasks are required by statute (e.g., property records, payroll, arrest records, etc.). For most of these tasks, the value of EDP is clear. But there is a far greater range of such tasks which have the potential to be automated. This range includes both increased information on existing tasks and also new data which support new information processing tasks.

In most instances, the marginal costs of expanding the information available for any information processing task are small. Where it is rather easy to collect and to store additional data, the "why not?" question is asked far more often than a "why?" question. Hence, a risk for local government activities is that EDP will stimulate the over-accumulation of information.[11] It has become axiomatic that more information is better than less information. Although we talk of information overload, we don't seem concerned about it, particularly when EDP can "manage" large amounts of data so stoically.

The problem is that the "more information, more manipulation is better" axiom is rather mindless and, at some point, is not true. For local government activities, there are currently no standards to distinguish the necessary from the desirable from the superfluous in the collection of data. Thus the argument here is that EDP is a two-edged sword regarding the management of information: EDP can indeed turn mountains of data into molehills; but it also has a tendency to turn mountains into mountain ranges.

3. EDP provides better information for decision making.

An important expectation among government actors has been that EDP would increase the usable information reaching decision makers. It is well known that there are substantial cognitive and time costs involved in the search for and analysis of information. Such costs drop significantly with EDP, particularly in handling large quantities of data. Moreover, it is assumed that the quality of available information will be enhanced, since it has been collected and analyzed more systematically than with most manual systems.

Those in decision-making positions usually observe that EDP has improved the quality and increased the quantity of usable information.

There is a subtle but important problem related to this canon. In the perceptions of many actors, computer-generated data have "special" credibility and reliability. In some cases, this means that data from the computer are viewed as more accurate and/or less doctored. For example, the head of the health department in a Southern parish (county) observed that federal auditors routinely accept her computer-generated statistics reporting service provision. Yet these same auditors had been extremely skeptical of the same reports when they had been prepared manually. In the cities and counties studied, this extra credibility granted to automated data was quite widespread.

Clearly, the generation of deceptive reports is no more difficult with the computer than without it. Indeed, some actors expressed a *prima facie distrust* of computer-generated data. This group includes both "old fashioned" persons and also sophisticates of computer technology, who realize the ease with which the computer can be made to generate data which misleads or distorts. For example, the planning department in one Eastern city assessed the complex computer simulations used by the county planning agency to justify an expansive highway program. After much sleuthing, they isolated the key parameter: a 1960 birth rate totally inappropriate for the area in the late 1970s. Only with the exposure of this assumption did local decision makers question whether the computer analyses might be "wrong."

A more extreme example of the potency attributed to EDP is the claim that computers can solve urban problems. One might object that this is merely hyperbole—no one really believes that the computer is more important in dealing with an urban problem, burglary for example, than factors like the amount and quality of resources committed to the problem. And yet, consider the experience of the deputy superintendent of police in a large city:

> The first exposure I had to anything at all about computers was in 1966 when I attended a two-week course at the University of Indiana. Then, I was very much impressed. But now, when I think back, it was just bull. . . .The computer guy told us—I'll never forget it, I was so impressed, I couldn't believe it—he told us he was able to tell that an accident was going to

occur on a certain corner, within a certain week, within a certain time period. Someone sat there for three of the six days and the accident did occur.

> That summoned up a brand new world for law enforcement. All we have to do now is get a couple of good computers and we'll be able to predict when a burglar is going to go into a building! If a guy can tell me when a car wreck will happen, he surely will be able to tell me when a robber is going to walk into a store. If I have an officer there, he'll make the arrest.

> That's the impression they gave. Then in 1970, when our department began to get some print-outs, I realized I didn't understand anything about what computers could and couldn't do. Now I'm learning by trial and, mostly, error.

In the cities and counties examined, there was a substantial number of such cases of "mystification via automation." Intrinsically, computer-based data and decision making should not be viewed with either more or less trust or hope than other forms of data and decisions. The problem is that many local government actors currently harbor some predisposition about the credibility of data and decisions where EDP has been employed. The idea is that, over time, these generalized, quasimoral positions about EDP will be replaced by accurate perceptions grounded in the realities of local computer use.

4. EDP increases the supervisor's ability to manage subordinates.

Downs has suggested that some of the most important organizational "power shifts" with EDP involve an increase in the power and control of higher-level officials over intermediate and lower-level personnel. In Downs' view, EDP facilitates the close monitoring of subordinates by capturing performance data from their routine reports.[12] In one example of this monitoring capability, a Southern sheriff used EDP to plot the times and locations of tickets written by his traffic wardens. The data revealed that the tickets were clustered at two times during the afternoon and in the streets adjacent to the town's movie houses. The sheriff made the logical inference about the afternoon activities of his wardens and forced an immediate change in their work habits.[13]

Work monitoring systems were employed in most of the cities and counties studied. In every area of local government operations that was examined, these systems were praised by supervisors. With few exceptions, they involve a minimal increase in data-entry activities and provide management information that did not exist prior to automation.

The problems with such monitoring systems are quite predictable. Most subordinates are uncomfortable if not unhappy with the increased measurement of their behavior. At one level, this is a reasonable response of people who have been accustomed to freedom from detailed scrutiny and who now believe they are confronted with the spectre of a Big Brother.

At a more subtle level, their malaise stems from the insensitivity of computer-based monitoring systems. The systems often monitor professional groups like policemen, whose activities are characterized both by a variety of roles and also by ambiguity and discretion in the performance of these roles.[14] But the systems tend to rely on quantitative and often uni-dimensional measurement. Those monitored are more or less consciously driven to "do well," as defined by the particular measures. Perceptive managers can blunt this effect; but there is an understandable tendency for both the monitors and the monitored to focus on these clear, quantitative measures when evaluation is otherwise subjective and ambiguous. In a characteristic example, police performance in one city is measured (and rewarded) on the basis of the number of arrests, not on the basis of the time and skill expended to maintain the peace, provide services, or improve relations with subcommunities.

The obvious solution is to develop work monitoring systems that utilize more sensitive measures; but none were evident in the systems studied, which included ones for police, property appraisers, social workers, and nurses.[15] To this point, EDP has provided the supervisor with easy access to performance data and enhanced his ability to manage his personnel. But the unintended consequences of current systems upon behavior and morale require attention. These systems have a tendency to supplant rather than supplement more qualitative criteria of control and evaluation and they might actually reduce the quality of service provision.

5. Inadequate utilization of EDP is primarily a function of either the user's resistance to or the user's failure to understand computers.

The reaction of most local government employees to the intrusion of the computer on their job space is a mix of anxiety, hostility, and intimidation. Moreover, most automated applications are neither smoothly implemented nor easily incorporated into the user departments' operating procedures. Many observers, particularly those in the EDP units, claim that the user's resistance to and misunderstanding of the computer is the primary obstacle to successful design, implementation, and utilization of many automated tasks.

This is at least partly true. Some managers and many staff and line personnel, perplexed or threatened by EDP, exhibit classic bureaucratic behavior—they resist change, they subvert innovations, they persist with old SOPs.[16] Within the user department, the best predictors of successful implementation and use of a new computer application seem to be: (1) the extent to which EDP has generally infiltrated the SOPs of the unit, and (2) the familiarity with EDP and/or the level of professionalism of the managers of the unit.

However, the case studies suggest that inadequate utilization of EDP in local governments is *not* primarily a function of failures and shortcomings internal to the user department. The most common source of problems is the unit in charge of EDP. A surprisingly large proportion of automated tasks are poorly designed. In some instances, this is due to the technical inadequacies of the analyst and programmer staff. Many local governments, hamstrung by civil service requirements regarding hiring, salary, and promotion, have an unexceptional technical staff.[17] In such settings, certain conditions are likely: (1) skill levels are inadequate to mount first-rate development projects; (2) projects are characterized by major delays, large cost overruns, or abandonment; (3) a large proportion of programmer and analyst activity concerns debugging and software maintenance rather than redesign or development; (4) documentation is insufficient or nonexistent; and (5) there is talk of a "credibility gap" between EDP and users.

The level of user involvement in design is another aspect of the utilization issue. Automated local government operations can be poorly designed, regardless of the technical competency of the EDP staff. This situation is manifest in two types of phenomena. First, decisions about the selection and priority of those information processing tasks to be automated are not informed by insight—the user lacks insight regarding the computer's capabilities and the technician lacks insight regarding the requirements and interdependencies of various user department tasks.

Second, the automation of some tasks either fails to fulfill the requirements of the task or fails to facilitate the task. For example, the billing systems used by the city treasurer in one Eastern city have no "balance forward" routines to credit partial payments on an account. And the controller's on-line ledger system files transaction records in a manner which makes audit trails extremely difficult. These omissions seem incredible to those who understand the requirements of each task. In an example of the failure to facilitate a task through EDP, a highly competent analyst in one Northeastern city designed an automated system which established a "rational" line of march for meter readers. Elegant in design, the lines of march are awkward and unusable in the real world of the meter readers, who view the automated system as a technological monstrosity.

There is no place in the local government bureaucracy where the "we"-"they" terminology is more common than between EDP users and the EDP staff. It is a relationship between foreigners, not adversaries —the differences are those of language and of work culture. In general, those sites where the two cultures gap is bridged are characterized by substantial user involvement in design and implementation. This takes a variety of forms. It tends to occur where programmers and analysts: (1) are decentralized to user departments and are in the user chain of command; (2) are personnel with actual job experience in the user department, for example, retrained policemen, planners, or finance people; or (3) are "programmed" by the EDP managers to have a fundamental user orientation.

Hence, there is no simple explanation of inadequate development and use of automated tasks for various local government units. To some extent, such problems relate to the fear and ignorance of computing among potential users. But in many cases the problems can be attributed to the quality of the EDP staff, to their misunderstanding of the user's task, or to overambitious technical designers.

6. Transfer of computer technology among local governments will prevent the continual reinvention of the wheel.

Given the increasing cost for developing automated systems, the transfer of standardized computer software has been widely advocated. Since many local governments perform the same tasks, it seems reasonable that the adaptation of well-designed software will be far less costly, on many automated applications, than inhouse design and implementation.

However, a striking finding when particular local governments are examined is that successful examples of software transfer are rare. For many cities and counties, serious exploration of transfer seldom occurs. When an EDP staff is undertaking a new application,

it will usually examine a few comparable systems or programs to discover their general nature. But a systematic search for such comparable cases is rare and the whole-cloth transfer of a system is seldom attempted. There are some packages, merchandized by vendors, consultants, government agencies, or clearing houses, that provide generalized software for a particular task.[18] Even these are adopted sporadically and, in many cases, are found by users to be unsatisfactory.

What explains the lack of extensive transfer? Ironically, the lack of adequate information is one problem. It is a difficult, often serendipitous, process by which a local government identifies other units which might have a transferable system. And as spatial distance increases, the chance of discovery is reduced and the costs of studying the system become prohibitive. Second, if a potentially transferable system is located, technical problems arise. Documentation for the system is often inadequate. Moreover, many EDP personnel argue that differences in hardware and/or languages between the two EDP units result in adaptation costs which eliminate the virtues of transfer.

A third obstacle to transfer is captured by Freud's notion of "the narcissism of small differences." Persons (here, local governments) who appear quite similar are motivated to stress their differences in order to maintain their own uniqueness. A frequent assertion is that "we are different from City A" or "our department does not do that function like County B." Reinforced by the patchwork of state and local statutes and by the particular pattern of their own SOPs, most user developments are unwilling to accept a system developed for the "different" situation in another local government. The attitudes of EDP personnel constitute a fourth obstacle. Most programmers and analysts view the design-development phases of automating a task to be a challenging, creative enterprise. However, the transfer-adaptation process is generally viewed as unstimulating, even drudgery.

Thus, both EDP and user department personnel are motivated to find shortcomings with transfer-in software. Each group argues, on technical grounds, that *local* development ought to occur. To the top decision makers, the combination of such technically based arguments is usually compelling. Broadly, there has been diffusion of the *concept* of the wheel—as ideas for EDP applications. But the desire of local government personnel to design and embellish their own particular wheel has stymied wide-scale utilization of the transfer process.

## CONCLUSION

Given the configuration of challenges and problems in urban/suburban America, the expanding role of EDP in the operations of local governments seems assured. It is clear that EDP has enhanced the efficiency, speed, and flexibility of some information processing tasks. The capabilities of computers for printing, record-keeping, record-searching, record restructuring, and sophisticated analysis can be utilized in a substantial number of operations.

There has been a rather uncritical acceptance that certain impacts of EDP are overwhelmingly beneficial. This acceptance has been a function of hope, of an information network heavily biased toward promotional EDP success stories, and of a lack of empirical research. This article has attempted to illuminate qualifications and complexities regarding certain aspects of this litany to EDP.

There is evidence that the impacts of EDP upon many local government operations are complex and might be, at least in part, negative. For many, perhaps most, information processing tasks, automation does not seem to result in cost reduction or staff reduction. EDP can stimulate the collection, coding, and storage of large amounts of data for which there is no compelling purpose. There can be important unintended and unsatisfactory consequences from the use of EDP to justify decisions or to monitor the action of subordinates. And there are organizational arrangements and role characteristics of users and EDP personnel that can lead to poor design of automated tasks and minimal use of technology transfer.

None of these observations is startling to those who have examined EDP in a variety of cities and counties. What *is* startling is the apparent absence of objective observers, whether practitioners or social scientists. Most of those publicly reflecting upon EDP in local government are committed to its success. Their attention is drawn to successful users, they confuse potential with performance, and they vigorously teach the EDP catechism.

The effect of such a favorable environment upon top policy makers is most important. In the absence of compelling negative evidence in their own jurisdiction, they are normally inclined to join with the EDP promoters and others who support the EDP litany. This research indicates that those actors who determine the uses of EDP in local government operations must consider the quality and biasing of information they have received about automated information systems. To the extent they accept the aptness of the litany metaphor, they should be prompted to reassess whether their responses to and decisions about EDP have been founded on balanced, objective information. These local government decision makers must free themselves from uncritical adherence to the EDP litany. Rather, they must attempt to identify the actual array of impacts from particular EDP activities.

Those social scientists who study EDP in local governments must direct their findings and insights to these local government actors. Research and analysis can specify the consequences of particular automated information processing tasks under specified conditions. For example, it might be that the impacts of EDP vary for different types of IPTs and for different mixes of political and administrative environments. Systematic analysis of such variations can provide local government actors with EDP policy advice which is both empirical and prescriptive. Such analysis is the desideratum of policy-relevant research.

## NOTES

1. This article is part of a larger research project, URBIS, which is evaluating information technology in local governments. It is supported by a grant from the RANN Division of the National Science Foundation (Grants GI-42038 and APR 74-12158-A01). The research is being undertaken by the Public Policy Research Organization of the University of California, Irvine. The ideas in this article owe much to my co-field researcher, Rob Kling, Department of Information and Computer Science, University of California, Irvine. Helpful commentaries were also provided by Ken Kraemer, John King, Joe Matthews, Bill Dutton, Mitch Modeleski, and anonymous reviews. I am also grateful for the helpfulness and patience of many local government personnel in the various research sites.

2. Examples include Kenneth Laudon, *Computers and Bureaucratic Reform* (New York: Wiley & Sons, 1974); Anthony Downs, "A Realistic Look at the Final Payoffs from Urban Data Systems," *Public Administration Review,* Vol. 27, No. 5 (September/October 1967), pp. 204–210; Rob Kling, "The Riverville Social Services Information and Referral System" (Irvine, Calif.: Public Policy Research Orga-

nization, 1975); Robert Quinn, "Computer Information Systems for Human Services: An Impact Analysis" (unpublished paper, University of Cincinnati, 1973); and Kent Colton, "Police and Computers: Use, Acceptance, and the Impact of Automation," *The Municipal Yearbook,* Vol. 39 (1972), pp. 119–136. *Municipal Information Systems: Evaluation of Policy-Related Research* (Irvine, Calif.: Public Policy Research Organization, 1974) is a helpful inventory of existing research and findings.

3. In each research site, the role of EDP was examined for a number of specific local government functions (primarily in finance, public safety, health and planning). Interviews were conducted with relevant actors in the EDP unit and in the user department units. Respondents were interviewed at all levels, from top managers to clerical personnel, and were selected by a "snowball" sampling technique. This procedure involves selecting initial respondents on the basis of the relevance of their administrative or political roles. These interviews lead to the identification of other important actors or types of actors who are also interviewed.

4. Most actual information processing tasks are a combination of the functions in this taxonomy. The classifications are based on the *primary modality* of a particular task. At this point, the taxonomy has heuristic rather than theoretical value. However, when it is refined, it might be viewed as a variable, with differential impacts hypothesized on phenomena like the quality of work environment.

5. Characteristic of the "social science wing" of this literature is the perspective of George Hemmens, *Impact Evaluation and Monitoring of the Charlotte Integrated Information System Project: A Baseline Report* (Chapel Hill: University of North Carolina, 1973).

6. It seems that most local government actors are aware of one or more bizarre computer blunders like the million dollar water bill. Such anecdotes are common responses to a question about negative impacts of EDP. These tales might function to short-circuit, for many actors, a more systematic and serious appraisal of pervasive negative consequences of computer use.

7. Interesting survey data on the current opinions about EDP among local government chief executives is presented in the special report by James Danziger, William Dutton, Kenneth Kraemer, and Sigfrid Pearson in *Nation's Cities,* Vol. 13 (October 1975).

8. This point is supported in Annabelle Sartore and Kenneth Kraemer, *Automation, Work, and Manpower Policy,* Vol. VI of Municipal Information Systems: Evaluation of Policy-Related Research (Irvine, Calif.: Public Policy Research Organization, 1974), pp. 2–10 to 2–13.

9. There are cases of increased productivity on more complex tasks, such as the units appraised per man-year where regression models are used for residential property appraisal.

10. For negative assessment of the actual use of cost-benefit and cost-effectiveness analyses for municipal information systems, see Edward Schrems and George Duggar, *Information Systems, Procurement, Computer Resource Allocation, and Finance Policy,* Vol. III of Municipal Information Systems: Evaluation of Policy-Related Research (Irvine, Calif.: Public Policy Research Organization, 1974), esp. ch. 2 and 5.

11. Available research varies on this point. Alan Westin and Michael Baker, *Databanks in a Free Society: Computers, Record-Keeping and Privacy* (New York: Quadrangle Books, 1972), claim that the introduction of computing did not increase the amount of information collected. Laudon, however, found examples of this proliferation of unused data. See Laudon, pp. 155 ff.

12. Downs, p. 208. Another aspect of Downs' argument is that automation reduces the ability of the subordinate to filter and bias the operations data which reach the supervisor.

13. This example is reported by Marshall Meyer.

14. James Q. Wilson, *Varieties of Police Behavior* (Cambridge, Mass.: Harvard University Press, 1968).

15. For another example, see Laudon, pp. 155–157.

16. This not to claim, of course, that the automation is inevitably opposed and resisted by operating agencies. Unit heads often support some use of EDP to support their own agendas. See, for example, Laudon, ch. 8.

17. The inability of the EDP unit to compete with the salary scales of local private industry for skilled technical staff was cited as a major problem in nine of the 12 research sites. This is supported by some research, such as that on county EDP salaries by Jack Bizzel, "EDP Personnel and Salaries," *American County Government,* Vol. 31 (1966), pp. 20–31. However, other studies claim salary schedules are competitive in the EDP area. See Public Administration Service, *ADP in Public Personnel Administration* (Chicago: Public Administration Service, 1969), esp. ch. V. Obviously, other factors than these can effect the quality and retention of an EDP staff.

18. An example of the clearing-house is Public Technology, Inc. (PTI), which provides a software system to its subscribers from time to time. Many transfers seem to be induced by the lure of outside funding support from government agencies, such as HUD and LEAA, which have used the grant carrot extensively.

# The Interests Served by Technological Reform
## The Case of Computing

Kenneth L. Kraemer
William H. Dutton

*This study explores the interests served by technological reform through an empirical analysis of power shifts stemming from the use of computer technology in American local governments. Alternative hypotheses concerning the existence and direction of power shifts are tested with survey and observational data collected in 42 U. S. cities. The findings indicate that computer-based systems tend to follow and reinforce the existing pattern of local government power relationships, whether that pattern be pluralistic or centralized in bureaucrats, technocrats, or politicians. Consequently, computing tends to support the interests of the status quo versus the interests of reform.*

Administrative reformers have always wanted to make government more businesslike by strengthening the professional management of government agencies (Banfield and Wilson, 1966). At the local level, the early reformers initiated structural reforms such as master planning, council-manager government, nonpartisan ballots, and at-large elections. At the state and national levels, they initiated the merit system, the executive budget, and the appointment versus election of department heads. Structural reform still emerges in contemporary mechanisms such as regional agencies for area-wide planning and coordination and mini-city halls for the decentralization of service delivery. Whereas the early reformers focused upon structural change as the primary means of implementing their goals, contemporary reformers increasingly turn toward technological change.[1] Thus, many governments have turned to the adoption and use of new technologies coincident with rapid advancements in the application of management science, computing, telecommunications, and other administrative technologies in the private sector.

Reprinted from *Administration & Society*, Vol. 11, No. 1, pp. 80–106. © 1979 by Sage Publications, Inc., with permission.

This trend is reflected in the widespread diffusion of computer technology in the government sector.[2] Computer technology might further the business goals of economy and efficiency through technical payoffs in the processing of information. Consequently, the success of computer processing of information might be evaluated as a reform mechanism by its impacts on saving money, staff, and other governmental resources. However, *the functions of technological reform may be political as well as technical.* Those who control technological reforms may shape the design and use of technology to serve their interests over the interests of others (Dutton and Kraemer, 1977). In doing so, political goals can supplant the business goals of economy and efficiency. Therefore, if one is to evaluate computer technology as a reform mechanism, one must first explore the interests served by the technology.

This paper investigates the interests served by computing as a technological reform. Specifically, it is about the power shifts which result from governmental computer use and the interests served by these power shifts. There are five hypotheses about the direction of power shifts which are empirically examined using survey and case study data on American cities.

## COMPUTERS AND POWER SHIFTS

There is considerable debate in the literature over both the existence and direction of power shifts and, therefore, whose interests are served by computing. On the one hand, some suggest that computing is apolitical in that it does not result in power shifts (Kling, 1974; Westin, 1972a). Computer-based information is claimed to be unsophisticated, of low quality, often conflicting, one of many sources of information, easily ignored by decision makers, often irrelevant, and, even if relevant to decisions, leaves great room for interpretation. In sum, decision makers would seldom develop or change their position on the basis of computer printouts.

On the other hand, information is viewed as a political resource within organizations much like status or positional authority and is closely akin to expertise. Because computers can change the character of information flows within organizations—including the speed, direction, content, and pattern of circulation—computers might influence the relative decisional effectiveness of different actors and therefore the relative influence of different interests in the governmental system.[3] Furthermore, those who control the technology might affect how the technology is utilized such as to enhance their decision-making effectiveness and interests within the organization.[4] That is, computing is likely to entail certain power payoffs or "power shifts." These power shifts are "gains in one person's decision-making effectiveness made at the expense of another person's. They are redistributions of the benefits of decision making" (Downs, 1967: 205). Among the most prominent expectations about the interest served by computing are the bureaucratic, technocratic, old-style, and pluralistic hypotheses.

## Bureaucratic Politics

A prevailing hypothesis is that computing is a tool of the administrative reform movement, is controlled by the professional bureaucrats through central administrative structures, and is used to improve their ability to manage subordinates and marshal information which supports their recommendations to top elected officials (Dutton and Kraemer, 1977; Ghere, 1978; Laudon, 1974; Downs, 1967). Computing serves the administrative reform movement by strengthening the role of lower level staff within the organization, and the general public. In local governments, the bureaucratic politics hypothesis suggests that computing tends to shift power to top managers (e.g., to the city manager in council-manager cities and to one or two department heads who informally serve the top management function in strong-mayor cities).[5]

## Technocratic Politics

Another common expectation is that computing, like most high technology, will be controlled by technical people (Danziger, 1977; Bell, 1973; Downs, 1967; Ellul, 1964).[6] Experts with specialized skills in the use of computing—technocrats—will control the design, development, and use of the technology for only they understand its operation, potential, and limits. Thus, computing will tend to serve their interests in the maintenance and enhancement of the technocrat's role in organizational decisions. In local governments, the technocratic politics hypothesis suggests that computing tends to shift more power to the "new urban planners," the modern counterpart of Taylor's "new class of urban managers" trained in the techniques of scientific management. In contrast to the traditional planner skilled in zoning and land use planning, the new urban planner is skilled in the use of computer-based analytical tools such as statistical analysis, urban modeling, and simulation. Often such planners are located in the research division of local planning departments, but they are also found in urban renewal, community development, and community analysis agencies.

## Old-Style Politics

Another expectation is that computing is a political technology which is largely controlled by and serves the elected officials through improving their capabilities to use and control information (Chartrand, 1967; Pool et al., 1964). In local governments, the old-style politics hypothesis suggests that computing tends to shift more power to the elected mayor and council who control computing through their legitimate and formal control over the organization. At the broadest level, public officials want to be reelected or advance to higher office and, therefore, might seek to use computing to advance these political ambitions. Depending on the official's election strategy, control over a government's computer-based information systems might be used to build public support indirectly, through improving the quality of governmental services, monitoring the bureaucracy, and cutting costs. Or, the politician might seek to use computing to build public support directly, through its use as a campaign tool for direct mailings, analysis of voting patterns, or data support justifying the official's decision to the public.

## Pluralistic Politics

A prominent rival hypothesis is that no single interest controls computer technology. Rather, a pluralistic array of interests—bureaucrats, technicians, and politicians—participates in the variety of governmental decisions which shape the adoption and use of computing (Pettigrew, 1975, 1973; Cyert and March, 1963). While a technological elite might tend to dominate many individual computing decisions, their influence is mediated by the numerous groups and interests which place demands on computing service providers and is further constrained by the bureaucratic politics of the government which sets the decision rules for the individual choices. In local governments, the pluralistic politics hypothesis suggests that computing will benefit elected officials, managers, and planners who all influence computing decisions.

## Reinforcement Politics

A final expectation is that control over computing will vary across organizations. Those who control the technology will shape it to serve their interests. However, because control over computer technology varies across organizations, computing does not systematically shift power to a particular kind of official. That is, *computer-based systems tend to follow and reinforce the existing pattern of power relationships, whether that pattern be pluralistic or centralized in bureaucrats, technocrats, or politicians.* Computing tends to be used or not used to the degree that it supports the position or interests of those who control the governmental organization. Computing reallocates power or influence only in the sense that it accentuates existing inequalities of influence. Computing seldom shifts power away from those who control governmental decision making (Hoffman, 1977, 1975, 1973). While the traditional hypotheses emphasize the impact of a technology on the organization which adopts it, *the reinforcement hypothesis emphasizes the impact of an organization on the technology which it adopts.*[7] The interests served by computing are likely to be the same interests served by the organization which has adopted the technology because computing simply enhances and extends the organization's capability of serving the interests of those who control the organization. In local governments, this hypothesis suggests that computing will increase the decision-making effectiveness of managers in reform governments, mayors in strong-mayor governments, and departments and planners in governments with departmental autonomy.

## METHODS AND DATA

Our strategy for empirically assessing the power shift hypothesis is to focus on those kinds of computer-based information systems which are most likely to affect the power relationships among organizational elites within a specific class of organizations— American cities.

While nearly any use of computer-based information can be viewed as increasing the decisional effectiveness of some official or agency in the government,[8] those systems which are most likely to affect the balance of power among bureaucrats, technicians, and politicians are those which better enable any of these officials to:

1. *manage*—control near term events by getting rapid and correct feedback about ongoing operations
2. *plan*—anticipate future uncontrollable events by getting analyses of current trends and predictions of future events
3. *persuade or coerce*—control decision situations by getting superior or sensitive information which is perceived as compelling.

Systems which serve these purposes can be distinguished by whether they are primarily oriented toward data about the urban environment or about the internal operations of the government. Table 1 arrays various illustrative systems which are likely to affect the decisional effectiveness of bureaucrats, technicians, and politicians by purpose (management, planning, and politics) and by the kind of data which supports their use (data banks versus operational systems).

Data banks pool facts about people and their environment (e.g., a jurisdiction's demography and its economy). In turn, this new information is aggregated and analyzed to determine environmental conditions (e.g., social indicators of the welfare of citizens and the health of the economy). These analyses can be used as a guide to public officials in identifying problems, determining needs, developing programmatic remedies, and applying for outside assistance. In some instances, information also is being fed into simulation and other models which mimic the behavior of some aspect of the environment (e.g., population growth and economic development). These analyses and models can be used to pretest the effects of various public actions as a guide to public officials in deciding among alternative policies. And, information about people (their demographic characteristics, likes and dislikes, and such) can be used to assess the political feasibility of development and financial plans.[9] As these examples illustrate, some data banks serve management, planning, and political purposes.

Operational systems are the functionally oriented computer systems which serve the internal operations of the government and which contain data about government employees and departmental operations. This information is variously aggregated and analyzed to determine revenue and expenditure patterns, personnel vacancies, turnover, vacations or sick leave, individual and departmental workloads, and selected indicators of performance. These analyses can be used by public

**TABLE 1**

**A typology of computer-based urban data systems, likely to affect the decisional effectiveness of bureaucrats, technicians and politicians**

| *Purpose* | Kind of system | | | |
|---|---|---|---|---|
| | **Data banks**<br>Contain data about the population/clientele and their environment | | **Operational systems**<br>Contain data about government personnel and operating departments | |
| *Management* | **Intergovernmental reporting** | | **Governmental reporting** | |
| | Uses: | Completing grant applications; preparing proposals; meeting intergovernmental reporting requirements | Uses: | Monitoring the activities of individuals and the operations of departments; monitoring revenues and expenditures, equipment and supplies. |
| | Example: | U. S. Census of population; housing survey, land use inventory | Example: | Budget monitoring systems, inventory control systems, activity reporting systems; accounting systems |
| *Planning* | **Environmental analysis** | | **Governmental analysis** | |
| | Uses: | Analyzing socio-economic characteristics of populations, geographic areas, and political districts; forecasting demand | Uses: | Allocating resources and manpower; scheduling activities, forecasting revenues & expenditures; forecasting cash flows; optimizing routes. |
| | Example: | Population, land use, traffic and economic inventory systems, urban development models; fiscal impact models | Example: | Manpower allocation models; emergency vehicle dispatch models; routing models, revenue and expenditure forecasting models |
| *Politics* | **Client persuasion** | | **Client and intergovernmental persuasion** | |
| | Uses: | Legitimation of policy positions to clients, political assessment of developmental plans; analysis of political constituency; analysis of distribution of costs and benefits of government services | Uses: | Handle client requests and complaints; document policy positions |
| | Example: | Social indicator systems; planning models and analyses (above), political analyses | Example: | Complaint monitoring systems; collective bargaining models; performance analyses |

officials in monitoring expenditures, identifying personnel problems, determining work assignments, and scheduling or rearranging departmental operations to improve performance. Sometimes information is fed into computer models which imitates some operation of a department such as handling emergency calls, dispatching vehicles, assigning personnel, or predicting cash flow. These analyses and models can be used to predict the effects of various departmental actions as a guide to public officials in deciding among alternative operational priorities and procedures. Also, individual and aggregated data from the operational systems can be used in support of particular policy positions, personnel actions, collective bargaining negotiations, or citizen requests and complaints. Consequently, operational data systems can serve management, planning, and political purposes similar to their data bank counterparts.

Given the different types of computer-based information systems in government and the different purposes they serve, our research strategy is first to empirically describe the use of data banks and operational systems by each type of decision maker for management, planning, and political purposes. This enables us to address the patterns of computer utilization characteristic of bureaucrats (city managers and administrators), technicians (new urban planners), and politicians (elected mayors and councils). These patterns of computer utilization allow us to speculate about the likely magnitude and direction of power shifts, for the use of computing seems to be a necessary if not sufficient condition for power shifts to occur. Second, we more directly explore the magnitude and direction of power shifts through an analysis of systematically coded case study observations regarding those officials whose influence was affected by the use of computing in 42 cities.

## The Sample

This study is based on data collected in 1976 in 42 U. S. cities over 50,000 in population. The cities were selected by a stratified sampling procedure such that all cities were automated and that the cities vary in the sophistication, extensiveness, and organizational arrangements of computing.[10] Thus, the average sample city is somewhat more automated than the typical U. S. city over 50,000; and the computing environments of these cities have somewhat more variation than would be the case for a random sample of automated cities.

## The Data

Within each city, data were collected using self-administered questionnaires, field-coded questionnaires, and case studies of the use of computing by top managers, mayors, councils, and planners. A pretested self-administered questionnaire was completed by the manager and several of the manager's staff, the mayor and several staff, a sample of council and staff, and those people responsible for maintaining and analyzing computer-based urban data banks and operational data—the planners and analysts.[11]

In addition to the self-administered questionnaires, the field work involved six investigators, including the authors, in case studies of each city for an average of three person-weeks in each of at least eight cities. Each site visit provided rich case study material as well as systematic judgmental ratings based on these case studies. This was accomplished by a series of structured questionnaires which were completed by the investigators during each site visit based on their case work, interviews, and archival research on each site. These questionnaires recorded their observations by a series of predetermined questions and response categories. This paper relies most heavily on these field-coded instruments as empirical data on the way in which computing is used by local government officials.

## Limitations

There are several important limitations to our analysis. First, this study is based on a limited group of U. S. cities, namely those with at least a moderate level of automation. Second, the concept of power shifts is controversial and its measurement is complex. Our study accepts a single definition of power shifts and is limited to systematic field observations and interviews at one point in time to explore a phenomenon which occurs over time. But, because power shifts raise important issues for the evaluation of technological reform, we have attempted to assess power shifts from computing by systematically integrating survey and case study methodology. We hope that other researchers will investigate similar issues in other settings and with other approaches and operational measures of power shifts. Third, this research does not deal with the interorganizational interests which may be served by computing. This study is focused on the intraorganizational, bureaucratic politics of computing and is only suggestive of the impact of computing on the relative influence of local governments vis-à-vis either the general public or other organizations.

## FINDINGS
### Do Power Shifts Occur?

The frequency and magnitude of power shifts are likely to depend on the degree and kind of use made of computers by bureaucrats, technocrats, and politicians. In order to describe the use of urban data banks and operational systems, we inquired about whether or not each kind of public official used either data banks, in each of six tasks displayed in Table 2, or operational systems, in each of four tasks displayed in Table 3. We then asked for examples and evidence of this use. The responses were used to categorize each official by whether computing was *not used, used only in exceptional cases,* or *generally used* (not just in isolated or nonspecific cases) for each task.

#### USE OF DATA BANKS

The patterns of data bank use suggest that power shifts are likely to occur but the magnitude of power shifts is likely to be less than predicted in much of the literature (Table 2). First, while each kind of official tends to use data banks, the overall use of data banks is low. In only about 10% of the cities does any given kind of public official *generally* use data banks. In about half the cities, the officials use data banks only in exceptional cases. For only two tasks, problem finding and problem legitimation, does any kind of official tend to generally use data banks in over 10% of the cities.

Second, there are more similarities than differences in use by role.[12] Planners are the major users of data banks given that their median level of use is highest on five of the six tasks. The planners are followed by the managers, mayors, and council, respectively. But, the total difference among roles on any task is less than 20% and most frequently is about 10%. This small difference in use among officials is unexpected given the predictions in much of the power shift literature.

Third, each kind of official tends to use data banks

TABLE 2
Levels of use of urban data banks by type of official

| | | Level of use by: | | | |
|---|---|---|---|---|---|
| Kind of uses | Level of use | Manager | Mayor | Council | Planners/ analysts |
| **Planning** | | | | | |
| Problem finding— | (1) Not used[a] | 27% | 40 | 41 | 18 |
| lead to new or clear | (2) Exceptional use | 63% | 49 | 46 | 60 |
| perceptions of | (3) Generally used | 10% | 11 | 13 | 22 |
| community problems | Median[b] | 1.87 | 1.69 | 1.69 | 2.04 |
| Changed or affected | (1) Not used | 57% | 72 | 67 | 57 |
| decisions | (2) Exceptional use | 43% | 25 | 33 | 38 |
| | (3) Generally used | 0% | 3 | 0 | 5 |
| | Median | 1.38 | 1.19 | 1.25 | 1.37 |
| Policy development | (1) Not used | 21% | 41 | 40 | 21 |
| | (2) Exceptional use | 4% | 0 | 0 | 3 |
| | (3) Generally used | 75% | 59 | 60 | 76 |
| | Median | 2.83 | 2.30 | 2.32 | 2.84 |
| **Politics** | | | | | |
| Legitimize existing | (1) Not used | 40% | 33 | 36 | 26 |
| problems | (2) Exceptional use | 43% | 33 | 51 | 38 |
| | (3) Generally used | 17% | 33 | 13 | 36 |
| | Median | 1.73 | 1.00 | 1.78 | 2.13 |
| Gain publicity | (1) Not used | 40% | 47 | 54 | 38 |
| | (2) Exceptional use | 50% | 50 | 38 | 50 |
| | (3) Generally used | 10% | 3 | 8 | 12 |
| | Median | 1.70 | 1.56 | 1.43 | 1.75 |
| Determine the | (1) Not used | 76% | 78 | 77 | 73 |
| political acceptability | (2) Exceptional use | 17% | 22 | 18 | 22 |
| of actions | (3) Generally used | 7% | 0 | 5 | 5 |
| | Median | 1.15 | 1.14 | 1.15 | 1.19 |

a. Percentage of cities where one or more data banks are automated, but not used in this way by role type.
b. Scored: 1 = not used; 2 = exceptional use; 3 = generally used.

in somewhat different ways. Other data indicate that planners focus on planning and political purposes.[13] Table 2 further indicates that while managers are more likely to use data banks for planning purposes (problem finding, decision making, and policy development), they are about as likely as are the elected officials to use data banks for political purposes (legitimizing their position, gaining publicity, and determining the political feasibility of different actions). Thus, while there is some specialization among roles in the purposes for which they use computing, no kind of official seems to have a monopoly over the use of computing in a specific area.

## USE OF OPERATIONAL SYSTEMS

The relatively low use of urban data banks by public officials might be due to the fact that data banks play a minor role in urban decision making when compared to operational data systems. Operational data systems *are* used more extensively than urban data banks, but overall use remains moderate (Table 3). In more than three-fourths of the cities, operational systems are used for management, planning, and political purposes. Also, there are somewhat greater differences in use by role. The managers' use of operational systems clearly dominates when compared to the use made by elected officials. In about one-half of the cities, the managers make general use of operational data systems for monitoring subunits, making decisions, and documenting policy positions. The only use which ranks low for the managers is responding to citizen complaints. In contrast, mayors most often use operational data for documenting policy positions and monitoring subunits. Thus, our general implication remains the

**TABLE 3**
**Levels of use of operational data systems by type of official**

| Kind of uses | Level of use | Level of use by: | | |
|---|---|---|---|---|
| | | Manager | Mayor | Council |
| **Management** | | | | |
| Monitor and control | (1) Not used[a] | 18% | 20 | 24 |
| departments and agencies | (2) Exceptional use | 33% | 63 | 61 |
| | (3) General use | 49% | 17 | 15 |
| | Median[b] | 2.44 | 1.97 | 1.93 |
| **Planning** | | | | |
| Changed or affected | (1) Not used | 18% | 38 | 46 |
| decisions | (2) Exceptional use | 32% | 34 | 27 |
| | (3) General use | 50% | 28 | 27 |
| | Median | 2.50 | 1.85 | 1.65 |
| **Politics** | | | | |
| Respond to citizen | (1) Not used | 35% | 55 | 59 |
| requests and complaints | (2) Exceptional use | 38% | 19 | 22 |
| | (3) General use | 27% | 26 | 19 |
| | Median | 1.90 | 1.41 | 1.34 |
| Document policy | (1) Not used | 26% | 28 | 47 |
| positions | (2) Exceptional use | 30% | 36 | 36 |
| | (3) General use | 44% | 36 | 17 |
| | Median | 2.31 | 2.09 | 1.58 |

a. Percentage of cities where operational data is automated, but not used by role type.
b. Scored: 1 = not used in this way, 2 = exceptional use, 3 = general use.

same. Power shifts are quite possible, but not dramatic in their intensity.

## Who Gains and Loses?

The direction of power shifts is also likely to be sensitive to the degree and kind of use made of computers by bureaucrats, technocrats, and politicians. The relative frequency with which each kind of official tends to use computing implies a loose hierarchy of officials who are more likely to gain in decision-making effectiveness (Tables 2 and 3). Planners tend to dominate the use of data banks; managers tend to dominate the use of operational data systems. This suggests that managers and planners generally gain somewhat more decision-making effectiveness than elected mayors or councils. However, the often small differences among officials in their frequency of use is suggestive of patterns expected by the pluralist interpretation.

## Patterns of Use

This loose hierarchy of officials with relatively greater and lesser gain from computing is based upon the percentage of cities in which a particular official rated high or low in the use of computing. It might be that in cities where the manager gains, the mayor and council

do not, and vice versa. In other words, the data could still support extensive power shifts if we find a tendency for high levels of use by one subset of officials. *But, as shown in Table 4, this is not a pattern of data bank or operational system utilization.*

Cities where one kind of official tends to have a high level of use, either of data banks or operational systems, are cities where all other kinds of officials will tend to have a high level of use. Rather than cities being distinguished by different kinds of officials dominating the use of computing, *cities are largely distinguished by those with and those without a high use of computing by planners, bureaucrats, and politicians.* Thus, the simple frequencies presented above do not mask more differentiated patterns of utilization. This finding tends to cast further doubt on the bureaucratic, technocratic, and old-style politics hypotheses and tends to add support to the pluralistic hypothesis.

## The Frequency of Power Shifts

While the frequency of utilization is suggestive of power shifts, a more direct measurement is available in the form of judgmental ratings made on the basis of extensive case study observations within each site. Table 5 shows the degree to which each type of public

178

**TABLE 4**
**Relationships among indicators of the use of computer-based operational and data bank information by role types[a]**

| Indicators | Manager use | Mayor use | Council use | Planner/ analyst use |
|---|---|---|---|---|
| | | **Operational data** | | |
| Manager use | | .36[b] | .34[b] | – |
| Mayor use | .51[b] | | .43[b] | – |
| Council use | .46[b] | .60[b] | | – |
| Planner/analyst use | .41[b] | .60[b] | .46[b] | |
| | | **Data banks** | | |

a. Pearson correlations among role types for use of operational data is presented in upper right and correlations for use of data banks is presented in lower left.
b. $p < .05$

official was judged to gain and lose influence as a result of computing in local government. These ratings further support the existence of power shifts and the same loose hierarchy of gainers described above. Computing is judged to have had *some effect* on the relative influence of at least one official in about 80% of the cities. Where there is an effect, computing has tended to increase rather than decrease the influence of public officials. While computing has decreased the influence of at least some officials in 27% of the cities, it has increased the influence of some officials in 54% of the cities. By rank, those who tend to gain (and not lose) influence are the planners (the technicians), the top managers and department heads (the bureaucrats), and the mayor and council (the politicians).

However, these rankings are less pronounced than either the technocratic or bureaucratic formulation of the power shift hypothesis suggests. Planners are not great beneficiaries of computing for they tend to gain influence in only about 27% of the cities. Likewise, managers have gained influence in only about 27% of the cities, while department heads and mayors gained influence in nearly as many, 18% and 19% respectively. Only the councils generally tend to have lost influence (in 20% of the cities) as a result of computing more often than they have gained influence (in 5% of the cities). Thus, no single official appears to be a general, substantial, and sole beneficiary of power shifts from

computing in cities. The shifts that occur are mainly gains rather than losses in the influence of officials, and the gains appear to be shared among nearly all officials. These findings, therefore, add support to the pluralist interpretation.

## Patterns of Power Shifts

While the marginals reported in Table 5 are supportive of the pluralist hypothesis, they are susceptible to a common problem with the aggregation of cross-sectional data. The same marginals could result from pluralistic patterns characterizing some subset of cities or the operation of different models of power shifts in different cities. Thus, it is important to evaluate the pluralist interpretation by testing whether it is the case that power gains on the part of one official are positively associated with power gains on the part of other officials—as would be the case for the pluralist model.

Surprisingly, in contrast to patterns of computer utilization, the patterns of power shifts are opposite the expectations of the pluralist hypothesis (Table 6). Power gains of one official are not positively associated with gains of other officials. Instead, there is a great deal of independence. Apparently, different models of power shifts operate in different cities, rather than pluralistic patterns being characteristic of a subset of cities in which power shifts are relevant.

179

## TABLE 5
**Percentage of cities where the use of computer-based data shifted influence among officials**

| | Effect on official | | |
|---|---|---|---|
| Official affected | Decreased influence | No effect | Increased influence |
| Data bank custodians and planners | 0 | 68 | 32 |
| Manager, CAO and staff | 3 | 70 | 27 |
| Departments | 10 | 72 | 18 |
| Mayor and staff | 14 | 67 | 19 |
| Council and staff | 20 | 75 | 5 |
| Any of the above officials | 27 | 19 | 54 |

a. Based on interviews at one-point-in-time, investigators developed a case history of the use of computing and its impacts on power shifts in each city. Each kind of official in each city was then scored as having had their influence decreased, unaffected, or increased as a result of computing. Disagreements between investigators (normally two per city) were resolved by reexamining the case histories.

### Power Reinforcement from Computer Use

The reinforcement politics hypothesis provides a plausible explanation for why the nature of power shifts might vary across cities. It may be that computing tends to reinforce the influence of those officials in control rather than to shift influence to a particular type of official. Because the influence structures of local governments vary, so might the nature of power shifts. In order to test the reinforcement hypothesis, we next explore the relationship between the structure of influence within a city and power shifts. If the reinforcement hypothesis is valid, then those in control should gain and certainly not lose power as a result of computing.

Table 7 describes the relationship between power shifts and several independent variables that tend to reflect the influence structures of local governments. Generally, power shifts tend to accentuate the existing structure of influence within the city, thereby supporting the reinforcement hypothesis. . . . In strong-mayor cities, computing tends to shift greater influence to the mayor, while in council manager cities, computing tends to shift greater influence to the manager. In larger cities with more complex and decentralized influence structures, computing tends to shift power away from the top manager and toward the planners and the operating departments, which already are likely to enjoy more autonomy than their counterparts in smaller cities. And where mayors and councils are influential in computing decisions, managers are less likely to gain power as a result of computing.

### SUMMARY AND DISCUSSION

Given the diversity of opinion regarding both the existence and direction of power shifts, we have examined the use of urban data banks and operational data systems as well as the power shifts to which they can be linked. From this examination, we can review the findings concerning the magnitude of power shifts and draw some conclusions as to the explanatory power of the five hypotheses regarding the direction of power shifts. We will then turn to the interests which are likely to be served as a result of these power shifts.

Power shifts occur in most automated local governments but these shifts tend to be subtle, limited, and complex in their patterns. While power shifts were judged to occur in over 75% of the cities investigated, the generally low to moderate use of computing for management, planning, or politics tends to limit the relevance of computing to the power relationships among bureaucrats, technocrats, and politicians. Across all governments, the relative decision-making effectiveness of no single kind of official is overwhelmingly enhanced by computer use.

The bureaucratic politics hypothesis suggests that managers will be major beneficiaries of power shifts. We did find that managers are the most frequent users of operational data systems and that managers were judged to have gained some influence in about one-fourth of the cities. However, managers are not the most frequent users of data banks and are not the most frequent beneficiary of power shifts. While managers are somewhat more likely to gain as a result of computing in the smaller city manager cities, they are not the dominant beneficiary in general. Consequently, the bureaucratic politics hypothesis is not descriptive of our findings.

The technocratic politics hypothesis suggests that the new urban planners will be the major beneficiaries of power shifts. We did find that planners both use data banks more than other officials for nearly every use investigated and are the most likely beneficiaries of power shifts. However, they have far from a monopoly over the use of data banks, are nearly irrelevant to the use of operational systems, and tend to gain influence in only about a third of the cities investigated. Furthermore, where planners tend to gain, so do mayors and other operating departments, generally in the larger cities. Thus, while the technocratic politics hypothesis predicts the relative dominance of the planners, it fails to explain the overall pattern of power shifts which include many shifts in favor of other officials.

### TABLE 6
### Relationships among power shift ratings for different officials

| Power shifts to: | Manager | Mayor | Council | Planner/ analyst | Departments |
|---|---|---|---|---|---|
| | | | Pearson correlations[a] | | |
| Manager | | .05 | .10 | −.13 | −.19 |
| Mayor | 27 | | .04 | .36 | −.19 |
| Council | 30 | 37 | | −.23 | −.06 |
| Planner/analyst | 30 | 37 | 40 | | .21 |
| Departments | 30 | 37 | 40 | 40 | |
| | | | Sample size | | |

a. Pearson correlations are presented in upper right and sample sizes are presented in the lower left.

The old-style politics hypothesis suggests that elected officials will be the major beneficiaries of power shifts. This is not supported. While mayors and councils use computing and sometimes appear to gain influence as a consequence, they least often gain and most often lose influence relative to planners and bureaucrats.

The pluralist hypothesis suggests that no single kind of official predominantly gains in decision-making effectiveness. This hypothesis finds substantial support in that each kind of official uses computer-based data and all appear to occasionally gain influence as a result. Further support is provided by the fact that where one kind of official tends to use computer-based data, so do the other kinds of officials. However, the patterns of power shifts are inconsistent with the pluralist hypothesis and suggest the operation of different power shifts in different cities.

Finally, the reinforcement politics hypothesis suggests that computer-based systems tend to follow and reinforce the existing pattern of power relationships. This hypothesis is most consistent with all survey findings and explains why we find the nature of power shifts to vary across governments. Each model of power shifts—the bureaucratic, technocratic, old-style, and pluralist—might be found to operate in some cities, depending on the existing structure of influence.

Thus, *planners and managers tend to be relative gainers because of the existing structure of influence in local governments.* In many cities the planning function is taking on a greater role with the increased importance of federal grants, needs assessment, evaluation components of programs, and more stringent reporting requirements. In the large cities, these factors come to play within an organizational setting which is more decentralized. Within such a system, planners have some autonomy and gain relatively more influence than they might otherwise have without the computing resource.

Likewise, managers clearly gain in influence in relation to their subordinates by the use of computing to monitor and control departmental operations. Yet, computing does not tend to shift greater influence to the manager in those cities where departments and agencies have a great deal of political autonomy from the manager—that is, in the large, strong-mayor cities. In contrast, computing tends to reinforce the power of the manager in the smaller city manager cities in which the mayor and council are less active and influential.

### Whose Interests Are Served?

The local government reform movement sought to make local government more efficient and rational through a series of structural and technological reforms. However, computing as an administrative reform has not had a large role in increasing the influence of professional managers in the operation of local government. Rather, those who control local government decisions have adapted this technology to serve the existing social and political structures. Thus, computing is a *malleable technology.* It can be shaped to serve the interests of administrative reform to the degree that administrative reformers control the operations of local government. Where they do not, computing is likely to serve other interests.

## TABLE 7
### Pearson correlations between selected independent variables and power shifts to managers, mayors, councils, planner analysts and departments

| Independent variables | Power shifts to:[a] | | | | |
| | Manager | Mayor | Council | Planner analyst | Departments |
|---|---|---|---|---|---|
| **Structure** | | | | | |
| Strong mayor city | −.22 | .38 | −.03 | .12 | −.13 |
| Council manager city | .22 | −.37 | .09 | −.23 | .05 |
| **Size & Complexity** | | | | | |
| Total population | −.31 | −.03 | −.20 | .39 | .41 |
| Government expenditures | −.26 | −.15 | .03 | .29 | .46 |
| **Control** | | | | | |
| Top manager influence[b] | −.21 | .25 | −.24 | .04 | −.29 |
| Mayor influence[b] | −.49 | .10 | −.16 | .04 | −.12 |
| Council influence[b] | −.34 | −.04 | −.16 | −.12 | −.03 |
| Department head influence[b] | −.11 | −.32 | −.19 | −.16 | .20 |

a. Marginals for these dependent variables are presented in Table 5.

b. Two or more informants in each city were asked "Consider a decision related to data processing, such as introducing computers to help perform a task. How often has each of the following officials had a major input into the final decision?"

Computing can be viewed as a malleable but certainly not an apolitical technology to the degree that it serves those interests which control its design and use. It is a means, a tool, for accomplishing the ends of those who use it. However, its impacts are not neutral. Given the current patterns of control over computing and use of the technology, computing as now implemented tends to serve some interests more than others. Most generally, computing supports the status quo of most local governments.[14] Specifically, urban data systems have been shaped to serve the interests of the planners, top managers, and department managers over elected officials. In large part, this bias of computing is a reflection of the success of the structural reform of local government. It may be that reformers have been successful in raising the influence of technocrats and bureaucrats in the operations of local government to the point that they can shape organizational change and innovation to further enhance their influence.

*Authors' names are listed randomly. We thank Debbie Dunkle, Eric Hoffman, and Alana Northrop for their helpful comments. An earlier version of this paper was presented at the Third Annual Hendricks Symposium on Administrative Reform and Public Policy, Department of Political Science, University of Nebraska, April 13–14, 1978.*

## NOTES

1. Danziger and Dutton (1977) indicate that reform structures promote technological innovations, such as computing, in local governments.

2. The federal government was first and has remained the most extensively automated level of American government. However, computing has broadly penetrated both state and local governments. A 1976 survey of 49 states shows that they are directly served by at least 603 separate computer systems (NASIS, 1977). At the local level, more than 90% of the cities over 50,000 population and counties over 100,000 population now utilize computers in their operations (Matthews et al., 1976; Kraemer, Dutton, and Matthews, 1975).

3. The power shift hypothesis has attained credibility by virtue of multiple predictions (Kraemer and King, 1976; Crecine and Brunner, 1972; Oettinger, 1971; Etzioni, 1970; Whisler, 1970a, 1970b; Downs, 1967; Leavitt and Whisler, 1958) and empirical research (Dutton and Kraemer, 1977; Hoffman, 1977, 1975, 1973; Laudon, 1974).

4. Who controls technology within public organizations has been shown to affect the adoption, development, and orientation of the technology (Danziger and Dutton, 1977; Dutton and Kraemer, 1977).

5. In most strong-mayor cities these officials tend to be the Director of Finance or the Director of Management and Budget. These officials tend to have professional management backgrounds and tend to be given the chief adminis-

trative roles of the mayor. These officials should be distinguished from another group of department heads whose management role is much more limited and from the mayor's political advisers who often fill one or two department head positions but serve little or no management role.

6. While both Danziger (1977) and Downs (1967) broadly suggest that technically educated officials are more likely to control high technology, they do not specifically deal with the planner analysts on whom we focus.

7. Studies of computing in organizations by Dutton and Kraemer (1977), Hoffman (1977, 1975, 1973), and Laudon (1974) point out the overriding influence of an organization on how a technology is used.

8. The use of computing to send utility bills has no obvious power implications for relations among managers, planners, and elected officials. However, it has very problematic and subtle implications for the relative control relationships between government and the general public.

9. Surveys of public preferences have been used for determining which projects would be supportable through bond elections.

10. This sampling procedure is described in detail in Kraemer, Danziger, Dutton, Mood, and Kling (1975).

11. In mayor-council cities there was often an official who served the role of manager such as the Director of Management and Budget. Also, many cities have no mayors or council staffs.

12. The self reports point even more clearly than the researcher's ratings to the greater similarities than differences in the use of computing by public officials. The mean level of computer use for *planning purposes* was 42, 44, 41, and 52 for managers, mayors, council, and planners, respectively. Planning uses included the identification of city problems, the identification of solutions to city problems, and the identification of changing city conditions. The mean level of computer use for *management purposes* was 46, 44, 39, and 30 for managers, mayors, council, and planners, respectively. Management uses included budget making, daily expenditure decisions, salary negotiations, determining the real costs of programs, controlling staff, setting realistic goals for subordinates, allocating manpower, monitoring subordinates and determining the efficiency of operating units.

13. These data are based upon open-ended responses in which public officials *mentioned* the use of data banks in ways conforming to our categories of administrative reporting, planning analysis, and political uses. Planners mentioned administrative uses in 90% of the cities, planning uses in 90%, and political uses in 22%. Managers mentioned administrative uses in 63%, planning uses in 47%, and political uses in 23%. Elected officials mentioned administrative uses in 40%, planning uses in 54%, and political uses in 47%.

14. The nature of our sample and observations limits the generality of our findings to American cities. However, the consistency between the findings of other studies and the reinforcement politics hypothesis adds credibility to this hypothesis as a description of the nature of power shifts beyond the local government level (Dutton and Kraemer, 1978; Hoffman, 1977; Laudon, 1974; Westin, 1972a, 1972b).

For example, Westin's (1972a, 1972b) case studies of computing in federal, state, and local agencies indicate that "computers have been a factor in consolidating rather than in redistributing governmental power" (1972b: 21). Westin also concludes that there is not "the slightest sign of a displacement of the traditional elites of top and middle management in government by information specialists" (1972b: 21). This is supported by Hoffman's (1977) study of computing in the Soviet Union which examines the classic case for those who forecast the rise of a technocratic elite with the emergence of modern information processing technologies. Hoffman concludes that:

native and imported information technology is not likely to alter the fundamental characteristics of the Soviet political system and the central values of the national Communist party leaders. Rather, computerized information systems are among the important new means to pursue traditional values and goals [1977: 429].

Also, a comparison of computer-based information systems in the United States and Western Europe illustrates how computing tends to reinforce existing structures. Computer-based systems serving local governments in the United States are relatively fragmented and decentralized whereas those in Germany and Scandinavia are relatively integrated and centralized, each reflecting their political and cultural setting (Kenneth and Maestre, 1974; Lenk, 1973).

## REFERENCES

Banfield, C. E. and J. Q. Wilson (1966) City Politics. New York: Vintage.

Bell, D. (1973) The Coming of Post-Industrial Society. New York: Basic Books.

Chartrand, R. (1967) "The role of automatic data processing in politics." Washington, DC: Science Policy Research Division, Legislative Reference Service, Library of Congress.

Crecine, J. P. and R. D. Brunner (1972) "Government and politics: A fragmented society, hard to govern democratically—from another vantage point." In The Conference Board Information Technology. New York: The Conference Board.

Cyert, R. and J. G. March (1963) A Behavioral Theory of the Firm. Englewood Cliffs, NJ: Prentice-Hall.

Danziger, J. N. (1977) "The skill bureaucracy and intra-organizational control." WP-77-36. Irvine, CA: Public Policy Research Organization.

Danziger, J. N. and W. H. Dutton (1977) "Technological innovation in local government." Policy and Politics 6: 27–49.

Downs, A. (1967) "A realistic look at the final payoffs from urban data systems." Public Administration Review 27: 204–210.

Dutton, W. H. and K. L. Kraemer (1978) "Management utilization of computers in American local governments." Communications of the ACM 21: 206–218.

Dutton, W. H. and K. L. Kraemer (1977) "Technology and urban management." Administration and Society 9: 305–340.

Ellul, J. (1964) The Technological Society. New York: Vintage.

Ghere, R. K. (1978) "Municipal data processing systems and shifting organizational power: The case of the computer technician." Unpublished manuscript.

Hoffman, E. P. (1977) "Technology, values and political power in the Soviet Union." In F. J. Fleron (ed.) Technology and Communist Culture. New York: Praeger.

Hoffman, E. P. (1975) "Soviets information processing." Soviet Union (II): 22–49.

Hoffman, E. P. (1973) "Soviet metapolicy: Information processing in the Soviet Union." Administration and Society 5: 200–232.

Kenneth, P. and C. Maestre (1974) Information Technology in Local Government. Paris: OECD.

Kling, R. (1974) "Computers and social power." Computers and Society 5: 6–11.

Kraemer, K. L., J. N. Danziger, W. H. Dutton, A. Mood and R. Kling (1975) "A future cities survey research design for policy analysis." Socio-Economic Planning Sciences 10: 199–211.

Kraemer, K. L., W. H. Dutton and J. R. Matthews (1975) "Municipal computers: Growth, usage and management." Urban Data Service Report II: 1–15.

Kraemer, K. L. and J. L. King (1976) "Computers, power, and urban management." Professional Papers in Administration and Policy Studies (Vol. 3). Beverly Hills, Calif.: Sage.

Laudon, K. C. (1974) Computers and Bureaucratic Reform. New York: John Wiley.

Leavitt, H. J. and T. L. Whisler (1958) "Management in the 1980's." Harvard Business Review 36: 41–48.

Lenk, K. (1973) Automated Information Management in Public Administration. Paris: OECD.

Matthews, J. R., W. H. Dutton and K. L. Kraemer (1976) "County computers: Growth, usage and management." In ICMA (ed.) The County Year Book. Washington, DC: International City Management Association.

NASIS (1977) Information Systems Technology in State Government. Lexington, KY: Author.

Oettinger, A. G. (1971) "Communications in the natural decision making process." In M. Greenberger (ed.) Computers, Communication and the Public Interest. Baltimore: Johns Hopkins Univ. Press.

Pettigrew, A. (1975) "Towards a political theory of organizational intervention." Human Relations 28: 191–208.

Pettigrew, A. (1973) The Politics of Organizational Decision Making. London: Tavistock.

Pool, I., R. P. Abelson and S. L. Popkin (1964) Candidates, Issues, and Strategies. Cambridge, Mass.: MIT Press.

Westin, A. (1972a) Data Banks in a Free Society. New York: Quadrangle.

Westin, A. (1972b) Information Technology and Public Decision Making, abstract in Harvard University Program on Technology and Society. 1964–1972: A Final Review. Cambridge, MA: Harvard Univ. Press.

Whisler, T. L. (1970a) The Impact of the Computer on Organizations. New York: Praeger.

Whisler, T. L. (1970b) "The Impact of information technology on organizational control." In C. A. Meyers (ed.) The Impact of Computers on Management. Cambridge, MA: MIT Press.

# Technical Information and Policy Choice
## The Case of the Resource Recovery Nondecision

Barry Bozeman
J. Lisle Bozeman

*Innovation is only one of a range of public policy responses to social and technological novelty and is not necessarily the most appropriate response. While a*

Reprinted from *Journal of Public Policy,* 1 (May, 1981): 251–267, by permission of Cambridge University Press.

*number of case studies have provided information about determinants of innovation and have traced processes leading to the adoption of innovation, there has been little attention given to the processes that lead to the rejection, deferral or avoidance of available innovations. This paper examines the technical and political controversy surrounding a proposed resource recovery steam plant in metropolitan Syracuse, New York. Although a report on solid waste management had been prepared in 1969 and a dozen consulting studies authorized over the next decade, by 1981 no decision had been reached. In analyzing twelve years of "nondecision," this study seeks to examine some of the difficulties of using technical information in complex policy problems. The case highlights a number of issues pertaining to the use of information in technology policy including: (1) the role of scientific and technical information in policymaking; (2) the interplay between technical information and political values, and (3) the reciprocal effects of information resources and decision processes.*

## INTRODUCTION

Public sector innovation is a topic that has been much on the minds of public managers in recent years. The scores of studies of social and technological novelty provide ample evidence of its perceived importance (see Kelly, *et al.,* 1978). But an understandable enthusiasm for the potential benefits of innovations has sometimes resulted in a pro-innovation bias. In embracing the new it is sometimes easy to forget that innovation is only one of a range of public policy responses and not necessarily the most appropriate response. There is an important gap in the public policy literature. While a number of case studies (for a review, see Yin *et al.,* 1976) have informed us about determinants of innovation and have traced decision processes leading to adoption of innovation, there has been little attention given to the processes that lead to the rejection, deferral or avoidance of available innovations. Clearly the avoidance of innovation can be just as rational (or irrational), just as practical (or impractical) as the adoption of innovation. Also, there are as many likely explanations for the avoidance of innovation: cost constraints, evidence (or lack of evidence) about the effects of the innovation in other sites, technical feasibility, political feasibility, decision-making inertia and so forth.

Our paper is a case study of a "non-innovation." We examine the technical and political controversy surrounding a proposed resource recovery steam plant. In 1969, the Onondaga County Legislature (metropolitan Syracuse, New York, USA) received the report of a special citizen committee regarding the County's solid waste management problem. Shortly after receiving the report the Legislature established the Solid Waste Disposal Authority to advise on alternatives to an increasingly unsatisfactory land-fill method of waste disposal. The Legislature thereby placed on its agenda a policy problem that would occupy its attention for many years. During the next decade the Legislature was to authorize more than a dozen consulting studies of the problem and review six technological approaches, six potential sites and three major financing schemes. The problem would be considered at four levels of government. To this point (1981) no decision has been reached and the County is presently employing the same land-fill method as in 1969.

In analyzing twelve years of "nondecision," this study seeks to examine some of the difficulties of using technical information in complex policy problems. The case highlights a number of issues pertaining to the use of information in technology policy including: (1) the role of scientific and technical information in policymaking; (2) the interplay between technical information and political values and (3) the reciprocal effects of information resources and decision processes.

## INFORMATION, INNOVATION AND PUBLIC POLICY

Certainly a great many factors impinge on public policymaking and by focusing on the role of information resources we do not intend to imply that information variables are more important than, say, organization structure, behavior of political coalitions, or economic constraints. Still, we argue that a focus on information resources and their use is helpful because: (1) such a focus serves to delimit the analysis; (2) information variables are often among the more important determinants of policy outcomes; and, most importantly, (3) information variables are closely interrelated with other determinants of policy outcomes and sometimes capture aspects of political, economic and technological variables.

Our chief concern here is with technical information but it is important to note that a variety of *types* of information are potentially important in policymaking and that different kinds of information resources often have quite different uses. Thus it is not reasonable to consider the effects of technical information in isolation. Given the difficulty in conceptualizing information types it is not surprising that distinctions remain crude. A recent article (Bozeman and Cole, 1982) presents a rough typology of information types important in policy processes. "Simple information" refers to coded observations (e.g. "raw data"); "political information" refers to knowledge of preferences; "expository information" refers to information that conveys an explanation (and includes scientific theory, systematic evaluation, analogies and so forth). Each of these categories may, in turn, be subdivided.

Where there has been little concern in the technology policy literature with the use of information resources in decisions that did *not* lead to innovation (our basic concern), a number of researchers have contributed to our understanding of the relationship of a variety of information resources to innovation. Several studies (Rogers, 1962; Rogers and Beal, 1957; Rogers and Shoemaker, 1971; Mansfield, 1963) have cited professional communication and inter-organizational communication as a major determinant of innovation. Mohr (1966) has shown that knowledge about the properties of the innovation itself is often critical. Information about other organizations' experience with an innovation is generally perceived as a significant determinant of adoption (Havelock, 1969; Hill and Bonjean, 1966; Marsh and Coleman, 1955; Waltman, 1974). The more one organization knows about the outcome of innovations in other environments, the less the perceived risk for the adopter (Crain, 1966; Walker, 1969). In some cases it is the information-seeking behavior of groups outside the organization that leads ultimately to innovation. Groups sometimes take it on themselves to gather information and bring it to the attention of policy-makers in hopes of spurring innovation (Havelock, 1969; Menzel, 1975). In addition to information about the innovation and its scientific and technical base, information about possible sources of technical assistance has been found positively related to innovation. Finally, while there is consensus that information-seeking (and supplying) behaviors play an important role in innovation, the role varies considerably according to the timing of the information (Rogers and Shoemaker, 1971).

One of the most important gaps in our knowledge of innovation/technological decision-making is the effect of numerous conflicting information resources. Our case study shows that this can be a significant problem.

## THE POLITICS OF RESOURCE RECOVERY TECHNOLOGY

After the solid waste problem had been placed on the agenda of the Onondaga County Legislature a promising approach to the problem emerged; an approach that seemed to effectively deal with the problem of solid waste disposal and, at the same time, provide economic benefits. But the resource recovery approach would present a variety of problems, political as well as technical.

## EARLY DEVELOPMENTS: SHREDDING TECHNOLOGY AND AN EXPANDED AGENDA

Having established a Solid Waste Disposal Authority in response to the special citizen committee's report on solid waste management problems, the Legislature's next order of business was to review the citizen committee's recommendation that a shredding technology be employed in disposal of waste. The newly formed Solid Waste Disposal Authority (SWDA) was quickly given responsibility for implementing the shredding technology on new landfill sites. The SWDA soon encountered problems. After considerable haggling over new landfill sites had been settled, the SWDA discovered that little information was available about the shredding technology and its effects. At that time (1970) only one other city in the United States was employing a similar technology and it was not possible to consult with engineering firms that had experience in this or closely related technologies. Since the social and environmental impacts of shredding seemed relatively limited and the capital costs were not great, the County proceeded with the establishment of the shredding plants. The first shredding plant began operation in 1973 (after some construction delays) and a second was in operation by 1977.

The experience with implementation of the minimally disruptive shredding technology was the County's early encounter with two problems that would reoccur as the solid waste agenda was expanded to include resource recovery technologies. This was the first of many instances in which the County would have to make a decision in the absence of an information base perceived as adequate. Also, early political controversies pertaining to the choice of solid waste disposal sites were portents of more serious and large-scale disputes that would emerge in consideration of resource recovery alternatives.

In addition to recommending the establishment of the SWDA and the implementation of the shredding technology, one of the citizen committee's formal recommendations was that the County immediately act to acquire additional technical information regarding rapidly developing solid waste management technologies, particularly resource recovery technologies.

## INITIAL RESOURCE RECOVERY PROPOSALS

The County moved to enlist the support of the State of New York in its attempt to sort out solid waste management alternatives. In 1970, the New York State Department of Environmental Conservation provided money to the Central New York Regional Planning and Development Board to assist Onondaga County in planning for solid waste disposal. The Board contracted with private consultants Malcolm Pirnie, Inc., to provide recommendations about effective approaches to solid waste disposal for a five county region that included Onondaga County. The chief recommendation of the consulting report was to consider mass burning technology as an alternative to landfill. The report included extensive information on projected population increases and anticipated quantities of waste generation and concluded that mass burning should prove an effective approach. Additionally, the possibility of pursuing a technology that combined solid waste disposal with resource recovery and power generation was first introduced.

In 1974, a study co-sponsored by the Onondaga County, Syracuse University and Carrier Corporation (the latter initiated the study), investigated the feasibility of a resource recovery project using mass burning. There was a complementarity of interests here. The Carrier Corporation officials had read the 1970 report of the Planning Board and concluded that there was potential for expansion into a new market: energy generation for the University and the County offices.

The two most promising technologies appeared to be water-wall incineration (mass burning) and refuse-derived fuel (RDF). The major by-product would be steam which could be sold to proximate customers. The report concluded that steam generating resource plants would be both technologically and economically feasible given the existence of shredder plants and the energy demand that would be generated by Syracuse University and County facilities. No specific site was chosen at that time but the criteria established (particularly close proximity to the County offices and the University) assured that the plant would be located in a downtown, predominantly black neighborhood.

After reviewing the report the County Legislature authorized Carrier Corporation to begin designing a system. The full-scale design study was completed in 1976 and recommended a refuse-derived fuel (RDF) process at a specific site: McBride Street, an inner-city, low-income and predominantly black neighborhood. Additionally, the report recommended that trucks be used to transport fuel to the resource recovery/steam plant facilities from the shredders and to transport ash residue from the facilities to the landfill.

## RESISTANCE TO A DOWNTOWN RESOURCE RECOVERY PLANT

Neighborhood opposition to the proposal began to crystallize in March 1977. At that time the opposition chiefly focused on the vast increase in truck traffic (80 to 100 truck trips per day was the report's projection). Early opposition was not sufficient to stall project planning but was partly responsible for the establishment of a County Task Force to further review the proposal. After a few months, the Task Force endorsed Carrier's earlier recommendation of the McBride Street site and by mid 1977 the County called for bids for a County-operated resource recovery plant.

As further details of the project became known, opposition to the proposed plant began to mount. By late 1977, however, a County Solid Waste Management Team had been established and had contracted with various consultants in an effort to move ahead with the project. In January 1978, the Management Team, drawing from the work of six consulting analyses that evaluated technical feasibility of various approaches at various sites, submitted the Onondaga County Comprehensive Solid Waste Management Plan. The report included a re-evaluation of all previous studies, estimated the amount of solid waste generation, projected energy demand and analyzed a range of technologies. The Plan recommended the mass burning of refuse using water-wall incineration, a county-wide landfill site, a method to control and administer the proposed system and, significantly, the use of the McBride Street site. The Management Plan also addressed several concerns that had been articulated by the growing opposition. A major recommendation was that refuse and fuel be hauled by rail rather than by truck. Additionally, a supplemental study was commissioned to address the social, economic and enviromental ramifications of an inner-city located resource recovery plant and this same report presented conceptual designs for neighborhood revitalization.

## ᴬDDITIONAL GOVERNMENTAL ACTORS PROVIDE NEW ALTERNATIVES

During this period two other major governmental actors became involved with the project. In March 1978, the Urban Development Corporation (UDC), a quasi-public arm of the state government, was asked by Governor Carey to evaluate the State Fairgrounds (located in Onondaga County) as a possible resource recovery site. The City of Syracuse, which up to this point had closely monitored developments but had taken no official part in planning, was mobilized by the increasing opposition of city residents. The city sent officials to Omaha, Nebraska, which had adopted a similar technology, to examine the operation of a resource recovery facility and the feasibility of a rail haul system (employed in Omaha). At about the same time, the City Commissioner of Public Works was dispatched to a US Environmental Protection Agency-sponsored Solid Waste Conference. After city officials compared notes, a consensus emerged that the proposed resource recovery technology was strictly at the experimental stage and involved substantial risk. Of the twenty plants in existence at that time across the United States, each seemed to have important operational problems. Additionally, operating expenses had been highly variable and there appeared to be little basis upon which to predict the cost of a Syracuse-based resource recovery plant. City officials agreed that the proposed technology was promising but it was an idea whose time had not yet come, that another ten years or so might be needed to work out technical and operational problems.

The City and its Democrat mayor disagreed with the County and its Republican county executive on other issues as well. In the first place, the City viewed the landfill situation as much less critical than County officials. Also, the City was highly critical of the County planning efforts and questioned the cost projections of the County, explaining that many of the figures appeared to have been "pulled out of the air." The City went on record as opposing *any* city site proposed without consultation of City officials. The position of the City was that delay would be beneficial and that the County should not rush ahead with the project.

In May 1978, the SWDA issued a report recommending yet another site, Ainsley Drive, for the resource recovery facility. This location would be about two miles from Syracuse University and the County Office Buildings Complex (the two major customers for the steam), whereas McBride Street was less than one-half mile. Moreover, while an Ainsley Drive site would have been somewhat less practical from economic and technical standpoints, it was viewed as superior in regard to social impact. Ainsley Drive was less populous and was relatively remote from residential areas. SWDA's recommendation listed "human considerations" as its chief reason for support of the site.

## THE IMPLICATIONS OF TECHNOLOGICAL DEVELOPMENTS

In the same month, the County Legislature had received a report from Kansas City-based Black and Veatch Consulting Engineers, a firm that had been hired to evaluate the Onondaga County Comprehensive Solid Waste Management Plan findings concerning waste generation, energy demand and technological feasibility. The report recommended a remote site for the plant and a mass burning water-wall incineration technology. It argued that the refuse-derived fuel (RDF) technology was not sufficiently proven and that rail haul did not appear financially feasible. Faced with conflicting opinion, the County Legislature again contracted with Black and Veatch for a supplemental report that focused in more detail on the siting problem and addressed inconsistencies in earlier findings. This supplemental report, interestingly, overturned its earlier recommendation for a remote site in favor of a recommendation for the McBride Street site. Also, the second report said that recent developments in the RDF technology—specifically development of a process for compressing shredded refuse in smaller, more compact pellets—enhanced the technological desirability of the process and, thus, the County should give further consideration to RDF. Using RDF and incinerating pellets rather than shredded refuse, the process would generate less pollution and less odor. Additionally, fewer trucks would be needed to haul the compressed pellets. Moreover, *technological developments that came to be visible during the relatively small interim between the first and second consulting reports lead to drastically different conclusions.*

The latest Black and Veatch report was viewed by City officials, as well as some of the County legislators (now controlled for the first time in history by a Democratic majority), as giving insufficient attention to the social costs associated with the project. While the Republican minority and the Republican county executive endorsed the report, administrative officials of the City and some Democratic county legislators argued that assumptions were biased and contradictory with the result that cost figures for the McBride site were understated and costs for other sites were overstated. Moreover, the report did little to settle the site controversy but did have one important effect: building some consensus around the RDF technology.

Further confusing matters, four more consulting reports authorized by the County Legislature were presented in 1978. The reports chiefly focused on the technological aspects of the problem but disagreed considerably as to costs and technological efficiency of various approaches. By this time four sites were contemplated—McBride Street, the State Fairgrounds, Ainsley Drive and Hiawatha Boulevard. The latter site involved a major change in direction. A private citizen (an engineer by training) suggested to county legislators that Hiawatha Boulevard, an industrial area relatively remote from residential neighborhoods, might be pursued and the plant's steam could be used to generate electricity which could be sold to the major public utility, Niagara Mohawk. This could entail a technology not presently in operation in the United States.

The McBride Street site still had strong support of the county executive, but appeared to have less support from the legislature and almost no support among City officials. Indeed, the Common Council of the City of Syracuse had, in September, 1978, passed a resolution expressing opposition to the McBride Street site or any other residential location in the city.

In December, 1978, the New York State Urban Development Corporation (UDC), an agency chiefly concerned with bonding and financing of public projects (but in this instance acting as the executive arm of Governor Hugh Carey), issued a study comparing the four major sites in regard to social impact of the technologies. In a study in which social criteria were viewed as most crucial, the State Fairgrounds was evaluated as most desirable because of the remoteness from residential and business areas; the McBride Street site was evaluated as least desirable. The UDC report also argued that the project might be most appropriate for the private sector, introducing still another decision point.

## NEW TECHNOLOGICAL AND POLITICAL DEVELOPMENTS ADD COMPLEXITY

By early 1979, the resource recovery issue was highly visible to the general public, was consistently in the headlines of the local papers and was a major item of business for the City of Syracuse, the Onondaga County Legislature, the Urban Development Corporation and the Onondaga County Executive. Generalized public opinion had begun to emerge in addition to the interest group/neighborhood politics that had continued for almost ten years. The legislature was being overwhelmed by solicited and unsolicited recommendations for particular technologies at particular sites. The response to this information overload was to request more information. Many legislators observed that their understanding of the technical dimensions of the proposed projects was inadequate and hoped that another study might resolve some of the uncertainty. Yet another study was authorized.

Private consultants O'Brien and Gere presented their report to the County Legislature in March 1979. Although it was clearly evident by this time that the McBride Street site was unacceptable to the neighborhood residents, the black community as a whole, a large proportion of the County Legislature, the City Council and the Mayor, the O'Brien and Gere report urged that a resource recovery plant using the RDF technology be built at the McBride Street site. The report argued that additional ramps could be built on a nearby interstate highway to relieve the traffic problem. Also a *newly developed* "fluff" technology could be empoyed for RDF that would be superior to the pellets or previous shredding. The advantages of the pellets were by this time known to be offset by the fact that they could only be stored for three or four days until they solidified. After a few days the pellets become so hard that they have to be blown apart by dynamite in order to be processed (hardly a desirable procedure in a residential neighborhood). The fluff approach, as the term indicates, turns the shredded waste into a fluff that can be stored a much longer period of time. O'Brien and Gere recognized the opposition to the McBride Street site but noted that their findings might be evaluated by the opposition and result in a more favorable view of that site.

At about the same time a neighborhood impact analysis was prepared by a group of consulting architects working with the (McBride Street) Citizens Neighborhood Advisory Committee. This appears to be the first attempt to formally include the residents of the affected area in the decision-making process. The architects' report indicated that major economic and commercial development might accompany the building of a plant at the McBride Street site; but the Citizens Neighborhood Advisory Committee recommended that the plant *not* be built there. Members of the Committee had visited resource recovery facilities around the nation, observed pollution, traffic and odor problems, and after public meetings had come to the conclusion that possible economic benefits would surely be outweighed by environmental and social costs. The Committee's report went into considerable detail and listed the following as the most serious problems: inability to remove gases and small respirable particles from the air; noise level created by truck traffic; high levels of carbon monoxide created by truck exhausts; dangers to pedestrians; other facilities' noncompliance with air pollution standards; frequent failure of air pollution control devices. The water-wall and RDF technologies were both viewed as unacceptable for a residential area.

The work of the Committee received more media attention than any previous studies and the legislature immediately moved to establish a Joint City-County Solid Waste Committee to review the O'Brien and Gere report and those of the architects and Citizens Committee. Subcommittees were set up to attack specific problems including social impact, traffic, economic benefit, public safety and community development.

One of the first actions of the Joint Committee was to go to the State to determine the possibility of obtaining funds for ramp construction on the interstate highway and funds for economic development for the McBride Street site. Both requests were denied. The State did, however, offer to participate at a remote site that the State owned, the Fairgrounds. The rejection of the funding requests was based on the previous Urban Development Corporation study of social impact. In June 1979, a formal agreement was reached between the County Legislature and UDC that entailed evaluation of the State Fairgrounds site in regard to possible energy markets. During this period, indeed throughout the period of the controversy, the county executive continued to maintain that the McBride Street site was the only feasible location and assigned county administrators to develop data to refute the feasibility of the Fairgrounds site.

## RECENT "NONDECISIONS" AND DEFERRALS

A decade had elapsed since solid waste management first appeared on the County policy agenda but a final decision did not yet seem to be on the horizon. The $2 million worth of studies had, however, helped the County Legislature frame the problem and set some decision criteria. Three basic criteria were agreed upon, all to be stated in terms of perceived risk: (1) what was the market risk at each site?; (2) what was the technological and capital risk at each site?; (3) what was the environmental and social impact and risk at each site? The legislature wanted to minimize the probability associated with a worse-case scenario which included a heavily damaged environment, unlivable neighborhoods around the facility, an eyesore dominating the city skyline, ineffective waste disposal and a tax drain that would bankrupt the county. If all problems encountered at other facilities were experienced in Syracuse, the worse-case scenario could be prophetic.

By late fall 1979, and after further consultation with UDC, the legislature made a major decision *not* to act or, more specifically, it ruled out further consideration of an inner city site for a resource recovery plant. The UDC report once again underscored the benefits of a privately managed (though perhaps state financed) remote site facility. The remainder of the fall was devoted to consideration of this option. As expected, the UDC report was strongly criticized by the staff of the county executive but the County Legislature, with its Democratic majority, voted to continue analysis of the UDC proposal. The County Legislature let two requests for proposals, to determine likelihood that private investors would be attracted to the project.

At this point, late fall 1979, the curtain came down on yet another act of this seemingly endless drama as elections swept the Democratic majority out of the

County Legislature. Negotiations with UDC ceased but, despite the efforts of the Republican county executive (in a strong executive system), the Republican majority decided not to revive consideration of the McBride Street site. In early 1980, the county executive began to push for another site, Rock Cut Road, which had been ruled out nearly ten years ago but which was made more attractive by subsequent technological developments. Previously it did not seem possible to transmit the steam through pipes for more than one or two miles without substantial heat loss. Recent developments in materials and technology had ameliorated this problem and, at the time of this writing the feasibility of delivering steam from a relatively remote site to major inner-city customers remained under investigation. While still further analyses were underway in late 1980, it is possible that the Rock Cut Road site may be able to deliver energy to downtown markets, minimize negative social impacts and efficiently dispose of waste. It is not fitting, however, that this convoluted story should have a fairytale ending. It appears that major problems must be resolved with the Rock Cut site since it is located in an area of steep hills, thereby complicating construction and contributing to much higher costs. This last in a series of "optimal" solutions may well be unaffordable.

## DISCUSSION

The on-going resource recovery controversy illustrates a range of problems in policymaking for technologically-intensive public projects. The plurality of perspectives and "multiple rationalities" of highly visible, politically-charged controversies are not conducive to quick, painless decisions. After more than a dozen analyses at a cost of $2 million, Onondaga County not only does not have a resource recovery plant but has still not achieved consensus as to site, economic feasibility or technology.

Can we draw lessons from this "nondecision"? Are there issues that transcend this case or even technology policy? We feel that many of the issues and problems discussed here have broader implications for public policymaking. Among these: (1) uses and limitations of technical information in policy-making; (2) interaction effects among technical, socio-economic and political variables; (3) decision-making for technological innovation; (4) relation of information, learning and "rational" policy.

## INFORMATION RESOURCES AND TECHNOLOGICAL CONTROVERSY

There is sometimes a presumption that public decisions for technologically-intensive projects can be made "more scientifically" than decisions about, say, social services policy or education policy. Many of the crucial issues revolve around technical considerations and, thus, there should be clear-cut and rational solutions to readily identifiable problems. This case illustrates the fallacy of such reasoning. At one point in the controversy a befuddled county legislator summed up the frustration of information overload: "If only we can get the *true* facts we'll be able to get moving and make a decision." But when facts are deeply embedded in values, when the "facts" sought are actually predictions of anticipated consequences, and when the facts are rapidly changing, there is little hope of plugging public policies into a convenient decision equation.

The question we wish to entertain is this: Why is it that the prodigious amount of technical information available to the County Legislature did not enable them to arrive at some consensus regarding the resource recovery problem? A continuing problem in the resource recovery case has been the difficulty of sorting through different types of information. A distinction has been made earlier in the paper between simple, political and expository information. The information resources compiled in this case included each type of information; indeed, each type was included in virtually every report. With the possible exception of simple information (coded, discrete observations) about such matters as the amount of refuse generated in past years, each type of information entailed a considerable degree of uncertainty. Additionally, the fact that much of the information (and each type of information) dealt with projections of future events rather than descriptions of past events, contributed to complexity. The voluminous technical information generated certainly appeared "scientific" and rigorous—it was quantitative and was laden with sufficient jargon to impress and confuse laymen—but in most cases the technical information made claims and projections about future events. It is not necessary to discuss here the differences between scientific analysis and "science-like" forecasts (see Helmer, 1959); it is sufficient to emphasize that this voluminous collection of technical studies could not precisely answer the questions most salient to the political actors: Will the pollution control devices break down? Will the market for energy be sustained?; Will there be cost overruns in construction? The "true facts" about future events simply are not available.

Another reason that available technical information was inadequate for decision consensus is that *consensus is not achieved through shared information but through shared values* (though, of course, information can clarify value issues). Our subjective interpretation, based on our analysis of behavior and not on statements of policymakers, is that the chief concern of the County Executive was making available a cheap source of energy to major institutional customers. While the County Executive never demonstrated great concern with the social and environmental impacts of a McBride Street plant, the City and, later, the County Legislature placed strong emphasis on avoiding highly undesirable spillover effects. Moreover, all the major parties—including UDC, neighborhood groups, Carrier Corporation—seemed to us to have a unique mix of priorities. Even if we assume (somewhat unrealistically) that the technical information provided in various reports and testimony was understood and interpreted similarly by each of the major parties, there is no reason to expect that a generally agreed upon "rational" decision should flow from the information even if there were not problems (i.e. uncertainty, inconsistency) with the information itself. The objective content of technical information is inevitably filtered by the actor's mix of priorities (Adams, 1961; Bem, 1965).

## INTERACTION EFFECTS

One reason that the resource recovery project proved so trying is that a variety of considerations—political, economic, technological and environmental—were central to the policy. Achieving the best mix of political, economic, technological and environmental impacts is sufficiently difficult even in cases where there is some consensus as to the importance of each. But in a case, such as this one, where there is relatively little consensus about the importance of particular variables, where this dissensus is spread out over many significant actors (some having veto power for certain approaches), and where almost all assumptions about impacts must be stated in probabilities, it is easy to understand slow progress. If we consider all the combinations of technologies, sites and associated values for the actors it is apparent that interaction effects are

considerable. It is in recognition of such interaction effects that individuals involved in technology assessment have developed such techniques as cross-impact analysis and computer modelling in order to anticipate effects of technological change (Turoff, 1972; Dalkey, 1972). Moreover, the information resources available to policymakers certainly did not enable them to deal with interaction effects; in calculating interactions policy-makers were left to their own (largely intuitive) devices. By conservative calculation, the impacts (even assuming certainty rather than highly conjectural assumptions about outcomes) of all the major technologies, for all the major sites, for all the major sets of variables, would yield a matrix of about sixty outcomes; when we consider those outcomes according to all possible orderings or priorities (i.e., social impact, technological efficiency), the problem is well beyond the grasp of the human mind.

## A NONDECISION FOR A "NON-INNOVATION"

Certainly a host of disparate factors played a role in this "non-innovation." It is likely that the changes in partisan control of the County Legislature (three changes during the period studied) and partisan conflict between the Republican county executive and the Democratic mayor of Syracuse played a role. The mayor and city council were responding to an inner-city electoral constituency that was vastly different from the largely suburban constituency of the county executive. Additionally, the conflicting interests of the state, regional, county and city governments might well have impeded decision-making.

If we focus primarily on the use of technical information and its role in the non-innovation, deferral and status quo reinforcement are understandable. A major determinant of adoption of an innovation is knowledge about the properties of the innovation (Mohr, 1969) and other organizations' experience with the innovation (Havelock, 1969; Waltham, 1974; Hill and Bonjean, 1966). In the case we have examined, studies of the application of contemplated technologies in other cities did not provide a favorable prospectus. There were technical problems with RDF and water-wall incineration technologies, including breakdowns and problems with operation of pollution control devices; the rail haul system seemed expensive and largely ineffective; undesirable social impacts had accompanied the adoption of resource recovery technologies at every site.

The non-innovation seems sensible from another standpoint as well. The technologies contemplated for the County resource recovery plant were developing, changing and improving at a rapid rate. As was pointed out, the Rock Cut Road site could not have been entertained a few years ago but technological and materials improvements now make that site technologically feasible. Also striking was the change in recommendations in the second O'Brien and Gere report. Technological developments that had occurred during the brief period between the first and second report led the consultants to provide completely different recommendations. In short, it appears that risk could be plotted against a learning curve with early innovators bearing a disproportionate risk (see Bozeman and Rossini, 1979). The issue, then, is at what point does objective need for an innovation offset the learning effects that can be derived by relatively late adoption? Obviously there is a point at which it is unreasonable to wait any longer before adopting an innovation (or otherwise taking positive action to address a problem), but it is not an easy matter to find that optimal mix of technological state-of-the-art, need and risk. A costly twelve-year nondecision may, from this perspective, be more sensible than a costly rush to innovation.

## CONCLUSIONS

In his presidential address before the American Association for the Advancement of Science, Frederick Mosteller (1981) observed that, "We need both to have a larger number of innovations and to be sure that they are beneficial; this requires both inventiveness and evaluation." Moreover, innovation and benefit do not always go hand in glove. Mosteller discusses his research seeking to evaluate the effectiveness of twenty-eight innovations, concluding that only half could be viewed as an improvement over previously existing techniques.

*Perhaps the most general conclusion that can be drawn from this analysis is that avoidance of innovation is not necessarily bad or unreasonable.* Even after acquiring a prodigious amount of information (albeit, much of the wrong type or in the wrong form), the Legislature still chose to avoid the resource recovery innovation. Certainly there was political resistance to the innovation, but there was an equal portion of political embarrassment to endure as the public continued to criticize the Legislature's nondecision. While one

can debate whether the slope of learning curve for information about the innovation had begun to descend by 1980, it is doubtless that considerable uncertainty remained about the costs and social impact of the steam plant.

It is instructive to compare the Legislature's behavior in respect to the shredding technology and the resource recovery technology. In both cases there was a high degree of uncertainty, the technologies were not widely adopted, and there were significant political controversies regarding siting. The fact that the Legislature was able to act quickly and decisively in the decision regarding the relatively inexpensive and non-disruptive technology is significant. It gives at least some strength to the argument that the deferral of the resource recovery innovation was largely in response to poor quality information rather than simple inertia.

In sum, we agree with Mosteller that innovations must be viewed in terms of their instrumental value and in connection with the range of policy options available to decisionmakers. There is little or no intrinsic value to innovation.

*A second general point is that information, including technical information, can play a minimal role in rationalizing policy processes where there are several competing interests.* Herbert Simon's (1965) classic *Administrative Behavior* provides a view of "bounded rationality" that is largely based on information search. In attempting to revise traditional concepts of rational decisionmaking, Simon considers the properties of the decisionmaker, the simplifications the decisionmaker may introduce in order to bring the situation within the range of convenient computation, and the decisionmaker's search for alternatives. Decisionmakers identify obvious alternatives based on recent experience and evaluate their expected payoffs in terms of satisfactory (rather than optimal) quality. Upon finding an alternative with satisfactory payoff the search process terminates. It is only when the expected payoffs from all the obvious alternatives fall below satisfactory quality that the decisionmaker searches for innovative alternatives. The Simon "satisficing" model has, along with Lindblom's (1959) closely related incremental model, long provided a standard for students of public policy. The resource recovery case serves to point up the limitations of the model.

A major inadequacy of the more familiar decision-making models (e.g., Simon's, the pure economic rationality model) is that they implicitly or explicitly assume a unitary decisionmaker. This assumption poses no great problems when decisions are made authoritatively by a dominant coalition. In cases (such as the resource recovery nondecision) where there are a large number of official and unofficial actors with highly divergent interests and values, a model relating information search to a concept of rationality is not particularly helpful. Additional technical information can do little to rationalize decisions in such instances because the "optimal" solution (and, thus, the optimal amount and quality of information) varies with the perceived interests of the actors. *Technical information plays a major role but that role is the reduction of uncertainty, not the rationalization of decisions.*

## REFERENCES

Adams, J. S. (1961) The reduction of cognitive dissonance by seeking consonant information, *Journal of Abnormal and Social Psychology,* 62, 74–78.

Bem, D. J. (1965) An experimental analysis of self-persuasion, *Journal of Experimental and Social Psychology,* 1, 199–218.

Bozeman, B. and E. Cole (1982) Public managers' use of scientific and technical information, *Administration & Society* 13, 479–493.

Bozeman, B. and F. Rossini (1979) Technology assessment and bureaucratic decision-making, *Technological Forecasting and Social Change,* 4, 310–322.

Campbell, D. T. (1975) Degrees of freedom and the case study, *Comparative Political Studies,* 12, 178–193.

Crain, R. L. (1966) Fluoridation: the diffusion of an innovation among cities, *Social Forces,* 44, 467–476.

Dalkey, Norman (1972) An elementary cross-impact model, *Technological Forecasting and Social Change,* 3, 147–157.

Havelock, R. G. (1969) *Planning for Innovation Through Dissemination and Utilization of Knowledge.* Ann Arbor: Institute for Social Research, University of Michigan.

Helmer, O. (1959) On the epistemology of the inexact sciences, *Management Science,* 6, 25–52.

Hill, R. J. and C. M. Bonjean (1966) Diffusion: a test of the regularity hypothesis, *Journalism Quarterly,* 41, 336–342.

Kelly, P. *et al.* (1978) *Technological Innovation: A Critical Review of Current Knowledge.* San Francisco: San Francisco Press.

Lindblom, Charles (1959) The science of muddling through, *Public Administration Review,* 19, 77–88.

Mansfield, E. (1963) Speed of response of firms to new techniques, *Quarterly Journal of Economics,* 77, 290–309.

Marsh, C. P. and A. L. Coleman (1955) The relation of farmer characteristics to the adoption of recommended farm practices, *Rural Sociology,* 20, 289–296.

Menzel, D. (1975) Scientific and technological dimensions of innovation in the American states. Paper presented at the Annual Meeting of the Midwest Political Science Association, 1–3 May 1975, Chicago, Illinois.

Mohr, L. B. (1966) Determinants of innovation in organizations, *American Political Science Review,* 63, 111–126.

Mosteller, Frederick (1981) Innovation and evaluation, *Science,* 211, 881–886.

Rogers, E. M. (1962) *Diffusion of Innovations.* New York: The Free Press.

Rogers, E. M. and G. M. Beal (1957) The importance of personal influence in the adoption of technical changes, *Social Forces,* 36, 329–334.

Rogers, E. M. and F. Shoemaker (1971) *Communication of Innovations,* Second Edition. New York: The Free Press.

Simon, Herbert (1965) *Administrative Behavior,* Second Edition. New York: The Free Press.

Turoff, Murray (1972) An alternative approach to cross impact analysis, *Technological Forecasting and Social Change,* 3, 168–174.

Walker, J. L. (1969) The diffusion of innovation among the American states, *American Political Science Review,* 63, 880–899.

Waltman, J. (1974) Some disjointed thoughts on diffusion. Working paper, Indiana University, Bloomington, Indiana.

Yin, R. K., K. A. Heald, M. E. Vogel, P. D. Fletschauer and B. Vladeck (1976) A review of case studies of technological innovations in state and local services. Santa Monica, California: Rand Corporation.

# PROBLEMS

# OF

# PUBLIC MANAGEMENT

Doing more with less is always difficult. Such is the plague that afflicts most public managers. And it will be worse in the future. The virtual certainty of a dismal financial future makes the job of tomorrow's public managers particularly onerous. Much of the fiscal fallout will be borne by public administrators at the state and local levels. The reason, quite simply, is that the era of bountiful financial resources from Washington has long since gone. Yet it would be inaccurate to say that with fewer federal funds, the intergovernmental ties that bind the federal government with state and local governments have been loosened. Levine and Posner ("The Centralizing Effects of Austerity on the Intergovernmental System") underscore the fact that intergovernmental problems don't go away as budgets shrink. One of the ongoing problems of public management is to fulfill existing federal policies in an era of less.

Fiscal austerity is not the only problem that plagues public managers. When former top level public administrators recount their experiences in public service, they invariably point to the various cross pressures they faced, along with the fact that their actions were usually open to public scrutiny. Both the cross pressures and their public exposure made their job difficult —at least, that is what they usually say in their "swan songs." A former top-level public administrator, Frank Carlucci, who was Deputy Secretary of Defense in the Reagan Administration and held positions in the Central Intelligence Agency, the State Department, and the Department of Health, Education and Welfare (now Health and Human Services), complained that

so much attention is being placed on rooting out waste and abuse in government that, often, the central missions of public agencies are lost sight of. In his view, a proper balance must be struck between performance and accountability.

Mr. Carlucci's point of reference is the post-Watergate era, where questions of ethical standards and overall accountability have resurfaced as very significant problems of public management. Can there really be *too much* concern for accountability? Mr. Carlucci says that mechanisms to ensure accountability can sometimes conflict with other public management purposes. Achieving a proper balance between, say, the desire for "open, accountable" government and efficient and effective administration requires judgments by public managers. The world of public managers is colored in gray.

In "Auditing Disputes in Federal Grant Programs," Fred Doolittle shows that attempts to alter control and accountability mechanisms sometimes give rise to serious problems. Recent efforts to shift auditing functions from the federal government to the state have had as many implications for quality control as for efficiency.

Similar problems afflict state and local government managers. Consider just one cross pressure. In the aftermath of the "taxpayers' revolt" of the late 1970s, state and local administrators are ever watchful of their budgets. Like their federal counterparts, state and local managers have interest groups, citizen commissions, and the like scrutinizing every penny-pinching move. Public employee unions, once thought to be the main beneficiaries of the public's largesse, are particularly concerned about decisions that affect their members. So while managers are being scrutinized for their financial prowess (or lack thereof), their actions are also being scrutinized by public employee unions who want to minimize the impact of the fiscal fallout on their members. Collective bargaining becomes even more difficult in a financially shrinking public sector, especially when one considers not only the direct cost of collective bargaining but, as does Anthony Pascal ("The Hidden Cost of Collective Bargaining on Local Government"), the hidden costs.

The articles in Part Four explore some of these themes. We learn about the changing intergovernmental system in an era of fiscal austerity, efforts to enhance the productivity of the public sector, and new directions in collective bargaining. One theme is paramount: Public management has been made more difficult now than in former times because of the need to achieve more with less. And efforts to make public managers more accountable for their actions will make their achievements and failures visible to all who care to scrutinize—and criticize.

# CHAPTER EIGHT

# Intergovernmental Management

## The Centralizing Effects of Austerity on the Intergovernmental System

Charles H. Levine
Paul L. Posner

Even though the attractiveness of devolving public decision making and policy implementation to state and local governments is widely acknowledged, changes are occurring in the U. S. system of intergovernmental relations that are eroding local autonomy and centralizing authority. This is not a new observation. In recent years, observers of intergovernmental relations have noted that the discretionary portion of local government budgets has been declining in proportion to the growing presence of federal funding. But now the processes of erosion of state and local autonomy and centralization of authority appear to be accelerating as resource scarcity and the structure of federal grants, *in combination,* are causing subtle, yet fundamental, changes in the scope and role of state and local governments.[1]

At the core of the issue are displacement effects that occur when local priorities are skewed and distorted by the need to generate and commit local funds to match federal categorical grants in program areas such as criminal justice and law enforcement, water pollution control, transportation, health, and education rather than using local funds for some other purposes that may have greater local priority. These displace-

Reprinted with permission from the *Political Science Quarterly,* 96 (Spring, 1981): 67–85.

ment effects threaten to undermine the advantages of decentralized government: its greater responsiveness to local needs and priorities, its greater accountability and access for citizens wishing to influence policy, and its greater variety of services for citizens and businesses making location decisions. Increased centralization promises to produce instead a homogenized package of services formulated in Washington by obscure bargains among nearly anonymous interest-group representatives, bureaucrats, and congressional committee staffs.[2]

Now that many state and local governments are entering a period of austerity, they are attempting to stretch locally generated resources as far as possible. One obvious means is to use local dollars to match federal grants. But this practice has a major pitfall: Even though local governments may have increased their revenues through these grants, they have also increased their dependency on external resources, thereby accelerating the erosion of their discretion over policy, program, and service decisions. As a result, local budgets have increasingly come to resemble the structure of the federal government's domestic program, and local decisions are being shaped by federal constraints and directives at an accelerating rate. In short, the joint impact of displacement effects and resource scarcity is creating a serious structural problem for local government autonomy and for the functioning of American federalism. The growing severity of this problem poses a number of political and administrative dilemmas that evidence the appropriateness of reform in both the intergovernmental grants system and the revenue-raising mechanisms of state and local governments. In a uniquely American fashion, the United States may be on the way to "buying" a unitary style of national government through the grants system by enticing states and localities to adopt the growing federal agenda of priorities and policies.

This article summarizes the forces leading toward centralization within the federal system and the erosion of local autonomy by the federal grants system and explains how resource scarcity accelerates the erosion of local discretion. Some administrative and policy dilemmas posed by the impact of resource scarcity on the federal system are discussed in the conclusion.

## THE FISCAL IMPACT OF FEDERAL GRANTS

The effects of federal grants on state and local budgets and priorities have become more pronounced over the past twenty-five years due to the growing dependence on federal funds. By virtue of general revenue sharing, federal assistance has been extended to nearly every state and local government in the nation. Furthermore, through the growth of block and categorical grant programs during the 1960s and 1970s, the federal government has become involved in the funding of services traditionally dominated by state or local governments. This growth in the scope of federal assistance led the Advisory Commission on Intergovernmental Relations (ACIR) to comment that by 1976 it had become difficult to identify "a single major state and local function in which the Federal Government was not involved."[3] Thus, the impact of federal expenditures has been felt by states and localities in an ever-growing number of program areas.

This growing range of federal assistance has been provided primarily through categorical grants, each serving a narrow purpose allowing the grantee only minimal discretion. Since 1962, the ACIR has recorded a 300 percent increase in the number of categorical federal grant programs available to state and local governments, placing at 492 the number of federal categorical grant programs available to state and local governments in January 1978. In budgetary terms even after the advent of the five block grant programs and general revenue sharing, categorical grants still constitute over 75 percent of total federal grant outlays to state and local governments.[4]

By 1980 federal grant outlays constituted 25 percent of state and local spending, capping a twenty-five year period of relatively steady growth. While federal grants of $2 billion in fiscal year (FY) 1950 constituted only 10.4 percent of state and local expenditures, FY 1980 federal grant outlays are estimated to be $88.9 billion, constituting 25.3 percent of total state and local expenditures.[5] Major cities are even more dependent on federal funds for support than the aggregate figures suggest. In 1957, forty-seven of the nation's forty-eight largest cities received only 2.6 cents from the federal government for every dollar raised locally. In 1978, these cities received 50 cents in federal funds for every locally raised dollar.[6] A recent Treasury Department study calculates that the nation's ten most distressed cities would have to raise property tax rates by an average of 65 cents per $100 of assessed valuation if federal funds were withdrawn.[7]

Federal mandates and grant requirements, such as match and maintenance of effort, have effectively extended the federal fiscal presence to a larger share of state and local budgets. Even though compliance with grant requirements may be questionable, nevertheless, state and local funds needed to satisfy these requirements can be substantial. According to Office of Management and Budget (OMB) figures, states and localities will spend an additional one dollar from their own funds in FY 1979 to match these dollars in federal grant money. Matching requirements effectively extend the influence of federal grants to 36 percent of aggregate state and local expenditures. Minimum nonfederal match is also growing as a percentage of state and local expenditures. Between FY 1971 and FY 1980, minimum match required for all federal grants increased from 8 to 12 percent of state and local expenditures. In some states, the federal influence is more pronounced. For example, at least 45 percent of Michigan's budget is tied to federal funds; 25 percent in direct federal funds and 20 percent in matching funds.

### Stimulative Effects

The federal grants system, by design, is a powerful mechanism for stimulating spending at all three levels of government. Grants stimulate spending in three ways. First, categorical grants are premised on the notion that state and local sectors are not spending enough for services with high external or national benefit. The system intentionally seeks to broaden the public-policy agenda of state and local grant recipients through price incentives and, thus, to add to expenditure pressures. Grants also stimulate expenditures because grants structures provide only weak incentives to economize; and by dividing financial management responsibilities among several layers of government, federal grants tend to short-circuit the normal management constraints on expenditures. Third, the grant system, through mandates, matching, and maintenance of effort requirements stimulates additional state and local expenditures as a condition for receiving federal assistance, while discouraging spending reductions in federally funded areas by penalizing reduced fiscal effort with the loss of federal funds.

In large part, the grants system is predicated on the need to induce state and local government participation in the service of national programs and priorities. In this way, the federal government can act on an expanding agenda of national concerns without bearing the full fiscal impact or political risks associated with implementing controversial national policies in a complex, heterogeneous society.

Federal grants entice state and local government participation and increase their expenditures for both economic and political reasons. In economic terms, a grant lowers the cost to the states and localities of performing the aided activity. A grant thus reduces the price that the recipient must pay for the service and hence increases the attractiveness of the funded activity. According to the theory of grants, state and local governments are encouraged to fund activities with high external benefits they otherwise would not fund.[8]

The response of the state and local governments to these price incentives is further influenced by the political process. The presence of federal grant funds encourages or stimulates the development of strong political constituencies at the state and local level, which often use the federal fiscal presence as a way to press for increased and long-term involvement of the state or local jurisdiction in the aided program. Federal funds flow to most grantees in a somewhat automatic fashion, presenting a grantee who chooses not to participate with the unenviable task of returning available federal money that could have been used to benefit local residents. State elected officials seeking to control their public-policy agendas in the face of the onslaught of federal grant funds are thus in a bind. As one state legislator perceptively noted, he would rather spend federal funds on nonessential projects in his state than have them reallocated to a neighboring state.[9]

Traditional management constraints on spending at the state and local level are typically not operative within federal grant programs. Grant programs produce a functional disjuncture in the tax and spending structure of local governments that removes a potential brake on expenditure growth. Both federal and local officials are largely spared dealing with the potential conflict between groups concerned with *how much* money is collected (revenue providers) and those groups concerned with how money is *spent* (service consumers). As Edward K. Hamilton has noted, the public sector does not know how to control expenditures in an era when so much public spending is dominated by banker transactions from higher to lower levels of government. He has argued forcefully that "we do not know what disciplinary forces can resist impulses to excessive spending when the spender bears no responsibility for raising the revenue being allocated."[10]

A recent General Accounting Office (GAO) study joined in this observation by noting that grantees have little or no incentive to improve productivity in federally funded programs, because dollar savings achieved through expenditure controls in federal grant programs largely accrue to the federal government. The study further noted that most nonfederal matching requirements are too low or too weak to stimulate state and local management interest and oversight for grant programs. As a result, for example, Wisconsin recently excluded federal programs from the purview of its productivity-improvement program. Similarly, a 1979 survey showed that state legislative fiscal officers in two-thirds of the states indicate that their oversight of federally funded programs is typically less intensive than their oversight of state funded programs.[11] Clearly, when the responsibilities for management and finance in a program are separated, the process of management and control tend to wither away.[12]

Federal grant programs also weaken the analytic controls normally exercised by state and local officials in deciding on alternative program strategies and levels of spending. State and local attempts to compare the costs and benefits of federally funded projects with nonfederally funded alternatives can be futile because of the fundamental economic incentives in grant programs. Federal grants dramatically reduce the costs of federally eligible alternatives without affecting the benefits. While the benefits of most grant programs are concentrated in the local recipient area itself, the costs are typically spread throughout the nation. For example, a study of the process leading to New York City's decision to rebuild its West Side Highway concluded that the federal funding formula strictly constrained the range of feasible alternatives considered.

In this case, the mayor argued that mass transit alternatives to a new highway could not be considered because of federal funding rules that gave the city more federal funds for highways. The author of the study concluded that while the project selected had substantial environmental and economic disadvantages compared with other alternatives, federal grant funds made the outcome inevitable: "From the city's perspective the funds are costless. From the state's perspective, the money is pretty close to costless [nine to one federal match]."[13]

Categorical grant programs often increase state and local spending over and above the amount of the federal grant. A 1977 nationwide survey of local officials indicated that over two-thirds of these officials believed that the spending of local funds over and above required match was stimulated by federal funds.[14] Much of the expenditure impact can be explained by the political processes of state and local governments. By arousing new expectations and dormant constituency groups, federal grants can induce state and local governments to spend more than required for programs. But even more of the expenditure impact can be attributed to provisions of the grants themselves or to the "strings" that require additional spending as a condition for receiving grants. The impact of three types of provisions—mandates, matching requirements, and maintenance of effort requirements—require detailed examination.

## Restrictive Mandates

The disjuncture between the functions of developing policy and raising revenues has also contributed to the rapid growth of federal mandates imposed on states and localities. The process of developing new mandates at the federal level does not often benefit from the discipline of having to raise revenues to cover the costs of these mandates. Again, benefit-cost analysis is impractical in cases where one level of government realizes the benefits without considering the costs.

A wide range of federal assistance programs impose burdensome and costly federal regulations as conditions for participation. While state and local governments are not directly required to comply, the potential loss of federal assistance is usually punishing enough to force compliance. For example, the Department of Housing and Urban Development (HUD) requires all local building codes in flood-prone areas to incorporate federal flood-control standards. If local govern-

ments fail to comply, the entire local area loses its eligibility for any federal subsidy for construction or acquisition of property. A similar program requiring local implementation of building energy conservation standards certified by HUD is currently being phased in, pursuant to the Energy Policy and Conservation Act of 1975. The Codes must be statewide, uprooting long traditions of local control over building codes in many states.

In 1977, Congress extended coverage of regular unemployment compensation to all state and local employees, requiring state and local governments to fund the necessary payroll costs. Instead of using directly the commerce clause in the United States Constitution to require state and local coverage, the Congress chose to use the grants system to enforce state and local compliance. States that refuse to cover public employees will lose federal certification of their entire unemployment compensation programs, resulting in direct federal administration and significantly higher payroll costs for private-sector employers within the state.

Similarly, the Education of All Handicapped Children Act of 1975 requires, as a condition for state receipt of federal handicapped grant funds, that local school districts integrate all physically and mentally handicapped children, including those with learning disabilities, into the public-school system. Besides the basic expense imposed, the act requires each district to prepare an individual education plan for each child, to consult regularly with parents, and to identify millions of children with hidden learning disabilities. The federally mandated costs involved in achieving this worthwhile objective are substantial, but federal grant funds are not expected to cover more than 12 percent of the anticipated costs, according to the Office of Management and Budget.[15] More generally, Section 504 of the Rehabilitation Act requires grantees to provide access by the handicapped to all facilities built with federal grant funds. A recent Congressional Budget Office study found that $6.8 billion would have to be spent by transit systems alone to comply with this mandate, even though relatively few handicapped persons would actually benefit.[16]

Other examples of the extension of federal regulatory control over state activity through grant strings abound. As a condition for receiving energy-planning money from the Department of Energy, states are required to make significant changes in their laws to conform with federal standards. The Federal Highway Administration forces states to control outdoor advertising by reducing the federal match by 10 percent for states that do not adopt appropriate regulation of billboards pursuant to federal law. As a condition for receiving federal juvenile justice grants, the Law Enforcement Assistance Administration (LEAA) requires that states develop programs to deinstitutionalize juvenile "status" offenders, resulting in major legal changes and new fiscal outlays by the states.

Most major federal grant programs also incorporate a number of non-programmatic guidelines for implementing national policy objectives. ACIR has estimated that thirty-seven conditions exist that are applied by most grant programs. In order to qualify for federal assistance, state and local governments must achieve a broad range of national social objectives in addition to specific grant program requirements.[17] Some of these include mandates to provide equal access to the handicapped and disadvantaged to services; to protect environmental quality; to ensure prevailing wages for construction workers under contract; and to implement civil-service systems based on merit.

These mandates are often formulated with little or no attention to the costs imposed on state and local governments. Costs of compliance with the Davis-Bacon Act, the Uniform Relocation Assistance and Real Property Acquisitions Policy Act of 1970, and the National Environment Policy Act of 1969, for example, have resulted in increased costs as well as nonparticipation in federal grant programs. In one instance, delays due to excessive federal monitoring of environmental impact increased the costs of local highway-improvement projects for Ogden, Utah, from $740,000 to $1,950,000.[18]

A recent comprehensive study found that 1,036 federal mandates exist in laws and regulations as conditions for the receipt of federal grant funds. The costs of implementing these mandates attached to federal grant programs were paid from local revenues in over 45 percent of the cases. The study found that over 900 of the mandates were enacted during the 1970s.[19]

## Matching and Maintenance of Effort Requirements

Over 60 percent of federal grant programs require some kind of nonfederal financial share as a condition for participating in federal grant programs. OMB estimates that in FY 1979 fully 10 percent of aggregate state and local expenditures were earmarked to match federal grant programs.[20]

Matching requirements stimulate both federal and nonfederal expenditures and enable the federal government to initiate complex new programs without bearing their full costs. They also encourage state and local governments to devote portions of their budgets to programs they might not have initiated on their own in order to draw available federal dollars. Because of the large number of federal programs with relatively low matching requirements, state and local budgets can become crowded with obligations of low local priority. The econometrics literature provides considerable evidence to indicate that grants with matching requirements stimulate state and local expenditures. In one widely cited summary of the literature, Edward Gramlich found that in the aggregate, categorical grants with matching requirements stimulated $1.12 of state and local spending for every dollar of federal grant funds.[21]

Maintenance of effort provisions exist to ensure that state and local governments do not substitute federal funds for locally generated revenues. To prevent substitution, many federal programs institute maintenance of effort provisions that require that the grantee maintain a fixed level of prior spending. Some programs include a "nonsupplant provision" that prevents grantees from using federal funds to supplant funds that they otherwise would have spent for the program in the absence of federal funds. According to GAO, thirty-seven of the fifty-two largest federal grant programs are covered by maintenance of effort requirements.[22]

Federal requirements vary considerably. For example, the Urban Mass Transit Operating Assistance (UMTA) program requires state and local governments to continue their prior two-years average level of funding for transit as a condition for federal operating subsidies. The Comprehensive Employment and Training Act (CETA) requires that federal funds be used to *supplement,* not supplant, local funds and services that would otherwise be available in the absence of federal funds.

Maintenance of effort provisions, if effective, can prevent fungibility and ensure that the federal grant is used by the grantees for the specific purpose intended, not as general fiscal relief. But effective implementation of maintenance of effort provisions is problematic. For example, early studies of public service employment programs indicate substantial substitution of federal grant funds for state and local funds.[23] More recently, however, this substitution behavior seems to be ebbing. Two major studies by the Brookings Institution of the experience with two major block grant programs—CETA and the Community Development Block Grant program (CDBG)—found surprisingly low levels of fiscal substitution. Indeed, one study found that 94 percent of CDBG funds provided to the sample jurisdictions were allocated for new spending.[24]

*Effective* maintenance of effort provisions have the potential to cause serious fiscal and policy problems for state and local governments. One problem is the requirement that a grantee maintain expenditures to reduce spending even after productivity gains have been achieved or the demand for a service has been reduced. The UMTA subsidy requirement that a state maintain its prior year's subsidy or risk losing the entire federal grant, for example, could discourage a state from raising its public-transit fare and decreasing its budgeted operating subsidy.

Maintenance of effort and nonsupplant provisions may result in higher levels of public services than are deemed necessary by state and local officials. State and local budgetary decisions may be distorted far in excess of the required match. State and local officials have reported desires to reduce their own effort in public services only to have HUD officials inform them that they would be in possible violation of Community Development Block Grant maintenance of effort requirements. In the case of CETA, state and local budgetary flexibility is even more severely inhibited due to the program's stringent nonsupplant requirements and protections for regular public employees incorporated in the program since 1978.

The erosion of state and local budgetary flexibility, as a result of maintenance of effort, can best be appreciated in the aggregate. A larger local government is required to maintain spending levels of the prior year as a condition for receiving federal assistance in the following areas, among others: law enforcement to qualify for LEAA funds; mass transit for UMTA operating subsidies; services to meet the needs of the poor for community action funds; pre-grant community health expenditures for community mental health staffing grants; general education for a host of federal education programs; child nutrition for several child nutrition programs; and local public services for the Community Development Block Grant program.

During the explosion of state and local government expenditures over the past twenty-five years, maintaining the expenditures of previous years rarely was burdensome. As the pace of growth in the state and local sector declines, however, and as tax and expenditure limitations force absolute budget reductions, local governments may increasingly be hard pressed to meet maintenance of effort requirements. In addition, by continuing to maintain local effort in federally favored issue areas, local officials may not be able to fund locally favored programs at desired levels. Furthermore, the prospects for state and local budget flexibility can become even more imperiled if maintenance of effort requirements rigorous enough to prevent grantee fiscal substitution were spread to incorporate each of the 492 federal grant programs for state and local governments.

### Generating New Clienteles

In addition to stimulating short-term spending, federal grants drive up future spending as well. Federal grants that start new services create a clientele that continues to be dependent on the service regardless of the availability of federal funds. When federal funds do expire, local officials face the painful dilemma of either increasing the budget to accommodate the new service or alienating a public that has grown accustomed to the service. A recent GAO report identified a number of federal programs whose avowed purpose is to stimulate new projects initially with federal funds and then to withdraw funds after a prescribed period of time. Evidence gathered by GAO indicates that many state and local governments are absorbing these federally inspired projects once grant funds terminate. For example, this has been the case in over 60 percent of LEAA-funded projects that are now terminated.[25]

A report of the South Carolina General Assembly points to a number of cases where federal grant projects, started without the knowledge or approval of the state legislature, became a permanent part of state government when federal funds expired. The report quotes one state agency boasting that it had never lost one employee initially funded through a federal demonstration grant: "Specifically this means that in the last five years over 400 highly trained staff members have been assimilated and absorbed by regular state appropriations."[26]

Finally, state and local governments must pay off the long-term operating costs of capital construction projects funded with federal grants. In the case of interstate highways and sewage treatment plants, for example, federal matching funds stimulate the construction of new facilities. However, while it is apparently in the national interest to build these new projects, Congress has not yet determined it to be in the national interest to fund the long-term operating and maintenance costs of these facilities. The costs to a locality can be substantial. The city of Wilmington, Delaware, for instance, recently rebuilt its sewage treatment plant with heavy federal funding to meet Environmental Protection Agency (EPA) water quality standards. To operate the new, sophisticated plant, however, Wilmington has had to increase its work force threefold, from twenty to sixty-two people, and has increased its locally funded payroll costs proportionately.

## FEDERAL GRANT POLICIES AND RESOURCE SCARCITY

The impact of these federally driven expenditure increases on state and local budgets is a combination of two effects: those that stimulate overall expenditures; and those that distort priorities. These effects are accelerated by fiscal stress. In a time of abundance, it is possible to finance federally induced costs from the growth increment of new locally generated revenues without having to reduce nonfederally funded services correspondingly. During a period of austerity, however, programs are forced into zero-sum competition with one another. Financing the costs of existing or new federally funded programs means sacrificing local programs not eligible for federal assistance.

There is evidence to indicate that local governments experiencing budget cuts will tend to protect federally funded programs at the expense of their own locally funded programs. There is a considerable economic reason for this—budget cuts are needed to reduce expenditures based on insufficient locally derived revenues. In order to live within a contracting local resource base, it is not nearly as productive to cut a program funded mostly from external resources, that is, federal grants. In a 75 percent federally funded program, for example, a cut that saves only 25 percent in local revenue would nevertheless have the consequence of reducing the program by a ratio of 4 to 1—for every dollar of local funds, four dollars of total program funds would be reduced. When a program is funded entirely from local revenues, however, a one dollar cut is less devastating in programmatic terms.

Thus it is likely that the tendency to protect federal grant programs in a time of budget cuts will extend the distortion of local priorities. A GAO study of the impact of federal matching provisions found that seventeen of the twenty-three state and local governments reviewed had to cut disproportionately nonfederally funded services to avoid losing federal grant funds in time of budget cuts; in some cases, the reduced services were basic services such as fire, sanitation, and street cleaning that were not eligible for federal funds.[27] A recent report on New York City provides some interesting support for this proposition as well. In New York, a marked shift was found in city spending, away from basic services such as police, fire, and sanitation toward social services and health areas with heavy federal funding. The study shows the following trend for city expenditures.[28]

The report shows that during periods of growth, the city decided to invest new revenues among competing functions based in part on the federal dollar return. Similarly, the city's budget-cutting experience in 1975 and 1976 indicates that major budget cuts occurred primarily in locally funded services not eligible for federal funds, for example, police, fire, and sanitation. The report concludes that the disproportionate reduction in the basic services and the shift toward federally funded services was a product of the federal categorical grant system and was counterproductive to New York City's long-term fiscal, administrative, and social well-being because services that attracted dependent groups

| Function | FY 1961 | FY 1976 | Percentage increase or decrease |
|---|---|---|---|
| Welfare (including social services) | 12.3% | 22.6% | +10.3% |
| Hospitals | 8.2% | 9.7% | + 1.5% |
| Higher education | 1.9% | 4.5% | + 2.6% |
| Subtotals | 22.4% | 36.8% | +14.4% |
| Police | 9.5% | 6.4% | − 3.1% |
| Fire | 4.9% | 2.8% | − 2.1% |
| Sanitation | 5.4% | 2.7% | − 2.7% |
| Education | 25.6% | 18.4% | − 7.2% |
| Subtotals | 45.5% | 30.3% | −15.1% |

to the city continued to be funded while basic "house-keeping" services that benefit the entire city were cut.

The phenomenon is not limited to New York. The recent budgetary experience of California local governments in dealing with the impact of property-tax reductions mandated by passage of Proposition 13 tends to confirm this hypothesis. In planning for the potentially large reductions, local governments proposed greater retrenchments in locally supported basic services than in social-service programs that receive higher federal and state funding but are low in voter approval.[29]

In short, the strictures and structures of the federal grant system cause problems for local governments experiencing resource scarcity. Resource scarcity, however, also poses problems for the federal government. Resource scarcity could lead some state and local governments to preserve local priorities and sacrifice federal funds that involve matching requirements, maintenance of effort, or mandates. This practice would, however, tend to distort the distribution of federal funds away from those areas that may need them most. Thus, the fundamental purposes of many grant programs—to promote equity and to encourage uniform minimum levels of services throughout the country—may not be achieved. Resource scarcity therefore can lead to zero-sum conflict between federal and nonfederal interests. If federal programs are retained during a cutback period, state and local interests suffer; if state and local programs are retained, the federal interest suffers.

In sum, the entire intergovernmental system is distorted at all levels by the confrontation of grant requirements premised on growth with the political and administrative realities of resource scarcity. The theoretical and public-policy issues raised by this confrontation cannot be easily ignored.

## Jurisdictional Conflicts

By design, the American system of intergovernmental relations contains cleavages, both among levels and within jurisdictions, that are made more apparent by resource scarcity and fiscal retrenchment. Essentially, resource scarcity diminishes the control by each level of government over its own boundaries. State and local governments lose discretion over their budgets and policy agendas in proportion to their dependence on federal aid. The federal government comes to rely more

on other sectors of the economy—including states and localities—to implement national policies that are too expensive to be done by the federal government alone. The political accountability of each government for policies and programs becomes muddled as a consequence of this intensified interdependence.

Yet, the blurring of institutional boundaries and "policy space" sows its own antithesis—the redefinition of core interests intrinsic to each level of government and a consequent sorting out of priorities. Conflict among and within all levels of government intensifies as a result. In fact, it can be argued that intergovernmental cooperation is predicated on abundance as well as on the nature of the grant mechanism itself. When the responsibility for the costs and benefits of public programs are institutionally separated among levels of government, a critical incentive to discipline the size of public programs may be removed. The rather undisciplined proliferation of the imposing costs of federal mandates and the rather unselective acceptance of new federally funded programs by state and local governments offer further support for this proposition. Resource scarcity accentuates the realization of costs at all levels of government, however, and can induce the kind of critical evaluation and oversight at state and local levels that naturally occurs when benefits and costs become institutionally joined.

The institutional ambiguity in intergovernmental relations that tends to obscure the dominance of the federal government could be a luxury during a time when state and local governments are seeking to redefine their mission to accord with reduced resources. Under conditions of austerity, states and localities typically attempt to sort out and to rank programs and priorities so that dwindling resources can be used in the most essential areas.[30] Because state and local budgets are heavily dependent on federal funds, these cutback strategies affect and are affected by the federal grants system, triggering two kinds of conflicts that may ultimately weaken and undermine the intergovernmental system: conflict among levels of government; and conflict within jurisdictions.

Under conditions of resource scarcity, state and local policymakers seek new ways to relieve their financial burdens, including the use of federal funds to supplant state and local funds and support services previously supported by state or local revenues. This process can conflict with the federal grant system itself, which seeks to provide funding for new programs of national interest that state and local governments would not otherwise fund on their own. Indeed, the rationale for the existence of mandates as well as maintenance of effort requirements is that state and local governments cannot be left to implement national policies without some kind of federal intervention. Operationally, this means that state or local projects should qualify for federal funding only if their local priority is low enough that they would not have been funded with nonfederal funds. Fiscally well-off jurisdictions can tolerate peaceful coexistence between federally supported projects of low local priority and locally supported projects. If jurisdictions undergoing fiscal stress are to continue to receive federal grant funds and continue to comply with the structures of these programs, however, they would be forced to witness an erosion in the levels and quality of their traditional locally funded services while maintaining federally funded services of relatively low local priority.

For example, during the period of severe budgetary retrenchment, New York City argued that LEAA regulations, including maintenance of effort, required the city to use LEAA funds for new, innovative projects to improve the criminal justice system at the same time that the criminal justice system itself was experiencing large cutbacks and employee layoffs. The city felt that it should have been allowed to use these LEAA funds to restore the basic intrastructure of the system before launching innovative projects to improve it.[31]

It becomes a matter of vital self-interest for local governments to avoid cuts in locally funded services by shifting federal funds away from projects perceived to be nonessential by local officials but which may, nevertheless, be part of a major federal program. Maintenance of effort provisions, however, can prevent this by requiring that the brunt of cuts fall on those locally funded services with no federal fiscal involvement. Thus, if federal grant purposes are to be achieved, a priority inversion must occur, as local governments may be forced to harbor federal programs and mandates with low local priority and cut programs and services with high local priority. In addition, when abundant state and local resources are no longer available to cushion the impact of displacement effects, federal agencies themselves may be faced with a new conflict: whether to withdraw funding from state and local governments to satisfy federal requirements and

priorities or to tolerate a significant amount of noncompliance and in doing so to sacrifice the federal interest.

Resource scarcity at the federal level can also intensify conflict with state and local objectives in a different way. In an era of tightened budget constraints, the federal government may be more tempted to implement national policies without paying for the costs through mandates and direct regulation. Of course, these federal attempts to shift costs to other levels of government are bound to meet resistance in direct proportion to the budgetary constraints faced by state and local governments.

Conflict within a jurisdiction is also stimulated during cutback periods as bureaucracies and interest groups compete for a share of a shrinking economic pie. As this occurs, policymakers soon realize that the percentage of their budget under their discretionary control is decreased drastically.

During times of resource abundance, central state and local managers can more easily tolerate program expansion by agencies heavily funded by federal programs since other agencies funded mostly by state and local revenues are likely to be growing also. The greater autonomy of administrators of federally funded programs is not so obvious when compared with administrators of state and locally funded programs. Under conditions of fiscal stress and retrenchment, however, conflict is stimulated between constituencies and bureaucracies dependent on federal funds and state and locally elected officials responsible for controlling the size of the public sector and ultimately financing the second-order cost impacts of federal grants.

State legislatures, for example, have moved in recent years to assert stronger control over federal grant funds received by states. According to the National Conference of State Legislatures (NCSL), legislatures in twenty-six states attempted to increase their control over federal funds in the past two years by appropriating federal grant funds or reviewing state grant applications prior to submission to federal funding agencies. In a recent report, the NCSL concludes that this recent development has been prompted by tax and spending limitations which have provoked legislative concerns over the following impacts of federal grants for state budgets: predominance of federal priorities; ability to comply with match and maintenance of effort requirements; stimulative effects of federal seed money grants on state budgets; and inadequate federal funding to implement fully federal mandates and programs.[32]

## THEORETICAL IMPLICATIONS AND POLICY DILEMMAS

Even though these conflicts between levels and within jurisdictions may be ultimately muted through traditional means of intergovernmental lobbying and bargaining, it is difficult to account for them within frameworks of intergovernmental relations that emphasize cooperative federalism. These theories tend to emphasize the collaborative aspects of federalism and downplay the sources and significance of conflict between and within levels of the federal system.[33] It is imperative to ask: cooperation among whom for what purpose, and under what conditions?

If the diminution and distortion of state and local discretion and priorities become as severe as expected, then a reformulation of these explanations of intergovernmental relations is clearly appropriate. Resurrecting traditional theories of federalism and reviving time-worn discussions of the attributes of sovereignty, albeit under new conditions of intense interdependence and extensive externalities, may be needed. It is important during a time of heightened intergovernmental conflict to understand not only how conflicts are resolved, but also *how they arise.* Under conditions of resource scarcity, it is important to understand better how each level of the system *redefines* its own interests, priorities, and institutional boundaries.

Another missing element of cooperative bargaining models of intergovernmental relations revealed by resource scarcity is the limited influence of the state and local political officials most responsible for dealing with these aggregate impacts. Mayors, city managers, budget directors, and legislative officials are not full partners in the implementation of the variety of ongoing federal grant programs. Rather, the dominant actors are the functional specialists who control the vertical links of the intergovernmental picket fence. As a result, the officials most sensitive to defining and preserving the boundaries of state and local government autonomy are overshadowed by officials more concerned with protecting narrow programmatic boundaries than with enhancing the systemwide problem-solving capacity.

It is therefore quite possible that the mutual bargaining relationships thought to characterize the implementation of intergovernmental programs by some prominent students of intergovernmental relations theory may not, in fact, adequately describe the political problems of dealing with the residual effects of that system under conditions of scarce resources. These displacement effects are not a function of direct transactions within the intergovernmental system, but rather represent aggregate residual effects of the system as a whole. In its present form, cooperative bargaining models of intergovernmental relations theory do not and cannot adequately account for the aggregate impacts of the intergovernmental grants system functioning in its entirety. Indeed, residual or second-order consequences of that system are not recognized as *inter*governmental problems at all, but rather are dealt with in theory and practice as *intra*governmental issues. For example, waivers of federal mandates and grant requirements for fiscally distressed jurisdictions are not widely available in federal programs; and these waivers have not been widely lobbied for either.[34] Instead, state and local governments, no matter how fiscally strong or weak, have been left to their own devices in order to meet compliance requirements. Rather than considering this a problem in the grants structure, the displacement effects of federal programs are often celebrated as a *positive* consequence of the design of intergovernmental programs.

Ironically, the period that spawned the explosion of fiscally destabilizing categorical grants has also been marked by the emergence of a series of countervailing federal policies that seek to give fiscal relief to state and local governments. It could be argued that the distortion effects of categorical programs are somewhat muted by these countervailing policies, such as general revenue sharing, which provides discretionary "no-string" federal funds to states and localities. These strategies, however, are a very roundabout and indirect way for the federal government to deal with the displacement problem.

If the phenomenon of resource scarcity becomes a permanent feature of the public sector, the federal assistance system will face several significant policy dilemmas. Should the federal government, for example, continue to reward increases in the size of the state and local sector? Or, alternatively, should it remain neutral or actually encourage decreases? If expenditure reductions are encouraged through the federal grants system, is there a risk that federal funding will merely displace state and local funding, thus encouraging greater dependency on federal funds and less local autonomy? Can the federal government moreover tolerate decreased participation in grant programs developed to meet nationwide needs by state and local governments undergoing fiscal retrenchment? Is the resultant distribution of federal funds skewed away from areas or groups especially in need of federally funded services?

If this skewed distribution is to be rectified, should the federal government adjust grant requirements through waivers and other variances for all governments in fiscal distress? Or should policy distinctions be made between fiscal distress caused by secular economic decline and fiscal crisis brought about through the voluntary actions of wealthier communities? How should these distinctions be operationally determined?

If participation in grant programs begins to fall off, should the federal government itself directly provide for areas in need that cannot or will not participate in federal programs? What impact might this have on a federal budget which is also feeling the force of the taxpayer revolt? And how can emerging federal policies to shore up the fiscal and economic vitality of state and local governments through such efforts as general revenue sharing, countercyclical assistance, and emergency public-works assistance be reconciled with federal grant requirements such as matching and mandated costs that exacerbate state and local fiscal pressures?

Paralleling these dilemmas facing the federal government are numerous policy dilemmas confronting state and local governments that are rooted in the federal grants structure and resource scarcity. One of these dilemmas is especially noteworthy: By trying to reduce local government expenditures, voters supporting tax limitation initiatives may have inadvertently helped to increase the cost of government by pushing decision making to higher levels of government. This could add to the alienation that contributed to the tax limitation movement at the outset. At higher levels government feedback on local problems is weak, inaccurate, and sluggish, making control and implementation more difficult and cumbersome. Furthermore, by forcing policymaking upward, the danger of overloading state and national policymaking bodies with problems that used to be the exclusive concern of governors, mayors, state legislators, and city councilmen is increased. This leaves the central question of intergovernmental administration: Is it possible to transfer responsibility for funding services upward in the political system—and thus remove the link between revenue-raising levels of government and levels which

expend and implement—without eroding traditional constraints on spending and the traditional responsiveness of local government?

Finally, the federal grant system and resource scarcity present a dilemma for the design and administration of the intergovernmental system considered as a whole: By increasing state and local reliance on federal grant programs, the state and local policy agendas are likely to become "cluttered" by programs of national but not necessarily local priority. During times of cutbacks, the national priority programs tend to be protected while locally funded programs suffer the brunt of cuts. From the local viewpoint, it can be argued that protected federal programs are wasteful because they support innovations and program initiatives that local citizens and public officials consider frivolous—especially when the basic service infrastructure of local government is being retrenched. Thus a basic question for democratic theory and practice remains: Will sheltering federally funded programs while locally funded programs wither eclipse state and local political discretion? And, in so doing, will such a policy also promote cynicism, alienation, and the loss of efficacy among citizens who fund and are dependent on the services state and local governments deliver?

*This article is a revised version of a paper originally prepared for delivery at the Annual Meeting of the American Political Science Association, Washington, D.C., 31 August–3 September, 1979. The authors wish to thank David B. Walker of the Advisory Commission on Intergovernmental Relations for his helpful comments on the earlier draft.*

## NOTES

1. For a recent discussion of the importance and methods of democratic decentralization, see Samuel H. Beer, "Federalism, Nationalism, and Democracy in America," *American Political Science Review* 62 (March 1968): 9–21; for a discussion of the debates of the Founders on federalism, see Samuel P. Huntington, "The Founding Fathers and the Division of Powers," in *Area and Power,* ed. Arthur Maass (Glencoe, Ill.: Free Press, 1959). For a discussion of centralizing trends in the intergovernmental system, see David B. Walker, "The New System of Intergovernmental Assistance: Some Initial Notes," *Publius* 5 (Summer 1975): 131–145, and idem., "A New Intergovernmental System in 1977," *Publius* 8 (Winter 1978); for a discussion of the erosion of state and local discretion, see Paul L. Posner and Stephen M. Sorett, "A Crisis in the Fiscal Commons: The Impact of Federal Expenditures on State and Local Governments," *Public Contract Law Journal* 10 (December 1978): 341–379.

2. See Beer, "Federalism, Nationalism, and Democracy in America," pp. 17–20; also idem., "The Adoption of General Revenue Sharing: A Case Study in Public Sector Politics," *Public Policy* 24 (Spring 1976): 127–195.

3. Advisory Commission on Intergovernmental Relations, *Categorical Grants: Their Role and Design* (A-52) (Washington, D. C.: Government Printing Office, 1977), p. 39.

4. U. S. Executive Office of the President, Office of Management and Budget, *Special Analysis of the Budget, Fiscal Year 1981* (Washington, D. C.: Government Printing Office, 1980), p. 254.

5. Ibid.

6. See Rochelle Stanfield, "Federal Aid for Cities: Is It a Mixed Blessing?" *National Journal Reports* 10 (1978): 869.

7. Ibid.

8. See Wallace Oates, *Fiscal Federalism* (New York: Harcourt Brace Jovanovich, Inc., 1972), esp. chap. 3.

9. See Comptroller General of the United States, *The Federal Grant Process Should Be Changed to Permit Greater State Legislative Involvement* (GGD-81-3) (Washington, D. C.: General Accounting Office, 1980).

10. Edward K. Hamilton, "On Non-constitutional Management of a Constitutional Problem," *Daedalus* 107 (Winter 1978): 111–128.

11. Unpublished data from the National Conference of State Legislatures based on responses from forty-eight states, Denver, Colorado.

12. See Comptroller General of the United States, *State and Local Government Productivity Improvement: What Is the Federal Role?* (GGD-78-104) (Washington, D. C.: General Accounting Office, 1978).

13. Regina Herzlinger, "Costs, Benefits, and the West Side Highway," *Public Interest* 55 (Spring 1979): 94.

14. Advisory Commission on Intergovernmental Relations, *The Intergovernmental Grant System as Seen by Local, State and Federal Officials* (Washington, D. C.: Government Printing Office, 1977), p. 19.

15. U. S. Executive Office of the President, Office of Management and Budget, *Appendix, Fiscal Year 1981 Budget* (Washington, D. C.: Government Printing Office, 1980), p. 365.

16. U. S. Congress, Congressional Budget Office, *Urban Transportation for Handicapped Persons: Alternative Federal Approaches* (Washington, D. C.: Government Printing Office, 1979).

17. Advisory Commission on Intergovernmental Relations, *Categorical Grants: Their Role and Design,* p. 297.

18. Commission on Federal Paperwork, *Federal/State/Local Cooperation* (Washington, D. C.: Government Printing Office, 1977).

19. *Federal and State Mandating on Local Governments: An Exploration of Issues and Impacts; Final Report to the National Science Foundation* (Riverside: University of California, Graduate School of Administration, 1979).

20. OMB, *Special Analysis of the Budget, Fiscal Year 1981.*

21. Edward Gramlich, "State and Local Governments and Their Budget Constraint," *International Economic Review* 10 (June 1969): 163–182.

22. See Comptroller General of the United States, *Will Federal Assistance to California Be Affected by Proposition 13?* (GGD-78-101) (Washington, D. C.: General Accounting Office, 1978).

23. See George Johnson and James Tomola, "The Fiscal Substitution Effect of Alternative Approaches to Public Employment Policy, *Journal of Human Resources* 12 (Winter 1977): 3–26.

24. See Richard P. Nathan, "The Brookings Monitoring Research Methodology for Studying the Effects of Federal Grant-in-Aid Programs" (Paper presented to the Annual Meeting of the American Political Science Association, Washington, D. C., 31 August 1979).

25. See Comptroller General of the United States, *Federal Seed Money: More Careful Selection and Application Needed* (GGD-78-78) (Washington, D. C.: General Accounting Office, 1979).

26. South Carolina General Assembly Legislative Audit Council, *A Study of the Impact of Federal and Other Funding on Legislative Oversight* (Columbia: South Carolina General Assembly Legislative Audit Council, 1977), p. 35.

27. Comptroller General of the United States, *Proposed Changes in the Federal Matching and Maintenance of Effort Requirements for State and Local Governments* (GGD-81-7) (Washington, D. C.: General Accounting Office, 1980).

28. Temporary Commission on City Finances (TCCF), *An Historical and Comparative Analysis of Expenditures in the City of New York* (New York: TCCF, 1976).

29. Comptroller General of the United States, *Proposition 13—How California Governments Coped with a $6 Billion Revenue Loss* (GGD-79-88) (Washington, D. C.: General Accounting Office, 1979). See also L. Cannon, "California Finds That Repealing the New Deal Is Not Easy," *Washington Post,* 5 June 1978.

30. For a more in-depth discussion of this process, see Charles H. Levine, "Organizational Decline and Cutback Management," *Public Administration Review* 38 (July–

August 1978): 315–325; and idem., "More on Cutback Management: Hard Questions for Hard Times," *Public Administration Review* 39 (March–April 1979): 179–183.

31. See statement submitted by Mayor Beame, New York City, in U. S. Congress, House, Committee on Banking and Currency, Subcommittee on Economic Stabilization, *Debt Financing Problems of State and Local Governments,* 94th Cong., 1st sess., 1975, pp. 898–902.

32. See Winnifred M. Austermann, *A Legislator's Guide to Oversight of Federal Funds* (Denver, Colo.: National Conference of State Legislatures, 1980).

33. See, for example, Daniel J. Elazar, *The American Partnership* (Chicago, Ill.: University of Chicago Press, 1962); Helen Ingram, "Policy Implementation through Bargaining: The Case of Federal Grants-in-Aid," *Public Policy* 25 (Fall 1977): 499–526; Deil Wright, *Understanding Intergovernmental Relations* (North Scituate, Mass.: Duxbury Press, 1978); and Catherine Lovell, "Where We Are in Intergovernmental Relations and Some of the Implications," *Southern Review of Public Administration* (June 1979): 6–20.

34. The GAO found that most grant programs with these requirements do not provide for waivers. See Comptroller of the United States, *Matching and Maintenance of Effort Requirements.*

---

# Bargaining Analysis in Intergovernmental Relations

## Donald B. Rosenthal

To the extent that the study of American federalism, as traditionally understood, has been replaced by the analysis of intergovernmental relations (IGR) as "an important body of activities or interactions occurring between governmental units of all types and levels within the federal system" the intellectual focus of the field has been rendered less certain.[1] Indeed, the recent extension of IGR to include the study of policies formulated and implemented through these "interactions" appears to have expanded the notion of legitimate participants in IGR beyond governments—including local governments and special districts—to count pri-

From *Publius,* (Summer, 1980), Vol. 10, pp. 5–44. Copyright 1980, the Center for the Study of Federalism. Reprinted by permission.

vate organizations, interest groups and citizens as important actors.[2]

Not only is it difficult to draw conceptual boundaries around the *structures* of IGR, but it is equally problematic how best to understand the *processes* associated with those relations. Thus, even while some effort has gone into describing "cooperative" patterns of behavior, much remains to be done in identifying the various factors which either promote cooperation or conflict.[3] Some suggestive work has been done in this regard which focuses either explicitly or implicitly on the process of bargaining. In particular, Jeffrey Pressman has written that "viewing intergovernmental relations as a bargaining process is useful in keeping us from over-emphasizing either the cooperative or conflictual elements of that behavior."[4] Yet, equating IGR with bargaining, as Pressman's statement appears virtually to do, would be misleading for it would obscure certain analytic and practical difficulties in the study of IGR.

This article begins to explore some of these difficulties. We will proceed by first examining several aspects of bargaining as a concept relevant to the study of American IGR and, second, by presenting a set of case materials that bear on federal-local relations. These illustrate the range of variables which need to be considered in using the study of bargaining behaviors as a major vehicle for understanding intergovernmental processes. The article closes with an examination of some of the factors which constrain bargaining behaviors and thus limit its utility as an independent focus of analysis.

## BARGAINING AS CONCEPT AND BEHAVIOR

At its simplest, a bargain may be conceived of as an understanding reached between two parties to a transaction, by which Party *A* agrees to exchange certain values for others provided by Party *B*. This definition suggests at least four problems to a student of political behavior. These are the problems of evaluation, intensity, perception, and number.

First, actors to an exchange may value the good(s) at issue quite differently. Indeed, it may be in the interest of parties to a bargaining process to misrepresent the value they place upon the good(s) they wish to obtain, or the good(s) they are willing to contribute. Thus, the study of bargaining behaviors may need to include not only a concern with weighing the objective values at issue (assuming such can be determined) but the bargaining values in operation.

Secondly, the values at issue may reflect quite distinct levels of intensity on the part of different actors. Commonly, a local government applying for a project grant will be one of many entered in a competition whose specific allocational outcome may be of less intense interest to a funding agency than to the prospective recipient. Thus, bargaining relationships may acquire an intensity quite independent of the particular goods at stake. Participants, for example, may expend quite different levels of resources on a particular transaction because of their different relationships to the transaction.

Thirdly, even if the goals of a transaction are understood in the same general terms by the parties to it, the analyst may discover considerable differences in perceptions among the actors in a bargaining process. Therefore, generalizations which bear only on the outcomes of bargaining processes may be insufficient in helping us to classify varieties of behavior in IGR. Who "won" or "lost" in a particular conflict may be less interesting and important than each actor's perception of the process. Indeed, in some circumstances, the parties may not even agree that a bargaining process has occurred. Like one hand clapping, what is one to make of a case in which one party describes a bargaining relationship, whereas another actor insists that it has been engaged simply in a process of applying the narrowly-defined requirements of a law passed by Congress directly to a particular instance? We shall deal with such a case later.

Finally, the notion of bargaining as a simple "two-person" transaction is commonly violated in reality by the existence of numerous parties to any intergovernmental activity. Not only are there likely to be many actors in any major transaction, but some of the most conflictual exchanges may occur among actors nominally on the same "side." Indeed, as several of the cases discussed later indicate, once complex negotiations among local participants were completed, bargaining relations between local and federal actors were actually relatively straightforward. To describe the overall process as purely "cooperative," however, would be misleading.

We shall return to some of these problems after presenting the case materials, but before doing so, it may be helpful to deal with two other aspects of analyzing bargaining: (1) delimiting the scope of bargain-ing behaviors and (2) the use and abuse of bargaining language.

## Delimiting the Scope of Bargaining

Let us paraphrase Wildavsky's question about planning: "If bargaining is everything, then is it nothing?" Thus, while references to "cooperation" and "sharing" abound in IGR, in practical terms many of the transactions which occur in IGR necessarily involve what might be termed modified cooperation. Even though values may be shared, organizational and personal interests vary. Therefore, though cooperation may be a pervasive attitude and, on occasion, may act as a value-constraining conflictual behavior, conflict is equally pervasive. For absolute cooperation would mean a unit of interests, including agreement upon the means by which common purposes were to be achieved. Even for Grodzins, who highlighted the "sharing" aspects of IGR, there was never assumed to be an absolute identity of values of the kind that even authoritarian regimes are rarely capable of creating. He described certain relationships as based on "antagonistic cooperation."

If there are limits to cooperation, there are also bounds to what is negotiable in any set of human relationships, including ones which are essentially congenial. Particularly in a political culture where personal and organizational autonomy are important values in their own right, unresolved interorganizational tensions are persistent if not endemic. Thus, in a sense critical to IGR, local and state politicians guard their autonomy zealously, even if only to use that autonomy as a bargaining chip in negotiations with other actors.

In principle, at least three conditions can be identified in the real world where an equation of IGR with bargaining might be inappropriate: (1) in a highly consensual set of relations where patterns of shared values have become so institutionalized that bargaining need not enter the picture; (2) in those highly conflictual situations where values are so much in conflict (as in some cases of school or housing desegregation) that the principal actors find very little room for negotiation; and (3) where actors believe that the threat of bargaining to some set of fundamental values so outweighs the benefits at issue that bargaining avoidance behaviors are preferable.

Fritschler and Segal take account of the first two conditions in their typology of behaviors in intergovernmental relations when they identify four types of relationships: (1) joint (or "routine") policy-making, (2) mutual accommodation, (3) innovative conflict, and (4) disintegrative conflict. The first, which accords with a highly consensual situation, involves "preimposed and generally accepted procedures"; the last, "severe intergovernmental disagreements".[5] If distinctions such as these come readily at the end points of this analytical continuum, many of the real problems for analysis arise in the middle where most of the interesting cases occur.

Thus, in this broad middle range, many cases occur which offer opportunities for bargaining activities to be carried on, but observers may actually witness bargaining avoidance by key actors. Curiously enough, given his emphasis on bargaining, Pressman's study of aspects of IGR in relation to the city of Oakland provides one of the better examples of a city government that consistently avoided intergovernmental bargaining. To cite one example, when given the opportunity under the Green Amendment to play a larger role in the direction of a community action agency which had assumed a fairly militant posture, the Oakland city government (in keeping with the general behavior patterns ascribed to it by Pressman) sought ways to evade involvement. It could be argued, somewhat ironically, that Pressman's attempt to apply bargaining theory did not work in the Oakland case because the city refused to bargain with anyone whether they were local, state or national actors. Indeed, in one of the few instances where the mayor of Oakland did attempt to strike an activist posture in relation to the operation of a federal program—a case involving direction of the local manpower training program—his bargaining skills were so feeble that the federal agency virtually ignored the mayor's efforts.

## Problems in the Use of Bargaining Language

Because there is a well-developed tradition within international relations of bargaining analysis and in the use of the language of "game theory," it is tempting to import those approaches into the study of American IGR. Thus, Pressman draws some interesting parallels between donor-recipient relationships in foreign assistance and the federal-local relationship in American fiscal federalism. Unfortunately, it is not a comparison grounded in true structural or functional equivalency, for federal actors clearly can feel freer, particularly since the 1960s, to speak "for" local interests on terms equal to those posed by local governments. Indeed, much of the controversy surrounding "creative federalism" turned on just this issue. Even during the 1970s, when the federal government stepped back a little from direct interposition between citizens and their local governments on some matters, much bargaining in IGR continued to involve the definition of terms on which local governments would administer federally-funded programs consistent with federal versus local government definitions of requirements, such as, citizen participation, affirmative recruitment policies, concern for the environment, and the application of professional standards of administration. Through these and related struggles, federal and other government actors have sought to mobilize non-governmental interests to their own positions. This hardly accords with the usual situation in international relations.

While the use of bargaining language in international politics originally was associated with "crisis bargaining" and with "zero-sum" games, most transactions in domestic IGR are of a "positive sum" character. Indeed, international relations has itself moved more recently in the direction of complexity in its appreciation of the factors that characterize a less polarized international world: system fragmentation, conflicts among "allied" nations, in-fighting among bureaucratic actors.[6]

The application of the language of games to domestic politics is explicit in the recent work on implementation by Eugene Bardach.[7] His concern with the problems involved in bringing about agreement among institutionally-distinct actors in order to promote a common program, and his emphasis on the need to develop mechanisms by which incentives can be manipulated to achieve certain ends are matters which should be of great concern to those interested in developing a more analytical approach to the study of IGR.

While he denigrates the theoretical utility of his own enterprise, Bardach points to his use of the language of games as a "master metaphor" that "directs attention and stimulates insight." At the same time, he writes: "Their interrelationships are so manifold and convoluted that it is impossible to say much about the system as whole except that the . . . games . . . are on the whole only loosely interrelated."[8] Nonetheless, Bardach identifies a set of concerns important to any student of bargaining in IGR when he outlines some of the factors which merit attention in the study of implementation "games."

It directs us to look at the players, what they regard as the stakes, their strategies and tactics, their resources for playing, the rules of play (which stipulate the conditions for winning), the rules of "fair" play (which stipulate the boundaries beyond which lie fraud or illegitimacy), the nature of the communications (or lack of them) among the players, and the degree of uncertainty surrounding the possible outcomes. The game metaphor also directs our attention to who is not *willing* to play and for what reasons, and to who insists on changes in some of the game's parameters as a condition to playing.[9]

While this statement points to some intriguing possibilities for the study of cases of intergovernmental bargaining, Bardach leaves open the question of how to go about reestablishing an analytical *system* of political behavior overall. It is quite consistent with his approach that no common framework exists, only individual games. It might follow that each independent game has its own rules for participation and for bargaining. This is an issue for the study of IGR to which we will return briefly at the close of this article.

In identifying the terminological difficulties surrounding the bargaining process in IGR, it is also necessary to avoid confusing assumptions about "planes" of government with participants in bargaining behaviors. As noted earlier, specific cases may involve complex sets of bargaining activities but some of the most difficult relations may take place among actors in the same "plane." If the literature of IGR has emphasized anything over the last thirty years, it is the need to avoid the assumption that there are distinct "levels" of the system. Equally important, it must be left to empirical examination how negotiating coalitions for and against particular actions are put together, and who bargains for particular interests. Indeed, one of the niceties of the American political system—though, by no means peculiar to it—is the institutionalized ambiguity built into certain roles, notably the role of a member of Congress, which can serve as a bridge across troubled bargaining relationships, albeit occasionally making those relationships more difficult rather than easier.[10]

While a few, fairly intense occasions may arise in which one "plane" is aligned against another, these are relatively rare. Not only do many of the significant actors in IGR share critical political values—procedural as well as substantive—but most instances of IGR involve transactions in which all participants see the benefits at issue as providing services to the same target constituency. Commonly, where they disagree

enough to require negotiations, those negotiations may involve a debate about the most desirable methods for achieving the agreed-upon ends rather than about the ends themselves. That is especially likely to be the case where issues involve the design or implementation of project grants.

As obvious as these points may appear to be, they do raise potential problems for the development of a theory of "intergovernmental" relations. Conventionally, an examination of federal-local bargaining relations, for example, might focus only on points of federal-local conflict and the tactics employed by the federal and local "sides" of a particular controversy toward each other. Such an approach, however, may illuminate only a portion of a total decision-making process. It may also misrepresent that process by underestimating the effects of internal contradictions within a "plane" with respect to valuation and perception of the outcomes of a bargaining transaction. Thus, for example, one might argue rigidly that descriptions such as the one by Frieden and Kaplan of conflicts among federal bureaucrats over the Model Cities program should be excluded from discussions of IGR except, perhaps, as an "input" to understanding the way relations between federal and local actors were subsequently arranged.[11] The analytical problem is equally serious when one deals with cases of the kind discussed in the next section, in which a variety of local actors—municipal governments, interest groups, special authorities—disagreed vigorously among themselves on a given issue. In pursuing their divergent goals, they may have drawn state agencies in on different sides of the conflict, and ultimately have implicated federal actors in ways the federal actors may have even struggled to avoid. When federal actors are forced to referee local differences (as in one case) or merely to ratify the terms on which local and state intergovernmental conflicts are resolved (as in another case), how should such cases be differentiated from those cases of IGR which follow more conventional "interlevel" distinctions? One approach might continue to give primacy only to cases involving bargaining between agencies of the national government, on the one side, and state and local governments, on the other. Still, some method would have to be developed to take into account these many cases in IGR, more broadly understood, where Rosencrantz and Guildenstern are the leading players and Hamlet simply a supporting actor.

## FEDERAL-LOCAL RELATIONS IN METROPOLITAN BUFFALO

The seven cases examined for the purposes of this analysis involved transactions between local governments in Erie County, New York (including the city of Buffalo) and agencies of the federal government. At one extreme of what may be viewed as a continuum of conflict was a case which involved such a rapid response by President Carter that relatively little time was available for bargaining—the declaration of a major snow disaster in western New York in the wake of the blizzard of early 1977. At the other end are two cases where sharp conflict occurred between agencies of the city of Buffalo and the federal government over school desegregation and the dispersion of housing opportunities for low-income persons. Drawn from a set of federal-local transactions that occurred during the period from 1973 to 1977, these cases involved a range of actors—various federal agencies, different local governments, distinct state agencies—and a multiplicity of bargaining encounters. Elsewhere, I have presented the case materials in some detail.[12] Here, only a few elements of each will be highlighted before proceeding to draw certain general lessons about bargaining in IGR from the group of interactions as a whole.

### The Snow Disaster of 1977

After the Buffalo metropolitan area and other sections of upstate New York were struck by an unusually severe series of blizzards during the winter of 1976–77, Governor Hugh Carey formally submitted a request for federal disaster relief on January 29. President Carter immediately responded with a declaration of "emergency," which triggered federal aid to deal with the immediate crisis. Such a declaration did not exhaust the range of benefits that would have been made available had a "major disaster" declaration been issued. The governor, members of Congress, and local officials pressed for the more extensive coverage.

While the Federal Disaster Assistance Administration (FDAA) had moved without delay to recommend emergency disaster relief to the president, there was some concern on their part about applying "major disaster" status to a blizzard-induced situation rather than to the more conventional emergencies associated with floods or hurricanes. Indeed, there was no precedent for a declaration for a snow-related disaster.

Nevertheless, the FDAA proceeded to gather what it regarded as the appropriate data from field staff in order to make a proper determination and on February 4 that field report was reviewed by the administrator of the agency, who supported a declaration of major disaster status. The president signed that declaration on February 5. At about the same time, however, the president refused to extend similar status to areas of Ohio and Pennsylvania which were suffering from severe weather conditions and fuel shortages. In his recommendations, the administrator supported the recommendation for western New York not only because of the severity of the immediate situation, but because of the "already depressed economic condition of the affected area," which demanded action "far beyond the effective response capabilities of the State and local governments."[13]

On the whole, the FDAA appears to have proceeded expeditiously to reach a decision favorable to metropolitan Buffalo by February 4, based largely on technical criteria. Yet, on the latter day, presidential aide Midge Costanza and the president's son, Chip Carter, visited Buffalo and observers later asserted that the visit and the political concerns that accompanied it were critical to the decision announced the following day. Thus, even in such a relatively straightforward case, where local actors did not instantaneously achieve their goal but that goal was realized within an unusually brief time, it is difficult to sort out all the conflicting perceptions of causal relationships. Whether intergovernmental bargaining even occurred is a matter of some uncertainty. Rather, this was a case in which there was insufficient time to organize an explicit bargaining process. As a result, while some local politicians continue to believe that local political pressure made a difference in the outcomes, agency personnel may be equally correct that all the technical procedures were followed that provided the proper basis for a recommendation of major disaster status. In a sense, the dual application of political and technical routines to the case may simply have reinforced the achievement of a single outcome. In the end, the locality got what it wanted and FDAA lost nothing by confirming its commitment to bureaucratic procedures— procedures which were subsequently tightened to limit similar cases in more recent winters.

## Sewer Plant Improvements

Federally-funded local sewer projects have become a routinized part of federal-local relations. Thus, when the suburban town of Amherst proposed to undertake a major expansion of one of its existing plants, little difficulty was anticipated in bringing negotiations to a speedy conclusion. Preliminary plans were prepared and presented at a public hearing in May 1973, at which time the plan received general support. The town then applied for a grant to the Environmental Protection Agency (EPA) which was expected to provide 75 percent of the funding; the New York State Department of Environmental Conservation (DEC) would contribute 12.5 percent and the town the remainder.

The routine character of the transaction broke down, however, when a small group of property owners, numbering perhaps forty households adjacent to the existing site, formed a group called the North Amherst Residents Protective Association (NARPA) and began to flood EPA regional offices in New York City with complaints about the threats the expansion of the sewer plant would pose to their area in terms of odor, construction noise, dangers from the chlorine associated with the purification process and the esthetic impact of the project design.

NARPA exercised little influence with the Amherst Town Board, but EPA chose to take their concerns seriously. In part, this was because EPA's independent examination of the town's preliminary plans led them to share some of the reservations advanced by NARPA. The agency was also prepared to raise questions about other, more technical, aspects of the plans. With NARPA playing a highly vocal role, however, EPA did not have to "go public" with its concerns. Nonetheless, the town was forced to redesign the facility taking the complaints both of NARPA and the EPA into account. The substantially-revised plan was presented to a new set of public hearings in January 1974. On this occasion, the town mobilized a large number of institutional representatives and representatives of various environmental groups on behalf of the project. They greatly outgunned NARPA.

On the basis of these hearings and additional preparatory work, the town submitted its revised plan in March and a favorable decision was reported by EPA in May. Significantly, the EPA abandoned its implicit alliance with NARPA at this point, when it refused to accept a NARPA demand that it require the town to submit an environmental impact statement, a process which would have required months of labor and considerable expense. NARPA proceeded to file a suit against EPA on this issue, but the suit was dismissed in July 1974—more than a month after EPA had declared its commitment to a project valued at $86 million.

That local proponents of the project were confronted with vocal local opposition may have been no bad thing in itself. As one town official later conceded: "There were some legitimate environmental concerns raised, so the project was probably better for having an active group like NARPA around. They forced the town to go back and review its original plans." Whatever EPA's own objections, it is pure conjecture how seriously they would have pressed the same issues had NARPA not been a party to the transaction. In a sense, however, EPA "used" NARPA to publicize some of the issues surrounding the project, while continuing to maintain relatively cordial relations with town officials. While additional negotiations between EPA and the town did require technical accommodations on the town's part, there was a sense of political cooperation surrounding their discussions of technical problems, whereas the relationship between NARPA and the town board had much more of a confrontational flavor. From the perspective of federal-local bargaining relationships, then, NARPA served the function of diverting the more conflictual elements of potential federal-local controversy entirely to the local political arena, thus allowing federal-local relationships to function rather smoothly.

## A Flood Protection Project

Ellicott Creek drains an extensive area in western New York including the town of Amherst. The history of the area is one of repeated flooding. In 1960, a flood inundated 3,220 acres; as recently as the summer of 1977, portions of the heavily urbanized town were under water.

Because of this continuing threat, various plans have been generated over the years to protect the area. For a time, the state's Department of Environmental Conservation (DEC) supported a recommendation for a multipurpose dam and reservoir upstream from Amherst in the rural town of Alden. That alternative was one of several recommended in a report prepared by the Army Corps of Engineers in May 1970. It was

214

favored by several state agencies with interests in Amherst including the State University of New York (SUNY), which was in the process of developing a new campus adjacent to Ellicott Creek, and the Urban Development Corporation (UDC), which was planning a "new town," Audubon, next to the campus.

Nevertheless, the residents of Alden were bitterly opposed to a solution which they regarded as coming at their expense. First, they prevailed upon their representative in Congress, Barber Conable, to require a more extensive study of alternatives by the Army Corps. That study was not completed until August 1973, when the Corps came forward with a report which highlighted four alternatives out of thirty-one examined. Two involved dams at points outside Amherst, including the Alden site. The third would have required that a major diversion channel 3.4 miles long be constructed in the immediate vicinity of the new campus and Audubon. The other would have necessitated major channelization—realignment, widening and deepening—of 7.8 miles of Ellicott Creek in the same general vicinity.

There were essentially two rounds of conflict in the course of reaching an acceptable solution. Significantly, both can be viewed as having been fought out without major federal-local conflict. Thus, in the first "round," the small band of Alden residents (approximately eighty-two families) were successful in convincing Congressman Conable that it was inequitable for them to suffer so that downstream residents of suburban Amherst (not in his congressional district) could benefit from the protection provided to them while living in a flood plain. Congressman Jack Kemp, who represents Amherst, deferred to Conable on this issue. He was willing to limit the choice to the two Amherst-centered alternatives and to recommend to the Army Corps of Engineers whichever solution state and local interests were able to agree upon.

With the Alden alternative dismissed, a second round of intense negotiations ensued among state and local interests. The corps identified the major diversion channel as its preferred solution but the UDC and its allies (SUNY and the DEC) much preferred major channelization which would mean lower costs because of less need for construction of roads, bridges and utility lines to ford a diversion channel. Local environmentalists strongly opposed major channelization, which they felt would destroy the environmental and

esthetic benefits of the creek. However, they were not really happy with either alternative.

Taking off from these two alternatives, the corps and state and local officials painfully hammered out a compromise which was unveiled at a public hearing in November 1974. It consisted of 1.5 miles of diversion channel and 4.4 miles of major channelization. As a result of this compromise, Governor Malcolm Wilson issued an official letter of intent to the Army Corps of Engineers on November 26, 1974, on behalf of the state of New York.

Despite this outcome, local dissatisfaction with certain aspects of the design continued to be a cause for further emendations of the plan. Environmental groups, in particular, pressured the Erie County government to make changes. As a result, by 1977, the plan had been revised to provide for two miles of diversion channel and only two miles of major channelization. This plan cut in half the amount of stream bed subject to widening and deepening. Major additions were also made in terms of recreational space. However, funding and implementation of the project have been slowed, most recently by President Carter's veto of water projects in 1978. Plans now call for construction to be underway by 1980.

Given the nature of rivers and harbors legislation, congressional involvement is critical in the activation of the work of the Army Corps of Engineers. Thus, in the initial "round" of negotiations, the veto exercised by Congressman Conable was pivotal. The support of state agencies and local groups in Amherst for the Alden alternative went for nothing once Congressman Conable decided to oppose an Alden site.

In the second phase, the corps was a more active participant but took a role largely as mediator and technical advisor in the course of negotiations among state and local agencies and interests. Critically, Congressman Kemp deferred to whatever results the state and local agencies might produce. Like the previous case, therefore, issues were negotiated less in terms of direct federal-local bargaining than as the resolution of differences among local and state acrods, although federal funding is critical to the project. Once a compromise was reached, funding would be provided almost automatically by the federal government on the basis of congressional priorities. Thus, this was a case involving an intergovernmental bargaining process without serious federal-local conflict. Indeed, more than the other cases, it resembles the "classical" model of federal-local relations in which federal resources are exploited on terms largely defined by nonfederal actors. Of course, that situation owes much to the historical approach to rivers and harbors ("pork barrel") legislation, an approach which President Carter attempted to change.[14]

## Health Maintenance Organizations in Erie County

Since the passage of the Health Maintenance Organization Act of 1973, the federal government has been encouraging the development of pre-paid health delivery organizations throughout the country on a demonstration basis. As an inducement to local groups, Congress made available a series of grants and loans to those undertaking such efforts. As a first step, a local group may apply for funding to conduct a "feasibility study," which may run to a cost of $75,000. If feasibility is established, a more intensive "planning grant" may be provided to conduct detailed marketing surveys, undertake preliminary site planning and develop an administrative structure including gathering commitments from local health providers. Grants for this phase may run up to $200,000. Toward the end of this second phase, an aspiring health maintenance organization (HMO) is expected to submit an application for an "initial development grant" which may be as much as $1 million.

In response to these federal incentives, two planning groups were formed in Erie County. One was based in the UDC's new town of Audubon; the other originated among personnel associated originally with the Erie County Health Department. For present purposes, the former will be referred to as the "Audubon group," the latter as the "County group."

One important aspect of this case, is the essentially non-governmental character of the two planning groups. Although both originated in personnel who were implicated otherwise in local or state government activity, once planning activity got seriously underway those connections were severed and the planning organizations became non-governmental recipients of federal funds emanating from the Public Health Service's Health Services Administration (HSA).[15]

Perhaps because of the non-governmental nature of the two planning groups, or more likely because of the values of those who administered the program, negotiations were marked by a certain political tension. While local planners greatly respected the technical

capacity of those HSA officials with whom they dealt —principally officials based in HEW's Region II offices in New York City—they resented the tutelary attitude that those officials assumed. To some degree, then, negotiations were characterized not only by disagreements over various technical issues but involved a struggle on the part of local planning organizations to establish a degree of political autonomy more characteristic of institutionalized local government agencies.

These tensions were reflected in the perceptions and attitudes of the two sets of actors. While local informants described what they viewed as the political aspects of negotiations over technical and organizational issues, HSA officials perceived their choices and behaviors as narrowly defined by the regulations under which they operated. At the same time, however, they insisted that their actions were essentially responsive to local initiatives rather than involving any effort to impose on localities a vision, of their own, of what a particular HMO should look like.

In the case of the Audubon group, a task force was created which included citizens from Amherst, local health care professionals, representatives of a suburban hospital, and of local governments. Despite some initial local opposition, the task force approved an application for a feasibility study which was funded by HSA to run from July 1, 1975 to June 30, 1976. The board of the Audubon group selected a man with strong credentials as study director in November 1975. However, his managerial style soon came under serious questioning by HSA. These differences came to the fore at the time local planners submitted their application for a planning grant in 1976. Region II officials made it quite clear that they were not prepared to proceed with funding so long as the director remained in place. As a result, he left Audubon to assume a position running an HMO outside Region II.

There were several technical aspects of the feasibility study that dissatisfied Region II officials, including a late shift to a proposal for several sites for the HMO after the original proposal had involved a single site to be located in Audubon. Despite their denial of the existence of a preferred model for HMO designs, local planners came away from discussion with Region II personnel convinced, as one informant described it, that those officials favored "one-stop, large-scale operations delivering both primary and secondary care."

Despite the confusion surrounding the controversy over the departure of the study director, the remaining staff were encouraged by HSA to put existing planning material into a better framework and submit their application. Revisions were made in only two to three weeks. Both HSA and local people concede that the product was weak. Nonetheless, the application was approved for funding. A new study director was not hired until October 1976. Her relations with the New York office proved to be much better than her predecessor's.

The second effort to design an HMO for Erie County was the result of the interest of the county's Deputy Commissioner for Health. Initially, he hoped to base an HMO in the community health centers operated by Erie County. However, Region II officials questioned the viability of an HMO tied directly to the county government. Their doubts reflected real concern about the budgetary problems of the county; the distinct personnel needs of the HMOs; dangers of political interference; and a certain concern about "distancing" the HMO from health centers, whose principal clients were low-income persons. Region II officials deny any insistence on their part on these matters, but they do concede that they "asked questions" about these features of the original design. Whatever the extent of pressure such "questions" represented, the County group abandoned its initial approach and developed a design for a single-site HMO entirely independent of the county government's health services.

By the fall of 1976, both planning organizations were moving toward submission of applications for large-scale development grants. Only at this point did it begin to become obvious that HSA might be forced to choose between the two. Given the demonstration nature of the HMO program and the uncertain demand in the area for HMO services, it became clear that only one design could be funded immediately. For a time, efforts were made by HSA to bring the two groups together for discussions of possible merger, but they failed to reach an accord. Since both had been funded to June 1977, to complete their second-year studies, there was no immediate incentive to the planners to seek a merger. Separate applications were duly submitted in anticipation of a funding cycle due to begin July 1, 1977.

Local informants suggest that HSA had considerable difficulty making a choice. Once again, it attempted to avoid the issue by holding a joint meeting of the boards of the two planning groups with the planning staffs absent in order to encourage a merger agreement.

This effort failed. Finally, with no other resources left, HSA selected the County group on grounds which involved certain marginal distinctions, including the availability of a prospective medical director with strong credentials, and the location of the facility at a site which promised greater access by target groups. The announcement made on July 22, 1977 assured the County group of nearly a million dollars in initial development funds. (The facility was in operation by late 1978.)

That Region II used their leverage over the release of federal funds to shape technical choices in the planning process does not mean that they were "wrong" in either some technical or political sense. Indeed, the quality of oversight exercised by Region II personnel has given them a reputation for high professional performance within HSA nationally. Whether viewed in political or professional terms, however, they were both able and willing to exercise considerable hierarchical control over the planning process in what might be regarded as a superordinate-subordinate style unusual in federal-local negotiations. Because of the nongovernmental nature of the local planning groups, especially after HSA weaned them away from their initial governmental attachments, this case contrasts rather sharply with the previous one of federal deference to local choices.

Equally important, local planning groups accepted the critical presumption that the design of HMO facilities should be left to discussions limited to professionals. Thus, while members of Congress were drawn upon to make "inquiries" during the course of negotiations and to provide letters of support for the two proposed HMOs, there is little evidence that these routine interventions had any effect upon the behaviors of federal actors or upon the final outcomes. Nor was there any effort by local planners to mobilize public opinion behind their efforts. Indeed, very little of the history of the events narrated here ever appeared in local newspapers, very much in contrast to the other cases examined in this study. Rather, local planners tacitly agreed to play by the technical standards and, consequently, within the political boundaries set by the HSA. In sum, the almost complete dependence of local planners on the goodwill of the HSA bureaucrats for funding, and their willingness to confine disagreements to narrow professional channels cut them off from access to some of the bargaining methods normally associated with federal-local relationships.

## The Mass Transit System

In June of 1976, the Urban Mass Transportation Administration (UMTA) announced an award of $269 million to the Niagara Frontier Transportation Authority (NFTA) to be used, along with a matching share of $67 million from New York State, toward construction of a fixed-rail mass transit system in the city of Buffalo. That decision culminated a process covering a period of planning and negotiation that began in 1969.

The proposal for a mass transit system originated with a report issued by the New York State Office of Planning Coordination in March 1969. In very general terms, it described a system which would run from downtown Buffalo to the new SUNY campus in Amherst, approximately twelve miles away. The proposal was subsequently developed by the NFTA, a regional authority created by the state to operate regional airports and the Port of Buffalo as well as to direct transportation planning for western New York. (Subsequent to its creation, the NFTA also assumed responsibility for the operation of bus systems in Erie and Niagara counties.)

In August 1969, the NFTA applied to UMTA and the New York State Department of Transportation (NYSDOT) for funds to conduct a feasibility study for a mass transit system. An award was announced in January 1970, with the federal government assuming two-thirds of the cost of the $786,000 study. NFTA conducted a public meeting in late March 1972. Despite local opposition, NFTA was supportive.

Once the NFTA began to get seriously into the process of planning, however, two major issues emerged: the precise route, and the type of grade. The first evoked a series of battles between NFTA and one particular neighborhood group, which opposed a route through its area. That conflict was further heightened by NFTA's preliminary study, released in November 1970, which proposed running an overhead monorail through the area. The result was the rise of a citizens movement which eventually became known as No Overhead Transit (NOT).

At first, the NFTA refused to concede ground to NOT, but the latter worked effectively at building a coalition which eventually came to include respected local institutions such as Sisters Hospital and Canisius College. While UMTA did not get involved directly in these local battles, they did indicate on various occa-

sions that Buffalo would need to resolve its local conflicts before any advanced application could be taken seriously. Such a resolution clearly had not been achieved by the time NFTA unveiled its revised plan at what proved to be a stormy public meeting in late March 1972. Despite local opposition, NFTA continued to work on completing that plan and the accompanying application for UMTA funds to undertake a major "preliminary design and engineering study." When that application was completed, another public hearing, as required by law, was held. Again, the proposal evoked considerable citizen hostility. That hostility, it should be noted, was directed basically at the design of the "middle corridor" of the system, rather than at either the section planned for the central business district, or the suburban portion of the route.

Even though the plan continued to meet with local opposition, NFTA's board approved the application for the engineering study in May 1972 and forwarded it to UMTA along with transcripts of the public hearings. UMTA delayed action for several months. In part, UMTA's delays were attributable to its own decision-making rules. In particular, the agency was coming under increasing pressure to take a stronger stand on the citizen participation issue. Criticisms were being heard from various cities where systems were either being planned or were under construction. The conflict at the time in Atlanta was particularly bitter.

After months of silence, NFTA and local interests prevailed upon members of Congress from the Buffalo area—who came to play an especially active role in subsequent transactions in this case—to arrange a meeting with UMTA officials. That meeting was held in October 1972. It was agreed that NFTA should further "refine" its pending application including giving due consideration to citizen complaints. In carrying forward this "refinement," however, NFTA received a major commitment of $1.8 million, most of which was borne by UMTA (with a small matching share from NYSDOT). This grant permitted NFTA to proceed with preliminary design work but on the understanding that serious alterations might need to be made in the more controversial aspects of the project.

In February 1973, NFTA was reorganized to reflect a greater commitment of staff to the development of the mass transit system. New personnel were brought in who moved to abandon the confrontational approach to NOT and its allies. This change was evidenced in a series of "community forums" held in October 1973. At the one held on the "middle corridor," NFTA announced major concessions on the route. Nevertheless, it continued to support the use of overhead construction in some portions of the corridor as a major cost-saving device. NOT did not accept this position and demanded further action on the grade. Ultimately, NFTA conceded defeat and agreed to a design that involved construction of an underground system along a major business artery rather than through the neighborhood represented by NOT. From an estimated cost of $257 million in 1971, however, the total cost being mentioned by 1974 was $480 million, reflecting partly rapid inflation in the component elements of the system, but also the major alterations in the design.

With this first phase of the process completed locally, NOT and others became as strong supporters of construction of the system as they had formerly been its opponents. It now became incumbent on UMTA to reach a decision about approving or rejecting the design. Only at this point did it become apparent that the agency was itself going through considerable internal debate over the procedures to be followed and its own goals. Faced with an increasing number of applications for expensive mass transit systems, UMTA began to hint at the desirability of such alternatives to fixed heavy rail systems as buses or modernized variants of trolley systems.

Through the summer of 1974, UMTA engaged in exchanges with members of Congress from the Buffalo area about its concern over the escalation of costs and the need for the examination of less expensive alternative modes. In July, for example, congressional representatives, NFTA representatives, and UMTA officials met in Washington. Rather than resolving outstanding issues, however, the meeting resulted in an agreement by UMTA to fund yet another study—this time by an independent consultant—to review alternative modes and routes.

At the same time, NFTA continued to work on its preliminary design and engineering study, pointing that effort toward the next stage—an application for a first-year grant for the final engineering design, and the beginning of land acquisition. On completion of that study, NFTA applied for $20.6 million from UMTA, a sum to be matched with $5.1 million from New York State. In connection with that application, public hearings were held on July 24–25, 1974. This

time, reflective of the new local mood, NOT representatives and other speakers were uniformly supportive.

The consultant's alternatives analysis was completed in December. It generally supported the route proposed earlier by the NFTA, although it recommended that only six and one-half miles from downtown to the northern part of the city be funded initially as "the best alternative on the basis of transportation benefits only."[16]

At this point, the factors contributing to delay become uncertain. Suggestions range from inadequacies in UMTA's staff to questions about UMTA's goals. Planners at NFTA were left to guess what was going on. In part, at least, UMTA's procedures for processing materials were inadequate. Until 1976, the agency had no formal guidelines for the submission and review of materials. As one UMTA informant admitted, "Buffalo was caught in the middle as the process evolved within UMTA."

While the agency temporized, it found yet another occasion for funding a study. It asked the outside consultant on the alternatives analysis to do a "refinement" of its report to include a more careful examination of alternative modes such as light rail and buses. As in the past, UMTA bought its way out of a decision by funding a large share of this $340,000 "refinement."

In the spring of 1975, regimes changed in the federal Department of Transportation and in UMTA. A new secretary, William Coleman, and a new administrator of UMTA, Robert Patricelli, expressed attitudes different from their predecessors. Where earlier leaders had emphasized cost-benefit relationships, based primarily on transportation activities alone, the new agency leadership was willing to put more stress on the use of transit projects as vehicles for promoting general urban development. Part of UMTA's previous non-decision-making stance in the Buffalo case had reflected the agency's serious doubts about the financial viability of the Buffalo system. In terms of economic benefits like employment opportunities for associated development, as several UMTA informants suggested, the Buffalo proposal looked somewhat better.

It was at this point that considerable political influence was brought to bear upon the agency by state and local actors. Commissioner Raymond Schuler of the NYSDOT, the Buffalo congressional delegation and local business, government, and citizen groups were mobilized to maintain continuous pressure on UMTA. This effort was further aided when the entire New

York State congressional delegation went on record for funding the system, a rare case of agreement within that quarrelsome delegation.

One of the major shifts that occurred in the course of the often implicit negotiations between UMTA and the NFTA was the substitution of a design involving light rail for the heavy rail system originally proposed. Typically, UMTA did not make a direct demand to the NFTA for such a substitution, but it did make it known generally that it might be interested in funding at least one such project as an experiment. This was a point at which not only Buffalo but other applicants like Denver suddenly began to take an interest in modifying their heavy rail approaches to conform to UMTA's "signals."

In February 1976, the "refined" alternatives analysis was finally issued. It reflected a general shift in design to a system of only 6.4 miles using a "light-rail rapid-transit" mode. It was this system for which Secretary Coleman announced a "commitment in principle" on June 10, 1976.

UMTA staff insist their reviews and re-reviews involved purely technical criteria, although several have hinted at other factors which they were notably unwilling to discuss. Their hesitance in acting reflected, in part, the mounting criticism surrounding some of the new mass transit systems including the (non-UMTA) BART system in the San Francisco Bay area and Washington's very expensive METRO, which had not become fully operational at the time.

The timing of the announcement in the Buffalo case has been the subject of much local speculation. Coming as it did shortly before the Republican national convention, when the commitment of the New York State delegation to the re-nomination of President Ford was by no means certain, rumors are common that the designation of the system was a concession to the more conservative upstate wing of the party, led especially by Congressman Jack Kemp, who had been active in promoting the NFTA application. In that connection, informants point to the timing of a Miami transit commitment by UMTA just before the Florida primary in which Ronald Reagan and President Ford were engaged in close combat.

The general perceptions of NFTA personnel toward their lengthy negotiations are suggested in the comments of one:

> It was an important factor that Buffalo had the local professional staff to keep on top of the situation . . .

UMTA was creating a series of hoops that they had to jump through and they were willing to stick to the job. After a while, UMTA simply ran out of hoops. In part, UMTA's actions were a protection to buy time because UMTA ran up against the problem of having to make a decision.

Thus, while this second phase of negotiations did involve bargaining, it was bargaining of a rather indirect variety. Many signals were issued by the federal agency. Some were only in response to proposals submitted by NFTA; others were directed at what UMTA was really looking for at any point. In an important sense, some of the agency's apparent indirections were used by UMTA both as a way to avoid making controversial and expensive choices in an environment of high uncertainty, and also as a means by which UMTA could use local applicants to act as experimental surrogates in developing a better technical approach to the design and implementation of mass transit systems—still a relatively new area of federal policy.

In the end, Buffalo was forced to move away from its original design in order to acquire as much of a system as it finally got. From a larger perspective, however, it can hardly be argued that the result clearly reflected a weak bargaining position on the part of the locality. For, after all, the process yielded a $320 million project. Currently under construction, it continues to reflect the basic agreements on routes and grades reached locally with neighborhood and institutional interests.

## Integration of Buffalo's School Staff

The history of school desegregation efforts in Buffalo has been a long and tortuous one. Efforts by the New York State Education Department and federal education officials to hasten movement toward integration were met with many local evasions.[17] It was not until April 1976 that an order was issued in the local federal district court mandating the Board of Education to move immediately toward developing a plan for integrating pupils and staff throughout the city. Efforts along those lines were initiated beginning in the fall of 1977.

During the several years that the integration case was being litigated, Buffalo was a participant in various federal and state programs which provided aid to local school districts. One of these, the federal Emergency

School Aid Act (ESAA), became the center of controversy in 1975 when the city applied for funds but was turned down when it refused to move immediately to the adoption of a plan for integrating its school staff.

This conflict between the federal Office of Education (OE) and Office for Civil Rights (OCR) within HEW, on the one hand, and the Buffalo Board of Education, on the other, was preceded by dissatisfaction among federal actors with respect to the city's prior performance under ESAA. In the first year of that program, 1974, the city had been funded at the last moment after considerable conflict over the maintenance of an all-black school for the mentally retarded. Buffalo had promised to eliminate the school as a condition for receiving the funds. However, this promise had been acted upon in what OE regarded as bad faith. The school in question had been closed but the handicapped students were dispersed to other heavily minority schools.

As early as 1973, when regulations for the program were being developed, the board had been informed of its obligation under the law to desegregate staff as well as students. The OE did not pursue that issue in connection with ESAA funding in 1974–75. Nevertheless, officials at OE had not forgotten Buffalo's prior performance or its inaction on the staffing issue when the city submitted an application for ESAA funds in 1975.

In its response to that application, OE reminded the board that it had failed to act upon OE's previous finding that the city continued to assign faculty in a manner that maintained the segregation of staff. It indicated that the city would be disqualified from participation in ESAA unless it moved immediately to correct the situation.

On their part, the board insisted that staffing patterns reflected the preferences of teachers rather than the actions of the board alone. Indeed, one of the schools with the highest proportion of black teachers was being run under contract with a militant minority organization founded with the aid of Saul Alinsky to promote black identity. The board also claimed that immediate action would only create confusion at a time when the outcome of the pending court decision on the fate of the entire system was expected momentarily.

When the conflict over ESAA emerged, Buffalo's school board consisted of three blacks and six whites. It was a relatively moderate board headed by a black. Despite conflicting backgrounds and attitudes, members of the board were united in opposition to the OE order.

The Office of Education first informed the board of its demands on June 17, 1975. The board met and responded, on June 20, with a request for a meeting in Washington, which was held on June 27. That meeting took place in the presence of staff representative of the three area members of Congress. It was relatively brief and amounted to little more than an affirmation of the two conflicting positions. Shortly thereafter, the city was formally given until September 30 to comply or lose the amount sought.

An exchange of telegrams ensued during the following month. From its side, the Office of Education, now joined by the Office of Civil Rights, merely affirmed its demands. The board responded by holding a public hearing, on July 23, at which various local groups argued against immediate action on the staffing transfer demand. Conflict was escalated when OE also notified the board in mid-July that the deadline for action had been shifted from September 30 to August 15. Another meeting was requested by the board with HEW representatives. Held in Washington on July 28, no resolution was achieved.

At this time, the three local members of Congress drafted a joint letter sent to OE on August 1, which reviewed the situation and argued against the decision to withhold funds. In particular, they objected to the decision to shift the deadline, contrary to what they regarded as a congressional mandate. In that connection, Congressman John La Falce wrote to the new secretary of HEW, F. David Mathews, condemning OE's behavior as "the height of absurdity," for OE and OCR were demanding a racial quota for teachers while none was yet required for pupils.

Despite these political interventions, OE remained adamant in its position. One senior official remarked, with respect to the general approach of his office:

> After all [ESAA] is discretionary money under federal mandates and is appropriated by Congress. Either a city must meet the requirements or withdraw its application. It is not fair for a city to apply and then complain when it does not do those things that are required by the Act.

In an effort to prevent OE from denying funds to the city, the board filed a suit in federal district court asking for an injunction against HEW which would prevent the agency from applying the $1.5 million earmarked for Buffalo elsewhere until the issue was resolved. A temporary restraining order was issued on August 21, and a hearing was held shortly thereafter on the basis of which HEW was ordered on September 29 to hold the funds in question until a decision was announced. That decision has never been rendered.

Instead, the federal district judge in this case apparently decided to wait for resolution of the larger school integration suit. In effect, the issue of funding for Buffalo was allowed to become moot for 1975–76. On the basis of the new desegregation order issued in 1976, however, Buffalo did qualify for $1.57 million in ESAA funds for the following year, and was also given priority status for an Emergency Special Projects program which applies to cities under desegregation orders.

This case is instructive because it illustrates the ability of a federal agency to take a tough position and stick to it, and for a local board to hold firm to its own quite distinct position. Not all intergovernmental conflicts lead to bargaining and satisfactory resolutions. Furthermore, the active intervention of members of Congress appeared to have little effect in promoting a mutually-acceptable outcome through bargaining processes. Given the history of Buffalo's past performance, HEW felt fully justified in demanding strict conformity to what it determined to be its responsibilities. Yet, in the longer run, this was only a temporary episode. The Board of Education and the Office of Education did not cut off diplomatic relations. Currently, the city appears to be treated much like other school systems in its dealings with Washington.

## Buffalo's Housing Assistance Plan

When Congress passed the Housing and Community Development Act of 1974, it made the receipt of Community Development Block Grant (CDBG) funds contingent upon the submission of applications which were to include Housing Assistance Plans (HAPs). The latter would identify the housing needs of low- and moderate-income persons and outline efforts that were planned by the locality to meet those needs using HUD resources. In the case of Buffalo the $11.7 million in CDBG funds promised for the first year came at a time when the city was particularly deep in financial difficulty. It was regarded as essential to maintaining even a minimal level of existing services.

At the outset of the CDBG Program, the HAP was understood by many local governments to be little

more than a symbolic activity.[18] This was in keeping both with the spirit of non-intervention associated with the New Federalism and the need to develop formal procedures for reviewing local applications. Thus, inadequacies in Buffalo's HAP might have gone uncriticized, as was the case elsewhere, had the area office of the Department of Housing and Urban Development (HUD) lacked an aggressive director. However, Frank Cerabone had been in charge of the Buffalo office since 1970 and had become very concerned with the failure of the city to develop what he regarded as a balanced housing program, providing sufficient opportunities for assisted housing for low- and moderate-income persons, particularly large families. In keeping with HUD mandates, that housing was expected to be located outside areas of minority and low-income concentration and away from those neighborhoods where public housing had been traditionally concentrated. These principles were unacceptable to many white citizens of Buffalo and to some of the members of the Buffalo Common Council who represented them.

As with the previous case, the conflict that arose around Buffalo's HAP reflected a history of difficulties between municipal leadership and a federal agency. In this case, Cerabone and the mayor of Buffalo had signed a "memorandum of understanding" in 1972, under which HUD promised to fund two senior citizen projects desired by the city in return for an agreement by the city to develop a plan for assisted family housing. The city was very slow to deliver on that commitment. One site discussed as early as 1971 involved an essentially white neighborhood in which thirty units of family housing were to be constructed. Announcement of selection of that site had stirred considerable opposition among residents. That earlier conflict had died down when a designated developer failed to move forward expeditiously. It was only in late 1974 that attention was drawn to that project once again, when Cerabone wrote to the city's Public Housing Authority and the developer about their plans on the project. Both indicated continued interest. This set off a new uproar among neighborhood residents, who demanded a meeting with Cerabone in February 1975, at which they complained about plans for the project. At that meeting, the newly-seated member of the Common Council from the district played a prominent role in opposition to the project. A temporary halt on the project was agreed to by Cerabone while the matter was reviewed by HUD, but on April 7, Cerabone announced that HUD still planned to proceed with funding.

It was against this background of conflict that work began on the city's application for CDBG funds. That document, incuding the city's HAP, was submitted to HUD on April 14. It contained a list of sites which might be developed using HUD housing assistance programs, but it did not indicate specifically which sites would be used to meet the needs of low- and moderate-income families, especially those of minority backgrounds. Furthermore, many of the sites were in areas which had been designated earlier for urban renewal or public housing construction (areas surrounded by blight). They were neighborhoods regarded by HUD as inappropriate for housing programs since they already were characterized by considerable "impaction." What turned out to be equally controversial was the inclusion on the list of the disputed site mentioned earlier.

It was because of the controversy surrounding selection of that particular site that Cerabone was invited to a meeting of a committee of the Common Council on April 18, at which time he was closely questioned about the selected site and about block grant and HAP processes. For three hours, members of the council assaulted him verbally for the sins of commission and omission by HUD over the years. After this direct confrontation, on April 29, the council moved to rescind the city's commitment to the proposed neighborhood project. This clearly angered the area director, who wrote to the mayor on May 5 warning that this action "must be taken into account" in HUD's review of the city's HAP. He asked the city to revise the HAP that had already been submitted and to submit alternative proposals by May 28, outlining "how it would provide a reasonable choice of housing for low- and moderate-income households."[19]

Unfortunately, no one in city hall moved immediately to do so. Therefore, on May 23, Cerabone met with the mayor and warned him that he would recommend the rejection of the city's block grant application if no action was taken. Indeed, Cerabone proceeded to prepare materials in support of a rejection and to consult with the central office of HUD in Washington about doing so. Nevertheless, city hall still seemed to be relying on the belief that HUD would not really come to a showdown on the issue given first-year uncertainties surrounding the requirements

of the program. It was also clear that the mayor was incapable of achieving an agreement among members of the Common Council about making non-impacted sites available in their districts.

Originally, the area office provided no directions about what would be necessary to satisfy its demands. In the course of discussions, however, Cerabone indicated that he would accept a commitment by the city to undertake the construction of ninety units of assisted housing for families. HUD staff and city housing officials met on June 3 to discuss the implication of this admittedly arbitrary figure. At that time, the city proposed four specific sites. After review, HUD rejected all four, three on the grounds of being in "impacted" areas and one as "environmentally unacceptable." Despite this rejection, the Common Council went ahead and affirmed its backing for a list which included two of the four rejected locations, both of which were long-vacant urban renewal sites. However, some room for maneuver remained since there was ambiguity built into HUD's position on whether all of the sites had to meet the "non-impaction" criteria or only a certain proportion.

On June 12, Cerabone met with the mayor, who argued that he was unable to come up with a commitment from the council that would be acceptable to HUD. Cerabone indicated that he was working against a deadline of June 27 for review of CDBG applications. This point was reinforced, on June 17, by a telegram in which he called upon the mayor to secure passage of a resolution by the council no later than June 24 in which it committed the city to putting sixty of the ninety units in "areas not having an undue concentration of assisted persons or low-income persons." This was the first time that HUD specifically had stated a willingness to accept a sixty-thirty division. The telegram was brought to the council at its next meeting on June 24. At this eleventh hour, the council passed a resolution of the kind requested by Cerabone. Even that resolution involved only a commitment "in principle" to a list of sites, not a definite commitment to the use of those sites for specific types of units.

On the same day, Cerabone was in Washington discussing the situation both with officials at HUD and with the three area congressional representatives. Interestingly, none of the three indicated any desire to play an active role in defense of the city's position. Indeed, one Washington-based HUD official later noted that "unlike other cities, what Buffalo did *not* do was come to Washington. No effort was really made by the city to go over the head of Cerabone."

Equally important, senior officials at HUD counseled Cerabone against pushing the city over the brink, for internal review of the legal position of the department had indicated that an action cutting off CDBG funds might have been untenable if the city brought a suit. At the time of the controversy, the act was not yet backed by regulations detailing procedures for implementing the HAP requirements. As one official remarked, "That is why we told [Cerabone] that he should work out the best deal he could. He had gotten into the crisis in the first place and he had to work himself out of it."

The result was a climb-down disguised as a compromise in which the area office director chose to accept the council's resolution of June 24 as an adequate sign of good faith on the city's part. However, he insisted that the city continue to refine the list of sites and to go forward with commitments on the ninety units.

Unable to exercise political leverage over members of the Common Council, the mayor retreated from the bargaining process and turned the matter over to the Majority Leader of the council for direct negotiations with HUD. One of the first things the latter did was to arrange a private meeting among Cerabone and his HUD staff and several members of the council. That meeting lasted six and one-half hours and turned out surprisingly well. As one HUD participant recalled, "For the first time we had someone in city hall who was willing to act responsibly. As a result, we worked closely with [the majority leader] over the next three or four months to come up with an acceptable set of sites."

One of the steps taken involved a further retreat by HUD from a strict definition of impaction in the case of one of the urban renewal sites that had been proposed earlier and had been rejected on impaction grounds. It is now to be counted as a location satisfying nonimpaction criteria and would house thirty families. Negotiations continued in order to identify sites for thirty additional units. A compromise was finally ratified on September 30, 1975, when the Common Council voted ten to four to accept a list moved by the Majority Leader.

Of all the seven cases, this one came closest to resembling a classic negotiating scenario: two fairly distinct positions grounded in quite different political values, the use of threats, the apparent breakdown of the negotiating process only to be saved at the last moment by external intervention, and then a retreat from the brink involving a settlement in which both parties agreed to terms they had rejected only a few months earlier.

## PROBLEMS IN THE ANALYSIS OF BARGAINING

The confrontational style depicted in the HAP case obviously went beyond the bargaining stereotype of actors sitting around a table to negotiate differences related to the design of policy, the implementation of a program, or the provision of specific resources to institutions or individuals. Nevertheless, a bargaining process was very much involved. To a greater or lesser extent, the other cases also had transactional components which involved either implicit or explicit bargaining processes including the use of various signals, threats, and bargaining maneuvers to achieve desired outcomes.[20]

My purpose here, however, is to suggest some of the constraints that operate in intergovernmental transactions to make use of bargaining analysis more difficult for researchers interested in developing a theory of IGR. In this section, I will focus on five such constraints drawing on the case materials as appropriate: (1) the existence of anti-bargaining values among participants; (2) how the different content of transactions may affect the character of bargaining; (3) a zone of indifference which marks many transactions; (4) the presence of indeterminancy in other transactions; and (5) a floating actor problem. Even where bargaining does go on, these factors add a considerable complexity to the analysis of intergovernmental transactions.

### Values Inhibiting Bargaining

We have already suggested various circumstances in which actors appear to avoid bargaining. In the case of Oakland, Pressman suggested that this phenomenon arose from political apathy among city officials as much as from any conscious choice. In contrast, Bardach remarks on bureaucratic values which operated in California to account for the "highly defensive" character of the implementation process he observed with respect to a particular mental health law. He characterizes that behavior as involving the expenditure of considerable bureaucratic energy "maneuvering to avoid responsibility and blame."[21]

In the Buffalo cases, most instances involved action on applications for project grants—cases which might have been expected to be most easily negotiated. Yet, part of the interaction process appeared to involve ambivalence over bargaining. As Bardach's remark suggests, some of this ambivalence appeared to grow simply out of the familiar bureaucratic phenomenon of "covering one's ass." At its simplest, this process was apparently at work in the snow disaster case where the FDAA sought to put together the most unimpeachable record possible before submitting a recommendation to the president. At a more complex level, UMTA's approach to negotiations over the mass transit system in Buffalo virtually took on the character of evasion of decision-making responsibility rather than merely pursuing a decision which flowed from the best technical advice available. A similar phenomenon seemed to be at work in the HMO case with respect to the final selection process.

There are related but distinct aspects of bureaucratic culture which inhibit bargaining. Where bureaucrats insist upon demonstrating their claims to technical expertise by adhering to procedures either defined in statutes or regulations, or prescribed in administrative routines, these may obviously be an important constraint on intergovernmental bargaining. This factor, which I would label *bureaucratic purism* was manifested, for example, in the HMO cases where HSA personnel insisted that their approach to relations with local planning groups was based entirely on their application of the rules. From such a perspective, proposals put forward by local planners were either correct or incorrect, but not negotiable. That does not mean that such bureaucratic behaviors are not warranted. Complaints against the federal bureaucracy might be even greater than they are, if bureaucratic discretion was allowed to operate free from responsiveness to legislative and presidential direction.[22]

Distinct from bureaucratic purism in limiting bargaining strategies or tactics, there is a professional or communal dimension that influences intergovernmental transactions. To the extent that a particular transaction involves contacts among professionals or among persons who share values of similar experiences, the bargaining process may be constrained, and the way actors move to exploit the range of resources available to them may be short-circuited. In the HMO case, for example, local health planners proceeded in a highly circumspect fashion in negotiating the development of

the HMOs. Despite a number of conflict points that developed in the planning process, they carefully avoided "going public" which might have put pressure on the federal agency to alter its behavior. This weakened their negotiating posture, but it was seen as appropriate by them and consistent with procedures for working out what were defined, essentially, as professional issues by both the federal and local actors.

Equally important, where bureaucratic or professional actors anticipate working together in the future, there is an incentive to pull one's bargaining punches and to restrain conflict within professional boundaries. In some instances, the softening of bargaining conflict may have more the character of a shot-gun wedding than of communal harmony. Thus, in the ESAA case, even while the Buffalo Board of Education pressed its suit, school administrators sought to avoid widening the conflict beyond the relatively narrow issue of gaining additional time to move toward the goal sought by the Office of Education.

If a certain communal sense may prevent pressing a bargaining position, it may also contribute to exacerbating conflict in some circumstances. As Coleman noted a generation ago, where communal relationships jump the tracks, they may result in particularly bitter exchanges which may undermine "normal" political relationships altogether.[23] Thus, relationships in the ESAA and HAP cases were made worse by the fact that both agencies were involved earlier in other controversies and transactions with Buffalo officials when these new conflicts emerged.[24]

Whatever the source of bargaining constraints, they may manifest themselves in an attitude that emphasizes strict legal construction. There may be good substantive grounds for such an approach, where agencies truly believe their statutes or regulations to be obligatory, but an appeal to this factor can also be tactical. Thus, in the HAP case, legal construction was clearly employed as a bargaining device rather than as a professional or technical imperative. The director proceeded as if his demands were fully legitimate, when there was, in fact, considerable doubt within HUD that those demands were backed by law. In that case, however, legal construction was used to encourage action by the city rather than to prevent negotiations.

There is an important sense in which bargaining is also a cost of intergovernmental relations, which actors can only enter into selectively. The behavior of an activist federal agency may run up against practical limitations of time, personnel, and money. Few federal agencies can afford to take on a great number of non-routinized relationships at the same time, even if most of those relationships are of a cooperative character. Conflictual transactions may need to be avoided simply to maintain other on-going program activities. Given the numerous occasions on which federal bureaucrats are forced to come into contact with representatives of other governments, they must be selective in going beyond the routine acceptance of applications, the superficial evaluation of performance, or minimal efforts to enforce compliance requirements linked to legislation. There may be selective action taken against the most flagrant violators of federal procedures, but even such limited actions have costs. Routinization of many intergovernmental relationships, therefore, results in bargaining being avoided in favor of an evasive attitude.[25]

If a federal agency has to be cautious in the number of targets it chooses for hard bargaining or conflict over intergovernmental transactions, local actors are likely to be equally cautious in their pursuit of conflicts with federal agencies, especially where the locality needs federal funds to support existing services.

In most situations, of course, this problem does not arise. Participants simply operate at the level of routine exchanges of project implementation responsibilities for federal dollars to be spent on plans preferred by local actors. In such cases, there may be negotiations on relatively narrow technical standards but the larger project selection decisions remain with the local actors.

When the performance of a local or state government is questioned by a federal agency, the reasons for the choice may vary. The agency may wish to demonstrate to a dissatisfied part of its clientele that it is serious about its regulatory obligations under the law; it may exercise its political muscle simply to provide an exemplary lesson to others without having any intention of following through. Why a particular "victim" is selected is by no means clear. Thus, Buffalo was one of the few jurisdictions to become directly involved with HUD in the first year of the CDBG program in a conflict over its HAP commitment, though many others could have been criticized as readily.[26]

Indeed, in that case, federal officials conceded that they supported Cerabone's efforts, so far as they went, as a way of indicating to other local governments that HUD would be serious about reviewing HAPs in the future. As one official remarked:

The small number of units and the character of the argument in the Buffalo case were useful in the department because it demonstrated better than any number of public statements that we meant business. It allowed us to broadcast the fact that we were willing to hammer communities on the head even when only a small number of units were involved . . . . We were also saying to other area office directors that if you want to play hardball, we will go with you.

Thus, the common phenomenon of selective enforcement of a legal "string" had turned up Buffalo's number and occasioned a more elaborate bargaining process than occurred elsewhere. Next time, it might be someone else's turn.

## The Distributive and Regulatory Aspects of Bargaining

On the whole, bargaining is likely to be easiest in those instances where what is at stake is the funding of a project which national actors simply review for technical compliance. Construction of a sewage plant is normally one such case; the development of a plan for a flood protection project is another. That does not rule out bargaining on "details," which may become difficult. At least in the Amherst sewer and Ellicott Creek cases, federal-local bargaining was low-keyed and accepted the basic premises of the projects. Conflicts involving non-national actors were less routine in those cases. Essentially, such cases involve the *distribution* of federal resources for use in cases where basic agreements on values exist. That does not rule out significant federal-local differences about the specifics of other project grants, as in the HMO or mass transit cases. In the latter case, however, UMTA was not entirely sure of its own procedures and value preferences, a fact which had important implications for both its ability and willingness to enter into direct negotiations with the NFTA. In the HMO case—although this was not highlighted in the presentation —federal and local actors were constrained both by values which they held in common about the proper delivery of health services, and by the existence of a hostile environment in which many individual health providers bitterly opposed the HMO concept. Federal-local bargaining in that case revolved, in part, around developing HMOs strong enough to survive the hostility of that environment.

There is clearly a difference, however, between such interactions and those involving *regulations of behavior.* Less room for maneuver and for bargaining may exist in such instances. In most distributive programs, the terms of the federal offer are a strong inducement for the locality or state to enter the process of participation and to sustain that participation. But negotiations involving regulation of behaviors and the substitution of national values for local ones may be particularly unpalatable to a local government. For financially-distressed local governments like Buffalo's, the "strings" attached to such grants as ESAA and CDBG are accepted as part of the "deal," often on the assumption that either the federal agency will not have the resources to enforce compliance or the local government will find ways to conform verbally while not needing to accept the spirit of the regulation.[27]

In the HAP case, a "string" was pulled against a city that was desperately in need of funds to relieve a very difficult fiscal situation. Consequently, the city was forced to bargain on terms preferred by the HUD area office, thus forcing a debate over values that were not shared in many city neighborhoods. In cases where wealthier local governments have found themselves under the same kind of HUD threat, they have simply chosen not to participate in the CDBG program. This option was virtually unthinkable in the Buffalo case and HUD knew it. Still, the city came very close to refusing to assume the commitment HUD sought because of the fundamental value cleavage involved, and what it finally did accept was largely a token programmatic effort.

## A Zone of Indifference

As noted earlier in this article, bargaining relationships may be affected by the asymmetry of interests among actors. Thus, in many intergovernmental transactions one set of actors may simply be less concerned with specific outcomes than the other. For example, as long as a federal agency can maintain itself or expand, its specific intergovernmental clientele or the particular project proposed for a grant may be of relatively little importance. On the other hand, a particular project may be of great importance to local actors.

The existence of this *zone of indifference* may operate as much on the local or state side of an intergovernmental transaction as it does on the federal side. Thus, following Pressman and Wildavsky's account, much of the effort made by the Economic Development Administration (EDA) in its relations with the Port of Oakland involved trying to convince the port that the incentives in construction funds being provided to it were worth the bother of compliance with federal employment goals. Similarly, Derthick's account of the failure of a program, initiated by the Johnson administration, to turn federal surplus land into "new towns in-town" revolved around the many considerations that caused local governments to resist rising to the bait. As noted earlier, Pressman also has shown how the city government of Oakland took a generally passive approach to a number of federal programs in which it might have taken a more active role.[28]

In practice, of course, indifference may be curbed by other considerations. The different modes of behavior of federal agencies are conditioned by political factors, including an awareness of the need to distribute the political and financial benefits of programs widely enough to maintain the support of important clienteles including relevant members of Congress.[29] Along with displaying sensitivity to the politics of distribution, many agencies limit their zones of indifference by developing strong program missions which predetermine some program choices to be more correct than others. While such missions may be achieved through laws and program regulations, they are more likely to be a function of the professional commitments shared by persons recruited to the agency or through the process of socialization that goes on within the agency. In effect, strict legal construction is one mechanism for trying to cope with bureaucratic indifference.

Nonetheless, every actor in IGR is bound to have a space in which value preferences are unclear or the options available are open to interpretation. In some of these situations, actors may enter intergovernmental negotiations with no fixed positions on certain issues and allow the negotiations themselves to yield a solution. Thus, a local government may seek federal funds with only the vaguest notion of how it expects to use those funds, but it will still go through the requirements associated with completing a grant application and profess an intention to carry out federal objectives. A federal agency may also have so unclear a definition of its mission that it may allow its project selection processes to be directed largely by the choices made by other actors. Only after funds have been granted may parties to the selection process recognize that a locality has neither the ability to achieve the goals it has set, nor is it clear that even the most competent local agency could achieve such goals. This phenomenon has been particularly common in HEW grants associated with compensatory education but also has been a feature of some of the more famous episodes in the history of Office of Economic Opportunity (OEO),

Model Cities, and, more recently, aspects of the Comprehensive Employment and Training Act (CETA) program. Even in a high technology area like mass transit, UMTA appears to have developed standards of evaluation for mass transit systems only in the midst of the process of negotiation itself.

The behavior of actors with respect to the existence of zones of indifference opens the analysis of intergovernmental transactions to even greater uncertainty than already exists for other reasons. Thus, the selection of one city over another for a categorical grant is often shrouded in political mystery only slightly camouflaged by the language of qualification. Even in the case of a single agency reviewing applications for a single program, there may be significant variations in the bargaining processes involved. Within the same field office, administrators may be indifferent to the transgressions of some local governments, while quite concerned about the performance of others. Thus, one of the matters that particularly bothered the city government of Buffalo in respect to its conflict with the area office of HUD was the perception that HUD was pressing the city to undertake the construction of housing for low- and moderate-income families, while it largely ignored the serious performance deficiencies over time of Buffalo's suburban communities.

## The Indeterminancy Problem

Closely related to the existence of a zone of indifference on the part of actors in IGR is the problem of *indeterminancy* both for actors and analysts. Of course, indeterminancy is the life-blood of bargaining and of the literature which has grown up about bargaining theory and practice in international relations.

Especially in the early stages of a program's history, but also when national administrations change or when new personalities take over an agency, there is likely to be considerable indeterminancy surrounding the operation of the system of inducements and threats associated with prototypical bargaining relations.[30] One consequence of this factor is the misapplication of resources. This author's interviews pointed to numerous instances in which actors not only misinterpreted each other's motives, but, because of those interpretations, managed to use the wrong tactical responses or inappropriate resources to overcome what they perceived to be the major problems in the way of a settlement. In one instance, at least, not only were local resources wasted in achieving political "overkill," but

some resentment was created on the part of federal actors who felt political pressures were being exerted unduly in an area where they were already inclined to move favorably.

To speak of misperception, of course, is to beg one important question that figures prominently in the difficulties of students of IGR in developing more systematic analyses of bargaining behaviors, that is, an agreement upon facts. Anyone familiar with the problems of conducting studies of intergovernmental transactions is aware of the Rashomon-like experience involved in trying to identify the factual foundation of a political conflict. Not only do participants describe the elephant in many different ways, but the researcher is easily led from the soft ground of event analysis to the quicksand of motivational interpretations and misinterpretations, where informants may identify quite different intentions with their own acts from those attributed to them by other participants. In such circumstances, not only do actors commonly disagree about why they agreed to do something, but they may even disagree about the terms of the outcome. It is not surprising, consequently, that students of policy implementation have reported the existence of a wide disparity between what federal program designers intended a program to accomplish and what it actually achieved.

Nevertheless, the ease or difficulty of a bargaining process may be unrelated to the degree of shared perceptions among actors. Indeed, there may be an inverse relation. An ideal bargaining outcome would presumably be one in which all parties believed they had attained their own ends. Even the broad terms of most IGR bargains might be unattainable if the conflicting goals and diverse value premises held by actors were really spelled out through bargaining. Here the factors of indifference and indeterminancy may work in tandem to allow for the attainment of outcomes which might be impossible if there were more explicit bargaining on matters of critical importance to particular actors. Thus, many "deals" are premised on actors talking past each other. One practical effect of this is to allow nonfederal actors the opportunity to use federal funds in a fashion alien to the supposed purposes of national programs.[31]

In an earlier era, local or state definition of project purposes may have dominated the way federal system transactions were perceived. This is no longer clearly the case. The argument has been made that one result of the shift from "cooperative federalism" to "creative federalism" has been the assumption by the federal government of a greater role in defining programmatic goals, the range of alternatives available to other actors in IGR, and the responsibilities that were to be assumed in return for fund commitments. By requiring local governments now to meet standards of affirmative action, citizen participation, Davis-Bacon wage rates, or environmental protection, new areas of intergovernmental conflict have been generated which only escalate the possibility of indeterminancies. However, the uncertain enforcement of such requirements, as well as disagreements about the operational standards to be employed in each case, opens IGR to as much indeterminancy as the less ambitious compliance standards of the past. The bargaining dance has become more complex in various respects but many of the basic steps are familiar. That these transactions take place in an environment cluttered with indeterminancy may be both frustrating to participants, and an opportunity for those seeking to deviate from federal expectations.

### The Floating Actor

In accounting for factors which lend uncertainty to bargaining in IGR, a final one worth mentioning is the *floating actor problem*—the existence of which has already been suggested in the course of the earlier presentation. If IGR were a simple two-person zero-sum game, one might need to account only for the goals and tactics of those two sides. In real life, an intergovernmental transaction may involve a great number and diversity of governmental and nongovernmental actors, whose interests vary from one element of a single transaction to another. While similar situations may be complex in international relations, it is quite possible that the mix of influences operating in American domestic politics is more complicated. Partly, this results from the problem of even identifying who the significant "actors" are in some cases; and partly, it is a function of the porosity of a transactional system which permits parties to play for very different stakes within the same game. Both of these are familiar problems to students of IGR, but they merit mention in the course of a review of impediments to the refinement of bargaining analysis.

The first problem has several components. First, only by a twist of words can "governments" be considered to be "actors" in IGR. Given the diversity of

administrative units in the federal government and in many state and local governments, this is hardly news. What it means, in practice, is that who speaks for a particular governmental interest in intergovernmental negotiations is by no means predictable. Elaborate "side deals" may also affect the relationships which are being conducted in the main arena. Thus, it may not be unusual for a federal agency to engage in conflictual relationships with one set of individuals "representing" a local government, while continuing to maintain positive informal contracts on the same or related matters with others in the same government.

Such multi-actor arrangements are not restricted to the local "side" of negotiations although that aspect has been emphasized in the Buffalo cases presented earlier. Other cases in the Buffalo area involved instances in which there were differences between the central office goals of HUD and the manner in which its field offices perceived those goals. This resulted in considerable variation in the way local program participants developed their applications. In one particular case, direct contacts between the central office and a municipal government were used as leverage for forcing a field office to modify its behavior. This occurred after direct instructions to the field office from Washington had failed to achieve the same goal.[32]

Not only is the attribution of solidarity to governmental actors on the same plane inappropriate, and their roles in intergovernmental bargaining less obvious than one might expect; but as Grodzins pointed out a generation ago, IGR in the United States provides innumerable opportunities for access and influence by both governmental actors and nongovernmental groups who are only nominally parties to a given transaction. Such a situation may be complicated when not only governments and quasi-governments (e.g., special districts and local planning bodies) participate in intergovernmental transactions, but when a plethora of political groups and private citizens take an interest in what is going on. The transaction may then be marked by complaints, expressions of opposition or support, mixed support and opposition, and kibitzing by a multitude of individuals and groups. In the general tumult, it may be impossible at some points to be sure that negotiations are still going on and who the principal parties to the transaction are. In some circumstances, it is not even clear when the major parties have reached a final understanding from which financial obligations are to proceed. Thus, the Ford administration publicly announced a "commitment in principle" to funding Buffalo's rapid transit system, shortly before the election of 1976. It was not until late 1978, however, that UMTA (operating under new political leadership) turned that "principle" into a financial commitment. Similarly, the gap between congressional authorization and appropriation has kept the "bargain" struck with respect to the Ellicott Creek project hanging for several years. The major consequence of such fluidity in the raising, negotiating, and resolution of program differences in IGR is that notions of a settled structure within which intergovernmental bargaining goes on, or a fixed set of actors participating in each transaction are untenable.

There are some governmental actors to whom the assignment of an identification by plane is in itself problematic. In particular, the role of members of Congress is an interesting one. A well-placed member of Congress can be a potent weapon for a local government. However, the nature of IGR is such that the same congressional representative may choose to represent the local perspective on one issue, the national perspective on another, and his/her own on yet another. Such flexibility would not be of concern in theory construction if there were an expectation that the selection of positions by these actors was consistent, but there is no evidence that more than personality determines such choices. Thus, one member of Congress who was clearly opposed to the demands of the Office of Education in the ESAA case was able to support HUD's effort to require Buffalo to meet its national obligation in the HAP case.

## CONCLUSION

This article has focused on seven cases in federal-local relations to suggest certain problems in the use of bargaining analysis as a central focus for understanding IGR. That does not mean that more systematic analysis of bargaining behaviors should not be one important element in the development of a theory of IGR. It does mean, however, that there are many other aspects of everyday interactions in IGR that must be recognized along with the ability and willingness of actors to bargain either explicitly or implicitly about the values at issue. In a certain sense, of course, even bargaining avoidance behavior of the kind discussed above can be conceived of as falling within the universe of behaviors that influence bargaining. This article

represents an effort to identify a set of considerations which need to be given attention in the course of developing a bargaining approach.

Aside from this review of factors that both detract from or condition bargaining behaviors, the cases presented illustrate a remarkably diverse set of resources and skills used by actors in federal-local transactions. Indeed, they represent such a diversity of situational factors that one shrinks from speaking of an intergovernmental "system" at work here. Following the different approaches of Lewis Carroll and David Easton, of course, an analytical system may be nothing more than what an analyst chooses to make it. Thus far, however, IGR remains a field marked by disagreement even about the basic units of analysis as well as about the behavioral patterns central to the characterization of a "system." In using bargaining behaviors as a point of departure, the complexities are numerous: bureaucratic or professional values which inhibit the desire or will to bargain; the variable content of the matters at issue; indifference; indeterminancy; and floating actors. So long as IGR remains a political process, however, bargaining will necessarily continue to form an element in any theory of action.

If the tone of this analysis has sounded unnecessarily discouraging for the analyst of political behavior, it has the important saving grace to supporters of the federal principle that some of the alarms sounded for the future of noncentralization may be unwarranted. For, despite the apprehensions which some observers of American IGR have expressed, the contemporary reality of intergovernmental relations is one of a multiplicity of actors and arenas in which intergovernmental transactions are conducted. There is very little that appears to be predictable about the outcomes of individual cases. Indeed, if any single theme emerges from this article, it is that the federal government, even at the height of its recent powers, has by no means been capable of exercising ultimate control over the outcomes of individual cases. Indeed, if any single theme emerges from this article, it is that the federal government, even at the height of its recent powers, has by no means been capable of exercising ultimate control over the outcomes of federal-local interactions. Even in the two cases which came closest to involving federal efforts to substitute "national values" for local ones, national "victories" were largely symbolic in the HAP case and transient in the ESAA conflict. Indeed, the federal court decision ordering integration of pupils and staff in the Buffalo schools was of much greater significance for the overall federal-local relationship than the ESAA-related action. Even while that court decision was premised on non-negotiable principles, the terms of enforcement of the order are still in the process of being bargained over between local and federal actors. Thus, in a curious way, even when the federal government expands its role in relation to local governments, new powers are so encased in procedural complexities and uncertainties shaped by IGR that most local governments have considerable room to maneuver in order to pursue their own ends.

## NOTES

1. This definition is from William Anderson, *Intergovernmental Relations in Review* (Minneapolis: University of Minnesota Press, 1960), p. 3, as cited in Deil S. Wright, *Understanding Intergovernmental Relations* (North Scituate, Mass.: Duxbury Press, 1978), p. 5.

2. Thus, in addition to the definition given above, Wright suggests that IGR involves "both citizens and public officials as well as governmental entities of all sizes and types," Wright, *Understanding Intergovernmental Relations,* p. 4.

3. Morton Grodzins, *The American System* (Chicago: Rand McNally, 1966); and Daniel J. Elazar, *The American Partnership* (Chicago: University of Chicago Press, 1962).

4. Jeffrey L. Pressman, *Federal Programs and City Politics* (Berkeley and Los Angeles: University of California Press, 1975), p. 12.

5. A. Lee Fritschler and Morley Segal, "Intergovernmental Relations and Contemporary Political Science: Developing an Integrative Typology," *Publius* 1 (Winter 1971): 102. They describe the second type as "slightly less cooperative" than the first but "characterized by low-keyed bargaining and harmonious compromise," whereas "innovative conflict" is characterized as starting in conflict and ending in compromise. Later, however, they suggest that in "mutual adjustment" "true bargaining involving compromise, side payments, log rolling, etc. does take place, but neither side takes a unilateral non-negotiable position" (p. 119).

6. For recent reviews of bargaining theory in international relations, see Glenn H. Snyder and Paul Diesing, *Conflict among Nations* (Princeton: Princeton University Press, 1977); and Oran Young, ed., *Bargaining: Formal Theories of Negotiations* (Urbana, Ill.: University of Illinois Press, 1975).

7. Eugene Bardach, *The Implementation Game* (Cambridge, Mass.: and London, Eng.: MIT Press, 1977). Also see, Wright, *Understanding Intergovernmental Relations,* pp. 191–192. For an early use of the game metaphor in the study of American politics, see Norton E. Long, "The Local Community as an Ecology of Games," *American Journal of Sociology* 64 (November 1978): 251–261.

8. Bardach, *Implementation Game,* p. 56.

9. Ibid. Italics added. A key issue hidden in the last sentence is the problem of how to treat the role of those who are *unable* to play because of their limited resources, including a lack of access to those governmental and nongovernmental arenas where decisions of major importance are made. This point goes to the issue of bargaining theory as a derivative of pluralist assumptions about the nature of American politics—an important issue but one which cannot be examined here.

10. For example, see the important linkage role assumed by members of the National Assembly in France, especially those who serve as mayors. See Mark Kesselman and Donald Rosenthal, *Local Power and Comparative Politics,* Sage Professional Paper in Comparative Politics (Beverly Hills, Calif.: Sage Publications, 1974).

11. Bernard J. Frieden and Marshall Kaplan, *The Politics of Neglect* (Cambridge, Mass.: and London, Eng.: MIT Press, 1975).

12. Donald B. Rosenthal, *Sticking-Points and Ploys in Federal-Local Relations* (Philadelphia: Center for the Study of Federalism, 1980).

13. Memorandum dated February 4, 1977, from the files of the FDAA. One estimate made subsequently of the outlays for snow disaster relief in the Buffalo area was $31.5 million by the FDAA and $3 million from other federal agencies. In contrast, first calculations for the 1977 Johnston flood involved $31.1 million in repairs costs alone.

14. See Elazar, *American Partnership*; and Samuel H. Beer, "The Modernization of American Federalism," *Publius* 3 (Fall 1973): 49–95.

15. Such arrangements are neither new to IGR nor peculiar to social services programs. Grodzins, for example, describes the work of the Department of Agriculture's Stabilization and Conservation Committees that bears a similarity to the present case. See Grodzins, *American System,* pp. 351–358. More typical, however, is the kind of relationship that prevailed at the outset of the poverty program when the Office of Economic Opportunity and local community action agencies established relations. See James L. Sundquist with David W. Davis, *Making Federalism Work* (Washington, D. C.: Brookings Institution, 1969).

16. Bruce H. Kirschner, "An Historical Examination of the Buffalo-Amherst Corridor Rapid Transit Project" (Paper prepared for the Department of Political Science Honors Programs, State University of New York at Buffalo, July 1975), p. 80.

17. For an earlier glimpse of Buffalo's battles over school desegregation, see Robert L. Crain, *The Politics of School Desegregation* (Chicago: Aldine, 1968), esp. pp. 59–71. Also

see Robert V. Watson, "Community Control of the Schools: A Case Study of Black Public School Teachers' and Principals' Attitudes in Buffalo" (Ph.D. dissertation, State University of New York at Buffalo, 1979).

18. On this point, see U.S. Department of Housing and Urban Development, *Block Grants for Community Development,* by Richard P. Nathan, et al., Washington, DC: Department of Housing and Urban Development, January 1977, p. 68, where they state, "Assistant Secretary Meeker adopted as a slogan, 'No second-guessing of local officials and a minimum of red-tape.'" However, former senior officials of HUD insist it was not their intention to give any locality a first-year "free ride." A more recent study of CDBG by Nathan and his associates indicates, however, the numerous occasions on which HUD raised objections to aspects of local plans during the first two years of the program and the way those intergovernmental issues were resolved. See Richard P. Nathan and Paul R. Dommel, "Federal-Local Relations Under Block Grants, *Political Science Quarterly* 93 (Fall 1978): 421–442. Nathan and Dommel suggest that local jurisdictions "tended to prevail on substantive issues, whereas on procedural issues HUD tended to prevail." (p. 430).

19. This quote and others used in this section come from materials in the Buffalo area office and central office files of HUD.

20. Elsewhere, I have discussed some of the bargaining devices—"ploys"—used in these cases. See Rosenthal, *Stickingpoints and Ploys.* Ingram's recent analysis of federal-state relations in respect to the implementation of planning for water resources policy highlights issues similar to those raised in this section. Despite the title of her article, however, its focus is less on the bargaining power per se than on the fact that federal legislation has created the conditions which *necessitate* bargaining between federal and state agencies if programs are to be implemented at all. For this, she holds Congress to be especially responsible, since its use of grants-in-aid rather than other devices encourage a bargaining rather than a hierarchical relationship. See Helen Ingram, "Policy Implementation Through Bargaining: The Case of Federal Grants-in-Aid," *Public Policy* 25 (Fall 1977): 499–526.

21. Bardach, *Implementation Game,* p. 37.

22. This issue is central, of course, to the argument made by Lowi in his classic attack on the abuses of bureaucratic discretion. See, Theodore J. Lowi, *The End of Liberalism* (New York: Norton, 1969).

23. James S. Coleman, *Community Conflict* (Glencoe, Ill.: Free Press, 1957). For a recent application of that analysis to neighborhood organizations, see Matthew A. Crenson, "Social Networks and Political Processes in Urban Neighborhoods," *American Journal of Political Science* 22 (August 1978): 578–594.

24. An important aspect of this conflict not highlighted in the text is the fact that a senior official in the Office of Education had formerly served as superintendent of the Rochester school system and was thoroughly familiar with the personalities and events associated with Buffalo's history of resistance to desegregation efforts fostered by several New York State Commissioners of Education.

25. Ingram refers to a process she describes as "bargaining at arms length." Of this phenomenon, she writes, "Certain prevailing attitudes and prejudices that federal bureaucrats and state agency people have about one another perpetuate separation and encourage independence. The ideology of states' rights is very strong, and federal officials wish to avoid the appearance of interference." Unfortunately, she does not spell out what these "prevailing attitudes and prejudices" are. Perhaps some of those discussed by Pressman, *Federal Programs,* esp. pp. 87–104 are what she has in mind. See Ingram, "Policy Implementation Through Bargaining," p. 502.

26. Conflicts over the HAP increased, later, particularly with respect to the "expected to reside" issue, as it bore upon suburban housing for low- and moderate-income families. See Nathan and Dommel, "Federal-Local Relations," pp. 435–436.

27. On the contrast between distributive and regulatory policies, see Theodore J. Lowi, "American Business Public Policy, Case Studies and Political Theory," *World Politics* 16 (July 1964): 677–714. Also see Beer, "Modernization of American Federalism."

28. Jeffrey L. Pressman and Aaron Wildavsky, *Implementation* (Berkeley and Los Angeles: University of California Press, 1973); Martha Derthick, *New Towns In-Town* (Washington, DC: The Urban Institute, 1972); and Pressman, *Federal Programs.*

29. For a study that begins to examine the politics of project selection processes, see J. Theodore Anagnoson, "Selecting Federal Projects: A Bureaucratic Perspective" (paper presented at the 1978 Annual Meeting of the Midwest Political Science Association, Chicago, Illinois, April 20–22, 1978). Also see Frieden and Kaplan, *Politics of Neglect,* esp. pp. 131–140, and 214–222.

30. Pressman and Wildavsky stress the importance of these discontinuities for program implementation. Also see Bardach, *Implementation Game.*

31. For an interesting account of how a local government in the South used an urban renewal program to convert an area from mixed racial population to one that was all white, see Lowi, *The End of Liberalism,* pp. 250–266.

32. Some of the problems associated with organizing the field staff of a federal bureaucracy to implement a program are described in Donald B. Rosenthal, "Joining Housing Rehabilitation to Neighborhood Revitalization: The Neighborhood Strategy Area Program" (paper prepared for the 1979 Annual Meeting of the American Society for Public Administration, Baltimore, April 1–4).

# CHAPTER NINE

# Procurement
# and
# Grants Management

## The Federal Contracting Process

Merrill J. Collett

In its October, 1975 issue *The Bureaucrat* carried an article entitled "The Federal Government Selection of Management Consultants," in which I presented the problem as a consultant saw it, of the federal contracting process.

Since then consulting, by individuals and firms, has taken a quantum leap. The Congress has become alarmed, and with cause. Senator David Pryor of Arkansas, chairman of the Subcommittee on Civil Service and General Services of the Committee on Governmental Affairs, concluded hearings on the federal government's use of consultant services. These hearings and the report which followed drew great media interest.

Contrary to an impression which may have resulted, securing and using of consultant services *is* governed by federal procurement regulations. Having been involved and affected by procurement practices for several years, I am very sure that most federal managers haven't the slightest idea of what contracting for consulting services involves. Certainly they will not learn from newspaper headlines. Therefore, I am laying the process before readers of *The Bureaucrat* because they constitute in large measure the government's program managers.

My focus will be on the procurement of *consulting services* rather than goods.

Summarized, and putting it as clearly as possible, the federal government will not get its dollar's worth from the procurement of services *until it manages both the process and the vendors properly. At present no one is responsible for doing so.*

### SOME REASONS WHY
### THE GOVERNMENT CONTRACTS

Historically, the Office of Management and Budget has set, through OMB Circular A-76, the federal government policy on contracting out. That policy has been, simply stated, that government agencies should contract for services if a particular government operation is more expensive than similar contractor services would be. The policy has been generally followed except in cases involving national security.

The fact remains that many government organizations need outside assistance from time to time for a variety of reasons. Some of the major reasons are:

1. *Shortage of expertise* among current staff, where the nature of the work to be done would not warrant hiring full time expertise, even for a temporary appointment.
2. *Shortage of staff,* usually because of employment ceiling restrictions. The "body shop" operations by which contracts furnish necessary manpower should be called labor contracting, not consulting.
3. *Shortage of time.* This can be due to a variation of the two preceding items.
4. *Need for an "outside" or "objective" viewpoint.*

## THE ACTORS AND THEIR ROLES

There are two principal actors and one important supporting actor—the "program" officer, the contracting officer, and the budget or finance officer.

The *program officer* has primary responsibility for determining the need for contractor assistance, developing the specifications, monitoring the contractor's performance, accepting the goods or services, and certifying the invoices for payment. The program officer may be any person, from any discipline, who needs consulting assistance, including authorized representatives.

The *contracting officer* has the overall responsibility for ensuring that the government's best interests are served through the contracting process. The contracting officer is the only official who has authority to obligate the government, i.e., to approve and sign the contract or to change its terms and conditions. Though having overall responsibility for the accomplishment of tasks involved in the contracting process, the contracting officer must rely heavily on the program officer for all input on technical matters related to the program. Additionally, though responsible for the legal sufficiency of the contract, the contracting officer may seek assistance from agency attorneys.

The *budget or finance officer* is generally responsible for fund control, and should be knowledgeable about sources of additional funds if a certain program officer lacks sufficient resources to achieve a contracting goal.

## ORGANIZATION FOR CONTRACTING

As in any other federal organizational matter, no set or standard approach governs procurement. Some common functional areas exist, however.

Procurement *policy* is set at a fairly high level in an organization. It may be coupled with grant policy and, in highly centralized operations, with procurement *operations* (actual contracting). These, however, are most often decentralized—both organizationally and geographically. On the other hand, *sole source approval* (discussed later), if formalized, is usually exercised at a fairly high headquarters level.

Each agency generally has a small business advisor and a minority business advisor.

A knowledge of where these functions are performed in a given agency is important, because the relative weight of the *actors* in the selection and monitoring of contractors is frequently determined by their organizational power base.

## THE PROCESS ITSELF

Ideally, a federal agency should try to plan its contract needs as early in the fiscal year as possible in order to allow sufficient time for orderly contracting. While program officers are beseeched by contracting officers to plan their programs and plan the necessary procurement actions to implement those programs, many program officers procrastinate until the last possible moment. In these situations lack of time may result in requests for proposals drawn up without adequate discussion between program officers and contracting officers, leading to studies or services not really dealing with needs, or to specifications hastily and loosely prepared. This latter is just as unfair to the contractor as to the federal government. Lack of time may also result in sole source contracting because the regular process requires, *at best,* 90 days of lead time: 30 days to prepare and announce the request for proposal; 30 days for contractors to prepare their responses; and 30 days for the government to evaluate bids and prepare, or negotiate and prepare, the contract. The time frequently exceeds this total of 90 days.

One of the most serious deficiencies in planning for contracting is that program officers frequently fail to consider first the elements essential to a decision on whether or not to contract. They do not evaluate their goals, the resource (personnel and funds) required, their in-house capability vs. that of contractors, a cost analysis (in-house vs. contractor), timing, and legal parameters.

Only if consideration of these and other factors leads program officers to decide that contracts are necessary and cost-effective should the process itself begin. *Unfortunately, department and agency executives, and the staff agencies having a functional responsibility— OMB and OPM—have failed to require and provide "how-to" training for the program officers making these decisions. For that matter, they have failed to require and provide program officers with training in the management aspects of the contracting process.*

The major tasks in the contracting process are:

- Preparation of the specification by the program officer.
- Preliminary meetings between program and procurement staff.
- Written request by the program officer for a contract.
- Determination by the contracting officer of the method of obtaining contracts.

- Preparation of a list of sources by the contracting officer with input by the program officer.
- Preparation of the solicitation (e.g., request for proposal).
- Publicizing the solicitation and award.
- Prebid conference chaired by the program officer and contracting officer.
- Receipt and evaluation of bids and proposals by an evaluation officer.
- Negotiations, contract preparation, and distribution by the contracting officer.
- Contract administration, or following the contractor's progress.

## FORMS OF CONTRACTUAL SERVICE

Too frequently the press, unions, and the Congress headline contracting horror stories without identifying properly what they are writing about. Differences exist in the business form and competitive status by which services are offered the federal government and the products which are offered. Identification of these differences permits focusing on the sources of problems and providing effective solutions for them.

### Business Form

This category deals with the different kinds of entities furnishing services to the government.

1. *Individuals.* These may furnish service in one of several ways, as follows:
   a. Reemployed annuitants who function as employees on reduced pay.
   b. Consultants and/or experts who are hired as individuals at (maximum) rates set by the government. Effectively, they are a kind of employee.
   c. Individual contractors who function at negotiated rates under contract. They equate more nearly to a business entity than to an employee. Many of them have firm (business) names under which they operate. Many are retired federal employees, retained under this form of contract.
2. *Partnerships/corporations.* These are "for profit" organizations that do business for the government under contract.
3. *Nonprofit associations/organizations/corporations.* These include universities and other institutions of higher learning, foundations, institutes,

and associations of public officials or units. They operate under contract, or, on occasion, under grants from the government.

### Competitive Status

Different organizations experience different forms of competition depending upon their size, ownership, basic structure, and sometimes purpose. These competitive forms include:

1. *Fully competitive.* Procurements that are large enough to require a contract rather than a purchase order (e.g., $10,000 or more). "For profit" organizations fall into this category.
2. *Excused from some forms of competition by law or regulations.* Section 8A forms (minority-owned and, in some cases, woman-owned). Nonprofit organizations also enjoy this status.
3. *Opportunities for occasionally restricted competition.* As an example, small businesses may compete only with one another when specific "set-asides" are made.

### Type of Product (Service)

Within the arena of consulting services, there are several large categories. These are:

1. *Advisory services.* Developmental, program studies, evaluations, and recommendations, and administrative management.
2. *Production services.* Essentially "body shop" efforts providing staff to perform a function otherwise performed by federal staff. Reasons given for contracting production services generally involve claimed savings or scarcity of available personnel.

I have specifically excluded from this classification the entire area of research and demonstration, which is unique enough to require a separate presentation.

## TYPES OF CONTRACTS

Contractors may be offered one of several types of contracts, although one contractor is not likely to experience all of them.

### Fixed-Price Contracts

These are of several types, so designed as to facilitate proper pricing under various circumstances.

The fixed-price contract establishes a price which is not subject to any adjustment by reason of the cost experience of the contractor in the performance of the contract. This places maximum risk upon contractors. Because contractors assume full responsibility for all costs under or over these fixed prices, they have a maximum profit incentive for effective cost control and contract performance.

Fixed price contracts may provide for escalation, the price fluctuating with the BLS (Bureau of Labor Statistics) index for a necessary commodity.

## Cost-Reimbursement Contracts

These provide for payment to the contractors of allowable costs incurred in the performance of the contracts. It establishes an estimate of total cost for the purpose of obligating funds, and a ceiling which the contractors may not exceed (except at their own risk) without prior approval or subsequent ratification by the contracting officer. There are several types of cost-reimbursement contracts:

1. *The cost contract.* The contractor receives no fee or profit, only costs.
2. *The cost-sharing contract.* The contractor receives no fee and is reimbursed for only an agreed portion of allowable costs.
3. *The cost-plus-a-fixed-fee contract.* The contractor is paid a fixed fee. Once negotiated, it does not vary with actual costs, but may be adjusted as a result of any subsequent changes in the work or service to be performed.
4. *The cost-plus-incentive-fee contract.* Provides for a fee adjusted by formula in accordance with the relationship which total allowable costs bear to target costs. Under this type of contract, there is negotiated initially a target cost, a target fee, a minimum and maximum fee, and a fee adjustment formula.

## Time and Materials Contracts

This provides for the procurement of property or services on the basis of (1) direct labor hours at specified fixed hourly rates (which include direct and indirect labor, overhead, and profit), and (2) material at cost. A handling fee may be included in the material charge or may be included in the overhead.

## Letter Contracts

This is a written preliminary contractual instrument which authorizes immediate initiation including but not limited to the procurement of necessary materials.

## Indefinite Delivery Type Contracts

One of the following may be used for service procurements where the exact time of delivery or amount of effort is not known at time of contracting:

1. *Definite quantity contract.* A definite quantity of specified property or performance of specified services for a fixed period, with deliveries or performance at designated locations upon order. Depending on the situation, the contract may provide for (1) firm fixed prices, or (2) price escalation.

2. *Requirements contract.* Filling of all actual purchase requirements of specific property or services of designated activities during a specified contract period, with deliveries to be scheduled by the timely placement of orders upon the contractor by activities designed either specifically or by class. Depending on the situation, the contract may provide for (1) firm fixed prices, or (2) price escalation. When large individual orders or orders from more than one activity are anticipated, the contract may specify the maximum quantities which may be ordered under each individual order or during a specified period of time. Similarly, when small orders are anticipated, the contract may specify the minimum quantities to be ordered.

## Basic Agreement

This is a written instrument of understanding executed between a procuring agency and a contractor which sets forth the negotiated contract clauses which shall be applicable to future procurements entered into between the parties during the term of the basic agreement. Use of the basic agreement contemplates the coverage of a particular procurement by the execution of a formal contractual document which will provide for the scope of work, price, delivery, and additional matters peculiar to the requirement of the specific procurement involved, and incorporates, by reference or appending, the contract clauses agreed upon in the basic agreement, as required or applicable.

## Basic Ordering Agreement

This is similar to a basic agreement except that it also includes a description, as specific as practicable, of the services to be performed, when ordered, and a description of the method for determining the prices to be paid to the contractor for services. Each order incorporates by reference the provisions of the basic ordering agreement.

## ABUSES AND MISUNDERSTANDINGS

A great deal of good work is done for the government by contractors at a reasonable price. Unfortunately, misunderstandings and abuses by the consultants, the government, or both have besmirched the process to the point that all consulting firms, good or bad, are viewed by some as "beltway bandits." These abuses and misunderstandings may be placed in the following categories: circumvention of the competitive process, improper management, and improper business practices.

### Circumvention of the Competitive Process

Let me state very frankly, at the outset, that competition for the sake of competition is not always in the best interest of the government. Low bidders or contractors accomplished in the art of writing slick proposals don't always give the government the most for its dollar. On the whole, however, the competitive process is the essence of the American marketplace and beneficial to the conduct of government business.

Tampering with the competitive process takes many forms. Among them are the following:

1. *"Wired" solicitations.* When a solicitation is publicized, knowledgeable contractors make phone calls to see if the results are "wired"—that is, the successful bidder has been secretly preselected. Bids and proposals take professional time and cost money. When competing proposals are requested by federal agencies merely as token indications of competition, knowledgeable contractors give this pseudo-competition a wide berth and mark the agency as questionable for future bidding.

2. *Sandbagging.* This occurs when an "undesirable" bidder seems to be gaining a competitive edge over the preferred bidder. The undesirable bidder is asked (off the record) to change the bid in some way that would in fact put the bid out of competition. For example, a government person might indicate that the price is too low: "Don't you want to increase it—(but don't say anything about this phone call)."

The other side of sandbagging involves the agency alerting the favored competitor on how to strengthen the proposal and thus acquire a competitive edge.

3. *"Sweetheart" solicitations.* On occasion agency staff will work with a favored consultant to develop solicitation requirements which can only be satisfied by one firm. Or, when a firm identifies a potential need for assistance in a given federal agency and submits an unsolicited proposal to that agency, the agency staff with a "sweetheart" contractor rewrites information from the unsolicited proposal into a solicitation that will, by its construction, either exclude the unsolicited proposal or benefit the "sweetheart."

4. *The "buddy" ("good ole boy" or "good ole girl") system.* This operates primarily through the hiring of individuals as "experts" or consultants. Competition is really not an issue because these selections are governed by personnel regulations and *not* by procurement regulations. It is frequently these individual hires, under regulated maximum pay arrangements, which break into news stories or speeches by members of Congress as indications of failures in or violations of federal regulations governing contractor selection. The "buddy" system can also apply in the negotiation of contracts with individuals.

5. *Use of other jurisdictions.* Some agencies, avoiding the complexities of the procurement process, arrange for a jurisdiction under their control, such as a state agency, to let a contract as an agent of the parent agency. For example, federal agency "A" wants to hire consulting firm "B" to perform a study. Agency "A" then contracts state agency "C" (which depends upon "A" for a large portion of its funds) and requests that "C" contract with "B" to perform work for "C" when, in reality, "B" will work for "A." This way "A" does not have to report the contract and can, if it wishes, take credit for the study as an internal effort.

6. *Use of multiple contract orders.* Federal procurement regulations permit contracting of small jobs on a sole source basis by use of purchase orders (or work orders) in amounts up to $10,000. I believe this to be generally a good, sensible, and economic way to procure services without costly and time-consuming competition.

Although this regulation has been in effect for some time, however, some federal agencies are either unaware of it or contracting officers in these agencies have not informed program officials of its existence.

In some agencies internal procurement regulations have retained a previous ceiling of $2,500.

The use of purchase orders under the $10,000 ceiling gives a distinct advantage to agencies when procuring training courses. However, even though Title 5, United States Code, Section 4105 also permits a federal agency to purchase training for government employees noncompetitively from nongovernment sources, some agencies take the position that this only involves purchasing a seat in a classroom or printed course material.

7. *Repetitive "sole source" contracts.* Sole source procurements meet a legitimate need on the part of the government to secure a product or service so unique that competition would be meaningless or costly, or where only one source can meet the government's needs on a timely basis. Undoubtedly, this form of procurement has saved much time and money and generally has been properly used. However, favored firms have secured sole source contracts because tight controls do not exist or because they perform one contract, possibly on a "buy-in" bid, and use the knowledge gained to establish a "unique" ability to perform another contract, and another, and another—and so on.

8. *The "feasibility study."* This is, of course, a study to determine whether further action is needed in a given area. If the study indicates that further work *is* required, a contractor should not be permitted to perpetuate itself by the "unique" knowledge it gained in conducting the feasibility study. Unfortunately, this does happen—and it may not be solely the fault of the contractor. Agency staff often feel more "comfortable" with contractors they know.

## Improper Management of the Process

When a federal staff complains, "We expected the study to come out differently," it may be due to unsatisfactory performance. It is more *likely* to be due to one of several other reasons:

1. The statement of work in the request for proposal did not represent the expectations of the government.
2. The government did not carefully follow the progress of the project.
3. The government did not respond to consultant requests for decisions.

4. The government changed the rules in the course of the engagement, creating a different climate or desired end product without a change in specifications.

A single phrase describes each of these: improper contract management.

Other deficiencies in management occur when *last-minute* decisions are made to "go contract," when staff with insufficient authority are asked to represent the government on a given consulting contract, or when the government representatives do not understand the proper role of consultants, expecting outside personnel to perform government functions or to make decisions that properly belong to government officials.

Most federal agencies cannot tell at any given moment just how much they are spending for the contracting of services. Many rationales are expressed for "excluding this" or "excluding that," but in reality they represent anticipated criticism for making too free use of the procurement process.

Every accounting system approved by the General Accounting Office could and should have the capability (say, through the use of a project code) to capture the data needed to identify types of consulting contracts as well as individual expert or consulting appointees, no matter what form the contract or employment takes. This has been done in the past and can be done in the future. It is ludicrous for a federal agency to reply to a congressional query by saying that it cannot tell the full costs or the number of all consulting engagements—broken down by contracts, purchase orders, reemployed annuitants, experts and consultants, grants, and so on.

## Improper Business Practices of Consultants

I would be naive were I to overlook that, in spite of the many restrictions of the federal procurement process, some few consulting organizations engage in practices that range from unsavory to questionable legality.

One such practice is to take advantage of the legislated advantages offered to disadvantaged, minority-owned firms and to nonprofit organizations. The result is well known. Some white-owned firms have created "8A" fronts; others have two organizations—one for profit, one not-for-profit.

Another common practice is the consulting version of "bait and switch." When bidding on competitive procurements, some firms will list their best staff in numerous proposals. These highly placed, highly qualified people will appear at the outset of each engagement, soon to be replaced by less qualified, sometimes inexperienced staff. This behavior is excused by citing the time it takes the government to receive, evaluate, negotiate, and approve contracts. "During that time, other proposals were accepted, and we had legal commitments." The surprise is that federal agencies have tolerated "bait and switch."

Some large organizations performing consultations at both the state/local level and the federal level—shift overhead costs away from the state and local work because contracts there tend to be smaller in amount, the size of overheads questioned more, and the competition composed of a different type of contractor—and charge those expenses to the federal projects where there is more money available and less questioning of a higher overhead.

A final practice, "buying in," is obviously restricted to large firms in sound condition. These may bid a project at a large loss for the purpose of making themselves known to the agency soliciting the work, or of securing the follow-on work they know to be involved. Having bought their way in by underbidding the competition, they plan to recover the losses in subsequent "wired" solicitations or sole source contracts.

## SUMMARY AND OBSERVATIONS

Regarding the weaknesses of the system and the faults which have been discussed, I suggest the following:

1. People responsible for procurement decisions and contract outcomes should be held strictly and publicly accountable for their efforts.

2. The system can and should be simplified. Many state and local jurisdictions function without all of the impedimenta related to most federal procurements. The technical requirements that apply to the procurement of scientific paraphernalia are applied by some federal agencies with equal fervor to the procurement of an administrative study. Proposal requirements are poorly and inconsistently defined. Cost indication forms supplied for proposals may make no distinction between producing services and producing goods. The bidding process is time consuming, and costly to the firms that bid. Payments are unconscionably slow, and federal agencies rule that *the cost of short-term loans required to meet cash shortages is unallowable in determining overhead!*

3. The request for proposal itself represents a fertile field for federal paperwork reduction. The "boiler plate" approaches telephone directory thickness. Too much and unnecessary cost detail is required. The federal government appears to favor excessive demands in connection with proposal submissions in lieu of careful evaluation of the past records of proposers.

4. The role of the various parts of the federal establishment should be more specifically defined, so that potential contractors know who does what, and where, among the procuring agency, OMB, GSA, GAO, and others.

5. Program officials who enter positions in which they will determine the need for outside services should be given brief but planned instruction in determining and specifying requirements, selecting methods to be used in contracting for assistance, and monitoring contract progress. Appropriate federal agencies should determine the specific amount and curriculum content and see to it that training is conducted.

6. Responsibility for determining whether a consulting contract is needed to carry out an agency's program better, for defining what is to be done, for selecting the consultant to be used, and for administering consulting contracts should be placed squarely on federal managers, at least at SES (Senior Executive Service) level and possibly as low as managers eligible for merit salary increases. Until they are held accountable for managing the procurement and utilization of consulting services as part of their total managerial role, including receiving the rewards for superior performance and the penalties for substandard performance, consulting "horror stories" will continue to hit the headlines.

7. The Office of Management and Budget and the appropriations committees of the Congress should interpret the word "management" as something other than organization studies, reporting systems, and human resource applications. OMB and its predecessor have, with one or two exceptions, limited their "management" focus on interagency, not internal agency, matters. No better time exists than during budget hearings for carefully phrased questions to be addressed to an agency regarding its management of personal service contracts—particularly if later budget and appropriation decisions reflect the answers given.

8. The General Accounting Office should establish, as one criterion for its approval of an agency accounting system, that the system have the capability to capture the data needed to identify types of consulting contracts as well as individual expert or consulting appointees, no matter the form of contract or employment.

---

## Auditing Disputes in Federal Grant Programs
## The Case of AFDC

Fred Doolittle

*Financial audits in federal grant programs are an important bureaucratic control technique but recently have provoked controversy. Three recent disputes in the AFDC program illustrate the delay in program review, federal efforts to shift review costs to states and lower costs through sampling of grantee operations, difficulties in decentralizing federal decision making and the need to define audit appeal procedures. This paper concludes with policy suggestions.*

### INTRODUCTION

Federal audits of grant programs are an important control tool designed to assure that grantees use funds according to standards established by the federal statute and regulations. Auditing is important because of the large number of federal grants to state and local governments,[1] as well as the problems other control techniques present.[2]

Audits are also important because the issues they pose arise in other aspects of intergovernmental relations; in the routine administration of grant programs or in federal programs requiring planning or the commitment of resources by state or local governments many of the same problems arise.[3] The federal government may have a poorly defined goal and confusing requirements, the states and cities may face a bureaucracy in which authority is divided among many offices with no clear line of authority and the states and cities

Reprinted with permission from *Public Administration Review*, (July/August, 1981). © 1981 by the American Society for Public Administration, 1225 Connecticut Avenue, N. W., Washington, D. C. All rights reserved.

may attempt to mobilize political support for their position. The lessons learned from examining audits in grant programs may also apply to other situations in which governments interact.

This paper examines these problems in financial audits[4] of grant programs through a case study of the Aid for Families with Dependent Children (AFDC) program, one of the largest categorical grant programs in existence.[5] The AFDC program has been administered by various federal agencies. Before 1976 the program was administered by the Social and Rehabilitation Service, a part of HEW. Between 1976 and 1979, the Social Security Administration, also a part of HEW, ran the program. In 1980 HEW was renamed the Health and Human Services Department (HHS). When discussing specific events before 1980 the federal agency will be designated HEW and when discussing recent events or generalizing HHS will be used. This section concludes by identifying the key issues in these auditing disputes; the following section then presents a brief history of auditing disputes between California and HHS. Next, is an analysis of the issues the case poses for auditing in grant programs. The paper ends with a brief discussion of several policy implications.

### Delay in Financial Review

Between the time grantees receive and use the funds and the final federal audit, there is often a long delay. Federal program officials in the regional offices conduct the initial review of grantee practices in the course of normal administrative contacts. The auditor, of course, is less likely than regional officials to accept debatable grantee practices which increase federal cost. If the dispute concerns a continuing practice, delay in financial review means that more money will be in controversy. As the practice becomes routine, others in the grantee bureaucracy (e.g., budget office) or among the beneficiaries of the grant may come to rely on it. To the extent that the grantee feels the initial program review was an approval of the practice, later audit rejection will appear to be retroactive disapproval; delay in review leads to increased resistance to audit exceptions.

### Federal Efforts to Shift the
### Burden of Proof to the Grantees

Given the high cost of detailed financial reviews, federal administrators have an incentive to shift some or all of the costs of evaluation to the grantees. In the best of all worlds, the grantees would be paid only after they had proven their program outputs to be proper. More realistically, however, federal administrators sometimes defer approval of claims until the grantees provide detailed information on their use of funds. The grantees have fought this funding procedure by protests to the federal agency and in congressional committee hearings and through litigation.

### Attempts to Lower Evaluation Costs Through Random Samples

Federal administrators have also attempted to use financial penalties to reduce the high cost of evaluation. Since it is particularly costly to audit programs in which grantees must determine the eligibility of many people for grant-funded services or case assistance, federal administrators have tried to impose financial penalties based on the error rate discovered in a sample of grantee eligibility determinations. This effort to create an administrative "quality control" system raises many issues concerning definition of the proper measure of program performance and setting of minimum standards and has led to challenges by states in the federal courts.

### Conflict Between Efforts to Decentralize and Auditors' Powers

Under the Nixon administration's "New Federalism," there was some effort made to assign certain federal program decision-making power to the regional office level.[6] The extent of decentralization of authority was unclear, however, because regulations did not state whether decisions of regional officials would be final. Later audits revealed the potential conflict between this decentralization and the power of the central audit office.

### Need to Define Appeal Procedures for Audit Disputes

Until the early 1970s, many federal agencies did not have formal procedures for appealing auditing decisions. With the increased importance of grants and audits, more disputes arose and some agencies developed more formal procedures for administrative review of audit decisions. Dissatisfied grantees began to sue in federal court for reversal of audit decisions, making the audit more like an adversary relationship. Both the federal agencies and the courts were thus forced to consider the best ways to structure review

procedures and to determine the relative decision-making capacity of the judiciary and administration.

## A CASE STUDY IN AUDITING: THE AFDC PROGRAM

Established by the Social Security Act in 1935, the AFDC program provides matching grants to the states for public assistance payments. During the late 1960s and early 1970s the AFDC caseload grew rapidly but has leveled off at about 10.5 million people since the mid-1970s.

### AFDC Administrative and Financial Procedures

Before receiving funds, a state must develop a "state plan" to use the grant which is consistent with requirements outlined in the federal statute and accompanying regulations. Legally, grantees must adhere to the plan and change program operations only with the approval of HHS. If a state refuses to operate its program in conformity with federal requirements, HHS officials can make a formal finding of nonconformity; grantees may appeal this finding to the secretary of HHS and in the federal courts. If upheld, HHS officials can cut off funds until they receive assurances that future grants will be used properly.

HHS's regional offices, which provide information on program requirements and review program operations, contain representatives of bureaus such as Assistance Payments and the HHS Audit Agency. Under regulations issued in January 1969, the regional commissioner of the Social and Rehabilitation Service (SRS) was designated the personal representative of the federal administrator of the Social and Rehabilitation Service for the region.[7] The extent of the regional commissioner's authority was uncertain, however, since he/she was empowered to act only when "in conformance with the policies, objectives, and guidelines established by the Administrator" and he/she could only approve state plans. In September 1973, new regulations gave regional commissioners the authority "to request, approve, and determine the effective date of a cost allocation plan." These cost allocation plans involve state formulas for determining what administrative costs the federal government should reimburse and at what matching rate.

Forty-five days before each quarter, the states must provide the regional office with an estimate of welfare payments, a justification of the estimate, and a request for the amount of federal money required to match the state funds.[8] After reviewing the request, the regional office recommends a disposition and forwards the material to the Washington office for computation. At the end of each quarter, the state submits a statement of actual expenditures and adjustments are made if the earlier estimate of expenditures was incorrect.

Though both the HHS Audit Agency and the General Accounting Office (GAO) audit the AFDC program, HHS audits are by far the most frequent and complete. Agency auditors operate independently of program officials; they release their reports simultaneously to federal and state officials. Auditors may discover people receiving aid who are ineligible under the state plan or eligible recipients who are receiving overpayments. They may also find administrative practices that are inconsistent with federal requirements or attempts to claim federal funds at a higher matching rate than is authorized.[9] If the auditors file "exceptions," they ordinarily submit detailed justifications to the state. If the state does not concur, it can submit further information in support of the claim or appeal any exceptions to the Grant Appeals Board. The regulations imply that the decision on the appeal is final and the statute makes no mention of judicial review of audit exceptions. If the appeal fails, future state claims are reduced by the amount of the remaining audit exceptions. If the auditors discover serious non-compliance with federal requirements, "the state agency is required to correct its practice so that there will be no recurrence of the problem in the future."

The following sections describe three simultaneous auditing controversies between the federal agency and the State of California. The effects of delay in review, confusion over lines of authority within the federal bureaucracy, and difficulty in fashioning an appeal procedure are illustrated by the first dispute over a cost allocation plan. The second dispute concerns the federal government's "deferral" of state claims in an attempt to shift to the states some of the costs of evaluating grant-funded activities. Federal attempts to lower evaluation costs through "quality control audits" based on samples of program operations are the subject of the third dispute.

## Disallowances of States Claims

In September 1968, the State of California instituted a new method of computing and allocating the costs of administering the food stamp and AFDC programs.

HEW audited this new procedure in 1971; at issue was whether the state had improperly shifted food stamp costs to the AFDC program where there was partial federal funding.[10] HEW auditors decided to require the state to revise its method of cost allocation and they ruled that the state had to return $3,279,520 in "overpayments" to the federal government; the state, in turn, chose to appeal the auditors' findings in informal administrative proceedings, the only recourse available at the time.[11]

When the informal appeal failed, California brought suit in federal court seeking to enjoin HEW from withholding the contested audit exceptions from future grants. The U. S. District Court dismissed the suit, holding that disallowances were not subject to judicial review. The state appealed, and in 1975, the U. S. Court of Appeals reversed the District Court's ruling, finding that Congress intended final administrative decisions on audit exceptions to be reviewable in court.[12] The case was sent back to the District Court for a hearing on the merits, and HEW was enjoined from withholding the alleged overpayments.

The first issue involved in the suit was whether the cost allocation plan was a part of the state plan and, therefore, had to receive federal agency approval before the state could legally receive the funds. Since funds had been distributed, the state argued, the cost allocation plan had implicitly been approved. HEW was forced to argue the cost allocation formula was not a part of the state plan, thus undercutting the usefulness of the state plan as a control device.[13]

There was also debate over whether HEW had approved the state cost plan. While the state cited assistance from the regional HEW staff in drafting the plan, HEW argued that this advice did not bind the regional office. Even if the facts did point to regional office approval, HEW claimed that the regional commissioner did not have the power to approve a plan that is in violation of the central office's interpretation of federal regulations or policy.

In 1976, the parties collected evidence and prepared their arguments; from 1977 to 1979 the case was inactive pending the result of a related case. During the period of this litigation, and in response to a growing number of audit disputes, HEW adopted formal procedures for administrative appeals. HEW first adopted regulations providing for somewhat less than a "formal adjudicatory hearing," requiring a written administrative record outlining the basis of the Social and Rehabilitation Service administrator's decision, full disclosure to the state of all evidence and a right of response, and a conference with the administrator at the option of the state. In 1976, with 160 cases under reconsideration, HEW issued new regulations allowing the deputy administrator to rule on appeals as well. By 1978, the case backlog led to another change: Jurisdiction over audit appeals was transferred to the HEW Departmental Grant Appeals Board.[14]

Action on the court appeal came in 1979. With the availability of the Grant Appeals Board procedures, the parties to the suit agreed to remand the case to HEW for a hearing. The case is currently before the board and no decision has been reached. Even after the board's decision, future state appeals in the federal district court are possible.

## Deferral of Approval of State Claims

Under the deferral procedure, HEW attempted to shift the burden of proof to the states, forcing them to bear the expense and cash flow problems of collecting detailed information concerning disputed claims. California's deferral controversy began with a 1973 change in regulations that allowed states to submit claims retroactively for additional federal funds to cover administrative expenses for 1970–72. When California submitted a quarterly statement of expenditures including these retroactive costs, the regional commissioner deferred approval for about $13 million of the claims and requested that the state provide detailed justification for the expenditures. The legal support for this action was a 1973 delegation of authority from the secretary of HEW that had never been adopted as a formal regulation. After receiving approval for $9 million in 1975, the state sued for the remaining $4 million.[15]

The issues the litigants raised had more far-reaching implications than merely this deferral dispute in that the logic of the deferral process applied to all state claims for reimbursement.[16] Relying on general arguments about the role of the states in a federal system and about the language in the federal AFDC statute, California attempted to establish that its claims should be assumed valid until proven otherwise. It argued that it should not suffer a cash flow problem while awaiting federal approval of its claims or submit to informal audits by federal administrators. The only review the state accepted was the formal, after-the-fact, federally financed audit. In response, HEW argued

that it had no authority under the Social Security Act to pay claims that the state could not prove valid. Since there was no presumption of validity of state claims, HEW maintained that it had general monitoring powers that are not limited to formal audits.

The court issued a summary judgment against the deferral procedure on the grounds that the practice was contrary to the regulations in effect at the time. The court did not decide, however, if the deferral procedure would be valid if there were supporting regulations.

On February 17, 1976, HEW formally adopted regulations that explicitly put the burden of establishing the validity of all claims on the states.[17] A regional commissioner can defer any claim but background material issued with the regulations suggested retroactive claims are automatically deferred. If the regional commissioner does not act within 90 days after receiving supporting material, the claim is automatically approved. Uniformly hostile to the new procedures, the states argue that they lack statutory authority and create excessive delays in the review process as well as unacceptable financial burdens.[18] No court challenges to the new regulations have been successful. Currently about 30 states have funds deferred pending a decision by regional commissioners.[19]

## Quality Control Through Sampling

In a conventional audit, federal administrators impose financial penalties only for violations of federal policy actually found. To create a more powerful incentive system, HEW officials sought to establish a "quality control" program of financial penalties based on information from random samples of each state's caseload. The effort has been long and difficult, and only recently has a system been put in place.

Starting in the mid-1960s HEW urged states to establish quality control systems. Because of continued high error rates, HEW published tentative regulations in 1972 that required quality control sampling in each state and reduced federal aid by the percentage of sample cases receiving overpayments or including ineligible recipients. Overpayments less than $5 were ignored. State reaction to the proposal was immediate and hostile. HEW chose to delay implementation of the quality control system and lower the proposed financial penalties; in 1975, after further negotiations with the states HEW finally announced it would implement the system complete with financial penalties.

Although error rates had generally dropped in the early 1970s, most states still were considerably above the target rates and thus faced cuts in federal funding.

Congress investigated the quality control system in hearings in late 1975 but action was delayed pending judicial review of the threatened funding cuts. This review came in mid-1976 in response to suits by California and more than 10 other states.[20] The court held that a quality control system is consistent with the purposes of the AFDC program and that the federal government has the power to deny state claims for erroneous payments. The court found the HEW's error rate targets, however, were unreasonably low and were set arbitrarily; it, therefore, held that the quality control system as implemented did not promote efficiency in the administration of the act.

Following this court case, HEW rescinded its quality control regulations[21] and again imposed penalties only for erroneous payments actually found in the sample. It also began a series of negotiations with state and local officials and welfare groups to fashion a compromise quality control system for the AFDC program, later expanding the discussion to include Medicaid and SSI quality control as well.[22] While these negotiations continued, Congress chose to combat high error rates in AFDC administration by offering incentive payments for states having error rates in dollars paid (not cases) below a certain percent.[23] In calculating the dollar error rate, underpayments and incorrect denials of eligibility are considered.[24]

Under the quality control system implemented in March of 1979,[25] a state with an overpayment dollar error rate equal to or below the weighted mean of all states' overpayment rates would receive full federal funding. All other states had to reduce their overpayment rate to the national standard or make satisfactory improvements in each audit period to avoid financial penalties. HEW also announced a study to determine a reasonable goal for funding reductions in the future. In spite of the extended negotiations and the changes in the quality control systems, many states and local governments still opposed the concept of financial sanctions and many details of the program.

During 1978–79, a more cost-conscious Congress was also taking actions affecting the AFDC quality control program. In October of 1978, it passed an appropriations bill that included a $1 billion cut in HEW funding, the savings to come from eliminating the waste and fraud identified in a report of the HEW

inspector general.[26] In the course of deliberations on the 1979 Supplement Appropriations bill (P.L. 96-38), Congress relaxed the previous year's cutback but directed the secretary of HEW to issue regulations requiring states to reduce their AFDC overpayment rate to 4 percent by September 30, 1982, or face a reduction in federal funding (unless the secretary determined that a state made a good faith effort to comply).[27]

In January 1980, the now redesignated HHS responded to the congressional directive by issuing new regulations that require states above the 4 percent target to make one-third reductions in the excess by September 1980 and two-thirds by September 1981.[28] In addition, however, the regulations excuse states from the performance standard if they can demonstrate "a good faith effort," e.g., through the commitment of top management, record keeping and data collection proficiency, and follow-up or corrective action plans. The congressional conference report states that this exception should be used only in "certain limited cases."

Currently, HHS is administering the incentive payments and collecting data for the initial fund cuts under the quality control system. Only four small states are receiving incentive payments for low error rates. Addition of the "good faith" exception to the target rates has also posed problems in that some states argue that exception should apply to the March 1979 system until the new system is in place. HHS is also continuing the study of the proper target error rate in hopes of encouraging Congress to reconsider the 1979 amendments.[29]

## ISSUES POSED BY THE AFDC CASE STUDY

The three disputes between California and HHS just described pose a number of important issues for the financial control and auditing of grant programs.

### The Disallowance Dispute

Audit of a state AFDC program may be far from the ideal of quick, clear program review. Bureaucratic control systems work best when the undesired action and the response are close in time. The actions being reviewed here, however, occurred between 1968 and 1971, the initial audit came in 1971, and the administrative appeal followed from 1971 to 1974. Court action began in 1975 and continued to 1979. The second round of administrative appeal is currently underway and further litigation can be expected if the state claim is not upheld.

Since there is no statute of limitations on state over-claims, federal officials are not under strong pressure to provide timely information on financing problems. States, on the other hand, have an incentive to get a quick and authoritative ruling, which is not always possible given the confusion over lines of authority in the federal bureaucracy. The amount of money at issue can thus continue to grow, and the states are forced to bear the risk of later disapproval. As the amount of money increases, the state's resistance to the eventual audit exception also grows.

The dispute between the State of California and HHS also illustrates an apparent conflict between efforts to decentralize authority to the regional level while retaining strong audit powers in the central office. Federal officials in HHS clearly recognized the issue when they wrote the regulations that limited the authority of regional officials to situations in which their decisions were found to be consistent with policy set at the Washington level. Once the states understood what this meant, they recognized the strong incentives to bypass the regional office and deal solely with Washington on matters not clearly covered under established rules.

The dispute also demonstrates the difficulties of establishing a system of administrative appeal of audit results. Since the statute did not require any particular approach, HHS experimented for several years with a variety of informal appeal procedures. With the increasing number and importance of audits and the likelihood of judicial involvement, the agency chose to establish more formal appeal procedures and finally to turn the decisions over to a specialized body with jurisdiction over a wide variety of appeals. The courts in recent years have also been careful to limit their jurisdiction over audit appeals,[30] and are quite willing to send disputes to the Grant Appeals Board.

Although judicial review of audits is inevitable, the courts are hesitant to enter the case any sooner than absolutely necessary. The factual issues are often very complex, requiring a detailed knowledge of the AFDC program. While this is true in other legal disputes, it has made the court refuse to accept an active role in audit appeals.

## The Deferral Dispute

Since the test for final approval of a state claim is the same under deferred and immediate approval, the two most important issues in the dispute are whether the states should hold the money pending resolution and how much of the cost of collecting information they should pay. Concern over potential cash flow problems under deferral led the states to focus on this issue in the litigation. While they attempted to establish a presumption of validity of state claims, HHS argued that under the federal statute it was not obliged to honor all claims until a formal audit could be conducted. To date, the federal government has been able to enforce deferrals and compel the states to finance operations fully during investigation, a process that can take up to six months even without problems.

The success of the deferral process means that the federal government has shifted a portion of program evaluation costs to the states. Even though the federal government subsidizes 50 percent of state AFDC administrative costs, the deferral process provides federal savings over audits which are completely financed by the federal government.[31]

The details of the deferral procedures pose a number of other problems. First, what types of claims will be deferred? In practice, current and retroactive claims are treated similarly.[32] HHS has so far issued no clear rules stating when the regional commissioner is justified in finding the claim is of "questionable allowability." Though a number of states have requested such a discussion in the regulations, HHS has responded that the wide variety of claims makes it impossible to present clear criteria.[33] The regulations are also unclear as to the burden of proof the states face in contesting a deferral, though presumably the usual civil law test of the preponderance of evidence would apply.

## The Quality Control Dispute

The quality control dispute illustrates the political vulnerability of major administrative initiatives to increase program review. From the late 1960s to the mid-1970s, Congress provided little support for quality control in AFDC; in 1975, however, it held a series of hearings at which the states aired their grievances. Once Congress did take note of poor program administration, it undercut HHS efforts by offering incentives to states rather than sanctions, and then by imposing a strict quality control system instead of the one carefully negotiated by HHS. Even this last apparent victory for quality control poses problems for HHS since it permits states to be excused from penalties if they make a "good faith effort," an exception that is certain to be difficult to administer. Congress substituted a strict but potentially avoidable rule for a more permissive but clear standard. While it can take credit publicly for clamping down on lax administration, Congress has also given the states a way to pressure HHS for relaxation of the penalties.

The dispute also shows the one-sidedness of HHS's monitoring efforts. Since only overpayments and payments to ineligible recipients are punished, incentives exist to risk underpayments to recipients. HHS claims that the reasons for overpayments are often the same as for underpayments so only overpayments need be addressed, but this assertion is backed by little data and analysis. When states face penalties only for errors of excess spending, they would logically respond by being less concerned that they provide proper assistance to everyone eligible; if they later discover an underpayment they can provide the assistance and suffer no financial penalty.

Finally, the dispute shows the difficulty of defining performance standards in control systems. The quality control measures were originally based on the percentage of cases in error, an inducement to focus on the easiest errors to avoid rather than the most costly errors. Measures based on the percent of dollars paid in error still allow states to change their regulations to define away certain troublesome errors rather than improve program administration.

## POLICY SUGGESTIONS

Several policy suggestions emerge from this research. First, allocating more money for auditing purposes could well lower the total federal cost of grant programs; since grantee errors would be discovered sooner, less money would be spent improperly. Greater financial incentives also could stimulate states to adopt new administrative techniques that have proven useful in lowering costs in other places.[34] In addition, Congress should consider imposing a statute of limitations on audit exceptions to encourage timely federal audits and to lessen the uncertainty which grantees face. If federal auditors later determine that a state initially provided deceptive or incomplete information, the statute of limitations could be suspended.

The deferral process that HHS currently employs is a sensible response to the problem of evaluating state claims for reimbursement. Deferring all expenditure claims would be inappropriate since this would increase the resources devoted to verifying claims without likely payoffs. But using the deferral process selectively when it is especially difficult for the grantor to audit after-the-fact and when abuse is suspected could well lower the cost of evaluation and improperly spent funds.

This approach, however, is not without problems. It seems necessary that federal officials "cross-examine" grantees and require production of documents as in the discovery phase of civil litigation. The political interest of congressional representatives would lead them, in turn, to police this process and protect the grantee from harassment. Clearly, the continuing controversy in grant programs suggests that further experiments may be worthwhile.

Legislation establishing grant programs should contain carefully designed quality control systems with financial penalties where feasible. Because a quality control system could provide timely and systematic review, it could reduce the amount of money spent improperly and lessen the political controversy surrounding financial reviews.

One final policy implication emerges clearly: To avoid further confusion and controversy, Congress should pay much closer attention to financial review procedures when it enacts federal grant programs. The inattention of the past has led to administrative, political, and legal battles that could have been avoided.

*I would like to thank Arnold Howitt, Kathryn Haslanger and Marcia Fernald for their help. All remaining errors are my own.*

## NOTES

1. See Office of Management and Budget, *Special Analysis of the Budget of the United States, Fiscal Year 1980* (Washington, D. C.: U. S. Government Printing Office, 1979).

2. See Fred Doolittle, "A General Theory of Categorical Grants-in-Aid," Harvard University, Department of City and Regional Planning, Discussion paper D78-30, October 1978, for a discussion of these problems.

3. Some other authors have considered the political and administrative problems with audits. See V. O. Key, *The Administration of Federal Grants to the States* (Chicago: Public Administration Service, 1937); E. L. Normanton, *The Accountability and Audit of Governments* (New York: Praeger, 1966); Bruce L. R. Smith (ed.), *The New Political Economy* (New York: John Wiley & Sons, 1975). *The Policy Circle* by

Aaron Wildavsky and Judith May (Beverly Hills, Calif.: Sage Publications, 1978) also contains an article by Floyd Stoner entitled "Federal Auditors as Regulators."

4. See Elmer Staats, "New Problems in Accountability for Federal Programs" in Smith (ed.), *The New Political Economy,* p. 64; and Michael Reagan, "Accountability and Independence in Federal Grants-in-Aid," also in Smith, pp. 184–185 for a discussion of financial, managerial, and program audits.

5. See U.S. Office of Management and Budget, *Special Analysis of the Budget of the United States,* Fiscal Year 1980 (Washington, D.C.: U.S. Government Printing Office, 1979), chapter H. AFDC is the third largest categorical grant program behind Medicaid and the Federal Aid Highway program.

6. See the discussion in Rufus Miles, *The Department of Health, Education and Welfare* (New York: Praeger, 1974), pp. 67–68, 277–280.

7. 34 F.R. 1286 (January 25, 1969).

8. See generally 45 CFR 201.5.

9. Another type of violation occurs when the grantee does not provide some service which is required as a condition of the grant. This may occur because the grantee wishes to avoid its share of the cost of the activity or because it feels the activity will have an undesirable local impact. Controlling this violation has proven much more difficult since the audit approach does not provide any appropriate penalty.

10. See 45 CFR 16 and discussion later in the paper.

11. See 40 F.R. 25599 (June 17, 1975) for a brief discussion of this.

12. See *State of California v. Weinberger,* 520 F. 2d 351 (1975).

13. This confusion was remedied by HEW in 1976 with the issuing of new regulations on cost allocation formulae. See 45 CFR 201.150.

14. See 43 F.R. 9264 (March 6, 1978).

15. *California v. Weinberger,* United States District Court, N.D.—Calif. #C-75-0391.

16. About $3 billion in claims from many states had been deferred when California sued. See *AFDC Quality Control Program,* hearing before the House Ways and Means Committee, Subcommittee on Oversight, 94th Cong., 1st sess., October 31, and November 3, 1975, p. 99.

17. 41 F.R. 7103 (February 17, 1976).

18. Comments on file, U.S. Department of Health, Education and Welfare.

19. Phone interview with Kent Dickson, deferral officer, Social Security Administration, August 27, 1980.

20. *Maryland v. Mathews,* 415 F. Supp. 1206 (D.D.C. 1976).

21. 42 F.R. 14717 (March 16, 1977).

22. 43 F.R. 29311 (July 7, 1978).

23. 42 U.S.C. Section 603(J).

24. See 43 F.R. 54105 (November 20, 1978) and 44 F.R. 67421 (November 26, 1979) for a discussion of the changes.

25. 44 F.R. 12579 (March 7, 1979).

26. P.L. 95-480 (October 18, 1978) Section 201. For background, see the House debate on HR 12929 in the *Congressional Record,* June 7 and June 8, 1978.

27. See *Congressional Record,* July 11, 1979, H 5778, and 44 F.R. 55314 (September 25, 1979).

28. 45 F.R. 6326 (January 25, 1980).

29. Phone interview with Sean Hurley, Division of AFDC Quality Control, Social Security Administration, August 27, 1980.

30. Under the Social Security Act, states may automatically appeal fund cutoff decisions to the U.S. Court of Appeals. These courts have closely examined the facts in state claims before them to be certain that the state is not trying to bring an audit appeal before them, merely labelling it a fund cutoff.

31. The normal matching rate for administrative expenses in AFDC is 50 percent.

32. Phone interview with Kent Dickson, deferral officer, Social Security Administration, August 27, 1980.

33. 41 F.R. 7103 (February 17, 1976).

34. For a discussion see Bendick, Lenine and Campbell, *The Anatomy of AFDC Errors* (Washington: Urban Institute, 1978).

# CHAPTER TEN

# Collective Bargaining

## Some Impacts of Collective Bargaining on Local Government
### A Diversity Thesis

Raymond D. Horton
David Lewin
James W. Kuhn

*The rapid growth of collective bargaining in the American public sector, especially local government, has sparked much concern with, but relatively little research of, union impacts on governmental management. Such impact analysis may most fruitfully be undertaken from a diversity perspective that envisions a multiplicity rather than a single pattern of bargaining outcomes. This diversity thesis is examined in relation to five dimensions of public management—compensation, personnel administration, service provision and delivery, government structure, and politics—and is tested in a preliminary way against relations in New York City, Chicago, and Los Angeles. The paper concludes with some implications of the analysis for policy and research in public sector labor relations.*

In recent years, government has grown faster than any other sector of the American economy. This growth has been accompanied by a major expansion of public employer unionism and collective bargaining. Consequently, widespread scholarly interest has developed in public sector labor relations, particularly the structure of collective bargaining and the process by which bargaining decisions are reached. Relatively little attention, however, has been paid to the impacts of collective bargaining on governmental management.

Utilizing a diversity-of-impacts theory, this paper discusses some of the conceptual and methodological approaches useful in an impact analysis of labor relations decisions in the public sector.[1] Central to the theory is the notion that the impacts of public sector labor relations decisions on governmental management reflect sharp differences that exist among and even within governments with respect to structural, political, organizational, and union variables.

## TRENDS IN GOVERNMENT EMPLOYMENT, PAY, AND UNIONISM

Between 1960 and 1973, public employment in the United States grew by more than 60% or approximately 25% faster than employment in the private nonfarm sector of the economy.[2] The increase was especially sharp in state and local government where employment rose almost 78% over this 13-year period. Employment advanced more rapidly in state than in local government (89 versus 74%), but more than two and one-half times as many persons, 8.3 million, were employed in the latter sector than in the former in 1973. Employment growth rates varied substantially among state and local government functions, with the largest increases recorded in public welfare (161%), health (120%), education (102%), corrections (91%),[3]

Reprinted from *Administration & Society,* Vol. 7, pp. 497–516. © 1976 by Sage Publications, Inc., with permission.

general control (72%), hospitals (63%), and police (57%). However, growth rates were large in virtually all public categories compared to the overall growth rate in the private economy (35%).

While the number of government employees has grown rapidly since 1960, public payrolls have risen even faster. For example, average monthly earnings of full-time employees of state and local governments increased 112.3% during the 1960–1973 period. Average hourly earnings in the private nonfarm sector rose three-fourths as much, 86.1%, and manufacturing earnings increased but 79.6%. Government workers who enjoyed the largest earnings increases over this period were employed in hospitals (132%), fire protection (123%), general control (119%), police protection (119%), health (115%), and highways (115%). These increases were all greater than earnings changes in the high-wage private construction sector (110%). So rapid and large have been the earnings increases for public employees that many of them now are paid more than their private sector counterparts (Perloff, 1971; Fogel and Lewin, 1974). These rates of pay increase may help explain why payroll costs represent well over half of all state and local government expenditures, and also why state and local governments accounted for more than 61% of all government purchases of goods and services in 1973, compared to 49.6% just six years earlier (Joint Economic Committee, 1974: 2). Government compensation expenditures now are claimed by some (Kuhn, 1972) to be an important element of modern inflation in the United States.

Finally, government workers continue to join unions and employee associations in record numbers, and to push for collective bargaining rights in public employment. In the federal sector, 52% of all employees were members of labor organizations in 1970, although much of this membership was concentrated in the postal service (Goldberg, 1972). More important, by 1972, slightly more than half of the 8.3 million full-time state and local government employees had enrolled in unions and employee associations (Labor Management Relations Service, 1975: 1; hereafter, LMRS).[4] The extent of employee organization in the public sector is particularly impressive when compared with private industry, where about 25% of all wage and salary workers belong to unions and employee associations, and 30% in the nonagricultural sector (U. S. Department of Labor, Bureau of Labor Statistics, 1972: 72).

In response to the heightened organizational activity of public employees, governments at all levels have attempted to formalize and treat labor relations as a functional specialty. In the federal government, the framework for labor relations was established in 1962 by President Kennedy's Executive Order 10988, and was subsequently modified by Executive Orders 11491 and 11616 in 1969 and 1973, respectively (see Taylor and Witney, 1975: 545–556). By 1973, two-thirds of American states had enacted legislation providing for some form of collective negotiations in their respective public sectors (U. S. Department of Labor, 1973), and in every one of the 50 states at least some governments engaged in such negotiations (LMRS, 1975: 1). In summary, government has been a major source of growth in the American economy since 1960 and an important arena of labor relations activity.

## ASSUMPTIONS ABOUT THE PUBLIC AND PRIVATE SECTORS

The aforementioned developments raise major questions about the role of collective bargaining in the public sector and the impacts of unionism and collective bargaining on various dimensions of governmental management and operations. In addressing these issues, both scholars and policy-makers generally have emphasized the peculiarities of the public sector; specifically, their analyses stress essential differences between the private and public sectors. Representative of this view are Wellington and Winter (1971: 8), who claim that "the public sector is *not* the private, and its labor problems *are* different, very different indeed." Differences indeed do exist, though to us some are not as pronounced as they appeared initially and others are more important than usually recognized.[5]

The difference identified earliest and to which the most attention has been paid concerns the legal position of government. Elected officials possess or are delegated rights that did not, at first glance, easily mesh with the concept and practice of collective bargaining. The problems of introducing collective bargaining and of adjusting legal perspectives to produce a tolerable fit with the "sovereignty" doctrine have been examined closely, and we have little to add to this literature. Suffice it to say that the sovereignty doctrine is withering away as the practice of collective bargaining continues to grow in government.

A second celebrated difference between the public and private sectors is the monopoly aspect of governmental services (Wellington and Winter, 1971).[6] Often, consumers have no, or few, alternatives; even if they choose not to avail themselves of a publicly provided service, they nevertheless must pay for it through taxes. However, not all state and local governmental services occupy a monopoly position. For example, alternative private services are typically available in sanitation and transportation. Some consumers have purchased protective services in the private market to supplement police protection. Given time for adjustment through relocation, some consumers can escape a government's high taxes. The costs and feasibility of alternatives to local government services cover a wider range than has been recognized and deserve further exploration, for they may be important determinants of manpower utilization and collective bargaining outcomes in the public sector. The diversity of government services needs to be emphasized, rather than being considered monolithic simply because they are publicly provided.

A third difference between public and private employment pertains to personnel administration. Civil service and the practices characteristic of it form a more common and broader personnel system than ever existed in private industry before, and probably even after, workers employed in that sector turned to collective bargaining. However, civil service systems vary markedly in operation from one government to another. The interaction of collective bargaining with civil service systems appears to produce a variety of outcomes that can be delineated, although much more work in this area is required.[7]

A fourth difference between the public and private sectors, only recently mentioned in the literature (see Fogel and Lewin, 1974; Lewin, 1974), but appearing to be one of signal importance, is governments' egalitarian pay structure: Pay differentials between high and low positions are narrower in the public than in the private sector. Individuals in low positions—unskilled, blue-collar, and entry level white-collar jobs—enjoy higher pay in public than in private employment, while the opposite appears to be true for those in high positions—professionals, managers, and executives. Significantly, these pay patterns antedate the development of unions and collective bargaining in the government sector. The egalitarian pay structure in government also provides a set of constraints and opportunities for negotiators on both sides of the bargaining table not present for bargainers in the private

sector. The effects of relatively well-paid public employees working in various capacities, directed by managers who are relatively poorly paid, deserve careful scrutiny by those concerned with collective bargaining in government.

## A DIVERSITY MODEL

Certainly as a consequence of the four major differences mentioned above, labor relations and patterns of manpower utilization in the public service display some features not found in the private sector. To focus on these differences as a key to understanding governmental labor problems, however, may mislead both scholars and policy-makers. It implies that government officials face unique problems and can expect little or no help from examining the solutions devised in the private sector. Similarly, it is unwise to assume that collective bargaining processes and solutions to industrial relations problems developed in the private economy provide "the answer" for public managers. In fact, managers and union leaders in private employment have elaborated a wide variety of roles, styles, procedures, and approaches to labor and manpower problems. They respond in many different ways because the situations in which they find themselves and the purposes they pursue are widely different.

Too often, observers of the labor scene implicitly assume a model of private sector labor relations and manpower management that describes only the manufacturing sector—and, more precisely, a model descriptive of large production firms and large industrial unions. In it, managers retain the initiative in directing employees, while the union concentrates its activities through grievance procedures on deflecting or modifying the thrust of managerial decisions. Alternatively, in other models, such as those provided by organized musicians and workers in the building trades and garment industry, union leaders have assumed a number of functions in decision-making areas usually regarded as strictly managerial, such as hiring, layoffs, and discipline. In some of these industries as well as in others, workers' representatives play important roles in strategic decisions affecting plant location, investment, subcontracting policy, and accounting methods, as well as wages, hours, and working conditions. Grievance handling plays a far less important part in labor relations patterned after the second model than the first.

If differences in labor relations and patterns of manpower utilization *within* the private sector are as wide and significant as suggested here, imputed differences *between* the public and private sectors may well be exaggerated and even misleading. For example, public employees not only bargain for benefits over the negotiating table, but through voting and other political activities may also punish or reward their employing managers. In the private sector, some unions occupy an analogous position. The coal miners' union, as a large stockholder in several coal-producing and transportation companies, has "sat" on both sides of the bargaining table; the garment unions and the Teamsters in local trucking are powerful enough in their respective industries to influence small employers directly as well as through collective bargaining.

Exaggeration of the differences between the public and private sectors arises not only from assuming more uniformity in private industry than actually exists, as noted above, but also from ignoring the diversity in the public sector with respect to control devices, organizational structures, services, and occupational and work groups. We believe this diversity, which is rooted in historical, legal, functional and political features of government, contains several implications for public sector labor relations. There may be no a priori reason to assume that labor relations in New York City ever will closely resemble those in Chicago or Los Angeles, even after formal collective bargaining has been introduced in Chicago and has matured in Los Angeles.[8]

The foregoing discussion suggests, then, that to conceive of governmental labor relations as sui generis and to hypothesize that only one pattern of union impact on public sector management will occur, overlooks the diversity of organizations, relationships, and impacts that may occur even within a single jurisdiction. Thus, a diversity model of public sector labor relations and collective bargaining impacts seems especially appropriate.

## THE IMPACTS OF COLLECTIVE BARGAINING ON GOVERNMENTAL MANAGEMENT

All but the most inconsequential political decisions produce impacts, latent as well as manifest, that change some patterns of relationships in the political system. The most important evidence in analyzing the impact of political decisions concerns the exchange or redistribution of resources that usually (but not always) accompanies a political decision. The process leading up to a political decision and the decision itself may permit hypotheses about decisional impacts, but observation of actual resource exchanges is necessary to translate hypotheses into findings (see Horton, 1974).

As noted earlier, labor relations and collective bargaining decisions appear to be playing an increasingly important allocative or redistributive role in American government, especially at the local government level. While some evidence and much speculation has surfaced concerning the impact of public employee labor relations on government, little systematic, comparative research has been conducted.[9] Five impact areas warrant particular analytical concern: compensation, service production and delivery, personnel administration, formal governmental structure, and informal politics.

### Compensation

The level of wages (or, more accurately, total compensation) which induces or maintains employment in a given organization represents perhaps the most important labor relations exchange. This is true in public or private organizations, and it is true whether or not employees are organized and bargain collectively with management to establish wages.[10]

Popular opinion is divided over the cause of the relatively rapid increase in public employee wages that has occurred in the United States during the last two decades. One school of thought emphasizes the emerging political strength of public workers, including their organization and, in some jurisdictions, the introduction of collective bargaining, while another branch of opinion interprets public sector wage developments as essentially economic phenomena whereby intersectoral wage differentials were erased or even reversed by exceedingly strong demand for public services (see Wellington and Winter, 1971; Hayes, 1972; and Ehrenberg, 1973).

Our inclination, at present, is to view both explanations, standing alone or in conjunction, as overly simplistic and incapable of explaining what appears to be an extremely diverse pattern of wages and wage development—not only within and between the aggregate private and public sectors, but within and between private and public industries.

There are, to be sure, considerable data which suggest that for certain occupations in the public sector wages are higher than for comparable positions in the private sector,[11] but this neither establishes the political explanation based on emerging public sector bargaining nor disproves the explanation centered around market considerations. That the causal scenario is more complex is indicated by the fact that some public workers were paid as much, if not more, than comparable private employees *before* public sector unionization and bargaining and *before* the strong demand for public services that emerged in the 1960s (see Smith, 1975).

## Service Provision and Delivery

Here we refer to collective bargaining impacts on work rules and procedures (broadly defined), manning schedules, job assignments, and the like. According to some industrial relations theorists (Kuhn, 1968: 284–309), organized workers in the private sector of the American economy are concerned primarily with protecting their "property in work" as reflected in the detailed provisions of collective agreements and the informal working rules of the shop, office, and factory. While this claim may be accurate as a generalization, it covers a wide variety of practices and relationships—ranging from a situation in which bargaining occurs only over wages and fringe benefits to one in which the union plays a major role in production, marketing, and financial decisions.

It has been argued (Wellington and Winter, 1971: 137–153) that workers in the public sector seek to negotiate over a broad range of employment-related issues, and that the impact of bargaining upon governmental management policy and decision-making will be greater than in industry. (For a contrary view, see Gerhart, 1969). Alternatively, however, our diversity thesis suggests major differences among and within local governments in the extent to which unions endeavor to bargain over or "control" so-called management rights. For example, in Chicago's local government, where formal collective bargaining does not exist outside of the educational sector, some public employee unions—the building trades, Teamsters, and Service Employees International Union (SEIU)—to a considerable degree control access to city jobs. None of the labor organizations in cities with more "developed" labor relations systems (for example, New York and Los Angeles) exercises similar control. In New York City, several important unions, including firemen, police, teachers, and municipally employed interns and residents, negotiate over hours of work and job assignments, but other unions limit their concerns to grievance procedures and/or compensation. In Los

Angeles, public employee labor organizations are also differentially concerned with service production and delivery issues; however, in response to the bargaining efforts of these organizations, the city and county governments now are attempting to identify more accurately public managers, devise incentive systems appropriate to their functions, and hold them more closely accountable for the performance of their departments, bureaus, and agencies. Further empirical work is necessary, of course, to fully identify the impacts of collective bargaining on governmental service production and delivery, but preliminary evidence supports the view that these impacts will be diverse rather than singular.

## Personnel Administration

Most students of the governmental labor relations-personnel interface see substantial conflict between the emergence of collective bargaining and traditional civil service (i.e., "merit") rules.[12] We neither see nor predict inherent pervasive conflict between collective bargaining decisions and merit rules, but, rather, diverse impacts on merit administration resulting in some instances in a strengthening and in other instances in a weakening of traditional merit rules.

Our central hypothesis is that labor relations conflict in this area is concerned not with merit rules per se, but with deep-seated divisions between labor and management regarding control over the rules by which employees are selected, promoted, and disciplined (see Lewin and Horton, 1975). Thus, where merit rules are supportive of control over the personnel process, management will assert and unions will attack traditional merit concepts in collective bargaining; but where management's personnel goals are inconsistent with merit rules, the positions of labor and management with respect to the validity or lack thereof of merit rules will be reversed.

This hypothesis appears to rationalize much of the seemingly contradictory discussion of union impacts on personnel administration recorded in the literature. Seniority, for example, clearly is not a merit rule, but it is gradually being implanted in personnel systems where unions possess substantial bargaining power. Many unions that have succeeded with respect to seniority also have succeeded in instituting the rule-of-one, an appointment procedure clearly more consistent with the merit concept than the rule-of-three, management's generally preferred position.

Adding additional validity to this diversity thesis is the fact that public managers and public unions appear to have differing degrees of allegiance to the merit principle.[13] Finally, we suspect that differences in the scope of bargaining and in bargaining power among and within jurisdictions further weaken the notion that collective bargaining and unionism in the public sector will lead to "zero-sum" impacts on merit rules.

## Government Structure

In order to promote and administer the public policy of collective bargaining, most governments have instituted structural as well as legal changes in their institutional make-up. In some instances, existing agencies such as personnel boards have been charged with the responsibility for representing management in collective bargaining, but for the most part new labor relations departments have been created specifically for this purpose. Furthermore, many collective bargaining programs create independent or quasi-independent agencies responsible for administering labor relations and providing third-party assistance in conflict resolution.

In addition to structural additions, accretions of power and responsibility to new agencies from traditional overhead and line agencies are likely to occur when formal collective bargaining programs are instituted in government. Personnel commissions, budget bureaus, line agencies, and even legislative bodies quite often lose authority (sometimes not reluctantly) to new administrative agencies.

The structural impacts of unionism and collective bargaining on government have received relatively little scholarly attention. Most academics (for example, Burton, 1972) who have studied this phenomenon have concluded that the impact of new labor relations programs has tended to centralize previously fragmented personnel decision-making systems.[14]

While fragmentation of managerial structure and authority is, in our opinion, an impediment to the development of effective labor relations in the public sector, for a variety of reasons we are not as sanguine as others about the presumed centralizing effects of new labor relations programs and institutions. First, the formal dispersion of political power, particularly at the local governmental level in American cities, is so well-advanced that political "end-runs" around newly designated labor relations agencies and actors remain possible. Second, and closely related to the above point, one must distinguish between formal and in-

formal power structures. The mere act of creating new labor relations institutions and delegating to them responsibilities to make decisions previously reached elsewhere in government does not mean, in fact, that the locus of control over decision-making also changes. Third, in certain cities where public employees are well-organized and politically strong, formal bargaining programs may result in a redistribution of power from public officials to municipal unions. This may represent a form of centralization, but not of the kind customarily anticipated by academics or public officials.

Again, we return to a more plausible hypothesis than the centralization thesis—namely, that diverse impacts on governmental structure will result from the promulgation of formal collective bargaining systems. In a sense, our focus here shifts from the concerns of industrial relations and economic analysis to those of political science and public administration.

## Politics

One rationale for the introduction of formal collective bargaining programs into government has been to insulate labor relations from the unwholesome reach of "politics," but we are struck with the vigorous and often successful attempts of political actors, particularly mayors, to use emerging labor relations systems for their own political purposes. This has occurred despite the wide differences in politics and public employee labor relations among New York, Los Angeles, and Chicago.[15]

At first glance, it might be assumed that the rapid growth of public employment and public employee organizations virtually dictates that mayors pursue policies of accommodation rather than conflict over not only the introduction of formal bargaining into government but also over bargaining itself. Collective bargaining settlements would appear to be a rich source of "patronage" for mayors seeking wider political constituencies.

Closer examination of the politics of municipal labor relations, however, discloses a number of quite varied mayoral reactions to public employee unionism. In Chicago, where a centralized party apparatus works closely with powerful private sector unions, Mayor Daley has vigorously opposed the formalization of bargaining. He has sustained this position by pursuing a high-wage policy under that city's "prevailing rate" system. In New York, however, where party organizations are fragmented, Mayors Wagner and Lindsay were influential proponents of extending bargaining rights to municipal workers, though not entirely for the same reasons. Both mayors reaped important electoral benefits from civil service unions during critical election campaigns. The Los Angeles situation is more complex, in part because of the chief executive's more diffuse governing responsibilities in that city; but it appears that Mayor Bradley, unlike his predecessor, Samuel Yorty, realizes both the potential managerial problems and political opportunities posed by public employee unionism. Bradley is emerging as a key actor in that city's youthful labor relations program.

## POLICY AND RESEARCH IMPLICATIONS

Public policies designed to regulate state and local government labor relations are in flux. To date, these policies largely have been constructed in the absence of impact analysis—a sequence which violates the policy scientist's admonition that policy-making should reflect, rather than precede, analysis of various policy options and their consequences.

While several policy implications ranging from the macro to the micro level are suggested by the aforementioned diversity thesis and discussion of collective bargaining impacts on government management, only two will briefly be considered here. The first is the issue of comprehensive labor relations. If, as the present analysis indicates, divergent labor relations processes and impacts reflect functional adaptations to the peculiarities of state and local governments, it is questionable whether a comprehensive federal law should be enacted to regulate labor relations at the state and local level. Instead, federal legislation based on the "minimum standards" concept may be preferable either to extending the National Labor Relations Act to the public sector or to instituting a "model" public sector labor relations law.[16]

A second important policy issue germane to this paper concerns public employee strikes. For various reasons, we are skeptical about the dominant (though not exclusive) view that favors blanket no-strike laws in the public sector. Once again, recognition of clearly disparate political and bargaining relationships within and among governments argues for a more sophisticated approach to the admittedly serious problem of public sector strikes than simply (and often unsuccessfully) prohibiting them. Similar difficulties are raised by the use of compulsory arbitration as a substitute for public sector strikes. The rationale for a no-strike/

arbitration law may be far stronger in one jurisdiction than another, and applicable only to some, not all, employee groups within a single jurisdiction.

With respect to research implications of the present study, perhaps the key point is that collective bargaining impacts on governmental management must be examined longitudinally, if they are to be understood and properly evaluated. This is particularly true in those impact areas which are at best only partially amenable to quantitative analysis—for example, service production and delivery, personnel administration, and government structure. This is not to gainsay the importance of cross-sectional studies or survey data in the examination of public sector labor relations; indeed, these methodologies dominate the current literature on this subject. Rather, it is to emphasize the special value of the longitudinal method in analyzing the dynamics of a public sector labor relations system.

Finally, the diversity thesis and the accumulating evidence regarding public sector labor relations, especially the impacts of collective bargaining on governmental management, could well be used as a basis for reexamining labor relations in (and public policies governing) the private sector of the American economy. Much of what we presume to know about the latter sector has taken on connotations of the conventional wisdom and rests, in part, on old evidence. The aforementioned reexamination not only would challenge this conventional wisdom, it also would represent a "revised sequence" of research in this field—i.e., using the accumulating knowledge about *public sector labor relations* to better understand those in industry.

## NOTES

1. This paper is based on an as yet uncompleted study of public sector labor relations in New York City, Chicago, and Los Angeles which is being supported by the Ford Foundation and U.S. Department of Labor and conducted under the auspices of the Conservation of Human Resources Project, Columbia University. The larger study relies on a variety of research methodologies and data sources to analyze the diversity-of-impacts thesis outlined in the paper. The central empirical concern, the impact of labor relations decisions on the five areas described in this paper, is being analyzed longitudinally through data collected in on-site research and cross-sectionally through a survey of 2,200 American cities. The survey questionnaire is designed by the authors and administered by the International City Management Association.

2. Unless otherwise indicated, all data presented in this section were obtained from U. S. Department of Commerce, Bureau of the Census (1961 and 1974).

3. For corrections, the change reported is for the 1961–1973 period; 1960 data for this function were not available.

4. Previous estimates had placed state and local membership at only about 33%. See Steiber (1973) and U. S. Department of Labor (1971).

5. Assumption of major differences between the public and private sectors leads to another familiar theme: prediction of dire outcomes resulting from collective bargaining in government. For a critique of these assumptions and additional insights into the approach followed in the present study, see Lewin (1973).

6. Wellington and Winter (1971) feel that the existence of such monopoly requires the imposition of restrictions on the bargaining activities of organized public employees.

7. A framework for analyzing these impacts is provided in Lewin and Horton (1975).

8. The development of collective bargaining in New York City government is reviewed in Horton (1973 and 1971). Chicago has received little analysis in terms of its municipal labor relations system, but see Derber (1968) and Jones (1972). The Los Angeles experience is analyzed in Lewin (1976).

9. For a general critique of the literature of public sector labor relations, see Lewin (1973).

10. It should be kept in mind, despite the heavy attention paid to the impact of collective bargaining on wages in both sectors, that wages of a substantial majority of private workers (75%) and more than half of public workers are not established by collective bargaining.

11. Publications of the regional offices of the Bureau of Labor Statistics comparing salaries and benefits of municipal workers with those of private sector counterparts show that in most metropolitan areas public workers are better compensated. These comparative surveys, unfortunately, were not begun until 1970.

12. For a thorough review of the literature, see U. S. Department of Labor, Labor Management Services Administration (1972). See also Morse (1973) and Stanley with Cooper (1971: 32–59).

13. For instance, the Lindsay administration in New York City for eight years attempted through a variety of administrative initiatives to circumvent certain strictures of the "civil service" system. One of Mayor Beame's first formal acts upon succeeding Lindsay in 1974 was to issue an executive order replacing the rule-of-three with the rule-of-one. Civil service unions also display divergent attitudes toward merit

rules. Unions based on departmental rather than citywide units often favor closed rather than open promotional exams.

14. For a different viewpoint emphasizing the fragmentation theme, see Kochan (1971), Horton (1973), and Lewin (1976).

15. New York City represents a "mature" system—that is, one in which the institutional and legal structures surrounding formal collective bargaining are well-entrenched (see Horton, 1975). Los Angeles, including both the City and County, may be characterized as a "transitional" system moving from an informal to a formal labor relations system (see Lewin, 1976). Chicago's public sector labor relations system for the most part remains underdeveloped. For a description of the Chicago system, see Jones (1972: 195–226).

16. A discussion of the minimum standards concept and various types of federal labor legislation for public employees is contained in Bureau of National Affairs (1974: B12-19 and F1-9).

# REFERENCES

Bureau of National Affairs (1974) Government Employees Relations Report 575 (October).

Burton, J. F., Jr. (1972) "Local government bargaining and management structure." Industrial Relations 11 (May): 133–139.

Derber, M. R. (1968) "Labor-management policy for public employees in Illinois: the experience of the Governor's Commission, 1966–67." Industrial & Labor Relations Rev. 21 (July): 541–558.

Ehrenberg, R. G. (1973) "The demand for state and local government employees." Amer. Econ. Rev. 3 (June): 366–379.

Fogel, W. and D. Lewin (1974) "Wage determination in the public sector." Industrial & Labor Relations Rev. 27 (April): 410–431.

Gerhart, P. F. (1969) "Scope of bargaining in local government labor negotiations." Labor Law J. 20 (August): 545–553.

Goldberg, J. P. (1972) "Public employee developments in 1971." Monthly Labor Rev. 95 (January): 56.

Hayes, F. O. (1972) "Collective bargaining and the budget director," pp. 89–100 in S. Zagoria (ed.) Public Workers and Public Unions. Englewood Cliffs, N. Y.: Prentice-Hall.

Horton, R. D. (1975) "Reforming the municipal labor relations process in New York City." Study prepared for the State Charter Revision Commission for New York City (January).

Horton, R. D. (1974) "Public employee labor relations under the Taylor Law," pp. 172–174 in R. H. Connery and G. Benjamin (eds.) Governing New York State: The Rockefeller Years. New York: Academy of Political Science.

Horton, R. D. (1973) Municipal Labor Relations in New York City: Lessons of the Lindsay-Wagner Years. New York: Praeger.

Horton, R. D. (1971) "Municipal labor relations: the New York City experience." Social Sci. Q. 52 (December): 680–696.

Joint Economic Committee, Council of Economic Advisers (1974) Economic Indicators, February 1975. Washington, D. C.: Government Printing Office.

Jones, R. T. (1972) "City employee unions in New York and Chicago." Ph.D. dissertation, Harvard University.

Kochan, T. A. (1971) City Employee Bargaining with a Divided Management. Madison: University of Wisconsin, Industrial Relations Institute.

Kuhn, J. W. (1972) "The riddle of inflation: a new answer." Public Interest 27 (Spring): 63–77.

Kuhn, J. W. (1968) "Business unionism in a laboristic society," pp. 284–309 in I. Berg (ed.) The Business of America. New York: Harcourt, Brace & World.

Labor Management Relations Service (1975) Labor Management Relations Service Newsletter, Vol. 6, No. 3. Washington, D. C.: Labor Management Relations Service.

Lewin, D. (1976) "Local government labor relations in transition: the case of Los Angeles." Labor History 16.

Lewin, D. (1974) "Aspects of wage determination in local government employment." Public Administration Rev. 34 (March–April): 149–155.

Lewin, D. (1973) "Public employment relations: confronting the issues." Industrial Relations 12 (October): 309–321.

Lewin, D. and R. D. Horton (1975) "Evaluating the impacts of collective bargaining on personnel administration in government." Arbitration J. 30 (September): 199–211.

Morse, M. M. (1973) "Should we bargain away the merit principle?" Public Personnel Rev. (October): 233–243.

Perloff, S. H. (1971) "Comparing municipal salaries with industry and federal pay." Monthly Labor Rev. 94 (October): 46–50.

Smith, S. P. (1975) "Wage differentials between federal government and private sector workers." (unpublished manuscript)

Stanley, D. T. with the assistance of C. L. Cooper (1971) Managing Local Government Under Union Pressure. Washington, D. C.: Brookings.

Steiber, J. (1973) Public Employee Unionism: Structure, Growth, Policy; Studies of Unionism in Government. Washington, D. C.: Brookings.

Taylor, B. J. and F. Witney (1975) Labor Relations Law (second ed.). Englewood Cliffs, N. J.: Prentice-Hall.

U. S. Department of Commerce, Bureau of the Census (1974) Public Employment in 1973. Washington, D. C.: Government Printing Office.

U. S. Department of Commerce (1961) State Distribution of Public Employment in 1960. Washington, D. C.: Government Printing Office.

U. S. Department of Labor (1973) Summary of State Policy Regulations for Public Sector Labor Relations: Statutes, Attorney Generals' Opinions and Selected Court Decisions. Washington, D. C.: Government Printing Office.

U. S. Department of Labor (1972) Directory of National Unions and Employee Associations. Washington, D. C.: Government Printing Office.

U. S. Department of Labor, Bureau of Labor Statistics (1971) "Labor union and employee association membership." News Release (September 13).

U. S. Department of Labor, Labor Management Services Administration (1972) Collective Bargaining and the Merit System. Washington, D. C.: Government Printing Office.

Wellington, H. H. and R. K. Winter, Jr. (1971) The Unions and the Cities, Studies of Unionism in Government. Washington, D. C.: Brookings.

# The Hidden Costs of Collective Bargaining in Local Government

Anthony H. Pascal

The spread of collective bargaining among employees of local government carries profound implications for the cost and quality of public services. A large fraction of all municipal, county, and school district employees work under negotiated agreements which materially raise the levels of municipal budgets and which significantly alter the nature of services provided to the public.[1]

Reprinted with permission of the author from Taxing Spending, Vol. 2, (Spring, 1980). © 1980 by the Institute for Contemporary Studies.

**TABLE 1**
**Work stoppages in state/local government and the remainder of the economy, 1946–1971**

| | State/Local Government | | | Remainder of Economy | | |
|---|---|---|---|---|---|---|
| | FTE Employees | Person-days idle | | FTE Employees | Person-days idle | |
| | | Number | Per 1000 | | Number | Per 1000 |
| | (000) | (000) | FTE Employees | (000) | (000) | FTE Employees |
| 1946–50 | 3393 | 22 | 6.7 | 44592 | 54778 | 1228.4 |
| 1951–55 | 4115 | 27 | 6.6 | 50163 | 32193 | 630.5 |
| 1956–60 | 5096 | 19 | 3.5 | 51059 | 32301 | 632.6 |
| 1961–65 | 6244 | 59 | 9.0 | 53402 | 19381 | 362.9 |
| 1968 | 7850 | 2536 | 323.0 | 61982 | 46482 | 749.9 |
| 1971 | 8832 | 893 | 101.0 | 62316 | 46696 | 749.3 |

Source: Burton and Krider, 1975

The fiscal limitation epidemic[2], which by now has struck in half of all states in the United States, may well engender more organizing and tougher bargaining as public sector unions seek to protect their turfs; and on top of that, increased militancy and diminished morale threaten to further reduce the productivity of public employees. Thus, the local government official may find himself or herself working with a smaller budget *and* a less manageable work force in trying to meet the public demand for services. Local fiscal controls also tend to exert a centralizing pressure as state governments step in to bail out local jurisdictions. As bargaining and lobbying action by public sector unions shifts from city hall to the state house, strikes by public employees may become more extensive.

How can today's public manager respond to these trends? What can taxpayers and voters do? At the conclusion of this article, some possibilities are explored.

The pace of organization among employees of local governments in the United States has accelerated in recent years: One serious effect of that—and a very visual one—is the dramatic increase in work stoppages. Table 1 indicates that at the local and state level from 1946 to 1971. Over this time span person-days of idleness due to stoppages increased by a factor of 40 for state and local employees while the figure actually fell for other workers.

These figures are particularly distressing considering the high levels of organization which have been attained in the state and local public sector. As Table 2 demonstrates, about half of state and local governments' full time employees were organized by 1974. For various functions of local government the fractions ranged considerably higher, with two-thirds of teachers

and three-quarters of fire fighters in employee organizations. (Generally the larger the jurisdiction, the higher the percentage of organized employees.) By contrast, fewer than one-quarter of private sector employees belonged to unions in the same year, although over 40 percent of manufacturing workers did. In nonmanufacturing industries, which perhaps come closest in terms of internal structure to the public service, only about 16 percent were union members. (Transportation workers were the most unionized.)

Of course, membership in an organization is not the same as involvement in collective negotiations; but of 3.7 million organized local employees, three-quarters worked under negotiated contractual agreements by 1976. Between October 1974 and October 1976 the number of local employees who were represented by bargaining units rose by 18 percent, to over 4,350,000. But the attempt to secure gains for employees extends well beyond compensation. Of the 350 local government work stoppages in 1975–76 about a quarter concerned issues other than wages, fringes and hours. Strikes ensued over job security, supervision, assignments, and other non-compensation items.[3]

Why has public sector unionism grown so rapidly in recent years and why has it become increasingly militant? Changes in the legal environment have obviously had some influence, but other factors may also be at play. Chickering concludes that the unions have taken the place of formal and informal government, i.e., political machines, which formerly preserved a "fragile order" among a diverse and fragmented urban population.[4] In a period marked by decline in the power of the urban machine and decrease in public confidence in government, the unions become, for their members,

**TABLE 2**
**Organization of employees in the private and state/local public sectors, 1974**

| Type and function of government | No. of full time employees (000) | Percent in organizations |
|---|---|---|
| *State/local government* | | |
| State and local | 9177 | 51.5 |
| State | 2470 | 39.3 |
| Local | 6707 | 56.0 |
| Education | 3640 | 67.0 |
| Welfare | 169 | 34.0 |
| Hospitals | 432 | 31.6 |
| Police | 448 | 56.1 |
| Fire | 204 | 74.4 |
| All Others | 1814 | 38.6 |

| Industry | No. on payroll (000) | Percent in unions |
|---|---|---|
| *Private Sector* | | |
| All | 78413 | 23.4 |
| Manufacturing | 20046 | 44.5 |
| Nonmanufacturing | 58367 | 16.2 |
| Transportation & public utilities | 4696 | 61.7 |
| Wholesale & retail trade | 17017 | 7.5 |
| Financial, insurance & real estate | 4208 | 0.8 |
| All others | 32446 | 13.4 |

State/Local: *Labor-Management Relations in State and Local Government*, 1977.
Private: *Handbook of Labor Statistics*, 1977.

a substitute repository of social trust and serve as mechanisms for participation and expression of public spiritedness. Unionism may also serve as a refuge for civil servants who are no longer highly esteemed by the public.

## PUBLIC VS. PRIVATE SECTOR

Certain considerations lead to the expectation that public sector contracts will generally be stronger than those in the private sector. First, public managers are not so consistently subject to periodic financial accountability as are those in private firms. In addition, the ultimate decisionmakers in government are elected officials, many of whom are dependent on public employees for votes and campaign assistance. Also, the ideology of managers in government may predispose them to rank "fairness" high relative to productivity when reacting to the demands of their employees.

Then, government agencies often supply services for which there are no ready substitutes, meaning that work stoppages are more discomforting to the public—and more threatening to politicians. Finally, many organized employees of local government feel themselves to be professionals and will therefore strive more vigorously for autonomy in their working lives.[5]

These characteristics of public sector contracts all translate into higher costs for government, and they affect the nature, costs and quality of services received by the public.[6]

## GAINS ACHIEVED BY ORGANIZED PUBLIC EMPLOYEES

Several studies have explored the effects of unionization and collective bargaining on the compensation received by local government employees. Victor concluded that teachers' unions succeed in raising salaries from 5 to 20 percent.[7] Schmenner finds that unionization is associated with positive salary differentials of about 15 percent for police and firefighters.[8] It has been ascertained that unions increase the share of the municipal budget which goes toward the labor costs.[9]

A recent study conducted at Rand for the National Institute of Education traced the extension of collective bargaining by public school teachers in a sample of 151 school districts.[10] These were the findings: Bargaining in education generally spread from large, highly urbanized districts in the Northeast and Midwest to surrounding suburban and rural districts and to the West and the South; over time, teacher contracts became stronger in provisions governing noncompensation items; the legal environment in a particular state—statutes and case law which regulate public sector bargaining—had a significant effect on the strength and scope of contracts; and interunion rivalry also appeared to lead to stronger contracts, as did a large membership. Gains in compensation and successes in the non-compensation areas were not traded as freely as had been hypothesized. Local factors—history, political climate, the use of lobbying and electoral action—played a major role in determining contract outcomes.

Even as regards the budgetary implications of collective bargaining in the public sector the existing literature largely fails to address two issues: One, negotiated additions to fringe benefit packages—pensions, vacations, insurance, etc.—are usually not costed out in empirical estimates of the union effect (largely as a result, I am sure, of the sparseness of data), and two, costs generated through provisions which cover entry requirements, assignment and promotion rules, case loads, "contact" hours, paraprofessionals, reduction-in-force, and professional development are almost never taken into account.

Given the absence of systematic research in these two areas, no accurate assessment of the relative costs of salary improvements and the sum of these other budgetary effects is available. For workers in non-manufacturing industries fringe benefits (leave time, retirement, health and unemployment benefits) ac-counted for about 20 percent of total compensation in 1972.[11] I know of no studies which have undertaken the detailed cost analysis of a large sample of contracts which would be necessary to calculate the impacts of working condition, job security and professional pro-visions on public budgets. My intuition, based on ar-guments advanced below, tells me that non-salary costs would loom large.

Our research on collective bargaining by school teachers produced the results shown on the accom-panying Figure I. The provisions listed there were chosen with the help of professional teacher contract

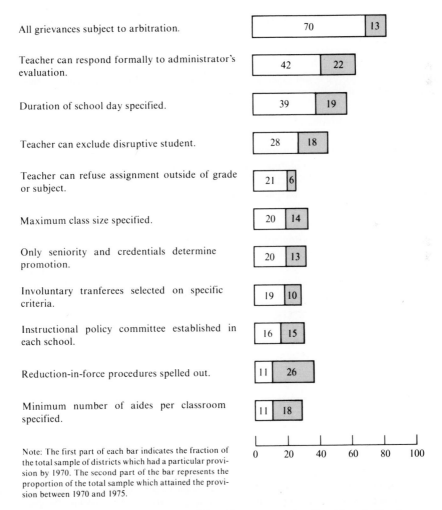

| Provision | | |
|---|---|---|
| All grievances subject to arbitration. | 70 | 13 |
| Teacher can respond formally to administrator's evaluation. | 42 | 22 |
| Duration of school day specified. | 39 | 19 |
| Teacher can exclude disruptive student. | 28 | 18 |
| Teacher can refuse assignment outside of grade or subject. | 21 | 6 |
| Maximum class size specified. | 20 | 14 |
| Only seniority and credentials determine promotion. | 20 | 13 |
| Involuntary tranferees selected on specific criteria. | 19 | 10 |
| Instructional policy committee established in each school. | 16 | 15 |
| Reduction-in-force procedures spelled out. | 11 | 26 |
| Minimum number of aides per classroom specified. | 11 | 18 |

0   20   40   60   80   100

Note: The first part of each bar indicates the fraction of the total sample of districts which had a particular provi-sion by 1970. The second part of the bar represents the proportion of the total sample which attained the provi-sion between 1970 and 1975.

**Figure 1**   Trends in Attainment of Key Noncompensation Provisions in Teacher Collective Bargaining Agreements, 1970 and 1975

negotiations to represent key items in each of the non-compensation areas. In the contracts we analyzed, the appearance of the key provision was correlated with the appearance of other, supporting items in the same bargaining area.

In examining the trends portrayed, one perceives that after grievance procedures (the necessary enforcement mechanism for the contract) successful bargaining seems to proceed from working conditions (length and composition of day, disruptive students, assignment refusal, class size) to job security (promotion, transfer and force reduction rules). On professional autonomy issues (teacher evaluation, instruction policy committees) no clear priority is apparent.

Where teachers go, police officers, social workers, nurses and firefighters will soon follow. Teachers were among the first to engage in collective bargaining and our research on them convinces me that as bargaining relations mature, contracts become wider in scope and stronger. Moreover, workers in health, protection, and social services also view themselves as professionals—with standards to protect and independence to maintain. These groups will learn from what teachers have accomplished. Organized teachers have lobbied for changes in the state education code, changes which often supplement victories at the bargaining table, and for broadening of statutes which govern bargaining in the public sector. Broad statutes result fairly inevitably in strong contracts, especially in the non-compensation area. What emerges at the bargaining table will, as in the case of teachers, affect the pocketbooks of taxpayers and the welfare of clients.

## BARGAINING ON NON-COMPENSATION ITEMS

Consider what might be attained, or has indeed already been won, in fields aside from compensation:

### Regulation of Hours

Public workers, like their private counterparts, bargain over the length of the work day, as well as the work year. And contracts may further reduce the period during which service providers are available to clients. The part of the working day set aside for ancillary duties (recordkeeping for nurses and social workers, lesson preparation for teachers) may reduce accessibility for clients or may result in additional hires to maintain a given degree of client contact.[12] And teachers

often receive bonus pay for extracurricular duties in school hallways or playgrounds. Will the police soon demand supplements for courtroom appearances and social workers for visits to the housing office?

### Case Load Ceilings

Just as teachers bargain over class size, nurses could negotiate over patient load, and police, over the extent of the beat. Though some ceiling generally accords with the preferences of the user of a given service, their establishment does increase costs to the taxpayer.

### Arrangements for Paraprofessionals

Study of bargaining by teachers reveals two tendencies —the demand for guaranteed numbers of aides and restrictions on the duties they may perform. Both of these tendencies increase costs by simultaneously expanding workforce and reducing flexibility across skill levels. The addition of paraprofessionals to agency staffs may also affect the quality of services rendered to the public.

### Assignment and Transfer Provisions

Assignment of a teacher to a new grade level, subject, or school site is often constrained by a contract. Credentials and seniority, rather than management judgment, then determine who teaches what and where. Police and firefighter unions have attempted to regulate transfers among precincts through their contracts. It seems that unionized local employees will increasingly demand a say in assignments to jobs and functions. Again, flexibility is reduced, with obvious implications for costs—and clients living in undesirable areas or with disagreeable problems may find themselves being served by inexperienced personnel.

### Standards for Entry, Promotion, and Reductions-in-Force

Through bargaining and influencing stipulations in the state education code, the standards for entry into the profession have been affected. Other local government professionals will, again, learn from the teachers. Such union-imposed barriers to entry will raise wages and simultaneously alter the characteristics of the eventual labor force.

While examining teacher contracts, we often found provisions which restricted promotions to the candidate with the proper credentials and the most seniority. Such rules limit management latitude. They may also, over time, change the nature of management itself as promotees filter upward. Consequences for service quality, although hard to predict, are probably significant.

Union contracts often specify that reductions-in-force (RIF) will be first visited upon the least senior employees. Prior to the establishment of bargaining, jurisdictions found it possible, during contraction, to retain lower paid employees and to terminate senior staff, at least where civil service regulations did not prevent it. The cost and staff quality implications of RIF rules are clear.

### Professional Development Provisions

Increasingly, local contracts require the employer to encourage the professional development of employees —through outside courses and the like—by arrangements for released time and by granting automatic salary increases for increments of additional education. Both types of benefits add to costs and may also affect the quality of the workforce.

## CONCLUSIONS

Unionism changes the employment level and the skill mix of the typical agency, for better or worse, and may alter the geographical distribution of a service. In some cases organization reduces accessibility of service providers to clients and the accountability of local employees to the public. Contract-induced restrictions constrain the decisionmaking latitude of managers in local governments, which may slow adaptation to changing circumstances.

What can the responsible local official do in an era characterized by both fiscal retrenchment and continuing union militancy? As the tax revolt rages and the tax base erodes, it will become increasingly necessary to uncover the hidden costs of bargaining. Some of the hidden costs show up in the local budget; others are felt in reduced quality of services.

Costs rise when contracts specify staffing of ancillary employees, such as paraprofessionals. Reducing individual caseloads means more employees. Granting sick leave and released time for staff development also pushes total employment up.

Overall service quality can fall when the most senior employees are allowed to pick their own assignments. "Safety" provisions may allow civil servants to refuse service to clients they find disagreeable. Rigid adher-

ence to detailed job descriptions may produce too fine a division of labor and result in incoherent service to clients.

The implications for such hidden costs must be evaluated before negotiations begin. Knowledge of full costs should lead to tougher bargaining on the management side. One device is to incorporate in the contract incentives for increased employee productivity.

But there are also devices which lie outside of collective bargaining. The contracting out of a service to the lowest bidder among private firms is becoming increasingly prevalent. Contracting may extend to the entire service, such as trash collection, or be limited to a particular input such as the maintenance of the auto fleet or the trimming of trees in parks. Some local governments have opted for privatization—abandoning a particular service in expectation that the private sector will offer a substitute (for a fee, of course). This happened with summertime schooling in California after Proposition 13 passed.

The citizenry will have to adopt a more active role in collective bargaining if it wants lower tax bills or continuation of current service quality. In our research on teacher organizations[13] we found that the ostensible advocates of the citizen interest—the members of the Board of Education—are less and less involved in the process of bargaining. Affairs are left to professional administrators who may cave in on costly provisions in the interest of harmony and smooth working relations. Some states have instituted full disclosure "sunshine" laws which inform the public on negotiations with government employees. Others have gone so far as to admit public observers to bargaining sessions. A few writers are even beginning to argue that full-scale, tripartite negotiations are the only solution.

It seems to me that the time has come to open the closet door and examine hidden costs; the process is bound to be illuminating to officials and, perhaps, liberating for taxpayers.

## NOTES

1. Past research has concentrated on the wage effects of public unionism. The costs of provisions governing fringe benefits have received much less attention. Studies of the costs of working condition and job security provisions and the consequences for the nature of the public product have been virtually ignored.

2. A. H. Pascal, et al., *Fiscal Contraction of Local and State Government,* R-2494-FF/RC, The Rand Corporation, September 1979.

3. U. S. Bureau of the Census, *Labor Management Relations in State and Local Government,* USGPO, Washington, D. C., 1974, 1976.

4. A. L. Chickering, *Public Employee Unions* (San Francisco: Institute for Contemporary Studies, 1976.)

5. H. H. Wellington and R. K. Winter, *The Union and Cities—Studies of Unionism in Government* (Washington, D. C.: The Brookings Institution, 1971). L. C. Shaw and R. T. Clark, Jr., "The Practical Differences Between Public and Private Bargaining," *UCLA Law Review,* 19, 1972. J. Steiber, *Public Employee Unions* (Washington, D. C.: The Brookings Institution, 1973.) D. S. Hamermesh, ed., *Labor Relations in the Public and Non-Profit Sectors,* (Princeton: Princeton University Press, 1975). A. L. Chickering, op. cit. R. D. Horton, D. Lewin, and J. W. Kuhn, "Some Impacts of Collective Bargaining on Local Government," *Administration and Society,* February 1976. A. H. Hopkins, G. E. Rawson, and R. L. South, "Public Employee Unionization in the States: A Comparative Analysis," *Administration and Society,* November 1976.

6. H. Kasper, "On the Effect of Collective Bargaining on Resource Allocation in Public Schools," *Economic and Business Bulletin,* Temple University, Spring–Summer 1971.

7. R. B. Victor, *The Economic Effects of Teacher Unions: An Appraisal,* WN-10045-HEW, The Rand Corporation, January 1978.

8. R. W. Schmenner, "The Determination of Municipal Employee Wages," *Review of Economics and Statistics,* February 1973.

9. J. Batterschneider, "The Impact of Collective Bargaining Laws Covering Police and Firefighters on Municipal Budgeting," (unpublished Cornell University Ph.D. dissertation, 1979).

10. L. McDonnell and A. H. Pascal, *Organized Teachers in American Schools,* R-2407-NIE, The Rand Corporation, February 1979.

11. I could find no data on aggregate fringe benefits restricted to either unionized or public sector workers, let alone to the overlap in these two categories. Chaiken and Walker in *Growth in Municipal Expenditures: A Case Study of Los Angeles,* The Rand Corporation, WD-175-RC, May 1979, show that, in 1978, fringe benefits to municipal workers in the city of Los Angeles averaged about 40 percent of salaries, depending on function. Bahl and Jump in "The Budgetary Implications of Rising Employee Retirement Systems Costs," *National Tax Journal,* September 1974, report that in the years 1962–72 negotiated pension benefits rose more than 50 percent faster than negotiated wage rates in the state and local government sector.

12. R. B. Victor, *The Effects of Unionism on the Wage and Employment Levels of Police and Firefighter,* P-5924, The Rand Corporation, August 1977. R. Ehrenberg, "Municipal Government Structures, Unionization and the Wages of Firefighters," *Industrial Labor Relations Review,* October 1973.

13. L. McDonnell and A. H. Pascal, *Organized Teachers in American Schools,* R-2407-NIE, The Rand Corporation, February 1979.

# PART FIVE

# PERFORMANCE

# AND

# PUBLIC ADMINISTRATION

Thus far, the watchword of the 1980s has been productivity. Productivity is a concern that knows no sector boundaries: The private sector has productivity problems of its own. The rate of productivity growth in the United States has been steadily falling since the mid-1960s. Problems of productivity and competitiveness crop up all across the board. As a result of a failure to retool and revitalize plants, many steel companies are in danger. An inability to compete with low-wage foreign labor has virtually demolished the shoe industry. A recent news report tells us that even the U. S. General Services Administration is purchasing thousands of Japanese typewriters because they are less expensive and just as durable as those provided by domestic manufacturers.

While productivity is much on the minds of public managers, political executives, and legislators, no one labors under the illusion that the productivity of public programs is easily measured. As Rosenberg and Straussman ("Maximization, Markets, and the Measurement of Productivity in the Public Sector") show, the nonmarket character of most public sector activities poses some problems.

*Program evaluation* is a term most often used in connection with evaluation research designs that approximate experimental method (though real world program evaluation often only faintly resembles experiments). Built on the belief that public administrators need to know if their programs are producing results, evaluation has been used by managers at all levels of government for several years. This should not be interpreted to mean that program evaluation is a sophisticated science. On the contrary, it is more ac-

curately described as an art. Besides, some government programs are inherently difficult to measure; many escape the methodological grasp of the evaluator; and some successfully avoid scrutiny because of reasons that have nothing to do with the ease or difficulty of subjecting them to the evaluator's wizardry. After all, evaluation takes place in the environment of bureaucratic politics.

Still, evaluation work has proceeded apace in government. Pressures for improved accountability and efforts to streamline a bloated public sector make it reasonable to expect program evaluation to survive and perhaps even prosper in the future. While "Shoot the evaluator!" may be a cry of the managers of tomorrow, it is unlikely to be successful. With the realization that fiscal austerity is a permanent condition of government comes the additional recognition that some programs must be terminated. And how could termination decisions be better informed? Evaluation to the rescue! It would be naive to assume that a concern for improved performance would eliminate irrational criteria (such as politics, for example); nevertheless, the hard choices that will have to be made by tomorrow's public managers could only be enhanced through the application of new knowledge. Is this not the ultimate purpose of Public Administration, after all?

The selection by Anderson and Ball ("Evaluation Purposes") provides a useful overview of reasons why public managers perform evaluations. In "Processing Citizens' Disputes Outside the Courts," Connor and Surette describe an actual evaluation.

The final section deals more systematically with a

topic that has cropped up throughout this book: Organizational decline and termination of programs. David Whetten ("Organizational Decline") synthesizes recent work on this topic. In "More on Cutback Management," Charles Levine not only demonstrates that cutback management is something quite different from routine or growth management, but also reviews some of the strategies and paradoxes that arise as public managers seek to cope with decline.

There is no need to end this book on a pessimistic note, however. Perhaps the "newest of the new" in Public Administration is revitalization management. The recent upturn in the economy may prove short lived; moreover, there is little reason except that a growing economy will (or even should) lead quickly to an expanded public sector. But there is some reason to hope that the next new direction in public administration will be organization resurgence and revitalization management.

# CHAPTER ELEVEN

# Productivity

## The Value of Measuring and Improving Performance

Paul D. Epstein

Efforts to measure and improve local government performance are not free. Officials must invest their own time and the time of their staffs. Their investment also may include the cost of additional staff, special training, consultants, capital equipment, or increased energy use. Unfortunately, the value of a measurement and improvement effort is usually less clear-cut than its costs. It is often difficult or misleading to put a dollar value on an improvement, which can still be extremely valuable to the community. Four types of measurable improvement value are the value of improving decision making; the value of improving service effectiveness; the value of improving service efficiency; and the organizational value of measurement and improvement efforts.

### THE ECONOMIST VS. THE ENGINEER

Since this article is about *value*, productivity in its strict economic sense is a useful idea to consider. In economic terms, productivity is the ratio between the value of a final product or service and the cost of the

resources used to produce it. However, many economists say public sector productivity cannot be measured. Economists have a problem with public sector productivity because they insist on putting a dollar value on the output and the input so they can compare and combine the productivity of producing apples and oranges. That's all right in the private sector, where the marketplace establishes those values. In the public sector, however, there's no market mechanism to determine the value of the output of government agencies.

Engineers, on the other hand, examine government services and often define their productivity in terms of efficiency. For each service, they try to define specific service units for the output side of their productivity, or efficiency, ratios. Engineers do not try to put a dollar value on the output of government agencies. However, they do try to improve the productivity (efficiency) of individual services, knowing they can either save money by providing the same amount of services at a lower cost, or give the community more services for the same cost. A dollar value can often be calculated for improving service efficiency. This "efficiency value" represents the differences in cost between more efficient and less efficient service delivery methods. This calculation can be useful, but it can also be misleading because it will change depending on the "quantity of service" used in the calculation. The greater the quantity of service provided using the more efficient methods, the higher the "efficiency value" calculated, even if money is wasted by providing more services than a community actually needs or can afford. The calculation of "effficiency values" and their associated problems are demonstrated in the following example, "The Asphalt Paradox."

## THE ASPHALT PARADOX

Like many other jurisdictions, City X was caught in a tight fiscal squeeze. The budget director called on all departments to make existing resources go as far as possible. One of City X's larger public expenditures each year went for resurfacing its streets and highways, which the city did with its own work force. The city government did not want to cut this program because poor street conditions were one of the biggest sources of citizen complaints. An industrial engineer was assigned to the resurfacing program to see if it could be made more efficient.

The engineer's analysis indicated that the program had an operating efficiency of $17,500 per lane-mile resurfaced; this unit cost was based on $10,000 labor cost per lane-mile plus $7,500 asphalt cost per lane-mile. Furthermore, at the current rate of productivity per labor hour, City X's resurfacing crews would be able to resurface seventy-five lane-miles in a year.

After carefully charting out the entire resurfacing process, work sampling the resurfacing crews in action, and analyzing the results, the engineer determined it was possible, in a relatively short time, to reschedule the delivery of asphalt, vary the size of resurfacing crews, and improve work methods. The engineer concluded such changes would increase the productivity of the resurfacing labor force by thirty-three percent in the first year alone. In other words, the existing resurfacing work force would be able to resurface 100 lane-miles in a year; the unit cost of labor would be reduced to $7,500 labor cost per lane-mile; and the program's operating efficiency would improve considerably, as the total unit cost would be reduced by $2,500. The new unit cost would be $15,000 per lane-mile resurfaced, based on $7,500 labor cost per lane-mile plus $7,500 asphalt cost per lane-mile.

In seeking approval to implement the proposed improvements, the engineer told the budget director the improvements would have an annual "efficiency value" of $250,000 to the city, based on the benefit realized by resurfacing 100 lane-miles at reduced unit cost, that is,

Benefit = Reduction in cost per lane mile ×
number of lane-miles resurfaced
Benefit = $2,500 × 100 = $250,000 "efficiency value"

Convinced by this argument, the budget director supported the engineer's recommendations to the mayor, who approved them. The mayor was pleased that they might get 100 lane-miles resurfaced by the same crews that resurfaced only seventy-five lane-miles the year before.

The operations improvements were implemented quickly and smoothly. Labor productivity increased as predicted, resulting in the projected $2,500 reduction in unit cost. By the end of the fiscal year the resurfacing work force, without adding any staff, had resurfaced 100 lane-miles of streets and highways.

At the end of the year, however, the budget director was angry at the engineer. In fact, he was livid. He had expected a $250,000 benefit. But when all the bills were added up, he decided the "improved" program had actually *cost* the city budget $187,500. Here is how it happened. Under the "original" program of resurfacing seventy-five lane-miles at a higher unit cost, the total costs would have been:

Labor: $10,000 per lane-mile × 75 lane miles = $750,000
Asphalt: $7,500 per lane-mile × 75 lane miles = $562,500
Total cost $1,312,500

Under the "improved" program of resurfacing 100 lane-miles at the lower cost, the actual total costs were:

Labor: $7,500 per lane-mile × 100 lane miles = $750,000
Asphalt: $7,500 per lane-mile × 100 lane miles = $750,000
Total cost $1,500,000

The result was a *net increase* in city expenditures of $187,500 (that is, $1,500,000 − $1,312,500 = $187,500). Was the engineer correct, who calculated a "benefit" of $250,000? Or was the budget director correct, who calculated an added cost of $187,500?

They were both right. If City X really wanted to have the additional twenty-five lane-miles resurfaced, then the program did save them $250,000 over what it would have cost to resurface 100 lane-miles using the old methods. This type of benefit is often referred to as "cost avoidance." However, the figures clearly add up to $187,500 more than City X had originally budgeted to resurface seventy-five lane miles. If City X were really in a fiscal squeeze, wouldn't it be poor management to spend $187,500 more than planned on the resurfacing program, even if it was being run more efficiently?

From yet another point of view, however, both the engineer and the budget director were wrong, because they did not take the extra step before implementation to determine how to take their benefits from improved efficiency. By reducing costs? By increasing services delivered? By doing some of both? If, in achieving the $15,000 per lane-mile unit cost, City X had reduced its resurfacing work force by twenty-five percent, it would have maintained its seventy-five lane-mile service level and cut its budget by $187,500, as follows:

Labor: $7,500 per lane-mile × 75 lane miles = $562,500
Asphalt: $7,500 per lane-mile × 75 lane miles = $562,500
Total cost $1,125,000

Thus, $1,312,500 (cost of old program) − $1,125,000 = $187,500 in savings. Of course, a twenty-five percent work force reduction may require politically or socially unacceptable actions. And what sounds better, $250,000 of increased services or $187,500 in savings? A jurisdiction could easily be tempted into taking a benefit it cannot afford.

Someone in City X must make a value judgment that despite the higher calculated dollar benefit of increasing services, the greater value to the city at this time is to take its productivity gains in the form of savings. More likely, City X's decision makers would have factored the problems associated with a large work force reduction into their value judgment and made some sort of compromise. They might have decided on increased services at no cost increase. For the original $1,312,500 budgeted, they could achieve the improved unit cost of $1,500 per lane-mile and increase service to 87.5 lane-miles resurfaced, if they reduced their labor costs by $103,550, or 13.8 percent. They might achieve that amount by normal attrition, without having to resort to layoffs. If attrition will not occur that fast, they might decide to implement a lesser increase in efficiency the first year and to achieve the full increase over a period of years as attrition gradually reduces the work force.

Efficiency benefits in the form of cost reductions can be difficult to achieve if they involve layoffs of public employees. Such layoffs could be considered politically or socially unacceptable, and can cause employees not to cooperate with attempted operations improvements. If a community has the foresight, three to four years before a potential fiscal crisis, to make the value judgment that it must reduce costs, it can take its labor cost reductions through attrition rather than layoffs. In this case, efficiency will increase gradually, the work force will be reduced gradually, there will be no big shock to the service delivery system, and a fiscal crisis might be avoided without reducing services or creating labor problems.

## SERVICE VALUE AS RESPONSIVENESS TO COMMUNITY NEEDS

The economist's "market value" cannot be determined for government services. The engineer's "efficiency value" can have perverse results, as suggested by "The Asphalt Paradox." Yet if value judgments are important in service improvement efforts, some useful notion of value is needed for local government services. One such useful notion may be that a service is as valuable as it is responsive to the needs and desires of the community. Community needs and desires for local services can be measured as can local government responsiveness to those needs and desires, all as forms of effectiveness measurement. Thus, measures of effectiveness can be helpful to public officials who must make value judgments concerning service improvements.

One strong citizen "desire" always seems to be the desire to pay no more taxes than necessary. From another viewpoint, this can be seen as the "need" to limit the burden of the costs of government on its citizens. Thus, cost and efficiency measurement are also important in making value judgments concerning service improvements. Since the community's needs and desires always exist in an environment of limited resources, basic policy decisions on allocation always involve value judgments concerning government responsiveness—whether or not service improvements are involved, and whether or not these value judgments are made consciously. These decisions include allocating resources among different service targets (e.g. different neighborhoods, different public facilities, different client groups). In essence, measures of effectiveness, efficiency, and cost can thus be useful for making value judgments concerning the allocation of resources to meet competing needs and desires. Just as helpful is some sort of systematic process for building information on community needs and desires into the resource allocation process, so public officials have a better understanding of the value judgments they are making. The data collection and decision-making process can be simple or elaborate and can take a variety of forms.

## The Value of Improving Policy Decisions

The value of using performance measurement to improve policy decisions will rarely be obvious to public officials in terms of clear good vs. bad judgments, definite savings, or benefits they would not otherwise have achieved. To a large extent, public officials notice this value in the form of increased confidence in the decisions they make. The value becomes clearer when large reallocations of resources are made due to an examination of performance data. Such redirection of resources represents an increase in the value received for public tax dollars, because they are shifted to meet community needs more closely.

## The Value of Improving Performance

If a service improvement concentrates on increasing effectiveness rather than efficiency, it is particularly difficult to establish a connection between the improvement made and a dollar value to the community. Cost-benefit analyses are sometimes made in which the cost of improvement is weighed against some dollar value of the benefits received by the community as a result of the improvement. For example, the number of accidents avoided as a result of street improvements might be estimated. The benefit would then be the estimated cost of medical and repair bills and of lawsuits from those accidents, if they actually had happened. Of course, no one can really tell how many accidents did not happen or what they did not cost, but if extensive "before and after" accident data is collected, one might be able to make a convincing case that a specific dollar value could be assigned to the street improvement. Usually, it is much more difficult to assign a dollar value to an improvement in service effectiveness. What is the dollar value of cleaner streets and sidewalks? The value in improved service effectiveness must be seen as an increase in the responsiveness to citizens' needs and desires. When a service is made more effective, the resources used for that service, and the public dollars that supply those resources, become more valuable because they are meeting community needs better. Often such improvements in service effectiveness are more valuable to a community than other improvements for which clear dollar values can be calculated.

When there is a measurable increase in service efficiency, and that increase is verifiable through careful performance measurement and cost accounting, it is often possible to calculate a dollar value for a service improvement. However, as shown in "The Asphalt Paradox," efficiency value taken out of context can be misleading and cause local officials to make poor judgments concerning service changes. Like City X, they may choose to take a higher valued benefit they cannot afford. Or, they may improve efficiency at the cost of effectiveness. Service quality may suffer as a result of crews working faster, but with no quality controls. Responsiveness may suffer if geographic distribution of services is based solely on the most efficient way to deliver them, without concern for the distribution of need. It is reasonable for public officials to calculate a dollar value for an increase in efficiency, so long as they understand the limited meaning of that efficiency value and consider it in its context of the impact on service effectiveness and the impact on the budget.

Local governments should not necessarily take their efficiency improvement benefits in a way that will cut a service's budget or hold it even. Sometimes improving fiscal conditions justify a service increase. To a growing jurisdiction (say a city that recently annexed a few square miles with additional residents and infrastructure), the cost avoidance benefits described in "The Asphalt Paradox" represent real savings even though the budget goes up, as the jurisdiction has to increase services to meet the demands of growth. Even a jurisdiction that is not growing physically or economically can still make a valid judgment to increase a service, if there is a real need or desire in the community for that increase, preferably supported by effectiveness measures or some process that documents community priorities. The jurisdiction can make up for that increase by reducing costs in other services through increased efficiency or actual service reductions. The important thing is for the community's officials to recognize the need for a value judgment and to make that judgment consciously rather than let it be made by default, as in "The Asphalt Paradox."

## THE ORGANIZATIONAL VALUE OF MEASUREMENT AND IMPROVEMENT

The learning process involved in establishing a performance measurement or productivity improvement program can result in important organizational benefits (see Table 1). Management improvement and increased productivity can occur at the legislative and chief executive levels as well as within operating de-

**TABLE 1**
**Forms of value associated with performance measurement and productivity improvement efforts**

| Type of improvement achieved | Form of benefit produced | Form of value received |
|---|---|---|
| Improved policy decisions | Reallocation of resources to more closely meet community needs. | Shifted resources increase in value to public, as needs are better met by public tax dollars. Not expressible as a hard dollar figure. |
| Improved service performance —effectiveness | Services made more responsive to community needs. | Services increase in value to the public, as needs are better met by public tax dollars. Not expressible as a hard dollar figure. |
| Improved service performance —efficiency | Increased amount of services delivered per dollar spent. Also expressible as decreased cost per unit of service delivered. | A dollar value of increased efficiency may be calculated, representing actual savings, cost avoidance, or both. This "efficiency value" can be misleading, particularly if it is in the form of cost avoidance. But it is a valid calculation. |
| Improved organizations | Managers and employees see their programs and jobs in a new light, becoming more creative as well as more efficient and effective (human development benefits). | Public organizations increase in value to the public as their ability to change and improve is enhanced. Not expressible as a hard dollar figure. |

partments. They can result from the processes of selecting measures, defining or reexamining public purposes and program goals, or analyzing decision processes. They can also result from the experience of using performance measures to help make decisions, and from implementing productivity improvement projects.

The organizational benefits of measurement and improvement essentially involve officials learning to think about public programs in new ways. Workers who have changed their work methods with the assistance of a consultant or management team are more likely to keep employing the new methods properly after the consultant leaves—if they are convinced these are helping them do their job better. New facts learned from measurement, or a new perspective gained from participating in a productivity improvement project, may cause a manager to see a program in a different light, leading to a much more creative approach to managing it in the future. In the best case, the manager's new perspective is picked up by others, so a creative approach to using measurement and improving performance lasts within the organization even after the manager leaves.

The organizational benefits of performance measurement and productivity improvement are not guaranteed. To achieve them, a jurisdiction must pay some attention to developing its human resources when implementing a measurement or improvement project.

But these benefits are well worth the extra effort needed, even though their full value will never be fully measurable in dollars. Organizational benefits are potentially the most valuable that a jurisdiction can gain from a measurement or improvement project because of their lasting effect on the organization.

# The Waste Collection Division and Its Incentive Plan

John M. Greiner
Roger E. Dahl
Harry P. Hatry
Annie P. Millar

## SOLID WASTE COLLECTION IN FLINT[1]

Flint had about 181,700 residents in 1973, reflecting a decline of about 4,000 persons per year since 1970. The city's Waste Collection Division serviced some 51,650 residential stops in 1975, about 2 percent fewer than the previous year. This decline reflected the demolition of nearly 900 housing units. Accompanying

From *Monetary Incentives and Work Standards* by John Greiner, et al. Copyright 1977, The Urban Institute. Reprinted by permission.

these changes was a decrease in the number of tons of solid waste collected between 1973 and 1975. Each collection stop was covered once a week, using curbside pickup. As of October 1975, the stops were divided into ninety-five residential pickup routes, each route involving between 550 and 585 stops. Nineteen of these routes were serviced daily. Bulk items were picked up on request.

In addition to the 95 residential collection routes, there were three commercial routes serving a total of about 177 establishments and a single route serving three public housing projects twice a week. Thus, altogether there were 100 collection routes to be completed each week, or 20 per day.

Overall, there had been no major changes in waste collection methods (except for route balancing) since 1965. However, city officials believed that passage of a strengthened "no burning" ordinance in 1972 was responsible for a brief increase in the amount of waste collected.

There were some equipment changes in the period of interest. In FY 1973, the year before the introduction of the incentive program, there were about fourteen 20-yard packers and thirteen 25-yard packers. As of October 1975, the city was operating twenty-two collection vehicles—two 20-yard rear-loading packers and twenty 25-yard packers, a figure that had remained relatively constant since December 1974.

Due to a shortage of trucks, the division began operating on two shifts in March 1973. As newer, more reliable trucks were phased in, the second shift was gradually reduced in size until it was eliminated entirely in September 1974. However, continuing problems with breakdowns and out-of-service vehicles soon led to the reintroduction of the second shift. As of late 1975, it was expected that two-shift operation would become permanent, for it allowed the division to eliminate six trucks. Flint used twelve crews on the first shift and eight on the second.

In June 1975, the city closed the municipal landfill and began to rely solely on a private landfill. Before the closing, the city used the private landfill only during the second shift. Since the private landfill did not have scales, the tonnage collected during the second shift had to be estimated. This led to complaints by union officials, since changes in the amount of waste collected affected bonus earnings. Union officials felt that the closing of the public landfill would increase the waste collection workload because fewer members of the general public would take their own refuse to the private landfill, which charged citizens who used it.

Each truck was manned by a crew of two who took turns driving and collecting. The members of each crew worked together regularly and were assigned the same truck and the same collection routes. Except for supervisors, all persons in the Waste Collection Division were classed as "waste collectors" and were represented by Local 1600 of the American Federation of State, County, and Municipal Employees (AFL-CIO). Supervisory employees belonged to AFSCME Local 1799.

As of October 1975, the Waste Collection Division had a total of fifty-nine employees (down from sixty-six at the beginning of FY 1973). These included the waste collection superintendent, the assistant superintendent, three foremen, a landfill attendant, and fifty-three driver-laborers.[2] A maximum of forty waste collectors was needed to staff the collection crews on any given day. The additional staff were used to fill in for absent crew members and to perform a few other duties, such as picking up dead animals. If not needed in those capacities, the extra staff were assigned to individual collection crews on the basis of the age and seniority of the crew members and the heaviness of the routes (the resulting three-man crews were sometimes expected to take on additional responsibilities). The collectors were paid on the basis of a forty-hour work week.

The crews did not usually handle collection complaints. Complaints were given to the employee responsible for picking up dead animals. In January 1974, the field foremen began driving over the collection routes several times a day to check the progress of the crews; to look for spills, missed collections, and late set-outs; and to take any needed remedial actions. Occasionally a truck was ordered to return to a collection area if its crew appeared to have been at fault, but this was usually avoided as too costly.

Collection rules were strictly enforced in Flint. Crews were not required to pick up refuse that was not properly bundled and wrapped, had been placed more than three feet from the curb, was not near a driveway, had been scattered by dogs, etc. (Collection crews were responsible for "tagging" stops at which a pickup was not made because of violations.) When a complaint was actually the fault of the complaining citizen, a foreman personally informed the citizen of collection rules, procedures, and schedules.

Overall expenditures for the Waste Collection Division in FY 1975, including revenue-sharing funds but excluding the operation of the landfill, were $1,422,662.

## THE INTRODUCTION OF THE INCENTIVE PLAN: THE PRODUCTIVITY BARGAINING PROCESS

Early in the summer of 1973, Flint's waste collectors sought to raise their pay classification by one level—a move which would have resulted in an average increase of about $250 per year per man. Although they were only one year into a three-year contract, the collectors maintained that they were not being adequately compensated in view of the increasing trash tonnage. When the requested change in pay classification was turned down by Flint's Civil Service Commission, the waste collectors took their case to the city administration in the form of a demand for a ten-cent-an-hour wage increase. They also began a slowdown.

City officials saw this as an opportunity to gain some needed changes in waste collection practices and procedures while being responsive to the collectors' demands for an increase in pay. Thus, the city reopened its negotiations with the waste collectors and introduced the issue of productivity.[3] The primary goal of city negotiators was to reduce overtime, which in FY 1973 had amounted to about 9,900 hours, including 3,200 hours of scheduled overtime to make up for holidays. The city wanted to reduce the 6,700 hours of unscheduled overtime. City negotiators therefore designed a productivity contract which would permit all sixty-six members of the division (including supervisors) to share on an equal basis in the savings which would accrue from reductions in overtime and improved productivity, defined as a decrease in the cost per ton collected.[4]

Under the settlement finally negotiated, the city promised the waste collectors an increase of eight cents an hour or a productivity bonus, whichever was larger —but in either case contingent on total overtime (including holiday makeup) being cut by 25 percent (equivalent to a 37 percent reduction in controllable, unscheduled overtime). The bonus was to be paid at the end of the fiscal year. The city also promised to introduce a modified task system whereby a crew could go home after six hours on the job if its route were finished. In accepting this proposal, the union agreed to drop its demand for a flat ten-cent-an-hour raise.[5]

The waste collectors ended their slowdown about the end of July and began to honor the incentive agreement about August 15. The program was formally ratified by the city council without opposition on September 17, 1973, retroactive to July 1.

## THE ORIGINAL DESIGN OF THE WASTE COLLECTION INCENTIVE PLAN

As originally conceived, the incentive plan had two main elements: (1) a "task system" under which a collection crew was permitted to go home after six hours if its collection route were completed, and (2) a bonus plan designed to share with division employees the savings that accrued from reducing overtime and increasing productivity. These two elements endured— with modifications—throughout the incentive effort.

### The Task System

Flint officials believed that a critical prerequisite for both the task system and the bonus plan was that collection routes be closely balanced among all crews and be designed to represent a "fair day's work." As such, a collection route was a kind of work standard. Prior to the productivity contract, routes were designed subjectively. However, between August 1973 and January 1974, all collection stops in Flint were surveyed and heuristic routing techniques were used to equalize the number of stops per day and per route, resulting in between 550 and 585 stops per day per route. Lighter routes were assigned to older collectors. Furthermore, if a crew felt that its route was too heavy, the route could be reexamined and adjusted if warranted. Similarly, if a crew was unhappy with the design of a particular route, its members were given an opportunity to redesign it themselves. The objective was to ensure that the standards which formed the basis of the task system and the bonus program were generally accepted as equitable by the waste collectors.

Prior to the productivity agreement, waste collectors in Flint were required to remain on the job for eight hours, no matter when they finished their routes. Under the July 1973 agreement, however, a crew was permitted to go home after six hours if its route were finished. If a crew's route were not completed, the crew was not eligible for overtime until it had worked a full eight hours. However, a crew assigned to complete another route after finishing its own would draw overtime after accumulating six hours of work for the

271

day (on the assumption that completing its own route constituted a fair day's work).

After the waste collection foremen expressed some dissatisfaction at not being able to leave as early as their subordinates (since they did not participate in the task system), a plan was established to permit all but one supervisor to leave after six and one half hours. The latter was required to stay the full eight hours. (This assignment was rotated among the foremen.)

## Incentive Bonus Formula

The other element of the productivity contract was the bonus plan. According to the original agreement, the bonus formula rested on the following principles:[6]

- Reduction of overtime hours was a savings to the city.
- Savings should be shared as part of an incentive program.
- A productivity coefficient should be included which weighed the efficiency achieved against the standards agreed on by labor and management.
- Any decrease in the cost per ton should be factored into the bonus formula and shared on an equal basis.

The bonus was not proportional to salary but was originally divided equally among all persons in the division, including supervisory personnel but excluding seasonal employees. Partial shares were awarded to employees who had retired or transferred from the division (the amount was based upon the fraction of the year during which they were members of the division). No penalty was assessed for absenteeism under the original incentive agreement. The bonus was to be computed after the close of the fiscal year and paid in a lump sum within the next thirty days.

The actual formula for the bonus was as follows:

$$PB = \frac{1/2 \times PC \times [OTS + (\Delta CT \times IT)]}{N}$$

where   PB = productivity bonus per person,
        PC = productivity coefficient,
   OTS = overtime dollars saved (average annual overtime hours for the period FY 1971 to FY 1973 minus the actual overtime hours for the current fiscal year, times the average overtime rate for the current fiscal year),

$\Delta CT$ = decrease in cost per ton (including overtime costs) relative to the preceding fiscal year),
    IT = increase in tonnage collected over that for the preceding fiscal year, and
    N = number of employees affected (adjusted as noted above).

The bonus was derived from a pool of savings (in brackets in the formula) determined by the value of the overtime saved and the imputed value of the increase in tonnage.[7] Half of these savings was shared by the eligible employees, after adjustment by the productivity coefficient for the degree to which collection standards were met (as discussed later). The overtime saved was based on the difference between overtime usage for the current fiscal year and average annual overtime usage for the three baseline years FY 1971 to FY 1973 (8,472 hours).[8] The savings from reduced overtime hours were valued at the average overtime rate for the current year. Overtime due to snow removal activities, spring cleanup week, vehicle breakdowns, and most other causes not the responsibility of the crews was not counted, but scheduled overtime to make up for holidays was included for purposes of computing the bonus.

The remaining factor in the savings pool—the product of the increased tonnage by the decrease in the cost per ton—was expected by city officials to provide only a small contribution, if any. The inclusion of the change in tonnage reflected the union's contention that workers should earn more for having to pick up more refuse.[9] However, no credit was given for extra tonnage unless the cost per ton decreased. The more that productivity improved, the greater the credit given for increased tonnage. (The formula provided no extra bonus if tonnage did not increase, even though unit cost went down.) In effect, this component of the savings pool was an index reflecting both the concern of the union that increased tonnage be considered and the concern of the city for increased productivity.

The change in tonnage was computed by comparing the tonnage for the current fiscal year with that for the preceding fiscal year. The cost per ton was based on the sum of direct labor costs (including overtime premiums) plus rental costs for collection and disposal equipment.[10] Due to bookkeeping idiosyncrasies, employee fringe benefits were not included.

The productivity coefficient was obtained by adding three components: overtime, route completions, and complaints. The three components were defined and evaluated as follows:

1. *Overtime Reduction Component*
   0.5 if total overtime were reduced by 25 percent with respect to the average for the past three fiscal years.[11]
2. *Quality Component*
   0.2 if the number of valid complaints were less than or equal to 5 percent of the number of collection stops.
   0.1 if valid complaints numbered greater than 5 percent but less than or equal to 10 percent of the stops.
   0.0 if valid complaints numbered greater than 10 percent of the stops.
3. *Route Completion Component*
   0.3 if seventeen of the twenty daily routes were completed without overtime being required.
   0.2 if sixteen routes were completed without overtime being required.
   0.1 if fourteen routes were completed without overtime being required.
   0.0 if fewer than fourteen routes were completed without overtime being required.

In each case performance levels were based on averages over the fiscal year. The "scores" achieved for each component were added together to yield the productivity coefficient.

As noted earlier, overtime had to be reduced by at least 25 percent before employees were eligible to receive the bonus; no increase of any type was to be granted if a 25 percent reduction were not achieved. In effect, this condition appeared to assure that the productivity coefficient in the bonus formula would be nearly one when any bonus was earned at all, since the required overtime reduction would assure a contribution of 0.5 from the overtime component, and the need for a high route completion rate (to achieve such a reduction in overtime) would effectively assure another contribution of 0.3.

In addition, the complaint rate for waste collection in Flint was historically around ten per day. Thus, the goal of holding valid complaints to less than 515 per day (5 percent of the approximately 10,300 daily collection stops) was practically guaranteed. Although the "quality" component may not appear to have had any incentive value for this formula, interviews with waste collection personnel indicated that they did try harder to "satisfy" the citizens on their routes because they knew that citizen complaints could affect their bonus earnings.

## Changes in Data Collection Procedures

The bonus formula affected some division data collection practices. Valid complaints, which were not tallied before the agreement, were reported quarterly beginning in July 1973. In early 1974, the foremen began driving over the collection routes to monitor the quality of the pickups; informal reports were maintained but were not used as part of the productivity contract.

Subsequent to the incentive agreement, overtime for waste collectors was recorded in a separate account (prior to April 22, 1973, it had been lumped with overtime for the disposal operation). Tonnage figures had always been collected; however, as noted previously, tonnage for the second shift had to be estimated until July 1975, when scales and an attendant from the Waste Collection Division were assigned to the private landfill used by that shift.

## RECENT MODIFICATIONS IN THE INCENTIVE PLAN
## FY 1975 Modifications

The productivity agreement negotiated for FY 1975 left the bonus formula and the task system intact, although both were specified more precisely. For instance, the baseline overtime level (8,472 hours) and the standard size of a collection route (550 to 585 stops per day) were formally noted in the contract. The minimum bonus (if overtime were reduced by at least 25 percent) was raised two cents an hour, yielding a total of $208 for each waste collector.

In a departure from the previous approach, it was decided that the bonus would not necessarily be distributed equally to all persons covered by the incentive plan. The total time each employee missed due to lateness or unexcused absences was to be multiplied by the hourly "bonus rate" (the maximum possible bonus divided by 2,080 hours) and deducted from the employee's bonus. (Absenteeism due to job-related injuries was excluded.) The purpose of this modification was to provide employees with an incentive to reduce absences.

Another innovation in FY 1975 was to broaden the focus of the bonus plan to include reductions of staff as well as of overtime and cost per ton. Under the agreement, the city would add $2,000 to the bonus pool for each waste collector eliminated below the level of sixty-three. (This $2,000 would not be shared with the city but would instead be divided among the remaining waste collection personnel.) The figure of $2,000 was reached after negotiations. (City and union officials subsequently noted that the real savings to the city from elimination of a waste collection position were closer to $12,000.) Although agreeing to a bonus for reducing the number of jobs appears contrary to traditional union policy, the position of the shop stewards was that the division intended to cut back manpower anyway and that this negotiated bonus would at least give the employees something to show for it.[12]

The FY 1975 agreement also formalized a number of work rules. Among other things, these rules fixed the daily number of residential collection routes at nineteen; assigned responsibility to the collection crews for completing their own routes, cleaning up spillage, and tagging stops not picked up because the trash had been improperly bundled or positioned; and provided that shop stewards would receive information relevant to the incentive plan (e.g, overtime figures and chargeable absences) on a regular basis.

Another development during FY 1975 is worth noting. Division management felt that the collection routes had become unbalanced—and somewhat lighter —since they were first established in early 1974, primarily because of the demolition of 900 dwelling units in the interim. Thus, the residential stops were recounted between December 1974 and February 1975. The revised total was 51,647, or an average of 544 stops per route. Management noted that with eighteen routes a day, the average number of stops per route would rise to only 574, still within the limits provided by the contract but eliminating the need for one crew. But management's attempt to implement an eighteen-route-per-day system ran into heavy union opposition, including a one-day walkout in March 1975.

## FY 1976 Modifications

The productivity agreement negotiated for FY 1976 incorporated a number of changes in the incentive program, many of which were attempts to resolve the problems associated with route reductions and the counting of collection stops. As a compromise, the standard number of residential collection routes was decreased to eighteen for the "winter" period (November through May), when less waste was usually collected, but was kept at nineteen during the "summer" period (June through October). The corresponding number of stops per route was set at 580 (±5 percent) during the "winter" period and 560 (±5 percent) for the "summer." Waste Division management believed that one full-time crew could be eliminated under this agreement by hiring an extra crew made up of temporary personnel during the "summer" months.

A second, related change involved the technique for counting collection stops. Previously, management did the counting and decided just how many stops should be credited under various circumstances. The furor over the revised stop count stimulated the union's interest in these decisions. Consequently, the FY 1976 agreement incorporated a negotiated formula for determining the number of collection stops:

1. Multiple families would be counted as follows:
   - Two families as one stop,
   - Three families as two stops,
   - Dwellings with four or more families as 85 percent of the total number of families.
2. Trailers would be counted as 85 percent of the total number of trailers in the park.
3. Apartments would be counted as 85 percent of the units in the apartment complex.

In addition, subsequent counts were to be conducted by a team consisting of one management and one union representative.

To compensate for the winter reduction in the number of collection routes, the city added $3,000 to the bonus pool (the $3,000 did not have to be shared with the city). The rationale behind the $3,000 figure was as follows. The employees' share of the savings from the elimination of one route per day for twelve months was determined to be $6,000—$2,000 for reducing expenses for vehicle rentals plus $4,000 for the elimination of one crew (two persons, each worth $2,000 to the bonus pool under the precedent set by the FY 1975 contract provision for rewarding a reduction in manpower). Thus the negotiated six-month reduction was valued at $3,000—half the value of a twelve-month reduction.

A major change was made in the task system for FY 1976 by permitting crews to leave after five hours on the job, provided their route was completed. In addition, the baseline bonus was raised to fifteen cents an hour (or $312 per worker). At the request of the union, the landfill attendant (previously guaranteed a fixed bonus) was included in the bonus agreement. Elimination of the municipal landfill had reduced the number of landfill personnel to one, and his inclusion under the bonus plan actually meant a savings to the city since his bonus no longer had to be paid out of the city's share of the savings.

Other changes included the revision of the baseline overtime level and the baseline manpower level (both of which were used to determine the bonus pool) to reflect the fact that supervisory personnel were no longer covered by the incentive agreement negotiated by Local 1600. (Supervisors subsequently received a similar incentive plan of their own.) There were also a number of additions and modifications to the work rules.[13]

## SUMMARY OF FINDINGS AND CONCLUSIONS

The major findings and conclusions regarding Flint's performance incentive program through October 1975 follow.[14]

### Productivity

1. Flint's productivity program appears to have been generally successful in terms of reducing controllable overtime, labor costs, and personnel requirements. For instance, controllable overtime dropped from about 6,700 hours in FY 1973, the year before the incentive program, to 2,200 hours in FY 1974 and to 45 hours in FY 1975. This sharp drop more than met the goal specified in the productivity agreement between the city and the waste collectors which stipulated that the combined total of controllable and scheduled (i.e., holiday makeup) overtime would be reduced at least 25 percent. Indeed, after the first two years of the incentive agreement, little additional reduction of controllable overtime appeared to be possible. (However, maintenance of this lower level continued to be an objective of the program.)

2. These reductions in overtime were matched by savings in personnel and labor costs. Relative to FY 1973, the year before the incentive agreement, the city realized a net savings in overtime costs (after subtraction of the bonuses paid and the administrative expenses of the program) of about $15,700 in FY 1974

(deflated to FY 1973 dollars) and $22,200 in FY 1975 (also in FY 1973 dollars). Overall personnel costs (excluding fringe benefits) declined 3.3 percent between FY 1973 and FY 1975 (the decline is 11.1 percent if deflated expenditures are used). During the same period, average division staffing dropped 7 percent (from 64.5 workers in FY 1973 to 60.0 in FY 1975).

3. Other factors unrelated to the productivity program may have contributed to these changes. For instance, during the three years of interest, the city introduced new and larger collection vehicles, redesigned and rebalanced the collection routes, and closed the municipal landfill. On the other hand, the continuing decline in both city population and number of housing units served may have counteracted the tendency of these factors to increase productivity. Indeed, taken together, the two elements of the productivity plan—the task system and the bonus program—appear to have played important roles in improving division productivity and effectiveness. Although the task system appears to have had the greatest impact, the combined use of the bonus plan and the task system was viewed by many members of the division as essential to their success in improving productivity.

4. The productivity program appears to have led to improved efficiency, although the results were not so clear as those on the resources saved. In FY 1974, the first year under the incentive agreement, there appeared to be a general improvement in efficiency. For instance, the tons of solid waste collected per hour rose 8 percent, tons collected per employee rose 2 percent, and units serviced per constant labor dollar climbed 6 percent. Meanwhile, unit labor costs (per ton of solid waste) fell 8 percent. On the other hand, a few measures (e.g., the number of units serviced per employee) indicated declining efficiency in FY 1974. In FY 1975, there appeared to be a general decrease in division efficiency relative to the preceding year. Declines were registered during FY 1975 in the tons of waste collected per employee and the units serviced per 1,000 deflated labor dollars, while the deflated labor cost per ton actually rose 9 percent. Nevertheless, relative to preprogram conditions, division efficiency generally showed a net improvement over the first two years of the incentive effort (e.g., in terms of the deflated cost per ton, the number of units serviced per 1,000 deflated labor dollars and per employee, etc.). These achievements were all the more remarkable because Flint's waste collection operation was

quite productive before the productivity program was introduced.[15]

5. The impact of the incentive program on service quality is not clear because little information was available on the quality of service before the introduction of the program. While the proportion of route completions increased and there was an initial trend toward fewer citizen complaints, the latter increased significantly in 1975 (city officials knew of no specific reason why).

6. Bonus payments totalled $17,787 in FY 1974 and $28,385 in FY 1975 (including bonuses paid to landfill personnel). The waste collectors received about $261 each in FY 1974 and up to $458 each in FY 1975. These sums were not large enough to compensate for the average loss in overtime earnings in each of these years. However, although a number of waste collectors indicated that without the extra time off provided by the task system the bonuses would not have been worth any effort on their part, slightly more than a majority of those interviewed indicated that the combination of the task system plus the bonuses was preferable to preprogram conditions. Note that the productivity bonuses exceeded the average wage increase originally sought by the collectors.

7. Total deflated costs for the program—including bonus payments and administrative expenses—came to $21,648 in FY 1974 and $33,279 in FY 1975 (FY 1973 dollars). In addition, the program required one to three weeks of effort each year by the city manager for program design and the associated negotiations. The redesign and balancing of the collection routes, viewed as a crucial prerequisite for the program by city management, required several hundred staff-days of effort every few years.

8. Management reported that daily truck use decreased, resulting in more preventive maintenance and fewer chances for traffic accidents. In the first year of the program, reductions were also experienced in fleet mileage and fuel costs.

9. Management reported that one of the biggest problems associated with the productivity program was the unavailability and unreliability of the collection vehicles. Increased employee concern over these problems was also reported. However, there were some reports from city officials that employees were harder on their vehicles than they were before the incentive agreement (although no quantitative evidence of such an effect was found). Management reported that waste collection crews on occasion deferred maintenance until they completed their route (e.g., by driving on a flat tire) and sometimes damaged the packers by overloading.

## Labor-Management Relations

10. Although the productivity program grew out of a period of labor conflict in the Waste Collection Division, labor relations were generally characterized as "good" after the introduction of the agreement. Nevertheless, the program has not been without labor problems. The chief of these was a one-day walkout on March 17, 1975, when management tried to reduce unilaterally the number of waste collection routes. The union subsequently filed a formal grievance, which ultimately went to arbitration and led to a ruling largely in favor of the union. The city was required to negotiate over the number of routes and procedures for counting collection stops, and a joint labor-management committee was ultimately set up to make such counts.

11. The negotiation of the productivity improvement program appears to have been facilitated by union officials' familiarity with such productivity efforts. Several months before the beginning of the productivity negotiations, the city sent management representatives and the president of Local 1600 to one of the first national conferences on productivity and labor relations (the conference emphasized productivity bargaining). In addition, union officials were well aware of a similar productivity program which had recently been introduced in nearby Detroit's Sanitation Department.

12. Within the Waste Collection Division, the productivity program appeared to have enhanced employee regard for union shop stewards and to have made the waste collectors a more cohesive group. The collectors appeared to exhibit confidence in their ability to handle their own problems by meeting together—with management, if needed—rather than relying on the traditional mechanisms provided by Local 1600. Indeed, the shop stewards believed that the productivity program had produced the first meaningful interaction among division employees, stewards, and management.

13. On the other hand, the incentive effort appears to have had a negative impact on relations between waste collection employees and the rest of Local 1600. Presidents of the local subsequent to FY 1973 saw the

program as creating problems of equity for union members not covered by the incentive agreement. During the program's first year, two grievances over this issue were filed by nonparticipating city employees, and waste collection employees reported criticism from other city employees. (These criticisms focused on both the bonus plan and the task system, although mostly on the latter.) Such criticism apparently led the president of Local 1600 to refuse to sign the incentive agreement negotiated (with his help) in FY 1975 on the grounds that it should have been approved by the entire membership of the local. The agreement for FY 1976 *was* submitted to the membership, where it passed (with few members—primarily the waste collectors—voting).

14. Three years of productivity bargaining appeared to have led to some changes in the focus of negotiations. Negotiators for the waste collectors became more sophisticated in their understanding of productivity bargaining. For instance, they began to look at total savings—both direct and indirect—associated with personnel and route reductions and to demand a full share of those savings for the waste collectors. Moreover, as productivity bargaining continued from year to year, union negotiators began to focus on features such as work content (e.g., how to count the collection stops) in addition to the more traditional concerns of wages, hours, and working conditions. As the productivity negotiations evolved, they appeared to address more items bearing on the definition of the elements of the job, the content of the work, and its organization. Thus, productivity bargaining appeared to be slowly increasing the area of joint decision making.

15. Some animosity appears to have developed between the waste collectors and first-line supervisors over the inclusion of the latter in the bonus plan. Although the task system apparently reduced the daily conflicts between the crews and their supervisors, line employees generally believed that they were bearing the brunt of the effort to improve productivity and reduce collection time and that the supervisors' jobs had become easier. Thus, nine of ten waste collectors interviewed felt that it was unfair to include the supervisors in the bonus plan. When the latter transferred from Local 1600 to another bargaining unit early in 1975, negotiators for Local 1600 moved to drop the supervisors from the incentive plan. However, the supervisors were subsequently given their own plan.

## Employee Job Satisfaction and Related Issues

16. The majority of the waste collectors interviewed perceived no change in job satisfaction or related items—job security and promotional opportunities—as a result of the incentive program. This result was generally supported by available data on separations, absenteeism, sick-leave use, injury days, and accidents. All but the accident rate declined between FY 1973 and FY 1975, the second year of the plan. The improvements were especially marked during FY 1974. A worsening in these indicators was generally evident during FY 1975 (although in most cases not exceeding preprogram levels). However, FY 1975 was a period of considerable labor unrest in the division over management efforts to reduce the number of collection routes, and this may account for the worsening trend.

17. An important exception to the FY 1975 worsening of the indicators of job dissatisfaction was the 16.8 percent reduction in the rate of absenteeism due to tardiness and unexcused absences. This appears to have been a direct result of the FY 1975 incentive agreement which for the first time provided that bonuses would be reduced by an amount proportional to the number of hours of unexcused absences recorded for each employee.

18. A majority of the employees interviewed reported that the task system had led them to work faster; seven of thirteen felt that the pressure on them had increased (primarily due to their superiors, although pressure from peers and from themselves was also noted). The collectors felt that the quality of service was the same or better as a result of the task system. On the other hand, most of those interviewed reported that the bonus plan had had little effect on their work pace, although several noted that the plan had had a positive impact on the quality of their work. (This was attributed to concern that citizen complaints might reduce the bonuses earned.) Clearly, the task system had the greatest impact on employee behavior but many reported that there was a need for both the task system and the bonus plan, since the latter made the loss of overtime in connection with the task system more acceptable.

19. Six of the ten employees who responded to a question on job safety indicated that their work had become more dangerous as a result of the productivity program (primarily because the task system caused many of them to hurry their efforts). Data on

accident rates and number of injury days per employee were inconclusive on the question of job safety. The accident rate fell in the first year of the program but almost doubled in the second year, the year to which employees were apparently referring in reporting increased danger in their work. However, injury days per employee—an indication of the severity of those accidents—fell 48 percent in FY 1974 and rose only modestly in FY 1975, never exceeding the preprogram level. (When a few especially serious injuries are omitted, the injury days per employee show a slow but steady decline after the introduction of the incentive plan.) Thus, no clear confirmation could be found for the contention that the incentive plan increased the danger of the job.

20. Employees and supervisors exhibited a reasonably good understanding of the incentive program. The waste collectors attributed this largely to efforts by the shop stewards to explain the program to them.

21. Among the waste collectors, there appears to have been a division of opinion regarding the desirability of the incentive program. From the beginning, a minority was critical of the idea. Its members complained about the loss in overtime earnings and the small size of the bonuses, and they indicated no desire for a shorter work day. Continuing efforts by management to reduce the number of collection routes while increasing the daily workload per employee added to this criticism. Frequently, opinion appears to have been divided between the younger employees (who favored the shorter working hours) and the older ones (who were more sensitive to the pressure and increased work pace needed to finish in five or six hours). Acceptance of the program over the first several years was apparently due to a sometimes slim majority of waste collectors in favor of the effort. Interviews with waste collectors reflected this split. Seven of the thirteen employees interviewed felt that, all things considered, they had done better after the introduction of the incentive plan than before; the other six felt the opposite. Similarly, seven of the thirteen felt that the decision to introduce the bonus plan and the task system had been a good one, while four felt it was bad, and two reserved judgment.

22. Perceptions of the fairness of the productivity program were mixed. Five of the thirteen interviewed felt that their collection routes were generally fair (older employees reportedly received the shorter,

lighter routes); the remainder generally disagreed. (Some felt that those who worked the fastest got the heaviest routes.) Eleven of twelve respondents felt that the bonus plan was unfair in one way or another. Among their objections were the size of the city's share of the savings (50 percent), the basis for computing the savings (some felt that only a portion of the actual savings was being put into the bonus pool), the problem of unreliable equipment, and the strain of the task system on older employees.

## Miscellaneous Findings and Observations

23. Both city and division management, as well as line employees, believed that the incentive program had eased the job of management. In effect, the task system apparently encouraged the waste collectors to "manage themselves." Thus, management was able to eliminate a field checkpoint previously used to monitor the progress of the work and to reassign crews as the need or opportunity arose. The waste collectors opted to forgo their coffee and lunch breaks in order to finish earlier; this eliminated what had frequently been a source of conflict between collectors and supervisors. The supervisors themselves believed that fewer foremen would be needed in the future.

24. Division management reported that the introduction of the task system was accompanied by a decrease in the amount of drinking on the job. The main reason was reported to be the shortened workday, which reduced the periods during which collectors had nothing to do.

25. Although apparently relatively straightforward, the incentive program had a number of complex ramifications and unexpected results. For instance, the selected performance criteria included in the "productivity coefficient" turned out to be strongly interrelated under the terms of the incentive agreement. This led, in effect, to an "all or nothing" situation in which, in practice, employees could qualify only for relatively low or relatively high rewards. The need for careful prior evaluation of the incentive program in terms of a wide variety of conditions appears to be clear.

26. Flint's incentive program appears to reflect the subtle strategy seen in other programs examined in the course of this project. Initial targets or standards were set relatively low, thus permitting employees to earn rewards with little additional effort. Subsequent adjustments of the targets—once employees had become

accustomed to rewards—were then more readily accepted and often led to even greater productivity improvements.

27. The Flint program points to the need for obtaining adequate baseline information before proceeding with a productivity program. Management should obtain complete, accurate baseline data on the performance criteria on which the incentive will be based. In this way, loose, self-fulfilling standards may be avoided (as in the case of the targets for citizen complaint rates used in Flint's incentive agreement).

28. A major unresolved issue is the extent to which the savings, especially of overtime pay, could have been achieved by the introduction of the task system without the accompanying incentive bonuses. The city government paid a price (in bonuses) for reduced overtime, but it might have been able to eliminate overtime simply by permitting crews to leave when their routes were completed.

*The assistance of the following persons in the Flint city government is gratefully acknowledged: Daniel Boggan, Jr., City Manager; Anthony DeBlaise, Public Works and Utilities Director; Kenneth Hammermeister, Superintendent of Waste Collection and Disposal; and Warren Vyvyan and Steven Kintz, Management Interns. The following AFSCME officials provided considerable assistance: Dennis Owens, Chief Steward, Local 1600; John Berryman, President, Local 1600; and Donald Newberry, President, Local 1799.*

## NOTES

1. The results of an earlier investigation of the effectiveness of Flint's incentive program have been reported in John M. Greiner, "Tying City Pay to Performance: Early Reports on Orange, California and Flint, Michigan," Special Report (Washington, D. C.: Labor-Management Relations Service, December 1974).

2. During the summer, the work force was supplemented by three seasonal employees who filled in for men on vacation.

3. This was not a new concern for city or union officials in Flint. For instance, early in 1973 the city sent management representatives and the president of Local 1600 to attend one of the first national conferences on productivity and labor relations. Several examples of productivity bargaining were presented at that conference.

For a background discussion of productivity bargaining in sanitation, see George W. Brooks, "Negotiating for Productivity in Sanitation," Strengthening Local Government Through Labor Relations, No. 15 (Washington, D. C.: Labor-Management Relations Service, June 1973).

4. The plan resembled the Sanitation Department incentive program in Detroit, Michigan, which formally went into effect on July 2, 1973. Flint officials consulted with officials in Detroit. For a discussion of the Detroit experience, see Leo Kramer, Inc., "Improving Municipal Productivity: The Detroit Collection Incentive Plan" (Washington, D. C.: The National Commission on Productivity, 1974); James Neubacher, "Detroit Sanitation Productivity—Everyone Wins," Strengthening Local Government Through Better Labor Relations, No. 18 (Washington, D. C.: Labor-Management Relations Service, November 1973); and Andrew Giovannetti and Theodore Opperwall, "Detroit's Sanitation Productivity Plan" (Detroit: Department of Public Works, City of Detroit, January 1974).

5. Four landfill attendants did not want to accept the productivity bonus plan; the city agreed to give them a ten-cent-an-hour increase (about $208 per year, exclusive of overtime).

6. A copy of the complete incentive agreement is included in the detailed project report available from NTIS.

7. Note that this pool does not necessarily include all of the savings which accrued to the city. Total savings might be estimated by multiplying the total change in the cost per ton (including overtime expenses) times the current tonnage collected.

8. A three-year average was used as the basis for comparison in order to compensate for the extraordinarily high overtime figures in FY 1973 (an all-time high due in part to an excessive number of vehicle breakdowns and thus the responsibility of the department). The same three-year average was to be used in each successive year as the basis for computing overtime savings.

9. A more appropriate way to reflect this concern might be to consider the change in the average tonnage per collector.

10. The trucks were rented from the city motor pool. The rate was $88 per shift as of January 1, 1975. The rate had been raised from $64 per shift to $72 per shift on February 24, 1974. Even though routes were usually completed in less than six hours, the division was billed for a full eight hours.

11. The coefficient was reduced by 0.1 for each additional five percentage points reduction in overtime. However, as explained later, 0.5 was the only value which could be achieved if a productivity bonus was to be earned. Hence, the scores defined for overtime reductions of less than 25 percent do not appear to be relevant to the bonus formula.

12. Another concession won by the union—as a condition for agreeing to the bonus for staff reductions—was that the city would not charge against the bonus any overtime made

necessary by up to three unexcused absences on a given day. The union's position was that if the city had not gone ahead with staff reductions subsequent to the new bonus arrangement, it would have had enough persons available to avoid such overtime.

13. The FY 1976 incentive agreement is included in the detailed project report available from NTIS.

14. The detailed findings and the data on which they are based are provided in Greiner et al., "An Assessment of the Impacts of Five Local Government Productivity Improvement Programs," chapter VI and appendix VI.

15. This assessment is based on the results of an earlier study comparing solid waste collection productivity in Flint and other cities. Flint's productivity was quite high relative to other similar waste collection operations. See *The Challenge of Productivity Diversity, Part II: Measuring Solid Waste Collection Productivity* (Washington, D. C.: National Commission on Productivity, June 1972). Flint was one of the cities covered in the above report, although the published results were tabulated without identifying the corresponding city.

---

## Maximization, Markets, and the Measurement of Productivity in the Public Sector

Jeffrey D. Straussman
Alexander Rosenberg

Imagine a public official proclaiming that he is *against* productivity improvement. Or perhaps that productivity is all rubbish (a view difficult to maintain even when the service in question is sanitation). In this age of "cutting government back to size," productivity improvement is universally embraced as one effort, albeit a modest one, to improve the performance of the public sector. More bang for fewer bucks, you might say. It is clearly nonpartisan, and it seems to have appeal at all levels of government.

At the risk of raining on everyone's parade, we wish to sound a pessimistic note concerning the prospects for genuine productivity improvements in the public sector. In so doing, we do not challenge the claims by some that real gains have been made. Perhaps more garbage has been picked up for the same cost in some jurisdictions. Or perhaps the number of arrests for a given law enforcement budget have really increased. Rather, we wish to make an argument that some of the

*inherent* features of nonmarket production present fundamental obstacles to productivity improvements in the public sector. At the same time, we argue that the obstacles may be overcome *if* marketlike mechanisms are adapted to the public sector.

The normative view that productivity improvement is desirable has a set of descriptive presuppositions. It is first necessary, we believe, to present these descriptive presuppositions and determine whether they are now satisfied, or even satisfiable, in a public sector setting. Unless this is accomplished, we cannot sensibly proceed to questions concerning the possibility or the desirability of specific efforts to improve productivity. At present, productivity discussions have it backwards. That is, the desirability of productivity improvement is asserted (again, who would deny that it is a nice thing?), and then we construct mechanisms to obtain productivity gains that rest on very shaky assumptions about economic and organizational behavior. This is not merely an abstraction. When productivity arrangements between public management and public unions break down, the source of the breakdown may rest in these shaky assumptions rather than in "bad faith" on the part of either side. Our effort, then, is simply to get the descriptive horse before the normative cart.

## A NECESSARY CONDITION FOR PRODUCTIVITY IMPROVEMENT

The quest for productivity gains must presume that we can at least improve public sector "output"—here defined as clean streets, safe streets, educated children, and so on. Productivity further means that these outputs *should* be maximized; that is, cleanliness, public safety, and education are worthwhile objectives to try to reach. But simply saying that clean streets are better than dirty streets, or that a mean reading score for sixth graders of, say, 6.2 is better than 5.6 is not enough. If we believe that productivity gains can in fact be achieved, we are implicitly making a crucial descriptive assumption. We are assuming that economic agents—civil servants in particular—do actually try to maximize some outputs such as utility, income, or a bundle of household commodities. For example, the teacher, while perhaps valuing education, really wants to maximize such things as income, prestige, leisure, and job satisfaction. Given the supposition that civil servants are already motivated to maximize something, the objective is to channel the *personal* goals of civil servants toward politically determined objectives—clean streets, public safety, or quality education. *This is where the normative dimension of productivity joins with the descriptive one.* For instance, pronouncements that we should improve performance in public education in itself provide no guarantee that teachers will actually try to mold their actions to achieve this goal unless we can make the attainment of their personal goals (income, prestige, etc.) contingent on the achievement of the politically determined objective. This is not to say that teachers do not "value" quality education. Nor are we suggesting that some, perhaps many, teachers have quality education as their primary objective. Rather, we are simply assuming that teachers most probably have personal objectives that are more important to them—provide them with more utility, if you will. (Those who doubt these assertions might simply reflect on the probable success of a productivity scheme that asks public employees to work harder, better, or longer for the "good of the community" without any divisible benefits.)

If we can make the political objective and the personal objectives of civil servants *by-products* of one another, we have a greater likelihood that productivity gains will be realized. Logically, this means that individual benefits for the civil servant are a *necessary condition* for productivity gains in the public sector. If we were discussing conditions of economic competition, we could end our argument here. For in the competitive model, the assumption that economic agents seek personal benefits is both necessary and sufficient for improvements in productivity. Nonmarket approaches to productivity must obviously search elsewhere for theoretical guidance.

The literature on the "economics of bureaucracy" is appropriate to cite here. Specifically, the factual assertion that civil servants try to maximize private goals—income and nonincome perquisites of public office—has been argued persuasively by others (Niskanen, 1971; Stockfish, 1976; Wolf, 1979). The empirical dimensions of what is the effort to expand the agency budget, according to Niskanen, essentially is an aggregation of the bureaucrat's utility functions (1971: 38). Budget expansion in turn, however, can affect productivity *adversely* since such expansion may drive agency budgets above their optimal level. According to Charles Wolf, budget maximization strategies can "boost agency *supply* curves above technically feasible

ones, resulting in redundant total costs, higher unit costs, and lower levels of real nonmarket output than the socially efficient ones" (1979: 117). The rationale for budget expansion lies not in the predisposition of individual bureaucrats to maximize budgets per se, but rather in the demand and supply characteristics of public sector products. The lack of a market "test," the difficulty of measuring output, and the unique relationship between agencies and their legislative overseers are well known to observers of the public sector. They create the environment for what Wolf has called "nonmarket failure"—the gap between objectives and actual implementation.

The problems of measuring productivity and, more important, stimulating productivity improvements are associated with these characteristics identified by Wolf. For example, the fact that bureaucrats do not necessarily maximize some unambiguous objective such as clean streets lies not in any deficiency of the bureaucrat. Rather, it lies in the absence of a clear consensus on what clean streets means. Nor is there agreement on the components of the production process (and the interrelationship among the components) that will achieve the objective. Given that bureaucrats are self-interested utility maximizers, their utility maximization may be unrelated or perhaps even inversely related to productivity. For example, Sterne, Rabushka, and Scott (1972) found that the ill-defined objective of "serving the elderly in need" through a lunch program was displaced by budget maximization, attained by feeding a high number of elderly regardless of need. In an important respect, productivity may have actually declined. Similarly, Staaf (1977) showed that educational personnel most clearly attempt to maximize salary schedules rather than any other output.

From the vantage point of neoclassical economic theory, markets would be an improvement as a way to organize economic activities. A market approach to public sector activities requires the assumption that all agents are rational, all maximize something in common. The trouble with this assumption is its great theoretical distance from data that can be collected and the ease with which it can be defended from falsifications. For purposes of illustration, let us assume that public agencies attempt to maximize their next budgetary allocation. On this factual finding can hinge schemes for improving their productivity, for we may make the next budgetary allocation contingent on some level of output of a mandated product (potholes filled, streets cleaned, cases covered), so that the maximization of the latter will be a *by-product* of the attempt to maximize the budget.

Linking the two outputs, of course, may not by itself increase productivity. This is the sense in which the descriptive assumption of maximization is normally a necessary condition for the desired aim of increasing productivity. But it is an important and necessary condition for the latter. If there is no actual maximization, there is nothing on which we can base economic and organizational changes that will affect the desired maximization. If it turns out that bureaucrats maximize things that cannot be linked to political objectives, then there is simply no hope of making the outputs joint by-products, thereby increasing productivity of the political objective. For example, if certain air traffic controllers maximize hours of on-the-job sleep, there is no way of improving their productivity in the provision of air safety. And again, if there is nothing that they can be determined to maximize (pay, prestige, vacation time, etc.), there is no way of improving their productivity.

## THE "NONISSUE" OF PRODUCTIVITY IN A PERFECTLY COMPETITIVE ENVIRONMENT

Maximization of a personal product is a necessary condition for maximization of a politically determined product, but not in and of itself a sufficient one, for it may be practically or theoretically impossible to link them. These impossibilities surface in the difficulties surrounding the operationalization and employment of productivity measures that are essential if we are to link personal and political objectives. And this is where the market approach derives its greatest strength, for *it obviates the construction and application of such measures by supervisory political agents.*

Consider the daunting problem of efficiency versus effectiveness. Productivity consists not only in minimizing cost per unit of output but also requires sufficiently high quality of the output to meet the need for which the good or service is ostensibly produced. If we measure productivity by cost per unit output alone, without adding a dimension to our measure that reflects its quality, our measure of productivity will produce artifactual readings of performance. For example, suppose we measure social service by numbers of cases processed per week. The result of introducing this measure is that using it to increase caseworkers'

income, or budget, or other benefits may simply serve to increase the number of cases "processed" while so decreasing quality of service as to make for what would be universally counted as a decline in productivity. Much of the work in public sector productivity theory focuses on measures that will not have this effect. But the obstacle that any successful measure must surmount is very great. The only measure that *cannot be corrupted* is one that is so inextricably linked to political objectives that the only practical way civil servants can increase their personal utility is by actually increasing productivity of the political objective itself. The measure must be constructed with ingenuity that is greater than the ingenuity of the civil servants whose activities are being measured!

The necessary prerequisites for productivity gains in the public sector are cumbersome. This cumbersomeness does not arise in the perfectly competitive model of an economy on which the market approach to productivity is founded. In the perfectly competitive world of neoclassical microeconomics, there is no problem of productivity because all economic agents and institutions always maximize the productivity of their inputs of land, capital, and labor. Where agents are numerous and rational, commodities divisible and infinitely substitutable, market entry and exit unrestricted, prices inelastic and returns to scale nonexistent, all factors of production are used at their highest level of productivity. The perfectly competitive market effectively assimilates issues of efficiency and effectiveness in production, since the demand for a firm's goods reflects buyers' assessments of the goods in terms of price and quality. A low-quality good must fetch a lower price, and so provide a smaller return, than a high-quality good. If firms can maximize their profits at the lower price, then of course the productivity of their factors has not declined but has remained at its optimum level.

By diminishing quality, a firm has simply entered the market for another good altogether. In the neoclassical model, the market provides an *information network* that producers use to fine-tune their mix of factors in order to provide consumer wants at the prices they are willing to pay. In a purely competitive market, we may be sure that the marginal productivity of every input or factor with respect to every output will be equal to its price. In such a market, the entrepreneur is provided with unambiguous signals when his productivity departs from the optimum: Sales fall, or receipts fall, or both. Of course, if the entrepreneur is perfectly rational and fully informed about production techniques and market prices, this will never happen, and the problem of productivity simply does not arise within the compass of the perfectly competitive model.

In the unreal world of perfect competition between rational agents, productivity and utility are both maximized as by-products of each other, not only by each individual agent but by the economy as a whole, up to the constraints of Pareto optimality. The proof that perfect competition generates a market-clearing equilibrium that is Pareto optimal both in production and consumption is of course one of the chief theoretical ornaments of contemporary economic theory. Long before this result was rigorously proven, the presumption that Adam Smith's beneficent "hidden hand" really existed made the real world appear much like the unreal world of perfect competition. Market-oriented approaches to public sector activities are a recent variant on this thrust. The thrust is of course parried by citing the deviation of the real world from the competitive model and the even greater divergence of the public sector from the economics of the market. Moreover, it is ironic that while our problems of measuring productivity derive from differences between the public sector and the perfect market, in a perfect market there is no need for the sort of measures of productivity we seek.

The welfare economic rationale for market mechanisms, either within the public sector or between the sorts of firms that actually exist and compete so imperfectly, has, of course, evaporated. Where agents are not rational, where there are indivisibilities, returns to scale, incomplete information, there is no certainty of Pareto optimas; indeed, there is every sign of the lack of equilibria necessary to such desired states.

What rationale, then, remains for the market approach in the real world of public and private endeavors? In fact, these considerations do not deprive market approaches of much of their attractiveness at all. For the appeal of these approaches does not rest on their welfare-economic aspects but on the strength of the market as an informational distribution system and as a force constraining the personally efficient use of the distributed information. Thus, a market of buyers and sellers will be sensitive to information about changes in prices (and changes in the supplies and demands they reflect) even when the sellers and buyers compete imperfectly. All that is required is that

they be at least intermittently rational and that they compete at all. For example, a pure monopolist in the supply of records and a pure monopolist in the supply of books may compete in the market for leisure products. As a means of decentralizing or disaggregating the needs and wants of the members of a society, the price system is unrivaled. In contrast to central planning, the price mechanism is simply a far superior means of communicating to producers how much of what to produce.

The price mechanism, then, is not defended on normative grounds. Rather, it is merely an effective way to provide individuals with information to aid decision making. And if productivity is of concern to economic agents, the price mechanism will be primary in the construction of indicators to monitor its improvement. Public sector producers lack this critical informational tool. The governmental environment in which most agencies operate separates the production of goods and services from information about the quality and quantity of their output. The electoral, legislative, and bureaucratic channels through which information relevant to optimal output is now channeled are long, noisy, misdirected, and subject to breakdowns. Market approaches in the public sector are nothing but the attempt to circumvent this poor information system in favor of one we know to be superior. Thus, attempts to introduce marketlike reforms in the public sector can be defended as a way of improving the bases of decision making, reforms that are necessary if productivity gains are to be detected.

## MARKETLIKE APPROACHES IN THE PUBLIC SECTOR

It may be useful, at this point, to summarize some key points. We have argued, in essence, that attempts to improve productivity in the public sector must direct individual maximizing behavior toward politically determined outcomes. But unless the two are by-products of each other, there is no reason to assume that what civil servants maximize will actually improve productivity. In particular, it is improbable that the maximization of some *intermediate* factor output—specified through collective bargaining negotiation, for example —will (1) necessarily produce desired final output, and/or (2) be sustained by the maximizing agents (e.g., civil servants). To put it another way, "second-best" solutions that surrogate the market are unlikely to resolve the problems surmounted by the market because they do not tap the best source of relevant market information and do not link it inextricably to agents' utilities or private production function.

Consider two simple case illustrations of this point. In the city of Flint, Michigan a productivity "bargain" was struck between the city and the union representing waste collectors. The city wished to curb waste collection cost primarily by cutting the amount of overtime pay. The union, in turn, wanted to increase the collectors' income. A productivity scheme was designed so that workers presumably had an incentive to reduce overtime pay since a pool of savings would be shared by the city and the workers—after adjusting for quantity (tonnage collected) as well as a quality (complaints) dimension (Greiner, Dahl, Hatry, and Millar, 1977: 50). Workers were supposed to maximize a "productivity coefficient" that consisted of an overtime reduction factor, a quality factor, a route completion factor, and tonnage collected. The maximization of these variables would increase the productivity bonus that, presumably, is what workers "really" wanted, instead of, say, overtime hours of work.

A similar case of productivity bargaining occurred between the city of Orange, California and the association representing the police. The agreement called for across-the-board wage increases that were tied to a reduction in the reported number of four "repressible" crimes: rape, robbery, burglary, and auto theft (Greiner, Dahl, Hatry, and Millar, 1977: 64). While the experiment was tried for one year and then discontinued, researchers from the Urban Institute considered that, on balance, the experiment *was* successful.

From the perspective of our argument, both cases are problematical. Consider the implicit assumptions: In both cases, workers were asked to maximize something. But what is put forth to be maximized is in fact, neither (1) what the workers ultimately wish to maximize (they want to maximize income but must maximize other variables to reach their real objective), nor (2) what the respective city governments wish to maximize—clean streets in the former case and public safety in the latter. It is an empirical question as to whether lower cost per ton of garbage is related to clean streets, or the reduction in reported crime is positively related to public safety. A great deal of literature has been written on the problems of measuring intermediate outputs and the distinction between outputs and the objectives (or consequences) of public pro-

grams (see Ross and Burkhead, 1974; also Levy, Meltsner, and Wildavsky, 1974). Suffice it to say here that a productivity bargain that commits workers to maximize an intermediate output may have disfunctional effects.

Consider the Orange, California case again. According to the Urban Institute report: "The department's response to the incentive program was to focus primarily on the prevention of burglaries, which historically had comprised about 80 percent of the four incentive crimes reported to police" (Greiner, Dahl, Hatry, and Millar, 1977: 63). From the standpoint of the productivity argument, this discussion seems rational. But as Lester Thurow (1970) has shown, the allocation of a law enforcement budget to achieve a given level of efficiency will create equity effects both for potential victims *and* potential perpetrators of crime (both of which should enter into a quality dimension of productivity). Thus, it is quite conceivable that the probability of being raped may increase if a decision is made to allocate law enforcement resources to maximize the reduction in burglaries. (This is simply one example of what Donald T. Campbell [1979: 84] calls the obtrusive and unintended effects of quantitative indicators.) Consequently, even if law enforcement personnel did indeed maximize the production of an intermediate good, it is by no means certain that the politically determined objective (such as public safety) will inevitably be improved or increased.

Consider a perhaps even more fundamental problem. In both cases, it is assumed that the intermediate outputs maximized and the politically determined objectives will be by-products of each other. But a simple point shows that this is not automatically so. Once a "productivity frontier" is reached, workers have no incentive to maximize intermediate outputs. Consider the example of Orange, California once again. According to the Urban Institute report: "After reducing the city's already low rate of incentive crimes enough to earn the maximum possible wage increases, police in Orange apparently felt that further reduction would be difficult, if not impossible. Indeed, most employees . . . felt that they had reached the point of diminishing returns and that if they continued with such a plan, they would, in effect, be competing against themselves (that is, against their own good record)" (Greiner, Dahl, Hatry, and Millar, 1977: 66). What this implies is that, at some point, workers may have no incentive to continue to maximize a negotiated indicator if the given indicator no longer is related to wage increases, utility, and the like. When this occurs, the variable that was previously maximized is neither sufficient nor necessary for the improvement of productivity in the public sector.

Where does this leave us? To restate an earlier point, the difficulty of improving productivity in the public sector is, to a great extent, *informational*. The problem of public sector productivity is not, as some would suggest, measurement, but rather the kinds of organizational arrangements that would allow maximizing agents—civil servants—to pursue their interests in ways that will lead to improved, politically determined outcomes. This, pure and simple, is the rationale for some of the market-based reforms that are receiving increased attention in public administration. This current attention comes from two basic sources. The marketlike reforms to be discussed here shortly have some appeal because they seem to be "reasonable" responses to growing fiscal scarcity—especially at the local level. Second, the reforms have conservative appeal in the current political climate because they seem to encourage "limited government." Our arguments are based on neither perspective. To reiterate: The justification for marketlike reforms in the public sector rests solely on the argument that they should improve the bases of decision making and thereby enhance productivity. The last part of the paper sketches out some of these market-based reforms and notes some special problems of implementation.

## Contracting

Governments, particularly at the local level, have for some time contracted with private firms, nonprofit organizations, and other jurisdictions for a range of services. The rationale for contracting is straightforward and the expected benefits include:

- cost savings
- choice of contractor(s)
- expertise of contractor(s)
- public management flexibility offered by the contracting method of service provision

The growing interest in contracting is related to the deterioration of the fiscal condition of many local governments. But this assumes only that contracting will be less costly than the direct (monopolistic) provision of services by local government agencies.

Whether contracting will actually improve public sector productivity is an empirical question. Still, we may make some inferences about the necessary conditions for potential productivity gains. First, the contractor must seek to maximize a private goal such as income or budget. Second, the local government must have some options available (choice) so that the availability of the contract (for the contractor) is by no means certain. Third, the local government must be able to act on these options. For example, a local government that contracts for a service must be able to choose among alternative bids and/or supply the service itself as an alternative to contracting. Under these conditions, demand and price factors make it possible to join maximizing behavior by the contractors with politically determined objectives. And under these conditions, productivity gains may be realized. The fact that, in practice, many contract arrangements fall short of such expectations means that factors intervene (often referred to as "political influence") to nullify the supply and demand factors.

## User Fees

Approximately 15 to 20 percent of locally raised revenue comes from user fees. The rationale for user fees is straightforward. First, fees presumably improve "allocative efficiency" since community residents can articulate their preferences for local public goods and services more accurately than through the voting mechanism. As one proponent of a greater reliance on user fees put it "If the government sets a price on the product—thereby opening up a market through which consumers can register their vote for or against, by either paying the price or not consuming the product—the price could guide the city in the production of its services" (Mushkin, Sandifer, Turner, and Vehorn, 1979: 126). Second, from the standpoint of bureaucratic performance, user fees are intuitively appealing since they avoid the bilateral relationship between agency and legislature. That is, the legislature is no longer faced with an all-or-nothing appropriation decision. On the contrary, the production of both quality and quantity of local government services becomes price sensitive—assuming that the local government agency does not enjoy a monopoly of the good or service that is nonsubstitutable. Under the conditions just outlined, the prospects for productivity improvement seem reasonably straightforward. However, the personal objectives of the civil servant are usually conspicuously absent from user fee mechanisms; consequently, a user fee approach is not in itself sufficient to ensure improvements in productivity.

## Public Sector–Private Sector Competition

Although there are analogous services provided in both the public and private sectors, consumers of public goods and services rarely have the opportunity to choose between the two. But if citizens could exercise such choice, the competition or even the threat of competition would make public producers (i.e., local government agencies) more efficient.

There are very few examples of this situation. A survey by the Urban Institute noted that in Wichita, Kansas and St. Paul, Minnesota private and public refuse haulers compete with each other. While public collection is slightly more expensive, the cost difference between public collection and private collection is trivial (Fisk, Kiesling, and Muller, 1978: 14–17). In contrast, a study by E. S. Savas found that private refuse collection in Bellerose, Long Island, comparable to collection in an adjacent area in the City of New York, was about one-third of the cost of municipal collection in New York City (1974: 478–479). While admittedly sketchy, these examples suggest that public-private competition may reduce the cost of provision by a public monopoly.

Creating a competitive environment is necessary but not sufficient. The information concerning efficiency must enter the public budgeting process so that public agencies are held accountable for cost containment or cost reduction. The legislature must use the cost information when making appropriations. While obvious, this requirement has not been easily accepted, given the routines of the typical budget process. An additional element is being introduced into budgetary decision making. But the history of budget reform suggests that information about efficiency does not automatically permeate budget routines (Straussman, 1979).

## Competitive Bureaus

The concept of competitive bureaus flies in the face of orthodox public administration theory, which views "coordination" and "centralization" as superior to organizational fragmentation. Yet there is little evidence to support this conventional wisdom.

Critics from the public choice school have seriously questioned this traditional view of bureaucracy. Specifically, coordination and centralization merely promote the monopoly position of bureaus. But why should competition between or among bureaus reduce this tendency? A bureau faced with competition from other bureaus will find that the elasticity of demand for its services may increase when citizen-consumers realize that there are alternatives available. For any single bureau providing the given good or service, the level of demand should decline. Two conclusions follow: First, bureaus faced with this situation will have an incentive to search for more efficient ways to produce their goods and services. Second, the legislature should be able to use the information to make appropriations that more accurately reflect the "true" costs of producing public goods and services.

Aside from obvious problems of political feasibility, there are three potential caveats that ought to be mentioned with regard to competitive bureaus. While bureaus often provide similar services, they usually do not provide identical ones. It is assumed that there is an elasticity of demand for like services among public bureaus. But bureaus try to reduce this possibility by stressing the uniqueness of their output. The empirical question is whether citizen-consumers perceive that the services of bureaus are indeed similar. For instance, would public assistance recipients who are declared employable recognize that job placement services are available from both a unit in a typical social services department (generally at the county level) and a state employment office? The consumer—in this case, the recipient of public assistance—needs to recognize that the services available are similar. Next, the bureaus, in turn, must acknowledge that the consumers will act as if choice is available to initiate a quasicompetitive environment. But while this would be sufficient in the private sector, it is not in the public sector. As in the case of the previous option—private sector–public sector competition—the legislature needs to see benefits in the competitive situation and incorporate such information into appropriations decisions. How else would gains from competition in the public sector be realized? As with the previous option, the funding arrangements for specific goods and services do not often provide the necessary fiscal atmosphere that encourages economizing. Returning to the example of job placement alternatives, federal funding of state employment agencies may remove part of the superficial competitive characteristics that seem to be present merely because both agencies provide similar services. But the similarities end once funding sources are considered. The legislature (as well as the respective agencies) may not have the required incentives to take advantage of competitive bureaus as a quasimarket option.

## CONCLUSION

We may close this discussion and review with some reiteration and qualification. Our argument for the implementation of market mechanisms has been resolutely nonideological and at least partially nontheoretical. Much of the resistance to such mechanisms stems from the perception that they reflect politically controversial perspectives and/or practically irrelevant theoretical possibilities. We have, however, suggested not that the decentralization fostered in a price system is good in itself or that a logically sufficient condition for a Pareto optimal must result in the public or private sector. Rather, exposing public service and its producers to a demand curve, to prices they do not themselves set, provides them with the *best available* information about how to increase productivity as well as with a strong motive to act on this information.

Some qualifications to our proposal must be kept in mind. Universally and invariably, the hopes of reformers overreach the actual improvements attained. Indeed, improvements are often overwhelmed by *unintended consequences* of the reform originally unknown to the reformer. We can have no assurance that market-inspired reforms would be different. Moreover, the market-based options by themselves offer no guarantee that the obtained informational advantages of the market will actually be utilized. In particular, the implementation problems of market-based options are perhaps the most difficult hurdle to overcome. The implementation of market-based reforms must itself be linked to—made a natural by-product of—the output maximized by political decision makers, especially legislators who appropriate public funds. Implementation presents a series of obstacles, some of which have been hinted at in our brief discussions of the four marketlike mechanisms. Yet implementation logically follows an understanding of the conceptual problems that make productivity difficult to achieve in the public sector. This prior state—the stage of conceptual clarification—has yet to be reached. Perhaps we have moved in the right direction.

*This article appears in a slightly different version under the title "Public Sector Monopolies" in* Productivity and Public Policy, *edited by Marc Holzer and Stuart Nagel, Beverly Hills: Sage Publications, Incorporated, 1984.*

## REFERENCES

Campbell, Donald T. "Assessing the Impact of Planned Social Change." *Evaluation and Program Planning* 2 (1979): 67–90.

Fisk, Donald; Kiesling, Herbert; and Muller, Thomas. *Private Provision of Public Services: An Overview.* Washington, D. C.: The Urban Institute, 1978.

Greiner, John; Dahl, Roger E.; Hatry, Harry P.; and Millar, Annie P. *Monetary Incentive and Work Standards in Five Cities: Impacts and Implications for Management and Labor.* Washington, D. C.: The Urban Institute, 1977.

Levy, Frank; Meltsner, Arnold; and Wildavsky, Aaron. *Urban Outcomes.* Berkeley: University of California Press, 1974.

Mushkin, Selma; Sandifer, Frank; Turner, Charles G.; and Vehorn, Charles L. "The Tax Revolt: An Opportunity to Make Positive Changes in Local Government." In *Proposition 13 and Its Consequences for Public Management,* edited by Selma Mushkin, pp. 119–140. Cambridge, Mass.: ABT Books.

Niskanen, William. *Bureaucracy and Representative Government.* Chicago: Aldine, 1971.

Ross, John, and Burkhead, Jesse. *Productivity in the Local Public Sector.* Lexington: Lexington Books, 1974.

Savas, E. S. "Municipal Monopolies Versus Competition in Delivering Urban Services." In *Improving the Quality of Urban Management,* edited by Willis Hawley and David Rogers. Beverly Hills, Calif.: Sage, 1974.

Schick, Allen. "The Road to PPB: The Stages of Budget Reform." *Public Administration Review* 26 (1966): 243–258.

Staaf, Robert J. "The Growth of the Educational Bureaucracy: Do Teachers Make a Difference?" In *Budgets and Bureaucrats,* edited by Thomas Borcherding. Durham: Duke University Press, 1977.

Sterne, Richard; Rabushka, Alvin; and Scott, Helen. "Serving the Elderly—An Illustration of the Niskanen Effect." *Public Choice* 13 (1972): 81–90.

Stockfish, J. A. *Analysis of Bureaucratic Behavior: The Ill-Defined Production Process.* Santa Monica: Rand Corporation, 1976.

Straussman, Jeffrey D. "A Typology of Budgetary Environments: Notes on the Prospects for Reform." *Administration & Society* 11 (1979): 216–226.

Thurow, Lester. "Equity versus Efficiency in Law Enforcement." *Public Policy* 18 (1970): 451–462.

Wolf, Charles. "A Theory of Nonmarket Failure: Framework for Implementation Analysis." *Journal of Law and Economics* 22 (1979): 107–139.

# CHAPTER TWELVE

# Evaluation
# and
# Analysis

## Evaluation Purposes

Scarvia B. Anderson
Samuel Ball

*There are references to other chapters not included in this volume. The material presented in this essay stands alone, however, and therefore is included separately.*

Chapter One listed six major purposes of evaluation. These purposes are stated in terms of a common element that runs through the writings of those identified with the field: namely, that evaluation bears, or should bear, some relationship to decision making. These purposes constitute our definition of *program evaluation*. At the same time, we indicated that there are many other definitions and "models" around, although we specifically disclaim any model status for our simple representation of the various purposes of program evaluation and of the kinds of situations that give rise to them. We recognize further that although these purposes can be separately described, they are not mutually exclusive, and we hope that they do not generate the kinds of confusion about their intent that Baker (1976, p. 2) calls attention to in other schemes. Specifically (and to paraphrase her statement), the six purposes are presented to help us organize the way we think about evaluation, not to control our

From *The Profession and Practice of Program Evaluation* by S. B. Anderson and Samuel Ball. Copyright © 1978, Jossey-Bass Inc., Publishers. Reprinted by permission.

actions or guide the specific ways in which evaluation is conducted.

Before we review each of these purposes in detail, it may be well to remind ourselves of some of the things that evaluation is *not*. It is not simply measurement and data collection, although measurement and data collection are usually important precursors to the process. It is also not decision making, although it must be useful for decision making to survive. It does not always qualify as research, although for some questions the closer the evaluation process comes to research the more valid and reliable it will be. It is not necessarily limited to determining how well programs achieve their objectives; it may begin before a program or policy is implemented, or it may touch on issues that were not envisioned at the time the goals or objectives of the program were formulated. It is not the exclusive province of social scientists, although psychologists, sociologists, economists, and others of similar bent have tended more than physical scientists or those in the arts and humanities to gravitate to the field.

The six major purposes of evaluation—or areas of involvement of evaluators—can each be broken down into a number of components. The major purposes and their components are listed down the left-hand side of Table 1. Table 1 also matches evaluation purposes and components to likely general methods of investigation, a matching which is the subject of Chapter Three.

The content of this list of evaluation purposes benefited from Scriven's (1974) "Product Checklist."

Scriven's list, however, is designed primarily for appraising completed educational products or evaluation proposals, while Table 1 is intended as an aid to overall evaluation planning. Now let us examine each of the six purpose categories in turn.

## I. TO CONTRIBUTE TO DECISIONS ABOUT PROGRAM INSTALLATION

Usually, the evaluation process has been thought to begin *after* the decision to implement an education, training, or social-action program. However, a number of the skills and techniques usually associated with existing or planned programs apply to what Harless (1973) calls "front-end analysis." Assessment of the needs for a program, evaluation of the adequacy of the conception, estimates of cost and of operational feasibility, and projections of demand and support are all important precursors to decisions about whether to implement a program and about the size and scope of the installation. Untold waste, wheel spinning, and harm can be prevented by sufficient advance attention to such factors.

Some of our colleagues in engineering have not been caught as often as we have with inadequate investigations into feasibility. They frequently start out by designing software instead of hardware, making plans instead of equipment, using simulations in place of the real thing. Many received their inspiration from advanced systems analyses in World War II, which doubled the chances of fighter planes intercepting Nazi bombers and increased the number of U-boats sunk by more than 50 percent (Pfeiffer, 1968). Our colleagues in publishing and manufacturing know what happens when their market research is inadequate. If nobody buys their products or books, they incur enormous losses as well as the wrath of stockholders and overstocked retailers. Experienced cooks try exotic new recipes on the family before they serve them to guests at a special dinner party.

But health officials attempt to distribute family-planning information to populations where the number of children in a family is an entrenched status symbol. A $45 million educational satellite is launched with no programs to be transmitted from it. Developers in countries where few people have cars build schools in locations far from public transportation lines. Legislation requires bilingual education in areas where the "native" language has never been written down. Elaborate experimental programs are launched in schools where, once the initial grant is spent, maintaining the program would take half of the school's total budget. Supplementary funds are allocated to school districts on the basis of the number of children diagnosed as "retarded"; is it any wonder that one county reported brain damage in 20 percent of its elementary school population? Reports indicate that the new closed-circuit TV training programs do not appear to be very effective; no one noted that the television sets were not delivered to some of the groups until the series had been underway for several months. (Guttentag and Struening, 1975, p. 4, have commented trenchantly that "evaluations continue without either raising or answering the primary question: 'Does the program exist?'") Employee-training programs are installed without determining whether organizational barriers will make it impossible for trainees to apply their newly acquired skills or whether supervisors' attitudes toward a program are so negative that it is likely to be scuttled or ignored. Elaborate licensing programs are pushed through as a means of eliminating competition in the occupation instead of protecting the public. Lengthy written procedures on how to qualify for special community health or economic assistance programs are distributed to a population verging on illiteracy. Horror stories? Yes. But each is an example of what can happen when programs are launched without appropriate concern for the context of the innovation.

It seems obvious to determine if there is a need for a program before one seriously considers installing it. There are at least two aspects to need: frequency and intensity (see IA, Table 1). In general, the more people who are presumed to have a need, the more likely it is that public support can be obtained for a program to fill it (for example, programs to reduce widespread illiteracy in developing countries). However, action may also be taken if the need, although not widespread, is seen as intense or grave. Recent extraordinary concern with mental retardation is a case in point (Anderson, 1973, p. 197).

Evaluators should be able to perform an especially important service in the area of needs assessment, because in the past relatively few program planners have approached degree of need directly, objectively, or even explicitly. If they have been explicit, they have tended to use their own and their colleagues' intuitions, second-hand reports ("Our social workers say that . . ."), general population indices that may not be

## TABLE 1
### Purposes and general methods of program evaluation

■ Likely investigation method

| | *Experimental study* | *Quasi-experimental study* | *Correlational status study* | *Survey* | *Personnel or client assessment* | *Systematic "expert" judgments* | *Clinical or case study* | *Informal observation or testimony* |
|---|---|---|---|---|---|---|---|---|
| I. To contribute to decisions about program installation | | | | | | | | |
| A. Need | | | | | | | | |
| 1. Frequency | | | | | | | | |
| a. Individual | | | | ■ | ■ | ■ | | |
| b. Society | | | | ■ | | ■ | | ■ |
| c. Other (that is, industrial, professional, governmental) | | | | ■ | ■ | ■ | | ■ |
| 2. Intensity | | | | | | | | |
| a. Individual | | | | ■ | ■ | ■ | | ■ |
| b. Society | | | | ■ | | ■ | ■ | ■ |
| c. Other | | | | ■ | ■ | ■ | ■ | ■ |
| B. Program conception | | | | | | | | |
| 1. Appropriateness | | | | | | ■ | | |
| 2. Quality | | | | | | ■ | | |
| 3. Priority in the face of competing needs | | | | | | ■ | | |
| C. Estimated cost | | | | | | | | |
| 1. Absolute cost | | | | ■ | | ■ | | |
| 2. Cost in relation to alternative strategies oriented toward same need | | | | ■ | | ■ | | |
| D. Operational feasibility | | | | | | | | |
| 1. Staff | | | | ■ | ■ | ■ | | ■ |
| 2. Materials | | | | ■ | | ■ | | ■ |
| 3. Facilities | | | | ■ | | ■ | | ■ |
| 4. Schedule | | | | | | ■ | | |
| E. Projection of demand and support | | | | | | | | |
| 1. Popular | | | | ■ | | ■ | | ■ |
| 2. Political and financial | | | | ■ | | ■ | | ■ |
| 3. Professional | | | | ■ | | ■ | | ■ |
| II. To contribute to decisions about program continuation, expansion, or "certification" (licensing, accredition, and so on) | | | | | | | | |
| A. Continuing need | | | | | | | | |
| 1. Frequency | | | | | | | | |
| a. Individual | | | | ■ | ■ | ■ | | |
| b. Society | | | | ■ | | ■ | | ■ |
| c. Other | | | | ■ | | ■ | | ■ |
| 2. Intensity | | | | | | | | |
| a. Individual | | | | ■ | ■ | ■ | ■ | ■ |
| b. Society | | | | ■ | | ■ | ■ | ■ |
| c. Other | | | | ■ | ■ | ■ | ■ | ■ |
| B. Global effectiveness in meeting need | | | | | | | | |
| 1. Short-term | ■ | ■ | | | | | | |
| 2. Long-term | ■ | ■ | | | | | | |
| C. Minimal negative side effects | ■ | ■ | | | | | ■ | |
| D. Important positive side effects | ■ | ■ | | | | | ■ | |
| E. Cost | | | | | | | | |
| 1. Absolute cost | | | | ■ | | | | |
| 2. Cost in relation to alternative strategies to fill same need | | | | ■ | | | | |
| 3. Cost in relation to effectiveness | | | ■ | | | | | |
| F. Demand and support | | | | | | | | |
| 1. Popular | | | | ■ | | | | ■ |
| 2. Political and financial | | | | ■ | | ■ | | ■ |
| 3. Professional | | | | ■ | | ■ | | ■ |

| | Experimental study | Quasi-experimental study | Correlational status study | Survey | Personnel or client assessment | Systematic "expert" judgments | Clinical or case study | Informal observation or testimony |
|---|---|---|---|---|---|---|---|---|

III. To contribute to decisions about program modification

    A. Program objectives
        1. Validity and utility (in meeting needs)
        2. Popular acceptance
        3. Professional acceptance
        4. Client acceptance
        5. Staff acceptance

    B. Program content
        1. Relevance to program objectives
        2. Coverage of objectives
        3. Technical accuracy
        4. Degree of structure
        5. Relevance to backgrounds of clients
        6. Effectiveness of components
        7. Sequence of components
        8. Popular acceptance
        9. Professional acceptance
      10. Client acceptance
      11. Staff acceptance

    C. Program methodology
        1. Degree of client autonomy
        2. Effectiveness of delivery methods
        3. Pacing and length
        4. Reinforcement system, if any
        5. Client acceptance
        6. Staff acceptance

    D. Program context
        1. Administrative structure, auspices
        2. Program administration procedures
        3. Staff roles and relationships
        4. Public relations efforts
        5. Physical facilities and plant
        6. Fiscal sources and stability
        7. Fiscal administration procedures

    E. Personnel policies and practices
        1. Clients
           a. Recruitment
           b. Selection and placement, if any
           c. Evaluation, if any
           d. Discipline, if any
           e. Retention
        2. Staff
           a. Selection and placement
           b. In-service training
           c. Evaluation for promotion, guidance,
             retention, and so on
        3. Administrators
           a. Selection
           b. Evaluation for promotion, guidance,
             retention, and so on

IV. To obtain evidence favoring program to rally support

    A. Popular

    B. Political and financial

    C. Professional

V. To obtain evidence against program to rally opposition

    A. Popular

    B. Political and financial

    C. Professional

VI. To contribute to the understanding of basic processes

    A. Educational

    B. Psychological

    C. Physiological

    D. Social

    E. Economic

    F. Evaluation (methodology)

applicable to the locale of interest, or "carrier" variables (for example, family income rather than actual appraisals of the needs of individuals in the income category). They have also tended to confuse possible solutions with problems; for example, in education, evaluators have defined needs in such terms as "individualization of instruction," "open classrooms," "differentiated staffing" (Blabolil, 1976). Scriven and Roth (1977a, p. 27) press for explicit distinction between needs described in performance-deficit terms (which we are stressing) and needs described in treatment-deficit terms. They suggest that the two kinds of needs have quite different implications for evaluation.

Needs may be defined at the level of individuals (the potential clients for an educational, economic, or social-action program) or at a higher level of government or organizational requirement. As an example at the governmental level, consider what happened following Sputnik, when we were afraid that we were not going to produce enough scientists, mathematicians, and engineers to meet the technological and defense demands the nation faced. Extraordinary educational and professional interventions, many well funded by the financial standards of the day, were launched. The results were so "successful" that we feared an oversupply of engineers in the decade that followed, but many individuals benefited from the opportunities provided. An organizational need is illustrated by an industry unable to establish plants in a certain area or keep existing installations open without undertaking massive training efforts to ensure an adequate supply of trained workers. In many such instances, partnerships with—and even sponsorship by—state development offices have made such efforts possible. The addition or maintenance of several hundred jobs contributed sufficiently to the economic welfare of the area to encourage such cooperation. And individuals profited from the chance to upgrade their earning ability.

Problems arise if the needs projected from above conflict with the needs of the individuals whom the program must ultimately reach. From time to time there have been proposals to redistribute the population of the United States to relieve congestion in the cities. Such plans have not materialized, not only because of the tremendous logistics and costs involved, but also because of a basic unwillingness of people in a democracy to be moved on any basis other than their own volition. Young and Willmott (1957) describe the

unhappiness of families in East London who were moved from their familiar neighborhoods to better housing in a strange district. Commenting on a similar kind of local redistribution effort, the Model Cities projects, Rothenberg (1975) suggests that "complicated social impacts of project activities on motivations, productive capacity, and decision-making processes may well have to be estimated, as well as more conventional notions of living standards, in order to predict continuing future consequences of . . . projects" (p. 87). But, in the past, program developers have seldom bothered to document their rights to inflict programs on others—or to justify the particular techniques they have chosen. In fact, Chazan (1968) and others point out that such value decisions are outside the scope of evaluative research. However, we suggest that assistance in clarifying the range of alternatives that underlie major value decisions related to possible program installation is an important function for the evaluator at the stage of front-end analysis and properly belongs under evaluation of program conception (item IB, Table 1).

But let us return for a moment to needs assessment "models" (as they are called), whether they are applied to individuals, groups, or institutions. The most usual definition of *need* is "a condition in which there is a discrepancy between an *acceptable* state of affairs and an *observed* state of affairs" (Anderson and others, 1975, p. 254). Scriven (and Roth, 1977a) rejects the definition of a need as a discrepancy between the actual and the ideal (although he admits it is a formula he used to like), "because we often need to improve and know how to, without knowing what the ideal would be like" (p. 25). Needs assessments may vary in their degree of objectivity, but they should at least qualify as systematic if they are to be discussed in the literature of program evaluation. Witkin (1976) provides a comprehensive review of approaches to needs assessment in the area of educational planning and evaluation. "Most writers agree," she says, "that a complete model should include at least these components: (1) consideration of goals; (2) procedures for determining the present status of those goals; (3) methods for identifying, describing, and analyzing discrepancies between goals and present status; and (4) methods for assigning priorities to those discrepancies. In practice, one or more of the components are often omitted, and the order of components 1 and 2 may be reversed" (p. 4). She also points to the dilemma that the broader the statement of the goal, the easier it will be to obtain agreement about its importance but the harder it will be ever to find out whether the goal is met.

Some of the key questions to ask in assessment of needs are: What made us think in the first place that there were any needs "out there" requiring mitigation? Whose needs are we talking about? How can we find out whether the needs are frequent or intense enough to justify intervention? How much frequency or intensity is sufficient—that is, how much discrepancy between acceptable state and observed state is intolerable, or at least undesirable? According to whose standards or what criteria?

The problem of standards is a particularly difficult one to deal with in needs assessment as it is in many other aspects of evaluation. We are all aware that standards change with circumstances, expectations, and who is setting them. They also vary with the perceived ability of a society or institution to influence the phenomenon to which they pertain. What is considered a minimum standard of living in this country has risen dramatically in the last generation and is much higher than that considered tolerable in less developed nations. Standards for employability go up during times of widespread unemployment; standards for nutrition go down during times of crop failure.

The field of literacy offers a fairly straightforward illustration of both changing standards and multiple definitions of them (see Corder, 1971). The U. S. Census Bureau definition of "literacy" is "ability to read and write a simple message in any language." For their purposes, individuals with more than five years of schooling are *assumed* to be literate; if people do not have five years of schooling, self-reports of ability to read and write are accepted (a person who claims to be able to read but not write is classified illiterate). In World War I, the U. S. Army adopted "the equivalent of a fourth-grade education" as its definition of functional literacy. Currently, the Army gives literacy training to those who score below fifth-grade level on a norms-referenced test (and "graduates" those who subsequently achieve at that level). Increasingly, objective measures of reading and writing are replacing years of schooling or self-reports, because performance associated with those criteria has been found wanting.

Thomas G. Sticht, of the National Institute of Education's Basic Skills Group, has plotted the relationship between criteria of literacy and the proportion of the population judged illiterate, where the criteria are

defined as follows (after Resnick and Resnick, 1977): (a) writing one's name; (b) reading familiar text aloud; (c) reading familiar text aloud and indicating recognition of content; (d) reading unfamiliar text to gain new information; (e) inferential reading of new text; and (f) interpretive and relational reading of texts. The curve, shown in Figure 1, corresponds closely to one that can be derived from National Assessment data (ECS, 1972), which includes items corresponding approximately to criteria b–f. One can readily see here how differences in standards can affect the size of a population judged deserving of "treatment."

Even after the case has been made that a particular kind of program is needed, we must be prepared to consider the priority for this particular program in the face of competing needs and limited resources. As a very simple example, should a school system assign its special remedial-reading teachers to the large number of eighth graders reading at fifth-grade level or to the handful of fifth graders reading at second-grade level? Such decisions about priorities probably should go hand in hand with evaluation of the conception of the program—its quality and appropriateness (see item IB, Table 1).

In the same vein, do we have the capabilities—financial, personnel, material, and operational—to deliver the goods? If not, can we obtain them by the

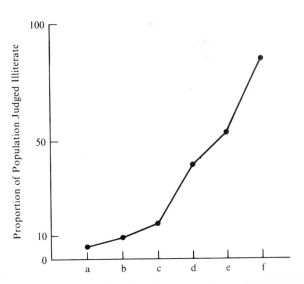

**Figure 1** Diagram of the Relationship Between Criterion of Illiteracy and Proportion of Illiterates

293

scheduled starting date and maintain them for the life of the effort? Whose support besides that of the "clients" and "staff" are we going to need to make a go of the program? The list might be long: community members, parents, educational associations, public officials, funding agencies, professionals. (Consider the difficulty of setting up a nationwide inoculation program when physicians disagree about its efficacy, or of installing a new mathematics curriculum that is considered technically unsound by the National Council of Teachers of Mathematics.) These are some of the elements of evaluation designed to contribute to decisions about program installation. None of them should be neglected. However, we should stress that evaluators tuned more to empirical investigation than to judgmental processes will be even more frustrated in front-end analysis than in pursuing the other five evaluation purposes outlined in Table 1, for Purpose I requires a full measure of wisdom, opinion, speculation, estimation, discretion, and political acumen. Economists talk about the "art" of cost projections at this stage (perhaps through simulation) as contrasted with the "science" they can employ after a project has already been installed. It is obviously easier to evaluate an existing program than one still on the drawing board (Sassone and Schaffer, 1977). However, front-end analysis is worthwhile if only a few potential clients, would-be program directors, and hard-pressed funding agencies are spared a dismal experience—or, conversely, promised a more rewarding experience than a poorly thought-out effort might have provided.

## II. TO CONTRIBUTE TO DECISIONS ABOUT PROGRAM CONTINUATION, EXPANSION (OR CONTRACTION), OR "CERTIFICATION" (LICENSING, ACCREDITATION, AND SO FORTH)

This purpose is the one usually served by what is commonly called "summative" or "impact" evaluation, which many people, especially those outside the profession, see as the essence of evaluation. For example, Briggs (1976) has said of educational evaluation, "When an administrator, school board member, teacher or parent says, 'X will be evaluated,' he or she usually means that at some future point the question, 'Was X worthwhile?', will be answered." Weiss (1975) allows that "many public officials in the Congress and the executive branch sincerely believe that policy choices should consistently be based on what works and what does not" (p. 18). Deming (1975) recognizes the widely shared view "that evaluation is a pronouncement concerning the effectiveness of some treatment or plan that has been tried or put into effect" (p. 53). That many people directly involved in evaluation take a broader view of evaluation processes—and the range of decisions they can contribute to—than do the decision makers they are trying to serve is one cause for tensions in the system. Even though we recognize that problem, our definition of evaluation even within the Purpose II category is somewhat more comprehensive than the general "summative" one (assessment of the overall effectiveness of a program in meeting its objectives).

Investigations under Purpose II may well include some of the same components as investigations under Purpose I. After a program is in operation, it is frequently important to monitor the continuing needs for the program. Some of them may change or even go away. In fact, the major criterion of success for some programs may be a drastic reduction in need for the services. Some health care delivery efforts whose goal is to minimize the need for treatment of disease through positive programs of health maintenance might fall into this category. Unfortunately, it is the nature of bureaucratic structures, which frequently house the kinds of educational and social-action programs we are interested in here, not to discontinue programs under any circumstances. And it is not easy for any structure to dismantle a program that has been shown to be successful. Yet in many cases, evaluation evidence of success, rather than of failure, should contribute to decisions about discontinuing a program.

Two other familiar items from Purpose I appear again under Purpose II: cost (E) and demand and support (F). Both need to be assessed against the estimations and projections made in the planning phase of the program, which may have been too optimistic or too pessimistic. Assessment of popular, professional, and other support for the operating program may help explain some of the impact or lack of impact the program had on its "targets."

Assessment of actual costs can now be related to the effects or benefits the program appeared to achieve: Have we spent $1 on a 10¢ problem? Or have we spent an average of $1000 a child to raise reading levels only one month? Of course, we may be pleasantly surprised to find that we have spent comparatively little and managed to effect important and substantial improvements. Much of the recent discussion of "accountability" in education and other fields assumes as an underlying premise that improved information and delivery structures can contribute to the productivity (and efficiency) of resource use. The economic principle of return on investment applies: Can the same benefits/effects be obtained at less cost? Can greater benefits/effects be obtained at the same cost? Such cost analyses have not figured prominently in many evaluations of education and social-action programs, partly because the evaluators were not sophisticated in the ways of economic analysis, partly because economists have been slow to communicate their techniques to evaluators in these fields and to help in applying them, partly because assigning values—monetary and otherwise—to the outputs of social and educational programs is very difficult. However, the situation seems to be changing. We are promised something beyond the fairly simple economic functions and relationships evaluators have tried to use in the past.

Jamison (1972), Rothenberg (1975), and Levin (1975) are among those who speak directly and understandably to the problems of economic analysis in education and social-action programs. Rothenberg, for example, immediately dispels the myth that cost-benefit analysis is "unitary or definitive," but he maintains that there is still a central focus that must be kept in mind. That focus is "the means-end relationship. . . . Its centrality stems from the existence of scarcity. . . . Under scarcity the productive resources—human and nonhuman—available to the society do not suffice to enable everyone's total wants (needs) to be satisfied. Every possible configuration of use of these resources makes possible a configuration of partial fulfillments. The target of the . . . system is to bring about the best configuration of fulfillments, or at least a configuration not inferior to any other" (pp. 58–59). Levin distinguishes among cost-benefit, cost-effectiveness, and cost-utility analysis. The first, requiring as it does the assignment of monetary values to both benefits and costs, is frequently difficult to apply in such areas as general education. However, it is the "father" of cost-effectiveness analysis, which allows the effectiveness of a strategy to be expressed in terms of "its actual physical or psychological outcome rather than its monetary value" (p. 92). Cost-utility analysis "incorporates the decision maker's subjective views in valuing the outcomes of alternative strategies" (p. 94).

In general, economists recognize the differential applicability of their constructs and analytic strategies to evaluating economic impacts (effects on national economic developments), environmental impacts (changes in physical and biological surroundings), and social impacts (effects on distribution of income and on the psychological, social, and physical well-being of people). It may be useful to sketch out in detail Sassone and Schaffer's (1977) formulation of cost-benefit analysis (CBA) and its relationship to cost-effectiveness and social-impact analyses. They trace CBA all the way back to an 1844 publication on "Measurement of the Utility of Public Works" by Jules Depuit, an engineer, and define CBA as an estimation of net benefits associated with alternatives for achieving public goals. They recommend six steps for a cost-benefit analysis: problem specification, identification of all costs and benefits, research design including development of assessment procedures, calculation of all elements in detail, data collection, and analysis-conclusions-presentation. At the problem-specification stage, the analyst chooses between assuming that the project takes place and estimating the consequences or assuming that the project is not undertaken and estimating the consequences. Although at first glance the second assumption would seem relevant only before a project is installed, analyses proceeding from it are also applied to projects already in operation. Cost-benefit problems are conceptualized in terms of the nature of the decision: accept or reject the project—accept if the "net present value" (NPV) is greater than zero; accept one of several alternatives—where the choice would be of the alternative with maximum NPV; or accept a few alternatives out of many—where capital constraints and dependencies among alternatives would have to be taken into account along with NPV. Other considerations figuring in the type of CBA approach advocated by Sassone and Schaffer include:

- Internal versus external effects, where the former accrue directly to the project; for example, elimination of mosquitoes as an internal effect of a mosquito-control project, with opening an area for recreation as an external effect.
- Measurables versus intangibles. So-called "incommensurables" would have to be made explicit to be included in the CBA, but there is a trade-off between quantification and credibility; some hard-to-quantify variables may be hypothesized to con-

tribute so little that it is not worth dealing with them from the economist's point of view. However, consultations and comments from interested parties are included in typical economic reports of environmental impact studies (see Levin's description of cost-utility analysis above).

- Direct verus indirect effects. Examples of indirect effects might include the cost of unemployed resources (negative) or the opportunities offered by freeing resources for use elsewhere (positive). The analyst might not choose to address certain secondary effects (for example, the effects of a metropolitan transit system on surrounding counties) if such effects would be unlikely to influence project decisions. However, such eliminations must be justified explicitly.
- "Double counting." A pitfall to be avoided is including essentially the same costs or benefits in the analysis under different names.

Cost effectiveness-analysis, according to Sassone and Schaffer, addresses these decisions: determining the least-cost means of achieving a specified level of performance of a given system, or determining the greatest level of performance that can be obtained for a specified cost. Social-impact analysis, on the other hand, deals with and stresses noneconomic effects that might be relegated to the "incommensurables" category in CBA.

As can be seen, cost-effectiveness relationships are a little easier to conceptualize in Purpose II evaluations when the design pits one approach to mitigating a social or economic problem against another, than they are in the situation where "absolute" appraisals of value received for money spent must be made. When we say, for example, that trainees in program A performed significantly better on criterion tests than trainees in program B and the costs of the two programs are about the same, the decision to continue A and terminate B is fairly straightforward. (We say "fairly straightforward" because nothing is really straightforward in the evaluation business. If influential political forces have some reason for pushing program B, then. . . . But that situation is covered in Chapter Seven.) However, if the cost of A is twice the cost of B, the evaluator and program director must ask: Is the difference in effectiveness worth the extra money? Here economic analysis, using the concepts of productivity and efficiency, may offer some help.

Along this line, Glass (1976) concludes that evaluation in the areas of law enforcement and criminal rehabilitation, with a fairly consistent record of "no difference" findings, has paid off better than evaluation in other areas. He notes: "One feature after another has been altered experimentally, and crime and recidivism rates have remained unchanged. . . . If cutting reformatory sentences in half does not produce increased recidivism, then shorter sentences are 100 percent more cost-effective, *ceteris paribus*. Doing as well as in the past but doing it more cheaply is a gain in value as surely as is doing better at a greater cost" (p. 11).

The more "usual" component of Purpose II evaluation is embodied in item IIB, Table 1: global effectiveness of the program in meeting need. This phrase is generally interpreted to mean effectiveness of the program in meeting the goals or objectives espoused for it, where the goals or objectives are themselves based on the perceived or documented need the program was designed to address. As suggested in the cost-effectiveness example above, evaluation efforts oriented toward component IIB may be conducted in either a comparative or absolutist framework. In a comparative framework, results will be judged in comparison with the performance of another group (perhaps exposed to an alternative program) or with earlier performance by the same group. In an absolutist framework, results will be judged according to some performance standard related to program objectives. Cronbach (1963), early on, discouraged curriculum evaluators from relying on a "horse-race" approach, which at that time generally involved comparing performance of one group exposed to the new curriculum in math, physics, or some other subject with another group offered traditional school courses in the subject. These curricula frequently were intended to accomplish different goals, and the problem of ensuring both comparable and valid measurement for two groups in such a situation—which is something like pitting a Clydesdale against a quarter horse—continues to loom large. However, Scriven (1967) consistently maintains that comparison is an important part of all evaluation and that even if the two curricula are designed for different purposes, the evaluator must attend to relative outcomes across many dimensions. Certainly there are cases when the most meaningful question to be addressed in evaluation is whether one treatment or delivery system accomplishes a certain effect better than an alternative system—especially if the systems differ profoundly in cost or in such factors as ease of execution, popularity, or potential for negative side effects.

The two subcategories under "Global effectiveness in meeting need" in Table 1 are "Short-term" and "Long-term." Ideally the decision whether to look for long-term or short-term effects should depend on the nature of the program and the needs it serves. The effects of a first-term algebra course might best be evaluated immediately at the end of that course, as students prepare to enter second-term algebra. However, the effects of a high-school training program on "parenting" can be determined only after the students have become parents. Short-term effects may be all that we are concerned about in evaluating certain television shows, audio-visual materials, billboard campaigns, and job-training programs. But it is hard to imagine many instances where long-term effects are not the object of community health, certification and licensing, rehabilitation, urban planning, or environmental protection programs. Bronfenbrenner (1975) noted, for example, that "two years was regarded as a minimum for gauging long-range aftereffects" of early childhood interventions such as Head Start (p. 520).

But four problems plague us. First, it is sometimes not feasible to measure the ultimate criterion of program effectiveness. For example, the ultimate criterion of a training course for firefighters is effectiveness in combating fire, but we hate to think of having to wait around for a three-alarmer to test the trainees' prowess (and it would be next to impossible to obtain valid and reliable assessment under those conditions anyway). Furthermore, it would be difficult and certainly destructive to try to simulate such conditions in the training center. Second, it is an awesome task to follow up for any considerable length of time adults who are free to move about the country. For that matter, longitudinal work with school children is not much easier, because moving parents tend to take their children with them. Weinstein (1975) points to some of the complexities involved in maintaining multiyear medical records and in locating medical patients who do not return for treatment. "Lifers" in prison, military personnel with long enlistments, institutionalized "incurables" offer better opportunities for long-term studies, but even there pardons, discharges, and miracles may alter the population. Besides, we spend comparatively little time inventing programs to im-

prove the social and economic welfares of such populations. Third, extraordinary problems of privacy and confidentiality attend many attempts to keep longitudinal records. Fourth, outsiders (government agencies, school boards, and elected officials, to name a few) want—and sometimes demand—evaluation results before the program has had a fair chance to take effect or before apparent effects can be interpreted. This problem alone has probably sent more evaluators screaming from the field than any other.

Evaluators seem more attentive to possible program side effects (items IIC and D, Table 1) than they were a few years ago, partly because of the emphasis placed on side effects by such authors as Messick (1970), Scriven (1967), and Suchman (1967). This concern with side effects is more novel among those working in the educational and social-action fields than those in medical fields, where researchers have long attended to the issue even when distributors and practitioners appeared to ignore their warnings. Of course, not all side effects are negative. When early Head Start advocates could find little comfort in the size of IQ increments among their charges (an inappropriate major criterion of effectiveness of that program in any case, but one used simply because "the tests were there"), they could point with some pride to the involvement of enormous numbers of parents and to the diagnosis and treatment of medical defects for many, many children (Temp and Anderson, 1966; Grotberg, 1969).

Side effects are included on the Table 1 checklist to remind evaluators once again that limiting themselves to estimating how effectively a program meets its intended outcomes may distort or impoverish the picture of the program's impact. Of course, it is not possible for evaluators to list—or measure—all potential side effects of a program. However, once evaluators are familiar with the program, they should be able to make some fairly good guesses about variables that, though not specified in the program objectives, deserve examination. For example, these classes of variables frequently figure in the search for side effects: drop-out (client drop-out, program-personnel turnover), attitudes (of those who receive the program, those who deliver it, and those who are excluded from it for one reason or another), transfer effects (to other content areas or areas of activity). (See Anderson and others, 1975, pp. 364–367.)

Results of investigations of continuing needs, costs, and demand and support should all be considered along with results of impact studies (focusing on both intended and unintended outcomes) in making decisions whether to continue a program, expand it or cut it back, or stamp it "approved" or "disapproved" when certification, licensing, or accreditation is at issue.

## III. TO CONTRIBUTE TO DECISIONS ABOUT PROGRAM MODIFICATION

Purpose III corresponds to the one usually ascribed to formative evaluation, although information about program components can also be obtained in the context of a global appraisal of effectiveness after a program is in full operation. Of course, if a program is cast in an unchangeable mold, the evaluator is wasting his time seeking information to help make it better. Fortunately, this is seldom the case. But the role of evaluation in program improvement has been less well sold than its role in overall appraisal of effectiveness, and sometimes the problem is simply to show program directors how useful feedback can be to them. One hypothesis advanced to account for the poor quality of evaluations under Title I of the Elementary and Secondary Education Act, in addition to the lack of technical sophistication in some of those thrown suddenly into evaluator roles, is that local education agencies have not seen any program-improvement benefits accruing to them from the effort. Thus they have done as little as possible to get by and "satisfy the Feds."

A major distinction between evaluation efforts devoted to Purpose III and those devoted exclusively to Purpose II is the emphasis on describing program processes in contrast to program products. As Table 1 indicates, the evaluator may seek information to guide program improvement in a broad range of areas, including:

### A. Program Objectives

Are the objectives valid and useful for attacking the needs the program is designed to serve? Do they meet with general acceptance from those who can be expected to influence, or be influenced by, the program? "Acceptance" criteria have acquired a bad name in some evaluation circles, because the "smiles test" has sometimes been the only form of evaluation. However, as the listing in Table 1 suggests, information about the acceptability of the program and its components to the parties involved is important for decisions pertaining to program installation, continuation, modifi-

cation, defense, or defamation (see items IE, IIF, IIIA, IIIB, IIIC, IV, and V).

### B. Program Content

Is the content relevant to the program objectives and does it cover those objectives adequately? Is it technically accurate and professionally acceptable (that word again!)? Is it overly structured or not structured enough for the sophistication and "styles" of those who must deliver the services and of those for whom the services are intended? Does the program fit the backgrounds of the clients? Are we asking clients to make assumptions or handle materials that are beyond their experience or over their heads? Or are we talking down to them? What about the effectiveness of each of the components and the order in which they are presented, prescribed, or delivered? It would usually cost more than it is worth to evaluate the effectiveness of each tiny program module separately. However, some components that program directors are least sure of probably deserve specific attention; for example, how long the four-year-old audience for "Sesame Street" could attend to TV presentations of letters and numbers (Palmer, 1976, p. 138). Sequence can also be important; for example, offering experience B before experience A could make all the difference in whether clients return for a second visit to a mental health clinic.

### C. Program Methodology

Here we are concerned not with the "what" but with the "how" of program presentation. How much control do clients have? How much does the staff have? How is the program delivered? Are there better methods than group discussion for dealing with the families of the mentally ill? What about the practice and length of the program? Would weekly sessions over six months be more effective than an intensive one-week "immersion course"? How are clients reinforced for participating in the program? Are the reinforcements adequate to sustain interest?

### D. Program Context

Weiss (1975), Tumin (1970), and Campbell (1972) all stress the significance of the political context in which educational and social-action programs are evaluated. Weiss summarizes: "Political considerations intrude in three major ways, and the evaluator who fails to recognize their presence is in for a series of shocks and frustrations. First, the policies and programs with which evaluation deals are the creatures of political decision. . . . Second, because evaluation is undertaken *in order to* feed into decision-making, its reports enter the political arena. . . . Third, . . . evaluation itself has a political stance. . . . It makes implicit political statements about such issues as the problematic nature of some programs and the unassailableness of others, the legitimacy of program goals, the legitimacy of program strategies, the utility of strategies of incremental reform" (pp. 13–14). However, under Purpose III, we are concerned primarily with the political and administrative stance and workings of the program itself. A program may be technically sound, but if it is administered badly, if staff working relationships are ill-defined or antagonistic, if facilities and resources are inadequate, if fiscal policies are unsound and support shaky, or if the program's own public relations efforts are insensitive, the program may be doomed. Ah, you say, but most of those things should have been worked out at the planning phase; what happened to evaluation under Purpose I? Of course they should have, we reply, but this is the real world. There may not have been any evaluator when the program was conceived; planning may have been haphazard; or conditions may have changed—the "cup and lip phenomenon" (Weiss, 1973). The evaluator, playing the role of an objective near-outsider, may be in a position to spot problems that program managers in their day-to-day involvement and proximity cannot see. Many management consultants continue to earn their keep because they can get from staff information that has escaped supervisors or can detect poor accounting practices that have slipped into the system. The evaluator may also be able to apply some empirical methods as well as subjective judgment in this general area. We should note that the opposite of the good-program—bad-context combination can exist. We know of instances where a program has received far better press than its merits warrant, because of the charisma of its director, because of enthusiastic if unenlightened support from the community, or because of Hawthorne effects.

### E.  Personnel Policies and Practices

Investigations and descriptions in this area go hand in hand with inquiries into program context. With respect to clients: Who is the program reaching? How is it reaching them? Do the clients represent the "needy" population the program was designed to serve? Or are they ever likely to be able to contribute to the societal or organizational needs that the program was designed to serve? With respect to staff: Who are they? How were they selected? Are they qualified to deliver the program initially? If not, is in-service training adequate to qualify them? With respect to both clients and staff: Who stays in the program? Who leaves? What efforts are made to retain "worthy" clients and staff? Are there any attempts to weed out clients who are not profiting from the program or staff who are incompetent? What effects do such personnel policies seem to have on the operation and effectiveness of the program?

### IV. AND V.  TO OBTAIN EVIDENCE FAVORING A PROGRAM TO RALLY SUPPORT, OR TO OBTAIN EVIDENCE AGAINST A PROGRAM TO RALLY OPPOSITION

These two purposes recognize the realities of program evaluation. Many evaluators shun evaluations with these purposes; many people who commission evaluations are unwilling to admit to their real motives. But occasions do arise when decision makers must rally support for a program in order to sustain it or drum up opposition in order to "kill" it and divert funds to other things. We must at least entertain the possibility that the public interest will be served on some occasions by declared efforts to seek support or opposition. We must also consider the possibility that the evaluator might perform a legitimate function on these occasions; that is, if the requirement is not sweeping contrary evidence under the rug, but simply collecting evidence (where none has been collected before) or disseminating existing evidence convincingly. With respect to disseminating evidence, some evaluator may have been at fault in the first place if reports were written in such a way that, even though they contained data favorable to the program director's position, the director could not interpret or use them. It should be noted here that the items listed under Purposes IV and V in Table 1 are all oriented toward the groups that the program director is trying to influence. And it is certainly true that the same evidence may be accepted or rejected, depending not only upon the initial inclination of the recipient but also on the way that evidence is presented.

In any case, it is better in the long run if the agency authorizing the evaluation faces up to its real motives and does not hide them from the evaluator. The evaluator's responsibilities, in turn, include defining clearly the nature of the evidence being presented, indicating any lack of representativeness, and ensuring the validity of the evidence even if it is only a partial picture of the total state of affairs.

The situation for the evaluator is happier when decision makers are willing to consider both negative and positive evidence about the effectiveness and operation of a program. The so-called adversary model of evaluation applies directly to this situation (Churchman, 1961; Stake and Gjerde, 1971). Usually, evaluators with roots in the social sciences operate on the assumption that they should gather the best and most relevant data they can, interpret it according to accepted criteria, and then present the results as fairly and openly as possible, no matter what the implications for the program. Thus, the evaluator is charged with both finding and presenting evidence. The adversary model of evaluation has its beginnings in the legal profession, which offers its own approach to reaching "truth." Specifically, the proponents of the adversary model (Kourilsky, 1973; Levine, 1973) suggest including in the evaluation process an adversary who will "cross-examine" all the evidence as it comes in or at least providing for later presentation of evidence on both sides of all important issues. We have tended in the past to reject the adversary model on the grounds that good debating techniques may prevail over good evidence (Anderson and others, 1975, pp. 21–22), but we have come around to the point of view that at times, especially when the results are truly equivocal and much is at stake, this approach may be best.

## VI. TO CONTRIBUTE TO THE UNDERSTANDING OF BASIC PROCESSES

Pursuing decision-oriented evaluation does not preclude investigating, within the context of the same study, basic processes in at least one of the disciplines listed under Purpose VI in Table 1. In the last chapter, we considered some of the overlaps between research and program evaluation. Nonetheless, evaluators cannot afford to lose sight of two key issues. First, if they have agreed to perform evaluation services for a program, those services must be the central focus of their efforts. It is unfortunate that a few social scientists have given program evaluation a bad name by trying to bootleg their theses, pet research projects, or tests of new methodologies on someone else's hard-gained evaluation funds. Second, in spite of any zeal they

may have to contribute to the basic disciplines, evaluators must recognize any limitations inherent in specific evaluations that undercut their ability to test hypotheses or make generalizations, processes important to fundamental contributions to knowledge. Many evaluation scenes present such limitations.

## REFERENCES

Anderson, S. B. "Educational Compensation and Evaluation: A Critique." In J. C. Stanley (Ed.), *Compensatory Education for Children Ages Two to Eight.* Baltimore, Md.: Johns Hopkins University Press, 1973.

Anderson, S. B., Ball, S., Murphy, R. T., and Associates. *Encyclopedia of Educational Evaluation: Concepts and Techniques for Evaluating Education and Training Programs.* San Francisco: Jossey-Bass, 1975.

Baker, E. L. "Lean Data Strategies for Formative Evaluation." Paper presented in the symposium "An End of Affluence: Educational Evaluation in Tight Money Times" at the annual meeting of the American Educational Research Association, San Francisco, April 1976.

Blabolil, G. J. "Emergence of Needs Assessment as a Basis for Title I Planning." Paper presented in the symposium "Evaluating Title I in an Urban School System—A Decade of Happenings" at the annual meeting of the American Educational Research Association, San Francisco, April 1976.

Briggs, R. G. "What Philosophic Questions for Educational Evaluators?" Paper presented in the symposium "Philosophical Perspectives on Educational Evaluation" at the annual meeting of the American Educational Research Association, San Francisco, 1976.

Bronfenbrenner, U. "Is Early Intervention Effective?" In M. Guttentag (Ed.), *Handbook of Evaluation Research,* Vol. 2. Beverly Hills, Calif.: Sage, 1975.

Campbell, D. T. "Reforms as Experiments." In C. H. Weiss (Ed.), *Evaluating Action Programs: Readings in Social Action and Education.* Boston: Allyn & Bacon, 1972.

Chazan, M. "Compensatory Education: Defining the Problem." In *Compensatory Education: An Introduction.* Occasional Publication, No. 1. Schools Council Research Project in Compensatory Education, Department of Education, University College of Swansea. Swansea, Wales: Schools Council Publishing, 1968.

Churchman, C. W. *Prediction and Optimal Decision.* Englewood Cliffs, N. J.: Prentice-Hall, 1961.

Corder, R. *The Information Base for Reading: A Critical Review of the Information Base for Current Assumptions Regarding the Status of Instruction and Achieve-*

ment in Reading in the United States. Washington, D. C.: U. S. Department of Health, Education and Welfare, 1971.

Deming, W. E. "The Logic of Evaluation." In E. L. Struening (Ed.), Handbook of Evaluation Research. Vol. 1. Beverly Hills, Calif.: Sage, 1975.

Education Commission of the States. National Assessment of Educational Progress Report 02-9-00: Reading Summary. Denver: Education Commission of the States, May 1972.

Glass, G. V. Evaluation Studies Review Annual. Vol. 1. Beverly Hills, Calif.: Sage, 1976.

Grotberg, E. (Ed.). Critical Issues in Research Related to Disadvantaged Children. Princeton, N. J.: Educational Testing Service, 1969.

Guttentag, M., and Struening, E. L. "The Handbook: Its Purpose and Organization." In M. Guttentag (Ed.), Handbook of Evaluation Research. Vol. 2. Beverly Hills, Calif.: Sage, 1975.

Harless, J. H. "An Analysis of Front-End Analysis." Improving Human Performance: A Research Quarterly, 1973, 2, 229-244.

Jamison, D. "Definitions of Productivity and Efficiency in Education." Appendix A in A. Melmed (Ed.), Productivity and Efficiency in Education. Washington, D. C.: Educational Panel of Federal Council on Science and Technology, Commission on Automation Opportunities to the Service Areas, 1972 (draft).

Kourilsky, M. "An Adversary Model for Educational Evaluation." UCLA Evaluation Comment, 1973, 4 (2), 3-6.

Levin, H. M. "Cost-Effectiveness Analysis in Evaluation Research." In M. Guttentag (Ed.), Handbook of Evaluation Research, Vol. 2. Beverly Hills, Calif.: Sage, 1975.

Levin, S., and Bishop, D. "An Evaluation Tool for Feedback and Leverage of Mental Health Delivery Systems." Canadian Psychiatry Association Journal, 1972, 17, 437-442.

Levine, M. "Scientific Method and the Adversary Model: Some Preliminary Suggestions." UCLA Evaluation Comment, 1973, 4 (2), 1-3.

Messick, S. "The Criterion Problem in the Evaluation of Instruction: Assessing Possible, Not Just Intended Outcomes," In M. C. Wittrock and D. E. Wiley (Eds.), The Evaluation of Instruction: Issues and Problems. New York: Holt, Rinehart and Winston, 1970.

Palmer, E. L. "Applications of Psychology to Television Programming: Program Execution." American Psychologist, 1976, 31, 137-138.

Pfeiffer, J. New Look at Education: Systems Analysis in Our Schools and Colleges. New York: Odyssey Press, 1968.

Resnick, D. P., and Resnick, L. B. "The Nature of Literacy: An Historical Exploration." Harvard Educational Review, 1977, 47, 370-385.

Rothenberg, J. "Cost-Benefit Analysis: A Methodological Exposition." In M. Guttentag (Ed.), Handbook of Evaluation Research. Vol. 2. Beverly Hills, Calif.: Sage, 1975.

Sassone, P. G., and Schaffer, W. A. "Cost-Benefit Analysis and Economic Evaluation of Business Activity." Seminar presented at Georgia Institute of Technology, March 10, 1977.

Scriven, M. "The Methodology of Evaluation." Perspectives of Curriculum Evaluation. American Educational Research Association Monograph Series on Curriculum Evaluation, No. 1. Chicago: Rand McNally, 1967.

Scriven, M. "Evaluation Perspectives and Procedures." In W. J. Popham (Ed.), Evaluation in Education: Current Applications. Berkeley, Calif.: McCutchan, 1974.

Scriven, M., and Roth, J. "Needs Assessment." Evaluation News: The Newsletter of the Evaluation Network, 1977a, 2, 25-18.

Stake, R., and Gjerde, C. An Evaluation of T City: The Twin City Institute for Talented Youth. Urbana: Center for Instructional Research and Curriculum Evaluation, University of Illinois, 1971.

Suchman, E. A. Evaluation Research: Principle and Practice in Public Service and Social Action Programs. New York: Russell Sage Foundation, 1967.

Temp, G., and Anderson, S. B. Final Report Project Head Start—Summer 1966, Section 3, Pupils and Programs. Princeton, N. J.: Educational Testing Service, 1966.

Tumin, M. M. "Evaluation of the Effectiveness of Education: Some Problems and Prospects." Interchange, 1970, 1 (3), 96-109.

Weinstein, A. S. "Evaluation Through Medical Records and Related Information Systems." In E. L. Struening (Ed.), Handbook of Evaluation Research. Vol. 1. Beverly Hills, Calif.: Sage, 1975.

Weiss, C. H. "Between the Cup and the Lip." Evaluation, 1973, 1 (2), 49-55.

Weiss, C. H. "Evaluation Research in the Political Context." In E. L. Struening (Ed.), Handbook of Evaluation Research. Vol. 1. Beverly Hills, Calif.: Sage, 1975.

Witkin, B. R. "Needs Assessment Models: A Critical Analysis." Paper presented at the annual meeting of the

American Educational Research Association, San Francisco, April 1976.

Young, M., and Willmott, P. *Family and Kinship in East London.* London: Routledge & Kegan Paul, 1957.

# Processing Citizens' Disputes Outside the Courts
## A Quasi-Experimental Evaluation

Ross F. Conner
Ray Surette

*Citizen dispute processing programs are becoming more common in the United States as an alternative to expensive, time-consuming litigation in court. Although no empirical evidence has been presented to date on the effectiveness of this type of mediation program, policy makers are calling for an increase in the number of such programs. This article reports on the results of an outcome evaluation of the Orange County (Florida) Bar Association's Citizen Dispute Settlement Project. The results indicate that complainants, respondents, and hearing officers are generally very satisfied with the hearings. In a three-week follow-up, complainant satisfaction increased, while respondent satisfaction stayed at the original high level. A quasi-experimental comparison of hearing and no-hearing groups of disputants indicated that mediation programs of this type may not be particularly effective for long-term solutions of underlying problems. The implications of these results are discussed for public policy-making and for theoretical refinement of the mediation concept.*

## INTRODUCTION

Occasional disagreements between people are a common occurrence in daily life. These disagreements sometimes escalate into longer-term disputes, which can escalate further into court cases. Recently, new approaches to dispute processing have been advocated as quicker, more effective means to dispute settlement

Reprinted from *Evaluation Review*, Vol. 4, No. 6 (December, 1980), pp. 739–768. © 1980 by Sage Publications, Inc., with permission.

than the traditional method of adjudication. This article reports the results of an evaluation research project conducted on the Orange County (Florida) Bar Association's Citizen Dispute Settlement Project. Although citizen dispute programs have become more common, the Orange County Project is unique in that it included an outcome evaluation component to determine whether the program was, in fact, settling disputes.

### Approaches to Dispute Processing

Americans are not hesitant to take their problems to court: Approximately ten million new civil cases are initiated each year (Johnson et al., 1977: 1). Courts, however, are not always the best forum for dispute resolution. Warren Burger, Chief Justice of the United States Supreme Court, stated the situation this way:

> The role of law, in terms of formal litigation with the full panoply of time-consuming and expansive procedural niceties can be overdone. . . . The notion that ordinary people want black-robed judges, well-dressed lawyers and fine-paneled courtrooms as the setting to resolve their disputes is not correct. People with problems, like people with pains, want relief, and they want it as quickly and inexpensively as possible [Hager, 1977: 4].

The trend away from the courts as agents of dispute settlement began about the middle of the nineteenth century when courts began to expand their role as facilitators of economic transactions (Friedman, 1973, cited in Nader and Singer, 1976: 282). This movement was accelerated by lawyers who were changing their primary activity from dispute settlement for individual clients to legal work for businesses, a shift related to the greater fees businesses paid to lawyers. Consequently, as Friedman states, "Courts turned their backs on what in most societies is their ordinary and primary function—dispute settlement—thus abandoning people to their own institutions and devices" (Nader and Singer, 1976: 282).

Short of a day in court (or, more accurately, a year or two), disputants have other options which they can use in their attempts to resolve their disputes (Johnson et al., 1977; McGillis and Mullen, 1977; Nader, 1975). Studies, primarily by legal anthropologists, have shown that different kinds of disputes require different modes of settlement (e.g., Collier, 1973; Gluckman, 1955; Gulliver, 1963; Nader, 1969; Nader and Metzger, 1963; Pospisil, 1967). In simple cases disputants can negotiate a settlement themselves (Gulliver, 1973). If the reasons for disagreement are complex, however, negotiation is more difficult to implement because of the inability of the disputants to weigh the facts—or even to agree on the important facts (Galanter, 1974).

Another approach open to disputants is avoidance; that is, the parties can simply ignore the disagreement or each other or exit from the situation (Felstiner, 1974). This model of resolution is more feasible for relatively unimportant disputes; if the dispute is complex and long-standing, however, avoidance may not be possible (Danzig and Lowy, 1975).

## Mediation

A more frequent mode of dispute processing, increasingly popular in the United States, is mediation (Felstiner, 1974; Fuller, 1971). In this case, a third neutral party aids the disputing parties in airing their disagreement and reaching a settlement. Unlike the adjudication process which also involves a third party, the mediation process can produce settlements only when the disputants consent to a solution proposed by the mediator or by the disputants themselves. Moreover, the mediation process usually does not depend on coercive power to enforce the settlement, as is the case with adjudication or arbitration.

The form and function of the third party in a mediation can vary. The third party can be a single individual, on occasion someone who is known to the disputants (Gluckman, 1955), or the third party can be a small group of individuals, a "community moot" (Danzig, 1973: 41-48). The specific functions of the mediator or moot can vary but their general approach to their mediational task is similar. Both complainant and respondent are given a chance to tell their sides of the story, then discussion ensues between the disputants to resolve differences. A solution to the dispute, if one is possible, arises from the discussion; ideally, the solution comes from one of the disputants but it can also be suggested by the mediator, moot, or by friends and relatives who may also be in attendance.

Unlike the adjudicative system, a mediation procedure is focused on obtaining peace and harmony rather than on assigning blame and determining guilt. The mediation setting is usually less formal than that for adjudication, without judicial robes, elevated platforms, and artificial customs. Also unlike the adjudicative system, the mediation procedure is inexpensive, quick and convenient for the disputants. It also is more

private, in that formal records are not kept which could be obtained later by credit firms, journalists, and the like. Finally, the mediation procedure is understandable to the disputants and offers them a chance for a just settlement, in contrast to the courts where a legal decision and a just decision are not necessarily the same thing (Mund, 1976; Nader, 1975).

Mediation has been promoted by social reformers because it has the potential for relieving the litigation overload of the courts, particularly at the lower levels. Mediation is not the first attempted remedy for this problem. Small Claims Courts, for example, received much attention, not only because they appeared to be an inexpensive and efficient system of justice but also because they offered the potential of reducing court overloads. Most early reports on the Small Claims Court were favorable. Closer evaluation of the available data, however, indicated that these courts were not as effective as their promoters had hoped (Yngvesson and Hennessey, 1975).

The Small Claims Courts, then, have not provided the kind of efficient, informal, and inexpensive dispute processing that reformers had hoped they would. This failure seems to be due, in part, to the fact that these courts remain part of the formal system and, as such, are susceptible to the limitations of this system, especially for elementary interpersonal disputes. Mediation forums, since they occur outside the formal system, may be able to avoid these limitations.

## The Need for Evaluation of Mediation Programs
### PROGRAM EFFECTIVENESS

Citizen mediation programs began to be implemented in the mid 1970s, at least in part because of articles like Danzig's (1973), which advocated such programs as a better alternative for the resolution of disputes than the present criminal justice system. Like any other social reform effort, citizen mediation programs need to be evaluated scientifically to determine whether the new programs are effective (Campbell, 1969). This becomes particularly critical for citizen mediation programs because leaders in the legal field (e.g., United States Supreme Court Chief Justice Warren Burger, as well as several recent past presidents of the American Bar Association) have advocated that the number of these programs be expanded. In 1976, the American Bar Association, the Judicial Conference of the United States, and the Conference of Chief Justices cosponsored the National Conference on the Causes of Popular Dissatisfaction with the Administration of Justice (the Pound Conference). A Task Force (under the direction of Griffin Bell) was subsequently appointed to carry out the recommended changes from this conference. One of the Task Force's main recommendations was for the development of neighborhood justice centers that would process disputes in a variety of ways, including mediation programs. The U. S. Department of Justice then initiated a new program to develop these neighborhood justice centers across the country.

In view of the rush to develop citizen mediation projects, the evaluation of the effectiveness of the programs which now exist is critical. Evaluative research on these current programs can provide valuable information on a variety of topics: What kinds of disputes are brought to the program? What kinds of mediators have been used? What hearing procedures have been used? Most importantly, does a mediation program really settle disputes? Before extra resources are committed, we need to analyze the mediation programs that are already underway.

Research on mediation programs in particular and grievance processing in general in the United States has been limited, with virtually no empirical research (Nader and Singer, 1976: 283). The most recent work on the effectiveness of citizen dispute processing has been limited to a description of the numbers of clients and types of problems. Evaluation research theorists have frequently stated that this type of input evaluation is an inadequate measure of program effectiveness (Suchman, 1969; Campbell, 1969; Gilbert et al., 1975). Although the number of clients who file complaints is certainly valuable information, these data tell nothing about what actually occurred at mediation sessions ("process evaluation"; see Freeman, 1977) or whether the disputes were, in fact, settled ("outcome evaluation"; see Bennett and Lumsdaine, 1975). It is this latter type of information that is most necessary before agencies such as the U. S. Department of Justice establish citizen dispute settlement programs across the country.

The limitations of current research on citizen mediation programs can be seen by reviewing the Columbus (Ohio) Night Prosecutor's Program. This program, one of the earliest large citizen mediation programs, was selected by the Law Enforcement Assistance Administration (LEAA) to be one of a select group of "exemplary projects" which LEAA promoted as a model for other cities to follow (LEAA, 1975). Consequently, this program has served as the model for others to follow, including the Orange County Citizen Dispute Project. In his Foreword to the manual on the program, Charles Work, Deputy Administrator for Administration of LEAA, states:

> The Columbus Citizen Dispute Settlement Program offers a constructive answer to a troubling problem: how to provide better service to the public without further burdening an already overloaded system. . . . During the project's first year, criminal affidavits were filed in only 2 percent of the cases handled and the average cost of diverting each case was approximately $20. When compared to the time and expense involved in normal criminal processing of such cases, the economy of the Columbus approach is obvious [LEAA, 1975: iii].

Although the economy of the Columbus program may have been obvious, the effectiveness was not. Data are provided on the number of hearings scheduled and the number of hearings held, as well as on the number of affidavits filed. Although provided as an indication of the effectiveness of the program, the first two kinds of data give information only on inputs to the project, not outcomes of the project. The fact that a hearing was held does not guarantee that the hearings solved the dispute, and the fact that a hearing was scheduled but not held (about one-third of the cases) does not indicate that the dispute was "resolved without intervention" (LEAA: 8). The number of affidavits filed is an outcome measure, in that successful hearings should lead to fewer affidavits, but it is an outcome measure of questionable validity in view of the types of cases brought to the project (i.e., the least serious kinds of interpersonal disputes). Although their problems were not solved, disputants may not have wanted to file complaints because the problems were not serious enough to warrant the expense, time, and prolonged procedure of the regular criminal justice system. Consequently, the one outcome measure that was provided for the Columbus Night Prosecutor Program is not a good indicator of the effectiveness of the program. The program personnel recognize some of these limitations; they advocate that future evaluations be "goal oriented and focus more on output than input or process" (LEAA: 25).

### THEORETICAL TEST

There is another important reason why the citizen mediation concept needs to be rigorously researched. There is a disagreement in the literature among theorists of dispute processing concerning the efficacy of citizen mediation programs in a developed society such as the United States. Danzig (1973) has advocated the creation of such programs as a useful adjunct to the traditional criminal justice system. Felstiner (1974) has challenged this view because of a basic incompatibility between our society's complex social organization and the requirements for successful mediation.

In a 1973 article, Danzig proposed a decentralized, neighborhood system of criminal justice to supplement the traditional adjudication system. Following a detailed discussion of the working principles which guide the community-based system, Danzig describes several specific innovations, including citizen dispute settlement programs. These community moots, as Danzig refers to them, are based on the model of the tribal moot:

> the moot emphasized the bonds between the convenor and the disputants, it encouraged the widening of discussion so that all tensions and viewpoints psychologically—if not legally—relevant to the issue were expressed, and it resolved disputes by consensus about future conduct, rather than by assessing blame retrospectively [Danzig, 1973: 43].

Danzig proposes that community moots be used to handle family disputes, some marital issues, juvenile delinquency, landlord-tenant disputes, and small civil suits between community members, as well as misdemeanors affecting community members. The method of operation of such community moots would vary but typically would involve a "salaried counselor" who would arrange sessions for complainants who either appear voluntarily or are referred by social agencies or the police. At the session, the complainant would state his grievance and his favored solution, following which the respondent would tell his view of the situation. The counselor would then lead a general discussion of the issues.

> It would be hoped that through such open discussion a range of grievances running in both directions would be aired and better understood; that the counselor might be able to suggest future conduct by both parties to reduce tensions; and that both friends and relatives invited by the participants might serve as "witnesses" and participants in the consensual solutions evolved, thus joining community officials in keeping the peace [Danzig, 1973: 47–48].

Felstiner (1974) challenges Danzig's view because it overlooks the critical influence of social organization in the proper functioning of a moot or neighborhood dispute settlement program. Felstiner (1974: 63) states that "dispute practices prevailing in any particular society are a product of its values, its psychological imperatives, its history and its economic political and social organization." In his article, Felstiner focuses specifically on the influences of social organization on dispute settlement mechanisms. He outlines two ideal types of social organization: a technologically complex rich society and a technologically simple poor society. Following a description of three types of dispute processing (adjudication, mediation, and avoidance), Felstiner explores the relationships between each type of social organization and each type of dispute processing. Mediation, Felstiner (1974: 73–74) believes, will not be a useful dispute processing mechanism in a technologically complex rich society such as the United States:

> Since mediation requires an outcome acceptable to the parties, the mediator . . . must construct an outcome in the light of the social and cultural context of the dispute, the full scope of the relations between the disputants and the perspectives from which they view the dispute. Mediation, then, flourishes where mediators share the social and cultural experience of the disputants they serve, and where they bring to the processing of disputes an intimate and detailed knowledge of the perspectives of the disputants. In the absence of such shared experience and such preprocessing knowledge, the effort a mediator would have to make to fill the gaps would be disproportionate to the social stakes involved in the dispute.

Felstiner believes that Danzig's community moots will not be effective because the mediator does not have sufficient intimate knowledge of and experience with the disputants. The typical mediator in an American neighborhood mediation program is not familiar enough with the disputants' perspectives and backgrounds and, consequently, will not be in a position to suggest acceptable, realistic resolutions. Felstiner (1974: 88) believes that mediators must be people "who are likely to share the social and cultural experience of the disputants and who have some preprocessing information about them as personalities—a neighborhood notable is preferable to a trained social worker or lawyer who is an 'outsider.'" Felstiner, however, is skeptical about the degree of significant primary group interaction in a technologically complex rich society such as ours. For these reasons, Felstiner believes that the effectiveness of neighborhood moots would be limited at best.

Danzig and Lowy (1975: 689), in a reply to Professor Felstiner, believe that Felstiner overestimates the importance of the mediator's role as well as the necessity for the mediator to have intimate knowledge of the disputants:

> the value of mediation is likely to be determined not so much by the third party's production function as by the conduct of the disputants, and "success" is to be assessed not so much by the outcome of a mediation as by the process by which the outcome was generated. . . . Insofar as the mediator does play a critical role, we think it is as an advocate for the process of discussion and bargaining, rather than for a particular settlement.

Felstiner (1975: 704) replied to Danzig and Lowy and discussed two problems with their model of mediation. First, the model overlooks the basic policy question of whether disputes which come to be aired at a mediation hearing "are a sensible crisis point at which to intervene with the limited public resources available for counseling." Second, the model assumes that disputes arise because disputants cannot communicate effectively. The more important factor, Felstiner believes, is the source of conflict. If the source of conflict arises from differing values and perceptions of reality rather than from competition over similarly prized objects such as money or property, then communication will be impossible; consequently, "mediation may be futile because people are reluctant to bargain away principles and cannot easily compromise on issues that they cannot cooperatively define."

Felstiner notes that he and Danzig and Lowy do agree on one point: that there is a need for empirical data on the effectiveness of dispute processing mechanisms. Felstiner (1975: 704) characterizes the absence of these data as "distressing." The findings presented below will help to remedy the absence of evaluative data on the neighborhood moots and dispute mediation programs. Moreover, the Orange County Bar Association's Citizen Dispute Settlement Project provides a unique opportunity to test in a quasi-experimental manner the Danzig community moot model and Felstiner's contention that community moots will not be effective. The Orange County Bar Association's program is remarkably similar to the community moot in organization, structure, and type of complaints. In addition, the program used lawyers as mediators—a group Felstiner specifically cites as unacceptable for the role. Although limitations on the research did not

allow an experimental test of the Danzig model, the evaluation design contained enough data on inputs and outcomes to permit some description of the cases brought to the program and an assessment of the effectiveness of the mediation sessions. Consequently, the results of this evaluation research project are directly relevant to the theoretical dispute between Felstiner and Danzig. This convergence of a policy-oriented social program evaluation and a theory-oriented quasi-experimental test demonstrates the ability of evaluation research to provide answers to policy-relevant questions and, at the same time, to theory-relevant questions.

## THE CITIZEN DISPUTE SETTLEMENT PROGRAM: DESCRIPTIVE AND PROCESS DATA

In early 1974, the American Bar Association (ABA) began a new program in criminal justice reform: BASICS (Bar Association Support to Improve Correctional Services). The BASICS program was intended to improve correctional services using a new method: bar association involvement and work on local criminal justice problems. The program solicited applications from bar associations across the country for small planning grants and funded 80 planning projects in 40 states. After approximately three months of planning, 62 bar associations applied for larger grants up to $35,000 to implement their correction reform efforts (Huff et al., 1975; Conner and Huff, 1979). Twenty "action" grants were awarded by the BASICS program, including an award to the Orange County (Florida) Bar Association to implement a Citizen Dispute Settlement Project.

The Citizen Dispute Settlement (CDS) Project was designed to provide impartial hearings for residents of Orange County, Florida, who have complaints involving ordinance violations and misdemeanors (e.g., simple assault). Those members of the Orange County Bar Association who were involved in planning their BASICS project were aware of the Columbus Night Prosecutor's Program. The bar association members' discussions with criminal justice personnel in the Orange County area convinced them that there was a need for a similar citizen dispute settlement project. The project planners decided to modify the Night Prosecutor model and use volunteer attorneys from the local bar association as hearing officers. Consequently, the action grant proposal submitted by the Orange County Bar at the end of the planning period met the requirements which the nationwide BASICS Program had adopted; that is, the plan was to improve the local criminal justice system using bar association resources. BASICS staff members were quite impressed by the Orange County Bar Association's project because it intended to involve bar members in social reform work in a very direct manner.

### Project Organization

The CDS Project began in the fall of 1975 when a project director was hired. The project was administered through the County Bar Association via an executive board, which directs general policy and long term development. Daily decisions and short term planning were under the control of the CDS Project Director.

The project staff was composed of a director, an intake counselor, and several part-time student aides. The director and counselor conducted intake interviews with all complainants. These interviews were usually held in the CDS office but occasionally were conducted over the telephone. The counselor scheduled hearings and notified both parties by mail of the date of the hearing. The part-time aides helped coordinate the mediation sessions and collect some project evaluation research data.

The largest part of the CDS "staff" was the group of volunteer attorneys from the Orange County Bar Association who served as hearing officers. Potential hearing officers participated in one-hour training sessions which consisted of a general discussion of mediation techniques. Specifically, the attorneys were instructed to allow each party to explain his side of the story, to remain neutral throughout the hearing, and to foster a participant-generated solution to the dispute. The attorneys were also reminded that the CDS hearings were an informal process, not a legal process, and that settlements did not preclude legal action by either participant.

### Project Operation

The main goal of the Orange County Bar Project was to conduct effective hearings for citizens involved in minor disputes. The kinds of disputes that the program mediates include these categories: simple assault, menacing threats, trespassing, disorderly conduct, harassment, breach of peace, property damage, neighborhood dispute, family dispute, petit theft, animal control, littering and bad checks. Citizens with any of these complaints are either referred to the program by city or county law enforcement officers or present their complaints at their own instigation.

When a citizen presents a complaint, he or she is interviewed by the CDS staff to obtain information about the dispute as well as information about the complainant. A date is then set for the hearing, usually within a week. The other party involved in the dispute, the respondent, is notified by mail of the date, place, and purpose of the hearing.

Hearings are held in the evening at a local traffic court in downtown Orlando. Complainant and respondent are asked to appear at specific times throughout the evening. If a respondent fails to appear for a hearing, the hearing is rescheduled. If a complainant fails to appear, the case is dropped.

Each hearing is unique. Some are as short as 30 minutes, others extend for two or three hours. Only the complainant, respondent, and a hearing officer are present at some hearings; at others, complainant and respondent are joined by family, friends, and witnesses, if permitted by the hearing officer. At a hearing, both complainant and respondent have a chance to tell their sides of the story without interruption. The complainant speaks first, then the respondent presents his or her view of the situation. Should either party begin to interrupt the other during the initial presentation, as frequently happens, the hearing officer quickly intervenes and reminds the parties that discussion will occur later. In the discussion period, the hearing officer may question both parties about discrepancies in their viewpoints, he may serve as a moderator as the parties discuss the issues between themselves, or he may suggest possible compromises. In the course of the discussion, one party may also suggest possible compromises.

Nearly all hearings end with at least an interim settlement to the initial complaint. The details of the resolution are written in triplicate by the hearing officer, then both parties sign the agreement and keep a copy. As they leave, the complainant and respondent separately make evaluative ratings; the hearing officer makes the same ratings before he begins the next hearing.

## EVALUATION PLAN
### Objectives

Several objectives underlay the evaluation plan developed for the CDS project. The primary objectives were (1) to monitor the clients and their complaints, and (2) to measure the effectiveness of the hearings. The secondary objectives were (1) to analyze the impact of the CDS Project on the local criminal justice system, and (2) to monitor the number of lawyers involved in the project.

### Method

To monitor the clients and their complaints, a client intake form was developed from a standardized form in general use in the Orange County criminal justice system. The client intake form was administered to all complainants by CDS personnel.

To measure the effectiveness of the CDS hearings, a two-part plan was developed. The first part of the plan involved ratings made at the conclusion of all hearings. Complainants, respondents, and hearing officers each made two ratings: (1) their degree of satisfaction with the settlement just reached and (2) their judgment of the likelihood that the underlying conflict had been solved. The parties made these ratings on 7-point scales, with three degrees of positive judgment to one side of a neutral point and three degrees of negative judgment to the other. A research assistant, who had not participated in the hearing, administered the scales; all judgments were made independently and confidentially by the three parties. The scales were extensively pilot tested; revisions were made both in the scales and in the instructions given to clients until we were confident that the scales' validity and reliability were high.[1]

The second part of the research plan to assess the effectiveness of the hearings involved drawing a random sample of complainant-respondent pairs for a follow-up which occurred approximately three weeks after the hearing. This time period was selected because successful resolutions were expected to be effected by this time. A sample of clients who had participated in a hearing was contacted, as well as a sample of complainants and respondents who did not have a hearing (although a complaint had been filed). Most people in both samples were contacted either by phone or in person by a research interviewer; a small number were reached by mail. The sample of people who had participated in a hearing was asked to rate their satisfaction with the settlement at this later time, using the same

7-point scale, and to make a forced-choice judgment of whether or not the problem which underlay the complaint was now solved. The sample of people who had not participated in a hearing was asked to make only the latter judgment. Data from these two follow-up samples permitted a quasi-experimental comparison of the longer-term effectiveness of the CDS hearing procedure.

## FINDINGS

The findings presented here are based on data collected between January and October 1976. Although the CDS Project began in late 1975, the program was not fully operational and the evaluation measures were not completely tested until January 1976.

### Complaints Filed with the CDS Project
#### TYPE AND NUMBER OF COMPLAINTS

A total of 306 complaints were presented for settlement during this period (see Table 1). The most frequent categories of complaint were harassment (28.4%) and simple assault (19.6%). When the small group of clients who presented multiple complaints (n = 37) was reclassified by primary complaint, it was found that harassment and simple assault constituted a majority of the cases (31.4% and 22.5% respectively).

#### CHARACTERISTICS OF COMPLAINANTS

When clients came to the CDS office to present their complaints, CDS personnel completed intake forms for each person. These forms included questions on a number of client characteristics. The median age of the 306 complainants was 36 years (M = 38.1, SD = 14.3; range: 17–81). More females than males filed complaints: 62% of the complainants were females; 38% were males. Information was collected on clients' race: 70% were Caucasian, 28% were Black, and 2% were members of other ethnic groups.

Data on marital status of complainants show that 49% of the clients were married, 20% single, 13% divorced, 12% separated, and 6% widowed. Data on employment status indicate that 57% of the complainants were employed full-time, 6% part-time, and 37% were unemployed. Complainants represented a variety of occupations: service (27%), laborer (20%), professional-managerial (15%), clerical (15%), crafts (10%), sales (5%), housewife (4%), other (4%). The monthly income of 47% of the complainants was between $300 and $800; 37% earned under $300 per

**TABLE 1**
**Types of complaints filed**
**(in percentages, n = 306)**

| Category | Percentage |
|---|---|
| Harassment | 28.4 |
| Simple assault | 19.6 |
| Neighbor dispute | 6.5 |
| Family dispute | 6.2 |
| Petit theft | 5.9 |
| Property damage | 5.9 |
| Menacing threat | 4.6 |
| Breach of peace | 3.9 |
| Animal control | 2.3 |
| Trespassing | 2.0 |
| Bad checks | 1.3 |
| Littering | .7 |
| Disorderly conduct | .3 |
| Multiple complaints | 12.4 |
| | 100.0 |

month. The remaining 16% reported monthly incomes over $800.

The typical complainant was an angry client, by his or her own admission. Complainants were asked whether they would have pursued a warrant if the CDS Project were not available, and 80% reported that they would. This figure is probably inflated by the client's need to convince the project staff of the seriousness of the problems and the intensity of the emotional involvement from the complainant's viewpoint.

### SOURCE OF CLIENTS

Through general announcements and special presentations, the CDS Project was publicized throughout the Orange County area. In this way, the Project hoped to attract clients from a variety of sources. The majority of clients who came to the Project between January and October were referred either by the Orange County Sheriff's Department (33%) or the Orlando Police Department (28%). The State Attorney's Office referred 14% of the clients, an additional 10% came on their own initiative, and private attorneys referred 8%. Police departments of communities surrounding Orlando were less frequent sources of referral, providing a total of 7%.

## Complaints Brought to a CDS Hearing

All complaints did not result in hearings between complainants and respondents. Of the 306 complaints presented, hearings occurred in 194 cases (63.4%). In the other 112 cases, no hearings occurred for a variety of reasons, the most frequent being the absence of respondents at the scheduled hearing (33.9%). Other

important reasons were that the complainant was referred elsewhere (for example, to a community agency) for settlement of this problem (18.8%) or that the complainant agreed to drop his complaint (17%).[2]

Comparisons between the type of complaint and the occurrence of a hearing showed, in general, the likelihood of holding a hearing was not significantly related to type of complaint, except for the category of neighbor dispute which was more likely to result in a hearing.[3]

### EFFECTIVENESS OF THE HEARINGS

Following each hearing, the complainant, respondent and hearing officer independently made two ratings: (1) their satisfaction with the settlement they had just reached, and (2) their judgment of whether the problem which caused the complaint was now solved. These judgments were made on 7-point scales, with the most positive rating equal to 1 ("very satisfied") and the most negative rating equal to 7 ("very unsatisfied").

Overall, complainants, respondents, and hearing officers were generally satisfied with the settlements reached at the hearings (see Table 2). Among complainants, 37.2% were "very satisfied" with the settlements; 68.6% gave positive ratings for the settlement. Only 8.4% of the complainants were "very unsatisfied"; 17.3% of the clients gave negative ratings. Among respondents, 48.4% were "very satisfied" with the settlements; 78.6% gave positive ratings. Only 6.8% were "very unsatisfied"; 9.4% gave negative ratings. In general, then, complainants and respondents gave quite favorable opinions. It is understandable that respondents would be even more satisfied than complainants, since respondents had just avoided potential legal battles with the complainants. Satisfaction ratings for complainant-respondent pairs were positively correlated (Spearman $r = .44$; $p. < .001$).

Hearing officer satisfaction ratings were also favorable, although slightly less so than complainants or respondents (see means in Table 2). The correlations between hearing officer ratings and complainant ratings and between hearing officer ratings and respondent ratings were high and positive ($r = .40$; $p < .001$ and $r = .42$; $p < .001$, respectively).

The three parties involved in each hearing also made independent ratings of the likelihood that the problem which underlay the complaint had been solved (see Table 3). Opinions were optimistic among complainants and respondents. Nearly 31% of the complainants and 41% of the respondents thought that it

**TABLE 2**
**Complainant, respondent, and hearing officer satisfaction ratings**
**(in percentages)**

| Scale | Complainant (n = 191) | Respondent (n = 192) | Hearing officer (n = 195) |
|---|---|---|---|
| 1 = Very satisfied | 37.2 | 48.4 | 27.7 |
| 2 = Somewhat satisfied | 21.5 | 20.8 | 21.0 |
| 3 = Just a little satisfied | 9.9 | 9.4 | 15.5 |
| 4 = Neutral | 14.1 | 12.0 | 12.8 |
| 5 = Just a little unsatisfied | 3.7 | 1.6 | 4.6 |
| 6 = Somewhat unsatisfied | 5.2 | 1.0 | 4.6 |
| 7 = Very unsatisfied | 8.4 | 6.8 | 13.8 |
| | 100.0 | 100.0 | 100.0 |
| Combined data (scale values) | M = 2.7 SD = 1.9 Med = 2.1 | M = 2.3 SD = 1.7 Med = 1.6 | M = 3.2 SD = 2.1 Med = 2.6 |

**TABLE 3**
**Complainant, respondent, and hearing officer ratings of the**
**likelihood of problem solution (in percentages)**

| Scale | Complainant (n = 191) | Respondent (n = 192) | Hearing officer (n = 195) |
|---|---|---|---|
| 1 = Very likely | 30.9 | 41.1 | 15.9 |
| 2 = Somewhat likely | 20.4 | 20.8 | 19.0 |
| 3 = Just a little likely | 6.3 | 8.4 | 11.3 |
| 4 = Neutral | 23.6 | 15.6 | 16.9 |
| 5 = Just a little unlikely | 4.2 | 2.1 | 9.2 |
| 6 = Somewhat unlikely | 4.7 | 2.1 | 10.8 |
| 7 = Very unlikely | 9.9 | 9.9 | 16.9 |
| | 100.0 | 100.0 | 100.0 |
| Combined data (scale values) | M = 3.0 SD = 2.0 Med = 2.4 | M = 2.6 SD = 1.9 Med = 1.9 | M = 3.8 SD = 2.1 Med = 3.7 |

was "very likely" that the problem was now solved. Optimistic complainant ratings tended to be associated with optimistic respondent ratings ($r = .33$, $p < .001$). However, overall judgments were cautious: the average complainant rating was 3.0 (that is, "just a little likely") and the average respondent rating was 2.6, only slightly more positive.

Hearing officers were significantly less positive than either complainants or respondents in their assessment of the likelihood of problem solution: their average rating was 3.8, only slightly optimistic (Complainant-Hearing Officer ratings: $x^2 = 13.54$, df = 2, $p < .01$; Respondent-Hearing Officer ratings: $x^2 = 29.30$, df = 2, $p < .001$). The correlations between hearing officer and complainant ratings and between hearing officer and respondent ratings were high ($r = .49$; $p < .001$ and $r = .45$; $p < .001$, respectively).

In sum, these post-hearing ratings by complainants, respondents and hearing officers indicate that all parties generally were satisfied with the solutions reached. In addition, complainants and respondents were cautiously optimistic that the problem which underlay the complaint really was solved. These favorable opinions were made regardless of the type of complaint presented.[4]

## Longer-Term Follow-Up of the Effectiveness of the Hearings

A random sample of hearing cases was selected to determine whether the longer-term effects of the hearings matched the positive short-term effects. Approximately three weeks following their hearing, pairs of complainants and respondents were contacted to obtain satisfaction ratings concerning the settlement they had reached earlier. In addition, complainants and respondents were asked whether the problem that caused the complaint had been solved. (Response rates were 91% for complainants and 93% for respondents. Comparisons of the follow-up sample with the entire hearing population verified the representativeness of the follow-up sample.)

Complainants and respondents continued to report high satisfaction ratings three to four weeks after their hearing (see Table 4). For complainants, the average rating at follow-up (M = 2.6) was similar to the average rating at the time of the hearing (M = 2.7). For respondents, the average rating at follow-up decreased from the average rating at the time of the hearing (2.8 and 2.3, respectively).

The average ratings for complainants and respondents tell only part of the story. It is also important to determine whether individual clients who were satisfied following a hearing remained satisfied three weeks later. Among the complainants, there was a moderate association between the two judgments (r = .30; p. < .03); among the respondents, there was a lower association between the two judgments (r = .11). When these judgments were analyzed more closely,[5] we discovered a significant change in complaint satisfaction toward more positive judgments ($x^2$ = 8.36, df = 2, p. < .05). The percentage of complainants making "satisfied" judgments increased from 58.6 to 75.2; the percentage of complainants making "unsatisfied" judgments increased much less from 13.6 to 19.5. A similar significant trend was not found for the respondents. The percentage of "satisfied" respondents remained high at follow-up (63.4). Although not significant, there was an increase in "unsatisfied" respondents (from 7.8% to 19.5%) which explains the lower correlation reported above of the respondent satisfaction ratings.

The follow-up sample of complainants and respondents was also asked to judge whether the problem which underlay the complaint had been solved (forced-choice judgments of either "yes" or "no"). A majority of both complainants (58.5%) and respondents (64.3%) reported that the problem was solved; however, a substantial minority of clients (41.5% of the complainants and 35.6% of the respondents) reported that the problem remained unsolved.

The meaning of these three-week follow-up ratings is unclear without a comparison group. Consequently, a quasi-experimental comparison group was included, drawn from the population of "potential" clients who

### TABLE 4
**Follow-up sample: complainant and respondent satisfaction ratings (in percentages)**

| Scale | Complainant (n = 41) | Respondent (n = 42) |
|---|---|---|
| 1 = Very satisfied | 51.2 | 38.1 |
| 2 = Somewhat satisfied | 22.0 | 26.2 |
| 3 = Just a little satisfied | 2.4 | 4.8 |
| 4 = Neutral | 4.9 | 11.9 |
| 5 = Just a little unsatisfied | 0.0 | 0.0 |
| 6 = Somewhat unsatisfied | 0.0 | 7.1 |
| 7 = Very unsatisfied | 19.5 | 11.9 |
|  | 100.0 | 100.0 |
| Combined data (scale values) | M = 2.6<br>SD = 2.3<br>Med = 1.5 | M = 2.8<br>SD = 2.1<br>Med = 2.0 |

had not participated in a hearing (i.e., complainants and respondents who were scheduled for a hearing but no hearing was held). A random sample of these "potential" clients was contacted and asked whether the problem they had reported earlier was now solved. "Solved" or "not solved" forced-choice ratings were obtained from 27 of the 29 complainants and from 21 of the 29 respondents in the quasi-experimental comparison group. These ratings were then compared with similar ratings made by clients in the follow-up sample who *had* attended a hearing. The objective was to analyze comparable groups who either did or did not have a hearing and thereby determine whether a hearing really helped to solve underlying problems. These comparisons need to be interpreted cautiously, however, because potential clients were self-selected into the hearing or no-hearing group.

The responses from the complainants in the two groups were similar. For the hearing group, 58.5% of the complainants reported that their problem was solved. For the no-hearing comparison group, 51.9% of the complainants reported that their problem was solved. These figures were not significantly different and indicate that the hearings may not be solving underlying problems. The ratings given by respondents are more difficult to interpret. Nearly all of the no-hearing group respondents (85.7%) reported that their problem was solved. In our opinion (based on interviewer reports), these ratings reflect a general desire to avoid the problem rather than a considered judgment about the problem. Consequently, no meaningful comparison can be made with the hearing group respondents.

311

## Impact of the Program on the
## Local Criminal Justice System

Because of the small number of cases involved in the CDS Project in its first year, the impact of the program on the local criminal justice system was minimal. During the period of this study, the CDS Project's average monthly intake was approximately 34 cases. During the same period, the average number of misdemeanors filed per month at the State Attorney's office was 141. During the same monthly period but one or two years prior to the time of the study, the average numbers of misdemeanors filed were 155 for 1975 and 202 for 1974 (see Figure 1). It would appear that there was a drop in the State Attorney's monthly intake from 1975 to 1976. However, during 1976, there was a 2.6% increase in the population of Orange County. If the State Attorney's intake is standardized for yearly populations changes, we see that there were 5.6 misdemeanor filings per 1000 residents in 1974, 4.2 filings per 1000 residents in 1975, and 4.1 filings per 1000 residents in 1976.[6]

As CDS intake increases, the impact of the program on the local criminal justice system may increase. During the first year of operation, however, the program's effect on misdemeanor filings and, hence, on the local court system was minimal.

## DISCUSSION

The findings on the effectiveness of the Orange County Bar Association's CDS Program have implications for the future conduct of similar citizen dispute programs. In addition, the results provide some empirical data for the theoretical dispute over the appropriateness of mediation in American communities.

### CDS Program Effectiveness

The CDS Program is involved with a variety of complaints. The majority of complaints which are both presented for a hearing and result in an actual hearing are serious ones: harassment and simple assault. Harassment was defined by the CDS Program as impugning the complainant's character, spreading rumors, or purposely creating a disturbance for the complainant. Although these kinds of charges would not automatically cause complainants and respondents to become involved in the criminal justice system, these problems can be precursors of the second largest category of complaint, simple assault. Verbal conflict, particularly if prolonged and unresolved, can easily escalate into

physical conflict. Simple assault often results in formal charges and processing by the criminal justice system. Although filed infrequently, other types of complaints presented (for example, neighbor dispute or property damage) also can lead to involvement in the criminal justice system. These evaluative data indicate that the CDS Program attracted a majority of cases involving serious problems—problems which could necessitate adjudication. If such problems are resolved out of court, the CDS hearings would be helping to reduce the burden on the judicial branch of the criminal justice system.

The project, then, has been successful in attracting the kinds of complaints which could result in involvement with the local criminal justice system. That a large majority of these kinds of complaints were presented implies that the CDS Program is not "creating" a new class of problems which normally would be handled outside any formal justice system. It might have been the case, for example, that the CDS Program attracted a number of clients with marital problems and, hence, served more as a free marriage counseling service for people who could have solved their problems via other means. This, however, was not the case.

During the nine-month period of the evaluation, 306 complaints were presented for a hearing and 194 resulted in actual hearings. On the average, then, 34 complaints were presented per month, and 22 hearings were held each month. It should be noted that these averages obscure the fact that the number of complaints presented and hearings held gradually increased over the period of the evaluation. Nonetheless, the fact remains the program was serving a small number of clients.

Findings indicate, however, that there does not seem to be a lack of need for CDS services. There are large numbers of misdemeanors filed in Orange County (see Figure 1) and an unknown but probably large number of similar kinds of problems which could be aided by a hearing. Instead, the case for low intake seems to be related to lack of referrals by law enforcement personnel or lack of interest on the part of citizens to follow the suggestions of police who refer them to the program. Throughout the project, the director has made presentations to all types of law enforcement personnel to explain the program. The project director has recently instituted a new procedure to increase the number of referrals by law enforcement officials. Police

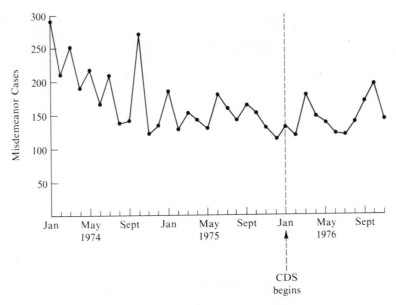

**Figure 1** Number of Misdemeanor Cases
Filed at the Orange County State Attorney's Office

Source: State Attorney's Office in Orlando, Florida.

are now informed about the disposition of each case they refer to CDS. The project director believes that this type of feedback will convince the police that their referrals actually do result in hearings and thereby encourage future referrals.

Possible solutions for the second cause of low referrals (citizen neglect to file complaints) might be to publicize the successes of the program more widely and to follow up police referrals more actively. The first potential solution is already occurring. With the release of the final evaluation report, the project had documented facts about program success to use in its publicity efforts. This information may help convince citizens and referral agents alike that the hearings generally help. In the case of the latter potential solution, police could be instructed to notify the CDS Program each time they make a referral. This might be done through the police supervisor so that police would receive "credit" for their referrals. In turn, the CDS staff could contact these potential clients to encourage participation in a CDS hearing.

The results are clear that complainants and respondents generally are quite satisfied with the short-term solutions reached and are convinced that the problem

which underlay the complaint is likely now to be solved. Hearing officers are a little more pessimistic but they too tend to rate the hearings positively.

The follow-up results three weeks after the hearings indicate that complainants and respondents generally remain satisfied with the settlements. Indeed, complainants tend to be more satisfied; however, about half the complainants and respondents report that the long-term problems remain unsolved. This result could mean that three weeks is too short a time for long-term problems to be affected, even though the immediate complaint is removed. Perhaps a follow-up at two or three months might indicate some change in the long-term problem. On the other hand, the program may not be affecting the long-term problems no matter what the time frame. It is probably asking too much of a one-hour hearing to expect fundamental problems to be solved.

An actual CDS case illustrates this point. A feud between neighbors had reached the point of open hostility among their children. At the hearing, a settlement was reached whereby the parents agreed to monitor closely their own children to prevent fights. The hearing had given both parties a chance to explain their

313

side of the story, and each party was quite satisfied with the settlement. Neither party, however, believed that much progress had been made in resolving basic differences that had existed for years. Consequently, both parties made high satisfaction ratings but judged the fundamental problems to be still unresolved.

On limited, specific complaints, the program has largely succeeded in helping complainants and respondents solve their problems. It should be noted, however, that the design used in this evaluation does not permit a definitive statement that it is the hearing alone that causes the settlements to be reached. It could be that complainants and respondents, left on their own to hold informal "hearings," may also find solutions. Data from the quasi-experimental comparison group of no-show complainants and respondents imply that this occurs to some extent. Indeed, one reason for the low intake may be that some complainants and respondents, once they are referred to the program by a police officer, decide to be a little more reasonable and solve their own problems. Intensive follow-up by the CDS staff of clients referred by the police and by others would indicate whether this is occurring.

A secondary goal of the evaluation was to analyze the impact of the project on the local criminal justice system. Because of the low client intake, the impact of the program on the corrections and court system was minimal. If all hearings had been completely successful and if all these hearings would have resulted in misdemeanor filings had the program not existed, the impact on the criminal justice system would have been only somewhat more pronounced (compare these statistics: average monthly Orange County misdemeanor filings in 1976 = 147; average monthly CDS *intake* = 34; average monthly CDS *hearings* = 22).

Although the program's impact on the Orange County criminal justice system is at present minimal, the program may be having more of an impact on the duties of the policeman on call. Very often it is a police officer who serves as an "instant" hearing officer to mediate neighbor disputes, harassment, and the like. These officers are confronted with two or more heated citizens who are not in the mood to present their side of the story calmly and rationally. The CDS Program provides an alternative to an officer who does not want to arrest anyone, but who does believe that the parties need to air their grievances. The CDS Program, then, may be reducing the police officer's or sheriff's burden. This issue was not addressed specifically in

the research reported here, but could be investigated in the future.

The other secondary objective of the evaluation was to monitor the involvement of the hearing officers—volunteer attorneys from the Orange County Bar Association. The project had hoped to involve a large number of the Bar's 750 members in the hearing. In meeting this goal, the project has been very successful. By the end of the nine-month evaluation period, 45 bar members had voluntarily served as hearing officers and another 55 were waiting to serve. In addition, the Bar's leadership actively supported the program and considered the effort a long-term public service project. This support and help from the Bar aided the project director in securing continuation funding for the project from LEAA and in securing funding for the expansion of the project into the area of juvenile dispute resolution. In addition, the Bar supported legislation in the Florida State Senate to institute CDS-like projects statewide.

The Orange County Bar Association's involvement in the CDS Program, then, included the use of members' services in the hearings themselves, as well as the use of members' services in promoting and continuing the project. Both of these types of involvement were important to the project's success. The Orlando experience provides a good example of a successful case of on-going public service via bar activation, a goal of the national BASICS Program of which the CDS Project was one small component.

## MEDIATION IN AMERICAN COMMUNITIES: THE THEORETICAL TEST

The CDS evaluation findings provide some clarification of the theoretical dispute over the appropriateness of mediation as a dispute processing technique in American communities. Danzig's idea of community moots is supported by these results, whereas Felstiner's assertion that mediation will be an unsatisfactory technique in a society like the U.S. is not born out by these data. CDS clients, both complainants and respondents, reported a high degree of satisfaction with the settlement hearings, both immediately following the hearing and approximately three weeks later. Indeed, complainants tended to be even more satisfied three weeks after the hearing. As a group, complainants could be particularly critical judges of the hearings, since they initiated the hearing procedure with high expectations for a successful outcome. Consequently, the positive ratings initially given by complainants and their subsequent, even more positive ratings are all the more impressive.

These quantitative ratings, as well as more qualitative data derived from discussions with CDS clients, indicate that clients like the hearings and believe that they are useful in airing the relevant issues. Felstiner's analysis of this type of hearing would lead us to expect dissatisfied clients who would be frustrated by the hearing process because the hearing officer did not know them personally. This was not the case in the great majority of hearings. The fact that the hearing officer was an unknown, neutral third party seemed to be an asset rather than an impediment. Each client could explain his side of the story and expect the hearing officer to listen with an open mind. Indeed, the hearing officer's unfamiliarity with the situation gave each client the opportunity to tell his story in great detail, occasionally revealing a seemingly unrelated issue which was, in fact, central to the cause of the problem.

Although clients are satisfied with the hearings, the follow-up results on longer-term problem solution indicate that the CDS hearings are not particularly effective in solving underlying problems. These results support Felstiner on one important assertion about this type of mediation: It is not suited for dispute settlement. If success is defined as solving underlying problems, then community mediation programs like the CDS Project will not be particularly successful, even though the process is satisfying to clients.

This conclusion needs to be qualified in two ways. First, the study reported here is only a quasi-experimental test of this assertion. The groups of hearing and no-hearing clients were not formed by the researchers but instead were self-formed. For this reason, we cannot be certain about the initial comparability of the two groups. Although we determined that the likelihood of having or not having a hearing was similar for most types of disputes, we could not be certain that, among clients with similar types of disputes, the degree of seriousness or complexity was not related to whether or not a hearing was held. Clients with less serious harassment problems, for example, may have been less likely to appear for a hearing than clients with more serious harassment problems. If this type of bias occurred, the results on CDS problem solution would be particularly conservative, since

clients with more serious problems and no hearing would have been compared to clients with less serious problems and no hearing. Alternatively, clients with the most serious, complex harassment problems may have decided that the CDS hearings would be useless and therefore did not appear. If this type of self-selection bias occurred, the inability of CDS hearings to solve underlying problems takes on new significance, since only the simplest problems would have been brought to the program. Although either of these biases is possible, it is impossible to know if one actually occurred because of the self-selection of clients.

There is a second qualification which is required to the conclusion that mediation programs are not successful in solving underlying problems. It must be remembered that mediation sessions are generally fairly short, with most CDS Project hearings lasting about one hour. To expect this short a session to solve underlying problems is asking a good deal. Moreover, it is an open question whether more time-consuming adjudication or arbitration programs are any more effective in problem solution. Perhaps we need to lower our expectations for mediation sessions and hope instead for a complete airing of issues and a renewed exchange of discussion between disputants. This is no small achievement and may be the necessary first step in changing the situation—a task which is left to the disputants to accomplish over a much longer period. Danzig and Lowy believe that the process of discussion during a mediation session is a more important outcome than a particular solution to a problem.

Future research in this area is needed to establish these findings more conclusively. Client satisfaction with the hearing process needs to be explored in greater detail. What is it about the hearing that clients like so much? Do complainants and respondents like different aspects of the hearing procedure? The hearings themselves need to be monitored more closely and more systematically to identify the dynamics involved. Most importantly, identical samples of clients who experience and do not experience hearings need to be compared over a long term to investigate ultimate problem solution as well as the extent of further disagreements between the parties.

There are other aspects of the mediation process which were not investigated in this research but which could be the focus of future work. The hearing officers were lawyers in the CDS Project. Are lawyers particularly good at mediating hearings or could other kinds of mediators be used? What type of mediator training is best for a hearing officer? Another important focus for future research would be the question of the impact of mediation programs on police officers' tasks. Does a mediation program provide a kind of diversion option which is desired and used by police officers for misdemeanor disputes? The relationship of mediation programs to the larger criminal justice system could also be analyzed in greater detail.

The study presented here begins to provide empirical data on the effectiveness of dispute processing mechanisms and to end the absence of evaluative research work in this area. Based on the results of this study, citizen dispute processing projects could be more widely instituted. However, policy makers need to realize that a CDS-type project may not solve long-standing problems. It will, however, probably give two disputants a chance to re-establish communication and to spend some time thinking about, rather than reacting to, a problem. In this way, CDS-type projects may be a limited but genuine source of relief for citizens who have turned their backs on the official, expensive, and intimidating court system, but who still, as Chief Justice Burger points out, want some quick relief from their disputes.

*The authors are grateful to William Felstiner, Michael Lowy, and Daniel Stokols for their comments on an earlier draft of this article. The research reported here was supported by an evaluation grant from the American Bar Association. The conclusions presented here are not necessarily those of the American Bar Association.*

## NOTES

1. During the pilot-testing, for example, the labels describing the anchoring endpoints of the 7-point scales were reversed (because clients reported that the best judgment ought to be associated with the number 1), the position of the scales was changed from horizontal to vertical (because clients said that the best judgment ought to be higher than the worst judgment), and "smiling faces" or "frowning faces" were added to orient the clients quickly to the valence of the scale points (because some clients reported that the labels looked similar).

2. Other reasons: complainant and respondent agreed to no hearing (14.3%), neither complainant nor respondent appeared (12.5%), and complainant did not appear (3.5%).

3. $x^2 = 6.25$, df = 1, p < .01; contingency coefficient = .49.

4. Further details can be found in Conner and Surette, 1977.

5. These analyses involved reclassifying ratings for easier inspection. Client ratings of 1 or 2 were reclassified as "satisfied"; ratings of 3, 4, and 5 were reclassified "neutral"; and ratings of 6 and 7 were reclassified "unsatisfied."

6. The reasons for the general downward trend in misdemeanor filings in 1974 and for the large increase for October, 1974, are unclear. Officials in the Orange County State Attorney's Office offered various explanations (the main one being that the October jump was the result of a seasonal influx of migrants and transients), but none was satisfactory (i.e., no similar seasonal jumps occurred in 1975 and 1976) nor substantiated by records.

## REFERENCES

Bennett, C. A. and A. A. Lumsdaine [eds.] (1975) Evaluation and Experiment: Some Critical Issues in Assessing Social Programs. New York: Academic.

Campbell, D. T. (1969) "Reforms as experiments." Amer. Psychologist 24: 409–429.

Collier, J. F. (1973) Law and Social Change in Zinacantan. Stanford, CA: Stanford Univ. Press.

Conner, R. F. and C. R. Huff (1979) Attorneys as Activists: Evaluating the American Bar Association BASICS Program. Beverly Hills, CA: Sage.

Conner, R. F. and R. Surette (1977) The Citizen Dispute Settlement Program: Resolving Disputes Outside the Courts—Orlando, Florida. Washington, DC: American Bar Association.

Danzig, R. (1973) "Toward the creation of a complementary decentralized system of criminal justice." Stanford Law Rev. 26: 1–54.

Danzig, R. and M. J. Lowy (1975) "Everyday disputes and mediation in the United States: a reply to Professor Felstiner." Law and Society Rev. 9: 675–694.

Felstiner, W. L. F. (1975) "Avoidance as dispute processing: an elaboration." Law and Society Rev. 9: 695–706.

Felstiner, W. L. F. (1974) "Influences of social organization on dispute settlement." Law and Society Rev. 9: 63–94.

Freeman, H. E. (1977) "The present status of evaluation research," pp. 17–51 in Vol. 2 of M. Guttentag (ed.) Evaluation Studies Review Annual. Beverly Hills, CA: Sage.

Friedman, L. M. (1973) "Some historical aspects of law and social change in the United States." University of California, Berkeley, Law and Society Program. (unpublished)

Fuller, L. (1971) "Mediations—its forms and function." Southern California Law Rev. 44: 305–339.

Galanter, M. (1974) "Why the 'haves' have come out ahead: speculations on the limits of legal change." Law and Society Rev. 9: 95–160.

Gilbert, J. P., R. S. Light, and F. Mosteller (1975) "Assessing social innovations: an empirical base for policy," pp. 39–193 in C. A. Bennett and A. A. Lumsdaine (eds.) Evaluation and Experiment: Some Critical Issues in Assessing Social Programs. New York: Academic.

Gluckman, M. (1955) The Judicial Process Among the Barotse of Northern Rhodesia. Manchester: Manchester Univ. Press.

Gulliver, P. H. (1973) "Negotiation as a mode of dispute settlement: towards a general model." Law and Society Rev. 7: 667–691.

Gulliver, P. H. (1963) Social Control in an African Society. Boston: Boston Univ. Press.

Hager, P. (1977) "Burger warns U.S. may be overrun with lawyers." Los Angeles Times (May 28): 1, 4.

Huff, C. R., R. F. Conner, and G. Geis (1975) Planning Correctional Reform: An Assessment of the American Bar Association BASICS' Program. Washington, DC: American Bar Association.

Johnson, E., Jr., V. Kantor, and E. Schwartz (1977) Outside the Courts: A Survey of Alternatives to Civil Cases. Williamsburg, VA: National Center for State Courts.

Law Enforcement Assistance Administration (1975) Citizen Dispute Settlement: The Night Prosecutor Program of Columbus, Ohio. Washington, DC: U.S. Department of Justice.

McGillis, D. and J. Mullen (1977) Neighborhood Justice Centers: An Analysis of Potential Models. Washington, DC: U.S. Department of Justice.

Mund, G. (1976) "The need for community arbitration." Arbitration J. 31: 109–115.

Nader, L. (1975) "Forums for justice: a cross-cultural perspective." J. of Social Issues 31: 151–170.

Nader, L. [ed.] (1969) Law in Culture and Society. Chicago: Aldine.

Nader, L. and D. Metzger (1963) "Conflict resolution in two Mexican communities." Amer. Anthropologist 65: 584–592.

Nader, L. and L. R. Singer (1976) "Dispute resolution." California State Bar J. 57: 281–286, 311–320.

Pospisil, L. (1967) "Legal levels and the multiplicity of legal systems in human societies." J. of Conflict Resolution 11: 2–26.

Suchman, E. (1969) Evaluation Research: Principles and Practice in Service and Social Action Programs. New York: Russel Sage.

Yngvesson, B. and P. Hennessey (1975) "Small claims, complex disputes: a review of the small claims literature." Law and Society Rev. 9: 219–274.

# CHAPTER THIRTEEN

# Terminating Programs

## Organizational Decline
## A Neglected Topic in Organizational Science

David A. Whetten

Organizational decline, though an important and ultimately unavoidable concern of organizations, has received little research attention. In this paper, I examine some reasons for this neglect, my intent being to stimulate additional discourse and research on organizational decline processes and their management.

### REVIEW OF THE LITERATURE

A review of the literature on organizational metamorphosis yields an extensive bibliography on organizational growth but few materials on decline. Little is available on the causes of decline, responses to decline, or the effects of decline on organizations. Furthermore, despite the fact that most of the standard organizational research topics (e. g., decision making, conflict, leadership, innovation, motivation, careers, and structural configuration) are affected by significant downward shifts in organizational size or profitability, seldom are these subjects researched in this context.

### Preoccupation with Growth

Organizational theories in general are based on an assumption of growth and hence researchers are pre-

From *Academy of Management Review,* Vol. 5, pp. 577–588. Copyright 1980, Academy of Management. Reprinted by permission.

occupied with studying growth and its effects [Scott, 1974]. Three common assumptions reflecting a bias in favor of growth are: (1) There is a positive correlation between size and age; consequently the greatest need of organizations as they mature is to manage growth. (2) Size is a desirable organizational characteristic— i. e., bigger is better. (3) Growth is synonymous with effectiveness.

#### COPING WITH GROWTH IS A
#### SERIOUS MANAGEMENT PROBLEM

This assumption is clearly evident in the work of Blau and his associates [Blau, 1968, 1970; Blau & Schoenherr, 1971], who have considered how organizations maintain coordination under conditions of expansion. As an organization grows, more extensive hierarchical structures emerge in order to properly integrate new personnel, product lines, departments, and so on. Interest in tracking this aspect of growth produced a spate of articles on administrative ratio [e. g., Indik, 1964; Pondy, 1969; Rushing, 1967]. Although interest in this particular research topic has waned, the influence of the early work relating size to structure has clearly left its mark, as is evident in the organizational design models proposed by Lawrence and Lorsch [1967] and Galbraith [1977]. The basic proposition of these models is that the greater the amount of task uncertainty, the greater the amount of information that has to be processed between decision makers during the execution of the task. One of the major sources of uncertainty (lack of needed information) identified by Galbraith is organizational differentiation: the greater the heterogeneity of tasks, product lines, and departments, the greater the need for coordination. The implication of this model is that an organization needs to overhaul its information-processing system at several critical points along the growth curve.

The assumption that coping with growth is one of management's most difficult problems also underlies much of the organization development literature. A common justification for OD interventions is that employees become alienated as a function of increasing organizational size. Large operations tend to produce depersonalized leader-subordinate relations, monotonous and specialized jobs, and bureaucratic organizational procedures [Bennis & Slater, 1968]. Hence, interventions are needed to transform the climate to that associated with small organizations. The creation of divisions or subsidiaries within a large corporation is one way of restoring the intimate climate of a small organization. Consultants supply numerous other remedies such as team building, morale surveys, conflict resolution techniques, and humanistic management training. The frequent use of a family metaphor in the OD literature suggests a perceived need to introduce a supportive, trusting, and sharing climate into large machine-like organizations to retard the natural tendency for employee commitment and satisfaction to deteriorate with increasing organizational size and age.

### SIZE IS A DESIRABLE CHARACTERISTIC

Large size is widely lauded as enabling an organization to function more efficiently, owing to economies of scale, and as enhancing its ability to absorb the shocks of environmental changes [Argenti, 1976; Kaufman, 1973; Perrow, 1979]. These benefits allegedly give large organizations a strong competitive advantage that overshadows the negative consequences of growth for management. The desirability of large size is clearly reflected in Selznick's *Leadership in Administration* [1975].

Some organizations are merely organizations—rational tools in which there is little personal investment and which can be cast aside without regret. Others become institutionalized. They take on a distinctive character: They become prized in and of themselves, not merely for the goods and services they grind out. People build their lives around them, identify with them, become dependent upon them. The process of institutionalization is the process of organic growth, wherein the organization adapts to the strivings of internal groups and values of the external society [summary by Perrow, 1979, p. 186].

This striving of mere organizations to become mighty institutions is guided by its administrators, who wish, in Selznick's terms, to be transformed into statesmen in the process.

### SIZE IS AN INDICATOR OF EFFECTIVENESS

If an organization is getting bigger then it is common to assume that it is being managed effectively. Hence, research on the "square cube" law of organizational scale [Haire, 1959] has shown that organizational size is a better predictor than profitability of the chief executive's salary. This finding adds credence to Persig's [1974] assertion that Americans have measured success quantitatively for so long that we are now insensitive to qualitative distinctions.

The practice of equating size with effectiveness is prevalent in the organization theory literature. Thompson [1967] proposed that organizations attempt to prove their fitness for future action by demonstrating historical improvement, or improvement relative to comparable organizations. The measurement of growth figures prominently in both assessments [Bogue, 1972].

The intertwined relationship between growth and effectiveness can be seen most explicitly in system theory. Because this perspective views an organization as a "living entity," growth becomes the preferred organizational state, since it connotes youth and vitality. A declining organization is considered ineffective since that is the equivalent of being unhealthy in an organic model [Scott, 1974, 1979]. Katz and Kahn [1966] have argued that, in order to avoid entropy (the tendency toward randomization), organizations must put in more "energy" (human and financial) than they consume in the production process. This additional energy is required to maintain a homeostatic balance between the organization and its environment. Organizational decline results unless sufficient energy is available to perform internal coordination and management activities and to properly map the complexity of the environment [Buckley, 1967]. Because environments are assumed to be increasing in turbulence and complexity [Emery & Trist, 1965; Terryberry, 1968], it follows that an organization must grow in order to maintain a steady-state relationship with its environment.

Scott has observed that, according to the management literature, organizational growth is not only necessary for maintaining effective organization-environment relations but also for effective administration-employee relations. According to a line of reasoning that Scott traces back to 1835 in the literature, management uses the surplus from production as currency for buying off internal conflicting interest groups. Frederick W. Taylor is credited with "recognizing that internal consensus is the outcome of growth-created surplus distributed by a scientifically enlightened management as a side payment for harmony of interest" [Scott, 1974, p. 245].

## Apparent Reasons for Emphasis on Growth

Having highlighted examples of the preoccupation with organizational growth, I now turn to a search for the underlying reasons for this singular focus on one half of the growth and decline cycle. Two possible explanations merit examination.

1. *Organization theories and research accurately reflect prevailing organizational reality.* One explanation for the strong interest in organizational growth is that it reflects our adaptation to the real world of organizations. As Boulding notes,

> For several generations, a considerable proportion of the human race, and the United States in particular, has enjoyed growth in almost all aspects of social life. We have had continuous growth in population, almost continuous growth in per capita real incomes, in productivity of the overall society, and in the gross national product. . . . All our institutions and ways of thinking have survived because they were well adapted to an age of rapid growth [1975, p. 8].

As a result of the unprecedented prosperity since World War II, growth has characterized American organizations. The factors stimulating organizational growth, especially during periods of economic expansion, are summarized by Boswell:

> The pressure to expand simply to satisfy an apparently insatiable market may be enormous. Moreover, in certain industries there may be conventions as to what is a respectable size, sufficient to impress potential customers, suppliers, or the trade in general. If this is true, then the "new boys" have an additional motive to grow in order to prove themselves. . . . As one [businessman] graphically put it: "Expansion is dictated to you; you simply try to plan and contain it" [1972, pp. 64–65].

Consequently, during the past 20 years the major concern of practicing managers has indeed been how to stimulate growth and simultaneously cope with its consequences [Kotter & Sathe, 1978].

A lack of interest in decline during periods of rapid growth is compounded by a relative lack of opportunity to study it. Moreover, those organizations that are declining are such a novelty that they are viewed as aberrations and are dismissed as examples of faulty management. Consequently, managers in these organizations have little to gain, and much to lose, by permitting outsiders to chronicle their organization's decline. Even if a researcher can gain entrance, the organization can little afford the luxury of sponsoring reflective research.

2. *The growth bias in organizational research reflects a broader social ideology.* Bendix [1956] argued that theories of administration typically reflect the prevailing ideology of a society. The use of organizational theories and managerial practices to reinforce dominant societal values and economic advantages has also been emphasized by Marxian theorists such as Heydebrand [1977] and Goldman and Van Houten [1977]. Following this logic it is not difficult to see how our organizational theories and research agendas reflect societal values that complement a pro-growth orientation.

For instance, our society inculcates values of determination and self-confidence. We are taught that no obstacle should deter us from reaching an objective. We are told that, through the *Power of Positive Thinking* [Peale, 1952], we can *Think and Grow Rich* [Hill, 1967]. It follows that if success can be willed, then failure must reflect a lack of desire. Hence, admitting failure is practically a national taboo. When people must discuss a failure (e.g., divorce, business bankruptcy, being fired), they tend to describe it as though it were a personal success. Personal credit is taken for being: perceptive enough to recognize that their spouse was ruining their life; capable enough to keep a business from losing any more than it did before they had sense enough to bail out; so ethical, smart, or experienced that their former employer felt threatened by their presence in the organization. This practice reflects a societal norm that someone must be blamed for every failure. In contrast, oriental cultures are far less concerned about affixing personal responsibility for failure. They are more likely to explain failure as the outcome of a malfunction in the "system," the will of the gods, or simply fate [Persig, 1974].

The fear of being blamed for failure increases the likelihood of large-scale failures because it reduces management's incentive to drop a new project or product at the first signs of significant trouble. Instead they tend to pour good money after bad in hopes of salvaging the operation—and their reputations. A related consequence of our failure paranoia is that managers frequently refuse to admit that their organization is in trouble. This tendency has been borne out in studies of businesses facing financial crises [R. A. Smith, 1963; Starbuck & Hedberg, 1977], and school districts experiencing shrinking enrollments [Rodekohr, 1974]. When forced to admit the existence of decline, managers tend to label it as merely a period of temporary consolidation, which is a forerunner of future growth [Scott, 1976].

The reluctance of managers to admit that their organization is in a state of decline is evidence of their substantial personal stake in growth. A colleague recently related an illuminating example of this proposition. This experience grew out of his work as a consultant for an electric utility company that services a geographical area with a rapid out-migration and an accompanying decrease in demand for power. Despite this trend, in an executive meeting the president presented a plan for expanding the structure of the organization. After the meeting, when the consultant confronted him with the seeming inconsistency between his optimistic speech and the pessimistic projections, the president replied that without the incentive of a possible promotion to a new vice-president position, his middle-level managers would become demoralized and quit. Because the upward mobility sought by most managers is not likely to be obtained in a declining organization, this president steadfastly presented an image of continued growth.

Hirschman [1970] has observed that some managers are reluctant to leave a declining organization to which they are morally committed because they feel that they can help minimize the negative consequences of decline. However, Scott [1976] argues that these cases are rare. He argues that competent managers avoid declining organizations. As a result, one of the major reasons it is difficult for organizations to effectively respond to crises is that the best hands are usually the first to jump a sinking ship and it is hard to sign on a new crew for a ship that is taking on water. Consequently, the central issue in organizational decline is not whether managers are *capable* of managing decline, but instead, will they be *willing* to?

Americans are not only willful, but also highly optimistic. Sutton, Harris, Kaysen, and Tobin [1956] have described the American business creed as comprising four key elements: practicality, austerity, individualism, and optimistic affirmation. This optimistic orientation is part of our Western heritage. Nisbit [1969] has noted that the Greeks studied only the growth part of the growth and decline developmental cycle. Fox traces the roots of our contemporary optimism even further:

> The vision of abundance, of enough to go around, has been part of the spiritual heritage of Western man for thousands of years. In biblical times, men dreamed of a land of milk and honey. In subsequent centuries, utopian writers looked back to a golden age behind them or forward to a golden age ahead. . . . In the eighteenth and nineteenth centuries, changes in technology and in the organization of production provided new grounds for optimism. The theory of economics was created to explain and justify this optimism [1967, pp. 177–178].

The oil crisis of 1979 presented a recent manifestation of American optimism. Most Americans refused to accept the possibility of a genuine crisis. Instead they accused the government and the oil companies of colluding to create artificial shortages to increase profits. One explanation for this logic is that it was a defense mechanism generated by the American public to preserve their faith in our society of abundance. By blaming the shortages on crooks who were trying to gouge the system for more than a fair share of its bounties, they did not have to admit that the system was at last fundamentally incapable of sustaining exponential growth.

## THE EMERGING ERA OF RETRENCHMENT

To this point, I have argued that organizational research and theory have been dominated by a growth orientation, and I have explored some of the sources of this influence, including the lack of incentive and opportunities to study declining organizations in a rapidly growing economy, and strong societal norms equating personal success with organizational accomplishment and organizational effectiveness with growth. It appears, however, that countervailing pressures are building in both the economic and social sectors.

Historically there has been a strong mediating effect of organizational size on organization-environment relations. Specifically, the high failure rate among the small has generally been due to the actions of the large [Perrow, 1979]. However, this pattern is beginning to change as major institutions find it more and more difficult to sustain their high rate of resource utilization and are forced to retrench. The industrial complex has been affected by an aroused public's concern about the rapid depletion of our natural resources [Commoner, 1976; Meadows, Meadows, Randers, & Behrens, 1972; Schumacher, 1973]; educational institutions have been forced to cut back because of declining enrollments [Cartter, 1970; Green, 1974; Trow, 1975]; and government's legitimacy and resource base have been eroded by a taxpayer's revolt over poor services and high taxes [Dvorin & Simmons, 1972; Fenno, 1966; B. L. R. Smith & Hague, 1971; Whetten, 1979].

The fact that a substantial number of old and large organizations are now faced with the need to substantially reduce the scale of their operations, or redefine their outputs, in order to maintain their level of effectiveness, makes it more difficult to explain away organizational decline as a failure to adhere to the principles of our growth-dominated management paradigm. Indeed, there are numerous examples of organizations that have failed to respond to declining environmental conditions because management was preoccupied with growth [Starbuck, Greve, & Hedberg, 1978].

The effects of these trends are to increase the salience of decline as an organizational phenomenon, and to provide researchers with access to larger numbers of organizations undergoing retrenchment. Recent changes in the cultural values of our society also provide legitimacy for research on organizational retrenchment as we see the values of the Bigger is Better era being challenged by the Small is Beautiful counterculture [Schumacher, 1973]. Just as many members of large organizations fondly recall when the organization was small and intimate, so too have members of our large and complex society begun to campaign for more humanistic fundamentals [Mathews, 1979].

For example, Berger and Neuhaus [1977] argue for the restoration of "mediating structures" such as the family, neighborhood, and voluntary associations, to serve as buffers between individuals and the megastructures of society. They argue that without them the larger social structure becomes detached from the realities of individual life. To counter the gradual deterioration of these mediating structures in our society, Berger and Neuhaus propose reformulating public policy by making mediating structures the principal instruments of social action. For instance, the government might pay a family a stipend each month to take care of its elderly members, thus reducing reliance on institutional care.

Several social critics view a retrenchment to smaller, more basic forms of organization as inevitable. For instance, Miles [1976] describes America as an *over-developed* country, noting that it is a high energy user and materialistically oriented. He argues that the most salient limit to continued growth will be the American psyche, not the fragile biosphere of our rapidly depleting natural resources. The most important "limits [to growth] are set by the already overstrained capacity of human beings to conceive, design, manage, support, and adapt to extremely complex systems of human interdependence. In short, it is the political limits that are likely to constrain the continuity of physical growth well ahead of all other factors" (p. 2).

If this prediction holds true, the outcome will exemplify what Forrester [1971] has labeled the counter-intuitive behavior of social systems. Miles [1976] and Fox [1967] have both argued that abundance has within it the seeds of its own destruction. If not used wisely it can precipitate new levels of scarcity as people and institutions fuel the growth machine with their insatiable demands for more goods and sevices. The result is that the machine finally blows up and its patrons are forced to accept drastically reduced levels of gratification. Another reason why overindulgence tends to be self-checking is that it produces a feeling of malaise. The economist Robert L. Heilbroner, reflecting on his work *An Inquiry into the Human Prospect,* observed:

> The malaise, I have come more and more to believe, lies in the industrial foundation on which our civilization is based. Economic growth and technical achievement, the greatest triumphs of our epoch of history, have shown themselves to be inadequate sources for collective contentment and hope. Material advance, the most profoundly distinguishing attribute of industrial capitalism and socialism alike, has proved unable to satisfy the human spirit . . . [1975, p. 26].

However, more than intellectual criticism of capitalism and nodding assent to changing values is required before day-to-day organizational practices will be altered. The difficulty of interrupting the ever-accelerating organizational growth cycle is illustrated in Molotch's work entitled "The City as a Growth Machine" [1976]. Molotch argues that the principal objective of local government is to increase the size of its municipality. Cities compete with one another for the preconditions of growth (e. g., new industry) by advertising their most desirable features, such as a low crime rate, low taxes, a large labor force, and abundant natural resources. Because of this growth orientation, local politics tends to attract those people who have a vested interest in the growth process, such as local businessmen. These people in turn reinforce the drive to increase city size so as to enlarge their share of the local resource pool. Molotch points out that the drive for municipal growth continues despite the fact that many of its supporting justifications are false. For instance, growth is frequently justified on the basis that it will increase employment. However, Molotch shows that in fact just the opposite is true—fast-growing metropolitan areas tend to have higher unemployment rates than do slow-growing ones. He predicts that the city growth machine will eventually be dismantled by no growth activists, but it is instructive to see the magnitude of their task. To reverse the cycle, a new cadre of administrators with a different set of vested interests will have to be cultivated, a new management ideology supporting no growth needs to be developed, and considerable research on the process of retrenchment must be conducted.

## AN AGENDA FOR ADDRESSING DECLINE

The organizational science profession has much to contribute in accomplishing these tasks. However, it is presently ill prepared to meet this challenge. We have no theories of organizational decline; relatively few articles have been published on managing an organization under crisis conditions; we are not prepared to provide data-based recommendations on how to manage the decline process; and the typical management curriculum does not teach prospective managers how to cope with decline-induced stress [Whetten, 1980]. As an initial step toward overcoming these deficiencies, I offer the following list of research, teaching, and consulting activities focusing on organizational decline.

### Research

1. *An important task for researchers is to improve the conceptual clarity of organizational decline.* Elsewhere, I distinguish between decline-as-stagnation and decline-as-cutback [Whetten, 1980]. The former is treated in the literature as a reflection of poor management, or noncompetitive market conditions; the latter as the consequence of environmental scarcity. In the first case the percent of market decreases; in the second case, the entire market shrinks. Organizational death prompted by stagnation is viewed as suicide, while

death due to cutback is treated as homicide. Although this distinction removes some of the ambiguity of this term, more work remains to be done on the operationalization of decline before extensive scholarly discourse can proceed. In the past, decline has been operationalized as a decrease in number of staff, profitability, budget, or demand for products or services. And, although decrease in staff size has been used as a *measure* of decline in some research reports, it is treated as an *effect* of decline in others.

2. *One of the most pronounced effects of decline is that it increases stress* [Levine, 1978]. Consequently, there is a significant need for more research on management under stressful conditions. It has been demonstrated that managers typically respond to crises by relying on proven programs, seeking less counsel from subordinates, concentrating on ways to improve efficiency, and shunning innovative solutions [Benveniste, 1977; Bozeman & Slusher, 1980; Dunbar & Goldberg, 1978; Smart & Vertinsky, 1977]. These habitual responses run counter to the prescriptions for self-designing organizations made by Hedberg, Nystrom, and Starbuck [1976, 1977], Weick [1977], Starbuck, Greve, & Hedberg [1978], Landau [1973], Toffler [1970], and Bennis and Slater [1968]. Smart, Thompson, and Vertinsky [1978] found that organizations characterized by a democratic leadership style, effective decision-making processes, and an aggressive marketing orientation performed better under both growth and decline simulated environmental conditions. However, the research on crisis management shows that it is extremely difficult to maintain this ideal organizational profile under decline-induced stress [Billings, Milburn, & Schaalman, 1980]. Further research on decline will, one hopes, help us understand how to reconcile actual with ideal behaviors under crisis conditions. The research on the physiological and psychological effects of stress provides a foundation for this research [Hall & Mansfield, 1971; Schuler, 1980].

3. *A key to understanding the management of declining organizations is the sense-making process* described by Bougon, Weick, and Binkjorst [1977]. Faced with a crisis, managers formulate a causal explanation that in turn dictates the domain of response alternatives they will consider. Faulty problem-identification procedures are frequently noted in case studies of organizational crisis mismanagement [Dunbar & Goldberg, 1978; R. I. Hall, 1976; Smart & Vertinsky, 1977;

Starbuck et al., 1978]. Boulding [1975] has suggested that managers in different institutional contexts tend to construct different explanations for resource cutbacks, which lead to stereotypic responses. For instance, in a therapeutic institution, administrators tend to interpret a budget cut as evidence that the legislature does not understand the social significance of the institution's function. As a result, they will likely respond with a strong informational campaign with heavy moralistic overtones. In contrast, a highly bureaucratic organization is likely to respond by producing statistics showing that the organization is already extremely efficient and therefore does not deserve a cutback. Cross-institutional research on the sense-making process during crises is essential to a clear understanding of the decline management process.

4. *Case studies of declining organizations point out the significance of management maintaining a balance between structural integration and loose coupling.* Much has been written recently about how loose coupling increases the adaptive potential of organizations [Aldrich, 1979; Weick, 1976]. However, in a recent study of 20 organizations that were badly mismanaged during crises, Dunbar and Goldberg [1978] noted that poor integration was a common characteristic. Top management had become isolated from their highly diversified and fragmented operations and were unable to formulate a coordinated response to environmental change. This finding underscores the significance of Lawrence and Lorsch's [1967] research, which focused on both integration and differentiation, and it suggests the need for additional research to ascertain how management can better maintain a balance between these twin systematic characteristics.

5. *Decline tends to exacerbate interpersonal and interunit conflict within an organization.* Levine [1979] observed that resource cutbacks sharply increase the incidence of conflict and make conflict more difficult to resolve by removing the "win-win" option. This suggests the need to develop new techniques for handling conflict in declining organizations. Research on this topic is especially critical because, in order to cope with decline, an organization needs to discourage its best people from leaving, and the conflict-resolution mechanisms utilized significantly influence an employee's choice between the Exit, Voice, or Loyalty options [Hirschman, 1970]. The effects of decline on other internal processes—such as goal setting, communications, and leader-subordinate relations—also

need to be examined. Yetten [1975] and Scott [1974] have argued that inasmuch as our theories of interpersonal relations were founded on observations from growing organizations it is necessary to re-examine these theories to determine whether they need to be recalibrated for declining organizations.

6. *It is important that researchers not examine decline exclusively from the perspective of top management or organizational owners.* In their recent book *Organizational America,* Scott and Hart [1979] argue that the hallmark of our age is the "organizational imperative"—that is, the social value that all that is good in humanity must be accomplished through organizations and therefore nothing must threaten organizational health. They argue that this impersonal force is even more powerful in shaping the course of organizational activities than is the desire of top management to perpetuate their regime. One can expect that during decline-induced crises the salience of the organizational imperative will be significantly increased. Hence, it would be useful for research on decline to examine ways of blunting the negative effects of this impersonal force on the personal rights of organizational members, especially lower-ranking employees. Such an examination would require shifting the unit of analysis from the organization to the individual. This shift would focus attention on research topics such as the effects on employee morale of various approaches to retrenchment (e. g., reduction in force, reduction in compensation), mechanisms for relocating and retraining displaced workers, and ways of sharing the burden of retrenchment equally between management and employees. Oi, in a recent article [1979] on tenure in universities with declining enrollments, exemplifies this orientation.

7. *Research needs to be expanded on the effects of decreasing organizational size on the ratio of administrative staff to total employees.* Studies in this area have been done by Akers and Campbell [1970], Freeman and Hannan [1975], and Ford [in press]. To date, this work has produced contradictory results. For example, Freeman and Hannan report that school districts with declining enrollments reduced their administrative component, whereas Ford counters that the declining school districts in his sample actually increased the size of their administrative staff. Researchers in this area should augment their analyses of changes in administrative ratios resulting from budget cuts with data on the personnel decisions producing the changes.

The addition of qualitative data on organizational histories described by Pettigrew [1979] would greatly increase the practical significance of this line of research as well as help reconcile the conflicting results previously reported. For example, it has been suggested that when local educational funding is cut back, school districts hire additional administrative personnel to secure more federal grants. This practice might account for an increase in a district's administrative ratio while its overall staff size was declining [Ford, in press].

8. *The effects of decline should also be studied beyond the organization's boundaries.* Interorganizational agreements, organizational network configuration, workers' family relations, and local labor market dynamics are all affected by retrenchment. An example of an important researchable issue in this area emerges from a study by Hage and Aiken [1967]. They postulated that resource scarcity encourages organizations to establish joint ventures to pool their resources for funding new programs. This has the secondary effect of increasing the density of the encompassing network, which in turn decreases its stability and adaptability [Aldrich & Whetten, 1980; Weick, 1976]. However, Aldrich [1979] and Hannan and Freeman [1977] have also argued that environmental scarcity will increase competition between organizations with similar resource needs. This suggests that the extent to which environmental scarcity will increase network density is a function of the complementarity of network members.

## Teaching

1. *The work of Molotch [1976], Boulding [1975], and Sutton et al. [1956] suggests the need for a new managerial ideology that supports no growth.* It is important that future managers believe that retrenchment does not necessarily reflect failure. Unfortunately, strategic retreat runs counter to the American business ethic [Sutton et al., 1956]. A common error committed in the management of crises is continuing to pursue a chosen course of action despite evidence that it is ineffective [Hedberg et al., 1976; Ford, 1980]. This management error is caused by faulty logic (i. e., what worked well under conditions of munificence becomes essential during conditions of scarcity), and a lack of understanding about how to terminate commitments effectively. Often programs are pursued long after their utility has been exhausted because people are not confident in their ability to effectively terminate relationships and agreements. The research by Albert and Kessler [1976] on terminating relationships and Harrigan's [1978] work on "endgame strategies" in business provide rich materials for classroom instruction on this topic.

2. *It is not enough to tell students how they should react in a crisis situation; we must also provide opportunities for practice.* By participating in crisis simulations, students can couple knowledge acquisition with skill development. Typical management cases and exercises do not simulate crisis conditions and therefore do not provide opportunities for this type of practice. As previously noted, it is much easier for managers to adopt ideal leadership styles, decision-making processes, and conflict-resolution strategies in growing organizations. To adequately prepare students for decline-induced crises, we must give them opportunities to perform under crisis conditions. Case studies of declining organizations are useful for presenting guidelines for effectively managing decline, but they do not provide exposure to actual battle conditions. These include the threat of losing the best personnel, the inability to get good information for problem identification —owing to stonewalling and blame-shifting—and the pressure to produce a quick solution to inspire confidence in one's leadership ability. For assistance in developing a crisis-management training program, it would be instructive to examine training programs in crisis-prone professions such as the airlines, law, and the military. The development of new materials couched in the context of decline will sensitize students to the negative consequences of relying on habitual responses under stress and help them develop alternative response patterns.

## Consulting

1. *Consultants can provide an important service to a client organization by diagnosing its potential for effectively dealing with a significant crisis.* Smart, Thompson, and Vertinsky [1978] have developed a diagnostic model that can be used for this purpose. In addition, Harrigan's [1978] model might be used as a forecasting device to help organizations identify potential sources of decline before they develop. Anticipating a downward shift in environmental munificence is naturally one of the most important crisis-prevention techniques.

2. *Consultants can also help organizations prepare for an impending crisis.* Smart and Vertinsky [1977]

propose that organizations should have a set of emergency procedures for managing crises. For instance, they suggest alternative decision-making structures for steady-state and crisis conditions. A central crisis management corps should be identified that is trained to deal with various types of catastrophes. This group would periodically conduct crisis simulations, or drills. These would serve the dual function of giving the staff experience in implementing emergency procedures, and unfreezing complacent attitudes. Consultants can serve a key role in these activities.

3. *There is a substantial need for a cadre of consultants that can aid practicing administrators during periods of retrenchment by pointing out decision-making errors and suggesting novel alternatives.* Boulding [1978] has noted that in our growth-oriented economy, knowledge about the experiences of declining organizations have not been widely disseminated in the management community. Hence, administrators forced to retrench do not have a compendium of "lessons learned" to direct their actions. Consultants who are experts in retrenchment management can partially make up for this deficiency in the management literature.

## CONCLUSION

Twenty years ago, managing growth was a dominant organizational concern. This stimulated considerable research and theory development on growth-related issues, which helped administrators routinize the growth process. During the late 1970s, managing decline has emerged as a significant organizational concern; unfortunately, the organizational sciences profession is ill prepared to provide significant insights or technical assistance. My objective in this paper has been to point out the urgent need for us to retool our theoretical orientations, research agendas, and teaching priorities so that they more closely reflect our changing environment.

*This project was completed during my appointment in the Center for Advanced Study at the University of Illinois. Their support was significant and is greatly appreciated. The opportunity to present an earlier draft of this paper to the faculty at the University of Calgary was very helpful, and I am also grateful for the comments of Gerald Salancik, John Kimberly, Robert Miles, and Bill Scott on an earlier version.*

## REFERENCES

Akers, R.; & Campbell, F. L. Size and the administrative component in occupational associations. *Pacific Sociological Review,* 1970, *13,* 241–251.

Albert, S.; & Kressler, S. Processes for ending social encounters: The conceptual archaeology of a temporal place. *Journal of the Theory of Social Behavior,* 1976, *6,* 147–170.

Aldrich, H. E. *Organizations and environments.* Englewood Cliffs, N. J.: Prentice-Hall, 1979.

Aldrich, H. E.; & Whetten, D. A. Organizational sets, action sets, and networks: Making the most of simplicity. In P. Nystrom & W. Starbuck (Eds.), *Handbook of organization design* (Vol. 1). London: Oxford University Press, 1980.

Argenti, J. *Corporate collapse.* New York: Halstead, 1976.

Bendix, R. *Work and authority in industry.* New York: Wiley, 1956.

Bennis, W. G. *Changing organizations.* New York: McGraw-Hill, 1966.

Bennis, W.; & Slater, P. E. *The temporary society.* New York: Harper & Row, 1968.

Benveniste, G. B. *Bureaucracy.* San Francisco: Boyd & Fraser, 1977.

Berger, P. L.; & Neuhaus, R. J. *To empower people.* Washington, D. C.: American Enterprise Institute for Public Policy Research, 1977.

Billings, R. S.; Milburn, T. W.; & Schaalman, M. L. A model of crisis perception: A theoretical and empirical analysis. *Administrative Science Quarterly,* 1980, *25,* 300–316.

Blau, P. M. The hierarchy of authority in organizations. *American Journal of Sociology,* 1968, *73,* 453–467.

Blau, P. M. A formal theory of differentiation in organizations. *American Sociological Review,* 1970, *35,* 201–218.

Bogue, E. G. Alternatives to the growth-progress syndrome. *Educational Forum,* 1972, *37,* 35–43.

Boswell, J. The rise and decline of small firms. London: Allen & Unwin, 1972.

Bougon, M.: Weick, K.; & Binkjorst, D. Cognition in organizations: An analysis of the Utrecht Jazz Orchestra. *Administrative Science Quarterly,* 1977, *22,* 606–639.

Boulding, K. E. The management of decline. *Change,* June 1975, pp. 8–9; 64.

Bozeman, B.; & Slusher, E. A. Scarcity and environmental stress in public organizations: A conjectural essay. *Administration & Society,* 1980, *11,* 335–356.

Buckley, W. *Sociology and modern systems theory.* Englewood Cliffs, N. J.: Prentice-Hall, 1967.

Cartter, A. M. After-effects of blind eye telescope. *Educational Record,* 1970, *51,* 333–338.

Commoner, B. *The poverty of power: Energy and the economic crisis.* New York: Knopf, 1976.

Cyert, R. M. The management of universities of constant or decreasing size. *Public Administration Review,* 1978, *38,* 344–349.

Dunbar, R. L. M.; & Goldberg, W. H. Crisis development strategic response in European corporations. In C. F. Smart &: W. T. Stanbury (Eds.), *Studies on crisis management.* Scarborough, Ontario: Butterworth, 1978.

Dvorin, E. P.; &: Simmons, R. L. *From a moral to humane bureaucracy.* San Francisco: Canfield, 1972.

Emery, F.; & Trist, E. The causal texture of organizational environments. *Human Relations,* 1965, *18,* 21–32.

Fenno, R. *Power of the purse.* Boston: Little, Brown, 1966.

Ford, J. D. The occurrence of structural hysteresis in declining organizations. *Academy of Management Review,* 1980, *5,* 589–598.

Ford, J. D. The administrative component in growing and declining organizations: A longitudinal analysis. *Academy of Management Journal,* in press.

Forrester, J. W. Counterintuitive behavior of social systems. *Technological Review,* January 1971, pp. 53–68.

Fox, D. M. *The discovery of abundance.* Ithaca, N. Y.: Cornell University Press, 1967.

Freeman, J.; & Hannan, M. T. Growth and decline processes in organizations. *American Sociological Review,* 1975, *40,* 215–228.

Galbraith, J. R. *Organization design.* Reading, Mass.: Addison-Wesley, 1977.

Goldman, P.; & Van Houten, D. R. Managerial strategies and the worker: A Marxist analysis of bureaucracy. *Sociological Quarterly,* 1977, *18,* 110–127.

Green, A. C. Planning for declining environments. *School Review,* 1974, *82,* 595–600.

Hage, J.; & Aiken, M. Program change and organizational properties. *American Journal of Sociology,* 1967, *72,* 503–519.

Hall, D. T.; & Mansfield, R. Organizational and individual response to external stress. *Administrative Science Quarterly,* 1971, *16,* 533–546.

Hall, R. I. A system of pathology of an organization: The rise and fall of the old *Saturday Evening Post. Administrative Science Quarterly,* 1976, *21,* 185–211.

Hannan, M.; & Freeman, J. The population ecology of organizations. *American Journal of Sociology,* 1977, *82,* 929–964.

Haire, M. Biological models and empirical histories of the growth of organizations. In Mason Haire (Ed.), *Modern organization theory.* New York: Wiley, 1959.

Harrigan, K. R. *Strategies for declining businesses.* Unpublsihed doctoral dissertation, Harvard University, 1978.

Hedberg, B. L. T.; Nystrom, P. C.; & Starbuck, W. H. Camping on seesaws: Prescriptions for a self-designing organization. *Administrative Science Quarterly,* 1976, *21,* 41–65.

Hedberg, B. L. T.; Nystrom, P. C.; & Starbuck, W. H. Designing organizations to match tomorrow. In P. C. Nystrom & W. H. Starbuck (Eds.), *Prescriptive models of organizations.* North-Holland/TIMS Studies in the Management Sciences (Vol. 5). Amsterdam: North-Holland Publishing Company, 1977.

Heilbronner, R. L. Second thoughts on the human prospect. *Challenge,* May–June 1975, p. 26.

Heydebrand, W. Organizational contradictions in public bureaucracies: Toward a Marxian theory of organizations. *Sociological Quarterly,* 1977, *18,* 85–109.

Hill, N. *Think and grow rich.* New York: Hawthorn, 1967.

Hirschman, A. O. *Exit, voice, and loyalty.* Cambridge: Harvard University Press, 1970.

Indik, B. P. The relationship between organization size and supervision ratio. *Administrative Science Quarterly,* 1964, *9,* 301–312.

Katz, D.; & Kahn, R. *Social psychology of organizations.* New York: Wiley, 1966.

Kaufman, H. The direction of organizational evolution. *Public Administration Review,* 1973, *33,* 300–307.

Kotter, J.; & Sathe, V. Problems of human resource management in rapidly growing companies. *California Management Review,* 1978, *21,* 29–36.

Landau, M. On the concept of a self-correcting organization. *Public Administration Review,* 1973, *33,* 533–542.

Lawrence, P.; & Lorsch, J. *Organization and environment.* Cambridge: Harvard University Press, 1967.

Levine, C. H. Organizational decline and cutback management. *Public Administration Review,* 1978, *38,* 316–325.

Levine, C. H. More on cutback management: Hard questions for hard times. *Public Administration Review,* 1979, *39,* 179–183.

Mathews, D. Practicing the art/perfecting the science of making public policy. *National Forum,* Winter 1979, pp. 3–8.

Meadows, D. H.; Meadows, D. L.; Randers, J.; & Behrens, W. R., III. *The limits to growth.* New York: Universe, 1972.

Miles, R. E., Jr. *Awakening from the American dream.* New York: Universe, 1976.

Molotch, H. The city as a growth machine: Toward a political economy of place. *American Journal of Sociology,* 1976, *82,* 309–332.

Nisbit, R. A. *Social change and history.* New York: Oxford University Press, 1969.

Oi, W. Y. Academic tenure and mandatory retirement under the new law. *Science,* December 21, 1979, pp. 1373–1378.

Peale, N. V. *The power of positive thinking.* New York: Prentice-Hall, 1952.

Perrow, C. *Complex organizations: A critical essay* (2nd ed.). Glenview, Ill.: Scott-Foresman, 1979.

Persig, R. *Zen and the art of motorcycle repair.* New York: William Morrow, 1974.

Pettigrew, A. On studying organizational cultures. *Administrative Science Quarterly,* 1979, *24,* 570–581.

Pondy, L. R. Effects of size, complexity, and ownership on administrative intensity. *Administrative Science Quarterly,* 1969, *14,* 47–61.

Rodekohr, M. *Adjustments of Colorado school districts to declining enrollments.* Unpublished doctoral dissertation, University of Colorado, 1974.

Rushing, W. A. The effects of industry size and division of labor on administration. *Administrative Science Quarterly,* 1967, *12,* 267–295.

Schuler, R. S. Definition and conceptualization of stress in organizations. *Organizational Behavior & Human Performance,* 1980, *25,* 184–215.

Schumacher, E. F. *Small is beautiful.* New York: Colophon Books, 1973.

Scott, W. G. Organizational theory: A reassessment. *Academy of Management Journal,* 1974, *17,* 242–254.

Scott, W. G. The management of decline. *Conference Board Record,* June 1976, pp. 56–59.

Scott, W. G. Organicism: The moral anesthetic of management. *Academy of Management Review,* 1979, *4,* 21–28.

Scott, W. G.; & Hart, D. K. *Organizational America.* Boston: Houghton-Mifflin, 1979.

Selznick, P. *Leadership in administration.* New York: Harper & Row, 1957.

Smart, C. F.; Thompson, W. A.; & Vertinsky, I. *The development of models for corporate crisis prevention.* Discussion paper, International Institute of Management, Berlin, 1978.

Smart, C.; & Vertinsky, I. Designs for crisis decision units. *Administrative Science Quarterly,* 1977, *22,* 640–657.

Smith, B. L. R.; & Hague, D. C. (Eds.). *The dilemma of accountability in modern government.* New York: St. Martin's Press, 1971.

Smith, R. A. *Corporations in crisis.* Garden City, N. Y.: Doubleday, 1963.

Starbuck, W. H.; Greve, A.; & Hedberg, B. L. T. Responding to crises. *Journal of Business Administration,* 1978, *9,* 111–137.

Starbuck, W.; & Hedberg, B. Saving an organization from a stagnating environment. In H. Thorelli (Ed.), *Strategy + structure = performance.* Bloomington: Indiana University Press, 1977.

Sutton, F. X.; Harris, S. E.; Kaysen, C.; & Tobin, J. *The American business creed.* Cambridge: Harvard University Press, 1956.

Terryberry, S. The evolution of organizational environments. *Administrative Science Quarterly,* 1968, *12,* 590–613.

Thompson, J. D. *Organizations in action.* New York: McGraw-Hill, 1967.

Toffler, A. *Future shock.* New York: Random House, 1970.

Trow, M. Notes on American higher education: Planning for universal access in the context of uncertainty. *Higher Education,* 1975, *4,* 1–11.

Weick, K. E. Educational organizations as loosely coupled systems. *Administrative Science Quarterly,* 1976, *21,* 172–181.

Weick, K. E. Organization design: Organizations as self-designing systems. *Organizational Dynamics,* Autumn 1977, pp. 31–46.

Whetten, D. A. *Organizational response to scarcity: Difficult choices for difficult times.* Unpublished manuscript, College of Commerce and Business Administration, University of Illinois, 1979.

Whetten, D. A. Organizational decline: Causes, responses, and effects. In J. Kimberly & R. Miles (Eds.), *The organization life cycle: Creation, transformation, and decline.* San Francisco: Jossey-Bass, 1980.

Yetten, P. W. Leadership style in stressful and non-stressful situations. In D. Gowler & K. Legge (Eds.), *Managerial stress.* New York: Wiley, 1975.

# Death by Reorganization

Alan P. Balutis

## INTRODUCTION

A tenet of our conventional wisdom in public administration has been a belief in the virtual indestructibility of government organizations. Indeed, a study by Herbert Kaufman has confirmed that government organizations do indeed display impressive powers of endurance. Thus, an announcement on March 8, 1977, marked a unique occurrence in our federal system—the obituary of a government agency.

On that date, the secretary of the Department of Health, Education, and Welfare, Joseph A. Califano, Jr., announced a major reorganization that he called "the most far-reaching in the Department's 24-year history." This reorganization was designed, in the words of the secretary, to "simplify and streamline HEW operations, and help make possible effective program management, sound financial control and coherent delivery of social services."

The changes announced included:

1. *The creation of a new operating division, the Health Care Financing Administration (HCFA).* This action placed under one head the oversight of the medicare and medicaid programs and related quality control staffs.
2. *Placement of all cash assistance programs under the Social Security Administration.* To achieve this goal, the aid to families with dependent children (AFDC) program was transferred from the Social and Rehabilitation Service (SRS) to the Social Security Administration (SSA).
3. *Placement of all human development and social services programs under the assistant secretary for human development.* At the time, these programs were divided between two components, the Office of Human Development (OHD) and SRS.
4. *Consolidation of student financial assistance programs in a new Bureau of Student Financial*

*Assistance.* At the time of the secretary's announcement, there were seven student financial assistance programs. The creation of a single bureau was undertaken "to provide the kind of leadership necessary if these programs are to be sensitive to student needs and accountable under sound financial practices."
5. *Simplification and strengthening of the departmental management structure.* Several separate offices were eliminated, reducing the number of personnel reporting directly to the secretary by about 30 percent. A new assistant secretary for management and budget was established as the departmental counterpart to the director of the Office of Management and Budget. Also created was an assistant secretary for personnel administration.

The result of the transfer of the medicaid, AFDC, and social services and child welfare programs from SRS to HCFA, SSA, and OHD, respectively, was the abolition of SRS.

Kaufman argued that more studies of the deaths of organizations are needed:

> . . . one must understand sickness and death to understand health; pathology contains many of the clues to normality. Information about failure is wanting in the study of public administration.[1]

That is what this study attempts to provide by examining the experience of the Social and Rehabilitation Service.

## THE SOCIAL AND REHABILITATION SERVICE

SRS was established on August 15, 1967, by then-Secretary of HEW John W. Gardner to carry out the functions of the Welfare Administration (composed of the Bureau of Family Services, the Children's Bureau, and the Office of Juvenile Delinquency), the Vocational Rehabilitation Administration, the Administration on Aging, and the Mental Retardation Division of the Bureau of Health Services of the Public Health Service. The long-time and distinguished commissioner of Vocational Rehabilitation, Mary E. Switzer, was put in charge of the new operation. The basic concept of SRS was to use the model of the "successful" vocational rehabilitation program to "rehabilitate" the poor through an integrated delivery of income maintenance, social services, and medical services. The objective was to establish "single state agencies," integrated and strengthened regional staff, and an integration of program policy development at the national level.

The combined 1967 appropriations of the HEW components joined in the SRS totalled $4.8 billion in federal funds. The new agency would have about 1,900 employees in five major divisions as follows:

> *Rehabilitation Services Administration:* responsible for programs aiding the handicapped, disabled social security applicants, crippled children, the mentally retarded, and for services for the blind and the permanently and totally disabled.
>
> *Children's Bureau:* responsible for studies and investigations of the status of children, and for federal-state child welfare, maternal and child health and juvenile delinquency programs, for health services to school children, and for family and child welfare services.
>
> *Administration on Aging:* responsible for administration of the Older Americans Act (OAA) and collecting and disseminating information on the status of older Americans, and for services for the aged (including insurance and assistance beneficiaries), standards for services to OAA beneficiaries, and the foster grandparent program.
>
> *Medical Services Administration:* responsible for medical assistance services by state and local agencies, including Title XIX programs.
>
> *Assistance Payments Administration:* responsible for the money-payment aspects of public assistance programs (aid to families with dependent children), old age (blind and disability) assistance and for the administration of work experience and community work training programs.

## WHEN IN DOUBT, REORGANIZE

There is a story in Washington of a new secretary of a large department who is left three envelopes by his predecessor, with instructions to open them in case of an emergency. After three months in office, facing numerous difficulties, he opens the first envelope. In it he finds a note: "Call a press conference and blame your predecessor." He proceeds to do so, and the difficulties become more manageable. But six months later,

he faces renewed problems and opens the second envelope. He is advised: "Announce a major reorganization of the department." Again he does so and the problems once more abate. But six months later they reemerge and, almost overwhelmed by the criticism and strain, the now-seasoned secretary opens the third envelope to find the admonition: "Prepare three envelopes."

While no doubt apocryphal, this story, and the instructions in the second envelope, provide an apt description of the problems SRS faced. Because of budget restraints, the formal organization to carry out the broad changes announced by Secretary Gardner was not established until 1970. Even before the new organization came into actual existence, however, changes were occurring. In 1969, a management study was undertaken by the consulting firm, Harbridge House, to develop recommendations for the organization and staffing of SRS. This study recommended a number of steps to strengthen the office of the administrator and to strengthen planning and evaluation capabilities, administrative and management services, and regional liaison.

While the study was underway, the largest original component of SRS, the Children's Bureau, was reorganized. The name and some of the staff were transferred to the office of the secretary, where it became part of the new Office of Child Development. Maternal and child health programs were transferred to the Health Services and Mental Health Administration (HSMHA). A few professionals in the child welfare field remained in SRS to assist in the child services aspect of the social services program and a small direct grant program for child welfare services.

In December, 1969 the Assistance Payments Administration was reorganized, producing new offices as well as changes in existing ones.

In March, 1970 the Medical Services Administration was reorganized to follow management principles recommended by a Secretarial Task Force on Medicaid and Related Programs, chaired by the president of the Blue Cross Association. In 1970, Miss Switzer retired and in June of that year the new administrator, John Twiname, undertook a reorganization of the office of the administrator and various staff offices. The major program units remained the same, with one exception —the Office of Juvenile Delinquency and Youth Development was raised to the status of a bureau and renamed the Youth Development and Delinquency Prevention Administration. Several other changes were made in the office of the administrator.

Because of unprecedented growth in program costs, 1972 was a year of transition. Congress approved 427 new positions for SRS to initiate a financial management program; the social services program was capped by federal law at $2.5 billion; a more rigorous AFDC quality control program was initiated; and Congress sought to legislate cost controls in medicaid.

In 1973, with the second Nixon administration, a new SRS administrator, James Dwight, initiated a series of formal and informal organization changes to centralize policy control and to streamline and strengthen the staff offices of the agency. The principal changes involved the transfer of policy, public affairs, and correspondence control from the bureaus to a new associate administrator for policy control and coordination and a comparable transfer of information systems staff to a new associate administrator for information systems. The concept of a strong staff structure reporting to the administrator had begun with the Twiname reorganization in 1971. The financial management and quality control initiatives moved further in that direction and the Dwight actions essentially established a structure in which the program bureaus were also staff units reporting to the administrator.

Effective April 1, 1973, the Administration on Aging and the Youth Development and Delinquency Prevention Administration were transferred from SRS to become—with the Children's Bureau—the nucleus of a new HEW unit, the Office of Human Development. Certain shifts in organization were mandated by congressional action as well. The original public assistance program had covered children and the aged, blind, and disabled. In 1973, when the proposed family assistance plan to reform federal welfare programs failed, the Congress federalized the aged, blind, and disabled program and placed it in the Social Security Administration under the title of the supplementary security income program. The transfer was effective January 1, 1974. In 1975, the vocational rehabilitation program, which had been the model around which SRS was formed, was transferred to the Office of Human Development. Also, a new title was added to the Social Security Act in late 1974. As a result, an Office of Child Support Enforcement was established in SRS to locate and obtain support payments from fathers who desert their children.

The summary above indicates only the major changes during SRS's ten years of existence. Many additional, minor changes occurred as well. In the Medical Services Administration, new units were es-

tablished for utilization control, long-term care, and EPSDT (early and periodic screening, diagnosis and treatment). Between 1970 and 1975, the Assistance Payments Administration was informally reorganized twice. The Community Services Administration was in flux between 1971 and 1977 as ad hoc organizational arrangements were established to deal with changes in program concept and program regulations.

There appears to be little doubt that SRS was in a state of almost constant change since its inception. A quotation sometimes attributed to Petronius Arbiter, a Roman satirist who died circa 66 AD, seems appropriate to some of the things that happened:

> We trained hard, but it seemed that every time we were beginning to form up into teams we would be reorganized. Presumably the plans for our employment were being changed. I was to learn later in life that perhaps we are so good at organizing we tend as a nation to meet any new situation by reorganizing; and a wonderful method it can be for creating the illusion of progress while producing confusion, inefficiency, and demoralization. During our reorganization, several commanding officers were tried out on us which added to the discontinuity.

After Miss Switzer retired, the course of SRS was charted over the next seven years by six new administrators or acting administrators.

One official present at the Califano press conference in March, 1977 put the problem more tersely: "We've been about reorganized to death in this agency."

## BREAKING UP THE COZY TRIANGLES

The Congress and the special interest and advocacy groups have long-established ties and lines of communication to specific programs (and agencies) and often are reluctant to alter the process in any manner that they fear may lessen their influence. These ingrown arrangements in various policy fields have been described as "subgovernments," "policy whirlpools," and "cozy little triangles." (Ed. note: current usage of "iron triangle" is, perhaps, a sign of the times.)

As the section above indicates, the structure of SRS gradually began to give way as the 1970's marched on. The programs that left were often those with highly effective lobbies who felt that their programs were not getting adequate support or attention in SRS. This was clearly the case in 1974 when the lobby for the handicapped played a major role in bringing about the transfer of the Rehabilitation Services Administration to the Office of Human Development. Combined with the earlier moves of the Children's Bureau, the Administration on Aging, the Youth Development and Delinquency Prevention Administration, and the Adult Categories of Maintenance Assistance (income maintenance for the aged, the blind, and the disabled), this shift left SRS with only two units from the original 1967 grouping—the Assistance Payments Administration (which handled AFDC, other emergency welfare, and refugees) and the Medical Services Administration (which ran medicaid)—along with the Public Services Administration (which provided social services and child welfare) which was established in SRS in 1969.

The effect of these changes was to leave SRS "even more conspicuously in the role of 'manager of the welfare mess.'" Put most starkly, SRS had lost those constituencies that were viewed as "the deserving poor," or "beneficiaries" of federal assistance programs, and was left with those who were "recipients" of public assistance. Moreover, it was stripped of support from those special interest and advocacy groups that championed the cause of the aged, the disabled, youth, and so on. Many observers would probably agree with Rufus Miles' assertion that SRS had been left with "an assignment with which it cannot possibly earn a good reputation."[2]

## KILLING THE MESSENGER

While the 1970's were years of organizational turmoil for SRS, they were also years of growth in program cost. In 1970 and 1971, the combined federal cost of the AFDC, medicaid, and social services programs was growing by more than $2 billion annually—from $7.6 billion in fiscal year 1970 to $12.1 billion in fiscal year 1972. Expansion was particularly marked in the social services area. Federal expenditures for social services were approximately $346 million in 1968. They reached $1.6 billion in 1972. An informal tally in the summer of 1972 of the potential state claims for federal matching funds for 1972–73 totaled nearly $5 billion. Seeing this multibillion dollar treasury raid, the Congress passed the State and Local Fiscal Assistance Act of 1972 which put a $2.5 billion ceiling on federal expenditures for social services.

The rapid increases in the costs of these SRS programs created considerable concern—in Congress, in state governments, and among competing purchasers of medical care services. Many states were facing major

budgetary problems in trying to plan for and meet these expanding, largely uncontrollable, expenditures. Congress also was unhappy with rising costs, uncontrollable expenditures, and continual requests for supplemental funds. As one report on the medicaid program noted:

> Congressional hearings have been repeatedly called on various aspects of the medicaid program—fraud, nursing homes, ESPDT, utilization control, prepaid health plans and program discretionary budgets. Few of these hearings have ended on a note which indicated congressional satisfaction that federal efforts were sufficient.[3]

SRS programs were also criticized for the failures to provide convincing systematic evidence of effective program management and administrative responsibility. More specifically, the agency was chastised for insufficient accountability for program operations; for not providing adequate leadership to the states; for failure to enforce statutory requirements; and, when specific penalties were enacted to reinforce these federal requirements, for both implementing *and* failing to implement these penalty provisions.

This last matter is illustrative of the "damned if you do, damned if you don't" position SRS occasionally found itself in. In an effort to ensure that federal requirements were adhered to, both Congress (by law) and the department (by regulation) introduced fiscal penalties to be imposed on states for such actions as failing to meet tolerance limits in eligibility, failing to maintain adequate utilization review systems, failing to conduct periodic reviews of nursing home patients, and so on. Several secretaries faced upbraiding by the Congress for not moving to impose those fiscal penalties. Others received critical letters from individual members when the penalties were imposed. As an SRS legislative liaison official described one case:

> Can you imagine the reaction when you tell some Senator that HEW will be withholding $10,000,000 from his state because our survey found two patients' files that didn't contain a plan of care? Why [a Senator] almost hit the roof. His letter was on [Secretary] Mathews' desk before I got back to my office.

The result, as a former SRS official noted, was that:

> Many Members of Congress just didn't want to see us, because everytime we came to their office it was carrying bad news. Mathews even said to us, "You guys from SRS, you're always getting me into trouble."

## ORGANIZATIONAL REPUTATION

Earlier, I noted Rufus Miles' observation that SRS had been left with an assignment with which it couldn't possibly earn a good reputation. In other parts of this article, I've described how SRS had struggled through a series of crises, problems, and reorganizations over the years. Regardless of the causes, it seems clear that by 1977 SRS had gained a bad reputation within the department and on the Hill, had created a number of problems, and was considered highly controversial.

The subject of reputation—how an agency acquires one, its impact on bureaucratic success or failure, its relationship to actual performance—might better be dealt with by an organizational anthropologist. It is not a subject that has been much discussed in the literature of public administration. Yet there was a clear consensus that SRS's "bad reputation" contributed to its demise. As a senior SRS official put it:

> SRS did not have a good reputation and therefore had no real supporters within the bureaucracy. It was an easy and vulnerable target. I think the prevalent view—in the department and on the Hill—was that it was best to just abolish it.

And one high HEW official who was a major architect of the reorganization said, "SRS' image was so bad that its disappearance was considered very useful."

In addition to the criticism noted earlier for program administrative problems, SRS had also been subjected to severe public criticism for alleged improper personnel management practices and failure to work in good faith with the union. The union took its case to congressional committees that examined the HEW budget and found allies there.

The reputation issue even surfaced in congressional oversight hearings on the implementation of the reorganization. Senator Herman Talmadge, who had previously introduced legislation to reform the administrative and reimbursement aspects of medicare and medicaid, asked the comptroller general to evaluate the reorganization and report his findings to the Subcommittee on Health of the Senate Finance Committee. Talmadge criticized SRS' record for personnel classification violation, terming it "a large and inefficient welfare bureaucracy." And he asked the GAO witness about SRS' reputation:

**Senator Talmadge:** Again, based on your experience with HEW, would you characterize the former SRS as being an efficient and well-managed agency?

**Mr. Ahart:** I do not think it was a terribly efficient organization . . .

**Senator Talmadge:** Which agency, SRS or BHI [the Bureau of Health Insurance in SSA ran the Medicare program], has a better reputation for administrative efficiency?

**Mr. Ahart:** BHI has a better reputation for that . . .

**Senator Talmadge:** If SRS were overstaffed, overgraded, and inefficient to begin with, why in Heaven's name would these positions be disproportionately allocated to the Health Care Financing Administration?[4]

The issue of organizational reputation warrants further study, but it is clear that many informed observers attribute the "death" of SRS to its poor image.

## ORGANIZATIONAL CONCERNS

The March, 1977 reorganization was not totally a response to a new secretary or a new president. The outline for the restructuring had emerged from a study of the department's structure initiated by then-Secretary F. David Mathews in December, 1975. A comprehensive organizational analysis was conducted by HEW staff between December, 1975 and December, 1976. The process by which this report came to serve as the basis for the 1977 reorganization has been described elsewhere by this author. Suffice it to say here that the completeness of the study—an historical and theoretical analysis, a pragmatic analysis, and a detailed peer review—heightened the chances of its being used by the incoming Carter administration.

The recommendations made by the work group would eliminate some fragmentation in the department. They were logical. It seemed that they would simplify management functions, increase policy consistency, and hopefully lead to substantial reductions in error rates. In addition, they were compatible with the expected studies of welfare reform and national insurance under discussion in the department.

Thus, the reorganization—and the resulting demise of SRS—also grew out of an analysis consistent with traditional public administration doctrine and characteristic of what Harold Seidman regards as "administrative orthodoxy." Seidman noted that this "dogma" views government organization as a "technological problem" to be analyzed "scientifically" and dealt with through the application of the principles of a single-headed executive, unity of command, limited span of control, and provision of authority commensurate with responsibility.[5]

## A PROGRAM THAT FAILED?

The question remains open as to whether SRS failed in its objective. Clearly, its activities affected the life, health, and welfare of millions of Americans. Its mission was an ambitious one and an assessment of its overall success is beyond the scope of this study and beyond the ability of this author.

Nonetheless, there was a perception on the part of many in HEW and in the Congress that SRS had failed.

The literature in public policy says little about how the political system responds to the failure of government programs. One of the few authors to address the subject, however, has fought to develop a clearer conception of policy or program failure. James Larson, in an unpublished paper, has outlined the major reasons for failure—all of which are in some way relevant to SRS.

A basic reason for the failure of many programs, according to Larson, is lack of clear and realistic goals. He argues that, "The clarity of larger goals is absolutely vital to the success of a program."

The mission of SRS was not well defined in its early days and attempts to define that mission further in the early 1970's produced only vague statements of goals. Moreover, by 1972 and the second Nixon administration, the mission of SRS changed dramatically as "the emphasis turned from helping the poor (albeit the working poor) to welfare cheats, reduction of social services, etc." SRS was never able to arrive at a consensus on clear and realistic program goals.

Larson also contends that poor implementation procedures are a cause of program failure. While there is no evidence available to compare program implementation in SRS to program implementation elsewhere in HEW or in the government, the organizational turbulence described earlier in this article drained limited staff resources from program management issues to focus on internal agency matters.

Associated with the problems of implementation are the problems of creating a policy which can survive intergovernmental action. A rule of thumb offered by

Robert Lineberry is that the greater the number of actors and agencies involved in a program, the less likely it is to succeed.[6]

The multiplicity of organizationally fragmented programs in HEW and in SRS has been illustrated earlier. Multiple relationships with Congress and special interest organizations helped to cause the proliferation of narrow categorical programs. Relationships between the department and state and local governments in the areas of medical assistance, AFDC, and social services were (and are) extraordinarily complex and difficult to manage. The medicaid program, for example, is not one program, but rather 53 rather different state programs.

The general state of the economy is a final impediment to the success of government programs. Larson argues that in a society plagued by inflationary pressures, "government programs which are associated with high costs are bound to suffer." The burgeoning costs in SRS' programs have been dealt with earlier. Certainly there can be little doubt that the "times" had changed since SRS' inception and that there was a greater concern in government and among the American people about controlling rising costs, improving governmental efficiency, and so on.

Even those such as Joseph Califano, who were closely associated with such Great Society programs as medicare and medicaid came, in the mid-1970's, to speak of managing during adversity, doing more with less, improving the management of federal programs, etc. Given the current environment—a serious economic depression, double-digit inflation, a national unemployment rate approaching 10 percent, and an erosion of faith in governmental institutions—it is doubtful that an agency like SRS could have long survived.

## CONCLUSIONS

As this article has shown, and as Charles Levine has noted, government organizations are not immortal. While agencies can and do die, the powers of organizations to endure are impressive. Thus, it seems important to offer some idea of the differences between SRS and other organizations that survive.

Among the most important may be the fact that SRS had not been established by statute and did not enjoy its own legislative base. One of the aspects attractive to Secretary Califano when he reviewed the task force's organizational proposals was the fact that all the changes could be accomplished *without* securing congressional approval.

Certain unique factors also coincided in a way that brought about the abolition of SRS. First, it had devolved into a politically vulnerable organization as a series of reorganizations had stripped it of support from special interest and advocacy groups and congressional committees. The effect of these changes was to leave SRS in the role of "manager of the welfare mess." Congress also was unhappy with rising costs, uncontrollable program budgets, and continual requests for supplemental funds. SRS programs were criticized for fraud, abuse, waste, and management deficiencies. The agency had gained a bad reputation within the department and the Congress, had created a number of problems, and was considered highly controversial.

SRS was also suffering from organizational atrophy caused by role confusion, political conflict, high turnover, and continuous reorganization. As Rufus Miles has noted, reorganizations may be analogized to surgical operations:

It is important that their purposes be carefully assessed and a thoughtful judgment reached that the wielding of the surgical knife is going to achieve a purpose that, after a period of recuperation, will be worth the trauma inflicted. And the surgical knife should not be wielded again and again before the healing process from earlier incisions has been completed.[7]

Many of SRS' difficulties may not have been organizational, but may have been partly the result of too much reorganization.

Third, the demise of SRS grew out of a departmental study consistent with the "scientific management" or "administrative management" doctrine. Of course, it is almost certain that included in any justification of reorganization is that it will bring about "streamlining" by "eliminating overlap and duplication" and result in greater "economy and efficiency." This rhetoric is used with complete sincerity by some policy-makers and with utter cynicism by others who use it as a smokescreen for other motives. HEW officials seem to have been about midway on such a continuum when they announced the 1977 reorganization.

Finally, while SRS may not have failed in its objective, its various program goals had become less politically popular. In part, this resulted from the diminished capacity of the environment (the government) and the economy to support SRS at its prevailing level. However, since the programs run by SRS continue under other or newly created agencies, these problems will continue until there is basic reform of the department's programs.

This case study raises several interesting issues. No organization is immune from the problems that afflicted SRS: role confusion; rationalization of performance failure by "killing the messenger"; high turnover; continuous reorganization; and so on. Few, however, appear to face them all at once or in such a heavy dose as SRS did. Moreover, SRS was an extremely vulnerable organization. Its programs did not enjoy widespread support—in Congress or from the public. The beneficiaries of the program are poor, lacking political clout. The important, efficacious constituencies had been lost in previous reorganizations. And the fiscal pressure on the states and the federal government caused by burgeoning program costs only served to diminish the capacity of the "environment" to support SRS.

Obviously, the specific factors found important in this case study of the Social and Rehabilitation Service will not necessarily be important in other agencies. However, other studies of organizational decline and death should focus on the relevance of organizational atrophy, political vulnerability, and environmental entrophy as major causes.[8]

*The research for this article was conducted as part of a larger study of the 1977 reorganization of the Department of Health, Education and Welfare which involved interviewing over 100 senior staff members in SRS and the Health Care Financing Administration and talking to a number of individuals outside the agency (e. g., in the Office of the Secretary, in the media, in the Congress, and in various public interest groups). The views expressed in the paper are solely the author's, and should not be attributed to the Office of Program Evaluation or the Department of Commerce.*

## NOTES

1. Kaufman, Herbert, *Are Government Organizations Immortal?* (Washington: The Brookings Institution, 1976), p. 78.

2. Miles, Rufus E., *The Department of HEW* (New York: Praeger, 1974), p. 128.

3. Medical Services Administration, *Medicaid, 1977–1981,* July, 1975, p. 35.

4. Hearing before the Subcommittee on Health, Committee on Finance, United States Senate, 95th Congress, 1st Session,

July 21, 1977 (Washington, D. C.: U. S. Government Printing Office, 1977), p. 19.

5. Seidman, Harold, *Politics, Position, and Power* (New York: Oxford University Press, 1975), pp. 3–14.

6. Lineberry, Robert, *American Public Policy* (New York: Harper & Row, 1977), p. 78.

7. Miles, *op. cit.,* p. 161.

8. Levine, Charles H., "Organizational Decline and Cutback Management," *Public Administration Review,* Vol. 38 (July/August, 1978), pp. 318–319.

## More on Cutback Management
### Hard Questions for Hard Times

Charles H. Levine

We are entering a new era of public budgeting, personnel, and program management. It is an era dominated by resource scarcity. It will be a period of hard times for government managers that will require them to manage cutbacks, tradeoffs, reallocations, organizational contractions, program terminations, sacrifice, and the unfreezing and freeing up of grants and privileges that have come to be regarded as unnegotiable rights, entitlements, and contracts. It will be a period desperately in need of the development of a methodology for what I call "cutback management."[1]

Let me explain why this will not be an easy time to manage government programs. Writing in 1965—in happier times—Robert Lane, in an article entitled "The Politics of Consensus in an Age of Affluence," observed that support for government and political tolerance were promoted by economic growth and government expansion: "Since everyone is 'doing better' year by year, though with different rates of improvement, the stakes are not so much in terms of gain or loss, but in terms of size of gain—giving government more clearly the image of a rewarding rather than a punishing instrument."[2] In 1969, Allen Schick added to this with an observation of his own:

If there were losers in American politics, there was no need for concern, for they, too, could look to a better tomorrow when they would share in the political bargains [and benefits].[3]

Cast against these observations, the challenge of *scarcity* and public sector *contraction* to the viability of our political and administrative systems should be obvious. Growth slowdowns, zero growth, and absolute declines—at least in some sectors, communities, regions, and organizations—will increase the probability of rancorous conflict, decrease the prospects for innovation by consensus, and complicate the processes for building and maintaining support for administrative systems and democratic processes. In this potentially turbulent environment, the dominant management imperatives will likely involve a search for new ways of maintaining *credibility, civility,* and *consensus*; that is, in an era of scarcity, we will need new solutions to problems of how to manage public organizations and maintain the viability of democratic processes.

I have no ready solutions for these hard questions. I do not know of anyone else with solutions either. For now, I can only pose some questions which may point the way to the development of a methodology for cutback management:

1. What is cutback management? Why is it different and difficult?
2. What are the unique problems and paradoxes of cutback situations?
3. What strategic choices must managers make in cutting back?
4. What do these questions and problems suggest as directions for future research?

### WHAT IS CUTBACK MANAGEMENT? WHY IS IT DIFFERENT?

Cutback management means managing organizational change toward lower levels of resource consumption and organizational activity. Cutting back an organization involves making hard decisions about who will be let go, what programs will be scaled down or terminated, and what clients will be asked to make sacrifices. These are tough problems that are compounded by four aspects of resource scarcity. First, behavioral scientists have demonstrated that change is most easily accomplished when the people affected have something to gain, but under conditions of austerity the acceptance of change will be unlikely because the rewards required to gain cooperation and build consensus will be unavailable. Second, public organizations are confronted with professional norms, civil service procedures, veteran's preference, affirmative action commitments, and collective bargaining agreements which constrain the ability of management to target cuts. Third, organizational contraction produces some serious morale and job satisfaction problems which make it difficult to increase productivity to make up for the cuts. Fourth, cutbacks reduce the enjoyment of working and managing in an organization because nearly everyone is forced into a position of having to do with less. Under these conditions, creativity diminishes, innovation and risk taking decline, and the sense of excitement that comes from doing new things disappears. Simply put, it just is not as much fun working and managing in a contracting organization as it is in an expanding one.

A declining organization confronts its management with several unique problems. The first problem I call *"The Paradox of Irreducible Wholes."* The problem refers to the fact that an organization cannot be reduced piece-by-piece by simply reversing the sequence of activities and resources by which it was built. The "lumpiness" of public organizations stems from the growth process in which critical masses of expertise, political support, facilities and equipment, and resources are assembled. Taking a living thing like an organization apart is no easy matter; a cut may reverberate throughout a whole organization in a way no one could predict by just analyzing its growth and patterns of development.

The criminal justice system provides one example of the complexity of scaling down public services. Over time, the criminal justice system has become increasingly interpenetrated and interdependent so that functional agencies like police, courts, parole, corrections, and juvenile services continually interact and depend on one another. Yet each of these units are usually controlled and funded by different decision-making bodies—local governments, state and federal agencies, independent boards, etc. If a cut is made in one function or funding source, it will likely impact on the other units in the system; but because of the fragmentation of political and managerial decision making, coordinating and planning these cuts on a multi-unit basis will likely be extremely difficult, if not impossible.

The second problem is *"The Management Science Paradox."* This problem is caused by the way public organizations invest in and use their data systems and analytic capacity. When organizations have slack resources, they often develop elaborate management information systems, policy analysis capabilities, and hardware and software systems. But, when resources abound, this capacity is rarely used because public agencies usually prefer to spend slack resources building and maintaining political constituencies. In a decline situation, on the other hand, maintaining and using this analytic capacity often becomes impossible for a number of reasons. The scenario goes something like this: First, the most capable analysts are lured away by better opportunities; then, freezes cripple the agency's ability to hire replacements; and finally, the remaining staff is cut in order to avoid making cuts in personnel with direct service responsibility. All the while, organizational decisions on where to take cuts will be made on political grounds with important constituencies fully mobilized to protect their favorite programs. Therefore, in brief, the management science paradox means that when you have analytic capacity you do not need it; when you need it, you do not have it and *cannot* use it anyway.

The third quandary is *"The Free Exiter Problem."* Economists have identified what they call "free riders"; i.e., people who take advantage of an organization's collective goods without contributing their share to achieving the organization's goals. When an organization is growing, the problem for management is how to prevent (exclude) free riders from enjoying the fruits of growth such as promotions, travel, training opportunities, and other available slack resources. During contraction, however, organizations must find ways to limit (include) *"free exiters"*; i.e., people who seek to avoid sharing the "collective bads" produced by the necessity to make sacrifices by either leaving the organization or avoiding its sacrifices. Some potential free exiters, like skilled technical people and talented managers, are vitally needed if the organization is to function well through a contraction. Yet, these people have the greatest employment mobility and their replacements are usually the hardest to attract to a declining organization. The problem which declining organizations have to solve is how to design mechanisms to limit free exiters and reward valuable people for remaining in the organization through its difficult times.

The fourth problem is *"The Tooth Fairy Syndrome."*[4] In the initial stages of contractions few people are willing to believe that the talk of cuts is for real or that the cuts will be permanent. The initial prevailing attitude in the organization will usually be optimistic; i. e., that the decline is temporary and the cuts will be restored soon by someone—in some cases as remote as the tooth fairy. Under these conditions, management's credibility suffers and resistance, cynicism, and sarcasm tend to dominate responses to calls for voluntary budget cutting. Top management appeals for voluntary sacrifice tend to be met with a "you first, then me" response from middle and lower levels in the organization. The preferred tactical response for nearly everyone is to delay taking action while waiting for someone else to volunteer cuts or for a bailout from a third party.

The fifth problem is *"The Participation Paradox."* The field of organization development teaches that the best way to manage change is to encourage the maximum amount of participation by all affected parties. But, a rational cutback process will require that some people and programs be asked to take greater cuts than others. By encouraging participation, management also encourages protective behavior by those most likely to be hurt the most. The participation paradox confronts management with a nearly insoluble problem: How does one single out units for large sacrifices who have people participating in the cut process? The usual answer is to avoid deadlocks or rancorous conflict and allocate cuts across-the-board.

*"The Forgotten Deal Paradox"* is the sixth problem. Ideally an organization or unit should be able to plan cuts and attrition on a multi-year basis. Such an optimum arrangement would allow an organization to plan its cuts so that six months, two years, or further on it will be allowed to fill *some* vacancies, replace some equipment, or restore some services when needed. In the private sector it is possible to make bargains for restoring some cuts later on knowing that they will likely be honored by the management team in the future. This kind of arrangement is much less likely in the public sector because the top management team usually lacks the continuity required to make and keep bargains with a long time frame. Most managers will resist multi-year bargaining if they fear that the other party to the bargain will not be around when the cuts are to be partially restored.

The seventh problem is *"The Productivity Paradox."*

Briefly stated, when dealing with productivity, it takes money to save money. Productivity improvement requires up front costs incurred by training and equipment expenses. Under conditions of austerity, it is very difficult to find and justify funds to invest in productivity improvement, especially if these funds can only be made available by laying off employees or failing to fill vacancies.

The eighth problem is the *"Mandates Without Money Dilemma."* This problem stems from the practice of legislative bodies and courts passing laws and issuing court orders without providing funds to offset the additional expense incurred by compliance. These mandates without accompanying financial assistance, ranging from occupational health and safety standards in public works to minimum education and social service requirements in correctional facilities, have had the effect of committing absolute levels of cost resources to programs that sometimes have low local priority or are already overfunded relative to other programs. Since these mandates rarely take into consideration the financial health of the government units affected, they can force managers and public officials into the uncomfortable position of choosing between responding to local public service preferences and retaining their flexibility to target cuts or noncompliance and the possibility of indictment and jail. In most cases, managers and public officials have chosen grudging acquiescence and exempted mandated programs from absorbing cuts. In some rare cases, however, where prevailing public sentiment is strongly on their side, officials have been willing to risk indictment rather than sacrifice local autonomy.

The ninth problem, *"The Efficiency Paradox,"* is perhaps the most important and most troublesome to public managers. This paradox stems from two ironies of public management. First, it is one of the hard realities of cutback management that it is easier to cut inefficient and poorly managed organizations than those that are efficient and well run. Inefficiency creates slack and waste that can be easily identified for cuts. Efficiency, on the other hand, tends to enmesh slack resources in the organization's core tasks by encouraging the commitment of spare resources to long-term planning and capacity-building activities. When cuts are to be taken across-the-board, efficient organizations are likely to be penalized more than their poorly performing peers because they will be forced to make much tougher decisions about who, what, and how cuts will be distributed. Also, efficient organizations have a difficult search for more productivity gains because they are likely to have already exhausted most of the easy and obvious productivity improvement strategies. For poorly performing organizations the task is much simpler: To achieve higher performance, all they have to do is borrow the management practices and productivity ideas already employed by high performing agencies.

Second, there are few rewards for conserving resources in public management. Too often, to conserve is to be irrational. In many agencies there are substantial *dis*incentives against saving or underspending resources. Early in their careers, most government managers learn that frugality will usually not bring them personal rewards or more resources for their programs. Instead, more often than not, they will be *indirectly penalized* for their frugality because the resources they save will likely be used to make up deficits incurred by other less efficient and self-sacrificing units and managers. To change this attitude, *managers will have to be shown that saving has rewards. In most government organizations this will require fundamental reforms in budgeting and personnel practices.*

These nine problems are illustrative of the difficulty involved in managing cutbacks. They tend to force management to rethink the process of organizational development and growth; and they force managers to make new kinds of strategic choices.

At the present stage of our knowledge about cutback management, strategies are easier to describe than prescribe. So at this point, we need to be satisfied to raise appropriate questions and hope that later their answers can help managers cope with austerity. A proper start, therefore, is to investigate the major steps in the cutback process; that is, the strategic choices that an organization must make about confronting, planning, targeting, and distributing cuts.

*Resist or smooth cuts?* When confronting possible cuts, managers and political leaders will have to choose between resisting these cuts or smoothing them out by limiting their impact on the organization's most important functions, procedures and long-term capacity. Since no organization accedes to cuts with enthusiasm, some initial resistance is likely. But resistance is risky because "stonewalling" financial stress may ultimately force the need to make cataclysmic cuts like massive layoffs; missed paydays; defaults on loans, bonds, and notes; and the selling off of physical facilities and equipment. No responsible manager or public official wants to be caught in that kind of a situation with its unpredictable long-term consequences and embarrassing short-term implications. Sometimes, usually quite early

in the planning process, an organization's or government's leadership will have to make the choice between struggling to resist cuts or struggling to minimize their negative effects.

*Deep gouge or small decrements?* This choice is affected by The Forgotten Deal Paradox; that is, the utility of taking deep cuts initially in order to rebuild the organization later is limited by the risk that the resources needed to build back capacity later will not be available. The alternative strategy is to take the cuts year-by-year in small decrements to minimize their impact in the hope that public support for the agency will increase and the cuts will stop. NASA, an agency which has had eleven consecutive years of budget cuts in real dollar terms, chose to follow the "small decrement strategy." People familiar with NASA in the late 1970's and who know something about the agency during the 1960's often comment about the detrimental effect the "small decrement strategy" has had upon the organization's management systems including some of the management innovations it pioneered, like project management. The deep gouge strategy tends to make the most rational *management* strategy, but, the small decrement strategy *may* make the only rational *political* strategy.

*Share the pain or target the cuts?* Sharing the pain of cuts by allocating them across-the-board to all units may minimize pain, help to maintain morale, and build a good team spirit in the organization; but it is not responsible management. Not every unit in an organization or every agency in a government contributes equally to the goals, purposes, and basic functions of that organization or government. In the initial stages of austerity, however, the preference of public officials will be to avoid conflict by asking for across-the-board cuts from every unit—usually to be absorbed by vacancies and voluntary attrition. Eventually, however, if an austerity situation gets bad enough, some leadership will emerge to identify and rank priorities and allocate cuts to units based on them. These hard choices will be accomplished by intense debates over such matters as the importance of different services, the method of ranking priorities, and the difficulty of maintaining excellence in an organization when it is declining. Targeting cuts is a difficult job that tends to be avoided by all but the most brave or foolhardy public officials. But, if things get bad enough, and the across-the-board strategy is no longer feasible, somewhere along the path of decline, top management will have to switch from across-the-board to targeted cuts.

*Efficiency or equity?* Perhaps the most difficult strategic choice to make in the cutback process involves the tradeoff between efficiency and equity. This dilemma stems from both the cost of delivering services to different populations and the composition of the public workforce. The most dependent parts of our population—minorities, the poor, the handicapped, and the aged—are often the most costly to serve. Blind cost-cutting calculated on narrow productivity criteria could do grave harm to them. The dilemma is also compounded by the recent rises in minority public employment and the salience of seniority criteria in laying off public employees; last-in, first-out criteria for layoffs usually means that minorities and women will be differentially hurt—*irrespective of their productivity.* Since there will always be a tendency to allocate cuts disproportionately to the politically weak, and productivity criteria *could* be used to disguise such an intent, we can expect cutbacks to spark much litigation as they become more widespread. The outcome of this litigation will, of course, greatly constrain, but never completely eclipse managerial and political discretion over the locus and extent of cuts.

## DIRECTIONS FOR FUTURE RESEARCH

To begin to answer these hard questions, a commitment must be made to develop a research program on the management of fiscally stressed public organizations. We know almost nothing about what works best under different kinds of cutback conditions. So, the first thing we need to develop is a baseline inventory of tools and techniques for managing cutbacks along with case studies of their application. With this information we can begin to sort out methods for scaling down public organizations and make some judgments about their appropriateness to solve cutback problems of different types and severity.

Second, we need to find methods for solving the credibility, civility, and consensus problems that plague organizations and governments during periods of large scale cutbacks. We need to invent and perfect democratic processes for allocating cuts which will make cuts effective yet equitable.

Third, we need to devote a great deal of thought to the ethical dimensions of cutbacks. We need to ask, for example, what the ethical responsibility of an organization is to its terminated employees and decoupled clients. No one to my knowledge has systematically struggled with this problem yet.

Finally, we need to understand how cuts affect public expectations and support for government, i. e., whether expectations about government performance will be lowered and toleration for poor services will be increased. If the post World War II era has been until recently characterized by rising expectations and optimism about an active public sector's ability to solve public problems, will this new era produce a downward spiral of expectations and a pessimism about the efficacy of government to help create a better society?

On a similar but more narrow note, how long and to what depths will Americans tolerate the effects of reduced public services on their lives? For example, how much will roads have to deteriorate from deferred maintenance before potholes become more than a minor irritation? At what point will drivers abandon poorly maintained highways and roads? How irregular and undependable will services become before there develops a movement in the citizenry to reorganize and reassign functions or refund and rebuild public services and facilities. In other words, if support for government services swings back and forth like a pendulum, how poor will services have to become before support for their improvement begins to build?

These are some hard questions we need to worry about. These, I predict, will be some of the dominant issues of public management in the decade ahead.

*The research for this article was conducted as part of a larger study of the 1977 reorganization of the Department of Health, Education and Welfare which involved interviewing over 100 senior staff members in SRS and the Health Care Financing Administration and talking to a number of individuals outside the agency (e. g., in the Office of the Secretary, in the media, in the Congress, and in various public interest groups). The views expressed in the paper are solely the author's, and should not be attributed to the Office of Program Evaluation or the Department of Commerce.*

## NOTES

1. For another explication of this theme see Charles H. Levine, "Organizational Decline and Cutback Management," *Public Administration Review* (July/August, 1978), pp. 316–325.

2. Robert E. Lane, "The Politics of Consensus in an Age of Affluence," *American Political Science Review* (December, 1965), p. 893.

3. Allen Schick, "Systems Politics and Systems Budgeting," *Public Administration Review* (March/April 1969), p. 142.

4. I credit Robert W. Wilson, Chief Administrative Officer, Montgomery County (Maryland) Government for first labeling this phenomenon for me.